The Radio Companion

THE RADIO COMPANION

Paul Donovan

HarperCollins*Publishers*

HarperCollins*Publishers*
77–85 Fulham Palace Road,
Hammersmith, London W6 8JB

Published by HarperCollins*Publishers* 1991
9 8 7 6 5 4 3 2 1

A catalogue record for this book
is available from the British Library

ISBN 0 246 13648 0

Set in Sabon

Printed in Great Britain by
Butler & Tanner Ltd, Frome and London

Contents

For my parents, who encouraged me to listen

Acknowledgements

This book would never have seen the light of day without the help of very many people, and I wish to place on record my gratitude for their patience and kindness. Almost every station in the land, BBC and non-BBC, provided information, and I am indebted to the whole of the wireless world.

I am particularly grateful to all the librarians who so willingly gave me access to their premises and their records: David Evans, Manager, Research Library (Broadcasting House); Yolande Harniess and the staff of Radio Programme Index; Neil Somerville of the BBC Written Archives Centre; Mark Jones of the BBC Sound Archives; and those of Times Newspapers and the British Library's Newspaper Library at Colindale. John Cain of the BBC's History of Broadcasting Unit and Anne Lount of News Biographies at Broadcasting House also went out of their way to help.

An array of resourceful publicists provided programme tapes, biographies and other documents, excavated elusive details and patiently dealt with a constant flow of inquiries. They include Sandra Chalmers, Head of Publicity and Promotions for BBC Network Radio; her deputy Sue Lynas; their colleagues Jeff Simpson (Radio 1), Taryn Rock (Radio 2), David Fraser (Radio 3), Marion Greenwood (Radio 4) and Sophie Toumazis (Radio 5); Robert Wilson, Senior International Press Officer for the BBC World Service; Steve Wall of Radio Luxembourg; Norman Divall of Capital Radio; Elsa Petersen-Schepelern of LBC; Helen Lord of BBC North; Keri Davies of BBC in the Midlands; Mary Parsons and Margaret Hale of BBC South and West; Alistair Clyde and Philippa Johnston of BBC Scotland and Catrin Lewis and Gwyn Griffiths of BBC Wales.

For their interviews, memoranda, suggestions or recollections, I would like to thank the following producers and departmental heads, past and present: Pete Atkin, Sharon Banoff, Peter Baxter, Tony Benn, Simon Brett, Michael Emery, Sally Feldman, Martin Fisher, Philip French, Ian Gardhouse, Jill Harris, John Harrison, Ray Harvey, Geoffrey Hewitt, Stuart Hobday, Larry Hodgson, Richard Imison, Chris Longley, Geoff Mullin, Stephen Oliver, Dan Patterson, Marlene Pease, David Rayvern Allen, Ernest Rea, Alec Reid, Susan Roberts, Marina Salandy-Brown, Carole Stone, John Tydeman, Michael Wakelin, Stephen Williams, Juli Wills and Anne Winder.

Broadcasters who kindly gave interviews, or provided material in writing, included Cliff Adam, David Allan, Charles Allen, Michael Aspel, Simon Bates, Tony Brandon, Douglas Brown, Peter Clayton, Alistair Cooke, Russell Davies, Simon Dee, Ferdinand Dennis, the late Charles Fox, Ray Gosling, Deryck Guyler, Gerald Harper, Ted Harrison, Jocelyn Hay, Bob Holness, Janice Long, Cliff Morgan, Nigel Rees, Gillian Reynolds, David Rider, Tony Shryane, Keith Skues, Peter Spence, Richard Stilgoe, David Symonds, Sheila Tracy, Paul Vaughan and Dick Vosburgh.

Outside the immediate world of broadcasting were people who took the trouble to track down lists and yearbooks, consult records and provide facts, figures and synopses. I am indebted to Simon Newton of the Open University; Dickie Arbiter at Buckingham Palace Press Office; Major Vyvyan Harmsworth of Associated Newspapers; Eve Keatley at Church House; Sue Anstruther, head of Spoken Word Home Entertainment at BBC Enterprises; Mark Le Fanu at the Society of Authors; Suzy Langford of Zafer; Sue Griffin of *Broadcast*; Ann James of the Radio Academy; and Anne Waterman of Ferguson. I must also thank Sandra Pronger, Maureen Winnall, David Glencross, Kevin Howlett, Geoff Sherlock, Mike Gilliam, George Eracleous, Stacey Clegg, David Welsby, Graham Ellis, and Gerry Wells, who educated me about early wireless at his unique museum in Dulwich.

Special thanks are due to four individuals who each took on the burden of checking the entire manuscript and making many helpful suggestions to improve, amend and correct where necessary. These were Sandra Chalmers and Robert Wilson of the BBC; Quentin Falk, the writer and son of sometime broadcaster Sir Roger Falk; and the broadcaster and light entertainment consultant Michael Pointon. Any mistakes which remain are, of course, mine and mine alone.

Books I have consulted include *British Radio Drama* edited by John Drakakis, *Let Truth Be Told* by Gerard Mansell, *Ball By Ball* by Christopher Martin-Jenkins, *The Goon Show Scripts* and *More Goon Show Scripts* by Spike Milligan, *Desert Island Discs* by Roy Plomley, *The Archers: The Official Companion* by William Smethurst, *The Best of Round The Horne*, selected by Barry Took, *Conversations with the World* by John Tusa and *The Church of the Air*, produced by the Religious Broadcasting Department of the BBC. I also consulted successive editions of the BBC Annual Report and Accounts, other official publications of the BBC and IBA, all seven volumes of the invaluable *Who Was Who*, and the first two volumes of Lord Briggs's epic *History of Broadcasting in the United Kingdom*.

The following autobiographies proved useful: those of John Arlott (*Basingstoke Boy*), Tony Blackburn (*Tony Blackburn 'The Living Legend'*), Bernard Braden (*The Kindness of Strangers*), Derek Jameson (*Touched by Angels*), Ian Messiter (*My Life and Other Games*), Bill Naughton (*On the Pig's Back*), Kenneth Williams (*Just Williams*) and Glyn Worsnip (*Up the Down Escalator*).

At HarperCollins I am much indebted to Katherine Everett for tracking down so many evocative photographs and cartoons.

Lastly, and most certainly not least, I thank my wife Hazel, without whose support and encouragement over the past two years this book would not have appeared.

June 1991

Introduction

My first radio memory is of sitting in my dressing gown in a pink armchair in the front room. I had been allowed up as a special treat to listen to the Light Programme with my elder brother. The wireless sat on top of a bookcase in the corner, and when switched on its dial glowed with soft amber light, illuminating exotic names like Hilversum and Luxembourg and Zeesen.

My brother was there too, in his pink armchair facing me. The set had warmed up. The words came floating out, an eerie disembodied boom. 'JOUR-NEY IN-TO SPAACE . . . ' Deep, mysterious, thrilling, forever part of a small boy's childhood.

A few years later I made up my mind to have my own portable radio. My heart was set on a small transistor, made by Ultra, which I had seen at the Radio Show. It was a little larger than a Walkman, in peach-coloured PVC and with a curved handle which fitted on with press studs. To save up the money, which I think was nine guineas, I subjected my family to the excruciating embarrassment of sitting through performances of magic tricks, which netted the odd half-crown and florin afterwards. In due course I bought that Ultra, cut down on the conjuring, and discovered a new sort of magic altogether.

The bakelite valve set, meanwhile, had been displaced by a hi-fi and was now upstairs in our bedroom. Then, as I turned fifteen in 1964, the North Sea pirates started to unleash a tidal wave of all-day pop on an unsuspecting nation. Listening to Radio Caroline and Radio London became *de rigueur,* a temptation to be resisted for the sake of O-levels and A-levels.

By the time I went to university most of the pirates had been driven from the air and Radio 1 was less than a fortnight old. Somehow I have no recollection of what set I listened to at Oxford, although I do remember copying down recipes from *The Jimmy Young Programme.* In this period I first discovered *The Archers,* when certain undergraduates flung themselves down staircases as soon as it ended in order to make dinner in hall before the doors shut on the dot of seven.

In the two decades since I have always had a radio close at hand and it has continued to provide unrivalled companionship both at home and, through programmes like *Radio Newsreel* on the BBC World Service, abroad. My first reason for writing this book, then, is simply to celebrate and chronicle a medium which has given me pleasure for almost as long as I can remember.

The other imperative is more objective. Since I started to write about radio, which happened more or less by accident at the end of the 1970s, I have noticed how difficult it can be to obtain even rudimentary information about programmes and their background. This does not reflect on those whom one asks, only on the lack of a central source of reference. The BBC has a multitude of departments, libraries, archives, regions and network production centres. Information is scattered and not always maintained in the same way and in the same detail.

In addition, there are dozens of stations outside the BBC; several radio prizes, which have never before been fully listed; and a mass of information which, as radio expands and competition intensifies, may be in danger of being lost for ever unless it is brought between the covers of a book. It seems strange, given radio's importance in British culture, its longevity and the affection in which it is held, that there has never been a one-volume encyclopaedia on radio as there is on cinema, television, jazz and so on. The Radio Companion is intended to help fill this gap and meet this need.

Fifteen years ago, radio was in the doldrums. Its future seemed dim, forever eclipsed by television. In media jargon it is now 'sexy' again, with a new awareness of its appeal, the launch of dozens of new stations and the occupant of Britain's first national commercial network due to be announced next month. (Two years ago, when I started to compile this book, London had a choice of seven stations: now there are sixteen.) Financial reorganisation within commercial radio, the government's plans for more choice and its creation of the Radio Authority, the launch of Radio 5 and the worldwide importance of radio manifested in the Gulf War, have all contributed to this. More does not mean better, and sadly often means worse, and the challenge of the future is to provide more *genuine* choice while preserving the high quality and traditional values of British radio, which we are always in danger of taking for granted.

The arrangement of this book is entirely alphabetical – one long index – so there is no index at the end. A word in capital letters has an entry in its own right. In the case of about twenty of the 400 biographical entries, it has proved impossible to ascertain dates of birth or death by the time of going to press, and in these cases the brackets contain a gap. I am keenly aware that any book of this sort will contain other omissions, too, if only by reason of personal preference. I trust they will not be regarded as glaring ones, but others will no doubt be the judge of that.

AA Roadwatch

From modest beginnings (one man and one telephone) in 1973, this has grown into Europe's largest road and traffic broadcasting service, operating round-the-clock from an office block in the middle of Stanmore, Middlesex, with seven regional offices. From its 47 studios, its staff broadcast about 230,000 reports a year which are heard on both BBC Local Radio and ILR. It also provides broadcasts on BFBS, the BBC World Service and Radio Luxembourg.

The ABC Quiz

Radio 2 game show devised by Neville Teller and presented by KEN BRUCE, beginning in 1986: contestants have to choose the right answer from a choice of three.

The Accordion Club

Weekly comedy series on the Light Programme from 1946–49, produced by CHARLES CHILTON and starring ex-RAF pilot JIMMY EDWARDS as a regular guest comic. FRANK MUIR cut his broadcasting teeth on the show, as the author of many of its gags. ROY PLOMLEY was compere and straight man.

Ack-Ack Beer-Beer

Comedy show which ran for most of the Second World War (1940–44) on the Forces Programme, intended for those in the Anti-Aircraft and Barrage Balloon units. Among those who appeared on it were Vera Lynn, KENNETH HORNE and ELSIE AND DORIS WATERS.

Acker's Away

Lunchtime Light Programme show with the former Somerset blacksmith, Acker Bilk, and his Paramount Jazz Band. It ran for three months in 1960. Compere: BRIAN MATTHEW.

Acoustic Roots

Radio 2 series from 1987–89 exploring the range and origins of acoustic music. Those featured included Gordon Lightfoot, Tracy Chapman and Steeleye Span.

Across the Line

One of Radio 5's six weekly youth magazines, live in the evenings from different cities across Britain. This programme comes from Belfast and goes out on Sundays.

An Actor's Life For Me

Delightful Radio 2 comedy series starring John Gordon-Sinclair as a fantasising, unsuccessful actor called Robert Wilson. Written by Paul Mayhew-Archer and running since 1989. It was welcomed by BBC Radio's then light entertainment head, Martin Fisher, as the network's first successful sitcom made in front of an audience for some years.

Ad Lib

A welcome break from the braying smartyboots and smug London dinner party ethos of STOP THE WEEK, this goes out in the same Saturday evening slot on Radio 4 when the chat show takes a break. It began in 1989. Chairman Robert Robinson leaves the metropolis and penetrates the provinces, where he has descended on undertakers' conventions, Scottish golf clubs, Cambridge senior common rooms and so on and joined conversations therein.

Adam, Cliff (1923–)

Founder of Radio 2's SING SOMETHING SIMPLE, and its conductor, since it began in 1959. A Cockney who first sang at his church in Bow, he became a musical arranger, formed the Star Gazers vocal group in 1949 and later created his own company of singers for the BBC Show Band in 1954. He disbanded the Star Gazers, with whom he often appeared on THE SHOW BAND SHOW, in 1960. Adam has made his mark and his fortune on television as well as radio, having composed the music for several celebrated and long-running commercials. These include 'The Lady Loves' theme for Cadbury's Milk Tray, Fry's Turkish Delight, and 'For mash – get Smash'.

Adams, Douglas (1952–)

Creator of a modern radio classic, THE HITCH-HIKER'S GUIDE TO THE GALAXY. Despite its brevity (only twelve episodes in all) it somehow captured the *zeitgeist* of the late 1970s, with a yearning for a better world wrapped in both melancholy and *Star Wars*-wonder. Largely through spin-off books, it also made a fortune for its author.

After Cambridge, Adams wrote bits and pieces for WEEK ENDING; met, and wrote with, Graham Chapman; then worked as a bodyguard (he is 6ft 5in) for part of the Royal Family of Qatar. He wrote a synopsis for a science-fiction comedy series and sent it to SIMON BRETT, who nursed it, got it commissioned and produced the first episode which went out on Radio 4 in March 1978. GEOFFREY PERKINS produced the rest.

The show lasted for two series, the second being in 1979. The following year it transferred to BBC-TV, and was not regarded as a success. But the Hitch-hiker books became a publishing phenomenon: they have all been Number One bestsellers in Britain and have sold widely throughout the rest of the world. Adams estimates their total worldwide sale to be about 10 million. So far there have been four: *The Hitch-hiker's Guide to the Galaxy*, *The Restaurant at the End of The Universe*, *Life, The Universe and Everything* and *So Long and Thanks for All The Fish*. A fifth, *Mostly Harmless*, is promised for the end of 1991.

Adams was briefly a staff producer in BBC Radio in 1978. In that capacity he produced an extraordinary pantomime on Radio 2 that year called *Black Cinderella II Goes East*, whose cast was composed of ex-Footlights members. Peter Cook played Prince Disgusting, John Cleese was The Fairy Godperson and others who appeared were RICHARD BAKER, RICHARD MURDOCH, John Pardoe and The Goodies. It was written by two youngsters who subsequently hit the big time, Clive Anderson and Rory McGrath.

Adams also presented the 1989 Radio 4 series about endangered species, LAST CHANCE TO SEE.

Adrian, Rhys (1928–90)

Playwright who had 32 plays broadcast on radio, mainly on the Third Programme and Radio 3, starting with *The Man on the Gate* in 1956. Twenty-seven of them were directed by John Tydeman, who became head of radio drama. He received several awards but only two plays were published in book form.

'His plays reflected a questioning mind and a sensitive ear for the agony and laughter of ordinary lives' – Roger Woddis.

Adult Education

The first education programmes for adults were broadcast in 1924, but there was no formal department making them until the 1960s when 'Further Education', as it was then called, was created. Programmes were broadcast first on Network Three in the early evenings; then on Radio 4 FM in the late evenings; and then,

from 1985, on Radio 4 FM on Saturday and Sunday afternoons under the umbrella title OPTIONS. The programmes are now made by 'Continuing Education' and go out on Radio 5.

Aeolian Hall

Ornate building in Bond Street, named after the Greek god of winds, through which has blown gales of laughter and a lot of hot air: it was the home of BBC Variety, and of THE GOON SHOW, HANCOCK'S HALF HOUR, TRAD TAVERN and JUST FANCY, for over thirty years.

The Grosvenor Art Gallery apparently stood on the site from 1877, and then the Grosvenor Club in 1883, before it became the Aeolian Hall in 1904. Here, in the concert hall upstairs, is where Caruso sang and William Walton's 'Façade' received its world premiere in the 1930s. Downstairs was a piano workshop.

BBC Variety's old headquarters was ST GEORGE'S HALL: when this was destroyed by bombing in 1941, it needed a new home. The BBC took over the Aeolian Hall for this purpose in March 1943 and was there for the next thirty years: in the early 1960s, twenty shows a week were being recorded or performed on its premises.

African Service

The BBC's African Service, part of the World Service, began in 1940 with programmes in English (and, for a time, Afrikaans) aimed exclusively at white expatriates, although some West African colonies, including The Gambia, had been given a limited type of cable radio service in the mid-1930s.

As well as English, the African Service broadcasts in a trio of African languages – Hausa, Swahili and Somali – all of which were introduced in 1957. This was the year the winds of change started sweeping through the continent when the Gold Coast became the first of Britain's African colonies to gain independence. The three new language services, however, began not in response to that but to counteract the anti-British output of Radio Cairo after the Suez crisis of 1956.

Their Somali broadcasts worried the Colonial Office, especially as Ethiopia was also trying to destabilise the British Somaliland Protectorate. The British government therefore made a formal request to the BBC to start broadcasts in Somali, along with Swahili (lingua franca of East Africa) and Hausa (widespread throughout West Africa). It is interesting to note that this was 15 years before Somali became a written language: even today, some of the correspondence from Somali listeners arrives at BUSH HOUSE on cassette, not paper.

The TRANSISTOR revolution of the 1960s enabled thousands of Africans to buy their own radio sets and laid the foundations of the BBC's popularity throughout the continent. This received a further boost when a new Indian Ocean transmitter opened in 1988, making reception throughout East Africa clearer and stronger, followed in 1989 by a new Ascension Island transmitter which did the same for listeners in West Africa. Today, Swahili programmes are on the air for an hour and a quarter a day and Somali for an hour.

Just as the three African language services were launched in response to a Whitehall request to the BBC, so too was a later and highly controversial part of the African Service's output. After Ian Smith declared UDI in Rhodesia in 1965, Prime Minister Harold Wilson asked Bush House to start beaming a special new service into the country and provided transmitters in Botswana for this purpose. Its main programme, *The World And Rhodesia*, was widely regarded as crude propaganda, and the illegal Rhodesian regime started jamming it. The BBC closed it down within three years.

The first head of the African Service was John Grenfell Williams: now it is his daughter, Dorothy.

After Dread and Anger
Six-part Radio 4 series in 1989 in which FERDINAND DENNIS brought listeners the experiences of African descendants in Britain.

After Henry
Bittersweet, neat and successful comedy series about three generations of women written by SIMON BRETT and running on Radio 4 since 1985. Centred on a fortyish widow, Sarah (Prunella Scales), and the never ending demands of both a cunning mother, Eleanor (Joan Sanderson), and a headstrong teenage daughter, Clare (Gerry Cowper). Escape is found in the more tranquil environment of Bygone Books, where she works for the homosexual bookseller Russell (Benjamin Whitrow). Scales and Sanderson, both brilliant, took the same roles when the series was snapped up by Thames TV – after BBC-TV foolishly turned it down.

Afternoon Play
See AFTERNOON THEATRE.

Afternoon Sequence
Radio 3 record programme from 1970–72.

Afternoon Theatre
Long-running drama slot on the Home Service which began in 1961 with *The First Train Home*, by R. Balls, and ran until 1984. Then a new title came into being – AFTERNOON PLAY – which in turn ran until 1987. Since then plays have been billed by the title only.

Against the State
Eight-part Radio 4 series on sedition and rebellion from Socrates onwards, presented by BRIAN REDHEAD in 1990.

Age to Age
Weekly history magazine on Radio 4, which began in 1989. Derek Wilson presented the first series but was then succeeded by Barry Cunliffe, Professor of European Archaeology at Oxford. It attempts to give a vivid historical perspective to current events, often showing that conflicts and problems are not nearly as new as they seem, and claims to be 'the programme where the past meets the present'.

Topics range from serious politics (comparisons between Tsar Alexander II, whose efforts to bring change got him assassinated, and the reforming zeal of Mikhail Gorbachev) and lighter snippets of social history (the history of pubs, how passive resistance to religious education before the First World War compares with contemporary resistance to the poll tax).

Appropriately, the programme itself has an interesting history.

Frank Delaney, the Irish broadcaster and author who invented BOOKSHELF, sent a proposal for a weekly history magazine programme to BBC Bristol in 1986 but had it turned down. When he discovered that a series similar to his proposal was in fact being made in 1988 (by the same part of the BBC to whom he had sent his original document), he took action in the High Court to prevent it going out. He claimed that *Age to Age* was based on his original outline, but his application for an injunction was rejected.

Ahern, Mike (1942–)
Liverpudlian DJ who had the shortest career on record at Radio 1. Although one of the original line-up in 1967, he left after only two shows because his programme, jointly hosted with JOHN PEEL, was not regarded as very successful. Thereafter he worked in Australia, and ILR, before joining the Capital Gold team in 1990.

AIRC
See ASSOCIATION OF INDEPENDENT RADIO CONTRACTORS.

Airport Information Radio
The station that tells you, while you are driving to Heathrow along the M4 or to Gatwick on the M25, that the KQ123 from Nairobi is due to arrive 25 minutes late and that roadworks on the such-and-such mean heavy congestion on the so-and-so.

It is a wholly-owned subsidiary of Crawley's Radio Mercury, whose managing director John Aumonier was seized by the vision of an eighteen-hour travel information service for the two airports when he heard a similar, pre-recorded, information service as he was driving to Disneyworld in Florida.

On the air since June 1990, when it was opened by the then Transport Secretary Cecil Parkinson, the

After Henry – **one of the few comedies on either radio or television in which all the principal roles were female ones, and also one of the best. Left to right: Gerry Cowper, Joan Sanderson, Prunella Scales. Benjamin Whitrow keeps his distance**

station – one of the new generation of INCREMEN-TALS – is aimed primarily at road users. (There were 60 million passengers at Heathrow and Gatwick in 1989, 70 per cent of whom arrived or departed by road.)

It has two studios, one in Hounslow for Heathrow and one in Crawley for Gatwick, and a low power transmitter in each provides a signal with a radius of about nine miles. Each studio receives data from the airport computers, police and AA ROADWATCH,

which is constantly updated and broadcast to travellers. By permission of the Department of Transport, all major approach roads to the airports carry several blue-and-white signs telling drivers of the station's frequencies.

Airs and Graces
Sunday morning programme of light orchestral music which ran on the Home Service for two months in 1960.

Alan, A.J.   (1884–1941)
Storyteller whose tales of mystery, popular throughout the 1920s and 1930s, were made all the more mysterious by the knowledge that this was not his real name: speculation as to his true identity did much to

quicken his appeal. He was a London civil servant, Leslie Harrison Lambert, but that was revealed only on his death.

Alan broadcast only about five times a year, in order not to dilute his impact, and displayed meticulous professionalism. He pasted the pages of his scripts on to separate pieces of card to avoid the smallest rustle at the microphone. He read his first story, *My Adventure in Jermyn Street*, in January 1924 and made his last broadcast in March 1940. *The Times* commented: 'Broadcasting has lost one of its most popular storytellers and one – possibly the only one – who maintained his anonymity until the end . . . around his personality and his stories the BBC had created an air of mystery, which was at the express desire of Mr Lambert.'

All American Heroes
Radio 1 series in the mid-1970s introduced by PAUL GAMBACCINI.

All For Your Delight
Musical series featuring the BBC CONCERT ORCHESTRA, produced by what was then the General Overseas Service at BUSH HOUSE, and broadcast on the Light Programme in the early 1960s.

All In the Mind
Radio 4 series about psychiatric topics presented by ANTHONY CLARE, which began in 1988.

All Join In
Wartime show on the Forces Programme between 1944–45 in which a different celebrity each week, who included Vera Lynn and Harry Welchman, sung popular songs, with the studio audience and preferably the listeners singing along as well – hence the title.

All Kinds of Music
Weekly record review which began on the Home Service and survived well into the Radio 4 era. It ran from 1964–73.

All the World's a Globe
A chronological history of the world, from amoeba to astronaut, was the modest theme of this eight-part Radio 3 comedy series in 1990 which starred the comedy duo of Jim Broadbent and Patrick Barlow, who together comprise the 'National Theatre of Brent'.

Allan, David (1940–)
Started in radio as a DJ on novelist Ted Allbeury's pirate station, Radio 390, from 1966–67; from 1968–82, presented a succession of country music shows on Radio 2, including *Country Style* (which in due course became COUNTRY CLUB); now presents Radio 2's

early show on Sunday mornings. His voice is also familiar to BBC2 viewers, as he is one of its continuity announcers.

Alldis, Barry (1932–82)
Australian-born presenter closely associated with both Radio Luxembourg, in its halcyon years before the pirates stole the audience, and Radio 1. Became an announcer at the age of eighteen in Tamworth, moving on to Brisbane before coming to London in 1955. Joined Luxembourg in 1956, and spent the next eight years hosting TOP TWENTY for an audience which may have reached ten million. Returned to Britain in 1964 and joined Radio 1 in 1967 as one of its original team of DJs, presenting LATE NIGHT EXTRA once a week. Returned to Luxembourg as general manager in 1976.

Allen, Charles (1940–)
Child of the Raj, born in India into a colonial family, who has become an oral historian of the British Empire. He began writing travel pieces and historical documentaries for Radio 4 in the mid-1970s and became researcher, interviewer and scriptwriter on PLAIN TALES FROM THE RAJ, *More Plain Tales From The Raj*, *Tales From The Dark Continent* and TALES FROM THE SOUTH CHINA SEAS. More controversial and contemporary was THE SAVAGE WARS OF PEACE, about Britain's campaigns since 1945. It concluded with a programme giving the Army's points of view on the conflict in Northern Ireland, HOLDING THE RING.

Almost Off the Record
Six-part Radio 3 series in 1990 in which Lyndon Jenkins went in search of, and played, the 'fillers' – short musical pieces, often by distinguished composers and none more than a few minutes in length – often included on the last side of 78 rpm record sets.

Alston, Rex (1899–)
Athlete and teacher (at Bedford School, from 1924–41) who became a BBC sports commentator during the Second World War and afterwards head of commentaries on cricket, rugby, tennis and athletics. He continued as a commentator and earned a reputation for fairness and precision, particularly in cricket.

AM
Amplitude modulation. A way of conveying the signal by varying the height of the radio wave so as to match the variation in the sound waves being transmitted. The modulation is reconverted into sound waves at the receiving end, i.e. the radio set. The first such transmission was in 1906 in Massachusetts, American physicist Reginald Fessenden (1866–1932) having carried out much of the pioneering work.

AM is used on all LONG WAVE and MEDIUM WAVE transmissions, but is vulnerable to storms and electrical interference (because they too can alter the height of the waves) and cannot easily be used to carry stereo broadcasts.

America – The Movie
Seven-part Radio 4 history of the US cinema, compiled and researched by Paul Wells, and presented by Christopher Frayling, in 1988.

American Countdown
Weekly show of hits from the American charts, launched in early 1986 with PAUL GAMBACCINI the presenter and Pepsi the sponsor. Produced by PPM and syndicated throughout ILR: by the end of 1986 it was being taken by eight stations and by the end of 1987, over twenty. Later, the host was Benny Brown (who described himself as 'an arrogant American jock') and Budweiser became sponsor. As part of the disposal of PPM by its new owners in 1990, the show was sold to UNIQUE BROADCASTING.

The American Way of Laughs
Larry Adler introduced, and Michael Pointon compiled, this eight-part Radio 2 series in 1980 analysing US humour.

Analysis
True to its name, this weekly current affairs series on Radio 4 offers serious dissection of issues – particularly new political ideas, such as national sovereignty – often before they reach the mainstream agenda. The format tends to consist of interviews threaded by a judicious narrative.

Launched in 1970, the creation of IAN MCINTYRE and a Hungarian-born former head of talks and documentaries, George Fischer, the programme was distinguished for over ten years by the presence of Mary Goldring (once business editor of *The Economist*) as its presenter. Her successors are David Walker and Peter Hennessy.

And Now, In Colour . . .
Late-night Radio 4 comedy series beginning in 1990, written and performed by a quartet of up-and-coming writers in their twenties who met at Cambridge: Tim Firth, Tim de Jongh, Michael Rutger and William Vandyck. Formerly they had been a revue group known as The Throbbs.

The show combines sketches and character-based humour and the team pretends that the Paris Studio, where they record the programme in front of an audience, is transformed each time into a different venue, such as the London Marathon, Salisbury Plain or a fairground.

And The Band Played On
Series of five afternoon plays on Radio 4 in 1990, each one making use of a particular tune. Six were made, but Al Hunter's *Alison* (its title taken from an Elvis Costello song) was banned because of its explicit sex and crude language. It was about two young lovers, played by Rosie Rowell and Kevin Whatley. It was promised a late-night slot but so far has not gone out.

Anderson, Marjorie (–)
Trained actress who became a much respected presenter, beginning with Second World War programmes such as FORCES' FAVOURITES and later WOMAN'S HOUR and HOME FOR THE DAY.

Andrew, Agnellus (1908–87)
BBC Radio religious commentator and programme maker, often working alongside RICHARD DIMBLEBY who later became the Vatican's head of social communication and a Bishop. He started his career on THE ANVIL and in 1946 became the first Roman Catholic priest in Europe to train as a television producer. In 1990 the Catholic Media Trust inaugurated an annual lecture which is named after him.

Andrew, Nigel (1949–)
Former Dulwich librarian who was the pungent and highly readable radio critic of THE LISTENER in 1983 and from 1986–90, and is now deputy radio listings editor on RADIO TIMES.

Andrews, Eamonn (1922–87)
Charming, relaxed Irish broadcaster who enjoyed a productive and varied association with radio before making his fortune in television in the 1950s with *What's My Line?* and *This Is Your Life.*

Son of a Dublin carpenter, he first came to the microphone at the age of sixteen, as a boxing commentator on Radio Eireann. He went on to commentate on rugby and soccer as well (and, in 1960, renewed his link with the company by becoming its chairman and helping to set up Irish television) before adding another string to his bow as radio critic of the *Irish Independent.*

In 1950 he succeeded STEWART MACPHERSON as host of the quiz show IGNORANCE IS BLISS and later took over Saturday's SPORTS REPORT.

Android, Seamus
Idiotic Irish chat show host on ROUND THE HORNE, incapable of saying more than 'Well now', 'Hallo there' and 'Alright'. This was a cruel mockery of EAMONN ANDREWS, whose Sunday evening show was proving popular with TV audiences but which failed to impress

either BARRY TOOK or his co-author Marty Feldman. Seamus was played by Bill Pertwee.

Announcers' Challenge
The name of two amiable quiz games on Radio 2, one at Christmas 1988 and the second at Christmas 1989, which enabled the announcers of Radios 2, 3 and 4 to emerge from their customary anonymity and display their personalities. MICHAEL ASPEL chaired both contests. Those who competed against one another included such pillars of their networks as James Alexander Gordon (Radio 2), Charlotte Green and Laurie MacMillan (Radio 4) and Susan Sharpe (Radio 3).

The Answerphone
Radio 5 phone-in series, on personal problems affecting the young such as leaving home and eating disorders, whose usual host is ALLAN ROBB.

Anthony Lawrence's Hong Kong
The BBC's former Far East correspondent (1956–74) presented this well informed, four-part report on the uncertain future of one of Britain's last colonies on Radio 4 in 1990.

The Anvil
Religious counterpart to THE BRAINS TRUST, on the air at the same time for most of the Second World War. About 4,000 questions were sent in during the first series of six programmes. Under a lay chairman, Prof. Victor Murray, a panel of four (two Anglicans, one Roman Catholic and one from the Free Churches) tried 'to give honest Christian answers to listeners' doubts, difficulties and enquiries'.

Any Answers?
Began in October 1954 to give listeners the chance to respond to comments made in the previous week's ANY QUESTIONS? programme. Likewise, it was produced in Bristol with the sister show's chairman (FREDDIE GRISEWOOD, then DAVID JACOBS, then JOHN TIMPSON) introducing this one as well.

This correspondence column of the air lasted until 1989, with actors reading out the letters. Objectors felt that, because it was based on letter writing, it was archaic and, more importantly, favoured the middle class who were supposed to have more time on their hands to write. Others felt that the style and accent of the readers made all the letters *seem* rabidly right-wing even when they were not.

In 1989, MICHAEL GREEN turned the programme into a live phone-in and moved it from its previous midweek slot so that it now immediately follows the Saturday repeat of *Any Questions?*. Listeners ring up about what they – and the wider audience – have just heard, and find themselves bouncing their comments off the *Any Questions?* presenter, Jonathan Dimbleby.

'People simply don't write letters any more. They're too busy. They tend to pick up the telephone to air their views' – Michael Green.

Any Questions?
(1) Original title of THE BRAINS TRUST when it began in 1941.

(2) Live, topical, Friday-night discussion programme on Radio 4 which began as a six-week filler in the BBC's West Region in October 1948, when it was launched by the region's then programmes head FRANK GILLARD. This origin explains why, for most of its life, it has been produced from Bristol.

Chairmen have been FREDDIE GRISEWOOD (1948–67), DAVID JACOBS (1968–84, axed because the BBC wanted the programme to be 'a bit sharper'), JOHN TIMPSON (1984–87) and Jonathan Dimbleby since then.

The first programme came from Winchester, and the first of what would be more than 11,000 questions asked on the programme was put by the city's lady mayor: 'What effect would it have in world affairs if women were able to exert more power in professional politics and diplomacy?' The answers do not appear to have been preserved but the names of the panellists are. Jack Longland, then chief education officer for Dorset; novelist Naomi Royde-Smith, who lived in the city; Honor Croome of *The Economist*; and JOHN ARLOTT, then a talks producer with the BBC.

Any Questions? has always dealt with political and social controversies of the day (though not to the exclusion of lighter topics) and its venue was twice switched when Enoch Powell was on the panel because of fears of violent disruption – once in 1968 shortly after his 'rivers of blood' speech, and again in 1984.

Powell was also one of the team when the programme suffered the one serious attempt to drive it off the air. At Basingstoke in 1976, 'anti-fascists' who protested at Dame Judith Hart sharing a platform with him succeeded in taking it off the air for twelve minutes (though when it resumed it had twelve extra minutes at the end, so the repeat the following lunchtime was of the normal length).

An episode in April 1990, from inside a women's prison called Askham Grange, near York, was the first in which inmates were able to ask questions themselves (previous episodes mounted behind bars had not permitted this).

The programme travels some 12,000 miles round Britain every year, visiting village halls, schools, churches, polytechnics, civic centres and festivals. The panellists most closely associated with it, apart from Powell, have included Lord Boothby, Mary Stocks, Ralph Wightman and Jack Longland (all of whom appeared on the 500th

7

edition in 1962), Russell Braddon, TONY BENN, Jeremy Thorpe and Denis Healey.

See also ANY ANSWERS?

Apna Hi Ghar Samajhiye

Asian-languages programme at breakfast time (8.10 a.m.) on Sundays in the Home Service in the 1960s, with an alternative on FM.

Applying the Micro

Four-part Radio 4 FM series in 1989 looking at small computers, presented by electronic novices DILLY BARLOW and Nigel Forde.

Appointment With Fear

Creepy and often macabre stories which chilled late-night audiences on the Home Service from 1943. Producers were VAL GIELGUD and Martyn C. Webster. The first tale was *Cabin B-13*, by John Dickson Carr, who wrote or adapted nearly all the early stories in this half hour of horror. THE MAN IN BLACK introduced them, and he later had a similar series of eerie tales under his own name in 1949.

Arabic Service

This was the BBC's first broadcasting service in a foreign tongue (apart from Welsh and Gaelic) when it began in 1938, and is thus the oldest foreign language output of the BBC World Service. It is also the biggest, normally on the air for eleven hours a day which is more than any of the other 35 foreign language services. It transmits to the Gulf, Middle East and North Africa.

The output was boosted from nine to 10 ½ hours a day when Iraq invaded Kuwait in August 1990, and further increased to 14 hours a day from the outbreak of the Gulf War the following January. Iraq attempted to jam the service from the time of the invasion of Kuwait until the following November, with the BBC's engineers tracing the jamming to a site south of Baghdad.

The BBC has claimed high levels of listening and during one survey discovered that 43 per cent of the adult population of Jordan, for example, were listening at least once a week, which is a higher proportion than any of its rivals. The BUSH HOUSE mailbag certainly provides evidence of enthusiasm. Letters in Arabic in 1989 numbered 69,291 – a total which, out of all the 36 foreign language services then operating, was exceeded only by Burma.

The service's first phone-in was to the then Foreign Office Minister William Waldegrave in March 1989, shortly after he became the first British Minister to meet PLO chairman Yasser Arafat (in Tunis). Live calls were taken at Bush House in Arabic and put to Waldegrave in English by the presenter, Hassan Muawad. Waldegrave's answers were simultaneously translated into Arabic as they went out on the air.

The Archers

Ambridge is hard to find on an Ordnance Survey map, yet countless radio fans know exactly where it is: just off the B3980, six miles south of Borchester and seventeen miles west of Felpersham and its magnificent cathedral. It's a typical Borsetshire village nestling in a valley below Lakey Hill, from which one can see across the Vale of Am as far as the Malvern Hills . . . and down into the home of the world's longest running broadcast serial.

The Archers was conceived at a time when the government was urging farmers to grow more food, and was keen to use the BBC to spread the word. Forty years ago Britain had many more farmers than now, and half the agricultural land was in holdings of 100 acres or less. The programme was intended as a device by which farmers would catch up with agricultural news and advice, on the basis that a serial would be more engrossing than dry, techniccaaal talks.

The seeds were sown in June 1948, at a meeting in Birmingham's council chamber between farming representatives and the BBC. One farmer got up and, referring to the programme that held the nation enthralled every night, suggested a DICK BARTON approach to putting over farming topics. On the platform was Godfrey Baseley, agricultural programmes producer for the Midland Region of the BBC (the region which has always produced the Corporation's farming output, on both radio and television). He took up the idea. Two years later, at Whitsun 1950, the first episode of the 15-minute serial began in the Midland region only. It made its national debut on Monday, 1 January 1951 at 11.45 a.m. on the Light Programme, billed in RADIO TIMES as 'The daily events in the lives of country folk.' On its advisory team in the early years were representatives of the National Farmers Union, Ministry of Agriculture and British Sugarbeet Corporation.

Baseley was the first editor. His family's home at Summerhill Farm in Hanbury, Worcs, was the inspiration for Dan and Doris Archer's home at Brookfield Farm, the emotional heart of the story. (It has been photographed many times for the BBC's publicity pictures of 'Brookfield'.) In other ways, too, Hanbury is the model for Ambridge: its parish church was where the BBC recorded the scenes of Phil Archer's wedding to Grace in 1955, his son David's wedding to Ruth in 1989 and Peggy Archer's wedding to Jack Woolley in 1991.

The first producer was TONY SHRYANE and the original writers the successful *Dick Barton* team of Geoffrey Webb and EDWARD J. MASON. Three months later (on Monday, 2 April) it replaced their earlier creation as the BBC's new early evening serial. From that day onwards it went out at 6.45 p.m., a slot that remained unchanged for many years. It moved from Light Programme to Home Service in 1967.

Although dedicated Barton fans such as TERRY WOGAN never forgave the new programme, it quickly

Tea at Brookfield, 1958, with Doris Archer playing
mother. Beside her, standing: Peggy (Thelma Rogers);
Paul Johnson (Leslie Dunn); Jack (Denis Folwell) and
Phil (Norman Painting). Seated: Dan (Harry Oakes);
Christine Johnson (Lesley Saweard, wide-belted dress);
Jennifer (Freda Hooper); Lillian (Margaret Lane, bottom
corner) and Jill (Patricia Greene, checked cape)

established itself in listeners' affections. By the 100th
episode at the end of May, its audience of 9 million
was (according to the BBC) already bigger than its predecessor's. Giles Romilly, radio critic on *The Observer*,
wrote on 27 May: '*The Archers*, celebrating their 100th
birthday last week, have gained confidence in themselves
and discarded the heavier banalities – "Don't let's look
on the black side till we have to" – which used to make
them a bit of a bore. They have grown enormously
popular.'

The serial has always ensured that it covers the
changing world of farming within the wrappings of
a soap opera. From Dan and Doris's shire horses
of 1951 to the four-wheel drive Range Rovers of
today, fowl pest, sheep worrying, organic vegetables,
milk quotas, shooting, animal diseases, rights of way,
chainsaw safety, gypsies, land use, agricultural ten-
ancies and rural poverty have all featured in successive storylines. But, like any other soap, it has
also chronicled the loves, lives, joys, squabbles, heart-
aches and tribulations of its gallery of characters, of
whom the Archers are the main but far from the only
family.

In addition to Dan and Doris's tribe (three children,
seven grandchildren and eight great-grandchildren) there
are the permanently grumbling Grundys of Grange Farm,
wealthy Lothario Brian Aldridge of Home Farm, plus
the Tuckers, Gabriels, Tregorrans, Perks and Snells and
dozens of other characters who drift in and out as
plots require. Details are preserved in the programme's
own comprehensive archives, which consist of 12,000
cross-referenced cards.

Several theories have been suggested to explain the

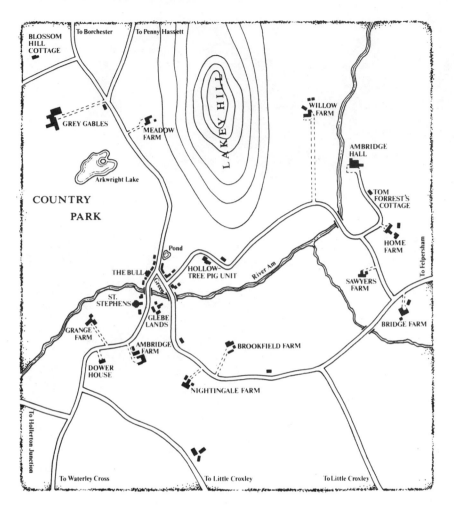

To Borchester
To Penny Hassett
BLOSSOM HILL COTTAGE
GREY GABLES
MEADOW FARM
LAKEY HILL
Arkwright Lake
COUNTRY PARK
WILLOW FARM
AMBRIDGE HALL
TOM FORREST'S COTTAGE
HOME FARM
To Felpersham
Pond
THE BULL
HOLLOW-TREE PIG UNIT
River Am
SAWYERS FARM
ST. STEPHENS
GLEBE LANDS
BRIDGE FARM
GRANGE FARM
AMBRIDGE FARM
BROOKFIELD FARM
DOWER HOUSE
NIGHTINGALE FARM
To Hollerton Junction
To Waterley Cross
To Little Croxley
To Little Croxley

Ambridge, home of *The Archers* since 1950. Phil and Jill live at Brookfield, Pat and Tony at Bridge Farm, the Aldridges at Home Farm and the Grundys at Grange Farm. The Tuckers rent Willow Farm from Dr Matthew Thorogood, who in turn rents Ambridge Farm, where he has his surgery. Mrs Antrobus lives at Nightingale Farm. Meadow and Sawyers Farm rarely feature in the storyline

programme's extraordinary longevity: a surrogate family for the whole nation; a memory link between the generations; a security blanket; a comforting folk memory of stability and order, harking back to an age when life was governed by the unchanging rhythm of the seasons. Certainly its appeal is potent. During the Gulf War, for example, the BBC said it had been 'deluged' with calls and letters protesting that neither the World Service nor BFBS was carrying it, whereupon BFBS promptly started to put out the Sunday omnibus edition as a reminder of home for the thousands of troops stationed in the desert.

The serial has also displayed a shrewd talent for self-publicity. Young and beautiful Grace Archer died in a stable fire in 1955, on the opening night of ITV (it did not, as has so often been said, knock that event off the front pages the next morning, but it became a national talking point and distracted attention from it). Gamekeeper Tom Forrest was charged with murder

– later reduced to manslaughter – after poacher Bob Larkin was shot dead with his own gun as the two men grappled with one another in a fight in the fields one night in early 1957. Ambridge breathed a great sigh of relief when, at his trial in July, he was acquitted. Doris Archer died in her armchair in Glebe Cottage in 1980, after a long and much reported battle against ill health on the part of the actress, Gwen Berryman. Lynda Snell, the *parvenu* from Sunningdale, had a partly ad-libbed encounter with Dame Edna in 1988. The 10,000th episode in May 1989 featured Dame Judi Dench, as the normally silent Pru Forrest.

Some of the best publicity *The Archers* has achieved has stemmed from the use of real people and, in particular, Royalty. The first real person to appear on the programme was Dr Percy Blount, an acknowledged poultry expert, in 1956. Phil Archer went to visit him at his poultry station near Aylesbury to learn more about broiler chickens, and they recorded a scene in one of the poultry houses. In the first decade of the serial all the real people who intruded into Ambridge were agricultural figures: two others were the Chairman of the Wool Marketing Board and Essex apple grower Giles Tuker.

Princess Margaret became the first member of the Royal Family to act on either radio or television when she played herself in the 8,715th episode in 1984. As president of the NSPCC, she dropped in to visit an Ambridge fashion show held to raise funds for the charity, and had all of 85 words in her script. The Duke of Westminster, who was chairman of the NSPCC's centenary appeal, also played himself in the same episode. (The BBC paid them £75 each, which they donated to the NSPCC.) And the Earl of Lichfield, a cousin of the Queen, took the pictures at the wedding of Shula Archer – the fairest rose in English soap – to solicitor Mark Hebden in 1985, only four years after taking the official snaps of Prince Charles's wedding to Lady Diana Spencer in 1981. One of his dreamy Shula-and-Mark pictures adorned the front cover of *Radio Times*.

The programme's signature tune, 'Barwick Green', is probably the most familiar piece of music in the whole of broadcasting. Far from being an homage to Borsetshire or anywhere else in the Midlands, it was composed by Arthur Wood in 1922 in honour of his native Yorkshire, and is the last segment of a four-part suite called 'My Native Heath'. There have been two fan clubs associated with the programme. EDDIE GRUNDY, the tenant farmer of charm and low cunning, had his own. Then in 1990 the cast formed its own appreciation society called Archers Addicts, which within a few months had 800 paid-up members. Subscribers pay £10 a year and receive a quarterly newspaper called *Ambridge Village Voice*.

'The position really is that *The Archers* has developed into a story of country life in which farming is incidental rather than basic' – *Birmingham Weekly Post*, 1951.

'That long series of love scenes with "Grace", the testing emotional scenes at the death of "Grace", "Phil's" two radio marriages, the period when he narrowly escaped going blind, the horrific occasion when he discovered "Uncle Tom" with the body of a poacher: all these and so many more scenes make me grateful to have had the chance to play such a wonderful part' – Norman Painting, at the time of the 3,000th episode in 1962.

'I suggest the name of the evergreen serial *The Archers* be changed to "The Guzzlers". It seems that it is impossible for two or more of these characters to be together for more than one minute without pouring some kind of liquid down their throats' – letter to

Radio Times in 1965 from Charles H.W. Groves of Oxford.

'Ambridge is a place always slightly nicer than our own' – William Smethurst, editor from 1978–86.

'It's a rural idyll in which secretly we would all like to live' – Jock Gallagher, head of Midlands network radio, 1970–89.

'Ambridge is more like the real world than it once was. The scripts are sharper, wittier, and listeners are invited to contemplate Pat's feminist views, the yuppie lifestyle of the Hebdens, marital crises, one-parent families and nervous breakdowns' – A.N. Wilson, 1990.

'It's a radio drug' – Timothy Bentinck, who plays David Archer, 1991.

Archive Feature
Goes out at 8.45 a.m. on Radio 4 on Mondays, when Parliament is sitting. For many years it had a dusty, unchanging mood, with JOHN EBDON plucking from the past all manner of remarks and exchanges found in the BBC SOUND ARCHIVES, poking fun at them all and coming to no very serious conclusion. He did this for 26 years, from 1961 to 1987. GLYN WORSNIP, who appeared every fourth Monday from 1981–87, had a similarly dry wit.

In 1989 their whimsical style was itself confined to the archives when a sharper edge was introduced. Items have included short re-creations of real-life events such as the Iranian Embassy siege and the mass gathering of women outside Greenham Common missile base, a celebration of ALISTAIR COOKE's genius and John Pilger on Australia.

'Gone are the days when people were quoted out of context and then made fun of' – Simon Elmes, senior producer of the archive slot, 1989.

Arden, John (1930–)
One of several playwrights with a particularly close association with radio, starting with his *The Life of Man* on the Home Service in 1956. About 20 plays have followed, including *Serjeant Musgrave's Dance* on the Third in 1962.

His radical vision of the world, and the feminist perspectives of his wife Margaretta D'Arcy, were channelled into a cycle of plays they wrote together about early Christianity called *Whose is the Kingdom?* It was set in the fourth-century Roman Empire and broadcast on Radio 3 in 1988.

'Are You Sitting Comfortably?'
The time-honoured question which always introduced LISTEN WITH MOTHER. It is also the title of a Radio 2 panel game, hosted by Leslie Crowther and beginning in April 1991, which takes a reminiscent look at children's radio and television programmes.

JOHNNY MORRIS and Sarah Greene have been among the guests.

Are You Still Awake?
Series of six Radio 3 late-night playlets in the mid-1980s, written by RUSSELL DAVIES. He is writing another six for a second series in late 1991.

Argument
Pungent Light Programme programme in 1951 in which two speakers of opposing viewpoints, such as Randolph Churchill and Tom Driberg, clashed in debate.

'In *Argument* we have something which exists nowhere else in the world – a radio forum in which supporters of Government and Opposition can tear each other's eyes out. It is an expression of British radio at its finest and frankest' – Jonah Barrington in the *Daily Graphic*, 1951.

Arlott, John (1914–)
Basingstoke-born policeman who, after eleven years in the force, left it in 1945 to join the BBC, in due course

'The voice of English summer' painting a picture of the national game as only he knew how. John Arlott, in action at the Gloucestershire v. New Zealand match in 1949; he was to continue as a cricket commentator for another three decades

becoming the best loved commentator in the history of cricket.

Aptly described as 'the voice of English summer', he infused his words with warmth, wit, love of language and a deep understanding of the rituals of the game, as well as an unmistakable melancholy.

The slow rolling richness of his Hampshire burr graced the airwaves from 1947 to 1980 when, at the Centenary Test at Lord's, he pulled the stumps on his commentator's career and retired to the pavilion, i.e. a more leisured life in Alderney.

His first job in the BBC had nothing to do with cricket but reflected his other love – poetry. He was hired as a Literary Programmes Producer in the BBC's Eastern Service, a post similar to the one GEORGE ORWELL had held a few years before.

'You could smell the grass when he was talking' – Michael Tuke-Hastings, one of his producers.

'He saw a game of cricket as something more than whether the ball was doing this or that. He would comment on the action going on all round the ground with a slight penchant for the pigeons feeding in the outfield. It was wonderful stuff and brought the cricket match alive. He always tried to imagine that he was talking to a blind person and coloured his commentary accordingly' – Brian Johnston.

Arnold
TONY BLACKBURN's big barking dog, which he brought with him to Radio 1 after finding him on a sound effects disc at Radio Caroline.

Arnold Brown and Company
Late-night Radio 4 comedy series starting in 1989. The star, Arnold Brown (1934–), stresses both his Glaswegian and his Jewish roots: he trained as a chartered accountant before gravitating to London's Comic Strip and eventually becoming what he describes as 'the grandfather of alternative comedy'.

Arnold-Forster, Val (1930–)
Radio critic of *The Guardian* since 1974. She is the daughter of the writer Naomi Mitchison and niece of the late J.B.S. HALDANE.

The Arthur Haynes Show
In his customary role as the all-purpose pest, comedian Arthur Haynes bothered his partner Nicholas Parsons in this Light Programme series written by Johnny Speight.

Arthur – The King
Dense, poetic, richly textured Radio 4 dramatisation in 1990 of the life of the mythical monarch and the Knights of his Round Table. Written by Graeme Fife, directed by John Powell.

The Arts Programme

Weekend arts strand which began on Radio 2 in March 1990, replacing ROUND MIDNIGHT at the behest of the new controller FRANCES LINE. The Friday show always comes from the regions; the Saturday programme is hosted by Sheridan Morley with a team of critics and pundits; and Sunday's is devoted to a different subject each week, which have ranged from Goldcrest to Glyndebourne. One key difference between the show and its predecessor is that the music is now more closely linked to the speech content than it ever was before.

The Arts This Week

Precursor of KALEIDOSCOPE, made by Philip French (who went on to devise and produce CRITICS' FORUM) with the aid of RUSSELL HARTY. It ran on Radio 3 from 1969–71.

As Others See Us

Friday-night Home Service series starting in June 1963 in which a foreign correspondent based here would give his thoughts on an issue of current importance in Britain. It stemmed from an edition of FROM OUR OWN CORRESPONDENT which had also turned itself inside out in this way, earlier in 1963.

As We Were

Four monologues on Radio 3 in 1989 selected from humorist E.F. Benson's book of reminiscences of the same name, and read by Sir John Gielgud.

Askey, Arthur (1900–82)

Highly inventive and innovative comedian from Liverpool whose work on radio established him as one of Britain's top stars. In BAND WAGGON, he and RICHARD MURDOCH were the first British performers to make radio a particular and distinctive vehicle for comedy, using nonsensical dialogue, quick gags and sharp ad-libbing, in contrast to previous entertainers who had tended to use the microphone as if they were on stage in a theatre.

He coined two immortal catchphrases: 'HELLO PLAYMATES' and 'Before Your Very Eyes', which was used as the title of both his first television series (in 1953) and his autobiography.

Asking the World

Monthly programme on the Home Service, from 1959–61, in which members of a studio audience in, for example, Chester, questioned academics and pundits linked up in, say, New York, Copenhagen, Hilversum and Birmingham – quite an achievement in 1960.

Aspel, Michael (1933–)

Versatile, popular and urbane presenter who started his radio career as an actor in 1954, playing a villain called Captain O'Hagerty in a CHILDREN'S HOUR serial.

In 1955 came the big one – he was cast as James 'Rocky' Mountain of the FBI in another *Children's Hour* serial called COUNTERSPY, and recalls that his most memorable radio moment was the look of disappointment on the faces of some children he met when they realised that *he* was rugged Rocky.

Presenting stints on JUNIOR CHOICE and HOUSE-WIVES' CHOICE led him to TWO-WAY FAMILY FAVOURITES, which he hosted from 1968–70, and later to Capital Radio, where he had his own show from 1974–84. He had a long-running series on LBC (which finished in 1989) and still appears on Radio 2 where, for example, he compered ANNOUNCERS' CHALLENGE, despite now being probably the highest paid presenter and chat-show host in the whole of British television.

Association of Independent Radio Contractors (AIRC)

Trade association for commercial radio stations in Britain, negotiating on their behalf matters like copyright, needletime rates, pay scales, industrial relations and agreements with bodies such as the Football League and Test and County Cricket Board covering the broadcasting of commentaries. It was created by the first ILR companies in 1973.

It makes representations to government on behalf of ILR and claimed a significant input in the Home Office's 1987 Green Paper *Radio: Choices and Opportunities* which paved the way for a less regulated regime. Its marketing arm, the Radio Marketing Bureau, promotes radio as an effective advertising medium and publishes the regular audience research carried out by JICRAR.

At Home and Abroad

Twice-weekly survey of current affairs on the Home Service from 1954–60, with speakers in London, the regions and overseas prognosticating on topical issues.

At Home with The Hardys

Radio 4 comedy series in 1990 which continued in the vein of *Unnatural Acts*, once again featuring Jeremy Hardy and his wife Kit Hollerbach. They co-wrote it with Paul B. Davies and Pete Sinclair (the regular author of Ned Sherrin's opening monologue on LOOSE ENDS).

At School on Our Holidays

Three-part Radio 4 series in 1989 looking at people who use their vacations to learn new skills, such as mountaineering.

At Your Request

One of the many series which SANDY MACPHERSON, 'at the BBC Theatre Organ', had on the Light Programme. This one ran for a long period, 1947–65.

Atlantic 252

Joint venture between Ireland's RTE and Radio Luxembourg which, when it began broadcasting pop and rock from its 500 kilowatt, 800-ft transmitter 25 miles from Dublin in September 1989, was the first legal, national, daytime commercial station in British radio history. Previous efforts had been either illegal (pirates), or local (ILR) or evenings only (Radio Luxembourg).

Claiming that DJs of Radio 1 (its main competition) were excessively chatty, it promised that music would come first and jocks would have to limit their prattle between records to an average of ten seconds a time. It also required them to keep on their toes – literally – having built all the control desks at standing height (36 inches above the ground, the same as a kitchen worktop). Making the presenters do it standing up is intended to make them feel more energetic and project their voices to good effect, just as the best singing can be achieved only by standing. The practice was imported from rock stations in the USA and American presenter CHARLIE WOLF helped to pioneer its use here – first on pirate ship Laser 558, and then as a presenter on Atlantic 252.

Because it is based outside Britain, Atlantic 252 escapes British jurisdiction and has always therefore been unrestricted in the size of its prizes it can offer in competitions. Within three months of its launch it gave away £27,000 over three weeks in a promotion with the *Daily Star*. Such generosity was forbidden under IBA rules, and ILR stations were quick to complain that Atlantic 252 offered unfair competition.

Within a year, the new station, which broadcasts on 252 kHz long wave, was claiming an audience of over one million 15 to 34-year-olds in its main target area – Wales, the Midlands, the North and Scotland – and it started to broadcast round the clock in the summer of 1991.

Australia

Radio 4 marked the Bicentenary in 1988 with this distinguished, 13-hour series written by Mike Walker which traced Australia's growth over the last two centuries (and did not forget its vast span of pre-European history) through interviews with scores of Australians, historical analysis, national songs and sounds and music from the BBC RADIOPHONIC WORKSHOP.

'Ay thang yew!'

The way ARTHUR ASKEY pronounced 'I thank you'. It became one of his catchphrases through years of radio comedy.

The A–Z of Britain

Radio 2 comedy which ran for one series in 1989: stars included June Whitfield, Kenneth Connor and William Franklyn in sketches about Britain past and present.

Bach's '48'

J.S. Bach's 'Well-Tempered Clavier', his 48 preludes and fugues in all the major and minor keys, were played in their entirety on Radio 3 in eight programmes in 1989, by the Hungarian pianist Andras Schiff. They were last heard complete some five years before this.

Back to Africa

FERDINAND DENNIS travelled to Liberia, Sierra Leone, Senegal, the Cameroons, Nigeria and Ghana for this six-part Radio 4 series in 1990 exploring topics ranging from corruption to the failure of democracy.

Back To Square One

(1) Ingenious method used by early radio commentators in which they indicated where on a football or rugby pitch the action was taking place by referring to a numbered section on a diagram printed in *Radio Times*. This enabled listeners to follow the progress of the match from the commentary on the wireless set. (The general phrase 'back to square one', meaning back to the beginning, has often been said to derive from this usage, but the *Oxford English Dictionary* cannot substantiate the claim.)

The idea of the squared plan of the field as an aid to commentators was pioneered by LANCE SIEVEKING, first head of Outside Broadcasts. But it was abolished by his successor SEYMOUR DE LOTBINIÈRE in 1935. He laid down the principles of effective commentating which enabled the practitioner to become the eyes of the listener without reference to numbered squares.

(2) Radio 2 quiz series which began in 1986, chaired by Chris Serle: two teams of celebrities try to uncover the correct origins of puzzling words, phrases, sayings and song titles.

Back to the Delta

Five-part Radio 3 series in 1990 in which Alyn Shipton (who also made THE CHEERFUL LITTLE EARFUL) traced the jazz revival in Britain from the late 1940s to the late 1960s.

Backchat

Sunday afternoon gossip programme on Radio 1 in the 1980s presented by LIZ KERSHAW.

Background to Music

Weekly series on Network Three for enthusiasts thirsting for more knowledge and understanding of music. It ran from 1958–66.

Backward Glances

Four talks by Sir John Gielgud, on Radio 4 in 1990, about some of the colourful personalities with whom his long life has brought him into contact, including the Sitwells, Queen Mary and Ralph Richardson.

Bakelite

Resin-based plastic used for the outer casings of radio sets from the late 1920s onwards. The first alternative to wood, over which it had one unassailable advantage – resistance to woodworm. Named after its inventor, L.H. Baekeland (1863–1944). EKCO was the first British company to use it on a large scale. Now highly fashionable, with the best reconditioned valve and bakelite sets fetching up to about £750 depending on age and condition.

Baker, Richard (1925–)

Although television has been the keel of former Royal Navy officer Richard Baker's career (his was the first voice heard reading the BBC-TV News in 1954, and he continued there for 28 years) his authoritative manner and comforting, dark brown voice has also been much in evidence on radio.

For three years he was an announcer on the Third Programme, for nearly ten years the host of BAKER'S DOZEN, for seventeen years the presenter of START THE WEEK, and he has introduced the PROMS every summer since 1963. Weekly Radio 4 record programmes have also included THESE YOU HAVE LOVED and RICHARD BAKER COMPARES NOTES; on occasion he has presented MAINLY FOR PLEASURE on Radio 3;

and his Sunday morning show on Radio 2, MELODIES FOR YOU, has been running since 1986.

Baker's Dozen
One of Radio 4's rare record programmes, hosted by RICHARD BAKER, which ran from 1978–87.

Baldwin, Peter (1927–)
First chief executive of the new RADIO AUTHORITY. A former officer in the Royal Signals who served in the Berlin Airlift and Korea, he retired with the rank of Major-General in 1979 and joined the IBA as its Deputy Director of Radio, succeeding JOHN THOMPSON as Director of Radio in 1987.

Band Waggon
Influential BBC comedy series – one of the very first sitcoms – which ran from January 1938 to December 1939, making stars of ARTHUR ASKEY and RICHARD MURDOCH.

They dominated the show with routines in which they purported to live in a flat at the top of BROADCASTING HOUSE, with visitors such as Mrs Bagwash and her daughter Nausea, and Lewis the goat. A regular spot was *Chestnut Corner*, creaky old jokes introduced by a whistle. Murdoch: 'I haven't seen your girl for a long time. Has she kept her figure?' Askey: 'Kept it? She's doubled it!'

Bandstand
Showcase of brass band music which originally began in 1942, later transferring to Radio 3, where it was axed in 1988.

Bannister, Miss Minnie
Character on THE GOON SHOW played by SPIKE MILLIGAN. Former can-can dancer at the Windmill Theatre and 'the darling of Roper's Light Horse' in the Naughty Nineties.

Barker, Eric (1912–90)
Whitgift-educated actor, comedian and writer best remembered for his gentle, whimsical, long-running series JUST FANCY.

He made his radio debut in 1933, gaining fame in the 1940 revue *Howdy Folks* in which he created the character of Lord Blockhead. During wartime service in the Royal Navy, he wrote and starred in the Navy's contribution to the comedy series MERRY-GO-ROUND, playing a shy, modest Englishman in charge of tough, surly sailors aboard HMS Waterlogged in Sinking-on-the-Ooze. 'Steady, Barker!' was what he said to himself, in the verbal equivalent of a cold shower, when feeling hot flushes for his lady friend (played by his wife, Pearl Hackney). Those words, epitomising unresolved and understated sexual tension, became one of the best known catchphrases of the war.

Britain's first great comedy partnership of the air. 'Stinker' Murdoch (left) and Arthur Askey in their wise-cracking *Band Waggon*, 1938

In 1948, with the series now split into three separate programmes, Barker continued in *Waterlogged Spa*, which carried on the tradition of Navy larks. This also helped to launch Jon Pertwee, who originally came into contact with the show when he was sent to investigate it as an Admiralty civil servant on suspicion that it was being too rude about the brass. Pertwee joined the cast and made his name as a postman with a country bumpkin accent. *Just Fancy* followed, in 1951. Other series included *Passing Parade*, *Barker's Folly* and *Law and Disorder*.

He used 'Steady, Barker!' as the title of his 1956 autobiography: his other notable catchphrase was 'Oh, I say! I rather care for that!'

Barker, Peter (1933–)
Radio 3's longest serving announcer, who first joined BBC Radio in 1962. Former actor, hired for his voice (soothing, friendly, yet authoritative). Says he has never taken his tie off at the microphone, apart from one occasion when he was in the open air and on a bandstand, simply because that is what he feels happiest in.

Barlow, Dilly (1953–)
Radio 4 announcer from the late 1970s to early 1980s, taking over WOMAN'S HOUR as a holiday relief and later the presenter of ENQUIRE WITHIN.

Barnes, Sir George (1904–60)
Dartmouth-educated, would-be sailor (rejected by the Royal Navy because of poor sight) who became Director of Talks for the BBC and then, in 1946, first Head of the Third Programme. He helped to give the new network its own distinctive identity, with music and speech of an uncompromisingly high tone. In 1948 he was appointed the BBC's Director of the Spoken Word, and in 1950 the first Director of BBC Television.

Barnes People
See PETER BARNES.

Barnes, Peter (1931–)
Playwright renowned for his dramatic monologues written for famous actors and broadcast on Radio 3. One of them, *No End to Dreaming*, specially written for Lord Olivier's 80th birthday, was the actor's first radio appearance in over thirty years (and was to be his last). He played Nathan Yavok, a Jewish American businessman born in a Polish ghetto and now at the end of his life.

The monologues have usually been grouped together in series of seven. They began with *Barnes People* in 1981 and continued with *Barnes People II* in 1984 and *Barnes People III* in 1986. The last collection, *More Barnes People*, started at the end of 1989. Janet Suzman played an old Romany fortune-teller, Alan Rickman a schizoid ventriloquist and Jeremy Irons a gravedigger.

Adaptations have formed the bulk of Barnes' other radio work, all of which has gone out on Radio 3.

Batchelor, Horace (1899–1977)
Football pools tipster who frequently advertised his 'infra-draw' system on Radio Luxembourg in the 1950s, making his home town of Keynsham, near Bristol, a household word by painstakingly spelling it out letter by letter in all his advertisements. He called his home in Bath Road, Keynsham, 'Infra-Grange', after the pools method which made him nationally famous.

Whether it also made him rich, however, is a matter of debate. Obituaries in the Bristol press claimed that it did, and that it was estimated that over 23 years it had also earned £12 million for his punters, who wrote off for details of the scheme at £1 a time. His son John was quoted as saying that his father was a very wealthy man from his pools winnings alone.

However, Radio Luxembourg itself says that as far as it is aware, nobody ever made a fortune from the method which he advertised so intensively. It was claimed in *The Guardian* in 1990 by Nina Webb of Manchester that Batchelor had bought the method from her father, Victor C. Webb, who had invented it in the 1940s, and apparently never paid for it.

A former insurance collector, whose first business venture was making cut-price, no-nicotine Batchelor cigarettes in Bristol's Old Market, Batchelor's first major pools win is recorded as having been in 1948, when he was presented with £11,321 by the old Sherman's Pools on the stage of the Rex Cinema in Bedminster.

Bates, Simon (1948–)
Bright, versatile broadcaster with a dark brown voice. The only broadcaster to have presented programmes on all five BBC radio networks.

On Radio 1, he has hosted the weekday mid-morning show since 1978. On Radio 2 he had the dawn slot in 1976–77. On Radio 3, in 1987, he introduced one of that year's most distinctive Proms – featuring Loose Tubes, a 21-piece jazz band. He chaired both series of THE YEAR IN QUESTION on Radio 4 (where he also worked for some months as a newsreader in 1976) and presented his own digest of the daily papers on Radio 5's MORNING EDITION for the first two months.

Worked as a DJ and announcer in radio and television in the USA, Australia and New Zealand (where he also played a Cockney cab driver in a radio play) before coming to the BBC, where the high-profile morning show which he inherited from TONY BLACKBURN has made him a household name.

Its most celebrated segment – sneered at by the intelligentsia and hugely popular with the audience – is the *Our Tune* spot, a daily sob story in which Bates reads out listeners' accounts of make-ups, break-ups, tender longings and tragic deaths. The background music which accompanies these outpourings is a BBC arrangement of 'The Love Theme' from Franco Zeffirelli's *Romeo and Juliet*, composed by Nino Rota. The spot was created in 1980 by the then producer, Ron Belchier, and attracts about 400 letters a week from listeners keen to share their joy or anguish with millions of strangers.

Bates and producer Jonathan Ruffle went round the world in 78 days in summer 1989, with portable satellite equipment. Each day they sent back a live, 30-minute report on Radio 1 about their travels. They also sent back weekly programmes for the BBC World Service. Although they did not fulfil their aim of going round the world without taking a plane (they had to fly over

17

Saudi Arabia) they nonetheless helped to raise £300,000 for Oxfam.

Baxter, Raymond (1922–)

Spitfire pilot in the Second World War who began broadcasting with BFBS in Cairo and became a commentator who excelled in all things to do with cars and engines – even managing to compete in a Monte Carlo Rally and commentate at the wheel at the same time. His voice has also been heard at several major state events.

BBC

The best known initials in broadcasting stood for British Broadcasting Company from 1922 to the end of 1926, and ever since then for British Broadcasting Corporation.

The company was formed on 18 October 1922, at a meeting of some 200 firms connected with wireless, including all the main manufacturers. Its purpose was to broadcast programmes 'to the reasonable satisfaction of the Postmaster-General', the final arbiter as to what could go on air. J.C.W. REITH was appointed the company's first General Manager (and became the first Director-General in 1927) and the BBC started broadcasting on 14 November 1922, with the 6 p.m. NEWS read by Arthur Burrows. It formally received its first licence to broadcast from the Postmaster-General on 18 January 1923, four months before moving into its first proper home in SAVOY HILL.

Lord Crawford's Committee of 1925 – one of the first of what seems an endless procession of committees on the BBC – approved the general tenor of Reith's approach. It therefore recommended that broadcasting should henceforth be conducted by a public corporation 'acting as trustee for the national interest'.

The BBC thus became the British Broadcasting Corporation as from 1 January 1927, the date its first Royal Charter came into force. The Charter has been regularly renewed and updated. The present one, granted in 1981, expires at the end of 1996.

The responsibilities of the Postmaster-General in his ultimate power over what the BBC could transmit were inherited by the Minister of Posts and Telecommunications, and in 1974 transferred to the Home Secretary.

BBC Big Band

Part of the BBC RADIO ORCHESTRA, embracing saxophones, trumpets, trombones, percussion, bass, guitar and piano. SHEILA TRACY works closely with them and presents their concerts and weekly Radio 2 programme BIG BAND SPECIAL. The band was saved (after a plea from DAVID HATCH) when the orchestra as a whole was axed in 1990. This made good sense: the BBC Big Band is hired regularly by theatrical promoters from Plymouth to Huddersfield, who pay the BBC for

its services and recoup their money from ticket sales. At each of these concerts the band manages to record two episodes of *Big Band Special* – so Radio 2 gets the programmes free.

BBC Choirgirl of the Year

Annual competition running since 1986, launched to recognise the presence of girls in choirs. It is open to girls aged between 11 and 17 inclusive, who have to be members of church or chapel choirs. About 200 such girls enter the contest each year and the judges always include a representative of the Royal School of Church Music.

The BBC gives the winner £500, an appearance on Radio 2 which hosts the competition, £1,000 for her choir and a trophy. Winning choristers in the first five years came from the Midlands (twice), Northern Ireland, Lancaster and Scotland.

BBC Concert Orchestra

Founded in 1952 and celebrated particularly as the backbone of Radio 2's FRIDAY NIGHT IS MUSIC NIGHT and MELODIES FOR YOU, although it is heard on Radio 3 as well. Its repertoire embraces classical, light opera, light music and popular song: it performed the entire Gilbert and Sullivan canon on Radio 2 in 1989. The figure most closely associated with it was Ashley Lawrence, principal conductor from 1970–89.

BBC Dance Orchestra

Formed in 1928 under the leadership of Jack Payne to play the sort of music then at the zenith of its popularity. He and the band enjoyed similar success. Later it came under the baton of HENRY HALL.

BBC Drama Repertory Company

This backbone of radio drama was formed at the outbreak of war on 3 September 1939, when actors and producers were evacuated to Evesham, and later Manchester, in order to keep drama alive 'for the duration'.

In Evesham, venues such as converted stables and bear pits were used to record a wide variety of plays. That range has been a characteristic of the 'Rep' ever since, and helps to explain its appeal for actors. CARLETON HOBBS, MARIUS GORING (who played Hitler in one play, a propaganda piece attacking the Third Reich), MARJORIE WESTBURY and VALENTINE DYALL were early members. The 21st anniversary of the Rep was marked by a production of *Carnival* by COMPTON MACKENZIE as a SATURDAY NIGHT THEATRE play.

In the 1980s, the company changed its title to the BBC Radio Drama Company, a name the BBC felt was more up-to-date. At any one time, it consists of 28 full-time actors and two students. Past members include Timothy

West, Andrew Sachs, Nerys Hughes, Martin Jarvis, Polly James, Richard Griffiths and Gavin Campbell (later of *That's Life*).

Bernard Shaw had in fact urged the creation of such a troupe in 1924 in the pages of RADIO TIMES, when he complained that it was 'absurd' for the BBC to 'persist in asking handsome actresses – and well known pictorial producers – to get up ordinary theatrical performances and allow the public to overhear the dialogue.'

BBC English
Title that came into being in 1988 to embrace all the teaching of English activities broadcast and promoted by the BBC World Service (radio and TV programmes, books and written material), 'with a brief to exploit more energetically the commercial opportunities offered by the growing demand abroad for knowledge of the language', to quote the BBC's Annual Report for 1988.

BBC Essex
Chelmsford-based BBC local radio station which was opened, in 1986, by the Marchesa Maria Marconi, widow of radio's founding father GUGLIELMO MARCONI who made Chelmsford his base (and from which he made Britain's first public radio broadcasts). It is one of a minority of local radio stations to broadcast regular ball-by-ball cricket commentary. All of Essex's Sunday matches are followed ball-by-ball, as well as important cup and championship matches.

BBC External Services
The name which for many years embraced both the round-the-clock English language service and the 36 foreign language services, all based at BUSH HOUSE and broadcasting to the world. It formally changed its name to BBC World Service on 1 September 1988.

BBC for Europe
Trilingual mix of French, German and English broadcasts from the BBC World Service which goes out on medium wave (648 kHz) for audiences all over North-West Europe. It began in 1987 under the name BBC 648. News bulletins and other programmes go out in all three languages, but sometimes the co-operation goes further: for example, Berlin was linked with London for a bilingual discussion the weekend after the historic breaching of the Berlin Wall in 1989.

BBC Gospel Choir of the Year Award
National contest, organised through BBC Local Radio, which has so far been held only twice – because the BBC feels there are not enough gospel choirs of a sufficiently high standard. In 1986 it was won by the Angelical Voice Choir of London, and in 1988 by The Merrybells of Manchester. Both choirs took part in concerts on Radio 2.

BBC Gramophone Library
One of the BBC's unique cultural resources, this now holds 1,250,000 recordings. Some of the earliest date from the birth of the recording industry in the 1890s. It lends 1,000 records a day to departments throughout the Corporation, supplying network, regional and local radio, World Service and television. It has had only four heads since it began in 1931.

BBC Hereford and Worcester
BBC local radio station serving the new fusion which is the County of Herefordshire and Worcestershire, with studios in both cities. It began in February 1989.

BBC Local Radio
Chain of 37 stations in England (Scotland, Wales and Northern Ireland have their own regional radio networks) which was initiated in 1967 with BBC Radio Leicester. It was the culmination of a long campaign headed by FRANK GILLARD, who on a visit to the USA in the 1950s had been persuaded of the value of local radio and brought the vision back with him. The decision as to where the first stations would be was made partly on the basis of the amount of support from local authorities.

The BBC has never completed its network of local radio stations: plans to build one in Dorset were scrapped in 1990 forr financial reasons. Also threatened in the late 1980s was the trio of metropolitan stations GLR, GMR and BBC Radio WM, but the BBC eventually decided to retain all three. The BBC's stations, in contrast to ILR, have traditionally been built around speech. At the end of the 1980s another dimension was added, when some of them began systematically to reflect a multi-cultural audience. Hindi, Urdu and Bengali programmes from the World Service were broadcast for their own Asian audiences by BBC Radio Leicester and BBC Radio WM from 1989 onwards; and later also by BBC CWR, GLR, GMR, and the BBC's stations in Stoke, Derby, Nottingham, Kent, Bedfordshire, Leeds, Sheffield, Merseyside, Lancashire, Cleveland and Newcastle.

BBC Midland Light Orchestra
Changed its name to the BBC MIDLAND RADIO ORCHESTRA in 1975.

BBC Midland Radio Orchestra
Dissolved in 1981, along with the BBC SCOTTISH RADIO ORCHESTRA and BBC NORTHERN RADIO ORCHESTRA, to save costs.

BBC Monitoring
One of the BBC's more interesting areas, given its wartime origins, government funding, and the fact that every day it exchanges information with an American body run by the CIA.

The BBC started monitoring and translating foreign radio broadcasts in 1938, when the Foreign Office asked it to listen to Italy's broadcasts to Arab listeners, questioning the British presence in the Middle East. This was done by members of the Arabic Service, the BBC's first foreign language service, which had been set up in the same year.

Monitoring produced its first Digest of Foreign Broadcasts (which today is called the Summary of World Broadcasts) on 27 August 1939, a few days before the outbreak of the Second World War. Its main item was a report from German radio on a new rationing decree. The service was first based at Evesham (where foreign radio broadcasts were received on wax cylinders, collected several times a day by staff carrying wicker baskets) but by 1943 it had grown so rapidly that there were then 500 monitors. In that year the entire operation moved to a larger home – an eighteenth-century Berkshire mansion, Caversham Park, which had once been used as a boys' school.

Today, about 140 gifted linguists, wearing headphones, work in shifts round the clock to listen to a total of over 600 broadcasts a day from 33 countries in 31 languages. (The government, which funds BBC Monitoring to the tune of £12 million a year, stipulates which countries are listened to.) There are several monitors for the USSR alone, listening not just to broadcasts in Russian but also those in Baltic languages and the Central Asian tongues of Turkmen, Kazakh, Uzbek and Kirghiz – reflecting the recent turbulence of Russia's regions and the importance of outspoken regional radio stations. All transmissions are received on high-powered receiving dishes and antennae at a base three miles north of Caversham.

BBC Monitoring and its American equivalent, the Foreign Broadcast Information Service, carve up the globe between them. The BBC listens to broadcasts from the USSR, Eastern and Western Europe, North Africa, parts of the Middle East and Afghanistan. The FBIS, based in Washington and administered and funded by the CIA, monitors about 100 countries in Central and South America, the Far East, Australasia and the Indian subcontinent. The two bodies co-operate closely and exchange information by satellite. Each day the BBC produces a 100,000-word digest, Summary of World Broadcasts. This is printed at Caversham and sent to a variety of paying customers including libraries, intelligence agencies, academics, embassies, oil companies, and the international and national press. Hot news is sped to newsrooms, including the BBC World Service.

BBC Monitoring claims it has frequently picked up – and revealed to the world – the first word on coups, wars, disasters and other major events. These have included many of the announcements on Baghdad Radio during the Gulf War; the deaths of Soviet leaders Chernenko and Gromyko and Ayatollah Khomeini's call to Moslems in February 1989 to kill Salman Rushdie for his 'blasphemous' novel *The Satanic Verses*.

In 1990, Monitoring acquired a £10 million computer and a new listening room, opened by the Duke of Kent, which replaced the one which had been in continual use since 1943. The revamp was an appropriate piece of modernisation for an operation enjoying a new lease of life, frequently playing a key role in bringing the first news of turmoil and change to a world audience.

How vivid this could be is illustrated in its report on the killing of the Romanian dictator, which included this passage: 'Concluding his reading of tonight's communiqué on the execution of Nicolae and Elena Ceausescu, the Bucharest radio announcer said: "Oh, what wonderful news on this Christmas evening. The Antichrist is dead." The announcement was followed by Christmas carols.'

The BBC is keen to dismiss any notion of links between its own trawl of the airwaves and the government's top-secret listening post, GCHQ, in Cheltenham. That unscrambles military and diplomatic signals – whereas BBC Monitoring (which also now monitors foreign television as well) listens only to those broadcasts in the public domain.

'BBC Monitoring has been Britain's ear to the world for over five decades. Often the only conduit for news, it has provided a unique insight into world events, often picking up the first reports of political upheavals, wars and natural disasters' – John Tusa.

BBC Northern Dance Orchestra
Manchester-based orchestra celebrated for its big band style; renamed the BBC NORTHERN RADIO ORCHESTRA in 1974, and given a more melodic feel, but dissolved seven years later.

BBC Northern Radio Orchestra
Disbanded in 1981 as a cost-cutting measure.

BBC Philharmonic
One of the Corporation's five main orchestras, based in Manchester since its inception.

BBC Radio Bedfordshire
Luton-based BBC local radio station, on the air since 1985, which covers parts of Herts and Bucks as well as its own county. As well as its regular shows for Asian, Afro-Caribbean and (unusually) Irish listeners, it is almost unique in English radio in also broadcasting an Italian programme – covering the activities of the Italian community in Bedford which forms almost 20 per cent of the town's population.

BBC Radio Bristol
BBC's local radio station for Avon and Somerset, based in Bristol. It has launched some well-known broadcasters:

Michael Buerk began his career here and was the first voice on the air on the opening day in 1970. Kate Adie reported on the Bristol Flower Show on the same day.

Somerset Sound is an opt-out part of the station which produces five hours a day of separate programmes from Taunton and Yeovil.

BBC Radio Cambridgeshire
Cambridge-based local radio station which, as a tribute to the role PYE has played both in the city and in radio, uses the company's famous 'Rising Sun' motif from the 1930s as its own logo.

In 1990 it hired its own science producer to cover the work of the city's 25 major research institutes – including the Royal Observatory, British Antarctic Survey and International Whaling Commission – as well as all its high tech companies and, of course, the University. He was the only specialist science producer in local radio.

As befits one of Britain's biggest and busiest concentration of cyclists (during term time), the station, which started in 1982, also has its very own Radio Bike.

Listeners to the station in the northern part of the county have been able, since 1990, to hear a separate service for nineteen hours a week called BBC Radio Peterborough, which features a twice-weekly programme made by and for that city's Asian community.

It was to BBC Radio Cambridgeshire that John Major (whose Huntingdon constituency is in the station's area) gave his first broadcast interview on the night Tory MPs elected him to succeed Mrs Thatcher in 1990.

BBC Radio Cleveland
BBC local radio station in Middlesbrough, which started in January 1971. It covers County Cleveland, the southern half of County Durham and the northern fringes of Yorkshire. Teesside's Ken Blakeson, author of the award-winning Radio 4 play *Excess Baggage*, presented a children's programme on the station in the 1970s. Another presenter from that era was Derek Hobson, who went on to host the ITV talent show *New Faces*.

BBC Radio Clwyd
See BBC RADIO WALES.

BBC Radio Collection
Classic BBC Radio shows released on audio cassettes at monthly intervals from autumn 1988 onwards. Part of BBC Enterprises, this was the BBC's first major attempt to make money in the marketplace to be ploughed back into radio programmes (previously, Enterprises had funded only television).

The initial batch of releases covered fifty years of wireless nostalgia and included HANCOCK, ITMA, THE GOON SHOW, CHILDREN'S HOUR and ROUND THE HORNE (which has proved to be the bestselling title).

Other popular titles have included LAKE WOBEGON DAYS, UNCLE MORT and the readings by ALAN BENNETT of *The Wind in the Willows*. More than 150 titles have now been released and over two million sets of cassettes have been sold.

In 1990 the operation launched another section, a series of cassettes called the BBC Audio Collection, for tapes derived both from television (e.g. *Oranges Are Not The Only Fruit*) and even non-BBC programmes (the first of which was *Poetry in Motion*, the Channel 4 series in which Alan Bennett read the work of six English poets).

BBC Radio Cornwall
One of the few British radio stations to have its own boat – on standby to cover nautical stories – and the only one to broadcast in the country's most obscure language, Cornish.

On the air since January 1983, the Truro-based station has found itself reporting on the decline of tin mining and the accidental dumping of tons of aluminium sulphate in the Camelford water supply.

The Cornish slot is a 15-minute programme on Sunday mornings, *Kroder Kroghen*. When translated from Cornish this means a bag full of useful odds and ends – an apt description of the programme, which is a mixture of English and Cornish speech and jointly produced with the Cornish Language Board.

BBC Radio Cumbria
Began in 1973 as BBC Radio Carlisle, where it is based, and adopting its present name in 1982 when it expanded to cover the whole of Cumbria. In that year also it launched BBC Radio Furness, its 'opt-out' station in the south which produces its own separate programmes at breakfast time.

The station is best known for its 'Lamb Bank' scheme, of key importance in a region whose economy is dominated by sheep farming. Ewes may die in childbirth, leaving orphan lambs which need to be fed and reared: lambs may die when young, leaving in-milk ewes. The Lamb Bank service, operating since 1973, marries the two. Farmers leave details in a tray at the station and twice a day a programme assistant reads out the details – giving the number of sheep involved, the breed (usually Suffolk Cross, sometimes Herdwick), the name of the farmer and his village or telephone number. This takes place throughout the lambing season of January to May and every spring some 4,000 lambs are fixed up with new mothers in this way. Buyers and sellers make their own financial arrangements.

BBC Radio CWR
Coventry-based local radio station covering Coventry and Warwickshire whose opening in January 1990

completed the BBC's chain of local radio stations in the Midlands. It was one of the first stations to go out on FM only. Later that year it started to broadcast THE ARCHERS simultaneously with Radio 4 – a local radio first – for the benefit of its own rural audience, and also launched its own soap opera, *Hillcrest*, about a health centre.

BBC Radio Cymru

Welsh-language service for the Principality, on the air since 1979 (although the BBC's first programmes in Welsh went out in March 1923). It goes out, on FM, seven days a week, for most of each day, though there are frequent breaks from the language when it goes over to Radio 4. There are magazine shows, interviews, discussions and sports coverage – all in Welsh – plus some music, particularly choral. Programmes are made mainly in Cardiff, with some at Bangor and Swansea.

Among its programmes has been *Nac yn Bagan Chwaith*, a thirteen-part series on the religious life of Wales 400 years after the Bible was first published in Welsh.

BBC Radio Derby

BBC local radio station based in Derby which jumped the gun. Officially it went on the air in April 1971, but two months before that it opened prematurely to cover the collapse of Rolls-Royce, the 'life blood of Derby'. The station broadcasts to Derby, Derbyshire and East Staffordshire and also runs an Asian programme, *Aaj-kal*.

BBC Radio Devon

Exeter-based station covering one of England's largest counties (and needing eight separate transmitters to do so), this began in the same week as its Cornish partner in January 1983. One of its more unusual, but vital, services is regular announcements of the firing times from the Army gunneries on Dartmoor.

One of the station's graduates is the BBC's man in Berlin, Ben Bradshaw, a former reporter in the newsroom.

BBC Radio Dorset

The station that never was. This would have completed the BBC's chain of local radio stations in England, had it been built as planned in 1991. But as part of a package of measures intended to save £3 million, the BBC announced in 1990 that the station was cancelled.

BBC Radio Durham

The only BBC radio station ever to have closed down (until Gwent in 1991, but that was an 'opt-out' and not a fully fledged station like this). It began broadcasting in July 1968 as one of the first eight local radio stations. Four years later, when the BBC was stopped from

having more than twenty local stations by the Heath government, it responded by choosing to close down Durham and open another on the other side of the Pennines, in Carlisle. See BBC RADIO CUMBRIA.

BBC Radio Foyle

'Opt-out' station from BBC Radio Ulster, based in Londonderry. Ever since its creation in 1979, it has been broadcasting to an audience split by the sectarian divide as well as by the river which provides its name.

Even the name of the city has provoked heated debate. Roman Catholics call it 'Derry', Protestants insist on 'Londonderry'. The station's Gerry Anderson, evidently a born diplomat, circumvented the problem by coining the name 'Derry-stroke-Londonderry', which he then shortened to 'Stroke City', a nickname he says seems to have worked. His daily show now goes out over the whole of BBC Radio Ulster.

In 1990 he earned the distinction of topping a BBC audience survey in two categories: most popular broadcaster *and* the broadcaster most people wanted to see removed. He made his national debut with five shows on Radio 2 in 1990.

Listeners to the station have been particularly hard hit by the Home Secretary's ban on broadcast interviews with certain specified Irish groups, dating from October 1988. This has meant that the voices of Sinn Fein members and supporters have not been allowed on the air since then. Sinn Fein had five seats on the city council during 1989, and the ban meant that Foyle was legally forbidden to broadcast the voices of those councillors even on local issues like the absence of post offices on council estates.

The station also houses the Irish Language Unit, and normally produces about three hours a week of programmes in the language (similar to Gaelic) which go out across the whole province on BBC Radio Ulster.

BBC Radio Furness

Part of BBC Radio Cumbria but based in Barrow-in-Furness which, with its heavy industry, is a strikingly different community from those of the Lake District: it thus opts out for about 90 minutes at breakfast when it broadcasts its own programmes for its own local audience.

BBC Radio Gloucestershire

BBC local radio station based in Gloucester, which started in October 1988. In 1990, in association with *The Gloucestershire Echo* newspaper, it launched an annual series of environmental awards. BRIAN REDHEAD presented the first year's trophies.

BBC Radio Guernsey

One of the BBC's local radio stations in the Channel Islands. Like its partner, BBC Radio Jersey, it began in March 1981. It covers the Bailiwick of Guernsey (Guernsey, Alderney and Sark) from its base in St Peter Port and broadcasts the same local radio mix of music and speech familiar on the mainland, and live coverage of the States of Guernsey parliament. It is on the air from 7 a.m. to 6 p.m., though six of those eleven hours are shared with BBC Radio Jersey. All 77 hours a week are in English apart from five minutes – devoted to Guernsey French, a particular dialect of the language which some wish to preserve.

BBC Radio Gwent
Formerly an 'opt-out' station within BBC Radio Wales, but closed in March 1991 to cut costs.

BBC Radio Humberside
Hull-based BBC local radio station serving a county in which 80 per cent of Britain's caravans and cucumbers originate. It went on the air in 1971 – adopting the 'Humberside' title three years before the uneasy creation of the county which shares its name. The station feels that, along with the Humber Bridge, it is one of the few real links between North and South Humberside, which otherwise have little in common. There are district offices in Grimsby, Scunthorpe, Bridlington and Goole.

Unusually for local radio, the station has been particularly active in drama. Thanks to significant funds from Humberside County Council, it has mounted many radio versions of local plays featuring professional companies such as Hull Truck. It has also been a regular broadcaster of locally written short stories.

BBC Radio Jersey
BBC local radio station in St Helier covering the island of Jersey. Like its Channel Islands partner BBC Radio Guernsey it began in March 1981; is on the air from 7 a.m. to 6 p.m. with six of the eleven hours in common; and broadcasts a familiar blend of music and speech with live coverage of its own assembly, the States of Jersey.

The station broadcasts twenty minutes a week in Portuguese for the thousands of hotel and restaurant workers on the island: some of it is local news, translated in the studio, and some is provided by the Portuguese Service in BUSH HOUSE. There is also five minutes a week in Jersey French, a local dialect.

Jersey and Guernsey are probably the most intensively listened-to local radio stations anywhere in the United Kingdom, partly because there is no ILR to provide local competition. Not for much longer, however: an ILR station is due to start on the Channel Islands early in 1992.

BBC Radio Kent
Chatham-based BBC local radio station. It began in 1970 as BBC Radio Medway, but in 1984 was given the expanded job of broadcasting to an area from the

English Channel to the Thames. It has made community participation a strong feature, as a result of which 150 village volunteers have become regular broadcasters.

BBC Radio Lancashire
Began in 1971 as BBC Radio Blackburn, broadcasting to the eastern side of the county. It changed its name and started covering the whole county in 1981, though the headquarters are still in Blackburn.

Howard Stableford of *Tomorrow's World* was once a programme assistant on the station and still has a family connection: his sister, Julie Webster, deputy head of a Preston primary school, presents the station's Sunday-morning show *Sunday Supplement*. The station also gave folk singer and comedian Mike Harding his broadcasting debut.

BBC Radio Leeds
BBC local radio station based in Leeds, which began in June 1968. Television newsreader Philip Hayton was once a journalist in the newsroom here.

BBC Radio Leicester
First local radio station in Britain, this went on the air on 8 November 1967, and has continued to be at the forefront of change.

In 1989, it was one of the BBC's first two local radio stations (BBC Radio WM was the other) to take 'mother tongue' programmes direct from the BBC World Service and put them out on its own airwaves for its own large Asian audiences. It began regular news bulletins in Hindi and Urdu and also its first regular programme in Gujerati.

The station has helped to launch several big names. David Icke, sports presenter and once a leading Green, started his broadcasting career on the station, as did Radio 1's ADRIAN JUSTE. BBC Radio's boxing correspondent Ian Darke and presenter Debbie Thrower were both news producers on the station, while Maggie Philbin used to be a reporter on its *Good Morning Leicester* programme.

BBC Radio Lincolnshire
Ten years old in 1990, this celebrated its birthday by handing out 10,000 iced cakes – made by a baker in Market Rasen – to listeners. Based in Lincoln, it estimates it has one of the three biggest areas to cover of any BBC local radio station, vying with Cumbria and Devon. Among its graduates is John Inverdale, the station's breakfast presenter before going to London, where he now anchors SPORT ON FIVE.

BBC Radio London
The BBC's local radio station for the capital, launched in 1970. It was relaunched as GLR in October 1988.

One of its best known and most influential programmes has been *Black Londoners*, devised by Ray

Cruickshank (then a community relations officer in Hammersmith) in 1974 and presented for the first ten years by Alex Pascall. It has helped to nurture a number of broadcasters of Afro-Caribbean extraction, including Juliet Alexander, Syd Burke and Mike Phillips, and was one of the first television or radio shows in Britain to offer regular coverage of black issues. It is still running today, under a slightly amended title of *Black London*, on Wednesday evenings.

BBC Radio Manchester
The BBC's local radio station for Manchester began in 1970, but was relaunched (as GMR) in 1988, at the same time as the two other big metropolitan stations BBC Radio London and BBC Radio WM.

BBC Radio Merseyside
Britain's third local radio station, on the air since November 1967. JANICE LONG began her broadcasting career here.

Eric Hardy, who every Tuesday evening presents a 25-minute programme about rural life, *The Countryside*, is now in his 80s and one of the country's oldest regular broadcasters. During the Second World War, in North Africa, he trained pigeons to fly with messages tied to their legs. He founded the Jerusalem Naturalists' Club in 1945 and has been secretary of the Merseyside Naturalists Association since 1938.

BBC Radio nan Gaidheal
Gaelic-language service in Scotland launched by the BBC in 1984 (although the BBC's first broadcast in Gaelic was in 1923, from Aberdeen). It transmits on FM for about thirty hours a week, all of which can be heard in the Hebrides, Orkneys and far North-West, and 75 per cent of which is available in the rest of the Highlands. Gaels in other parts of Scotland are able to hear about six hours a week.

Most of the output, which ranges from news and light entertainment to poetry and pop, is from Stornaway and Inverness, with some originating in Glasgow. There is also a studio at Portree on the Isle of Skye. (The name is pronounced 'Radio nan Gayle'.)

BBC Radio Newcastle
Believed to be the only pink radio station in the world – not a reference to the BBC's supposed political leanings, but the colour of the hi-tech building in which it is housed. Since 1987 it has occupied the BBC's regional headquarters in Fenham, Newcastle upon Tyne, known locally as 'The Pink Palace' on account of its pastel exterior.

The station went on the air in January 1971 and covers an area which includes Northumberland, Tyne and Wear and much of Co. Durham.

BBC Radio Norfolk
One of the first BBC local radio stations to cover a county, not a city or town, this was launched in 1980 with headquarters in Norwich. It was also the first to broadcast in stereo. Among the original broadcasters were David Clayton and Neil Walker, presenters of THE LOCAL NETWORK.

BBC Radio Northampton
BBC local radio station based in Northampton and covering the whole of its county. On the air since 1982, it sponsors the Northamptonshire County Youth Orchestra and awards two music scholarships every year to outstanding young musicians.

BBC Radio Nottingham
The station that started the first radio PHONE-IN programme on the British mainland, in 1968, and thus launched something we all now take for granted – putting listeners on the air. The station, which began in January of that year, still runs a daily phone-in which is sometimes a free-for-all and sometimes an encounter with experts.

SIMON MAYO, a graduate of Nottingham University, joined the station and was a presenter on it before going to Radio 1.

BBC Radio Orchestra
What was thought by many to be an indelible part of Radio 2, playing the music for STRING SOUND, *Songs From The Shows*, NIGHTRIDE and much more, frequently heard in concerts hosted by DAVID JACOBS and STEVE RACE and chosen to play at a BBC gala banquet in 1988 before Prince Edward, was killed off in 1990 to make an annual saving of £1 million.

This followed the Phillips Report on cost-cutting as a way of paying existing BBC staff more and thereby retaining talent. The 17-strong BBC BIG BAND, the brass section with its own conductor in Barry Forgie, was however saved. The orchestra's abolition reduced the total number of musicians employed in the BBC orchestras by 39, to 411.

The orchestra was formed in October 1964 from an amalgamation of the BBC REVUE ORCHESTRA and the BBC VARIETY ORCHESTRA. Their conductors, Malcolm Lockyer and Paul Fenoulhet, became joint musical directors. After their deaths (in 1976 and 1979 respectively) the orchestra was guided by no permanent baton until 1989, when Iain Sutherland was appointed principal conductor. The Revue and Variety Orchestras each had 28 players before their fusion and the Radio Orchestra thus became a body of 56 players, often augmented by horns and other musicians.

Its hallmarks were versatility through the whole range of popular music (shows, big band, light classics, adaptations of popular songs) and the presence within it of a number of fine jazz musicians. It gave its first public concert (under the baton of Robert Farnon, one of many top musical directors to have worked with the orchestra) in 1971 and its first public concert outside London in 1987.

BBC Radio Oxford

Oxford-based BBC local radio station, on the air since 1970. It sponsors the Oxford Music Festival and the Oxford Young Musicians' Platform. LIBBY PURVES, and Radio 5's breakfast host Jon Briggs, are among the broadcasters the station has helped to train.

BBC Radio Scotland

National network for listeners in Scotland, its output a mixture of speech, music, religion and education. Begins each weekday with *Good Morning Scotland*, the tartan equivalent of *Today*, and goes on to feature a range of programmes examining Scottish issues and sport. It gives regular weather reports for the country, as well as drive-time travel news. Its three main centres are Glasgow, Edinburgh and Aberdeen.

The network has four community stations on the peripheries: BBC Shetland at Lerwick; BBC Orkney at Kirkwall; BBC Solway in Dumfries and BBC Tweed in Selkirk. Intended to give people on the edges of the country a greater voice, they broadcast for their own areas for up to 90 minutes every weekday, contributing to the network as appropriate. BBC Highland, in Inverness, is another area station which 'opts out' with its own programmes for the Highlands as well as contributing to BBC Radio Scotland.

BBC Radio Sheffield

Britain's second oldest local radio station, which began in November 1967, only days after BBC Radio Leicester. It prides itself on both the quality of its journalism, pointing to its coverage of the miners' strike and the Hillsborough tragedy, and on its encouragement of creative writing: two of its presenters created Radio 4's comedy series THE BLACKBURN FILES and a third, Rony Robinson, is a novelist and playwright. In the late 1980s the station started a hypothermia helpline which proved sufficiently successful for Sheffield City Council to take over the project.

Among the station's original quartet of producers when it started was MICHAEL GREEN, later Controller of Radio 4.

BBC Radio Show

Nine-day extravaganza held at Earl's Court in autumn 1988, the first RADIO SHOW for 22 years, to celebrate the 21st birthdays of Radios 1, 2, 3 and 4 and BBC Local Radio. About 93,000 people visited it. More than 100 shows (including Sue Lawley interviewing TERRY WOGAN for DESERT ISLAND DISCS) were broadcast from the gala, whose central feature was a *son et lumière* exhibition called *The Story of Radio*, an entertaining trip from MARCONI to RDS.

BBC Radio Shropshire

BBC local radio station based in the county town of Shrewsbury, on the air since April 1985. It nurtured SYBIL RUSCOE, one of the journalists in the newsroom until she left to find fame and fortune on Radio 1, and Sheila McLennon, who hosted the breakfast show and now co-presents BBC1's *Prime Time*.

BBC Radio Solent

Southampton-based BBC local radio station, covering Hampshire, the Isle of Wight, West Sussex, East Dorset and South Wiltshire. On the air since 1970. Debbie Thrower used to be a reporter here.

BBC Radio Stoke

The first local radio station in Britain to be run by a woman (SANDRA CHALMERS, in 1976), this covers North Staffordshire and South Cheshire. It is based in Stoke-on-Trent and began in 1968. BRUNO BROOKES started as a teaboy here, eventually getting a show of his own before moving to Radio 1.

BBC Radio Suffolk

BBC local radio station which, when it started in April 1990, was one of the first BBC radio stations to go out on FM only. Based in Ipswich, its output, like that of most BBC local stations, is speech-based, interspersed with middle of the road music.

BBC Radio Surrey and Berkshire

As part of a series of measures to save £3 million, the BBC announced in 1990 that instead of being a separate station as originally intended, this would now be set up as two news centres in Guildford and Reading, and operate as opt-out services from BBC Radio Sussex and BBC Radio Oxford for 37 hours a week each.

BBC Radio Sussex

BBC local radio station which, when it went on the air in 1968 (two months early, to cover snowstorms) was called BBC Radio Brighton. Although its headquarters continue to be in Brighton (next door to the Pavilion) it changed its name in 1983, following an expansion of its brief to cover the whole county.

It was believed to be Britain's first radio station to give up-to-date bulletins on air pollution, when, in 1990, it started broadcasting daily readings of the county's ozone levels. Also that year it began its first weekly programme for Asian listeners, *Rang Tarang* (Hindi for colour and joy).

Famous ex-employees include Kate Adie and Desmond Lynam.

BBC Radio Ulster

Regional service for the whole of Northern Ireland, on the air since January 1975 (although broadcasting in the province began in the 1920s). Speech-based, it is strong on news and current affairs but also embraces music, sport and religion. It takes Radio 2 at night. It contributes a regular flow of programmes to Radio 4, particularly drama.

The network helped to launch both GLORIA HUNNIFORD, a reporter on its *Good Morning Ulster* programme at the end of the 1960s, and her daughter, EUROMIX host Caron Keating.

BBC Radio Foyle is its 'opt-out' station for Londonderry. The popularity of Foyle's best-known presenter, Gerry Anderson, led to his show being taken up by the network as a whole and he is now heard throughout the province.

BBC Radio Wales

Similar in output to Radio 2 – mostly music, with some discussion and talk programmes – this began in 1978 as the BBC's English-language network for the Principality. It goes out on medium wave and about 95 per cent of the output comes from Cardiff, though it goes over to Radio 2 at night.

In North Wales, BBC Radio Clwyd, on the air since October 1981, is an opt-out station providing thirteen hours a week of local programmes for listeners in the Mold area. The same service used to be provided for listeners in South-East Wales by BBC Radio Gwent, which began in April 1983, but this was shut down in March 1991 as part of a major cost-cutting exercise.

BBC Radio WM

BBC local radio station for the West Midlands, run from the Corporation's Midlands headquarters at Pebble Mill in Birmingham. It began as Radio Birmingham in 1970, adopting its present name ten years later. In 1988 the station was told, along with the two other metropolitan stations GLR and GMR, to increase its audience or face closure. The threat was formally lifted in 1990.

Nick Owen was once sports editor on WM, but the station also has a more embarrassing connection with sport. In autumn 1989, the station's sports reporters were banned from Wolverhampton Wanderers Football Club for several weeks after breakfast presenter Tony Butler, one of WM's biggest names, made crude racist jibes about black Wolves player Shane Westley, referring to a 'cage' and 'bananas' and 'swinging from the crossbar'. By contrast, WM also that autumn became one of the BBC's first two local radio stations (the other being BBC Radio Leicester) to put out some of the World Service's Asian-language programmes for its own listeners. It transmits the news in Urdu five nights a week and, in 1990, extended the Asian service with a Wednesday night programme in Bengali.

BBC Radio York

York-based BBC local radio station covering the whole of North Yorkshire, a region with many sheep and few people. It began in 1983. Bill Hanrahan of television's *Watchdog* was once a journalist here.

Unusually, it has a direct link with the main BR station in the city and the information shown on monitors on the platforms at York station comes up on video screens in the studios at the same time – enabling Radio York to operate a bang up-to-date rail information service.

BBC Radiophonic Workshop

This department of the BBC was created in March 1958 to meet the needs of radio drama and some pioneering playwrights. Among them were SAMUEL BECKETT, whose first radio play *All That Fall* had been broadcast the previous year, as had *The Disagreeable Oyster* by GILES COOPER. Both plays had suggested the desirability of a unit dedicated to the production of a wide variety of sound effects to stimulate the listener's imagination.

BBC Revue Orchestra

Orchestra consisting of 28 musicians, which played in a host of music and variety shows like TAKE IT FROM HERE. Similar to the BBC VARIETY ORCHESTRA: the two were amalgamated in 1964 to form the BBC RADIO ORCHESTRA.

BBC Scottish Radio Orchestra

One of the three BBC regional radio orchestras axed in 1981 in one of the Corporation's periodic financial purges.

BBC Scottish Symphony Orchestra

Founded in 1935 by Ian Whyte, then musical director of BBC Scotland, who was its chief conductor until his death in 1960. In tribute to him the Ian Whyte Award is given every three years to a composer – a £1,000 commission which is broadcast on BBC Radio and given four performances by the Royal Scottish Orchestra.

BBC Scottish Variety Orchestra

Became the BBC SCOTTISH RADIO ORCHESTRA in the 1970s.

BBC Singers

Formed in 1924 as the Wireless Singers, this assembly of 28 men and women is one of the oldest established bodies within the Corporation and also Britain's only full-time professional chamber choir.

It performs regularly on both Radio 3 and Radio 4, but is now heard only once a week on the DAILY SERVICE following a decision by a former head of religious broadcasting, the Rev. David Winter, that the Singers' sound was too clinical for worship.

The Singers also appear regularly at international festivals and in 1991, for instance, are making their first visits to the USSR, Spain and Finland.

BBC Somerset Sound
See BBC RADIO BRISTOL.

BBC Sound Archives
Repository of over 500,000 recordings, kept at BROAD-CASTING HOUSE. The earliest, such as the squeaky voice of Florence Nightingale in 1890 originally recorded on a wax cylinder, were made before broadcasting was invented. The vast bulk, however, are of BBC programmes of all types, beginning with an extract from the opening of a British Empire Exhibition in 1924. About 3,000 hours of programmes a year are added to the collection, though this is only a tiny fraction of what goes out.

The Sound Archives has kept all Radio 4's SIX O'CLOCK NEWS bulletins since 1982 and all its 8 a.m. news bulletins since 1984.

It supplies hundreds of recordings a week for use throughout the BBC. It has also been used to compile most of the cassettes of gems from the past which form the BBC RADIO COLLECTION. Despite its meticulously indexed vastness, however, it does have gaps: there is no voice of GEORGE ORWELL, nothing at all from RIDERS OF THE RANGE, nothing from the first year of THE ARCHERS, only one episode of JENNINGS and only one of NORMAN AND HENRY BONES.

BBC Symphony Orchestra
Its first concert, in October 1930, was conducted by Sir Adrian Boult (1889–1983) who was its chief conductor until 1950. Evacuated to Bedford during the Second World War. Today, it broadcasts only on Radio 3 but is often heard on tour and abroad, and at the PROMS.

BBC Theatre Orchestra
Forerunner of the BBC CONCERT ORCHESTRA.

BBC Topical Tapes
The part of the BBC World Service in which programmes in English are made for local use in foreign countries and then airmailed to them. In 1989, 260 tapes were despatched every week to a total of over fifty countries.

The section also has another function, making programmes which reach out a hand of comfort to British people abroad during emergencies. It made *Calling the Falklands*, broadcast to the South Atlantic during the war of 1982, and the daily *Gulf Link* for those trapped in Iraq and Kuwait in 1990. Both these programmes carried messages from people in the UK for their relatives or friends trapped in the emergency zones, and the BBC stressed that both were to give not just information but also support.

Gulf Link received a hundred calls a day when its lines first opened and people used it to remember birthdays, anniversaries and even just to say that someone was looking after the garden. It was broadcast continuously while hostages were held in Iraq and came off the air only after they were all freed, having broadcast some 6,000 messages which included one proposal of marriage (accepted).

BBC Transcription
Part of the BBC World Service, which sells BBC Radio programmes to stations in over 100 countries for broadcasting on their own frequencies.

It is the world's biggest distributor of radio programmes – like TOP OF THE POPS, nothing to do with the BBC1 programme but a showcase of British chart hits, presented since 1964 by BRIAN MATTHEW, sent to forty countries from Abu Dhabi to Zimbabwe. This, like many of the programmes it sells to the radio stations of foreign countries, is produced by the World Service. BBC Transcription (which used to have the word 'Service' at the end of its name), issues 350 hours of programmes annually ranging from pop to PROMS, plus serials, plays and light entertainment shows such as MY MUSIC. It maintains a permanent catalogue of 7,000 hours of programmes.

BBC Variety Orchestra
Orchestra with 28 players which performed an identical function to that of the BBC REVUE ORCHESTRA, with which it was fused in 1964 to form the BBC RADIO ORCHESTRA.

BBC Welsh Symphony Orchestra
One of the BBC's five house orchestras, and the only symphony orchestra in Wales. It now broadcasts only on Radio 3.

BBC West of England Light Orchestra
Long defunct band which made the music for long defunct Light Programme shows like OLD WINE IN NEW BOTTLES. In 1960 it was renamed the BBC WEST OF ENGLAND PLAYERS.

BBC West of England Players
Regional radio orchestra disbanded in 1966.

BBC Wiltshire Sound
BBC local radio station based in Swindon, with studios also in Trowbridge and Salisbury, which was launched in April 1989.

BBC World Service
The official name, since September 1988, for the entire output of BUSH HOUSE, i.e. the 24-hour World Service

Some of the most stirring broadcasts in history were the calls to his fellow countrymen by General de Gaulle, on the French Service of the BBC World Service. The first, on 18 June 1940, was in the wake of the sorrowful fall of France: the last, on 6 June 1944, was made at Bush House in the euphoria of D-Day

in English (which claims an audience of about 25 million regular listeners, regular being defined as listening at least once a week) plus all the 35 foreign language services (which between them account for another 95 million listeners). This estimated global audience of 120 million fits in neatly with the Foreign Office's grant of about £120 million a year, enabling the BBC to make the vivid claim that its huge worldwide operation costs a mere £1 per year per listener.

Prior to September 1988, Bush House's output was officially called the BBC External Services, and the term 'World Service' referred only to the familiar English-language service, carrier of programmes like

OUTLOOK and MERIDIAN. Unlike the rest of the BBC, the World Service is financed direct by the government. There is one other measure of State control: the Foreign Office stipulates which languages are broadcast and the number of hours devoted to each one. Beyond this, Bush House jealously guards the editorial independence of its programmes, and in recent years the upheavals in the USSR, Eastern Europe and China have all borne witness to the high respect which they command.

The BBC's 1990 estimate of its global audience, 120 million, represents a 60 per cent increase over the 1980 estimate of 75 million (and is 30 per cent ahead of its closest challenger, Voice of America). The sharp rise over ten years seems to suggest that the opening up of the USSR and Eastern Europe has sharpened, rather than diminished, the appetite for BBC services, which have an enviable track record of truthfulness, authority and reliability and amount to one of Britain's most valued exports. (Students in Tiananmen Square, and prime ministers behind what used to be called the Iron Curtain, have alike paid public tribute to the World Service, and in 1988 and 1990 it was nominated for the Nobel Peace Prize.)

In addition, the BBC has derived great benefit from the opening of its powerful new transmitters – resulting in much clearer reception, which has boosted audiences – and from the ending of jamming in the wake of glasnost.

The 120 million estimate, however, almost certainly falls short of the real total. It does not take into account audiences in several Asian countries (most importantly China) or the people who listen to local rebroadcasts – 500 stations in 60 countries, from Poland to Peru, incorporate World Service programmes into their own schedules either simultaneously or after they have already gone out from London on short wave.

In Britain, about 1.5 million were estimated to be regular World Service listeners even before the birth of Radio 5, listening on either 648 medium wave in the South-East or Radio 4 long wave in the small hours.

Each language service, e.g. ARABIC SERVICE, RUSSIAN SERVICE, has its own entry. For programmes made for Britons abroad in times of crisis, see BBC TOPICAL TAPES. See also BBC MONITORING, BBC TRANSCRIPTION, PHONE-INS.

'World Service programmes are designed to give a broad picture of Britain's life and thought'– official brochure.

'It's marvellously relaxing to listen to people telling me things I don't have to worry about' – Brian Mulroney, Canadian Prime Minister (who found it so relaxing he admitted falling asleep while listening).

'I read the papers when Margaret Thatcher was going to cut the BBC World Service down. That would be the greatest disservice to peace, love and understanding. From India to Capetown to everywhere it's very important and people appreciate it all over and not just English people living abroad or whites living in Australia but all the races on earth listen to that. Everybody's listening' – John Lennon, interviewed on Radio 1 in 1980.

'It must be the single most prestigious foreign policy asset we have left, so naturally it is kept short of funds' – Michael White in *The Listener*, 1989.

BBC Written Archives Centre

One of Britain's greatest treasure troves, this contains many millions of files, scripts, letters, artists' contracts, news bulletins, memorandums, publications and Press articles logging the BBC's programmes, policies and activities from the 1920s to the present day (though material after 1962 is sadly withheld from public view).

Thousands of the best-known people in Britain have at least part of their lives enshrined here: there are 100,000

files alone on the entertainers, writers, speakers and other contributors engaged by the BBC since its earliest days. The repository was established in 1970 and attracts a regular flow of researchers and historians to its premises, a short step from the BBC MONITORING building in a leafy road in Caversham, near Reading.

Be My Guest

BRIAN MATTHEW hosted this show, which began on the Light Programme in 1966 and ceased on Radio 2 in 1983.

Beachcomber . . . By the Way

Comedy series on Radio 2 in 1989 in which Richard Ingrams (as Beachcomber), helped by John Wells (Prodnose), Patricia Routledge and John Sessions brought to life the comic inventions of J.B. Morton's 'By The Way' column which appeared in the *Daily Express* for forty years. These included Mr Justice Cocklecarrot, Captain de Courcy Foulenough, the brilliant inventor Dr Strabismus of Utrecht and the inmates of Narkover School. It returned in July 1991.

Beacon Radio

ILR station on the air since 1976 which covers one of the largest of all ILR territories, from Birmingham to the Welsh borders and Staffs to Worcs. It split its frequencies to launch WABC, an easy listening service on medium wave, in 1989. The station's headquarters are in Wolverhampton and Shrewsbury and it derives its name from the presence within its area of four of the historic beacons (The Wrekin, Barr Beacon, Sedley Beacon and Kinver Beacon) once used for spreading news of national emergencies such as the Spanish Armada.

'Beau Chant' and Virtuosity

Six-part Radio 3 series in 1989 featuring the sonatas of Jean-Marie Leclair (1697–1764) which were imbued with both Italian and French influences.

A Beat In Time

Are conductors necessary? When did people first start beating time? These and plenty more questions from the world of the baton were explored in this six-part Radio 3 series in 1990 written and presented by Brian Wright, himself a choral conductor as well as a regular presenter of MAINLY FOR PLEASURE.

Beat the Record

Weekend Radio 2 show, originating on South African radio, in which listeners can win up to £200 in cash by ringing up and identifying instrumental versions of certain tunes. Don Davis bought the rights to broadcast the format in Britain and became its first presenter in 1972. After ten years he handed over to KEITH FORDYCE, who is still doing it.

Beaten Tracks
Four explorations by Roger Worsley of ancient high-ways, on Radio 4 in 1990.

The Beatles At The Beeb
Radio 1 series in 1982 which unearthed archive record-ings of music made by The Beatles at the BBC in the very early 1960s. But it was made up of only a fraction of the 53 hours of recordings the group had made. A further search was mounted for this material, thought to have been destroyed or taped over. After six years this yielded sufficient for another series of unique recordings called THE BEEB'S LOST BEATLE TAPES.

The Beatles Story
Radio 1 documentary series on the most successful group in pop music history, written and produced by JOHNNY BEERLING and broadcast in 1971.

Beckett, Samuel (1906–89)
The Irish playwright had a close association with radio, dating from *All That Fall*, commissioned by the BBC and broadcast on the Third Programme in 1957. This was not only the first of his radio plays but also the first play he published which was written in English after years of writing in French.

The cast included several of the best interpreters of his work, including J.G. Devlin, Mary O'Farrell, Jack MacGowran and Patrick Magee. Produced by DONALD MCWHINNIE, the play required such an array of subtle and dreamlike sound effects – a blind man's tapping stick, animals, distant railway noises – that it helped to lead to the creation of the BBC RADIOPHONIC WORKSHOP the following year.

More than two dozen works of Beckett, including poems, prose readings and plays, followed, all of them on the Third or Radio 3.

The Beeb's Lost Beatles Tapes
Radio 1 series in 1988 playing little known clips of the Fab Four from shows such as SATURDAY CLUB, and archive material – both songs and interviews – previously thought to be lost.

Excavated gems included The Beatles singing songs by Bill Haley and Eddie Cochran. The 14-part series followed on from THE BEATLES AT THE BEEB.

Beerling, Johnny (1937–)
Controller of Radio 1 since 1985. He produced its very first show (TONY BLACKBURN's breakfast pro-gramme on 30 September 1967) and his whole career since has been spent in the network. He made THE BEATLES STORY and conceived and launched the RADIO 1 ROADSHOW.

Like many, he had his first taste of radio while on National Service, becoming a station engineer and presenter for Aden Forces Broadcasting at the age of nineteen after being conscripted into the RAF in 1955.

Before the Ending of the Day
Fifteen-minute devotional programme which, every sixth Sunday on Radio 4, closes the day's programmes with a celebration of the Catholic service of Compline, the last service of the day. It was first broadcast on the Home Service in August 1944.

'Before Your Very Eyes'
Catchphrase of ARTHUR ASKEY.

Behind the Headlines
Radio 4 series in 1989 in which Robert Kilroy-Silk interviewed individuals who had suddenly been thrust into the headlines, allowing them to hit back at what they often regarded as distortions and exaggerations by the press.

Behind the Ritual
Six-part Radio 4 FM series in 1989 in which six young Londoners (a Buddhist, a Jew, a Muslim, a Pentecostal Christian, a Hindu and a Sikh) discussed their religions and cultures with Ronald Eyre.

Belfast Community Radio
One of the new generation of INCREMENTAL stations, this FM service for Northern Ireland's capital began in April 1990.

Bells on Sunday
These few minutes of bell ringing now go out before 7 a.m. on Sundays on Radio 4, but for many years were heard an hour later. It used to be a programme in its own right but is now part of MORNING HAS BROKEN.

Bengali Service
Part of the BBC World Service since October 1941. In 1989 it was on the air for one hour and twenty minutes each day, for an audience not only in Bangladesh (esti-mated at eight million, or 13 per cent of the population) but also in India and the Gulf States. Most of the output is news and current affairs, concentrating on the subcontinent.

In 1988 it was attacked by Bangladesh's President Ershad for interference in the country's politics. 'The reports were too detailed and authoritative for the regime's taste, their impact too significant', was JOHN TUSA's explanation.

Benn, Tony (1925–)
Has had a long and varied association with radio, stretching back more than forty years. Based at BUSH

HOUSE, he was a staff producer in the BBC's North American Service at a salary of £475 a year from 1949–50, when he left to fight Bristol South-East. He won, and became a Labour MP. (He remembers producing Wimbledon in the summer of 1950, and being 'too slow' to be effective as a commentator himself.)

Later, as Postmaster-General under Harold Wilson, he was instrumental in driving the PIRATES off the North Sea. He described them on television as 'a menace' and accused them of stealing copyright and endangering ship-to-shore radio. Has appeared on ANY QUESTIONS? on 57 occasions, which is probably as often as anyone in the show's history. He is proud of the fact that his archives include either a transcript or a tape-recording of every one of those 57 programmes. When FREDDIE GRISEWOOD retired, he wrote an affectionate poem in praise of him which has been broadcast on the air.

Bennett, Alan (1934–)
Poignant and gentle, Bennett's style as both actor and writer has graced several BBC programmes. He gave what many regarded as the definitive readings of *Winnie-the-Pooh* and regaled listeners with the sad and touching saga of THE LADY IN THE VAN.

Benno Moiseiwitsch
Seven-part Radio 3 series in 1990 marking the centenary of the birth of the Odessa-born virtuoso pianist.

Berlin, Sir Isaiah (1909–)
Oxford philosopher and man of the arts who contributed much to the early years of the Third Programme. His six lectures on the sources of Romanticism were broadcast in 1966. His 80th birthday was fêted with a special series of programmes on the network.

Berry, Colin (1946–)
One of the first pirates, in Radio Caroline's administration department in 1964; became a newsreader and presenter on the ship in 1965. A stint on BBC Radio Medway led in 1973 to Radio 2, where he has understudied most of the network's leading lights and often ushered in the dawn.

Best Avoided
Hairdressers, car maintenance, aeroplanes and estate agents were the pet hates of Leeds media studies lecturer Laurence Alster, as described in four humorous talks on Radio 4 in 1990.

The Best of English
Radio 2 series in 1988 in which comedian Arthur English reminisced with Michael Pointon and a studio audience.

Better Halves
Three comic duologues by Christopher Hope, billed as 'historical travesties', and based on the principle that

behind every great man stands an even greater woman. Patricia Routledge played Mrs Xanthippe Socrates, Anna Massey played Mrs Cosima Wagner and Prunella Scales was Mrs Marietta Machiavelli. Broadcast on Radio 3 in 1988.

The Betty Witherspoon Show
Comedy running from 1972–73 starring KENNETH WILLIAMS, TED RAY and Miriam Margolyes.

Between the Lines
Series on newspapers from 1976–78 on Radio 4, which spawned STOP PRESS.

Beyond Our Ken
Weekly comedy show which enlivened the Light Programme from 1958–64, written by BARRY TOOK and Eric Merriman.

KENNETH HORNE, KENNETH WILLIAMS, Hugh Paddick, Betty Marsden and Bill Pertwee starred, with music by the Fraser Hayes Four. All of them continued in the show's successor, ROUND THE HORNE, which developed its risqué revue into even something riskier.

'Keep it clean – precious rather than poofy' – instruction from the programme's producer, Jacques Brown.

BFBS
See BRITISH FORCES BROADCASTING SERVICE.

Big Band Sound
Nostalgic Radio 2 series hosted by ALAN DELL, which first went on the air in 1974.

Big Band Special
Radio 2 series beginning in September 1979 played by the BBC BIG BAND and celebrating their kind of music. SHEILA TRACY has introduced it from the beginning. The show's future appeared to be guaranteed when, in 1990, the band escaped the BBC's cost-cutting axe – unlike the BBC RADIO ORCHESTRA of which it was a part.

Big Ben
Chimes from the nation's most famous clocktower were first broadcast on radio in 1923, and have usually gone out daily since 1924. But despite their familiarity, the bongs of Big Ben are not heard very frequently today – a mere seventeen times a week, compared with 181 times for the PIPS. Radio 1, Radio 2 and Radio 5 never broadcast Big Ben, and Radio 3 does so only once a week (at 7 a.m. on Sundays). Radio 4 broadcasts the bongs at 6 p.m. and midnight every night of the week, and at 10 p.m. on Saturday and Sunday.

Absence of Big Ben from the airwaves generally causes a stir, as in 1990 after the hammer arm was

Rustic sage Arthur Fallowfield ('The answer lies in the soil'), moronic pop star Rikki Livid and gushing cook Fanny Haddock were all *Beyond Our Ken*. The team included (top to bottom and left to right) Bill Pertwee, Pat Lancaster, Hugh Paddick, Kenneth Williams, Betty Marsden and Kenneth Horne

replaced by the Department of the Environment. This altered the tone of the bong. Radio 4 presentation considered the new sound 'awful' and for several weeks ceased to broadcast it, substituting the pips. It was reinstated on 22 December, only three days before the Queen's Christmas message which it traditionally introduces.

The Big Fun Show
Radio 4 comedy series in 1988 written and presented by Paul Merton and John Irwin, and starring Josie Lawrence.

The Big White Chiefs
White musicians who played jazz, despite its having been created mainly by black Americans, were featured in this six-part Radio 3 series in 1990: they included bandleaders Paul Whiteman, Benny Goodman, Eddie Condon, Mulligan and Dave Brubeck.

The Billy Cotton Band Show
The famous cheery bandleader and ex-racing driver was the star of this Sunday lunchtime series on the Light Programme from 1949. By 1962 he had bellowed his weekly 'Wakey-Wakey!' 500 times, and the show still had six more years to run. Alan Breeze and Kathy Kay appeared as well. 'Somebody Stole my Girl' was the signature tune.

'I don't try to please everybody. That's impossible. But I try to please the majority' – Billy Cotton.

The Birth of Babel
Eight-part series on Radio 3 in 1989 in which COLIN TUDGE interviewed specialists in different areas of linguistic research and surveyed the current state of scientific knowledge on the origins of human language.

The Birth of Europe
Five-part documentary series on Radio 4 in 1991 which tried to uncover the links between the physical nature of Europe – rocks, mountains, soils and climate – and the development of civilisation, starting with the early hunters of the Ice Age 750,000 years ago.

Black, Alan (1942–)
Scots DJ who became the regular host of Radio 1's *Rock On* in 1974.

Black Sheep
Three-part series on Radio 4 in 1989 in which Jenny Cuffe spoke to people who had broken the unwritten rules of their tribe, family or workplace.

The Blackburn Files
Comedy series about a redundant young miner, Stephen J. Blackburn, who starts up a private investigation agency in South Yorkshire and gets involved in a succession of improbable and tragi-comic cases. Broadcast on Radio 4 in 1989. Written by a Yorkshire-based trio, Ian McMillan, Martin Wiley and Dave Sheasby (who also directed). A new series went out in 1991.

Blackburn, Tony (1943–)
Doctor's son from Bournemouth who started his disc-spinning career as breakfast host on pirate ship Radio Caroline in July 1964, made his mark on rival pirate ship Radio London (which he still describes as 'the best station we've ever had in this country') and won instant

Cherubic Tony Blackburn was only 24 when the BBC chose him to say the first words and play the first record on Radio 1, on 30 September 1967. 'On that day I was determined to be brighter and breezier than a hundred redcoats', he recalled in his autobiography

fame as the first voice ever heard on Radio 1 on 30 September 1967.

By the following year, he records in his 1985 autobiography *The Living Legend*, he was earning £60,000 a year. But gradually he fell from favour and slipped down the schedules: from the breakfast slot to 9 a.m. to 12 noon (in 1972), and then to the afternoons. He took over JUNIOR CHOICE from ED STEWART in 1980: when the programme's name was dropped two years later, he continued to present its successor, *Tony Blackburn's Saturday Show*.

In 1984, he left Radio 1 and moved to BBC Radio London where he presented a morning show for housewives and mixed soul with smut — daring jokes about getting out his '12-incher' (i.e. extended play record). Eventually he was dismissed for repeated naughtiness

in 1988, promptly taking up residence at Capital Gold, playing golden oldies six days a week in his old breakfast slot from a quarter-of-a-century ago.

He is quite open about the fact that he chooses none of the music he plays, apart from on Sunday. 'On Sunday I have a Motown show, for which I choose all the music,' he explained in *Music & Media* magazine in December 1990. 'But otherwise I do not have any input into that at all. But then I would not want it because if I selected all my favourite records they might well crop up in the next person's show. I have always been a great believer in the idea that no DJ should be able to choose his own music. That is the programmes director's job.'

Noted for outspokenness on the air, especially on emotional subjects such as the break-up of his marriage to the actress Tessa Wyatt, blood sports, radio bosses and trade unions. Also noted as Britain's most inexhaustible fount of corny jokes ('Why do woodworms like picnics? — Because they enjoy eating out of doors'). Has an indefatigably cheerful sense of humour, most of it directed at himself, and a good line in non-stop chatter.

Blackmore, Tim (1944–)
Radio 1 producer from 1967–77; worked for Capital Radio from 1977–82, leaving as head of programmes. Later a director of PPM, from which he resigned in 1989 following the Miss World takeover. Then helped to form the UNIQUE BROADCASTING COMPANY. Founder member, and first director, of the RADIO ACADEMY.

Blackwood, Algernon (1869–1951)
Distinguished author of supernatural tales who acquired extra fame as 'The Ghost Man' on radio, from 1934 until his death. He also appeared on television in its early years, again as a storyteller.

Blandings
Radio 4 adaptation of P.G. Wodehouse's comic stories with IAN CARMICHAEL as the Hon. Galahad Threepwood and Richard Vernon as Lord Emsworth. *Summer Lightning*, in six parts, was broadcast in 1987; *Heavy Weather*, in four parts, in 1988; and *Pigs Have Wings*, also four parts, in 1989.

Blofeld, Henry (1939–)
Cricket captain at Eton who went on to win a blue at Cambridge as a batsman and is now the plummiest, and most loquacious, member of the TEST MATCH SPECIAL team.

Blood and Bruises
Waspish Radio 3 sitcom in 1988 mocking the antics of an agitprop street theatre collective and its humourless,

feminist, autocratic, ex-librarian boss (Helen Atkinson Wood). Written by Colin McLaren.

Blood on the Prairie

The bitter story of the Sioux Indian wars was told in this Light Programme series in 1963, written and produced by CHARLES CHILTON. Its central figure was William Russell, one of the war correspondents despatched from Europe to cover the struggle.

Bloodnok, Major Denis

Character in THE GOON SHOW played by Peter Sellers. 'Born 1867 and 1880, Sandhurst NAAFI. Served in S. African war, taken prisoner on first day under strange circumstances. Released by Boers after three days as being "unreliable". Cashiered seven times – a world record.'

Blue, Rabbi Lionel (1930–)

Popular presenter of homespun religious homilies in Monday morning's THOUGHT FOR THE DAY on Radio 4. Also presents PAUSE FOR THOUGHT on Radio 2 from time to time. Talks frankly of his own spiritual doubts and uncertainties, as well as more mundane matters like baked beans. Avoids preachiness, and generally cracks a wry joke. Fifty of his Thoughts were released in 1990 on the BBC RADIO COLLECTION.

Bluebottle, Jim 'Tigernuts'

Character made of cardboard and string who appeared in THE GOON SHOW and was played by Peter Sellers. His catchphrase: 'You filthy rotten swine, you.'

Bob Hatton Rattle

Billed as 'radio's first and only football fanzine', this soccer magazine series began on Radio 5 in 1990.

Bogarde, Dirk (1921–)

The film actor and author has also worked occasionally as a disc-jockey – on I PLAY WHAT I LIKE on the Light Programme in the 1950s (he was nicknamed 'Dirge' Bogarde by EAMONN ANDREWS because of the romantic music he liked) and as holiday relief for DAVID JACOBS on Radio 2 in 1989. On the latter he played several of his personal favourites, including Marlene Dietrich's 'I Wish You Love' and (more oddly) 'I've Got a Brand New Combine Harvester' by The Wurzels. For his radio drama work, see THE FORSYTE CHRONICLES.

Bones, Norman and Henry

Boy detectives from CHILDREN'S HOUR, possessed of an amazing ability to solve knotty problems. They lived in Norfolk but, just like the Famous Five, had a habit of getting embroiled in exciting mysteries the minute they went on holiday. Clues woven into the plots enabled bright young listeners to match their own wits against those of the juvenile crimebusters.

The first of their 130-plus adventures was in July 1943; their creator was Anthony C. Wilson. Charles Hawtrey, and later Harold Reese, played Norman and PATRICIA HAYES was always his cousin Henry. Sadly, only one episode is preserved in the BBC SOUND ARCHIVES.

A Book at Bedtime

A venerable institution which lulls the nation to sleep with a wide variety of literature, from Dickens to Dick Francis and *Huckleberry Finn* to LAKE WOBEGON DAYS, but which can never get settled itself.

When it began, in January 1949 (with a reading of John Buchan's *The Three Hostages*) it went out on the Light Programme at 11 p.m. Now it adorns Radio 4 at 10.45 p.m. Over the intervening four decades it has constantly tossed and turned position: to 11.05 p.m. in 1952, back to 11 p.m. in 1955 and on to 11.45 p.m. in 1957 when it finished with a reading of Alan Paton's *Cry, The Beloved Country*. After a gap of five years, it returned in 1962 at 11.02 p.m. with David Beaty's thriller *The Proving Flight*, moving back to 10.15 p.m. in 1973. So many listeners complained that this was now more like A Book at Bathtime that it was pushed on to 10.30 p.m. a few months later and then to 10.45 p.m. a few months after that. By 1983 it was back at its original hour of 11 p.m.

Radio 4 changed its mind once more and moved the British bedtime back to 10.15 p.m. in the following year, despite further protests from night owls for whom this was again too early. In 1989, in the wake of evidence that the British people were going to bed later and also (more significantly) that a rising proportion of ABs was listening to the radio between 10 p.m. and midnight, MICHAEL GREEN gave it its present time slot of 10.45 p.m.

B at B is ruthless as well as restless. On average books are cut to one-third of their original length. Nonetheless, it can hurtle a title into the bestseller lists and helps to generate huge publicity when it coincides with publication. An example was John Le Carré's *A Perfect Spy*. He read it himself, though most readings are by actors. The programme's policy, traditionally, was to read books (mostly fiction) which were either accepted classics or regarded as likely to attain classic status. Within that remit, there was much variety: Rudyard Kipling's *Kim* to John Gale's *Clean Young Englishman*. However, this shifted slightly in 1989 after the retirement of Maurice Leitch, himself a respected novelist, who had been running the programme. David Benedictus, also a novelist, took over and tried to make the programme 'less Eng. Lit.' by choosing more contemporary titles. They have included Frederick Forsyth's

The Negotiator and Kazuo Ishiguro's Booker Prize winner *The Remains of the Day*, as well as Joseph Heller's *Catch 22*.

The programme hit the headlines with the reading in 1990 of the unexpurgated version of D.H. Lawrence's *Lady Chatterley's Lover*, unsuccessfully prosecuted for obscenity at the Old Bailey in 1960. The adaptor, Alan England, cut the book to the usual third of its original length but did not excise either the four-letter words or the explicit sex. Because it was so well publicised in advance (*A Bonk at Bedtime*, as *The Sun* put it) it therefore lacked any element of shock by the time it got on the air. Consequently there were very few (21) complaints. In addition, many episodes were preceded by clear warnings as to content and language. 'I loved Lady Chatterley – a nice change to have something a little naughty', was how one member of the Listening Panel (the BBC's own audience research body) was quoted in an internal BBC Broadcasting Research bulletin in May 1990.

In 1990–91 the programme repeated, as a 'listeners' choice' season, the three books which had achieved the highest appreciation figures on the Listening Panel over the previous six years. Out of some 240 Books at Bedtime, the three which had proved the most liked – and were therefore repeated – were the H.E. Bates short stories about the glorious wine and women existence of *My Uncle Silas*, read by David Neal; *In My Wildest Dreams* by Leslie Thomas, read by Hywel Bennett; and *The Warden* by Anthony Trollope, read by Jeremy Nicholas. All strong narratives, reassuring in flavour, and both written and read by men.

In July 1991 the programme launched a second edition in the Parliamentary recess – a so-called 'Book at Midnight' going out at 11.45 p.m. for more difficult or contemporary novels, leaving the earlier slot for traditional stories.

Bookshelf

Weekly Radio 4 programme launched by Irish broadcaster and author Frank Delaney in 1978. It looked outside the narrow, Hampstead-dominated literary establishment and brought a news and current affairs element (which was Delaney's own background in Dublin) to the subjects of books and reading. It also looked at what people actually *buy*, instead of what critics think is good for them. Consequently the programme had a very wide scope: one edition covered both Snoopy and James Joyce.

Delaney left to make a BBC-TV series on Celtic culture in 1983 and was succeeded first by Susan Hill and then Hunter Davies. Nigel Forde is the fourth and current presenter.

The Box of Delights

Much acclaimed serialisation on CHILDREN'S HOUR, first broadcast in 1943 and then again in 1948 and 1955, of John Masefield's book, with John Gilpin as Kay Harker. It was adapted by John Keir Cross.

Boyle, Andrew (1919–91)

Joined the BBC as a scriptwriter on RADIO NEWSREEL in 1947, becoming its assistant editor in 1954. Founded, and was first editor of, the influential lunchtime news programme THE WORLD AT ONE in 1965, on which he nurtured both the irreverent style and a number of talented reporters including SUE MACGREGOR and MARGARET HOWARD. His book *The Climate of Treason* led to the exposure of Anthony Blunt.

Boyle, Katie (1926–)

Italian aristocrat's daughter who worked as a fashion model for *Vogue* in the 1950s before moving into broadcasting, appearing on POP OVER EUROPE. She hosted her own Radio 2 show on Saturday afternoons in 1990.

Braden, Bernard (1916–)

Vancouver-born actor who came to Britain with his wife Barbara Kelly in 1949 and within a few months (helped by success on stage in Laurence Olivier's West End production of *A Streetcar Named Desire*) had become a major star.

His radio shows began with STARLIGHT HOUR and continued with JOHNNY WASHINGTON ESQUIRE and, most importantly of all, BREAKFAST WITH BRADEN. Before 1950 had ended he had found time to make two more: LEAVE YOUR NAME AND NUMBER and MR AND MRS NORTH.

In the 1950s they gravitated towards the increasingly glamorous world of television, where they were soon billed as 'a gay couple', but continued to make radio series such as *Braden on Toast*, *Braden on Thames* and *The Bradens* (Light Programme, 1961).

Bradford City Radio

Asian music station in Bradford, one of the new wave of INCREMENTALS, on the air since December 1989. Fifteen hours a day (9 a.m. to midnight) are given over to Asian music, with another two hours (5 a.m. to 7 a.m.) devoted to Moslem and Hindu religious output. There is black music from midnight to 5 a.m., and mainstream pop from 7 a.m. to 9 a.m.

The Bradman Tapes

Series of radio interviews with the normally reclusive cricketer Sir Donald Bradman made by the Australian Broadcasting Corporation (interviewer: Norman May) which was sold to the BBC and broadcast on Radio 3 in 1989.

It was the first time that a mainstream cricket programme had ever gone out in Radio 3's normal evening schedules; a rare example of an imported series; and came with an unusual history. When first offered to the BBC, in 1988, the BBC was unwilling to pay the asking price. This provoked Conservative MP Robert Hicks, an MCC member, to table a motion in the House of Commons asking the BBC to reconsider its decision 'on the basis of both historical and public interests as well as sporting criteria.'

The great man's three hours of reminiscences were duly bought by the BBC, but only because they were also released on cassette by the BBC RADIO COLLECTION (under the original Australian title of *Bradman – The Don Declares*). This meant ABC received royalties from the sales as well as a transmission fee, which together added up to a sum closer to what they originally wanted.

Brady, Pete (1941–)

One of Radio 1's original team of DJs, with a six days a week pop show when the station started in 1967. Canadian-born, he started his career with Radio Jamaica, before coming to Europe and working on the pirate ship Radio London and on Radio Luxembourg. He started a Radio 2 series in 1971.

Brain of Britain

Radio 4 quiz show which evolved in 1967 from WHAT DO YOU KNOW?, with Robert Robinson asking a variety of often rather difficult general knowledge questions. The annual winner is awarded the title 'Brain of Britain'; every three years the three such Brains compete against one another for the title 'Brain of Brains'. Every *nine* years the three Brains of Brains fight one another for an even more rarefied honour, 'Top Brain'. Listeners have an opportunity of putting their own questions in a spot called 'Beat the Brains': if their questions leave the contestants stumped, they win a prize.

Brain of Sport

Radio 2 sports quiz on the air since 1975. For many years its chairman was the much missed commentator PETER JONES.

The Brains Trust

Although always under the Variety Department, this unscripted discussion programme on the Home Service was unsurpassed at stimulating debate and encouraging curiosity among a wide variety of citizens about a wide variety of subjects.

It began on 1 January 1941 (confusingly, under the name *Any Questions?*) in the middle of a London blitz. BBC studios had been hit and glass crunched underfoot. Dr Julian Huxley, one of the panellists, arrived from London Zoo, which had just been bombed and from which a stallion zebra had escaped as a result. The programme changed its name to *The Brains Trust* in September 1942 and continued under that title until it finished in May 1949.

The first producer, Howard Thomas, hired Huxley for his brain, Commander A.B. Campbell for his heart and C.E.M. JOAD for his tongue. This trio was always the core, but over the years there were also many guest panellists including, for example, Kenneth Clark, Barbara Ward and Hannen Swaffer.

Going out at 8.15 on Tuesday nights, the programme soon became a national institution, famous both for the range and interest of its questions and the idiosyncrasies of the panellists in answering them. The most celebrated examples of these were Joad's 'It all depends what you mean by . . .' and Campbell's 'When I was in Patagonia . . .'.

Questions ranged from the opaque ('What is the fourth dimension?', 'What is the difference between fresh air and a draught?') and physical ('How does a fly land upside down on the ceiling?') to the moral ('Do we think this world is worthwhile?') and political ('Is civilisation advancing westwards?') not forgetting the trivial ('Why are so many women cats to one another for no apparent reason?')

Another, recalled in a *Radio Times* article by the programme's first chairman Donald McCullough, was: 'What are the most beautiful words in the language?' Joad said 'Over the hills and far away'; ROSE MACAULAY answered 'Oblivion'; while the down-to-earth Campbell replied: 'I choose words for sound rather than sense. I think the most beautiful word is "paraffin".'

The programme encouraged, and received, many questions from the Forces. Indeed, one of the earliest questions recorded was from an RAF airman: 'What are the seven wonders of the world?' (The panel's answers do not seem to be recorded.) It is rightly regarded as an educative as well as an entertaining institution which helped to keep minds alert and alive during the darkest years of the century.

In the 1950s it transferred to BBC-TV, with the soundtrack going out on the Home Service the following week. Panellists included A.J. Ayer, Noël Annan and Egon Ronay, the Hungarian-born restaurant owner.

Brambles, Jakki (1967–)

Made history in 1989 by becoming Radio 1's first female DJ in a daytime slot (as well as one of the youngest presenters in its history) when she took over the dawn show from Monday to Friday. She was promoted the following year to become the early evening DRIVE-TIME host four days a week. Alone among Radio 1's two dozen presenters, she always broadcasts on her feet — an American practice designed to project the voice properly and enable its owner to dance round the studio bursting with energy.

Brandon, Carter

Nephew of UNCLE MORT, the character created by PETER TINNISWOOD. Uncle and nephew have now had 26 adventures together on Radio 4.

We think, therefore we are – *The Brains Trust*. The nation listened as they expounded. Left to right, in 1941: Julian Huxley; Donald McCullough (partly hidden), chairman; C.E.M. Joad; Malcolm Sargent; Ellen Wilkinson; Commander A.B. Campbell. Standing at the back is Howard Thomas, first producer

Brandon, Tony (1933–)

Disc-jockey with an enthusiastic manner who started out as a variety artist, on Canadian Carroll Levis's show on the Light Programme. In 1966–67 he worked at Radio Luxembourg, followed by a few months on pirate ship Radio London; joined Radio 1 in November 1967, staying until 1971; hosted various shows on Radio 2 for twelve years (1971–83) and since 1987 has been at County Sound, where he now plays golden oldies.

Breakaway

Live, jolly, Saturday-morning holiday show on Radio 4 which began in September 1979, with BARRY NORMAN the first presenter. He left after eighteen months to concentrate on cinema programmes for BBC-TV and was replaced by cheery BERNARD FALK, who hosted it for the next nine years despite being (in his own words) 'more tabloid than your average Radio 4 presenter'.

At first the programme embraced not only holidays but also leisure and even DIY, running items on servicing lawnmowers and how to hang wallpaper. After MICHAEL GREEN took over in July 1986, however, it changed: the TODAY programme gained a Saturday edition and *Breakaway* was consequently trimmed by about ten minutes. It axed its TV previews hosted by Patrick Stoddart and became not only shorter but sharper, making a point of sticking up for the holidaymaker against the big battalions of the travel companies, who are regularly mauled on surcharges, overbooking, a cavalier attitude to complaints, and so on. (It did this while also accepting their free trips, just like almost every other travel programme, newspaper or magazine.)

The first producer, Jenny Mallinson Duff, was still there ten years later but then left to produce Channel 4's first travel series *Travelog* which started in February 1990 and which Falk also presented. She it was who selected Breakaway's bouncy signature tune ('Let's do the break-away, Get hot and shake-away, It's got the snapp-iest synco-pation . . .') which is a song from the

1920s also entitled 'Breakaway' and written by Gottler, Mitchell and Conrad.

When it became clear that Falk was going to present a second series of Channel 4's *Travelog*, the BBC said there could be 'a possible conflict of interest' and dropped him in June 1990. Julian Pettifer stepped in for two months before KEN BRUCE took over in September. (Falk died of a heart attack in the century's hottest weather in August.)

Breakfast Special
Popular series which began on the Light Programme in 1965 and carried on until 1972, by which time it was Radio 2. JOHN DUNN hosted it from 1967.

Breakfast With . . .
Radio 4 summer series in 1989, filling in for START THE WEEK during its eight-week break. Different hosts (including Ludovic Kennedy, Roy Hattersley and the Bishop of Durham) invited guests into their homes, or to places close to their hearts, for leisurely morning conversation.

Breakfast with Braden
'*The New Yorker* of the air' was how the *Daily Express* hailed this bright, popular BERNARD BRADEN comedy show of 1950, whose verbal dexterity owed everything to its writers FRANK MUIR and DENIS NORDEN (and, later, Braden's fellow Canadian Eric Nicol). It also featured singers Pearl Carr and Benny Lee, Ronald Fletcher and bandleader Nat Temple. Match manufacturers Bryant & May once asked permission to use some of the show's witticisms on the side of their boxes, but the BBC declined.

In the autumn of 1950 it was turned into an evening programme, *Bedtime With Braden*, and the star's wife Barbara Kelly joined the cast. Targets of the sharper jokes included Senator Joe McCarthy's political witchhunts in the USA.

Brett, Simon (1945–)
Creator and writer of AFTER HENRY, one of Radio 4's best comedies of recent years. He was a staff producer in BBC Radio's light entertainment department for nine years (1968–77) during which he worked on WEEK ENDING and THE BURKISS WAY and was the first producer of THE NEWS HUDDLINES. His last major job before leaving to be a producer at London Weekend TV was to make both the pilot and first episode of THE HITCH-HIKER'S GUIDE TO THE GALAXY. He has been a full-time writer since 1979.

Brett co-wrote (with FRANK MUIR) all of Frank Muir Goes Into . . . which ran to more than 100 editions, and more recently has had his own series on Radio 4, DEAR DIARY.

Bridgebuilders
'Britishers and Americans get together over a radio bridge of understanding', was how LONDON CALLING billed this interesting series which began on the North American Service of the BBC World Service in November 1941 – a month before Pearl Harbor.

The programme originated in a wartime scheme by a London paper manufacturer, Lancelot Spicer, to start a correspondence club between England and the USA. People in Britain would send in their names to the Stationers' Association and people in America would do the same, and they would then be allotted correspondents. (Conceivably, his motive might also have been to increase paper sales.) This resulted in the birth of the Stationers Overseas Correspondence Circle, which soon had 200 members on both sides of the Atlantic.

On the first anniversary of the Circle's formation, Spicer gave a broadcast in which he admitted, rather jocularly, that his building – situated by a bridge over the Thames, and packed with paper – was a 'lovely target' for the Luftwaffe, and that he was part of his staff rota who kept watch for fire bombs each night. He urged Britons to build from the east, and Americans from the west, so they would meet halfway 'on our bridge of understanding'.

Other trades and professional groups followed, from both countries, to make a series of broadcasts. They included Rotary, soroptimists, the blind, policemen and the Association of Teachers of Domestic Subjects.

The series not only spawned a young version (JUNIOR BRIDGEBUILDERS) but helped to cement friendship between the two main countries of the English-speaking world while they were fighting a common enemy. In March 1944, for example, when the programme was going out to North America every Wednesday evening, *London Calling* carried a photograph of a group of people standing on the edge of a crater in a bomb-damaged city. The caption explained: 'In one of the programmes a family of Londoners, Mr and Mrs Sydney Ing, and their children Geoffrey (14) and Marion (12), broadcast to a family of New Yorkers, Mrs Helen Lee and her seven children: Helen, Ruth, Carolyn, Bob, Bill, Tom and Mildred of Long Island, New York. The eighth member of the family, Corporal Peter J. Lee, now serving with the US Forces in Great Britain, introduced the Ings to his family back home during the broadcast. Here, left to right, inspecting the bomb damage near the Ings' home in the City of London you see Mr Ing, Geoffrey, Cpl. Lee, Mrs Ing and Marion.'

Britain Radio
Pirate station in 1966–67 which, unusually, broadcast light music and shared its North Sea ship with another pirate station, RADIO ENGLAND. Their vessel, fitted out in Miami, had the appropriate name of MV Laissez

Faire. Between them the two stations had twelve DJs, nine of them American.

Britannia – the Film
Eight-part history of British cinema, compiled and researched by Paul Wells and written and narrated by Christopher Frayling, which went out on Radio 4 in 1989.

The British Disease
Not homosexuality, but the other one – class. Helen Boaden, who started on FILE ON 4, presented this six-part series on the national obsession with class divisions, tracing it from 1918 to the present, on Radio 4 in 1990.

British Forces Broadcasting Service
Forces Broadcasting began in 1943, recognising the vital role radio played in military morale and the national war machine. It was present in every theatre of operations, following the soldiers in the Italian campaign and alongside the troops in Burma. Different sections operated in different areas. SEAC, for example, based in Ceylon, broadcast to South-East Asia, while the British Forces Network was launched in Hamburg. The organisation was called the Forces Broadcasting Service until the mid-1960s, when the present title was adopted.

Wherever British troops have come to be stationed – Germany, Gibraltar, Cyprus, Hong Kong, the Falklands, the Gulf – BFBS is also present, broadcasting programmes for their information and entertainment. Since 1982 it has been part of a quango called the Services Sound and Vision Corporation headed by Alan Protheroe, a former assistant director-general of the BBC, which also produces television services and live shows for British troops. BFBS has launched several big radio names, including DAVID JACOBS, CHARLES CHILTON, BRIAN MATTHEW, DAVID HAMILTON and Sarah Kennedy, who made her debut at the microphone in Singapore (where she had been private teacher to Lee Kuan Yew's fifteen-year-old son).

Britten, Benjamin (1913–76)
Composer who had a lifelong association with the BBC, at its most productive in the years 1937 to 1947 during which he produced 25 scores for wartime propaganda, radio drama and features, including THE DARK TOWER.

BRMB
Birmingham-based ILR station, covering Birmingham and the Black Country. The initials were taken from its parent company at the time it began, in 1974. Brummie comedian Jasper Carrott, frequently mentioning the station on his television shows, has helped to put it on the map.

BRMB split its frequencies in 1989, launching Xtra-AM on medium wave (run jointly with its sister station Mercia Sound) and continuing as BRMB FM on FM. Xtra-AM's breakfast host, Les Ross, is said to be the longest-serving breakfast radio presenter in Britain – having done the job, on more than one station, for over twenty years.

In 1983 the station began an annual Walkathon, which it says is the largest sponsored walk in Britain. Held every May, it benefits local charities and has raised, on average, £300,000 a year. Previous walks have been 25 miles long, but this year's (1991) was 20 miles.

Broadcasting Act 1990
Laid down the framework to allow what the then Home Secretary, David Waddington, officially called 'a massive expansion in choice' in both radio and television. It set up the RADIO AUTHORITY and empowered it to issue up to three licences for new national commercial radio channels, which would each be different from one another. One would be 'speech-based', and one 'devoted to music other than pop music' (rock music was defined in such a way that it could not be considered as distinct from pop). There would be a quality requirement for independent radio as a whole. Up to 300 new local and community stations could come on air in the 1990s, licences to be allocated on the basis of whether they would extend choice. The Act also extended the application of the Marine Etc Broadcasting (Offences) Act 1967.

Broadcasting House
Headquarters of BBC Radio since 1932, when the Corporation moved from SAVOY HILL. The external carvings of Prospero and Ariel (the latter the invisible spirit of the air, later adopted as the title for the BBC's own weekly magazine) are the work of sculptor Eric Gill.

Almost as soon as it moved in, the BBC found its new home too small, a continual complaint ever since. Sir John REITH was said to dislike it and Richard Lambert, first editor of THE LISTENER, called it 'a Leviathan of a building', saying its crest should have been a white elephant. In addition, rumblings from the Bakerloo Line which runs underneath have caused decades of frustration. But for all that the building has continued to be a solid and much loved symbol of the Corporation and all it stands for. Originally rented, its freehold was purchased by the BBC in 1936.

The Second World War inflicted much damage: it was hit by a bomb in October 1940 during the nine o'clock news (the newsreader, Bruce Belfrage, carried on reading the bulletin). The bomb destroyed thousands of gramophone records, plus some libraries and studios.

Two months later a bomb exploded outside in Portland Place, puncturing a water main and flooding part of the building as well as setting it on fire.

In 1981 Michael Heseltine, in his first stint as Environment Secretary, announced that Broadcasting House was being made one of three dozen listed buildings of the interwar period.

Later that decade, an outbreak of Legionnaires Disease caused by a wet cooling tower on top of the building caused the deaths of three people. The BBC was corporately prosecuted and in 1988 was fined at Bow Street magistrates' court for breaches of the Health and Safety at Work Act.

In the 1980s the Corporation decided to move BBC Radio's headquarters, and most of the studios, to the new complex at White City, but this was cancelled in 1990 to save money.

Broadcasting in the Seventies

Controversial BBC policy paper of 1969, strengthening the practice of giving the four national radio networks separate and distinct identities rather than the mixed assortment which both the Home and Light, to varying degrees, had been before 1967. It also paved the way for the dissolution of the Third Programme.

Bromley, Peter (1929–)

Owner of one of the world's most familiar voices: he has given the BBC Radio commentary for every Grand National and every other big race since 1961, and his commentaries go round the globe on the BBC World Service. For millions of listeners throughout the world, his is the voice of racing.

A former King's Hussars officer, he excelled at sport in the Army, winning the Bisley Cup for rifle shooting as a subaltern and almost qualifying for the British Olympic pentathlon team.

After the Army, he fractured his skull which drove him away from active sport. He gave racecourse commentaries for five years (1955–59) before joining the BBC as its first sports correspondent in 1959. The following year RAYMOND GLENDENNING retired, and Bromley succeeded him in that top sports role.

The televising of racing in Britain is divided between BBC and Channel 4. BBC Radio, however, has an all-embracing contract which allows it to cover any race and any number of meetings. This means that Bromley, unlike his BBC-TV counterpart Peter O'Sullevan, covers not half but *all* the main races a year (about 180, though it used to be over 250) and estimates that he has so far commentated for radio on over 6,000 races.

Brookes, Bruno (1959–)

Radio 1 disc-jockey who for four years (1986–90) hosted the top rated TOP 40 every Sunday afternoon, until MARK GOODIER displaced him. Son of a Staffordshire

car wash businessman, he started work on BBC Radio Stoke at seventeen and was signed up by Radio 1 in 1984. He continues to co-host the weekend breakfast show, and was also the first broadcaster to be heard on Radio 5. (Real name: Trevor Brookes.)

Brooks Aehron's Serenade

Radio 2's first major piano series since SEMPRINI SERENADE was this six-part melody showcase in 1990 for virtuoso Brooks Aehron, accompanied by Harry Rabinowitz and his Orchestra (who also played for Semprini).

Dedicated to Semprini's memory, it had an equally broad mix: programme one ranged from Chopin to Chopsticks, and Strauss and Gershwin to Andrew Lloyd Webber and the theme from *EastEnders*.

Brough, Peter (1916–)

Ventriloquist from a ventriloquial family, who appeared in NAVY MIXTURE before making his name in EDUCATING ARCHIE.

Brown, Douglas (1917–)

The BBC's first religious affairs correspondent, from the late 1960s to 1977, now freelance. An Anglican, he had formerly been a general radio reporter. Prior to the BBC he was a staff journalist on the *Eastern Daily Press* in Norwich, where he shared an office with Frederick Forsyth and on which JOHN TIMPSON also worked.

Browne, Tom (1944–)

Actor (RADA graduate in 1965) who presented Radio 1's Sunday afternoon TOP TWENTY SHOW in the late 1970s.

Bruce, Ken (1951–)

Quirky, amiable and wry-humoured Scot who has presented Radio 4's weekly BREAKAWAY since 1990 but is best known for his long association with Radio 2. In 1985 he succeeded TERRY WOGAN as the breakfast host, only to be displaced a year later by DEREK JAMESON and shunted to mid-mornings, where for four years he presented the network's only record request show.

In 1990 he was moved again, to host the new 10 p.m. to midnight show four days a week designed as a major project to boost Radio 2's late-night audience. This was an appealing blend of music and speech which featured a nightly short story (often by Saki, the prolific master of the genre, although the first was Ronald Seth's *Footprints in the Dust*); a look at the first editions of next day's national and regional papers; light features on topics like snoring and coincidences; an album of the week and a 'classic closer' to finish the show at midnight.

Nine months later, in 1991, he swapped places with CHRIS STUART and is now the early morning presenter – in the slot once occupied by RAY MOORE.

Born in Giffnock, Glasgow, Bruce began in hospital radio in Glasgow, before becoming a presenter on BBC Radio Scotland in 1978. His move to Radio 2 came in 1984, when he took over a late Saturday slot, and on which he has also chaired THE ABC QUIZ and POP SCORE.

Buggins Family
Name of a fictitious, working class family which popped up on radio at various times from 1925 onwards. During the Second World War, in KITCHEN FRONT, they showed the nation how to make economical fare such as Connaught Pie ('5oz of lard, one pint of water, one leek . . .').

Building a Library
Component of RECORD REVIEW on Radio 3 which features a different musical work every Saturday morning, analysing the various versions available on record and CD. It began on Network Three, in 1963.

Building Matters
Network Three series devoted to construction and do-it-yourself topics which ran from 1960–61.

Bulgarian Service
Programmes in Bulgarian on the World Service began in February 1940. Today, the service is on the air for 1 hour and 45 minutes a day. A grim and unsolved chapter in its history concerns its employee GEORGI MARKOV, murdered with a poisoned umbrella in 1978.

The Burkiss Way
Radio 4 comedy series produced by DAVID HATCH and starring Jo Kendall, NIGEL REES, Chris Emmett and Fred Harris. Broadcast from 1976–80, it was written by Andrew Marshall and David Renwick, later the authors of London Weekend TV's *Whoops Apocalypse* and *Hot Metal*.

Burmese Service
Programmes in Burmese began in the BBC World Service in September 1940 and today are on the air for 65 minutes a day. Little as it is, it is sufficiently potent for the military regime to discourage listening. However, evidence exists that it is much more popular than Rangoon's official service. BUSH HOUSE received 10,000 letters from Burma in 1983, but in the first half alone of 1989 more than 77,000. JOHN TUSA commented that this was a reflection on 'the terrible plight of listeners in Burma, where the domestic media are manipulated by the regime. Without the BBC, millions of people would be deprived of news', he said.

Burnett, Paul (1943–)
Enduring disc-jockey now at Capital Gold, where he was one of the first presenters when it began in 1988.

Son of travelling variety artists who lived in a caravan, he started broadcasting while in the RAF in the Persian Gulf in 1964.

In 1966 he joined pirate Radio 270 off Scarborough, switching briefly to Manx Radio in 1967. Later that year he started a seven-year stint on Luxembourg, where he hosted the weekly charts show (and discovered several boxfuls of records of LORD HAW-HAW's wartime propaganda broadcasts to Britain).

He returned in 1974 to join Radio 1, where he stayed for eight years, and then Radio 2. In 1985 he went back to commercial radio, as breakfast host on Pennine, before going south to Capital later that year. See also DAVE LEE TRAVIS.

Bush House
Imposing landmark in London's Aldwych which has been the headquarters of parts of what is now called the BBC World Service since the Second World War and where, at any time of day or night, programmes are being written or transmitted in three dozen tongues to some far-flung corner of the planet.

Famous for its massive stone pillars and echoing marble halls, it was built by US businessman Irving T. Bush in the 1920s and planned originally as a trade centre. The BBC took over much of it in 1940 and built the studios – many of them still in daily use – for its wartime broadcasts.

It is now Japanese-owned (the BBC having been prevented by the Treasury from buying the freehold) and the annual rent the BBC has to pay has risen sharply. The lease expires in 2005 and the BBC's new White City complex is being considered as the World Service's future home.

Business Matters
BBC World Service series on commerce and finance which now goes out on Radio 5 as well.

Bussey, Dave (1952–)
Former electrician on the aircraft carrier HMS *Ark Royal* who spent eleven years in the Royal Navy before entering civilian life in 1979. He started broadcasting with Radio Tay in Dundee and since 1986 has been presenting Saturday's dawn show on Radio 2. He also hosts a regular show on BBC Radio Lincolnshire.

Butler, Billy (1948–)
One of Merseyside's best known radio personalities, who hosted a weekly series of Liverpool and Lancashire music and comedy for Radio 2 in 1989–90. He sang with The Merseybeats in the 1960s and worked as a resident DJ in the Cavern Club – world famous for its associations

with The Beatles – from 1964–69. He joined BBC Radio Merseyside in 1971, defecting in 1978 to join the commercial rival, Radio City, but returning to the BBC four years later and still with them today. He has also presented several television shows, mainly in the north-west.

Buzz FM
Birmingham-based INCREMENTAL station which started in May 1990. Under its promise of performance made to the IBA when it was given the contract, 60 per cent of the music it broadcasts is obliged to be performed or written by black artists, but it interprets this in a popular and mainstream way (Tina Turner, George Benson, Motown) and has never been, in its own words, 'a ghetto station'. Every weekday night there is also an hour of programming in a mixture of Asian languages.

Byron in Exile
Eight-part Radio 4 series in 1989 which charted the poet's last eight years of life (1816–24) during which he was in exile in Europe. Robert Powell read from some of his hundreds of letters, culled from the seven volumes of them compiled by the great Byron scholar Leslie Marchand.

C

Cabaret Upstairs
'Alternative' comedy series on Radio 4, which ran from 1985–88. Chairman was Clive Anderson, who later became a household name from the success of WHOSE LINE IS IT ANYWAY?

Call Nick Ross
Phone-in on Radio 4 every Tuesday morning, hosted by journalist Nick Ross since 1986 as the successor to TUESDAY CALL.

Calling the Falklands
See BBC TOPICAL TAPES.

Cambridge Circus
The name of the 1963 revue of the Cambridge Footlights, whose cast included DAVID HATCH and John Cleese. Extracts from it formed a show on the Home Service in December 1963, marking the radio debut of the team who would soon be on the air with I'M SORRY I'LL READ THAT AGAIN.

Cameron, James (1911–85)
The celebrated newspaper journalist was once a regular presenter of Monday morning's ARCHIVE FEATURE, and was much less whimsical than his colleagues in that slot, but when he left he claimed he had been sacked because his false teeth whistled too much.

Campbell, Nicky (1961–)
History graduate of Aberdeen University who started in radio as a jingle writer, joining Radio 1 in 1987 to present a late evening Saturday show. His late evening show now, on three other nights of the week, features mainly album and CD music.

'Can I Do Yer Now, Sir?'
Celebrated wartime catchphrase of MRS MOPP, cleaning lady of ITMA.

Can I Help You?
A series which ran for a generation – on Sunday afternoons from October 1939 to September 1970. Dudley Perkins was the presenter for much of its life. It advised the unwary on such matters as going to law, the sort of predicament which even respectable Home Service listeners might find themselves embroiled in from time to time.

Can I Take That Again?
The radio equivalent of DENIS NORDEN's popular ITV series *It'll Be Alright On The Night*, this weekly fusillade of bloopers, fluffs and gaffes ran on Radio 2 from 1985–90 and was culled from JONATHAN HEWAT's vast collection of taped broadcasting blunders. (Newsreaders referring to a computer's 'floppy dicks', DJs introducing 'Simon and Gungfunkel', and so on.)

'Can You Hear Me, Mother?'
See SANDY POWELL.

Cantabile
One of the few acts to have appeared on Radios 1, 2, 3 and 4 – evidence of the wide appeal of this male comedy harmony group consisting of a baritone (Michael Steffan), a counter tenor (Richard Bryan) and two tenors (Stewart Collins and Paul Hull), accompanied by pianist Andy Read. Their usual network is Radio 2, where they have had three series of their own.

The Canterbury Tales
Four of Chaucer's pilgrims' stories (those of The Pardoner, Wife of Bath, Miller and Franklin), designed as a cross section of the reverent and the rude, were dramatised as afternoon plays on Radio 4 in 1991. The dramatisations were by Colin Haydn Evans, with a score by folk musician Sue Harris.

Cantonese Service
Part of the BBC World Service, dating from May 1941. See CHINESE SERVICE.

Capital Radio

Britain's second oldest ILR station (on the air eight days after LBC) which is now the biggest and richest, having grown from a pop and rock service for London into a shrewdly managed, diversified and profitable business. It accounts for nearly a quarter of the total income of British commercial radio.

The first words to be heard (at 5 a.m. on 16 October 1973) were those of Sir Richard Attenborough, who has chaired the company from the beginning; the first record played was Simon and Garfunkel's 'Bridge Over Troubled Water'; and the debut commercial was for Birds Eye fish fingers, the first of some 20,000 different products to be advertised on the station.

Britain's economic crisis in its early years, characterised by the three-day-week, almost killed Capital off. It just managed to survive and has been profitable every year since 1976.

In 1979, Capital bought the Duke of York's Theatre in St Martin's Lane and also launched Britain's first traffic spotting plane, known as the Flying Eye, which is the only aeroplane authorised to fly over London below 1,500 feet. Now sponsored by British Airways, it provides peak-hour traffic reports seven days a week.

The station organises the annual Capital Radio Music Festival, which began life as the Capital Jazz Festival in July 1980, at Alexandra Palace – shortly before the building suffered its second devastating fire. The festival returned there in 1988. Now held in several venues, the event is Europe's largest popular music festival and has attracted performers such as Stevie Wonder, Chuck Berry, Fats Domino and Queen.

It is also known for its annual campaign Help a London Child, which it launched in 1975 (in 1990 it raised £750,000, distributed to 519 Greater London charities), and for its off-air service Helpline.

Capital acquired the West Country ILR station Devonair in 1987 and, in 1988, a 60 per cent holding in Riviera Radio, an FM station broadcasting in English in Monte Carlo and Ventimiglia. It has shareholdings in several other radio stations and has formed MAC-TV, a television production company. In 1987 it secured a listing on the Stock Exchange.

Nigel Walmsley, who joined Capital as its managing director in 1982 from the Post Office, was almost certainly the highest paid executive in British radio during his period with the station: his salary was stated in the company's 1990 Report and Accounts to be £161,000. In April 1991 he left the company to take charge of a bid by Carlton Communications for a Channel 3 (ITV) franchise area.

Caribbean Magazine

Weekly thirty-minute World Service programme which talks to people in Britain's West Indian communities.

Presented by Annemarie Grey, it is now also broadcast on Radio 5.

Caribbean Service

Part of the BBC World Service, which fell victim to economies in 1974. Brought back in 1988, and in its first year after that found itself covering six general elections, two coups, Hurricane Gilbert and an attempted takeover in Haiti.

Carmichael, Ian (1920–)

Actor whose skill has often been in evidence on Radio 4: roles have included the Hon. Galahad Threepwood in BLANDINGS and LORD PETER WIMSEY.

Carrington, Desmond (1926–)

Made his debut on Rangoon Radio in 1946 while in the Army; seconded to Forces Broadcasting and joined Radio SEAC in Ceylon along with his friend DAVID JACOBS. Demobbed, he went into acting (and played Dr Anderson in ITV's *Emergency – Ward Ten*) and combined it with broadcasting on Luxembourg and later the Light, hosting shows like MOVIE-GO-ROUND and HOUSEWIVES' CHOICE. Since 1981 he has presented Sunday morning's *Radio 2 All-Time Greats*, based on letters from listeners requesting their musical favourites.

Carry On Up the 50s

Domestic nostalgia was the essence of this nine-part Radio 4 series in 1989 with Harry Thompson playing clips from the BBC SOUND ARCHIVES.

The Cartoonists

The personalities behind the squiggles exchanged one studio for another when, in this Radio 4 series in 1990, they revealed how they worked and where their inspiration came from. Interviewer was Frank Whitford, *Sunday Mirror* cartoonist and art historian. Subjects included Mel Calman and Paula Youens (both of *The Times*) and Terence Parks, who signs himself 'Larry' in *Private Eye* and *Punch*.

Cash, Dave (1942–)

One of Radio 1's original team of DJs who launched the station in 1967, joining it from pirate ship Radio London, where he had become famous for his *Kenny and Cash* show, jointly presented with KENNY EVERETT. Helped to coin the phrase 'Groovy, baby'. Later went to Invicta Radio in Kent. Later he joined Capital Radio.

Catlett, John (1941–)

Ohio-born pioneer of precisely targeted, single format radio in the USA. He started broadcasting on the radio station at Princeton University and later spent eight years with CBS, eventually running FM stations in New York and Chicago. He then bought, with a group of black investors, a black music station in Hartford, Connecticut, which he still co-owns.

In 1984 he was invited to put his skills to work on the American-owned pirate radio ship Laser 558 in the North Sea, which he managed for eighteen months, and was later hired as the main consultant when Atlantic 252 was being set up. He became general manager of Radio Luxembourg in London in 1991.

Cat's Tails

Filling the gap between the end of CAT'S WHISKERS in June 1990 and the beginning of Radio 5 two months later was this short Sunday-evening series hosted by Julie Mayer which included stories, features, updates on the coming network and repeats of popular items from *Cat's Whiskers*.

Cat's Whisker

A fine wire, an inch or two long, which had to be twiddled on primitive wireless sets in the 1920s until it made contact with a crystal (usually made of galena, i.e. lead sulphide). When that happened it enabled the radio signal to be heard by the listener, through earphones.

Cat's Whiskers

The first systematic attempt to woo children back to Radio 4 since CHILDREN'S HOUR was axed in 1964: a Sunday teatime magazine for the under-twelves, with stories, puzzles, competitions, whodunnits and birthday interviews.

It was launched on an irregular basis in 1986 with different presenters (starting with Paul Nicholas and continuing with Bernard Cribbins) and went out in the school holidays, but came into its own in autumn 1988, with three series a year coinciding with school terms. Richard Briers and a sixteen-year-old assistant, Jenny Luckraft, presented the first run. Adrian Moorhouse, then the only man alive to have swum 100 metres in under a minute, followed, along with Julie First. The first serial was Enid Blyton's *The Castle of Adventure*, but most of those which followed were aimed at a slightly older audience.

Going out early on Sunday evenings when there was no competition from television, the programme even developed its own Cat's Whiskers Club, which more than 4,000 children joined.

Sadly, *Cat's Whiskers* was not to have the longevity of a cat's nine lives. It ran for only two years and was axed in June 1990. Two months later, the new Radio 5 became the home for all children's programmes, but its first controller PATRICIA EWING felt this one was difficult to dovetail into the new schedules. However, she hired its producer, Mary Kalemkarian,

to make other children's programmes for the network.

Celebrity Stories

Junior book at bedtime (7.20–7.35 p.m.) broadcast on Radio 5 when it began, with stories ranging from *Little Women* to *Stig of the Dump* chosen by the likes of Buki Armstrong, Nick Berry and Willie Rushton.

Celluloid Rock

Radio 1 series in 1988, introduced by STEVE WRIGHT, tracing pop in the cinema.

Central FM

See CENTRESOUND.

Centre Radio

Station that once had the ILR franchise for Leicester, but was hit by financial difficulties. The IBA readvertised the franchise and the Radio Trent group won it.

CentreSound

Falkirk, Stirling and Clackmannan in Central Scotland are served by this Stirling-based INCREMENTAL station, on the air since June 1990. It was relaunched after only five months as Central FM, three of its four journalists having been shed to cut costs, and is now run by Radio Forth. It broadcasts golden oldie pop hits from the 1960s to the 1980s for a target audience of 25 to 55-year-olds.

A Century Remembered

Unique ten-year project, continuing until the millennium and aimed primarily at a teenage audience, in which Radio 5 is broadcasting an archive series about each decade of the twentieth century every winter until the year 2000. The recordings come mainly from the BBC SOUND ARCHIVES as well as from other historic collections such as the Imperial War Museum. Clearly there are similarities with the old SCRAPBOOK series on the Home Service, except that those were portraits of one particular year as opposed to a whole decade.

It began in February 1991 with a five-part series on 1900–10, featuring the voices of Christabel Pankhurst, Caruso, Asquith, Bleriot and Baden-Powell and reminiscences of Queen Victoria's funeral fleet sailing up the Solent. In 1992 a second series will be mounted, covering the years 1910–20, in 1993 a third on 1920–30 and so until the final series in 2000 looks back at the 1990s, which will just have ended.

Chalfont, Lord (1919–)

First chairman of the RADIO AUTHORITY from 1 January 1991, a position he is to hold for an initial period of five years. As deputy chairman of the IBA from

1989, he was midwife to the birth of over twenty new INCREMENTAL stations. Born Alun Gwynne Jones, he has been a soldier, defence correspondent of *The Times* (wherein he made several broadcasts on the Third Programme in the 1960s), Minister of State at the Foreign Office under Harold Wilson, and an author and businessman with companies ranging from aerospace to public relations.

Challis, Jean   (1934–)
Actress whose voice is one of the most familiar on Radio 2, as a continuity announcer and presenter of shows such as NIGHT RIDE and STRING SOUND. She used to present FAMILY FAVOURITES and also spent five years with BFBS in Cyprus.

Chalmers, Judith   (1935–)
Manchester-born presenter who started her career as a child actress on the Northern edition of CHILDREN'S HOUR, aged thirteen. Some years later, in the late 1950s, she helped to introduce a teenage slot on the programme called *Out of School*. Later, in a career more dominated by television, she deputised for JEAN METCALFE on TWO-WAY FAMILY FAVOURITES and presented WOMAN'S HOUR from 1966–70; but she did not land her own show until 1990 when she followed KEN BRUCE in the mid-mornings on Radio 2. Her speciality is getting people to ring in with details of their club reunions, anniversary get-togethers and so on. A member of the Peacock Committee on Broadcasting in 1986, she is the elder sister of Sandra.

Chalmers, Sandra   (1940–)
First woman to run a local radio station in Britain (BBC Radio Stoke, 1976–83). Then editor of WOMAN'S HOUR (1983–87), presiding over the special 40th birthday edition which included not only an interview with Winnie Mandela but also one of the most extraordinary items in the programme's history – on the problem of flatulence, complete with sound effects and first person accounts of windy discomforts. Launched IT'S YOUR WORLD as a joint venture with the World Service: MICHAEL CHARLTON chaired the first series, followed by SUE MACGREGOR. Head of BBC Radio Publicity and Promotions since 1987. Younger sister of Judith.

Change and Decade
Thoughtful, three-part Radio 4 series at the end of 1989 looking at some of the social and economic trends of the 1980s, and pondering what sort of society Britain had consequently become.

Changing Churches
Radio 4 series in 1990 on radical new approaches to worship and liturgy in some of Britain's churches, from

video screens and slide projectors to the evangelical Catholic movement known as The Way and the healing, tongues and prophesy of the 'happy clappies' of the House Church movement.

The Chapel in the Valley
Sunday morning organ music series which began on the Light Programme in May 1949 and carried on until the Radio 2 era in December 1969, hosted by SANDY MACPHERSON.

Charlton, Michael   (1927–)
Australian-born broadcaster who started his career as a cricket commentator with the Australian Broadcasting Corporation, coming to Britain in the 1950s to commentate on Test matches for his listeners back home. He stayed on to fashion a career as a serious journalist on both television (where he presented *Panorama*) and radio (with IT'S YOUR WORLD).

Almost uniquely, he has used radio systematically to analyse issues in contemporary history. In a clutch of heavily researched series, mainly on Radio 3, he has explored Vietnam, the Falklands, Iran, America's National Security Council (SAILING WITHOUT AN ANCHOR, 1989) and the collapse of communism in Eastern Europe (FOOSTEPS FROM THE FINLAND STATION, 1991). He is less interested in speculations about the future than in pinning down the key players from tumultuous events of the recent past.

Chart Quiz
Radio 1 series hosted by MIKE READ, starting in 1988.

Chartbusters
Radio 1 series hosted by BRUNO BROOKES, from January 1986 to September 1988.

Checkpoint
Celebrated and influential Radio 4 consumer watchdog which ran from 1973–85, attracting much publicity on account of its assertive presenter ROGER COOK and the physical injuries he received in the course of confronting a variety of dubious characters.

In 1985 he was poached away by Central TV to present a similar, but flashier, investigative series for ITV called *The Cook Report*. Radio 4 replaced Cook's programme with FACE THE FACTS, starting in 1986.

Checkpoint spawned an imitative series on Capital Radio called *PDQ* (the initials stood for Pretty Damn Quick as well as Problems That Demand Questions) which was created and hosted by former *Checkpoint* researcher John Stonborough.

It was on this programme that, probably for the first and only time in British radio history, a person was arrested on air. This happened in March 1983 when a man called Derek Barnes recorded an interview with Stonborough at Capital's studios about his minicab company. When an accusation of fraud was put, Barnes tried to walk out. But Stonborough, a former policeman, made a citizen's arrest and grabbed him. The scuffle was not broadcast at the time as it would have been *sub judice* but had to be delayed until the following October when Barnes was jailed for four years at Reading Crown Court for obtaining money by deception. It was then played on the programme, so listeners were able to hear the moment of arrest.

The Cheerful Little Earful

Influential Harlem composer and pianist Fats Waller, who wrote 'Ain't Misbehavin'' and 'Honeysuckle Rose', was profiled in this four-part Radio 3 series in 1989 by his biographer, Alyn Shipton.

Chester, Charlie (1914–)

Veteran radio comedian, nicknamed 'Cheerful Charlie', who has presented his own Radio 2 show – a remarkable affair of his own invention in which he redistributes goods from those who no longer want them to those in dire need of them – since 1969.

Made his radio debut in 1937 on a music hall programme alongside TOMMY HANDLEY and George Robey in ST GEORGE'S HALL in Portland Place, later destroyed by bombs. Came to prominence in STAND EASY, when he invented catchphrases like 'Wotcher Tish, Wotcher Tosh' as one half of a pair of barrow boys, and became a regular on WORKERS' PLAYTIME, MIDDAY MUSIC-HALL and *Calling All Forces* opposite TONY HANCOCK.

His first Radio 2 show in 1969, a daily programme, later moved to Sunday evenings and developed into the current SUNDAY SOAPBOX which helps those in need of advice and assistance. He has helped, with others, to ship 6,000 hearing aids to a deaf school in Tonga and 2,000 unwanted fur coats to Poland.

The Chesterian

Six-part Radio 3 series in 1990 in which Edward Blakeman presented extracts from the strongly independent musical journal of the 1920s.

Children Calling Home

Emotionally draining Second World War series presented by Enid Maxwell (1908–90), previously assistant to UNCLE MAC, which enabled parents in Britain to hear the voices of their sons and daughters, evacuated far away in the United States and Canada. It was broadcast between September 1941 and May 1944.

Children in Need

Today, and for some years, this has been primarily a television charity extravaganza, but its origins lie firmly in the defunct CHILDREN'S HOUR.

From the early 1920s, young listeners who subscribed to the programme's RADIO CIRCLE helped to put funds into children's charities. When the Circle was disbanded in 1933, DEREK MCCULLOCH started regular appeals on the programme, under the title 'Uncle Mac's Christmas appeal for invalid and crippled children.' It continued regularly throughout the Second World War and in one year raised as much as £18,000.

This spot grew into the annual Children's Hour Christmas Appeal for Children in Need of Help, with big names such as Sir Malcolm Sargent, DAVID DAVIS and WILFRED PICKLES making the appeals, and in 1951 it was taken into THE WEEK'S GOOD CAUSE. In 1955, a five-minute spot started on BBC Television as well as radio.

The total raised between the early 1930s and 1979 was £630,898: in 1980, BBC-TV mounted the first all-singing, all-dancing Telethon gala, which raised £1 million in *one night*, which had grown to over £20 million ten years later.

Children of the Cloth

David Frost, Jon Snow, Roy Hattersley, Penelope Mortimer, John Wells and Virginia Wade were the six personalities, all of them offspring of clergy, who were featured in this Radio 4 series in 1990. They spoke to Trevor Barnes about how their upbringing had shaped their lives.

Children's Choice

Junior version of HOUSEWIVES' CHOICE, beginning on the Light Programme on Christmas Day 1952 and presented by Donald Pears. It was Britain's first national record request programme for children and ran from 9.05 to 9.55 a.m., giving way to A STORY, A HYMN AND A PRAYER. Its name was changed to CHILDREN'S FAVOURITES in 1954, when UNCLE MAC took over.

Children's Favourites

Long-running (1954 to 1967) Saturday morning series on the Light Programme which succeeded CHILDREN'S CHOICE. UNCLE MAC, or DEREK MCCULLOCH as he was calling himself by now, was the regular presenter from 1954 to 1964. Although he had various stand-ins the programme will forever be associated with him and carried his stamp – decent, proper, well-behaved, wholesome, formal.

His opening words 'HULLO CHILDREN EVERYWHERE' and the string orchestra signature tune of 'Puffing Billy', became symbols of the Fifties every bit as evocative as Dan Dare, Meccano and grey flannel shorts: to have one's name read out on the air was one of the ultimate thrills.

The music played on Children's Favourites was genuinely requested by the children, but it also carried

47

– until the final years when pop reared its head – the Uncle Mac and Auntie BBC seal of approval. Today it may seem extraordinary that youngsters of twelve could write in and ask to hear Mantovani's 'Swedish Rhapsody', Roy Rogers's 'A Four-Legged Friend' and Rosemary Clooney's 'Me And My Teddy Bear', but they did, and in huge numbers.

Max Bygraves says that on occasion between 3,000 and 4,000 postcards (which then cost only one old penny) arrived asking for 'You're A Pink Toothbrush, I'm A Blue Toothbrush', which was one of many discs to be played over and over again. 'Every time I hear you whistle, It makes my nylon bristle . . .'

The programme catered for a broad age range – the whole span of what used to be known as childhood. Uncle Mac interspersed light classics like 'The Skaters' Waltz' and 'The Bluebell Polka' with novelty songs such as 'The Ugly Duckling' and 'Davy Crockett, King of the Wild Frontier' and nursery rhymes for the very youngest, along with 'Sparky's Magic Piano' and 'Little Red Hen'.

As the years went by, many of the children who had grown up with the programme in the 1950s started to experience pubescent stirrings. This corresponded with the onset of the pop age, Beatles and Stones. Thus it was that McCulloch and company started getting requests for songs about teenage love and fast cars in addition to 'The Laughing Policeman' and 'Nellie the Elephant'. These requests came from teenagers, not children, and McCulloch did not feel that this was his scene at all.

When Cliff and Elvis started to replace teddy bears' picnics and runaway trains in the affections of the audience, the programme could not continue to be safe and square. Although, in 1965, it was extended to Sunday mornings as well as Saturdays, it died with the Light Programme. Its successor, JUNIOR CHOICE, was launched on the very first day of Radio 1 in 1967.

'Part of the appeal of *Children's Favourites* was its thumb-sucking security, each week the same old welcome friends singing the same old welcome songs' – Jeremy Nicholas, presenter of the radio documentary *Hullo Children Everywhere* in 1988.

Children's Hour

For millions of people now in their middle years, no programme has ever woven a spell as powerful as this or provided so much pure and unalloyed pleasure over such a long period.

For more than forty years (although for only two of them, 1937–39, was it actually a whole hour) it enriched their lives by opening a window on all sorts of wonderful worlds: serials, plays, historical adventures, nature study, TOYTOWN, songs, music with Helen Henschel, finding out, quizzes, competitions, books, careers, Bible stories, travel, appeals and talks on world affairs.

It began in December 1922, only a few weeks after the BBC came into being. It ended on Good Friday, 27 March 1964 (two days before Radio Caroline went on the air, in a memorable weekend that snuffed out one age and ushered in another). Furious protest, including questions at Westminster and scathing attacks in the Press, achieved nothing.

In the beginning the programme was organised on a regional basis and it did not acquire a single boss until 1938, when UNCLE MAC took over. (Almost as soon as the programme had started in the 1920s, listeners wrote in to call the presenters 'uncles' with themselves as their nephews and nieces. The presenters soon included Uncle Caractacus (Cecil Lewis), Uncle Rex (Rex Palmer), Auntie Cyclone (Kathleen Garscadden) and Auntie Sophie (Miss Cecil Dixon), but the BBC was never particularly keen on the practice and in the early 1930s it was phased out.)

Despite having a single head, the Organisers in each of the seven regions commissioned and prepared their own programmes so they could opt out from London if they wanted. For example, one edition a week that was produced from Cardiff was always in Welsh, and Scotland had its own Zoo Man. North of the border, Kathleen Garscadden presented the programme for over three decades – from 1923 to 1960, during which time she produced sixteen adventure serials including several especially thrilling ones about the Lost Planet, written by Angus MacVicar.

The Children's Hour Sunday edition began in October 1939, having been delayed almost eight weeks by the start of war. It was here that Princess Elizabeth, then fourteen, made her first broadcast, in October 1940. She was introduced by Uncle Mac from Windsor Castle. It was also on the Sunday Children's Hour that THE MAN BORN TO BE KING went out.

The title 'Children's Hour' was dropped in 1961 when staff such as DAVID DAVIS were also forbidden to broadcast their own programmes. The programme's identity gradually dimmed. 'Junior Time', a title introduced in October 1960 for the first quarter of the hour each weekday, was dropped in March 1962. 'For the Young' was the new title introduced at the end of 1962.

There was furore – questions in Parliament and anger throughout the Press, with an attack by Dennis Potter in the *Daily Herald* headlined 'Slamming the Door to Wonderland' – when the BBC announced in 1964 that the programme would end. This was the most controversial decision which FRANK GILLARD ever took, and was allegedly made because of its shrinking audience (the figures were bitterly contested by some of the programme's supporters).

The very last programme ended, apart from in Scotland where Kathleen Garscadden gave a talk about her childhood, with a fifteen-minute story. A sorrowful

Children's Hour, 1951. **Recording a Northern Region production of** *The Adventures of Samuel Poppleton* **are (left to right) Brian Trueman (later a familiar face on Granada TV), Joyce Palin, Herbert Smith and Peter McKendrick**

David Davis read *The Selfish Giant* by Oscar Wilde. This was a tale about a large and insensitive bully who prevented children from coming into his garden after school not because they did any harm but because it was his garden and he wanted to keep it all for himself. The symbolism was there for those with ears to hear it.

Children's Hour launched many young talents, among them MICHAEL ASPEL, JUDITH CHALMERS, BRIAN REDHEAD, Julie Andrews, Robert Powell and James Galway. It influenced countless more, as Roy Hattersley indicated in *The Listener* in 1981: 'The wind that whistled around "Hilltops of Britain" blew right into my bedroom and the gulls scavenging in the wake of the Roman galley that sailed into Romney and Rye for episode one of "Castles of England" flew just above

my head. I was there with Hereward the Wake, Alfred, Simon de Montfort and the barons at Runnymede.'

See also NORMAN AND HENRY BONES, CHILDREN'S NEWSREEL, JENNINGS, NATURE PARLIAMENT, JOSEPHINE PLUMMER, RADIO CIRCLE, ROMANY and THE ZOO MAN.

Children's Newsreel
Part of CHILDREN'S HOUR, this began in 1945 in the Northern edition based in Manchester. It went national in 1954 and lasted until 1963.

Chiltern Radio
ILR station based in Dunstable and Bedford, which has been covering Herts, Beds and Bucks since 1981 and Bedford and Cambs since 1982. The group that owns it has been quoted on the Stock Exchange since 1989. In 1990 Chiltern launched a satellite 'sustaining' service called Supergold, which plays golden oldies from the last 35 years. Several other ILR stations take it and play it on their own airwaves.

Chilton, Charles (1918–)
Has an assured place in radio history as the creator and writer of one of its true classics, JOURNEY INTO SPACE, as well as many other shows including RIDERS OF THE RANGE and BLOOD ON THE PRAIRIE. He also wrote the original stage show *Oh What A Lovely War!* for Joan Littlewood.

A Cockney, he joined the BBC as a fourteen-year-old messenger boy in 1932 and worked his way up to a producer. During the Second World War, working for the RAF as an instructor of aircrew and teaching navigation using the stars, he first gained that interest in the solar system and astronomy which, years later, blossomed into the adventures of Jet Morgan and his crew in Operation Luna, Red Planet and The World in Peril. (It was also during the war, while he was at Radio South-East Asia, that he shared an office with a young naval lieutenant called DAVID JACOBS: the friendship that sprang up resulted in Jacobs being hired on *Journey Into Space* a few years later, playing all the minor voices.)

Back at the BBC, still a member of staff, Chilton wrote *Riders of the Range* and then turned his imagination to inventing a story which would blend the thrills and spills of the Western with the awe and mystery of outer space. *Journey Into Space* was the result. He wrote a ninety-minute sequel to it in 1981 and a new serial in the same vein, SPACE FORCE, in 1984.

Chinese Service
Programmes in both Mandarin (three and a half hours a day) and Cantonese (45 minutes a day) constitute the Chinese Service of the BBC World Service.

During the events that led up to the massacre in Tiananmen Square in 1989, the Chinese authorities started to jam the Mandarin output (sent from the BBC's powerful new transmitter in Hong Kong) which had been stepped up in response to demands for more coverage of China's turmoil and the welcome given to it (students had carried banners saying 'Thank You BBC' in the protest rallies in Peking). China's jamming, its first systematic interruption of any World Service programme, was intended to ensure that only the official version of the military crackdown reached Chinese ears. The BBC protested strongly. JOHN TUSA said there was 'no possible justification' for it, adding: 'It clearly indicates the impact the World Service is having inside China as far as the authorities are concerned.'

In 1989, Elizabeth Wright, a former Foreign Office diplomat in Peking in the wake of the Cultural Revolution and a fluent speaker of Mandarin, became head of the Chinese Service. She became known to listeners that autumn as writer and presenter of *The Chinese People Stand Up*, a major documentary series to mark the 40th anniversary of the Chinese revolution, produced jointly by the World Service and Radio 4 and also published as a book.

Chinstrap, Colonel
Drunken old Army wallah who was the longest running character on ITMA, played by Jack Train from 1942 to 1949. Catchphrase: 'I DON'T MIND IF I DO . . .'

Choice FM
'You can tune in and chill out to the hardest and coolest in Dance, Reggae, Soca, Hip-Hop, House and Calypso', promised this INCREMENTAL based in Brixton, South London, when it went on the air in March 1990.

It carries all types of black music: all the above plus soul to gospel (every Sunday morning) and rap to R and B. It started no fewer than three chart shows, all of them with national sponsors (Special Brew, Carlsberg and Old Jamaica Ginger Beer).

Choral Evensong
The weekly broadcast of this much cherished Anglican service is, according to the BBC's Radio Programme Index, the longest running programme of all – apart from the Sunday appeal slot THE WEEK'S GOOD CAUSE.

It was first broadcast on 7 October 1926, two years before the DAILY SERVICE which the BBC has usually stated to be its most venerable programme.

The series has moved about in its 65-year existence: it started on the National Programme, was later in the early evenings on the Home Service in the early 1960s and transferred to Radio 3 in 1981. For the next seven years it had a regular time of 4 p.m. on Fridays. Protests flooded in when Radio 3 controller JOHN DRUMMOND moved it in 1988 to a new and, for many, much less convenient time of 10.30 p.m. on Sundays. He later bowed to public wish and moved it back to 4 p.m. – but on Wednesdays.

The Christian Centuries
Twelve-part Radio 4 series in 1988 about a theological relay race, in which BRIAN REDHEAD showed how the flame of the Christian faith had been passed on down the centuries by a succession of larger-than-life characters (emperors, geniuses, holy prostitutes, hermits, abbesses, madmen and murderers) from Constantine and the end of the classical period to Dante and the beginning of the Renaissance.

Christian Outlook
Home Service series which ran for almost the whole of 1949 and then re-emerged as a weekly programme of Christian news, views and comment from 1957–64 on Network Three.

Christmas Rapping
Clever title for Radio 1 series in 1983 in which followers of Christianity ranging from Malcolm Muggeridge to Nick Beggs of pop group Kajagoogoo talked about their faith.

The Churchill Years
Six drama documentaries written by David Wheeler on Radio 4 in 1990 to mark the 50th anniversary of Winston Churchill becoming Prime Minister. They were designed to assess various critical turning points in the statesman's life. Daniel Massey played Churchill.

Cinema Scrapbook
Radio 2 film series presented by Chris Kelly, which began in December 1983.

Cinema 2
Weekly film programme on Radio 2, presented by Charles Nove since 1988, whose ancestors were MOVIE-GO-ROUND and STAR SOUND CINEMA.

Citizens
Twice-weekly soap opera, with an omnibus edition on Saturday evening, launched in October 1987 as BBC Radio's first new soap opera since WAGGONERS' WALK and the first on Radio 4 since THE ARCHERS.

It centred on the permanently bickering occupants of a house in fictional Limerick Road, Ditcham Heath, London SW21, whose landlady Alex Parker (Kate Duchene) was an unmarried mother who worked at the local Bread Street Arts Centre. Her lodgers, who had met her when they were all at college in Leicester, were twins Julia and Michael Brennan from an Irish Catholic family in Liverpool; Anita Sharma, a doctor from a Hindu family in Birmingham; and Hugh Hamilton, a yuppie merchant banker from Kilmarnock, who moved into one of the attic rooms. The sitting tenant, Ernest Bond, was played by Brian Murphy. The jangly signature tune was written by Harvey Brough, former leader of Harvey and the Wallbangers.

Critics, and most of the Radio 4 audience, found it grey, drab and miserable – soap box, never soap opera. Changes in the production team were to no avail and, not before time, it was killed off in July 1991.

'We hope to present a colourful, humorous and truthful picture of what life is like for many people living in different parts of Britain now' – statement by co-producers Marilyn Imrie and A.J. Quinn, on launching the serial in 1987.

'It would be foolish to pretend that radio was not encouraged by the success of *EastEnders*. We were, and we hope we have learnt things from its success' – John Tydeman, head of BBC Radio drama, in his statement launching *Citizens*.

Clancy of the Outback
Australian Dick Bentley took the title role in this Light Programme drama series from 1963 about a heroic figure from his country's folklore who lived in the pioneering and gold rush days of the 1880s.

Clare, Dr Anthony   (1942–)
Probing, articulate Irish psychiatrist who gained prominence as a regular guest on Radio 4's STOP THE WEEK and then as the man who persuades celebrity guests to sit back and unlock themselves IN THE PSYCHIATRIST'S CHAIR. In 1988 he began a new series, ALL IN THE MIND.

Classes Apart?
Six Radio 4 programmes in 1990 about the contrasting lifestyles of three Somerset families.

Classic Albums
Two series on Radio 1 in which the late ROGER SCOTT talked to the stars and musicians who had made some of the world's bestselling LPs. The first series of one-hour shows in 1988 featured 'Brothers in Arms' (Dire Straits), 'Beggars' Banquet' (The Rolling Stones), 'Pet Sounds' (The Beach Boys), 'The Joshua Tree' (U2), 'Rumours' (Fleetwood Mac), 'Synchronicity' (The Police) and 'Hotel California' (The Eagles).

The second series, made in 1989 and broadcast posthumously in 1990, included Tina Turner talking about 'Private Dancer', Elton John on 'Captain Fantastic' and Dave Gilmour of Pink Floyd discussing the band's 'Dark Side of the Moon'.

The Classic Buskers
Six-part Radio 2 series in 1989 in which Michael Copley and Jeremy Sams played classical tunes on tin whistles, plastic saxophones and so on, assisted by RICHARD STILGOE. In 1991 the Buskers, by now Copley and Ian Moore, returned for another series of eight shows.

Classic Serial
A general term, rather than a programme title, which has often been used to cover Radio 4's fine serialisations of established books. These have included, for example, Dickens's *A Tale of Two Cities*, *That Hideous Strength* by C.S. LEWIS, and THE FORSYTE CHRONICLES.

Clayton, Peter   (1927–)
Knowledgeable, softly-spoken presenter of jazz programmes for almost thirty years: few have done more to keep the flame burning. Sadly, he ceased to be a regular voice in July 1990, when a mysterious spinal affliction seized him at a jazz festival in Grimsby. Since then he has been in pain, paralysed below the waist and confined to a wheelchair at home, although he has been broadcasting on Radio 2 at intervals.

Spent seven years in public libraries, stamping books. Then became a sleevenote writer for Decca, an advertising copywriter and editor of a jazz magazine; made his radio debut in 1962 on the magazine show THE JAZZ SCENE. Given his own late-night programme, *Jazznotes*, in 1970, which ran on both Radios 1 and 2. Became a presenter of Radio 3's JAZZ RECORD REQUESTS and Radio 2's SOUNDS OF JAZZ, both of which he was hosting when he was struck down. Jazz correspondent for the *Sunday Telegraph* since 1964 and, following his near-stroke in 1990, its radio critic also.

The Clever Dick-athlon

Radio 2 comic quiz show chaired by Don Maclean, in which three other comedians tried to win the title of 'Clever Dick of the Week'. It ran from April 1988 to May 1989.

Cleverdon, Douglas (1903–87)

Producer of the immortal UNDER MILK WOOD, which he commissioned from Dylan Thomas and then spent seven years in badgering him to get on and write it. One of the BBC's most spirited and imaginative features producers from the mid-1940s to the mid-1960s, his love of both pubs and poetry nurtured a fruitful association with Thomas, and he also cast him as Satan in a twelve-part serialisation of *Paradise Lost*.

Cleverdon, a wheelwright's son from Bristol who joined the BBC in 1939 and worked briefly as a war correspondent, also helped to discover Donald Swann in the early 1950s and produced the HILDA TABLET satires.

Click

Playwright Ken Blakeson (who later had an award-winning play about Army wives, *Excess Baggage*, banned from an afternoon repeat on account of its strong language) wrote and presented this four-part Radio 4 series on photography which went out in 1984–85.

The Clitheroe Kid

An extremely short (4ft 3in) Lancashire comedian acted the part of a naughty schoolboy in this famous Light Programme sitcom which ran from 1958–72. Peter Sinclair played his Scottish grandad, Patricia Burke and Renee Houston his mother and Diana Day and JUDITH CHALMERS his long-suffering elder sister, Susan.

By a bizarre coincidence James Robinson Clitheroe, or Jimmy Clitheroe as he was better known, did actually come from the town of that name although it happened to be his own family name also. From a family of weavers, he went into showbiz and joined a touring troupe. He later settled in a bungalow in Blackpool, where he lived with his mother and his tame frog, Freddie.

Clough, Gordon (1934–)

Freelance who has presented THE WORLD THIS WEEKEND since 1972 and ROUND BRITAIN QUIZ since 1977. On the second, he took over from Jack Longland and his fellow chairmen on the panel game have been Anthony Quinton and now Louis Allen.

A fluent Russian speaker, he was Russian programme organiser in the BBC External Services from 1963–68 and travelled widely through the USSR to make his Radio 4 documentary series THE INDISSOLUBLE UNION.

CN.FM

ILR station for the Cambridge and Newmarket area, based in Cambridge, which has been on the air since 1989. It was the first ILR station to go out exclusively on FM. Mary Archer, a former chemistry don at Cambridge and wife of author Jeffrey, is among the directors. Another is broadcaster Chris Kelly, who owns a restaurant in Cambridge.

Coates, Eric (1886–1957)

Prolific composer of light music with many signature tunes to his credit, after earlier work as principal viola with the QUEEN'S HALL ORCHESTRA.

'By the Sleepy Lagoon' was chosen for DESERT ISLAND DISCS, and still accompanies the mewing seagulls at the beginning and end of every programme; 'Knightsbridge March', extracted from his London Suite written in 1933, was taken for IN TOWN TONIGHT and 'Calling All Workers' was the stirring introduction to MUSIC WHILE YOU WORK.

Cobblers, Willium 'Mate'

Character on THE GOON SHOW epitomising the sort of surly, petty, unhelpful commissionaires SPIKE MILLIGAN encountered while recording the programme at BBC theatres. 'Born Shoreditch 1900, son of Fred "Chopper" Cobblers, OBE, road sweeper . . . mentioned in dispatches, as "always moaning" . . . now uniformed doorman at BBC Aeolian Hall . . . informs all visitors to the BBC, "It's nothing to do with me, mate."'

Cock-a-Doodle Disc

Breakfast show on the Light Programme with EAMONN ANDREWS spinning the records, billed as 'a free and easy programme with more discs than doodle.' Despite its wonderful title it lasted only a month – from April to May of 1960.

Collectors' Corner

Radio 3 music series from October 1972 to April 1980.

Collins, Norman (1907–82)

Creator and first Controller of the Light Programme in 1945, on which he inaugurated several classic programmes including WOMAN'S HOUR and HOUSEWIVES' CHOICE. He also made his mark in a wide

Lancastrian midget Jimmy Clitheroe's alter ego, school-boy Jimmy, played gooseberry for years with his elder sister Susan and her boyfriend Alfie Hall. Here, in 1961, Diana Day plays Susan and Danny Ross is Alfie

range of other areas: as a novelist, whose best-known work was *London Belongs To Me* in 1945; as the BBC's Controller of Television from 1947–50; as one of those who paved the way for the establishment of ITV, breaking the BBC's broadcasting monopoly; as vice-chairman of ATV, under Lew Grade, from 1955–77; and as chairman of the Loch Ness Investigation Bureau.

Colour Supplement
Sunday-morning Radio 4 magazine programme lasting 100 minutes, introduced as a summer filler in July 1984 with Sarah Kennedy the first presenter. When it returned the following year, former Scottish Nationalist MP Margo MacDonald was the host and she and DEREK JAMESON appeared together – hardly the

network's usual mixture of voices! It ran until December 1985.

Comedy
Part of the schedules from the earliest days of wireless, which suddenly enabled comics to entertain more people in one evening than in an entire lifetime of live performances in the halls. One of the first shows to pioneer and polish specifically *radio* comedy techniques was BAND WAGGON. In the Second World War, production moved to Bristol, and then Bangor in North Wales, to avoid bombing, and comedy shows like ITMA, WORKERS' PLAYTIME, MERRY-GO-ROUND and ACK-ACK BEER-BEER proved of vital importance in maintaining morale.

Peacetime hits, in the so-called 'golden age' of radio comedy, spanned TAKE IT FROM HERE, launching the careers of FRANK MUIR and DENIS NORDEN (creators of THE GLUMS), and the surreal innovations of THE GOON SHOW. ERIC BARKER and JOYCE GRENFELL enjoyed success as mild satirists and

53

husband-and-wife newcomers BERNARD BRADEN and BARBARA KELLY became major stars through radio within a year of their arrival from Canada.

EDUCATING ARCHIE attracted audiences as high as 18 million, which is as many as tune to *Neighbours* or *EastEnders* today, and TONY HANCOCK became perhaps the greatest comedy star of all.

Postwar, post-Goon irreverence found a home in BEYOND OUR KEN, which paved the way for the robust vulgarity of ROUND THE HORNE. THE NAVY LARK, another classic which began in the 1950s, sailed for eighteen years: for a long time it held the record for the longest running comedy series in BBC history, an honour which now belongs to WEEK ENDING.

The tradition of funny, whimsical talks was represented by Grenfell, Basil Boothroyd of *Punch*, and later JOHN EBDON and GLYN WORSNIP.

Undergraduate humour, particularly from Oxbridge and later laced with satire, came to the fore in the 1960s with CAMBRIDGE CIRCUS, paving the way for I'M SORRY I'LL READ THAT AGAIN, *Week Ending*, THE NEWS HUDDLINES and RADIO ACTIVE. Producers such as JOHN LLOYD, GEOFFREY PERKINS, SIMON BRETT, Jimmy Mulville and Griff Rhys Jones all cut their teeth on radio before moving on to graze richer pastures in television.

Some television hits have been adapted for radio, such as *Steptoe and Son*, DAD'S ARMY and *Rumpole of the Bailey*, but a more interesting list is those which have started on radio before being snapped up by television – not always the BBC. These include HANCOCK'S HALF-HOUR (BBC), AFTER HENRY (Thames), WHOSE LINE IS IT ANYWAY? (Channel 4), DELVE SPECIAL (Channel 4), SECOND THOUGHTS (London Weekend), UP THE GARDEN PATH (Granada), THE NEWS QUIZ and THE MARY WHITEHOUSE EXPERIENCE (both BBC).

Comment
Weekly review of the arts on the Third Programme, from July 1955 to September 1960. It returned in June 1961 as *New Comment*.

Community Matters
Radio 4 series of 1987–90 which tried to assess the social trends of the 1980s (e.g. the retail culture of spend, spend, spend) which might also be significant in the 1990s.

Community Radio
Feelings that both BBC Local Radio and ILR were failing to represent and reflect their local communities led to the growth in the early 1980s of pirate stations and a movement for non-profitmaking community radio, to be owned and managed by local people and financed by trusts and from the public purse. This was crystallised by the creation in 1983 of the COMMUNITY RADIO ASSOCIATION.

Leon Brittan, then Home Secretary, caused great excitement when he announced in 1985 that the government was going to initiate a two-year experiment in community radio. The CRA was closely involved in working out the details, and 266 applications were submitted (186 from London) for 21 stations scattered throughout Britain.

Disappointment as great as the initial euphoria set in when the Home Office cancelled the experiment in 1986, before it had even begun. The official reason was that more legislation was needed because the Wireless Telegraphy Act 1949 was an inadequate framework in which to proceed. But there were persistent rumours that the Home Office was fearful that community radio stations in sensitive areas could be seized by agitators, black militants and terrorists in the event of riots, or used to spread the gospel of insurrection.

The abandonment by the Home Office of community radio sparked a further upsurge in pirate radio, particularly those playing black music, but legal community radio re-emerged on the political agenda with the Home Office's Green Paper in 1987, which envisaged perhaps hundreds of small community radio stations in the future (though with a ban on public funding of them) as well as three new national commercial channels. These proposals found expression in the BROADCASTING ACT 1990, with local authorities still not allowed to contribute to stations' general running costs.

Pre-empting this new world, and in its last major act before its own dissolution (to be replaced by the Independent Television Commission and the RADIO AUTHORITY), the IBA set up a new generation of over twenty INCREMENTAL stations in 1989–90 which provided specialised music, different language services and programmes for ethnic groups. The IBA's initiative did something to meet the aspirations of the community radio movement, which had been frustrated by what seemed like endless delays.

Community Radio Association
Created in 1983. Its own brochures record the fact that 50 per cent of the people at its first meeting were pirate broadcasters, clear evidence of its pedigree! See also COMMUNITY RADIO.

The Compleat Collins
Five-part Radio 1 series in 1990 in which MIKE READ talked to singer Phil Collins, probably Britain's most successful solo male performer of the 1980s.

Composers of the Week
Daily Radio 3 programme in which the composer featured at breakfast time one week is repeated at

night the following week, so that every week two different composers are included. It began in 1988, replacing THIS WEEK'S COMPOSER.

One of the more unusual weeks in *Composers of the Week* featured 'British Film Music 1930–55', which played pieces by William Walton (e.g. *Henry V*), Vaughan Williams (*Scott of the Antarctic*), Arnold Bax (*Oliver Twist*), BRITTEN, Bliss and many others in that golden age for movie music when they were wooed by the film studios.

Concert Hall
Radio 3's lunchtime concert or recital which comes live each Wednesday from the Concert Hall in BROADCASTING HOUSE. It has been running since January 1972.

Concert Hour
The hour was between noon and 1 p.m., on weekdays on the Home Service from March 1946 to December 1964, when music was commonplace on the Home Service – as opposed to the much rarer event which it is today. The music generally came from one of the BBC's orchestras.

Concerto
Series on Radio 4 which features a complete performance of a concerto on record preceded by a wide-ranging conversation with the soloist. JUNE KNOX-MAWER is the usual interviewer. Examples have included Vladimir Ashkenazy (Beethoven's Piano Concerto No. 4) and Thea King (Mozart's Clarinet Concerto). It has been running since May 1987.

Consequences
The familiar parlour game in which every instalment of a story is written by a different person has enjoyed several manifestations on radio. For a chronology, see under the most recent version, LITERARY CONSEQUENCES.

Consuming Passions
Devoted to upmarket consumerism and lifestyle topics, this magazine show, made by the WOMAN'S HOUR unit, ran on Radio 4 for two series in 1988–89. The first presenter was SARAH DUNANT: too busy to make the second one, Brenda Polan of *The Guardian* stepped in.

A Consummate Conductor
Seven-part series on Radio 3 in 1990 examining the work of the mighty Austrian conductor Herbert von Karajan, which blended recordings of his performances with contributions from musicians, critics and music producers. Presented by Richard Osborne, author of *Conversations with Karajan*.

Contact Point
Yvette Fielding and Arabella Warner have been the presenters of this Radio 5 series for twelve-year-olds and under in which they discuss problems sent in by children themselves including fear of the dark, bullying and brothers and sisters. It has been running since the network began.

Continental Serenade
Ran from 1942–53 and then re-emerged on Saturday afternoons on the Light Programme from 1958–62, 'with Luigi and his Continental Players'.

Conversation Piece
Occasional series of thoughtful, 25-minute interviews running on Radio 4 since 1978, in which SUE MACGREGOR interviews a person of her choice. Guests are from a variety of professions and have included Dame Alicia Markova, bookseller Timothy Waterstone, jeweller Gerald Ratner, author Adele Geras and (in Hollywood, in 1988) Walter Matthau and Steven Spielberg.

Conversations with Scientists
Radio 3 series in 1989 in which Lewis Wolpert, Professor of Biology as Applied to Medicine at London University, talked to a different specialist each week. Chemists, mathematicians and zoologists were among the interviewees.

Cook, Christopher (1946–)
Presenter of THIRD OPINION since it began (and chairman of the final edition of its predecessor, CRITICS' FORUM) who is also frequently heard on its stablemate THIRD EAR.

Now the most frequently used arts broadcaster on Radio 3, he first broadcast on the network in 1970 – in a discussion with critic Richard Mayne about the films of Samuel Fuller – and went on to appear on THE ARTS THIS WEEK, *The Lively Arts* and *Scan*. A former head of the liberal studies department at the Central School of Art and Design, he still teaches but now to American students in London.

'Someone should compile a Roget's Thesaurus of critics' clichés. Top of the list would be "stimulating", "marvellous", "enterprising", "provocative" and "thought-provoking". Then of course there is "challenging". That means "difficult, angry, and I don't quite understand it"' – Christopher Cook.

Cook, Roger (1943–)
Antipodean journalist (born in Auckland, New Zealand, but raised in Australia) who has become a star performer with foot-in-the-door techniques and aggressive confrontations pioneered on Radio 4's CHECKPOINT.

Although it was patient research and teamwork which exposed the swindlers and conmen, it was presenter Cook – who always remembered to leave his tape-recorder running when he was thrown downstairs – who got the publicity.

In 95 per cent of the programmes, the encounters with villains left him unscathed, but it is the 5 per cent that stick in the memory: the rip of a coat sleeve in a car door, the barking Alsatian in the background, the crashes, pantings, scufflings and raised voices. In one incident his ribs (concealed inside a plump fourteen-stone frame) were cracked and in another he was run over by a car in Somerset. He also had hot water poured over him by men he was seeking to interview.

The resulting publicity gave him the reputation of being something of a caped crusader of the airwaves. He himself pointed out, however, that he was 'only the pointed end of a hard-working team'.

Cook cut his teeth on a Sydney radio station, 2GB, in 1959, before coming to Britain in 1968. Joined THE WORLD AT ONE as a reporter and worked there several years before graduating to his own series in *Checkpoint*, of which he made some 500 editions. In 1985 he was lured away by Central TV, where he presents a pugnacious investigative series for the ITV Network called *The Cook Report*.

Cooke, Alistair (1908–)

Doyen of foreign correspondents, Manchester-born but a US citizen since 1941. No-one has done more in revealing each country to the other. Much influenced by H.L. Mencken (1880–1956), one of the USA's most influential critics, author of *The American Language* and founder of the national literary review *American Mercury*. Most famous for LETTER FROM AMERICA, running since 1946, but has done much else besides.

His first major BBC series, in 1938, was I HEAR AMERICA SINGING. He traced the history of American folk songs from the War of Independence through rural Appalachia, the Gold Rush, cowboys and labour struggles. After many exchanges of internal memos, the BBC agreed to pay Cooke the princely sum of 25 guineas for each of the twelve talks, which were illustrated with an extraordinary range of music including Indian chanters, negro hucksters, glee clubs, songs of the lone prairie, cattle round-ups, railroads and Depression. Each programme began with 'The Star Spangled Banner'. The penultimate programme was entitled *Songs of Five Wars* – the Revolutionary, the War of 1812, the Civil War, the Spanish–American War and the First World War.

For one of the programmes, Cooke travelled to the Deep South and recorded the songs of workers on cotton fields and citrus plantations ('Boll Weevil Blues', 'Shack Bully Holler'). But all this precious material went up in smoke when part of the BBC archives was destroyed by German bombing.

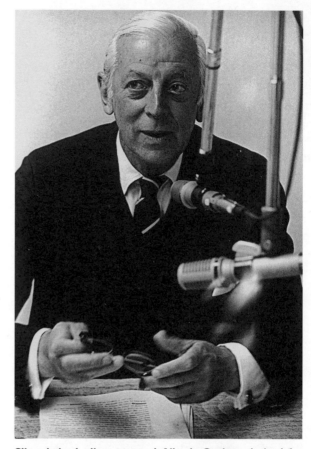

Silver-haired, silver-tongued Alistair Cooke, admired for shrewd insights and elegant prose since the 1930s. He has sent more than 2,000 *Letters From America* since his first in 1946, as well as written and presented several other programmes on jazz and popular song

Between 1974–87 he and producer Alan Owen made several series which alternated between Radio 2 and Radio 4. One showed how American popular song had developed from 1919–50. Another was a history of jazz from Louis Armstrong to Art Tatum. (Cooke thought then, and still does, that jazz ended when be-bop arrived in the late 1940s.) A third consisted of a five-part look at one of the greatest of US composers in *The Life and Music of George Gershwin* and yet another, *The First Half Century*, illustrated highlights of social history with music from the period.

In the past he has also worked for American radio: from 1935–37 he was NBC's London commentator, during which he reported on the momentous events in the Abdication Crisis, with NBC getting the Post Office to set up a microphone in his flat. He provided a weekly commentary for NBC from 1937–38 and in 1939–40 was theatre and film critic for the New York radio station WQXR.

See also FRANKLY SPEAKING.

Cooper, Derek (1925–)
Creator of THE FOOD PROGRAMME in 1979 and its presenter ever since. Other series include *Prophets Returned* and ISLANDERS, and he has appeared on many other programmes. He spent the whole of the 1950s with Radio Malaya, leaving as controller of programmes.

Cooper, Giles (1918–66)
Innovative radio dramatist whose play *The Disagreeable Oyster* (Third Programme, 1957) helped to lead to the formation of the BBC RADIOPHONIC WORKSHOP, because of the way in which it required sound effects to create aural images.

Cooper's first broadcast play was *Thieves Rush In* (Home Service, 1950) and he followed it with sixty more works, broadcast on Light, Home and Third. They included adaptations (ranging from *Lord of the Flies* and *The Day of the Triffids* to Dickens and Kipling) as well as disquieting, pessimistic, highly original creations such as the macabre *Unman, Wittering and Zigo* (Third, 1958), later made into a film starring David Hemmings.

Cooper died after falling out of a railway carriage as he was returning by train to his home near Midhurst after a dinner in London. The inquest was told the alcohol level in his blood was the equivalent of half a bottle of whisky. The jury returned a verdict of death by misadventure. Twelve years later, he was commemorated with an annual series of radio drama awards, the GILES COOPER AWARDS, named after him.

Costa, Sam (1910–81)
Portuguese-descended dance-band crooner of the 1930s who rose to fame in ITMA playing an office boy, and maintained it through MUCH-BINDING-IN-THE-MARSH. His catchphrase: 'Good morning, sir, was there something?' Later, he was the affable host of Radio 2's RECORD RENDEZVOUS.

Costello, Jenny (1969–)
DJ who became Radio 1's youngest when she took over the dawn slot at weekends in 1990. She started on hospital radio in Coventry and also works for RTM in South-East London.

Counterpoint
Musical quiz game on Radio 4, with questions ranging from Bach to The Beatles. Devised by Edward Cole, it has been running since July 1986, and the chairman is NED SHERRIN.

Counterspy
Exciting series about two security men which was part of CHILDREN'S HOUR – on the Wales edition only when it began (January–April 1953) and then nationally from 1955 to 1962. The 1955 run helped to launch the acting career of a young MICHAEL ASPEL, who has never forgotten the name of his character – 'Rocky Mountain'.

Country Club
Radio 2 folk series with WALLY WHYTON as its regular host, on the air since 1974. EDDIE GRUNDY stood in for him once in 1988.

Country Parliament
Began on the Home Service in 1966 on Sunday afternoons as a fusion of COUNTRY QUESTIONS and NATURE PARLIAMENT, both of which had been running since 1946. Derek Jones and Vincent Waite alternated as chairmen.

Country Questions
Sunday lunchtime programme on the Home Service in which listeners' questions about the countryside were answered by Ralph Wightman, Ernest Neal and Eric Hobbis. The chairman was Jack Longland. In 1966 it merged with NATURE PARLIAMENT to form COUNTRY PARLIAMENT.

The Countryside In . . .
Gentle, affectionate look at rural Britain on Radio 4, which began as a monthly programme on the Home Service in 1952 with the name of the month completing the title. It is now a quarterly programme, with the name of the season completing the title. MICHAEL GREEN has trimmed its length from 45 to 30 minutes.

C. Gordon Glover, who had already been responsible for a series on seasons in CHILDREN'S HOUR in 1949–50, presented it in the 1960s. His successor, the great WYNFORD VAUGHAN-THOMAS, presented it until his death in 1987. Since then it has been actress Molly Harris, who plays the quintessential countrywoman Martha Woodford in THE ARCHERS. Subjects have ranged from osier-cutting to the work of a Lake District postbus.

County Sound
Surrey's ILR station, on the air since 1983 with its headquarters now in Woking, which in June 1988 became the first ILR station to split into two separate services for the whole week. It launched a 'golden oldies' service of records from the 1950s, 1960s and 1970s aimed at the over-35s on medium wave, called Gold AM – the first such station in the UK – and gave a new name, Premier, to its FM service. Gold

AM has since been renamed First Gold Radio. In 1990 it launched a third and highly localised service, for Haslemere, called Delta Radio (also on FM) which was claimed to be the smallest station in Britain.

All the music on all three services is planned and selected by the station's computer, which is programmed to produce lists of songs of particular types and specific themes (e.g. Easter, summer holidays, money, loneliness) and which can match the music to the time of day and the age group listening. The DJs therefore have no say at all in what they play.

'Some people will argue that the computer takes individual creativity out of the presenter's hands. Frankly, I believe it does a better job. It works within the parameters we set which means we can control the whole sound of the network. That is far better than leaving it to a personal choice of one individual whose idea of good music may be totally out of tune with what the public wants' – Paul Owens, the station's head of music.

Crack the Clue
Quiz show hosted by DUNCAN JOHNSON in the early days of Radio 1.

Crazy People
Forerunner of THE GOON SHOW, in 1951–52. Its name was chosen to indicate that its four performers (SPIKE MILLIGAN, Peter Sellers, Harry Secombe and Michael Bentine) were akin to a junior Crazy Gang. Others who appeared in the show included Hattie Jacques and Max Bygraves.

Crime at Christmas
Collection of traditional whodunnits which made a festive entertainment on Radio 4 at Christmas 1987.

The Critics
Highbrow (and influential, with a peak audience of seven million) Sunday lunchtime symposium on the Home Service and its successor Radio 4, from September 1947 to December 1968, with critics such as J.W. Lambert, Cyril Ray, A. Alvarez, STEPHEN POTTER and Pamela Hansford Johnson discussing the latest plays, films and books.

Peter Sellers lampooned it with a wonderfully funny spoof, available on record (chosen by Noel Coward as one of the records he would take to the desert island) in which it transpired that each of the assembled critics had read a different book.

Critics' Forum
Weekly arts discussion on Radio 3 which, almost uniquely, had the same producer throughout the whole

of its long life, from 1974 to 1990 – Philip French, who is also film critic of *The Observer*.

Successor to THE CRITICS, its formula was unvarying: unscripted critical conversation about a book, play, film, exhibition and broadcast. There were a number of differences between the programme and its precursor, which French had also produced in the early 1960s: its length was extended but the number of speakers reduced from five or six to four. Having people from different disciplines was deliberate and enabled an art critic, for example, to bring fresh insights to a novel or a novelist to offer a fresh perspective on works of sculpture. In the first programme, when the speakers were Dilys Powell, Julian Mitchell, Edwin Mullins and Paul Bailey, there was such a fierce attack on one particular item that wits reckoned the programme should not have been called *Critics' Forum* but *Critics Against 'Em*.

French exercised untrammelled power. He selected both the topics to be discussed and the critics who would discuss them. He also wrote the introductory section to each topic which the chairman read. The programme was thus fashioned in his image and, when he retired, Radio 3 took the opportunity of retiring the programme with him.

Critics pointed out that it never covered music, design or architecture, and virtually never moved out of London. Few Scots or Continental critics ever appeared on it. Even JOHN DRUMMOND publicly conceded that for some listeners it epitomised all that was wrong with Radio 3: metropolitan, sniffy, exclusive and excluding.

The critics on the last edition, in July 1990, had all been regular contributors: Michael Billington, Marina Vaizey and John Carey. Chairman was CHRISTOPHER COOK. They discussed PAUL FERRIS's biography of Huw Wheldon, *Sir Huge*; a new RSC production of *King Lear* with John Wood in the title role; the Warren Beatty film *Dick Tracy*; Victor Passmore's *Artist's Eye* at the National Gallery; and ALAN BENNETT's Channel 4 series *Poetry in Motion*.

Cook went on to present the successor programme, THIRD OPINION, which makes sure that music, dance and architecture *do* get covered.

'It preserved the idea of there being a number of possible views on any given subject, and that civilised discussion can take place even when there are disagreements of an extreme kind' – Philip French.

Crown House
Soapy saga of the upper middle classes, beginning in 1988 on Radio 4, set in the 1920s and tracing the fortunes of the fictional Minster family whose lives intertwine with those of the Royals. Written by Peter Ling and Juliet Ace, and starring Jane Asher, Gayle Hunnicutt, Richard Pasco and Martin Jarvis.

Crun, Henry
Character on THE GOON SHOW, played by Peter Sellers.

Crystal sets
Early wireless sets in which crystals were used to act as rectifiers, allowing current to pass in only one direction. They were superseded by sets containing VALVES.

Culture Rock
Reggae series on Radio 1 presented on Sunday nights from March 1985 to March 1989 by THE RANKING MISS P.

Curtain Up
Drama slot on the Light Programme, running from October 1947 to December 1956.

The magic of wireless in the early 1920s brought the world to one's fingertips. Here, 'listening in' on a cat's whisker and crystal set

Cutforth, Rene (1909–84)
One of the most distinctive of radio correspondents – his gifts most in evidence while covering the Korean War – whose breadth of experience, passion for rotund, resonant, almost oratorical English and an eye and ear for telling detail characterised many of his generation. (During the Second World War he had enlisted in the army, served with the Sherwood Foresters, and been captured in the Western Desert in 1942.)

After Korea he worked as a freelance, specialising in travel, for both radio and television. In his obituary *The Times* remarked that he had brought to the airwaves 'the essentially literary quality of a vanished world, that of an essayist of the days before electronic news gathering.'

Cutler, Ivor (1924–)
Eccentric Scots songwriter, poet, painter and comedian who has developed a cult reputation in recent years. He entered radio in 1959 and has written several Radio 3

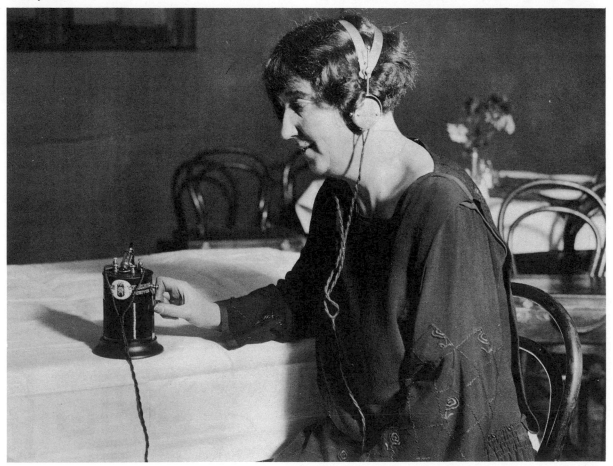

plays. In 1990 he started his first Radio 3 comedy series, KING CUTLER.

Czechoslovak Service
Czech-language output of the BBC World Service, which began in September 1939.

D

Dad's Army
Radio 4 broadcast its own version of BBC-TV's much loved comedy series from January 1974 to September 1976, with the scripts slightly altered from the television originals. The cast was the same: Arthur Lowe, John Le Mesurier, Clive Dunn and so on, with JOHN SNAGGE joining them as an announcer.

Daedalus
Independent production company which has made SHERLOCK HOLMES dramas for British Airways' in-flight entertainment. Founded by writer and management consultant Grant Eustace (who dramatised the stories) and Michael Bartlett, a former radio drama executive.

Daily Disc Delivery
Name of TONY BLACKBURN's breakfast show on Radio 1, whose first edition launched the new network at 7 a.m. on 30 September 1967.

Daily Mail
Has had a longer association with radio than any other publication: it was the *Mail* which sponsored Australian opera singer Dame Nellie Melba's historic concert (in English, French and Italian) at the Chelmsford studios of MARCONI in June 1920 which was heard as far away as Newfoundland, as well as throughout Britain, and showed beyond doubt that radio had arrived. At the end of the 1920s the paper organised what sounds in retrospect to have been a bizarre precursor to pirate radio, involving a yacht sailing round the coast of Britain and playing gramophone records (see STEPHEN WILLIAMS).

In the 1950s the newspaper sponsored a series of annual prizes, the NATIONAL RADIO AWARDS, revived as a one-off event in 1988 as part of the BBC RADIO SHOW. In 1979 it set up the Lord Rothermere Radio Awards, to encourage accurate research into radio advertising.

Daily Service
Fifteen-minute act of Christian worship every weekday morning on Radio 4 which is one of the world's longest-running programmes.

Its basic formula of prayer, hymns, a psalm and Bible reading has remained unchanged since it began in 1928 after a dogged crusade by a remarkable woman called Miss Kathleen Cordeux of Watford, who wrote to RADIO TIMES in 1926 proposing a daily service 'of a little sacred music, hymns, a brief reading or address to comfort the sick and suffering and the lonely.'

She proceeded to bombard SIR JOHN REITH with letters and organised a petition signed by 5,000 like-minded people who, as she put it in one of her many letters, longed 'to hear something *daily* of God and His love'. Among them were 'blind, bedridden and aged folk' and another who begged for a daily service was a paralysed girl who 'wrote a long letter with a pencil held in her lips'.

Reith may have been a committed Christian (and the son of a minister) but it still took nearly two years for the BBC to accept the idea. Eventually it bowed to the pressure and the first Daily Service – then, as now, fifteen minutes long – was broadcast in January 1928 from a studio at SAVOY HILL. It was not the first service the BBC had broadcast (that was shortly after the BBC had started in 1922, with microphones simply eavesdropping at a normal church service) but it was the first to be created specifically for broadcasting.

Within a fortnight, 7,000 letters of praise arrived at the BBC. Cordeux's persistence was clearly vindicated and in 1937 she was given the 100,000th copy of the service book which the programme produced for its listeners, *New Every Morning*, personally inscribed by a grateful Reith.

With the move in 1932 to BROADCASTING HOUSE, the religious broadcasting department acquired its own consecrated studio (3E) which was used by the Daily Service until the outbreak of war. From 1939 to 1945 the programme was evacuated first to Bristol and then Bedford (along with many other BBC activities) and continued to be a source of comfort and fortitude by broadcasting from churches in those two places.

Studio 3E suffered such severe bomb damage that it could not be used again after the war. When the Daily Service returned to London, therefore, its new venue became St Peter's in Vere Street, off Oxford Street. This church was linked to All Souls', outside Broadcasting House. All Souls' was in fact the BBC's first choice, but was undergoing major restoration.

All Souls' was rededicated in 1951, was being used for more Daily Services than St Peter's by the mid-1950s, and has been its permanent home since 1963. Today the programme comes once a week from a studio in Broadcasting House and once a week from outside the capital, but All Souls' remains the heart of this congregation of the air. The occasional muffled roar of traffic or road drill acts as a reminder of its location on one of the busiest roads in central London, and the fact that it goes out live. It was here that the 60th birthday service was held in 1988, led by the Archbishop of Canterbury.

Until 1951 the hymns sung on the programme (usually by the BBC SINGERS, but their role has been sharply reduced in recent years, and they now appear only once a week) were taken from two books, *Ancient and Modern* and *Songs of Praise*. But in that year the Corporation published its own *BBC Hymn Book* (thirteen years after it was first conceived, when a committee was set up by Henry Walford Davies, first Music Adviser to the BBC's Head of Religious Broadcasting). It was originally produced for church use but its 1981 supplement *Broadcast Praise* featured words and music specifically suited to the Daily Service.

'It is, and has always been, ecumenical, so it reflects what Christians have in common, rather than what divides us. I hope that the Daily Service will continue to hold its honoured place in the BBC's schedules, and provide a moment of reflection and worship in the very centre of our daily concerns' – Dr Robert Runcie, Archbishop of Canterbury, in 1987.

Dalby, Barrington (1893–1975)
Amateur referee for the British Boxing Board of Control who became a frequent radio sports commentator.

The Dales
See MRS DALE'S DIARY.

Dan Dare
The hero of *Eagle* was also Radio Luxembourg's first post-war daily serial, from 1951 to 1956 (the golden age both of radio and the boys' paper coincided). The show was sponsored by Horlicks with the Pilot of the Future played by Noel Johnson, who only a few years before had starred as that other square-jawed hero DICK BARTON.

In April 1990, Radio 4 adapted the very first of Dan Dare's thrilling adventures – the trip to Venus and the discovery of the cold, technocratic Treens run by the evil Mekon – as a four-part, late-evening serial going out in stereo to make the most of the interplanetary sound effects.

These, which included the Mekon's flying chamberpot and the death throes of a Venusian dinosaur, were created with digital equipment by Wilfredo Acosta, son of Walter Acosta, Uruguayan drama producer on the World Service.

The serial went out forty years to the week since *Eagle* first hit the streets. Mick Ford played Dan; Donald Gee his loyal Lancashire batman Digby; Terence Alexander Sir Hubert Guest; and Zelah Clarke that early feminist Professor Peabody.

Dance Party
Friday night show on Radio 1 in the late 1980s, hosted by JEFF YOUNG. Later it became *Jeff Young's Big Beat*.

Daniels, Bebe (1901–71)
See BEN LYON.

The Daring Dexters
Serial about a circus family which went out in the summer of 1947, while DICK BARTON was taking a break.

The Dark Tower
Celebrated parable about a spiritual quest, written as a fantasy by LOUIS MACNEICE and broadcast in 1946. The music was composed by BENJAMIN BRITTEN.

Date With Carole
Singer Carole Carr and the BBC WEST OF ENGLAND PLAYERS appeared in this Light Programme series which ran for three months in 1962.

Daventry
Site of the BBC's first major LONG WAVE transmitter, outside the Northamptonshire town, which opened in July 1925.

Davies, Gary (1957–)
Mancunian who joined Radio 1 in 1982, presenting a late night show on Saturdays from his native city. Now, he hosts a weekday lunchtime programme on the network – one of whose ingredients, consisting of back-to-back classic records, carries the elegant title of 'Gary's Gobsmackers'. Other items include the 'Sloppy Bit' and 'Your Most Embarrassing Moment'. Once branded a 'medallion man' and 'macho sex symbol', Davies prefers to think himself as a specialist in live outside broadcasts. Radio 1 regards him as its hitmaker, discovering records (particularly from Europe) and helping to put them in the charts.

Davies, Russell (1946–)

Actor turned comic writer, whose versatility has been well in evidence on BBC Radio. For two years on MIDWEEK (1979–81), when Desmond Wilcox was compere, he had a regular spot in the form of a five-minute round-up of silly stories. As a presenter, he was heard on WHEN HOUSEWIVES HAD THE CHOICE, RADIO FUN and SEVEN DEADLY SINGSONGS and a number of Radio 3 documentaries on jazz and American culture. As a playwright, he wrote both series of ARE YOU STILL AWAKE?

Davis, David (1908–)

Much admired, long serving and devoted presenter of CHILDREN'S HOUR, who took over as head of the programme in 1953. With his assistant head JOSEPHINE PLUMMER he was its guiding spirit through some of its greatest years, and still in charge of it when the BBC killed it off in 1964, a decision which left him broken-hearted. Real name: William Eric Davis.

The Day Job

Six-part Radio 4 series in 1982 in which TERRY WOGAN (then presenting the breakfast show on Radio 2) tried other people's jobs for a day – including those of a Concorde steward, AA patrolman and weather forecaster.

Day, Sir Robin (1923–)

Presenter of the phone-in programme IT'S YOUR LINE in the 1970s and THE WORLD AT ONE from 1979 to 1988.

de Lotbinière, Seymour (1905–)

Influential pioneer of sports coverage and outside broadcasts, supervising the entire coverage of King George VI's Coronation in 1937 and providing evidence of his own first-hand skills with his commentary on the great Crystal Palace fire the previous year.

An Old Etonian, he joined the BBC staff in 1932 and became widely known by the nickname 'Lobby'. He was the first to analyse and describe the radio commentator's art and the guidelines he drew up were given by him, and his successors such as ROBERT HUDSON, to all prospective commentators. Among those he brought forward were HOWARD MARSHALL and JOHN ARLOTT.

In 1952 he left BBC Radio to take over outside broadcasts in BBC Television – in time for the Coronation.

De Manio, Jack (1914–88)

Larger-than-life John Bull character, son of an Italian father and Polish mother, who worked as a trainee chef at the Ritz and won the Military Cross in France before becoming a national celebrity as presenter of TODAY from 1958 to 1971, during which he was chosen by Buckingham Palace as the person to whom Prince Charles gave his first broadcast interview, in March 1969.

He was famous for a rich, rotund, rather hoarse voice, a friendly and personable manner and an almost legendary inability to tell the time. One would think this was a drawback on a breakfast show, but it did nothing to dent his popularity.

De Manio, who started at the BBC in 1946 as an announcer, once said that he only landed the job on *Today* because nobody else was willing to get up at 5 a.m. BBC legend, however, has it that he was banished to the early mornings after yet another gaffe, made when he introduced a talk by Sir John Macpherson, former Governor of Nigeria. It was called 'Land of the Niger', which De Manio announced as 'Land of the Nigger'.

He made his reputation by misreading the studio clock: in an interview, played on Radio 4 just after his death, he recalled that he had once received a letter from a listener demanding compensation after he crashed his car in sheer surprise at hearing a spectacularly wrong time announced on his car radio.

De Manio presented the programme on his own from 1958–70, when JOHN TIMPSON joined him. After he left *Today* in 1971 he started presenting a new Radio 4 afternoon series, JACK DE MANIO PRECISELY, but this was axed in 1978 to make way for the new broadcasts from Parliament. His last major broadcasting job was a brief, not very happy, spell on WOMAN'S HOUR. His 1967 autobiography was called *To Auntie With Love*.

Dealing With Daniels

Radio 2 game show devised by IAN MESSITER, running from 1986–89, and hosted by Britain's most successful conjuror Paul Daniels. It combined general knowledge with a test of memory, as panellists (Anneka Rice, John Junkin, Patrick Moore, Duggie Brown and so forth) tried to recall which cards had already been dealt. The show evolved from FAIR DEAL, which Messiter also devised.

Dear Diary

Writer SIMON BRETT, editor of *The Faber Book of Diaries* and someone who has kept a diary himself from the age of nine, presented this Radio 4 series in 1990 in which he delved into history to see how famous diarists had spent their October 10ths or January 23rds.

Dear Jenny, Dear Julie

Radio 4 comedy series in 1990 about two penpals who meet up after twenty years. Written and performed by, and loosely based on the personalities of, comics Jenny Eclair (from Blackpool) and Julie Balloo (from Australia), who first mounted the show on the Edinburgh Fringe in 1988.

The clock always gave the right time, and sometimes Jack De Manio did too. But there was always plenty to smile at when he presented the *Today* programme. This was October 1967, just after the Home Service became Radio 4

Dear Radio Two
Regular letters column of the air on Radio 2, starting in April 1990, presented by VIVIEN STUART and Bob Sinfield. It finished in June 1991.

Dear Sir
Correspondence column of the air in the early years of the Light Programme, starting in 1950. It attracted so many letters (800 a week during its first run) that its editor, Leslie Baily, took on an assistant, Adrian Thomas, to whom he handed over in 1951 to make more time for his job in the Korda Film Organisation.

This switch did not meet with universal approval. Frank Allaun, later a Labour MP, later wrote to various papers criticising the programme for becoming more trivial and turning its attention away from weighty issues of peace and war to questions such as 'Do women like fat husbands?'

Debut
Radio 3 series running since January 1984 which gives listeners the opportunity to hear musical stars of tomorrow, such as soprano Lynne Dawson.

Dee, Simon (1935–)
The original pirate disc-jockey, uttering the first words on Britain's first pirate radio ship, Radio Caroline, on Easter Sunday 1964. He stayed with the ship until mid-1965, when a disagreement with the captain, he recalls, had him charged with mutiny.

He departed the high seas for a desk job at Caroline's command centre on shore – in Chesterfield Gardens, Mayfair – and thence the BBC. By 1966 he had a marathon Saturday-night show on the Light Programme, on the air from 11 p.m. until 1.30 a.m., and also hosted

MIDDAY SPIN and HOUSEWIVES' CHOICE. On Radio Luxembourg at the time he presented shows like *Simon's Scene*, *Battle of the Giants* and *Night and Dee*.

His move into television with the BBC chat show *Dee Time*, attended by all the hullabaloo of fame and fortune, led to a series of much publicised personal difficulties, and a succession of different jobs. His first regular radio slot since the crazy decade in which he played such a leading role was when he took over Radio 2's SOUNDS OF THE SIXTIES in 1987–88. Real name: C.N. Henty-Dodd.

Dell, Alan (c. 1930–)
Born in Capetown, of an English father and French Huguenot mother, and started in radio with the South African Broadcasting Corporation. He was one of the first announcers on Springbok Radio when it began in 1950, before going to the USA to study acoustics. He has been broadcasting on the Light Programme since the early 1950s and now presents Radio 2's weekly SOUNDS EASY.

Delve Special
Radio 4 comedy series running from 1984 to 1987 with Stephen Fry poking fun at the self-important, aggressive style of investigative journalism associated with ROGER COOK. It was adapted by Channel 4 in 1988 and renamed *This Is David Lander*. Stephen Fry remained the star.

Denham, Maurice (1909–)
Versatile actor, once called 'the man with the thousand voices', who has played everything from pigs in *Animal Farm* to the title role in JOHN MORTIMER's *Rumpole of the Bailey*, plus spivs, gypsies, bishops, Army officers and English gentlemen. NED SHERRIN, on LOOSE ENDS, neatly summed up his appeal as 'an inimitable blend of puckishness and gravitas'.

Formerly an apprentice engineer who used to maintain the lifts at BROADCASTING HOUSE, he then turned to acting and his first radio broadcast, in 1938, was a dramatisation of the history of flight from Icarus onwards. He was Mrs Lola Tickle in ITMA, the char who was so keen to look after all her gentle-maine, and Dudley Davenport ('Oh! I say, I am a fool!'), Ivy Clingbine and Winston the dog in MUCH-BINDING-IN-THE-MARSH. He appeared in both THE FOUNDATION TRILOGY and THE FORSYTE CHRONICLES.

To celebrate his fiftieth year in broadcasting in 1988, Radio 4 mounted a new production of Molière's comedy *The Imaginary Invalid*, in which he played the title role. The following year he notched up his 1,000th radio appearance (counting each episode as a separate one) in Radio 4's serialisation of *A Tale of Two Cities*, in which he played Dr Manette. He estimates that he has been in about 800 different radio programmes, mainly plays, serials, comedies and readings, as well as about 100 feature films and over 200 television roles.

His eightieth birthday was marked by a play specially written for him by PETER TINNISWOOD called *The Sitter*. He starred as a retired aviator, Bulldog Templeton. It was broadcast on Radio 4 in 1990.

Denning, Chris (1942–)
One of Radio 1's original line-up of DJs in 1967, presenting MIDDAY SPIN until 1969. Previously he had worked on radio in Kenya, Radio Luxembourg and the pirate ship Radio London. After the BBC he turned to voiceovers, which brought him considerable success.

Dennis, Ferdinand (1956–)
Journalist with an inquiring mind, nice turn of phrase and dislike of cant who has presented several entertaining Radio 4 series reflecting some of the experiences connected with his own background: born in Jamaica, brought up in London from a young age. They started with *African Encounters* (five ten-minute talks, 1986) and have continued with JOURNEY ROUND MY PEOPLE (two series, 1987 and 1988), AFTER DREAD AND ANGER (1989), BACK TO AFRICA (1990) and *Work Talks* (1991).

Department of Trade and Industry
The DTI exercises an important influence on the shape of British radio. It is responsible for the allocation of radio frequencies; for amateur, marine, cellular radio and Citizens' Band; for taking action against pirates via its Radio Investigation Service (rudely called a 'hit squad'). The RIS carried out 444 raids in 1988 and 259 raids, on 76 stations, in the first half of 1989 alone.

The DTI, keen to push its enterprise spirit, sponsors the Young Amateur of the Year Award, an annual competition open to under-eighteens and organised by the Radio Society of Great Britain, which is aimed at encouraging interest in amateur radio (Morse, call signs, antennae, building equipment and so on) as a breeding ground for the electronic and radio communications engineers of the future. The winner receives a prize of £250.

Desert Island Discs
Created by ROY PLOMLEY in 1942, this most celebrated of all record programmes has now cast away almost 2,000 celebrities – Royals, Prime Ministers, stars of stage and screen, legions of the great and the good – and invited each to choose the records to spend the rest of their lives with.

From the beginnning, the number of records has been eight and the theme music (augmented by herring gulls) has been ERIC COATES's 'By the Sleepy Lagoon': but the music chosen has covered all styles and tastes, from Puccini to Pink Floyd, Dido's Lament to Zorba the Greek.

'I believe *Desert Island Discs* adds a dimension to a listener's mental picture of a well-known person, giving the same insight he would receive from visiting the celebrity's home and seeing the books, pictures and furniture with which he surrounds himself,' Plomley wrote in his 1975 book *Desert Island Discs*.

The BBC has not compiled any tally of castaways' favourite music. But in that book Plomley indicated that, not surprisingly, popular classics were the most requested pieces – works such as Handel's *Messiah*, Mozart's *The Marriage of Figaro*, Rachmaninov's Second Piano Concerto, Beethoven's Fifth, Sixth and Ninth and Schubert's Unfinished Symphonies, Richard Strauss's *Also Sprach Zarathustra*, arias from *Carmen*, *Madame Butterfly* and *La Bohème* and so on. Only one person has come close to taking only her own records, and that was Elisabeth Schwarzkopf (partly, as she admitted, to be outrageous). Of her eight records, all but one featured her own voice. The selections do not have to be confined to music: ANTONY HOPKINS, for instance, chose as one of his records the sound of D-type Jaguars roaring down the Mulsanne Straight at Le Mans.

After about 100 programmes, Plomley invited his castaways to take a luxury with them. It was not allowed to be of any practical value. He ruled it had to be 'an inanimate object purely for the senses, which is not going to help you to live'. Thus, if castaways chose pianos, he would allow them only uprights on the grounds that they could always take shelter under a grand.

Luxuries have varied greatly. Former Polar explorer and actor Duncan Carse, the second Dick Barton (who once spoke on CHILDREN'S HOUR about his lonely winter nights on the tiny Atlantic island of South Georgia), raised a few eyebrows when he requested an inflatable rubber woman, which was also the choice of Oliver Reed. Sir Alec Guinness wanted apricot brandy and Norman Mailer 'a stick of the finest marijuana', which prompted an elegant rebuke from Plomley. Glenda Jackson opted for the Queen's dolls' house and JOYCE GRENFELL pencils and paper, so she could write plays. Margaret Thatcher played safe and asked for a photograph album of her children. Roald Dahl, evidently an optimist, chose a packet of tobacco seeds and a bunch of grape-cuttings from Burgundy; Artur Rubinstein, clearly a pessimist, wanted a revolver, since he was sure he would kill himself after only a few days of solitude.

One memorable argument about a castaway's luxury occurred when Princess Michael of Kent asked for another Oriental cat to replace her beloved Burmese, Kitty, a wedding present from her husband, which had been run over by a car. Plomley reminded her that luxuries had to be inanimate. She didn't budge, and

neither did he, so it was still stalemate by the time the show went out.

After another 300 editions Plomley allowed the guests to take a single book. Not the Bible or Shakespeare, since these happened to be on the island already. Because some castaways opted for multi-volume encyclopaedias (technically, a single work) these too were banned in due course. Favourite desert island reading has included Gibbon's *Decline and Fall of the Roman Empire* (the choice of both Terence Rattigan and Jeremy Thorpe) and Proust's *A la Recherche du Temps Perdu*. Alfred Hitchcock opted for a much less mighty tome – a Continental timetable, so he could go on imaginary journeys. The only pornographic book to date has been *Route 69* by Floyd Carter, chosen by David Hockney. Otto Preminger is remembered for the ultimate vanity: he chose his own autobiography.

The first castaway was Viennese comedian Vic Oliver (29 January 1942). The first woman was actress Pat Kirkwood, who became the fifth castaway. The first 200 programmes, in accordance with wartime practice, were scripted – Plomley himself writing out all the dialogue in advance on his typewriter.

Eddie Calvert was on the 500th programme, Viscount Montgomery of Alamein on the 1,000th, Bulgarian bass Boris Christoff on the 1,500th and actor John Thaw on the 2,000th. Princess Margaret and Princess Grace of Monaco were both cast away in 1981 and Princess Michael of Kent in 1984.

ARTHUR ASKEY has been the only castaway to make four separate appearances. A handful, including Robertson Hare, Celia Johnson, Emlyn Williams and Earl Hines, have made three and well over 100 celebrities have made two. Plomley himself was cast away twice: Leslie Perowne interviewed him in the 15th programme, in 1942, and EAMONN ANDREWS did so in 1958.

Two shows which Plomley recorded were not broadcast. The one with E. Arnot Robertson (1961) was spiked because he died just before it was due to go out. The one with Muhammad Ali (1980) was scrapped at an earlier stage because the speech of the former world heavyweight champion was a slurred, incoherent mumble – it was recorded when he was jet-lagged, and not long after the battering he received at the hands of Larry Holmes.

Plomley died in 1985, having transported over 1,500 castaways to his mythical isle. One of his regrets was that he had never succeeded in coaxing Lord Olivier there, having first asked him in 1943. Albert Finney and the Prince of Wales have also turned down invitations, as did George Bernard Shaw in 1942. He returned Plomley's letter with a note scribbled in the margin: 'No. Too busy with more important things. G.B.S.'

Plomley's successor, after JOHN DUNN turned down an approach, was the highly controversial Michael Parkinson (who had himself been a castaway in 1972). He was accused by some of turning the show into a series of chats with his sporting and showbiz pals, in which music was regarded merely as an irritating interruption. He presented about 90 programmes between 1986 and 1988.

His replacement, Sue Lawley (also an ex-castaway), proved much more popular. She has conducted sensitive, elegant interviews with guests who have included Arthur Scargill, John Ogdon, George Carman QC, Barbara Windsor and the Duchess of Kent, and mined a rich vein of prominent politicians, including Enoch Powell and TONY BENN, none of whom had appeared on the programme before. Under Lawley and her producer Olivia Seligman the show changed: castaways ceased to be chosen simply in order to celebrate their lives, and from then on were selected at least partly for their news value. The programme transferred from the music department to current affairs magazines, a sign of how it was perceived.

This emphasis on newsworthiness was the justification for the most bitterly criticised guest in the show's history, Lady Diana Mosley (widow of Sir Oswald Mosley, founder of the British Union of Fascists) in 1989.

There had been moments of controversy before: Pamela Stephenson's comments about her experiences under LSD were cut from the programme in 1982, and comments by Paul McCartney that year produced a writ from the late impresario Larry Parnes, who claimed (successfully) that he had been defamed. But the fuss over these was as nothing compared with the furore over Lady Mosley, which provoked vehement correspondence in the Press and more than 200 critical calls from listeners who felt the programme was the wrong forum for her views (the figure was revealed in the BBC's Annual Report). DAVID HATCH responded that the show was 'no longer an honours list'.

The BBC's embarrassment was compounded by its ineptitude in scheduling the programme: three separate dates were announced, each one turning out to be a sensitive day in the Jewish calendar, before it finally went out. BBC chairman Marmaduke Hussey sent a written apology about the scheduling to the Board of Deputies of British Jews, saying that the original dates were 'certainly inappropriate'.

Lady Mosley's tastes were mainstream classical, though she also chose Procol Harum's flower-power classic from the 1960s, 'A Whiter Shade of Pale'. She expressed her disbelief that the Nazis had murdered six million people. For many listeners this was a most unsavoury episode, and (thankfully) quite uncharacteristic of the series as a whole.

The following is a complete list of castaways up until May 1991. The number before each name is that of the *programme*, and *not* that of the castaway except in the first 200 or so cases. Thus, Deborah Kerr was on the 60th programme and was also the 60th castaway. But Evelyn Laye, on the 212th programme, was only the 211th castaway because by then Valerie Hobson had appeared twice.

1942:

1 Vic Oliver, comedian; 2 James Agate, critic; 3 Commander Campbell, mariner; 4 C.B. Cochran, showman; 5 Pat Kirkwood, actress; 6 Jack Hylton, bandleader; 7 'Sinbad' (Captain A.E. Dingle), explorer; 8 Joan Jay, glamour girl; 9 Canon W.H. Elliott, Precentor of Chapels Royal; 10 Arthur Askey; 11 Eva Turner, soprano; 12 Harry Parry, clarinettist; 13 Tom Webster, sports cartoonist; 14 Ivor Novello, composer; 15 Roy Plomley (interviewed by Leslie Perowne); 16 Beatrice Lillie, actress; 17 Leslie Howard, actor; 18 Nathaniel Gubbins, author; 19 BARRINGTON DALBY; 20 Emlyn Williams, actor; 21 Lord Elton, author; 22 Richard Tauber, tenor; 23 Jonah Barrington, musician; 24 Michael Powell, producer; 25 Admiral Sir Edward Evans; Antarctic explorer.

1943:

26 Donald McCullough, broadcaster; 27 Ian Hay, author; 28 Tom Driberg, MP; 29 Frank Swinnerton, author; 30 Beverley Baxter, MP; 31 Herbert Hodge, taxi driver; 32 C.A. Lejeune, critic; 33 Ivor Brown, author; 34 Tom Harrisson, anthropologist; 35 Lady Eleanor Smith, author; 36 Sir Stephen Tallents, administrator; 37 C.H. MIDDLETON; 38 J.B. Morton, journalist; 39 CHARLES HILL.

1944:

40 Alan Dent, critic; 41 Pamela Frankau, author; 42 Ralph Reader, director; 43 Wing Cmdr Guy Gibson, leader of the Dam Busters raid; 44 Mabel Constanduros, author.

1945:

45 FREDDIE GRISEWOOD; 46 Peter Fettes, announcer; 47 Jill Balcon, actress; 48 Michael Harrison, soldier; 49 Joan Edgar, announcer; 50 Roy Williams, announcer; 51 ALVAR LIDELL; 52 Pat Butler, announcer; 53 Margaret Hubble, announcer; 54 Michael Redgrave, actor; 55 Claire Luce, actress; 56 C.E.M. JOAD; 57 Celia Johnson, actress; 58 Valerie Hobson, actress; 59 Bobby Howes, actor; 60 Deborah Kerr, actress; 61 H.C.E. Wheeler, Naval signalman; 62 Eileen Joyce, pianist; 63 Stewart Granger, actor; 64 Richard Goolden, actor; 65 Nova Pilbeam, actress; 66 Sonia Dresdel, actress.

1946:

67 Barbara Mullen, actress. (There was then a gap of five years.)

1951:

68 Eric Portman, actor; 69 Monica Dickens, author; 70 Robertson Hare, actor; 71 Yvonne Arnaud, actress; 72 Donald Peers, vocalist; 73 Peter Scott, naturalist; 74 Constance Cummings, actress; 75 Jack Buchanan, actor; 76 Kay Hammond, actress; 77 Peter Ustinov,

actor; **78** Joan Hammond, soprano; **79** John Clements, actor; **80** TED KAVANAGH; **81** ANONA WINN; **82** Muir Mathieson, conductor; **83** Peter Fleming, writer; **84** Margaret Lockwood, actress; **85** Petula Clark, singer; **86** Larry Adler, harmonica player; **87** Denis Compton and W.J. Edrich, cricketers; **88** Ann Todd, actress; **89** Maggie Teyte, soprano; **90** Tommy Trinder, comedian; **91** Gracie Fields, singer; **92** ERIC COATES; **93** Bill Johnson, actor; **94** Stanley Holloway, actor; **95** Cicely Courtneidge, actress; **96** Leslie Henson, actor; **97** Jean Kent, actress; **98** JIMMY EDWARDS; **99** JOYCE GRENFELL; **100** A.E. Matthews, actor; **101** Phyllis Calvert, actress; **102** Vivian Ellis, composer; **103** Anne Crawford, actress; **104** Freddie Mills, boxer; **105** Sally Ann Howes, actress; **106** George Robey, comedian; **107** Mai Zetterling, actress; **108** Henry Kendall, actor; **109** Gerald Moore, accompanist; **110** Clemence Dane, author; **111** Ronald Shiner, actor; **112** Diana Wynyard, actress; **113** George Formby, comedian; **114** Kathleen Harrison, actress; **115** Elisabeth Schumann, soprano; **116** John Mills, actor; **117** Vera Lynn, singer.

1952:

118 Jack Hulbert, actor; **119** Carroll Gibbons, bandleader; **120** Dame Sybil Thorndike, actress; **121** Spike Hughes, writer; **122** Jeanne de Casalis, comedienne; **123** PETER BROUGH; **124** SIR COMPTON MACKENZIE; **125** Elisabeth Welch, actress; **126** Roger Livesey, actor; **127** Hermione Gingold, actress; **128** Fred Emney, actor; **129** Anna Neagle, actress; **130** Richard Hearne, actor; **131** WYNFORD VAUGHAN-THOMAS; **132** Delia Murphy, folk singer; **133** RICHARD MURDOCH and KENNETH HORNE; **134** Kirsten Flagstad, soprano; **135** Fay Compton, actress; **136** Robert Beatty, actor; **137** Dorothy Dickson, singer; **138** GILBERT HARDING; **139** Googie Withers, actress; **140** Godfrey Winn, author; **141** Ellaline Terriss, actress; **142** Boyd Neel, conductor; **143** Fred Perry, tennis champion; **144** HENRY HALL; **145** Gladys Cooper, actress; **146** Christopher Stone, broadcaster; **147** Joan Greenwood, actress; **148** Michael Denison and Dulcie Gray, actor and actress; **149** Trevor Howard, actor; **150** Anne Shelton, vocalist; **151** Richard Attenborough, actor; **152** Vivien Leigh, actress; **153** TED RAY; **154** Winifred Atwell, pianist; **155** Esmond Knight, actor; **156** Binnie Hale, comedian; **157** Joy Worth, announcer; **158** Florence Desmond, actress; **159** W. Macqueen-Pope, writer; **160** Tessie O'Shea, actress; **161** Nigel Patrick, actor; **162** Ada Reeve, actress; **163** Sonnie Hale, actor; **164** Gordon Harker, actor; **165** WALLACE GREENSLADE; **166** Joy Nichols, broadcaster.

1953:

167 WILFRED PICKLES; **168** Margaret Rutherford, actress; **169** Ralph Lynn, actor; **170** Belita, actress; **171** Duncan Carse, actor and explorer; **172** Donald Wolfit, actor; **173** Jean Carson, actress; **174** David Tomlinson, actor; **175** Sheila Sim, actress; **176** Richard Todd, actor; **177** Pamela Brown, actress; **178** Max Miller, comedian; **179** Moira Lister, actress; **180** Webster Booth, tenor; **181** Yolande Donlan, actress; **182** Norman Wisdom, comedian; **183** Isabel Jeans, actress; **184** JOHN ARLOTT; **185** Jack Hawkins, actor; **186** Naunton Wayne, actor; **187** Arthur Wint, athlete; **188** Pamela Kellino, actress; **189** Sir Ralph Richardson, actor; **190** Robert Helpmann, dancer; **191** Leo Genn, actor; **192** Lizbeth Webb, actress; **193** Geraldine McEwan, actress; **194** Cecil Parker, actor; **195** Brian Reece, actor; **196** Cyril Ritchard, actor; **197** Nora Swinburne, actress; **198** Hugh Williams, actor; **199** Alfredo Campoli, conductor; **200** Leslie 'Hutch' Hutchinson, singer; **201** Hugh Sinclair, actor; **202** Peggy Cummins, actress; **203** Jack Warner, actor; **204** Bernard Miles, actor.

1954:

205 Mary Ellis, actress; **206** Vivian de Gurr St George, Piccadilly shoeblack; **207** Jessie Matthews, actress; **208** John Betjeman, poet; **209** T.E.B. Clarke, screenwriter; **210** Valerie Hobson (second appearance); **211** Nigel Balchin, author; **212** Evelyn Laye, actress; **213** Robert Henriques, author; **214** Celia Johnson (second appearance); **215** Captain Mike Banks, Arctic explorer; **216** Reginald Dixon, organist; **217** Fred Hoyle, physicist; **218** Margaret Leighton, actress; **219** Dorothy Ward, actress; **220** Bobby Howes (second appearance).

1955:

221 Dorothy Tutin, actress; **222** Sir Cedric Hardwicke, actor; **223** Harriet Cohen, pianist; **224** Eric Ambler, author; **225** Robert Harris, actor; **226** Osbert Lancaster, cartoonist; **227** Christopher Chataway, athlete; **228** Pat Smythe, showjumper; **229** Pat Kirkwood (second appearance); **230** A.P. Herbert, writer; **231** Tod Slaughter, actor; **232** Arthur Askey (second appearance); **233** Sir Malcolm Sargent, conductor; **234** Anthony Asquith, film director; **235** Tommy Farr, boxer; **236** BARBARA KELLY; **237** Emlyn Williams (second appearance); **238** Tony Mottram, tennis player; **239** Nicholas Monsarrat, author; **240** Michael Redgrave (second appearance); **241** Yehudi Menuhin, violinist; **242** Lionel Gamlin, broadcaster; **243** Ursula Jeans, actress; **244** Edward Allcard, yachtsman; **245** Isobel Baillie, soprano; **246** Michael Ayrton, artist; **247** Claire Bloom, actress; **248** R.C. Sherriff, playwright; **249** Herbert Wilcox, film director; **250** Eileen Joyce (second appearance); **251** Philip Harben, cook; **252** Leslie Welch, memory expert; **253** John Gregson, actor; **254** Max Bygraves, entertainer; **255** James Robertson Justice, actor; **256** Sidonie Goossens, harpist; **257** Frances Day, actress; **258** VALENTINE DYALL; **259** Vic Oliver (second appearance); **260** Beverley Nichols,

'The irony of it is that I should be with Roy Plomley on Desert Island Discs.*'*

So far over 1900 men and women have managed to be with Roy Plomley or his successors on *Desert Island Discs*. A few of them even had connections with remote spots surrounded by sea, such as Duncan Carse (programme 171) and the evacuated inhabitants of Ascension Island (312)

author; **261** Jack Train, broadcaster; **262** BERNARD BRADEN; **263** Bob Monkhouse and Denis Goodwin, comedians; **264** Anton Dolin, dancer.

1956:
265 Laurence Harvey, actor; **266** SAM COSTA; **267** Dora Bryan, actress; **268** David Nixon, magician; **269** Terry-Thomas, comedian; **270** Robert Fabian, ex-detective superintendent; **271** Kenneth More, actor; **272** Nancy Spain, writer; **273** Donald Sinden, actor; **274** Vanessa Lee, actress; **275** Cyril Smith, actor;

276 BEBE DANIELS; **277** Stan Kenton, bandleader; **278** Marie Burke, actress; **279** John Neville, actor; **280** Athene Seyler, actress; **281** Len Harvey, boxer; **282** Dora Labette, singer; **283** David Hughes, tenor; **284** Robert Atkins, actor; **285** Stirling Moss, racing driver; **286** Ted Heath, bandleader; **287** Eartha Kitt, actress; **288** Eric Maschwitz, writer; **289** Leslie Caron, actress; **290** Jim Laker, cricketer; **291** Eva Turner (second appearance); **292** Tex Ritter, actor; **293** Shirley Abicair, singer; **294** Peter Ustinov (second appearance); **295** Dennis Brain, French horn player; **296** Dennis Price, actor; **297** Bernard Newman, writer; **298** HUMPHREY LYTTELTON; **299** Harry Secombe, entertainer; **300** Valentine Britten, BBC gramophone librarian; **301** Turner Layton, singer; **302** Kenneth Tynan, critic; **303** Ada Cherry Kearton, singer; **304** Peter Katin, pianist; **305** Anthony Steel, actor; **306** Isobel Barnett, broadcaster; **307** Donald Campbell, world water speed record holder; 308 Dennis Noble, baritone; 309 Malcolm Muggeridge, journalist; 310 John Watt, broadcaster; 311 SPIKE MILLIGAN; 312 Inhabitants of Ascension Island, eight of same; 313 Peter Finch, actor; 314 Janette Scott, actress; 315 Tyrone Power, actor.

1957:

316 George Cansdale, zoo broadcaster; 317 GERARD HOFFNUNG; 318 Dilys Powell, critic; 319 Zena Dare, actress; 320 Peter Sellers, actor; 321 Dame Peggy Ashcroft, actress; 322 Jack Solomons, boxing promoter; 323 EDGAR LUSTGARTEN; 324 Anthony Quayle, actor; 325 Elizabeth Bowen, author; 326 Alan Melville, playwright; 327 Bud Flanagan, comedian; 328 Christopher Brasher, athlete; 329 Cicely Courtneidge (second appearance); 330 Ralph Wightman, countryman; 331 Tommy Steele, singer; 332 Gwen Catley, soprano; 333 David Attenborough, zoologist; 334 Rawicz and Landauer, piano duettists; 335 Dick Bentley, comedian; 336 Victor Borge, entertainer; 337 Alec Robertson, music critic; 338 Count Basie, bandleader; 339 PERCY EDWARDS; 340 Mantovani, musician; 341 Harold Hobson, critic; 342 Tamara Karsavina, prima ballerina; 343 FRED STREETER; 344 Blanche Thebom, mezzo-soprano; 345 Audrey Russell, commentator; 346 TONY HANCOCK; 347 Owen Berry, actor; 348 Leopold Stokowski, conductor; 349 David Farrar, actor; 350 Alma Cogan, vocalist; 351 ERIC BARKER; 352 C.A. Lejeune (second appearance); 353 Christopher Stone (second appearance); 354 Marius Goring, actor; 355 Moura Lympany, pianist; 356 Johnny Dankworth, bandleader; 357 Commander Ibbett, broadcaster; 358 Belinda Lee, actress; 359 Bransby Williams, actor; 360 Jack Teagarden, trombonist; 361 Joan Cross, soprano; 362 James Fisher, naturalist; 363 Moira Shearer, dancer; 364 Eric Sykes, comedian; 365 Earl Hines, pianist; 366 Sir Thomas Beecham, conductor; 367 Lupino Lane, comedian.

1958:

368 Wendy Toye, dancer; 369 Lionel Hale, critic; 370 MAX JAFFA; 371 Victor Silvester, bandleader; 372 Anton Walbrook, actor; 373 Rex Palmer, broadcaster; 374 BEN LYON; 375 Margaret Rawlings, actress; 376 Michael Flanders and Donald Swann, entertainers; 377 Beryl Grey, prima ballerina; 378 Frankie Vaughan, singer; 379 Flora Robson, actress; 380 Geraldo, bandleader; 381 IAN CARMICHAEL; 382 Cleo Laine, vocalist; 383 Billy Mayerl, pianist; 384 Ruby Miller, actress; 385 Oliver Messel, stage designer; 386 Roy Plomley (second appearance, interviewed by Eamonn Andrews); 387 Agnes Nicholls, soprano; 388 Kay Smart, circus performer; 389 Eric Robinson, conductor; 390 Naomi Jacob, novelist; 391 Jean Sablon, singer; 392 DEREK MCCULLOCH; 393 Sarah Vaughan, vocalist; 394 Tito Gobbi, baritone;

395 Wilfrid Hyde White, actor; 396 Jean Pougnet, violinist; 397 Elisabeth Schwarzkopf, soprano; 398 EAMONN ANDREWS; 399 ELSIE AND DORIS WATERS; 400 Dr Ludwig Koch, ornithologist; 401 Hephzibah Menuhin, pianist; 402 Jack Payne, bandleader; 403 Percy Kahn, composer; 404 Dickie Valentine, vocalist; 405 Alicia Markova, prima ballerina; 406 Hardy Amies, fashion designer; 407 Harry Belafonte, actor; 408 RICHARD DIMBLEBY; 409 Elizabeth Seal, actress; 410 Benno Moiseiwitsch, pianist; 411 Edmundo Ros, bandleader; 412 Elena Gerhardt, mezzo-soprano; 413 June Paul, athlete; 414 G.H. Elliott, music hall artist; 415 Paul Robeson, actor; 416 Stanley Black, composer; 417 Aaron Copland, composer; 418 Charlie Drake, comedian; 419 SANDY MACPHERSON.

1959:

420 Ronnie Boyer and Jeanne Ravel, dancers; 421 Ronald Searle, illustrator; 422 John Osborne, playwright; 423 Frederick Ashton, choreographer; 424 June Thorburn, actress; 425 Chris Barber, bandleader; 426 John Morris, mountaineer; 427 Peter Cushing, actor; 428 Cyril Fletcher, comedian; 429 Judy Grinham, swimmer; 430 Ernest Thesiger, actor; 431 Malcolm Arnold, composer; 432 Laurens van der Post, writer; 433 Sylvia Syms, actress; 434 Edric Connor, actor; 435 TYRONE GUTHRIE; 436 MARJORIE WESTBURY; 437 Lord Brabazon of Tara, aviation pioneer; 438 Ray Ellington, jazz musician; 439 Dame Rebecca West, writer; 440 Alfred Marks, comedian; 441 Robert Farnon, composer; 442 Brian Vesey-FitzGerald, naturalist; 443 Henry Sherek, theatrical manager; 444 Lotte Lehmann, soprano; 445 Uffa Fox, yachtsman; 446 Hermione Baddeley, actress; 447 Harold Abrahams, athlete; 448 George Melachrino, conductor; 449 Ivor Newton; 450 B.C. Hilliam (FLOTSAM); 451 Norman Fisher, quizmaster; 452 Bessie Love, actress; 453 Charles Mackerras, conductor; 454 JOHN SNAGGE; 455 Sir Leonard Hutton, cricketer; 456 Douglas Byng, revue artist; 457 Peggy Cochrane, pianist; 458 Frankie Howerd, comedian; 459 Robertson Hare (second appearance); 460 Dave Brubeck, jazz musician; 461 Alfred Hitchcock, director; 462 George Thalben-Ball, organist; 463 STEVE RACE; 464 Sir Arthur Bliss, composer; 465 Benny Hill, comedian; 466 Joan Sutherland, soprano; 467 Billy Cotton, bandleader; 468 John Paddy Carstairs, novelist; 469 Andor Foldes, pianist; 470 Eve Boswell, singer; 471 TED MOULT.

1960:

472 S.P.B. Mais, author; 473 ALBERTO SEMPRINI; 474 Joan Heal, actress; 475 Antonia Ridge, writer; 476 Barrington Dalby (second appearance); 477 Herbert Lom, actor; 478 Leon Goossens, musician; 479 Sir Arthur Bryant, historian; 480 JACK JACKSON;

481 Marty Wilde, singer; 482 Prince Chula-Chakrabongse of Thailand; 483 Russ Conway, pianist; 484 Michael Somes, dancer; 485 Sir Adrian Boult, conductor; 486 Sid James, actor; 487 John Freeman, interviewer; 488 Ann Heywood, actress; 489 Anthony Newley, novelist; 490 David Langdon, cartoonist; 491 Shirley Bassey, singer; 492 Brian Rix, actor; 493 Liberace, pianist; 494 Marie Rambert, dancer; 495 Dickie Henderson, comedian; 496 Bernard Lovell, scientist; 497 Julian Slade, composer; 498 Sir Alec Guinness, actor; 499 Claudio Arrau, pianist; 500 Eddie Calvert, musician; 501 C. Day Lewis, poet; 502 Antal Dorati, conductor; 503 JOHNNY MORRIS; 504 Lord Boothby, journalist; 505 Danny Blanchflower, footballer; 506 Pat Suzuki, actor; 507 Godfrey Talbot, journalist; 508 Paul Beard, Leader of the BBC Symphony Orchestra; 509 Gladys Young, actress; 510 Michaela and Armand Denis, explorers; 511 Lionel Bart, composer; 512 Diane Cilento, actress; 513 Alec Bedser, cricketer; 514 SYDNEY TORCH; 515 Ernest Lough, ex-choir soloist; 516 Cliff Richard, singer; 517 Freddie Grisewood (second appearance); 518 Ursula Bloom, novelist; 519 Edmond Hockridge, actor; 520 FRANK MUIR and DENIS NORDEN; 521 Oda Slobodskaya, soprano; 522 Don Thompson, athlete; 523 Harry Mortimer, conductor; 524 Dave King, comedian.

1961:
525 Victor Gollancz, publisher; 526 KENNETH HORNE; 527 The Beverley Sisters, singers; 528 Ted Williams, horseman; 529 Cyril Mills, director; 530 Mary Ure, actress; 531 Antonio, dancer; 532 Jimmy Edwards (second appearance); 533 June Bronhill, soprano; 534 James Mason, actor; 535 Carmen Dragon, conductor; 536 Michael Wilding, actor; 537 Kenneth McKellar, singer; 538 Peter Scott (second appearance); 539 Barbara Jefford, actress; 540 Brian Reece (second appearance); 541 Adam Faith, singer; 542 Finlay Currie, actor; 543 Ralph Reader (second appearance); 544 Pietro Annigoni, artist; 545 KENNETH WILLIAMS; 546 Kingsley Amis, author; 547 Julian Bream, guitarist; 548 Richard Murdoch (second appearance); 549 Dr W. Grey Walter, scientist; 550 Ann Haydon, tennis player; 551 ROY HAY; 552 Anna Massey, actress; 553 Joe Davis, snooker player; 554 Nelson Riddle, orchestra leader; 555 Yvonne Mitchell, actress; 556 Gerald Durrell, zoologist; 557 Jack Fingleton, cricketer; 558 Diana Dors, actress; 559 Edward Ward, foreign correspondent; 560 John Slater, actor; 561 Coral Browne, actress; 562 Stephen King-Hall, sailor; 563 E. Arnot Robertson, author (programme not broadcast due to his death); 564 Tommy Reilly, harmonica player; 565 Canon Noel Duckworth, chaplain; 566 Hattie Jacques, comedienne; 567 Francis Chichester, yachtsman; 568 Sir Gerald Beadle, BBC administrator; 569 Wee Georgie Wood, music hall artist; 570 Rupert Davies, actor; 571 Virgil Thomson, composer; 572 Joan Collins, actress; 573 Paul Gallico, author; 574 Sir Michael Balcon, producer; 575 Bob Hope, comedian; 576 Gracie Fields (second appearance).

1962:
577 James Gunn, painter; 578 Hughie Green, talent show host; 579 STUART HIBBERD; 580 Ken Sykora, guitarist; 581 Sir John Gielgud, actor; 582 Kay Cavendish, pianist; 583 Stanley Holloway (second appearance); 584 Frank Chacksfield, conductor; 585 H.E. Bates, author; 586 Irene Handl, actress; 587 Col. A.D. Wintle, soldier; 588 Louis Kentner, pianist; 589 RAYMOND GLENDENNING; 590 Frank Launder and Sidney Gilliat, film makers; 591 Leslie Phillips, actor; 592 Bill Butlin, showman; 593 Robert Morley, actor; 594 Christina Foyle, bookseller; 595 Leslie Crowther, entertainer; 596 Sir Fitzroy MacLean, politician; 597 Sidney Nolan, artist; 598 Sir Alan Cobham, aviation pioneer; 599 Eric Hosking, ornithologist; 600 ALISTAIR COOKE; 601 Giovanni Martinelli, tenor; 602 John Allegro, authority on Dead Sea Scrolls; 603 FRANKLIN ENGELMANN; 604 Stephen Spender, poet; 605 Bruce Forsyth, comedian; 606 Paul Rogers, actor; 607 Merfyn Turner, prison social worker; 608 CHARLIE CHESTER; 609 Lionel Tertis, violist; 610 Edith Day, musical comedy star; 611 Mario del Monaco, tenor; 612 R.F. Delderfield, playwright; 613 Stanley Unwin, inventor of nonsense language; 614 L. Hugh Newman, butterfly farmer; 615 PETER JONES; 616 ANTONY HOPKINS; 617 Gwen Ffrangcon-Davies, actress; 618 Fanny and Johnny Cradock, cooks; 619 Norman Tucker, opera director of Sadler's Wells; 620 Pamela Hansford Johnson, author; 621 George Shearing, pianist; 622 VAL GIELGUD; 623 Dr Robert Stopford, Bishop of London; 624 Jack Warner (second appearance); 625 Peter Saunders, impresario; 626 Anna Russell, entertainer; 627 Acker Bilk, clarinettist; 628 A.G. Street, writer; 629 Lord George Sanger, circus owner; 630 Clarkson Rose, actor; 631 George Mitchell, choirmaster.

1963:
632 Dorothy Squires, singer; 633 Basil Boothroyd, humorist; 634 Gerry Lee, animal impersonator; 635 Richard Lewis, tenor; 636 Noel Coward, writer; 637 Sir Learie Constantine, cricketer; 638 Michael Bentine, comedian; 639 Quentin Reynolds, writer; 640 Cyril Ornadel, composer; 641 Percy Thrower, gardener; 642 Arthur Haynes, comedian; 643 Dudley Perkins, broadcaster; 644 Illingworth, cartoonist; 645 'Sir Harry Whitlohn' (April Fool's Day hoax); 646 Ted Willis, author; 647 David Frost, broadcaster; 648 Marjorie Proops, agony aunt; 649 Vivienne

Chatterton, broadcaster; **650** George Chisholm, trombonist; **651** Prof. L. Dudley Stamp, geographer; **652** Frank Worrell, cricketer; **653** Rowland Emett, artist; **654** Birgit Nilsson, soprano; **655** Barry Bucknell, DIY expert; **656** Eva Bartok, actress; **657** JOE LOSS; **658** Beryl Reid, actress; **659** Boyd Neel (second appearance); **660** Juliette Greco, singer; **661** KEN DODD; **662** Geraint Evans, baritone; **663** Vivienne, photographer; **664** CARLETON HOBBS; **665** Ian Fleming, author; **666** Sir Charles Maclean, Chief Scout; **667** Graham Hill, racing driver; **668** Scobie Breasley, jockey; **669** Reginald Jacques, conductor; **670** Sophie Tucker, entertainer; **671** RAYMOND BAXTER; **672** Norman Del Mar, conductor; **673** Group Captain Leonard Cheshire, founder of Cheshire Homes; **674** Bernard Cribbins, actor; **675** Pat Moss, showjumper; **676** NORMAN SHELLEY; **677** Sir Michael Maynard Denny, Admiral; **678** Patrick Moore, astronomer; **679** Joan Bennett, actress; **680** STEPHEN POTTER; **681** Gordon Pirie, athlete; **682** Ron Grainer, composer; **683** T.R. Robinson, expert on clocks; **684** Millicent Martin, actress; **685** H. Montgomery Hyde, author; **686** Nicolai Poliakoff, Coco the Clown; **687** Cyril Smith (second appearance) and Phyllis Sellick, pianists.

1964:
688 Dorita y Pepe, singers; **689** Ethel Revnell, comedienne; **690** Leslie Baily, writer; **691** Richard Attenborough (second appearance); **692** Regina Resnik, soprano; **693** Julie Andrews, actress; **694** Wilson Whineray, captain of the All Blacks; **695** Wilfred Brambell, actor; **696** Sir Miles Thomas, industrialist; **697** Stan Barstow, author; **698** Ian Wallace, bass; **699** REX ALSTON; **700** Jim Clark, racing driver; **701** David Kossoff, actor; **702** Dame Edith Evans, actress; **703** DAVID JACOBS; **704** Richard Wattis, actor; **705** Harry Wheatcroft, rose grower; **706** Paul Tortelier, cellist; **707** Kenneth Connor, actor; **708** Glen Byam Shaw, actor; **709** Dorian Williams, commentator; **710** Vanessa Redgrave, actress; **711** David Wynne, sculptor; **712** Roy MacGregor-Hastie, historian; **713** Dick Chipperfield, animal trainer; **714** Stephen Grenfell, writer; **715** Percy Merriman, concert performer; **716** Cilla Black, singer; **717** Lord Thomson of Fleet, newspaper proprietor; **718** Stratford Johns, actor; **719** Russell Brockbank, cartoonist; **720** Robbie Brightwell, athlete; **721** DIRK BOGARDE; **722** John Bratby, painter; **723** Jon Pertwee, actor; **724** The Rev. W. Awdry, creator of Thomas the Tank Engine; **725** William Douglas-Home, playwright; **726** Harry Brittain, writer; **727** Hardie Ratcliffe, trade union official; **728** Honor Blackman, actress; **729** FRANK PHILLIPS; **730** Brian Epstein, manager of The Beatles; **731** George Malcolm, harpsichordist; **732** Tallulah Bankhead, actress; **733** Lavinia

Young, matron; **734** JACK DE MANIO; **735** John Clements (second appearance).

1965:
736 Marlene Dietrich, actress; **737** Dawn Addams, actress; **738** Frank Ifield, singer; **739** Sir Basil Spence, architect; **740** Owen Brannigan, bass; **741** GALE PEDRICK; **742** Sir Paul Dukes, musician; **743** Arthur Fiedler, conductor; **744** Dick Richards, journalist; **745** Sir Richard Woolley, Astronomer Royal; **746** Bert Weeden, guitarist; **747** Anatole de Grunwald, film producer; **748** George Baker, baritone; **749** Dr W.E. Shewell-Cooper, horticulturalist; **750** Dame Margot Fonteyn, prima ballerina; **751** AL READ; **752** Bill Shankly, football manager; **753** Sheila Hancock, actress; **754** Hayley Mills, actress; **755** Julian Herbage, writer; **756** Robert Marx, underwater archaeologist; **757** Joseph Szigeti, violinist; **758** MAURICE DENHAM; **759** Hugh Lloyd, actor; **760** HAROLD PINTER; **761** Ginette Spanier, fashion house director; **762** Maxwell Knight, naturalist; **763** Mary Stocks, teacher; **764** Sir Lewis Casson, actor; **765** Sir William Walton, composer; **766** Annie Ross, singer; **767** Ambrose, bandleader; **768** Harry Corbett, children's entertainer; **769** Macdonald Hastings, journalist; **770** William Hartnell, actor; **771** William Connor ('Cassandra' of the *Daily Mirror*); **772** Rae Jenkins, conductor; **773** Ian Hunter, impresario; **774** Rita Tushingham, actress; **775** The Rev. David Sheppard, England cricket captain; **776** Robert Carrier, cook; **777** Adele Leigh, soprano; **778** Nadia Nerina, prima ballerina; **779** Peter Hall, theatre director; **780** Sir John Rothenstein, art historian; **781** Constance Shacklock, soprano; **782** Sir Robert Mayer, musical patron; **783** Hildegarde, singer; **784** Lord Robens, chairman of the National Coal Board; **785** JOHN HANSON; **786** General Frederick Coutts, Leader of the Salvation Army; **787** Sir William Coldstream, painter; **788** The Earl of Harewood, writer; **789** Michael Flanders (second appearance); **790** JIMMY SHAND.

1966:
791 Prof. W.E. Swinton, expert on prehistoric animals; **792** Patience Strong, poet; **793** Charlton Heston, actor; **794** Tommy Simpson, cyclist; **795** Christopher Hopper, manager of the Royal Albert Hall; **796** Andrew Cruickshank, actor; **797** Marie Collier, soprano; **798** Cyril Connolly, writer; **799** Bill Fraser, actor; **800** Sir Frank Francis, Librarian of the British Museum; **801** G.O. Nickalls, oarsman; **802** Sara Leighton, painter; **803** HUBERT GREGG; **804** Terry Scott, actor; **805** Alan Bullock, historian; **806** Bob and Alf Pearson, duettists; **807** Lord Soper, Methodist minister; **808** Inia Te Wiata, singer; **809** Henry Cooper, boxer; **810** Emily MacManus, retired matron; **811** Bill Simpson, actor; **812** Charles Craig, tenor; **813** Nina and Frederik, singers; **814** Lilli Palmer, actress; **815** Wilfrid

Andrews, chariman of the RAC; 816 Dame Ninette de Valois, prima ballerina; 817 Stanley Rous, football administrator; 818 Jennifer Vyvyan, soprano; 819 Virginia McKenna, actress; 820 Nat Gonella, bandleader; 821 Michael Craig, actor; 822 Peter Diamand, director of the Edinburgh Festival; 823 Bryan Forbes, film director; 824 Morecambe and Wise, comedians; 825 David Hicks, designer; 826 Derek Oldham, musical comedy artist; 827 June Ritchie, actress; 828 Peter Wilson, auctioneer; 829 Talbot Duckmanton, Australian radio administrator; 830 Katherine Whitehorn, columnist; 831 Jacques Brunius, writer; 832 Danny La Rue, comedian; 833 Mitch Miller, oboist; 834 Arnold Wesker, playwright; 835 Stephen Bishop, pianist; 836 Sarah Churchill, actress; 837 Anthony Burgess, author; 838 Captain John Ridgway and Sergeant Chay Blyth, Transatlantic oarsmen; 839 Leonard Cottrell, radio and TV producer; 840 Jack Brabham, racing driver; 841 Gwendolyn Kirby, matron; 842 George Solti, conductor.

1967:

843 Anne Sharpley, journalist; 844 RENE CUTFORTH; 845 Sheila Scott, pilot; 846 Richard Goolden (second appearance); 847 Gerald Moore (second appearance); 848 Renee Houston, actress; 849 GERALD HARPER; 850 Clement Freud, gastronome; 851 Arthur Negus, antiques expert; 852 Hugh Griffith, actor; 853 Barry Briggs, speedway champion; 854 Alan Whicker, reporter; 855 Dick Francis, author; 856 Rolf Harris, entertainer; 857 John Schlesinger, film director; 858 Sir Neville Cardus, music critic; 859 Eric Porter, actor; 860 The Rev. Walter Matthews, Dean of St Paul's; 861 Derek Nimmo, actor; 862 George Woodcock, TUC General Secretary; 863 John Barry, composer; 864 David Ward, bass; 865 Fenella Fielding, actress; 866 Xenia Field, gardening editor; 867 Raymond Huntley, actor; 868 Lord Ritchie-Calder, writer; 869 Roy Hudd, comedian; 870 Henry Longhurst, authority on golf; 871 Henryk Szeryng, violinist; 872 Tom Courtenay, actor; 873 Heather Jenner, marriage bureau owner; 874 Miriam Karlin, actress; 875 Jeremy Thorpe, MP; 876 Richard Briers, actor; 877 ALAN BENNETT; 878 John Ogdon, pianist; 879 Michael Hordern, actor; 880 Captain William Warwick, captain of the QE2; 881 Doris Arnold, broadcaster; 882 Roy Castle, entertainer; 883 Andre Previn, conductor; 884 Kenneth Wolstenholme, commentator; 885 Prof. Sir Denis Brogan, teacher; 886 Denis Matthews, pianist; 887 Sir Hugh Casson, architect; 888 Warren Mitchell, actor; 889 Irene Worth, actress; 890 Jacques Loussier, pianist; 891 The Rev. P.B. 'Tubby' Clayton, founder of Toc H; 892 Sir Edward Boyle, MP; 893 Robert Merrill, baritone; 894 Dame Gladys Cooper (second appearance); 895 Colin Davis, conductor; 896 Ann Mallalieu, first woman president of the Cambridge Union.

1968:

897 Desmond Morris, zoologist; 898 John Williams, guitarist; 899 JOHN MORTIMER; 900 John Bird, actor; 901 Susan Hampshire, actress; 902 Marilyn Horne, mezzo-soprano; 903 Bill Boorne, columnist; 904 C. Day Lewis (second appearance); 905 Rosalinde Fuller, actress; 906 Archie Camden, bassoonist; 907 T. Dan Smith, Newcastle-upon-Tyne councillor; 908 Jon Vickers, tenor; 909 Alfie Bass, actor; 910 Russell Braddon, writer; 911 Dame Maggie Teyte (second appearance); 912 Sir Nicholas Sekers, industrialist; 913 Sir Michael Tippett, composer; 914 Margaret Drabble, author; 915 Leslie Sarony, singer; 916 Trevor Nunn, artistic director of the RSC; 917 Janet Baker, mezzo-soprano; 918 Sir Gordon Russell, designer; 919 Colin Cowdrey, England cricket captain; 920 Henry Hall (second appearance); 921 Eleanor Bron, actress; 922 Sir Gilbert Inglefield, Lord Mayor of London; 923 Francis Durbridge, thriller writer; 924 Thora Hird, actress; 925 Eric Shipton, explorer; 926 Edward Chapman, actor; 927 Louis Armstrong, bandleader and trumpeter; 928 Sir Francis McLean, BBC Director of Engineering; 929 Carlo Maria Giulini, conductor; 930 Edwige Feuillere, actor; 931 Dame Ngaio Marsh, author; 932 Richard Rodney Bennett, composer; 933 Dame Anne Godwin, trade union official; 934 Marty Feldman, scriptwriter; 935 Richard Lester, film director; 936 Billy Russell, comedian; 937 Raymond Postgate, historian; 938 Barbara Murray, actress; 939 RICHARD BAKER; 940 Peggy Mount, actress; 941 Dan Maskell, tennis player; 942 Lt-Col C.H. Jaeger, music director, Brigade of Guards; 943 SANDY POWELL; 944 Sir Paul Gore-Booth, diplomat; 945 Des Wilson, director of Shelter; 946 Prof. Asa Briggs, Vice-Chancellor of Sussex University; 947 Arthur Askey (third appearance); 948 Rosea Kemp, weather forecaster; 949 Bob Braithwaite, clay pigeon shooting champion.

1969:

950 Heather Harper, soprano; 951 Alan Pegler, owner of the *Flying Scotsman*; 952 Maurice Jacobson, adjudicator at music festivals; 953 Maggie Fitzgibbon, actress; 954 Lord David Cecil, biographer; 955 Hylda Baker, actress; 956 Edward Downes, conductor; 957 Angus Wilson, author; 958 Zena Skinner, cook; 959 Mary Wilson, poet and Prime Minister's wife; 960 L. Marsland Gander, broadcasting correspondent; 961 Lady Diana Cooper, actress; 962 Jill Bennett, actress; 963 Sir Alec Rose, round-the-world sailor; 964 Hetty King, male impersonator; 965 Mary Stewart, author; 966 Dr Elsie Hall, pianist; 967 Alvar Lidell (second appearance); 968 Nicolai Gedda, tenor; 969 Virginia Wade, tennis champion; 970 Ginger Rogers, actress; 971 Lady Antonia Fraser, author; 972 Stanford Robinson, conductor; 973 John Trevelyan, film censor; 974 Evelyn Laye

(second appearance); **975** Kenneth More (second appearance); **976** Leonard Henry, comedian; **977** Vincent Price, actor; **978** Peter Pears, tenor; **979** Rachael Heyhoe, women's Test cricket team captain; **980** Cyril Harmer, philatelist; **981** Stanley Rubinstein, lawyer; **982** Hermione Gingold (second appearance); **983** Olivia Manning, author; **984** Des O'Connor, entertainer; **985** ROBIN DAY; **986** Donald Zec, columnist; **987** Sir John Wolfenden, Librarian of the British Museum; **988** Cliff Morgan, Rugby player and broadcaster; **989** Thea Holme, actress; **990** Henry Williamson, author; **991** Max Adrian, actor; **992** Raymond Mays, car designer; **993** Anthony Grey, foreign correspondent; **994** Evelyn Rothwell, oboist; **995** Dudley Moore, actor; **996** Irmgard Seefried, soprano; **997** Lillian Board, athlete; **998** Godfrey Baseley, countryman; **999** Moira Anderson, singer; **1000** Viscount Montgomery of Alamein, Field Marshal; **1001** Tommy Steele (second appearance).

1970:
1002 Fyfe Robertson, writer; **1003** Leonard Sachs, actor; **1004** Val Doonican, singer; **1005** A.S.C. Ross, Professor of Linguistics; **1006** Stanley Baxter, comedian; **1007** Isidore Godfrey, conductor; **1008** FRANK GILLARD; **1009** Richard Church, poet; **1010** Isobel Baillie (second appearance); **1011** Roy Strong, Director of the National Portrait Gallery; **1012** Richard Chamberlain, actor; **1013** Judy Hashman, Badminton singles champion; **1014** Nyree Dawn Porter, actress; **1015** Sheridan Russell, cellist; **1016** DERYCK GUYLER; **1017** James Lockhart, Musical Director of Welsh National Opera; **1018** Sir Gavin de Beer, scientist; **1019** Gina Cigna, soprano; **1020** Carol Channing, actress; **1021** Graham Usher, dancer; **1022** Andy Stewart, entertainer; **1023** Keith Michell, actor; **1024** Monica Dickens (second appearance); **1025** Barbara Windsor, actress; **1026** Ida Haendel, violinist; **1027** Vidal Sassoon, hairdresser; **1028** Robin Knox-Johnston, solo round-the-world sailor; **1029** Barbara Cartland, novelist; **1030** John Piper, artist; **1031** Joan Hammond (second appearance); **1032** Terry-Thomas (second appearance); **1033** DAVID DAVIS; **1034** Erich Leinsdorf, conductor; **1035** Freya Stark, explorer; **1036** Dick Emery, comedian; **1037** Ellen Pollock, actress; **1038** Helen Watts, contralto; **1039** A.P. Herbert, poet and politician; **1040** Harry Carpenter, commentator; **1041** Carrie Tubb, soprano; **1042** Lynn Redgrave, actress; **1043** Sari Barabas, singer; **1044** John Lill, pianist; **1045** Joan Whittington, Red Cross worker; **1046** Vilem Tausky, conductor; **1047** Margaret Powell, writer; **1048** David Hughes (second appearance); **1049** Diana Rigg, actress; **1050** Wally Herbert, polar explorer; **1051** Arthur Lowe, actor; **1052** Ivan Mauger, speedway champion; **1053** Quentin Poole, head chorister (age 13).

1971:
1054 Sacha Distel, singer; **1055** James Fitton, painter; **1056** Robert Bolt, playwright; **1057** Lilian Stiles-Allen, soprano; **1058** Laurie Lee, writer; **1059** ALAN KEITH; **1060** Harvey Smith, showjumper; **1061** Wendy Craig, actress; **1062** Ravi Shankar, musician; **1063** Ludovic Kennedy, broadcaster; **1064** Patrick Cargill, actor; **1065** Sir Louis Gluckstein, President of the Royal Albert Hall; **1066** Clodagh Rodgers, singer; **1067** Peter Daubeny, producer; **1068** Geoffrey Boycott, cricketer; **1069** Mrs Mills, pianist; **1070** Jonathan Miller, theatre director; **1071** Billie Whitelaw, actress; **1072** Reginald Foort, organist; **1073** John Braine, author; **1074** Joyce Grenfell (second appearance); **1075** Ronnie Corbett, comedian; **1076** Vernon Bartlett, broadcaster; **1077** Elizabeth Ryan, tennis champion; **1078** Clive Dunn, actor; **1079** Maurice Woodruff, clairvoyant; **1080** Michael Crawford, actor; **1081** Laurence Whistler, glass engraver; **1082** John Cleese, actor; **1083** James Laver, fashion writer; **1084** Lorin Maazel, conductor; **1085** Ian McKellen, actor; **1086** Richard Gordon, author; **1087** Sylva Stuart Watson, licensee of the Theatre Royal; **1088** Artur Rubinstein, pianist; **1089** Glenda Jackson, actress; **1090** David Shepherd, painter; **1091** Kenneth Allsop, author; **1092** Mollie Lee, broadcaster; **1093** Caterina Valente, entertainer; **1094** Sir Sacheverell Sitwell, writer and poet; **1095** Ivy Benson, bandleader; **1096** Sibyl Hathaway, Dame of Sark; **1097** C.A. Joyce, prison worker; **1098** Sir Vivian Dunn, former Musical Director of the Royal Marines; **1099** Nicolette Milnes-Walker, lone sailor; **1100** Alfred Brendel, pianist; **1101** Steve Race (second appearance); **1102** Graham Kerr, cook; **1103** Barbara Mullen (second appearance); **1104** Julia Trevelyan Oman, designer; **1105** David Frost (second appearance).

1972:
1106 Gwen Berryman, actress; **1107** Isaac Stern, violinist; **1108** Christopher Plummer, actor; **1109** Richard Ingrams, editor of *Private Eye*; **1110** Stuart Burrows, tenor; **1111** David Hockney, artist; **1112** Alice Delysia, actress; **1113** Michael Parkinson, broadcaster; **1114** Hammond Innes, author; **1115** Raymond Leppard, conductor; **1116** David Storey, playwright; **1117** Elizabeth Harwood, soprano; **1118** Robertson Hare (third appearance); **1119** John Noakes, *Blue Peter* presenter; **1120** Sir Geoffrey Jackson, diplomat; **1121** Wendy Hiller, actress; **1122** Leonide Massine, choreographer; **1123** Elizabeth Jane Howard, author; **1124** David Bryant, world bowls champion; **1125** Joan Bakewell, broadcaster; **1126** Geoffrey Parsons, piano accompanist; **1127** Tony Bennett, singer; **1128** Alec Robertson (second appearance); **1129** Francis Camps, Professor of Forensic Medicine; **1130** Judi Dench, actress; **1131** Jean Plaidy, historian; **1132** Charles Groves, conductor; **1133** Henry Cecil, novelist; **1134** Joe

Henderson, pianist; **1135** Marcel Marceau, mime artist; **1136** Sir Arthur Bliss (second appearance); **1137** Edward Ardizzone, water colourist; **1138** Stephane Grappelli, jazz violinist; **1139** Barry Cunliffe, archaeologist; **1140** Jimmy Tarbuck, comedian; **1141** David Franklin, broadcaster; **1142** Anthony Lawrence, BBC Far East correspondent; **1143** Margaret Lockwood (second appearance); **1144** John Reed, comedian; **1145** Terence Cuneo, painter; **1146** MICHAEL ASPEL; **1147** Christopher Gable, actor; **1148** Jackie Charlton, footballer; **1149** Imogen Holst, conductor; **1150** Dennis Wheatley, novelist; **1151** Maggie Smith, actress; **1152** Beverly Sills, soprano; **1153** Group Captain Peter Townsend, writer; **1154** Adelaide Hall, entertainer; **1155** Johnny Speight, writer; **1156** Tom Harrisson (second appearance); **1157** Doris and Elsie Waters (second appearance); **1158** Noel Rawsthorne, organist.

1973:
1159 Tony Britton, actor; **1160** Mike Yarwood, impressionist; **1161** Denise Robins, novelist; **1162** Robert Nesbitt, director; **1163** ANTHONY SMITH; **1164** Rita Hunter, soprano; **1165** John Le Mesurier, actor; **1166** Leslie Thomas, writer; **1167** Alexander Gibson, conductor; **1168** Dame Veronica Wedgewood, historian; **1169** George Melly, jazz singer; **1170** Cathleen Nesbitt, actress; **1171** Christopher Serpell, BBC diplomatic correspondent; **1172** Florence de Jong, organist; **1173** Harry Loman, stagedoor keeper; **1174** Chris Bonington, mountaineer; **1175** Edith Coates, mezzo-soprano; **1176** Norman Thelwell, cartoonist; **1177** John Huston, director; **1178** Joseph Cooper, pianist; **1179** Baroness Summerskill, doctor; **1180** Joe Bugner, boxer; **1181** Basil Dean, producer; **1182** Georgie Fame, singer; **1183** Brenda Bruce, actress; **1184** Wilfred Van Wyck, impresario; **1185** Sir Michael Ansell, show-jumper; **1186** Andrew Lloyd Webber, composer; **1187** Ruskin Spear, painter; **1188** Colin Welland, actor; **1189** Gervase de Peyer, clarinettist; **1190** June Whitfield, actress; **1191** Bert Foord, weather forecaster; **1192** Earl Wild, pianist; **1193** Joyce Carey, actress; **1194** Bill Sowerbutts, gardener; **1195** Leontyne Price, soprano; **1196** Ian Hendry, actor; **1197** Mary Peters, athlete; **1198** Edward Robey, barrister; **1199** Peter Rogers, producer; **1200** Prof. Sir Alister Hardy, zoologist; **1201** Arnold Ridley, actor and playwright; **1202** Trevor Philpott, reporter; **1203** Vic Feather, former TUC General Secretary; **1204** Barry Humphries, entertainer; **1205** Marghanita Laski, writer; **1206** Gareth Edwards, Rugby player; **1207** Alexander Young, tenor; **1208** John Mills (second appearance); **1209** Marion Stein, musician.

1974:
1210 Dr Jacob Bronowski, scientist; **1211** Sir Terence Rattigan, playwright; **1212** Bernard Haitink, conductor; **1213** John Brooke-Little, Richmond Herald of Arms;

1214 Fay Compton (second appearance); **1215** Brian Inglis, journalist; **1216** Roy Fox, bandleader; **1217** Eddie Waring, commentator; **1218** Maureen O'Sullivan, actress; **1219** Eileen Fowler, physical exercise teacher; **1220** BRIAN JOHNSTON; **1221** Edward Woodward, actor; **1222** Philip Hope-Wallace, writer; **1223** John and Boy Boulting, film-makers; **1224** Dr Thor Heyerdahl, anthropologist; **1225** Patricia Routledge, actress; **1226** David Dimbleby, broadcaster; **1227** ARTHUR MARSHALL; **1228** Antoinette Sibley, prima ballerina; **1229** T.C. Fairbairn, centenarian impresario; **1230** James Stewart, actor; **1231** Leslie Mitchell, broadcaster; **1232** Susan Hill, writer; **1233** Mark Lubbock, composer; **1234** Max Wall, entertainer; **1235** Osian Ellis, harpist; **1236** Richard Walker, angler; **1237** Sheridan Morley, writer; **1238** Sir Keith Falkner, singer; **1239** Valerie Singleton, broadcaster; **1240** Roland Culver, actor; **1241** Michael Levey, Director of the National Gallery; **1242** Dodie Smith, playwright; **1243** Dandy Nichols, actress; **1244** Phyllis Barclay-Smith, ornithologist; **1245** Graham Hill (second appearance); **1246** Denholm Elliott, actor; **1247** Frank Swinnerton (second appearance); **1248** David Munrow, musician; **1249** Cyril Ray, wine writer; **1250** William Hardcastle, journalist; **1251** Polly James, actress; **1252** Dr Magnus Pyke, scientist; **1253** Alan Ayckbourn, playwright; **1254** Elisabeth Frink, sculptor; **1255** ROBIN RAY; **1256** Bruce Tulloh, runner; **1257** Oliver Reed, actor; **1258** P.J. Kavanagh, novelist; **1259** Betty Kenward, writer; **1260** Angela Baddeley, actress; **1261** Percy Press, Punch and Judy man.

1975:
1262 Alan Civil, French horn player; **1263** James Prior, MP; **1264** Charles MacKerras (second appearance); **1265** Bernard Hailstone, painter; **1266** Celia Johnson (third appearance); **1267** Lord Longford, politician; **1268** Emlyn Williams (third appearance); **1269** Valerie Masterson, soprano; **1270** Jilly Cooper, writer; **1271** Duncan Grant, painter; **1272** Eric Thompson, actor; **1273** Stanley Dangerfield, dog show judge; **1274** Lionel Blair, dancer; **1275** Sir John Betjeman (second appearance); **1276** PATRICIA HAYES; **1277** John Hillaby, naturalist; **1278** Matt Monro, singer; **1279** Ben Travers, farceur; **1280** John Arlott (second appearance); **1281** Gordon Jackson, actor; **1282** Tom Hustler, photographer; **1283** Norman St John-Stevas, MP; **1284** Sammy Cahn, entertainer; **1285** Sir Maurice Yonge, marine biologist; **1286** David Hemmings, actor; **1287** Helen Bradley, painter; **1288** Dave Allen, comedian; **1289** James Herriot, vet; **1290** Anthony Dowell, dancer; **1291** C.P. Snow, author; **1292** Jean Simmons, actress; **1293** Robert Robinson, broadcaster; **1294** The Marquess of Bath, owner of Longleat; **1295** JIMMY JEWEL; **1296** Alec Waugh, author; **1297** Esther Rantzen, broadcaster; **1298** Bevis Hillier,

historian; **1299** Lord Carrington, politician; **1300** Paul Jennings, writer; **1301** Doris Hare, actress; **1302** Lord Norwich, writer; **1303** Stanley Holloway (third appearance); **1304** William Frankel, editor of *Jewish Chronicle*; **1305** Rumer Godden, author; **1306** Vince Hill, entertainer; **1307** Graham Thomas, National Trust gardens expert; **1308** Ron Moody, actor; **1309** Frederick Forsyth, author; **1310** Margaret Price, soprano; **1311** Bing Crosby, singer.

1976:

1312 Julia Foster, actress; **1313** Sherrill Milnes, baritone; **1314** Noel Streatfeild, author; **1315** Gavin Lyall, novelist; **1316** Ronnie Scott, jazz club owner; **1317** Lynn Seymour, ballerina; **1318** Luciano Pavarotti, tenor; **1319** Tim Rice, lyricist; **1320** Sir Robert Mark, Metropolitan Police Commissioner; **1321** Vincent Brome, writer; **1322** Noel Barber, writer; **1323** Rosina Harrison, lady's maid; **1324** Paul Theroux, novelist; **1325** Charlotte Rampling, actress; **1326** John Pardoe, MP; **1327** Dr Christian Barnard, heart surgeon; **1328** Glynis Johns, actress; **1329** Sir William Gladstone, Chief Scout; **1330** John Napier, anatomist; **1331** John Laurie, actor; **1332** Tony Grieg, cricketer; **1333** Douglas Fairbanks Jr, actor; **1334** Eric Simms, naturalist; **1335** Malcolm Williamson, Master of The Queen's Musick; **1336** Len Deighton, author; **1337** Philip Jones, trumpeter; **1338** The Rev. Stuart Blanch, Archbishop of York; **1339** Alan Pascoe, hurdler; **1340** Philip Larkin, poet; **1341** Mel Torme, singer; **1342** George Guest, organist; **1343** Melvyn Bragg, novelist; **1344** James Galway, flautist; **1345** Penelope Keith, actress; **1346** Tolchard Evans, composer; **1347** George Cole, actor; **1348** Michael Bond, creator of Paddington Bear; **1349** David Wilkie, swimmer; **1350** Peter Quennell, editor of *History Today*; **1351** Frank Muir (second appearance); **1352** Alan Bates, actor; **1353** Anthony Powell, author; **1354** Norman Bailey, baritone; **1355** Lt-Col John Blashford-Snell, explorer; **1356** Anthony Quayle (second appearance); **1357** Christopher Milne, the original Christopher Robin; **1358** Anna Moffo, soprano; **1359** Eric Idle, comedian; **1360** Igor Kipnis, harpsichordist; **1361** Gemma Jones, actress; **1362** Sir Denys Lasdun, architect; **1363** Charlie Cairoli, clown.

1977:

1364 Kenneth McKellar (second appearance); **1365** Robert Dougall, newsreader; **1366** James Blades, percussionist; **1367** Michael Holroyd, biographer; **1368** Roy Dotrice, actor; **1369** Barry Tuckwell, French horn player; **1370** John Curry, skater; **1371** Egon Ronay, writer; **1372** Merle Park, prima ballerina; **1373** Oliver Ford, designer; **1374** James Bolam, actor; **1375** Jacqueline du Pré, cellist; **1376** Mary Martin, actress; **1377** Brigadier Peter Young, military historian; **1378** Rod Hull, Emu owner; **1379** Yehudi Menuhin (second appearance); **1380** Magnus Magnusson, broadcaster; **1381** David Niven, actor; **1382** Lord Home of The Hirsel, former Prime Minister; **1383** Peggy Lee, singer; **1384** P.L. Travers, creator of *Mary Poppins*; **1385** Marisa Robles, harpist; **1386** Sir Oliver Millar, Surveyor of The Queen's Pictures; **1387** Mirella Freni, soprano; **1388** Derek Randall, cricketer; **1389** Jack Parnell, bandleader; **1390** Miss Read, author; **1391** Clare Francis, sailor; **1392** Shirley Conran, designer; **1393** Arthur C. Clarke, author; **1394** Billy Connolly, comedian; **1395** Jessica Mitford, author; **1396** A.L. Rowse, historian; **1397** Deborah Kerr (second appearance); **1398** Dannie Abse, poet; **1399** Dame Daphne Du Maurier, novelist; **1400** Robin Richmond, entertainer; **1401** Michael Croft, director of the National Youth Theatre; **1402** Mike Brearley, cricketer; **1403** Louis Fremaux, conductor; **1404** Molly Weir, actress; **1405** Barry Sheene, motorcycling champion; **1406** CLAIRE RAYNER; **1407** Wayne Sleep, dancer; **1408** Richard Adams, author; **1409** Prof. Alan Gemmell, botanist; **1410** Peter Ustinov (third appearance); **1411** Winston Graham, author; **1412** Grace Bumbry, soprano; **1413** Phil Drabble, countryman; **1414** Dennis Potter, playwright; **1415** Sir Alec Guinness (second appearance); **1416** Dorothy Edwards, author.

1978:

1417 Franco Zeffirelli, director; **1418** Omar Sharif, actor; **1419** Alan Coren, editor; **1420** Raymond Mander and Joe Mitchenson, theatre historians; **1421** Spike Milligan (second appearance); **1422** The Amadeus String Quartet, musicians; **1423** Margaret Thatcher, MP; **1424** Prof. J.H. Plumb, historian; **1425** Paco Peña, guitarist; **1426** The Rev. Gerald Ellison, Bishop of London; **1427** George MacDonald Fraser, author; **1428** David Wall, dancer; **1429** Felicity Kendal, actress; **1430** Les Dawson, comedian; **1431** Sir John Glubb, author; **1432** Robert Hardy, actor; **1433** Itzhak Perlman, violinist; **1434** Charles Aznavour, singer; **1435** Sir Lennox Berkeley, composer; **1436** Lord Shinwell, politician; **1437** Anna Raeburn, writer; **1438** Victoria de los Angeles, soprano; **1439** Derek Jacobi, actor; **1440** Sir Clifford Curzon, pianist; **1441** Dr Catherine Gavin, novelist; **1442** Mel Brooks, director; **1443** Jane Grigson, cook; **1444** Rita Streich, soprano; **1445** Patricia Batty Shaw, chairwoman of WI; **1446** Barbara Pym, author; **1447** Simon Rattle, conductor; **1448** Janet Suzman, actress; **1449** Fred Trueman, cricketer; **1450** Denis Healey, MP; **1451** Gian Carlo Menotti, composer; **1452** Tennessee Williams, playwright; **1453** Cathy Berberian, soprano; **1454** Alan Jay Lerner, lyricist; **1455** Alec Clifton-Taylor, architectural historian; **1456** Christopher Fry, playwright; **1457** NOEL EDMONDS; **1458** Colin Wilson, author; **1459** Jule Styne, composer; **1460** John Wain, author; **1461** Michael Crawford (second appearance); **1462** David Bellamy, botanist; **1463** Joan Fontaine, actress; **1464** Vladimir

Mrs Margaret Thatcher was still Leader of the Opposition when she was Roy Plomley's castaway on *Desert Island Discs* in February 1978. The other former Prime Ministers who have appeared are Lord Home and Sir James Callaghan

Ashkenazy, pianist; **1465** Barry John, Rugby player; **1466** Dinsdale Landen, actor; **1467** Sir Robert Helpmann (second appearance); **1468** Norman Parkinson, photographer.

1979:
1469 Robert Powell, actor; **1470** Allan Prior, novelist; **1471** Elia Kazan, director; **1472** Benjamin Luxon, baritone; **1473** Robert Stephens, actor; **1474** Norris McWhirter, editor of *The Guinness Book of Records*; **1475** Sir Arthur Bryant (second appearance); **1476** Nana Mouskouri, singer; **1477** Lauren Bacall, actress; **1478** David Attenborough (second appearance); **1479** Ileana Cotrubas, soprano; **1480** Ray Reardon,

snooker champion; **1481** Burl Ives, actor; **1482** Sir Adrian Boult (second appearance); **1483** Sir Edmund Hillary, mountaineer; **1484** Patricia Highsmith, author; **1485** Edward Fox, actor; **1486** Peter Blake, artist; **1487** Alec McCowen, actor; **1488** Jack Brymer, clarinettist; **1489** Sir Robert Mayer (second appearance); **1490** Ian Carmichael (second appearance); **1491** Irene Thomas, broadcaster; **1492** Ed McBain, author; **1493** Tito Gobbi (second appearance); **1494** Glen Tetley, choreographer; **1495** C. Northcote Parkinson, writer; **1496** Dick Clements and Ian La Frenais, scriptwriters; **1497** Moura Lympany (second appearance); **1498** Sir Ralph Richardson (second appearance); **1499** Lady Longford, historian; **1500** Boris Christoff, bass; **1501** Barry Norman, writer; **1502** Peter Barkworth, actor; **1503** June Mendoza, portrait painter; **1504** Richard Buckle, writer; **1505** Ted Allbeury, novelist; **1506** Pam Ayres, poet; **1507** Wilfred Thesiger, explorer; **1508** Josephine Barstow, soprano; **1509** Rex Harrison, actor; **1510** Roald Dahl, author; **1511** Sian Phillips, actress; **1512** Marti Caine, entertainer;

1513 Michael Palin, actor; 1514 Peter Shaffer, playwright; 1515 Charles Causley, poet; 1516 Elizabeth Soderstrom, soprano; 1517 Norman Mailer, author; 1518 Sir Osbert Lancaster (second appearance); 1519 Kyung-Wha Chung, violinist.

1980:
1520 Reginald Goodall, conductor; 1521 Sir Peter Parker, chairman of British Rail; 1522 Dizzy Gillespie, trumpeter; 1523 Sir Cecil Beaton, photographer; 1524 Otto Preminger, producer; 1525 Claudio Abbado, conductor; 1526 Timothy West, actor; 1527 Fay Weldon, author; 1528 Susannah York, actress; 1529 Kiri Te Kanawa, soprano; 1530 Geoffrey Household, author; 1531 Frances Perry, gardener; 1532 Donald Pleasence, actor; 1533 Catherine Bramwell Booth, Salvation Army commissioner; 1534 Leonard Rossiter, actor; 1535 Erich Segal, scholar and author; 1536 Salvatore Accardo, violinist; 1537 Lindsay Anderson, director; 1538 Natalie Wood, actress; 1539 Lord Denning, Master of the Rolls; 1540 Earl Hines (second appearance); 1541 Robert Tear, tenor; 1542 Freddie Jones, actor; 1543 Clive James, broadcaster; 1544 General Sir John Hackett, soldier; 1545 Barbara Woodhouse, dog trainer; 1546 V.S. Naipaul, author; 1547 Tom Lehrer, composer; 1548 Daley Thompson, decathlete; 1549 David Scott Blackhall, blind broadcaster; 1550 Gregory Peck, actor; 1551 William Trevor, author; 1552 Stephen Sondheim, composer; 1553 Tristan Jones, sailor; 1554 Renata Scotto, soprano; 1555 Lord Snowdon, photographer; 1556 Antal Dorati (second appearance); 1557 Michael Powell (second appearance) and Emeric Pressburger, film producers; 1558 Andrea Newman, novelist; 1559 Ronald Lockley, naturalist; 1560 Sir John Tooley, of the Royal Opera House; 1561 Brian Glover, actor; 1562 Catherine Gaskin, author; 1563 Derek Tangye, author; 1564 Mark Elder, conductor; 1565 Jacquetta Hawkes, archaeologist; 1566 Tom Conti, actor; 1567 Alan Minter, boxer; 1568 José Carreras, tenor; 1569 Neville Marriner, conductor; 1570 Arthur Askey (fourth appearance); 1571 Placido Domingo (tenor).

1981:
1572 Robin Cousins, ice-skating champion; 1573 John Fowles, author; 1574 Princess Margaret; 1575 Joan Plowright, actress; 1576 Jeffrey Archer, author; 1577 Mary O'Hara, singer; 1578 David Broome, showjumper; 1579 Frederic Raphael, author; 1580 Carla Lane, comedy writer; 1581 Daniel Massey, actor; 1582 Peter Nichols, playwright; 1583 RUSSELL HARTY; 1584 Patricia Ruanne, ballerina; 1585 Gary Glitter, singer; 1586 Sir Fitzroy MacLean (second appearance); 1587 Princess Grace of Monaco; 1588 Stewart Granger (second appearance); 1589 Sir Frederick Ashton (second appearance); 1590 Buddy Rich, bandleader; 1591 Sir John Gielgud (second appearance); 1592 Edmund Rubbra, composer; 1593 Eric Shilling, bass; 1594 William Whitelaw, MP; 1595 Richard Leakey, anthropologist; 1596 Giuseppe di Stefano, tenor; 1597 Morris West, author; 1598 Gloria Swanson, actress; 1599 Gillian Lynne, choreographer; 1600 Carl Sagan, astronomer; 1601 Roger Moore, actor; 1602 Julian Lloyd Webber, cellist; 1603 Terry Hands, producer; 1604 Sebastian Coe, athlete; 1605 Paul Eddington, actor; 1606 Frank Oz, puppeteer; 1607 Alan Jones, racing driver; 1608 Jessye Norman, soprano; 1609 Malcolm Muggeridge (second appearance); 1610 James Mason (second appearance); 1611 The Beaux Arts Trio, musicians; 1612 Montserrat Caballe, soprano; 1613 Elspeth Huxley, author; 1614 Joseph Cotten, actor; 1615 Lord Lichfield, photographer; 1616 Prof. Glyn Daniel, archaeologist; 1617 James Clavell, novelist; 1618 Diana Dors (second appearance); 1619 Sir Douglas Bader, pilot; 1620 Alan Howard, actor; 1621 Jack Higgins, author; 1622 Helene Hanff, author; 1623 Lord Harewood (second appearance).

1982:
1624 Trevor Brooking, footballer; 1625 Martin Gilbert, historian; 1626 ANGELA RIPPON; 1627 Frankie Howerd, comedian; 1628 Paul McCartney, musician; 1629 Prof. J.K. Galbraith, economist; 1630 Sir Christopher Leaver, Lord Mayor of London; 1631 Petula Clark (second appearance); 1632 John Osborne (second appearance); 1633 Dame Eva Turner (third appearance); 1634 George Chisholm (second appearance); 1635 Bernard Miles (second appearance); 1636 Sir William Walton (second appearance); 1637 Richard Armstrong, conductor; 1638 Julia McKenzie, actress; 1639 Brian Aldiss, novelist; 1640 Dorothy Dunnett, author; 1641 Jenny Agutter, actress; 1642 Lucia Popp, soprano; 1643 Julian Symons, author; 1644 Marti Webb, actress; 1645 Desmond Hawkins, founder of the BBC Natural History Unit; 1646 Delia Smith, cook; 1647 Sir Anton Dolin (second appearance); 1648 Eric Newby, author; 1649 Joss Ackland, actor; 1650 John Mortimer (second appearance); 1651 Captain Jacques Cousteau, oceanographer; 1652 Pamela Stephenson, actress; 1653 Lyall Watson, marine biologist; 1654 George Martin, record producer; 1655 Dame Janet Baker (second appearance); 1656 Donald Sinden (second appearance); 1657 Carl Davis, composer; 1658 Duke and Duchess of Devonshire; 1659 Claire Bloom (second appearance); 1660 James Loughran, conductor; 1661 Carlo Curley, organist; 1662 Wilbur Smith, author; 1663 David Lloyd Jones, artistic director of Opera North; 1664 Four members of the London Philharmonic Orchestra; 1665 Geoffrey Grigson, poet; 1666 Mike Harding, comedian; 1667 George Thomas, Speaker of the House of Commons; 1668 Thomas Allen, baritone; 1669 Rosamund Lehmann, author; 1670 P.D. James, author; 1671 Helen Mirren, actress; 1672 Alan

Price, composer; **1673** Gyorgy Ligeti, composer; **1674** Mary Ellis (second appearance).

1983:
1675 Rachel Billington, author; **1676** Steve Davis, snooker champion; **1677** Baroness Maria von Trapp, inspiration for *The Sound of Music*; **1678** Gwyneth Jones, soprano; **1679** Tim Severin, explorer; **1680** Beryl Reid (second appearance); **1681** Zandra Rhodes, fashion designer; **1682** James Ivory, director; **1683** Tom Keating, artist; **1684** Kenneth MacMillan, choreographer; **1685** Alexander Kent, author; **1686** Michael Wood, flying doctor of East Africa; **1687** Jan Morris, writer; **1688** James Fox, actor; **1689** Ruggiero Ricci, violinist; **1690** Geoffrey Moorhouse, author; **1691** Max Boyce, entertainer; **1692** A.N. Wilson, author; **1693** Arthur English, actor; **1694** Alan King-Hamilton, retired Old Bailey judge; **1695** TERRY WOGAN; **1696** Sinead Cusack, actress; **1697** Raymond Briggs, author; **1698** Sir Peter Pears (second appearance); **1699** Fleur Cowles, writer; **1700** Peter Maxwell Davies, composer; **1701** Terry Jones, writer; **1702** Julian Bream (second appearance); **1703** Sir John Pritchard, conductor; **1704** John Gunter, theatrical designer; **1705** Keith Waterhouse, author; **1706** Sir Frederick Gibberd, architect; **1707** Peter Bull, actor; **1708** Malcolm Bradbury, author; **1709** Cindy Buxton and Annie Price, photographers; **1710** Paul Jones, singer; **1711** Charlotte Lamb, author; **1712** Lionel Hampton, musician; **1713** Ian Richardson, actor; **1714** Rosemary Sutcliffe, author; **1715** Mollie Harris, author; **1716** Topol, actor; **1717** Linda Esther Gray, soprano; **1718** Sir Ranulph Fiennes, explorer; **1719** Shirley MacLaine, actress; **1720** Sir Hugh Greene, broadcaster; **1721** Thomas Keneally, author; **1722** Marvin Hamlisch, composer; **1723** John Piper (second appearance); **1724** James Stewart (second appearance); **1725** M.M. Kaye, author.

1984:
1726 Beatrice Reading, singer; **1727** David Gower, cricketer; **1728** Quentin Crewe, author; **1729** Princess Michael of Kent; **1730** Stubby Kaye, comedy actor; **1731** Lord Elwyn Jones, academic; **1732** Woody Herman, musician; **1733** Michael York, actor; **1734** GERALD PRIESTLAND; **1735** Don McCullin, journalist; **1736** Michael Quinn, head chef at The Ritz; **1737** Ed Mirvish, owner of the Old Vic; **1738** Paul Tortelier (second appearance); **1739** Christopher Reeve, actor; **1740** Lucy Irvine, real castaway for one year; **1741** David Lodge, author; **1742** Leo McKern, actor; **1743** Rosalind Plowright, soprano; **1744** Hugh Johnson, author; **1745** Zubin Mehta, conductor; **1746** Lord Rothschild, zoologist; **1747** Vlado Perlemuter, musician; **1748** Natalia Makarova, ballerina; **1749** A.J. Ayer, philosopher; **1750** Gayatri Devi, Maharani of Jaipur; **1751** Ron Goodwin, composer; **1752** William Rushton,

entertainer; **1753** Ved Mehta, writer; **1754** George Abbott, dancer; **1755** Catherine Cookson, author; **1756** Gerry Cottle, circus owner; **1757** Alfred Eisenstadt, photo-journalist; **1758** John Hurt, actor; **1759** John Surman, saxophonist; **1760** Michael Ffolkes, cartoonist; **1761** Jonathan Lynn, actor; **1762** David Rendall, tenor; **1763** Tom Sharpe, author; **1764** Vernon Handley, conductor; **1765** David Puttnam, producer; **1766** Robin Hanbury Tenison, explorer; **1767** Miklos Rozsa, composer; **1768** Sir John Burgh, Director-General of the British Council; **1769** Ray Cooney, director.

1985:
1770 Sir Michael Tippett (second appearance); **1771** TOM STOPPARD; **1772** John Harvey Jones, chairman of ICI; **1773** Madhur Jaffrey, cook; **1774** Julie Walters, actress; **1775** Elly Ameling, soprano; **1776** Michael Elkins, journalist; **1777** Anthony Hopkins, actor; **1778** Jorge Bolet, pianist; **1779** Alison Lurie, English professor; **1780** Gordon Beningfield, philatelist; **1781** Richard Eyre, director; **1782** Charlotte Duffy and Jimmy Savile, who fixed it for her; **1783** Doris Stokes, medium; **1784** Joseph Allen, astronaut; **1785** Robert Burchfield, lexicographer; **1786** Barbara Taylor Bradford, author; **1787** David Steel, MP; **1788** Sheila Steafel, actress.

1986:
1789 Alan Parker, director; **1790** Nigel Kennedy, violinist; **1791** Maureen Lipman, actress; **1792** Dennis Taylor, snooker player; **1793** Bruce Oldfield, fashion designer; **1794** Ben Kingsley, actor; **1795** Selina Scott, journalist; **1796** Johnny Dankworth (second appearance); **1797** Beryl Bainbridge, author; **1798** Ron Pickering, commentator; **1799** Shirley Williams, politician; **1800** Jane Glover, conductor; **1801** Arthur Hailey, author; **1802** Bobby Robson, England football manager; **1803** Elton John, musician; **1804** Ismail Merchant, producer; **1805** Max Hastings, editor; **1806** Jackie Stewart, former Grand Prix driver; **1807** Anne Sophie Mutter, violinist; **1808** BRIAN REDHEAD; **1809** Sir David Wilson, Director of the British Museum; **1810** Sir Geoffrey Howe, MP; **1811** Roger Vadim, director; **1812** Norman Lewis, author; **1813** Virginia Holgate, horse riding champion; **1814** Jane Lapotaire, actress; **1815** Stan Barstow (second appearance); **1816** Auberon Waugh, writer; **1817** Andrew Davis, conductor; **1818** James Herbert, author; **1819** Suzy Quatro, singer; **1820** Richard Condon, actor; **1821** Sir Ian MacGregor, former Chairman of the National Coal Board; **1822** Fred Hoyle (second appearance); **1823** Phil Edmonds, cricketer; **1824** Albert and Michel Roux, chefs; **1825** Jeremy Irons, actor; **1826** Kingsley Amis (second appearance); **1827** Hal Prince, impresario; **1828** John Ridgway (second appearance); **1829** Nigel Hawthorne, actor; **1830** Jackie Collins, author; **1831** BENNY GREEN.

1987:
1832 Tony Bennett (second appearance); 1833 Jeremy Lloyd, comedy writer; 1834 Sue Ryder, philanthropist; 1835 Peter Fluck and Roger Law, puppeteers; 1836 Victoria Wood, entertainer; 1837 Sir Michael Hordern (second appearance); 1838 Ken Russell, director; 1839 Sir Nicholas Goodison, Chairman of the Stock Exchange; 1840 Johnny Mathis, singer; 1841 Dora Bryan (second appearance); 1842 David Penhaligon, MP; 1843 Peter Alliss, broadcaster; 1844 Anthony Andrews, actor; 1845 Julian Critchley, MP; 1846 Michael Bogdanov, director; 1847 Frank Bough, broadcaster; 1848 Jane Glover (second appearance); 1849 Terence Stamp, actor; 1850 Robert Maxwell, publisher; 1851 Elaine Paige, singer; 1852 Lucinda Green, showjumper; 1853 Kenneth Williams (second appearance); 1854 Maya Angelou, author; 1855 Frances Edmonds, journalist; 1856 Susan George, actress; 1857 Edna O'Brien, author; 1858 Lord Montagu, peer; 1859 Kitty Godfree, tennis player; 1860 Joanna Lumley, actress; 1861 Peter West, broadcaster; 1862 Jacques Loussier (second appearance); 1863 Lulu, singer; 1864 Lord Killanin, former President of the International Olympic Committee; 1865 James Callaghan, MP; 1866 Bernard Levin, broadcaster; 1867 Bamber Gascoigne, broadcaster; 1868 Sue Lawley, broadcaster; 1869 Robert Carrier (second appearance); 1870 Barry Cryer, entertainer; 1871 Vernon Scannell, poet; 1872 Antony Sher, actor; 1873 Lord Grade, impresario; 1874 Victoria Wood (second appearance).

1988:
1875 Jeremy Lloyd (second appearance); 1876 Adele Leigh (second appearance); 1877 Michael Heseltine, MP; 1878 Gemma Craven, actress; 1879 Lord Donoughue; 1880 William Davis, writer; 1881 Dennis Potter (second appearance); 1882 Stephanie Beacham, actress; 1883 James Burke, scientist; 1884 Brendan Foster, athlete; 1885 Maya Angelou (second appearance); 1886 Sue Lawley (second appearance); 1887 Lord Hailsham, Lord Chancellor; 1888 Jane Asher, actress; 1889 Arthur Scargill, President of the National Union of Mineworkers; 1890 Mary Archer, don; 1891 Michael Gambon, actor; 1892 Neil Kinnock, MP; 1893 Evelyn Homes, agony aunt; 1894 Rowan Atkinson, entertainer; 1895 Anita Roddick, founder of The Body Shop; 1896 RABBI LIONEL BLUE; 1897 Anton Mosiman, chef; 1898 Douglas Hurd, MP; 1899 Gwen Ffrangcon-Davies (second appearance); 1900 Jeremy Isaacs, founder of Channel 4; 1901 David Owen, MP; 1902 David Essex, singer; 1903 Dame Edna Everage, megastar; 1904 Lord Armstrong, former Cabinet Secretary; 1905 Joan Turner, comedienne; 1906 The Rev. Ian Paisley, MP; 1907 Patricia Neal, actress; 1908 Lord Dacre, historian; 1909 Anita Dobson, actress; 1910 Wainwright, fell walker; 1911 Peter Donohoe, pianist; 1912 Salman Rushdie, author; 1913 The Rev.

Trevor Huddlestone, clergyman; 1914 Athene Seyler (second appearance); 1915 Terry Wogan (second appearance); 1916 Cilla Black (second appearance); 1917 Michael Foot, MP; 1918 Germaine Greer, writer; 1919 Sir Claus Moser, former Chairman of the Royal Opera House; 1920 Bob Hoskins, actor; 1921 Bob Champion, jockey; 1922 Stephen Fry, entertainer; 1923 Lady Warnock, philosopher; 1924 Charles Dance, actor; 1925 Edward Heath, former Prime Minister.

1989:
1926 Dr Robert Runcie, Archbishop of Canterbury; 1927 Twiggy, actress; 1928 TONY BENN; 1929 Boy George, singer; 1930 Joan Armatrading, singer; 1931 Rocco Forte, businessman; 1932 Jeffrey Tate, conductor; 1933 Enoch Powell, politician; 1934 David Hare, playwright; 1935 Dame Josephine Barnes, gynaecologist; 1936 Gerald Scarfe, cartoonist; 1937 Sir Stephen Spender, poet; 1938 Leslie Grantham, actor; 1939 Lord Jenkins, politician; 1940 Miriam Rothschild, biologist; 1941 Rachel Kempson, actress; 1942 Lenny Henry, comedian; 1943 Thora Hird (second appearance); 1944 Katherine Hamnett, fashion designer; 1945 Sir Nicholas Henderson, former diplomat; 1946 Richard Branson, tycoon; 1947 Jonathon Porritt, Diiirector of Friends of the Earth; 1948 Maria Aitken, actress; 1949 Joan Collins (second appearance); 1950 Mark McCormack, sports promoter; 1951 NED SHERRIN; 1952 Sir Thomas Armstrong, of the Royal Opera House; 1953 Dame Vera Lynn (second appearance); 1954 Eric Clapton, guitarist; 1955 Penelope Lively, novelist; 1956 John Ogdon (second appearance); 1957 Lucinda Lambton, conservationist; 1958 Jack Lemmon, actor; 1959 Alan Plater, playwright; 1960 Colin Thubron, author; 1961 Ian Botham, cricketer; 1962 Michael Codron, impresario; 1963 Seamus Heaney, poet; 1964 Lady Mosley, widow of Sir Oswald Mosley; 1965 Nigel Lawson, MP; 1966 Pauline Collins, actress; 1967 The Duchess of Kent; 1968 Dirk Bogarde (second appearance).

1990:
1969 Dennis Skinner, MP; 1970 JOHN PEEL; 1971 Sir Robin Day (second appearance); 1972 Lord Weidenfeld, publisher; 1973 Sarah Miles, actress; 1974 Michael Tilson Thomas, conductor; 1975 John Pilger, journalist; 1976 John Sessions, comedian; 1977 SIR IAN TRETHOWAN; 1978 Prof. Sir George Porter, chemist; 1979 Richard Rogers, architect; 1980 John Biffen, MP; 1981 Sir Crispin Tickell, diplomat; 1982 Mary Wesley, novelist; 1983 June Whitfield (second appearance); 1984 Prue Leith, restaurateur; 1985 Molly Keane, writer; 1986 Jonathan Pryce, actor; 1987 David Blunkett, MP; 1988 Ken Dodd (second appearance); 1989 Maeve Binchy, writer; 1990 Harold Fielding, impresario; 1991 George Carman, QC; 1992 Kaffe Fassett, knitwear designer; 1993 Peter Jonas, of English National Opera;

1994 Jean Rook, columnist; 1995 Robin Knox-Johnston, yachtsman; 1996 Lord Charteris, former Private Secretary to The Queen; 1997 Dr Ruth Westheimer, sex therapist; 1998 Barbara Windsor (second appearance); 1999 Gary Lineker, footballer; 2000 John Thaw, actor; 2001 Clive Jenkins, trade unionist; 2002 Ernie Wise (second appearance); 2003 Nicholas Snowman, Artistic Director of the South Bank Centre; 2004 Lord Annan, former Vice-Chancellor of London University; 2005 Barbara Castle, politician; 2006 Elizabeth Welch (second appearance); 2007 Lady Trumpington, politician; 2008 Eduardo Paolozzi, sculptor; 2009 Brian Keenan, former hostage in Beirut; 2010 Keith Floyd, cook.

1991:
2011 Lord Goodman, lawyer; 2012 Adelaide Hall (second appearance); 2013 Fred Zinnemann, director; 2014 Brian Eno, musician; 2015 Prof. Ralf Dahrendorf, social and political philosopher; 2016 Paddy Ashdown, MP; 2017 Dame Ninette de Valois (second appearance); 2018 Richard Eyre (second appearance); 2019 Sir Denis Forman, former Chairman of Granada TV; 2020 Jeffrey Bernard, journalist; 2021 Sir Trevor Holdsworth, Chairman of National Power; 2022 Marti Caine (second appearance); 2023 Naomi Mitchison, writer; 2024 Lord King, Chairman of British Airways; 2025 Dr Jonathan Sacks, Chief Rabbi-elect; 2026 Dame Shirley Porter, former Leader of Westminster City Council; 2027 Cecil Lewis, First World War pilot and BBC pioneer; 2028 John Simpson, BBC-TV Foreign Affairs Editor.

Devonair
Exeter, Torbay, East Devon, West Dorset and South Somerset are covered by this Exeter-based ILR station, now owned by Capital Radio, which began in 1980.

The managing director and programme controller until January 1991, David Cousins, is lead singer of The Strawbs pop group (whose biggest hit, 'Part of the Union', reached Number 2 in 1973) and always banned his own records from being played on the station to avoid any accusation that he was using it to line his own pockets with royalties.

Dial M for Pizza
Comedy series on Radio 4, from November 1987 to December 1988.

Diary of a Somebody
Splendidly written and read by Christopher Matthew, this creation of a modern Pooter in the shape of Simon Crisp – foolish, humourless, pompous, small-minded and yet for all that not entirely without sympathy – was broadcast as a Radio 4 MORNING READING in September 1979. It was widely regarded as a funny, mordant and successful updating of the George and Weedon Grossmith original, *Diary of a Nobody*.

Dick Barton – Special Agent!
Captain Richard Barton, late of the Commandos, was fearless, straight as a die and a natural leader of men. With his trusty sidekicks Snowey White and Jock Anderson, sergeants both but decent enough chaps all the same, he thrilled a grey and tired nation with cliff-hanging, crimebusting adventures from 1946 to 1951, injecting breathless escapism into the long grey years of rationing and austerity. 'Has the plane crashed? . . . Can Barton survive?? Don't miss the next episode of DICK BARTON – SPECIAL AGENT!' Followed by the thundering excitement of Charles Williams's celebrated signature tune, 'Devil's Galop' . . .

This, the BBC's first daily serial, instigated by NORMAN COLLINS and written by EDWARD J.

'Take that, you swine!' Villainous Flash Faraday reels from a straight right thrown by the gallant Captain Barton in a rehearsal for one of Dick's earliest adventures, *The J.B. Case*, in 1948. Sydney Vivian is Flash, Noel Johnson Dick and the damsel in distress Violet Loxley

MASON and Geoffrey Webb, was conceived as a fast-moving strip cartoon of the airwaves. It was dismissed by the *Daily Worker* before two weeks had elapsed as 'so bad as to be almost beyond criticism'. But listeners loved it. Dick's success reflected a national yearning, for the second time this century, to build a land fit for heroes.

Originally aimed at adults, it quickly caught on with youngsters for whom it was a welcome distraction from homework. When the BBC realised this, it promptly made Dick teetotal and laid down new guidelines: 'Barton has now given up drink altogether. No reference should be made to its existence in the Barton circle. The villains may drink, but never to excess ... Dick should have no flirtations or affairs and his enemies no molls or mistresses.'

At the peak of its popularity some fifteen million listeners tuned to the Light Programme every night. Noel Johnson, the first actor to play Barton, says he ended up getting 2,000 fan letters a week.

Listening to the first adventure on cassette, it now seems extraordinarily dated: the dialogue, spattered with 'rum coves' and 'queer old birds'; the Bulldog Drummond mannerisms lifted straight from the 1920s; the downtrodden women, like War Office secretary Jean Hunter with whom there was an initial hint of romance; the sinister foreign agents with their thick mid-European accents, suggesting a deep distrust of foreigners in the wake of the Second World War.

Nonetheless, with its cracking pace and constant excitement, it enthralled a generation of thrill-hungry youngsters, some of whom have never forgiven the BBC for displacing it by an altogether more gentle daily serial called THE ARCHERS. (That began on 1 January 1951, going out between 11.45 a.m. and 12 noon. *Dick Barton* continued at 6.15 p.m. on the Light Programme until its final episode on 30 March 1951. The following Monday, at 6.45 p.m., *The Archers* were pitchforked into the early evenings.)

Noel Johnson played the smooth, masterful Barton until 1949. He hung up his trilby and trenchcoat because (as he revealed in the Radio 4 documentary *Still a Special Agent* in February 1990) he felt underpaid and the BBC refused to give him a rise. Duncan Carse (the former explorer and ex-boxer who asked for an inflatable woman on DESERT ISLAND DISCS, and whose son-in-law is BBC-TV newscaster Martyn Lewis) took over the role until 1950. Gordon Davies played him for the final year. In 1951, Captain Barton was recalled to the Army and 711 episodes of a radio legend came to an end.

Alex McCrindle, who played Jock and died in 1990, and John Mann (Snowey White) met up again for the BBC's Golden Jubilee in 1972 to re-record the first adventure. It concerned the theft of a devilish secret weapon – a ray gun which could fire bubonic plague at people and shoot through walls. This 1972 version was released in 1989 as a cassette on the BBC RADIO COLLECTION, but this was made possible only by a member of the public in Carlisle. A devoted Barton fan, Pat Hetherington (a spina bifida sufferer for whom Barton was a hero because he always managed to extricate himself from physical difficulty), taped all of it at the time. Unlike the BBC she did not throw hers away, and lent it to BBC Enterprises in 1989 so that they could produce the cassette. Her name appears on the label, under the credits. This was the first time that the BBC had put on sale material recorded off the air by a member of the public.

'He was whiter than white, old Dick.' – Noel Johnson.

'As a young boy I never missed an episode. I've never been able to listen to *The Archers* with any degree of affection because they replaced Dick Barton and I've never really forgiven Ambridge for it.' – Terry Wogan.

Dimbleby, Richard (1913–65)

The outstanding broadcaster of his age and, for some, the greatest Britain has so far produced. Long before television made him a national celebrity, radio was the medium with which he seized the nation's attention.

As the BBC's first war correspondent, he conveyed by voice alone the impact and horror of some of the century's most momentous events. They included Alamein, D-Day, the bombing of Cologne and the liberation of Belsen. The peacetime years in radio, in sharp contrast, were spent mainly in light entertainment: he presented DOWN YOUR WAY for five years and was a TWENTY QUESTIONS panellist for eighteen years. At the same time he became much revered as a television commentator at great State occasions, notably the Coronation, and also anchored *Panorama*. He is said to have been the first person in Britain to have a telephone in his car. In 1990 he certainly became the first broadcaster to have a memorial dedicated to him at Westminster Abbey.

Two of his four children, David and Jonathan, followed him into broadcasting: the latter chairs ANY QUESTIONS? on Radio 4.

Disc jockey

In Britain, the first DJ was COMPTON MACKENZIE, who sat down and played a pile of gramophone records in 1924 at SAVOY HILL. The first DJ on Radio Luxembourg was STEPHEN WILLIAMS in 1933, the first DJ on the North Sea pirate ships was SIMON DEE, and the first to be heard on Radio 1 was TONY BLACKBURN.

The North Sea pirates of the 1960s injected new life and first made a practice, now commonplace, of DJs playing their own records rather than relying on an engineer to do it.

Discord In Three Flats
Clever title for Home Service comedy series about a landlord and his tenants, starring Cicely Courtneidge, Jack Hulbert and Vic Oliver.

Discovatin'
Late night Saturday show on Radio 1 from November 1978 to March 1980, presented by AL MATTHEWS.

Discovery
Weekly series on scientific research made by the BBC World Service, and now on Radio 5 as well.

Disgusted Tunbridge Wells
Daring Radio 4 show in 1978 which paved the way for FEEDBACK: presented by West Country author Derek Robinson, it enabled listeners to have a go at BBC programmes and policies.

This did not always endear itself to the top brass. Criticism of THE SPAM FRITTER MAN, for example, that 'it limped along like an arthritic elephant', drew an angry letter from DAVID HATCH saying that one BBC programme had no business sabotaging another BBC programme in this way. When AUBREY SINGER gave his backing to producers who refused to co-operate with the show, its fate was effectively sealed. It lasted for only nine months.

How the phrase 'Disgusted Tunbridge Wells' originally came about is a matter of some debate, and one suggestion is that it was coined in the comedy series TAKE IT FROM HERE.

The Doctors
Radio 4 documentary series in 1988 which, for the first time, went inside surgeries and eavesdropped on GPs as they saw their patients (made with the permission of both parties).

Dodd, Ken (1931–)
One of the comedy institutions of Radio 2, where he has appeared in numerous series including *Ken Dodd's Palace of Laughter*.

Does He Take Sugar?
Weekly Radio 4 series, running since 1978, which claims to be the world's first national radio programme for disabled people. Disabilities featured are mainly physical, though depression and dementia are examples of mental ones which have been discussed. Flatteringly, it has already been copied abroad, and a Danish radio network launched a similar series in 1983.

Does He Take Sugar? was devised by a broadcaster with BBC Radio London, Marilyn Allen, for whom physical handicap was an important subject because her brother suffered from Hodgkin's Disease. She also became the first presenter. John Mills took over after three years and then Kati Whitaker in 1986.

Disabled reporters used on the programme have included Kevin Mulhearn (who went on to front Central TV's disability series *Link*), Martin Duffy (Channel 4's *Don't Just Sit There*) and David Williams (later to take the role of a wheelchair-bound character in *EastEnders*).

The clever title originated as a phrase by social workers to denote an unthinking attitude in which we shy away from talking directly to disabled people but speak instead to their companions or relatives. The long life and high standards of *Does He Take Sugar?* have done much to counteract this.

Does The Team Think?
One of radio's longest running comedies, this was a farcical spoof on THE BRAINS TRUST and ANY QUESTIONS? in which four comics tried to outdo one another in spontaneous wit in answer to listeners' queries. Cheap to make, because off-the-cuff improvisations meant there was no scriptwriter to pay, it became a regular feature of Sunday lunchtimes on the Light Programme from 1958 to 1976.

JIMMY EDWARDS, who devised it, was nearly always on the panel, along with TED RAY, Tommy Trinder and ARTHUR ASKEY. Others who made appearances included Cyril Fletcher, Leslie Crowther and RICHARD MURDOCH.

Thames TV later mounted an unsuccessful television version and the formula was resurrected in PULL THE OTHER ONE.

Dogs
Several celebrated canines have barked their way over the airwaves: Winston in MUCH-BINDING-IN-THE-MARSH, played by MAURICE DENHAM; Psyche the dog, played by PERCY EDWARDS in LIFE OF BLISS; RUSTLER, who gave a woof at the end of every episode of RIDERS OF THE RANGE; ARNOLD, the faithful companion of TONY BLACKBURN. Those in THE ARCHERS have included Jack Woolley's Captain and Mrs Antrobus's Portia.

Donaldson, Peter (1945–)
Chief announcer on Radio 4 since 1988, with fifteen years in Radio 4 presentation before that. From 1970 to 1973 he was an announcer on Radio 2.

Don't Look Now
Basil Boothroyd of *Punch* compered this Home Service series of 1962–63 which continued the spirit of MONDAY NIGHT AT HOME, with music and witty sketches.

Double Bill

Radio 2 series starting in 1988 in which each show featured two famous movie stars whose careers had something in common which was not immediately apparent. Pairs included James Mason and Phyllis Calvert; Bette Davis and Ann Baxter; Michael Caine and Christopher Reeve.

Double Spin

Weekday afternoon record show on the Light Programme in 1966 featuring a 'Newly Pressed' spot featuring latest releases and 'Playtime' for younger listeners.

Double Your Money

Quiz show originally on Radio Luxembourg. Hughie Green later presented it on ITV (where it was produced by Associated Rediffusion) from 26 September 1955 until the end of the Rediffusion franchise period in 1968.

Douglas, Joe (1953–)

Founder of the Tottenham-based black pirate station WNK, in 1986, which two years later jointly won the Haringey INCREMENTAL contract. Born in Jamaica, and coming to Britain at the age of eleven, he also founded the now defunct London pirate station RJR.

Downtown Radio

Unique in being the only ILR station whose area exactly matches that of an ITV company and a national region of BBC Radio. Based in Newtownards, County Down, it covers the whole of Northern Ireland and began broadcasting in 1976.

It is one of only a handful of ILR companies to make drama, which has been a (tiny) part of its output since 1987. From that year onwards it has broadcast one home produced drama-documentary every year, starting with the sinking of the *Titanic* – which was built in Belfast – and continuing with the Australian bicentenary, French Revolution, Battle of the Boyne and, in 1991, Battle of the Somme. It is also carrying the winning plays in the Woolwich competition run by IRDP.

In 1990, like the vast majority of ILR stations, Downtown split its services. It launched Cool FM as a 'hot adult rock' service, based on contemporary album tracks, for 18 to 35-year-olds. This has a Belfast address, to convey the idea that it is fresh and different, but in fact comes from the same studios as the rest of the station's output.

The main service embraces a variety of music (country, dance, jazz, heavy metal, classical) and what it claims to be more specialist programmes than on any other ILR station (including motoring, amateur theatre, folklore, social issues, churches and nostalgia).

Down Your Way

Veteran Radio 4 series which has undergone radical surgery since it started on the Home Service in 1946 (an *annus mirabilis* which also saw the birth of DICK BARTON, LETTER FROM AMERICA, HOUSEWIVES' CHOICE and the Third Programme). Only the name has remained the same.

Presenters STEWART MACPHERSON (1946–50), RICHARD DIMBLEBY (1950–55), FRANKLIN ENGELMANN (1955–72) and BRIAN JOHNSTON (1972–87) all preserved the original formula of going to a different town or village each week, talking to colourful local figures about their community and hobbies, and then inviting them to choose a piece of music.

This unchanging format, with its staunchly patriotic signature tune of 'Horseguards, Whitehall', was a feature of Sunday teatime listening for almost forty years and gained a strong following. When it came off the air in 1975 as an economy measure, hundreds of distressed listeners rang or wrote in. The BBC said later it had been touched and influenced by all the letters from blind and disabled people who were unable to travel, and for whom *Down Your Way* was their only means of getting to know their own country. So the programme which travels 13,000 miles a year carried on.

In 1987, however, when Johnston stepped down at the age of 75, Radio 4 controller MICHAEL GREEN decided to 'refresh' its formula, bringing in different presenters each week and matching them to the places they visit. Instead of Down Your Way, the programme became a Down My Way.

Peter Ustinov, for example, went to Leningrad (where he was conceived), Sian Phillips returned to Swansea (where she was born) and actor Nigel Hawthorne (Sir Humphrey Appleby in *Yes, Prime Minister*) made his way to Whitehall, where he met Mrs Thatcher. The old signature tune was scrapped and the guests no longer have a say in the music, which is all chosen by the producer.

'It's not a knocking programme. We never look under any carpets. We only try to find nice things and nice people' – Brian Johnston, 1981.

Dragnet

'The story you are about to hear is true – only the names have been changed to protect the innocent . . .' Those words, and the bars of music which followed, introduced a hugely popular US radio show starring Jack Webb as Los Angeles police sergeant Joe Friday. It ran on NBC from 1949–56, sponsored by Fatima cigarettes: Webb continued the role in the hit television series from 1951–58, plus the 1954 feature film and the 1969 made-for-TV movie. The character was famous for the laconic utterances 'My name's Friday. I'm a cop' and 'Just the facts, mam', which goes to show that British radio does not have a monopoly of famous catchphrases.

Richard Dimbleby (right), presenter of *Down Your Way* in the early 1950s, and his producer John Shuter (holding microphone) at Southfleet, Kent, interviewing a pub landlord and his family

The radio series arrived in Britain for the first time some forty years later when the original serial was broadcast on the late-night Radio 2 show of KEN BRUCE in 1990. The show started a run on Radio 5 in 1991.

Drama

One of BBC Radio's greatest contributions to both high culture and popular entertainment has been its 'National Theatre of the Air'. The phrase may not have been coined until 1961 (when it was the umbrella title of an ambitious Home Service season covering 400 years of English drama, from Miracle and Morality plays to Oscar Wilde), but such was the vision from early days –

with a menu that included the classics, serious original works which exploited the unique qualities of the radio medium (its dependence on one sense only, its ability to reach inside the imagination with silences, pauses and the tiniest linguistic subtleties) and translations of Continental plays.

Pioneers such as LANCE SIEVEKING, TYRONE GUTHRIE and VAL GIELGUD laid the foundations of radio drama as did Laurence Gilliam, for thirty years head of the FEATURES DEPARTMENT, which produced UNDER MILK WOOD and the plays of LOUIS MACNEICE. They exploited the essential point of radio drama – that by providing only sounds, each listener has to create his or her *own* mental pictures – and developed this in both theory and practice, paving the way for the interior monologues and influential work of SAMUEL BECKETT and later HAROLD PINTER and GILES COOPER. Other writers to whom radio has extended invaluable help and encouragement include TOM STOPPARD, BILL NAUGHTON and JOHN MORTIMER.

In the 1980s, BBC Radio's Drama Department was often on the receiving end of complaints that its plays were too gloomy or too preoccupied with marital splits and sexual infidelity. Hence cartoonist Cathy Balme's comment in *The Listener*, February 1990

Dramatic milestones:

The first drama broadcast (February 1923) consisted of three scenes from three different Shakespeare plays.

The first complete play to go out (May 1923) was Shakespeare's *Twelfth Night*. (To mark the BBC's diamond jubilee in 1982, a new production was mounted on Radio 4 featuring Alec McCowen, Dilys Laye and Andrew Sachs.)

The first play to be broadcast which was written specifically for radio (January 1924) is generally regarded as *Danger* by Richard Hughes, although *The Truth about Father Christmas*, a children's play by Phyllis M. Twigg, has also been put forward.

It was set in the dark, in a coalmine, and began with the line: 'The lights have gone out.' Hughes hoped people would listen in the dark, and therefore find themselves sharing the experience of the characters and bound to them in their plight. (A new production for the diamond jubilee was also made of this, recorded in binaural stereo to show just how far wrap-around sound effects had progressed in sixty years.)

The first novel to be adapted (April 1925) was *Westward Ho!* by Charles Kingsley.

The first move to encourage new writing was in 1937, when VAL GIELGUD introduced *Experimental Hour*.

The first soap opera was THE ENGLISH FAMILY ROBINSON in 1937.

The first time the BBC commissioned an author to write a novel especially for broadcasting was in 1939, with *Let the People Sing* by J.B. PRIESTLEY.

The first daily serial was DICK BARTON – SPECIAL AGENT! in 1946.

The first living dramatist to have a major season of his work performed was the Irish playwright Brian Friel (1929–) on Radios 3 and 4 in 1989.

The first dramatisation of a James Bond novel was *You Only Live Twice*, broadcast on Radio 4 in 1990 with Michael Jayston as 007.

BBC Radio's drama department has grown into the largest commissioner and producer of plays in Britain – about 350 every year, in addition to over 260 episodes of THE ARCHERS. It offers about 1,000 writing opportunities a year, with about 9,000 for actors.

Drama has always maintained a very much smaller and more fragile presence within ILR: see RADIO CLYDE, DOWNTOWN RADIO and INDEPENDENT RADIO DRAMA PRODUCTIONS.

Most actors, including the greatest, have been happy to work in radio even at the peak of their careers. They do not have to learn the lines by heart, wear make-up or get dressed up in uncomfortable costumes. The only really notable exception is Laurence Olivier, who never showed very much interest in radio. Olivier made his radio debut in *A Winter's Tale* in 1935 and

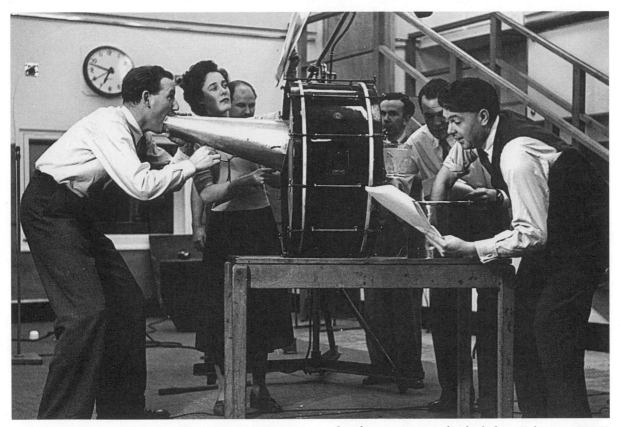

When the Martians invaded England in 1951, it sounded like this. The eerie noises in H.G. Wells's *War of the Worlds* (not to be confused with Orson Welles's famous production on American radio thirteen years before) were the outcome of a fortnight of experiment with mangles, megaphones, cymbals, sheets of glass, tin cans and vocal chords. John Chillingworth recorded the scene for *Picture Post*

his swansong in the monologue *No End to Dreaming* in 1987. This, his first radio appearance in more than thirty years, was specially written for him by PETER BARNES to mark his 80th birthday. Olivier played Nathan Yavok, a Jewish American business-man born in a Polish ghetto and now at the end of his life.

'One of the most magical properties of radio as a medium for drama is the way it enables playwright and performers to conjure up on the one hand great intimacy and on the other hand echoing spaces and vast crowds. The radio playwright can indeed be bounded by a nut-shell yet count herself, or himself, a monarch of infinite space' – Geoffrey Strachan of Methuen, co-organisers of the GILES COOPER AWARDS each year.

See also: entries on individual playwrights (e.g. RHYS ADRIAN); on the various slots (e.g. A BOOK AT BEDTIME); RADIO TIMES; BBC DRAMA REPER-TORY COMPANY.

Drama Now

Weekly Radio 3 slot for contemporary plays, initiated in 1988. One of its offerings, Nick Ward's *Trouble Sleeping*, in May 1990, about a couple living in rural isolation and the disruption to their lives caused by a delinquent young girl, marked the first ever collab-oration between BBC Radio drama and the National Theatre. The play was refined and rehearsed over six weeks in a workshop at the NT.

Drive-time

Radio industry jargon for the morning and afternoon rush hour slots, when stations traditionally mount some of their strongest offerings for their captive audience sitting in tens of thousands of cars.

Drummond, John (1934–)

Driving, ebullient, half-Australian and highly commit-ted Controller of Radio 3 who took over in 1987 with

Valentine Dyall, best known for providing the voice of _The Man in Black_. From Harrow and Christ Church he went to the Old Vic, where he began his acting career in 1930, later moving into radio (from 1936) and films (from 1941)

a mission to increase its audience without diluting its quality. Among his innovations were THIRD EAR in 1988 and OPERA NEWS in 1990, and special events such as the Australian and Scandinavian Seasons and the Berlin and Minnesota Weekends.

Drummond, Pete   (1943–)
One of Radio 1's original team of DJs when it began in 1967. Now a freelance.

du Garde Peach, Lawrence   (1890–1974)
University lecturer in English who became probably the most prolific radio playwright ever: he had 400 radio plays broadcast from the 1920s onwards. Many of these went out on CHILDREN'S HOUR, from 1928 until after the Second World War. He also contributed exciting features to the programme on the castles of England, Greek heroes, the mystery of the _Mary Celeste_, Knights of the Round Table, and other colourful historic themes.

Dunant, Sarah   (1951–)
Presenter of CONSUMING PASSIONS in 1988. Producer on KALEIDOSCOPE from 1974–76 and then worked on arts programmes for BBC Radio London, Capital Radio and the BBC World Service.

Dunn, John   (1934–)
Highly polished Radio 2 presenter nicknamed the 'gentle giant' partly because he is 6ft 7in tall and also to describe his soft, smooth approach. 'My programme is unashamedly bland,' he once said in a BBC information bulletin. 'That sounds derogatory but I defend the description because the most popular radio programmes are those in which people are apparently being nice to one another.'

Dunn served with the RAF during his National Service days before joining the BBC as a studio manager, moving into newsreading and annnouncing for all the networks. Joined Radio 2 when it was created in 1967. Hosted BREAKFAST SPECIAL for six years (1967–73) and then took up residence in the early evening slot which he still occupies. It offers the familiar blend of music and interviews – except that the guests are often boffins, explorers, architects and authors.

Dunn created his popular 'Mystery Voice' feature, in which listeners can win up to £300 in book tokens, record tokens or TV licence stamps by identifying a famous voice, of which only a short extract is played on the air. The voices are supplied by the BBC SOUND ARCHIVES.

Duran, Lucy   (1948–)
American specialist in music from faraway places, from Paraguay to Sudan, who has introduced it to listeners on both Radio 2 (Latin American) and Radio 3 (Greek and African). Born in New York of an English mother and Spanish father, she is also Curator of the International Music Collection at the British Library's National Sound Archive.

A speaker of Mandinka (a language of Gambia and Senegal), her first programme was on Radio 3 in 1986, in which she presented recordings of Gambian music. Several more Radio 3 series have followed, particularly on West African music such as _Songs of the Savannah_ in 1990. On Radio 2, she compiled and hosted two series, in 1988–89, of _The Latin Quarter_, which featured musicians from Panama and Cuba. She has also appeared on KALEIDOSCOPE and the BBC World Service and co-presents _Sidetracks_ on Jazz FM.

Dyall, Valentine   (1908–85)
Old Harrovian actor who made his radio debut in 1936 and was best known for playing THE MAN IN BLACK, the menacing-voiced narrator of APPOINTMENT WITH FEAR from 1941 to 1953.

Early Music Network
Eight-part Radio 3 series in 1990 featuring songs sung by, and music composed by, semi-courtesan Italian women in the sixteenth and seventeenth centuries.

Earshot
Live youth magazine show from Scotland, broadcast each week on Radio 5.

East End Radio
Funded initially from public purses, including Urban Aid and Strathclyde Community Business, East Glasgow's INCREMENTAL station went on the air, on FM, in June 1990, broadcasting both speech (including some Asian programmes) and music. It can be heard throughout the city and in the new towns of Cumbernauld and East Kilbride.

Eastern Beat
Long-running programme strong on the Asian pop music called bhangra, on both BBC Radio WM and BBC Radio Leicester, which in 1990 became the Midlands contribution to the evening youth strand on Radio 5.

Eastern Service
Began in May 1940, with the launch of a Hindustani Service which included programmes in both Hindi and Urdu as well as English. The object was to win over the hearts and minds of India, and to counteract Nazi propaganda broadcasts.

Before the end of the year services in Burmese and Persian had also been launched. Today it transmits in nine languages (those original four, plus Tamil, Bengali, Sinhalese, Pashto and Nepalese) for tens of millions of people throughout Southern Asia.

Its half-century was celebrated in November 1990 with a live concert which linked musicians in six cities (Dhaka, Delhi, Peshawar, Katmandu, Lahore and Madras), situated in four countries (Bangladesh, Pakistan, Nepal and India) using two satellites and three relay stations (on Cyprus, in the Indian Ocean and at Kranji in Singapore) to relay the signals halfway round the world from the Indian subcontinent to London and back again. This 2½-hour concert was one of the most elaborate international musical link-ups ever achieved.

Easy Beat
'New on the Light on Saturday night' was how this was billed when it began in January 1960: BRIAN MATTHEW both produced and presented the show, which featured teenagers' comments on the latest discs in the Hit Parade. The John Barry Seven were regulars. It ended in September 1967, six days before the Light became Radio 2.

Easy to Remember
Sunday evening show on Radio 2 in 1970 in which Paul Martin recalled 'familiar melodies from the past'.

Ebdon, John (–)
Humorous, plummy presenter of Radio 4's Monday-morning ARCHIVE FEATURE for over a quarter of a century (1961 to 1987) and remembered for the whimsical musings with which he threaded carefully excavated conversational snippets. Also for his two scrupulously polite catchphrases: 'How do you do?' (at the beginning of each programme) and 'If you have been, thanks for listening' (when he signed off). He presented another run of twenty-minute programmes from the archives on the Home Service in 1965–66, called *Nonsense at Noon*. Among other accomplishments, he was also the Director of the London Planetarium.

'His facetious patrician tones every third Monday morning, his sense of the absurd, his ear for a word mistakenly out of context, his famous cat Perseus, delighted much of middle England as much as it infuriated a small minority'– Glyn Worsnip.

Eccles
One of the best known creations of THE GOON SHOW, played by SPIKE MILLIGAN and inspired by Walt Disney's lovable cartoon character Goofy.

Mahogany-voiced John Ebdon was responsible for London Planetarium's stars and became one himself on Radio 4, where he combined observations on his feline company with quirks from the BBC Sound Archives

'Born 1863 ... at birth he was round and full of currants, and was baptised Eccles Cake ... part-time human being, height varies between 2ft 6in and 18ft 3in, depending upon food, environment and bed size.'

Eckersley, Peter Pendleton   (1892–1963)

The BBC's first chief engineer, appointed by JOHN REITH in 1923. Previously he was at the MARCONI company. Pushed out of the BBC in 1929 because he was cited in a divorce action, he later worked part-time as a consultant for one of Sir Oswald Mosley's companies, Air-time, using his exceptional engineering skills to help Mosley (founder of the British Union of Fascists, and

effectively banned from the BBC airwaves) pursue his plans for a commercial radio station on either continental Europe or an offshore island.

Eckersley's family made their mark in radio of an embarrassingly different kind from that of the BBC. His second wife Frances Eckersley and his stepson James Clark, then 22, pleaded guilty at the Old Bailey in December 1945 to 'conspiring to assist the enemy' by making Nazi propaganda broadcasts from Germany during the war. She was jailed for a year and he was bound over. James, Mrs Eckersley's son by her first marriage, had been sent to school in Germany by his mother, a fanatical Nazi supporter, and the two of them had then worked alongside WILLIAM JOYCE in that band of British, Irish and Germans who broadcast Hitler's propaganda, in English, over the airwaves during the Second World War.

The Edge of Fear

Twist-in-the-tale, half-hour plays presented every Friday evening in the Light Programme from June 1964. The first, *Requiem for a Nobody* by Gene Crowley, starred Noel Johnson and Ian Wallace.

Edmonds, Noel   (1948–)

Joined Radio 1 in 1969, making trailers. His first broadcast on the network was on 21 July that year, the same day as man stepped on the moon. One small step for mankind, perhaps, but one giant leap for Edmonds: within three years he had replaced TONY BLACKBURN as presenter of the breakfast show, where he stayed until 1977. Later, he helped to form UNIQUE.

Educating Archie

Not quite the first radio ventriloquist in Britain (see ALBERT SAVEEN), but the first to seize the popular imagination and help launch so many performers – including TONY HANCOCK, Max Bygraves, Dick Emery and teenage singer Julie Andrews, all of whom appeared on this popular Light Programme series which was part of Sunday afternoons throughout the 1950s.

The star was Archie Andrews, a ventriloquist's doll cast in the role of naughty schoolboy: the name was invented by TED KAVANAGH, who heelped to create the show. His operator was PETER BROUGH, son of Arthur Brough, a Jaeger rep and part-time ventriloquist.

Beryl Reid, who played Archie's girlfriend, was another who got her first big break on the programme. To put herself in the right mood at the microphone, she often dressed up in her old school uniform, complete with black stockings and a hanky tucked into her knickers.

Archie was a great favourite at the Palace, and was invited to Royal Christmas parties. Brough has recalled that once, King George VI and Queen Elizabeth, and the Princesses Elizabeth and Margaret as they were then,

Archie Andrews (left) was the naughtiest schoolboy of the 1950s until Jimmy Clitheroe came along, although he never looked any younger than his creator Peter Brough (right), and was always impeccably turned out

asked for the dummy's head to be taken off while they had a good look at the controls. Afterwards the King remarked: 'That's the only fellow I've ever beheaded in my reign.'

'People always said, why a ventriloquist on the radio? I always used to say "why not?" Radio is all about painting pictures for the mind' – Peter Brough.

Education Matters
Radio 4 FM series covering news and views in the world of education, which moved to Radio 5 when the new network began in 1990.

Edwards, Jimmy   (1920–88)
Whiskery, Falstaffian comedian with a love of fox-hunting and the tuba, best remembered on radio for playing Pa Glum in TAKE IT FROM HERE and also for regular appearances on his spoof panel game DOES THE TEAM THINK? He entered showbusiness, as did many, after service in the armed forces: he was shot down over Holland as a Flight Lieutenant in the RAF.

Edwards, Percy   (1908–)
Broadcaster with an almost unique talent – impersonating the calls of birds and animals, which he was first hired to do on radio in the series *Vaudeville* at SAVOY HILL in 1930. He made four broadcasts from there, followed by hundreds from BROADCASTING HOUSE until he retired in October 1989.

Among his general repertoire of 600 wild birds and a complete farmyard were two celebrated animal characters, Gregory the chicken in RAY'S A LAUGH and Psyche the dog in LIFE OF BLISS. His extraordinary ability to reproduce the sounds of living creatures has also been much in evidence in the cinema: he played the title role in *Orca – Killer Whale* and was heard on many other films from *The Belstone Fox* to *The Dark Crystal*, but was only rarely credited because, he says, the film companies were coy about owning up to the use of an animal impressionist.

Born and brought up in Ipswich, he first started to replicate the calls of the creatures of his native Suffolk at the age of seven and, he says, he still loves the countryside just as much today.

The Egypt Project
Five-part SCHOOLS RADIO series on Radio 4 FM in 1989 for nine- to eleven-year-olds which, in conjunction with a similar series on BBC2, looked at the country of the Nile both ancient (Pharaohs, pyramids, Old Testament stories of Moses and Israelite slaves) and modern (everyday life today as seen through the eyes of Cairo children).

Ekco
Former radio manufacturer based in Southend, whose name was an acronym of its creator Eric Kirkham Cole (1901–66), which did much to popularise the use of BAKELITE. The company, which Cole founded in 1922, imported from Germany the equipment needed to make bakelite cases. It became celebrated for its circular radios built between 1934 and 1945, which can now fetch hundreds of pounds.

Empire Service
What the BBC World Service was first called, when it was launched by JOHN REITH in December 1932.

Encounters in France
Six-part Radio 4 series in 1989 with Daniel Snowman sampling the contrasting views of French writers and intellectuals as the country got ready to celebrate the bicentenary of the French Revolution.

End of a Line
Touching series on Radio 4 in 1991 in which Paul Heiney met four men whose work would die with them:

the keepers of the Longstone Lighthouse overlooking the Northumberland coast, which was becoming fully automated; the man who guides travellers over the treacherous quicksands between Morecambe and Ulverston; one of the few freshwater pearl fishermen left in Britain; and the sailors of the flat-bottomed coble boats in Whitby.

The End of the Day

Five minutes of 'Christian words and music' which brought the curtain down on Sunday evenings on the Light Programme for several years. It began in 1957 and ended in 1964, when the network started to stay on the air until 2 a.m.

Engelmann, Franklin (1908–72)

BBC Radio broadcaster for over thirty years, admired for a deep, firm, unhurried voice and for long associations with two old favourites. He presented DOWN YOUR WAY for seventeen years (1955–72) and GARDENERS' QUESTION TIME for eleven years (1961–72). He would have chaired the 1,000th edition of the latter, at the Royal Horticultural Society in London, but died in the week of its recording. Producer Ken Ford stepped in.

Nicknamed 'Jingle', he also presented WHAT DO YOU KNOW? and its successor BRAIN OF BRITAIN and was the original host of PICK OF THE POPS, in 1955.

The English

Eight-part Radio 4 series in 1991, spanning the fall of the Roman Empire in the fifth century to the Industrial Revolution in the eighteenth, in which broadcaster Malcolm Billings and Jonathan Riley-Smith (Professor of History at London University) set out to explore the distinctive qualities and history of the English people.

The English Family Robinson

First British soap opera, in 1937.

English Now

Radio 4 series in 1990 in which David Crystal looked at the language of Shakespeare and Milton.

Enquire Within

'How heavy are clouds?' 'Who was Kilroy, as in Kilroy woz 'ere?' 'How did be-bop and boogie-woogie get their names?' The questions on this Radio 4 series, all of them sent in by listeners, have ranged from the curious to the wildly eccentric, but all of them get an answer.

Created (and presented) by the late Neil Landor, the programme began in March 1978 and has now clocked up over 500 episodes. DILLY BARLOW took over as host in 1987 when Landor fell seriously ill, and has presented it ever since.

Enterprise

Radio 4 series launched in 1977 when the economic recession was hitting many big companies but the growth of many small ones was, by contrast, a success story. The programme celebrates and monitors the activities of small firms and has carried profiles of more than 200. It organises the ENTERPRISE AWARD FOR SMALL BUSINESSES contest each year. Presenter: MARJORIE LOFTHOUSE.

Enterprise Award for Small Businesses

Annual competition organised by Radio 4 and RADIO TIMES, designed to winkle out Britain's most enterprising small firms. It has been mounted every year since 1984 and carries a £10,000 first prize. Firms can enter if they have an annual turnover under £1 million and been trading for no more than five years. In 1990 a second award of £5,000 was introduced for companies under two years old.

Winners – always announced on the ENTERPRISE programme – have ranged from fabric designer Georgina von Etzdorf to Dart Pottery and Encrypta Electronics, manufacturers of security seals which prevent goods from being stolen from lorries.

The Epilogue

Stemming from the deep Christian commitment of JOHN REITH, and his reverence in particular for the Sabbath, this began in 1926 as the programme with which transmissions finished on a Sunday. Initially it consisted of verses from the Bible, later being augmented by a psalm or hymn. By 1960 it was a ten-minute programme of Bible readings and hymns, late on Sunday nights on the Home Service. It finally ended on Good Friday of 1980.

Essex Radio

ILR station based in Southend-on-Sea, covering an area from Havering to Colchester and the Thames estuary to Bishop's Stortford. On the air since 1981. Breeze AM, an easy-listening service with Mantovani, the Carpenters and Tony Bennett, was launched on its medium wave frequency in 1989.

Alumni include *Grandstand* presenter Helen Rollason, who started as a secretary on the station.

Euromix

Radio 5 series exploring the European youth scene, presented by Caron Keating.

Europhile

Cleverly punning title for innovative weekly series on Radio 4 focusing on life in the 36 countries of Europe. When it began in November 1989, it was presented mainly from Paris by experienced European journalists who spoke fluent English with pronounced mid-Atlantic accents, and it had the honourable aim of covering stories which too often went unreported in Britain, like the fate of the gondola or Polish soup kitchens.

As soon as it started, however, the Berlin Wall came tumbling down and the programme had bigger concerns on its hands. It covered Eastern Europe's political turmoil with vivid colour but was heavily criticised for its presenters' mannerisms and ponderous links.

The only woman in the original trio of presenters was sacked after one programme, on the grounds that she was not easily understood. She was Christiane Collange, former editor of *Elle*, former editor of Antenne 2's breakfast television show *Telematin*, and author of several books on modern women and changing family relationships.

Her male colleagues lasted longer and went on to co-present the second series. They were Josef Joffe (foreign editor of *Suddeutsche Zeitung*, West Germany's biggest quality paper) and Phillipe Chatenay (deputy foreign editor of the French news weekly *Le Point*). Since June 1990, the series has been presented regularly by Max Easterman, with contributions from other European journalists. It goes out on Saturday mornings for half the year and there was much bitterness within the BBC that it kicked out the excellent FROM OUR OWN CORRESPONDENT from that favoured slot.

Everett, Kenny (1944–)

Liverpudlian funny man who loves to shock, both with characters (like his Cupid Stunt on television) and years of dubious jokes. After a stint on the pirate ship Radio London, he joined the BBC as a DJ but was sacked from Radio 1 in 1970 for suggesting on the air that the wife of then Transport Minister John Peyton had passed her driving test only 'because she slipped a fiver' to the examiner. The BBC said it regarded the joke as 'indefensible'.

Eleven years later the Corporation welcomed him back by giving him a Saturday morning show on Radio 2. Within two years, however, they were already apologising for a joke he made about Mrs Thatcher. Everett later became one of the first broadcasters on Capital Radio's Capital Gold, where he now presents an entertaining weekday afternoon show.

Everybody Step

Successor to TRAD TAVERN on the Light Programme, this began in 1962 and put the emphasis on instrumental

In the early 1970s Kenny Everett had his very own 'Wireless Workshop', a well-equipped studio at his medieval farmhouse home in Cowfold, Sussex, which he shared with his then wife Audrey Lee and their Great Dane, Bosie

music. Adriano evoked 'Continental moods and memories' on the accordion: Norrie Paramor and The Big Ben Banjo Band also appeared.

Ewing, Patricia (1939–)

First Controller of Radio 5. Previously she was Head of BBC Radio Sport, having joined the BBC in 1973 after twelve years in the WRNS.

The Eye-Witness

Saturday morning compilation of 'reports from Britain and overseas' presented on the Home Service. It ran from May 1946 to December 1968.

F

Face the Facts

Radio 4's major investigative and watchdog series began in 1986 as successor to CHECKPOINT. It continued in the same vein, though less aggressively. Former Scottish National Party MP Margo MacDonald presented the first series. She was succeeded, in January 1987, by John Waite (cousin of Terry Waite, the Archbishop of Canterbury's envoy who vanished in Beirut that same month) and he has done it ever since.

Investigations derive from listeners' letters. They have ranged from the plight of elderly British expatriates in Spain to pollution and financial chicanery. The BBC describes the programme's remit as 'to pursue individual allegations of injustice, sharp practice and the abuse of authority'.

Fair Deal

Magician David Nixon dealt cards with questions on them in this show devised by IAN MESSITER. It ran on Radio 4 from 1972–75. Panellists who had to answer the questions, and remember which cards had already been played, included William Rushton, June Whitfield and Patrick Moore. The game's successor was DEALING WITH DANIELS.

Falk, Bernard (1943–90)

Rumbustious, populist, cheerful and highly effective Liverpudlian who from 1981 to 1990 hosted Radio 4's holiday show BREAKAWAY (leaving because his company, Falkman, had been commissioned to make the Channel 4 travel series *Travelog*, which he was also going to anchor, and the BBC thought he would not be able to do both).

He was due to become the full-time presenter of GOING PLACES, but died of a heart attack (his second) on his speedboat in Bray, Berkshire, in a 90 degree heatwave, on the day after the hottest day of the century.

Fallen Arches

Late-night Radio 4 comedy series whose central character was a Victorian aristocrat called Lord Cliffhanger. It ran from 1988–89.

False Evidence

Panel game which has evolved into HOAX! Devised by the prolific IAN MESSITER, whose original suggested title of 'Spot the Liar' was rejected by the BBC as unpleasant, it had three people telling a story about themselves, two of which were true and the third a deliberate fabrication. A 'jury' of members of the audience had to vote as to who was telling the truth and who wasn't.

GILBERT HARDING was the 'judge' and FRANK-LIN ENGELMANN and Leslie Mitchell prosecuting and defence 'counsel'. The same format – three panellists, one of whom is making everything up – is the basis of HOAX!

Families and How to Survive Them

John Cleese and his former psychiatrist Robin Skynner broadcast this six-part Radio 4 series in 1990–91, based on their book about growing up, bringing up children and personal relationships. It was illustrated with extracts from familiar soaps and sitcoms, e.g. *In Sickness and In Health* and *Fawlty Towers*. It had the melancholy distinction of being the last programme ever reviewed in *The Listener*.

Family Choice

Successor to HOUSEWIVES' CHOICE after the birth of Radio 1 in 1967.

Family Favourites

Weekly record request show on the Light Programme, linking London with the British Forces Network in Germany. It started in 1945, changing its title to TWO-WAY FAMILY FAVOURITES in 1960 and continuing until 1984. JEAN METCALFE first met her future husband CLIFF MICHELMORE on the air, while they were on opposite sides of the Channel presenting the programme.

'It is doubtful whether any civilians who do not have relations in the Armed Forces can realise just how much her (Metcalfe's) record programmes mean to servicemen and their families and sweethearts – and especially to

It was love at first hearing for Jean Metcalfe and Cliff Michelmore. Normally on *Family Favourites* they were hundreds of miles apart – she in London, he in Germany – and talked on the air for eighteen months before finally meeting in 1949. They married the following year

people serving overseas' – Eve Sharpe, a Services wife, writing in *Radio Times* in 1963.

Family Footsteps
Racing driver Jackie Stewart and his son Paul, who has followed him into the business, and agent Mark McCormack and his tennis-playing wife Betsy Nagelson, were among those who spoke on this Radio 4 series on sporting families, talking to Gerald Williams, in 1989.

Family Fortunes
Exploration of three generations of working class family life in Northern England by PHIL SMITH in a six-part Radio 4 series in 1991.

A Family History
Four-part Radio 4 series in 1989 which traced the roots of four individuals – two pupils and two old boys – connected with Bolton School for Boys. They included British Coal chairman Sir Robert Haslam.

Famous for Fifteen Minutes
Revealing Radio 4 series beginning in 1988 in which people who have tasted instant fame speak of its effect on their lives and the obscurity to which they have often returned. The title was taken from Andy Warhol's famous aphorism of the late 1960s, 'In the future everyone will be famous for fifteen minutes.'

Interviewees have included 'Oi'll give it foive' pop girl Janice Nicholls, pop singer Twinkle, round-faced Billy Bunter actor Gerald Campion and British Leyland shop steward Derek 'Red Robbo' Robinson. The first was Erika Roe, who became an overnight sensation when she ran topless across the pitch at Twickenham during a rugby international in 1982.

She told the interviewer, Jenni Mills: 'I wouldn't streak again for a million quid. I'd rather be poor. Fame isn't worth the price.' She revealed that she had earned only £8,000 in the whole six-year period from her fame, mainly from newspapers, and was now living on social security.

Describing the streak as 'a dare to myself', she said: 'One always dreams as a little girl of being famous, like a ballerina. You want to know what it's like. I tasted it in a big way for two or three weeks when the media went crazy and it knocked it out of me.'

Famous Players in Famous Plays
Drama series which began in 1942.

Fanshawe On Five
Live arts programme for teenagers on Radio 5 hosted by Simon Fanshawe, offering a weekly audition slot.

Farming programmes
Over sixty years of daily farming programmes on BBC Radio began in March 1929 with a solemn recitation of the Fat Stock Prices, a phrase which became something of a music hall joke. Occasional talks on agricultural topics can be traced back to 1923, only two years after what appears to be the world's first ever farm broadcast, in Pittsburgh in 1921. A specialist service for farmers and gardeners was launched in 1934 by John Green, who joined the BBC from the office of the Ministry of Agriculture and whose career demonstrates one of the central aspects of the Corporation's farming output – its close links with Whitehall.

The first regular farm broadcaster was John Morgan (agriculture correspondent of the *Daily Herald* and Labour MP for Doncaster) who was succeeded after a year by James Scott Watson, an Oxford professor. The broadcasts of 'Scotty', in a programme called *For Farmers Only* on Wednesday evenings, proved popular at a time of acute depression in agriculture. Scotty gave way to Anthony Hurd (whose son Douglas later became Home Secretary) of *The Times* and by 1937 a programme called FARMING TODAY had emerged – then only once a week but, since 1964, daily.

During the Second World War, when efficient farming was crucial to Britain's survival, Churchill's agriculture minister R.S. Hudson wanted to exercise direct editorial control of BBC farming programmes. A compromise was reached whereby the farming output became subject to an advisory body operating under the Ministry of Agriculture's Publicity Committee, and known as the Broadcast Planning Sub-Committee. (Its chairman was Anthony Hurd, now straddling the two worlds of the BBC and the Ministry.) This sub-committee has survived until the present day and is now known as the Central Agricultural Advisory Committee of the BBC.

After 1945 (when Anthony Hurd was elected to the Commons as a Tory MP) the farming programmes continued to try and educate farmers as to what was in the national interest. It is no coincidence that THE ARCHERS was conceived, and has always been produced, in the Midlands, which is where the other farming programmes also hail from: it was created after one farmer called for 'a farming Dick Barton' at a meeting between the BBC and farming representatives in Birmingham in 1948.

The bulk of the audience today are town dwellers. As the Annan Committee remarked in 1977: 'Good agricultural programmes can explain the importance of agriculture and forestry to our largely urban community, who consume agricultural products without understanding much about the toil and hazards of production. They can also awaken in the audience a feeling of the life, traditions and beauty of the countryside.'

Farming Today
Heffers, yearlings, daffodils, potatoes all feature in Radio 4's digest of agricultural news, every weekday morning just after 6 a.m. The *Daily Telegraph* once described it as a 'daily symposium of agrarian delights' and the programme certainly exerts a strong appeal for the lay audience. The BBC estimates that only a minority of the audience consists of farmers. See FARMING PROGRAMMES.

The Farming Week
Radio 4's agricultural programme early every Saturday morning. See FARMING PROGRAMMES.

Fear on Four
Creepy stories on Radio 4, broadcast from 1988–91, performed by actors and introduced by Edward de Souza who resurrected THE MAN IN BLACK character with a chilling sense of menace.

Features Department
Source of some of BBC Radio's most memorable programmes in the so-called golden age of the 1940s and 1950s, such as UNDER MILK WOOD and the work of LOUIS MACNEICE. (Also the source of innumerable morale-boosting wartime programmes.)

It began life as an offshoot of the Drama Department in the 1930s. Its leisurely spirit eventually proved too much for an increasingly cost-conscious BBC, and it was disbanded in 1964. In the late 1980s, features gained a new lease of life with experiments in programmes eavesdropping on their subjects like fly-on-the-wall television documentaries, or painting sound pictures which spoke for themselves without narrators. SOUNDTRACK was one of the innovations.

Feedback
Weekly Radio 4 series running since 1979, which in the past has been presented by Mary Whitehouse, among

others. Today it is Chris Dunkley, television critic of *The Financial Times*, who ventilates complaints from listeners regarding the programmes and policies of BBC Radio. BBC executives then respond to these complaints on the air. Dunkley was chosen because, in his words, he was seen to 'stand with the audience rather than the broadcasters.'

It stemmed from DISGUSTED TUNBRIDGE WELLS.

Fergie Award
Annual award presented by the RADIO ACADEMY, and sponsored by Ferguson, for 'outstanding contribution to music radio'. The first, in 1987, went to ALAN FREEMAN; JOHN PEEL won it in 1988. In 1989 the trophy went posthumously to RAY MOORE and in 1990, again posthumously, to ROGER SCOTT. The winner in 1991 was BRIAN MATTHEW.

Ferris, Paul (1929–)
Radio critic of *The Observer*, 1954–88. Also an occasional broadcaster, and author of several novels and biographies.

A Festival of Nine Lessons and Carols
Annual Christmas Eve service from King's College, Cambridge, which has been broadcast live by BBC Radio every year since 1928. The service was originated in 1880 by the then Bishop of Truro, Edward Benson, but moulded into its present format with nine Bible readings (five from the Old Testament and four from the New) and a varying number of carols by the Dean of King's, Eric Milner-White, in 1918. Since 1919 the first carol has always been Once in Royal David's City.

File on 4
Pithy, weekly current affairs programme on Radio 4 created by MICHAEL GREEN when he was BBC Radio's boss in Manchester in 1977, and produced there ever since. Its essence is vivid, first-hand reporting on topical issues both at home and abroad – from the war in Nicaragua to women priests, interest rates to child sexual abuse – which stresses the effect on individuals of official policies and tries to avoid the Westminster agenda. Helen Boaden and Stuart Simon have been among its reporters.

Film Star
Radio 4 series in which *Evening Standard* film critic and author Alexander Walker profiled the greatest names of the cinema. It began in 1984 and finished in 1988.

The Financial Week
Introduced on Radio 4 in October 1989, presented by Vincent Duggleby, to replace the Friday edition of THE FINANCIAL WORLD TONIGHT.

The Financial World Tonight
Radio 4's nightly round-up of business and finance: claims to have been radio's first daily business programme when it began in 1974. When it moved to an earlier slot of 9.45 p.m., in October 1989, it also changed its agenda: less obsessed with the City, more concerned with broader topics of business and the economy.

The Finer Things
Radio 4 series in 1990, full of amusing anecdotes, which explored some of the ordinary things in life (making trips to the supermarket, buying shoes and so on) and the way they can provide solace and pleasure.

Finnish Service
Finnish-language programmes on the World Service were launched in March 1940. Today, they are on the air for about an hour and a quarter each day and, in addition, are rebroadcast on thirty local stations in Finland – boosting the audience considerably.

Fiona and Charles
Terribly, terribly English, and frightfully, frightfully stupid couple in ROUND THE HORNE, played by DAME CELIA MOLESTRANGLER and BINKY HUCKABACK, who in their turn were played by Betty Marsden and Hugh Paddick.

The First Day of the Week
Five-minute programme of Christian words and music which began transmissions on the Light Programme, and Radio 2, on Sunday mornings from 1951–74.

First Person
Innovative series beginning in 1988 in which first-time broadcasters with a story to tell give ten-minute talks on Radio 4. They have included a man who spent twelve years in a Turkish jail and another who taught English in Verona.

MICHAEL GREEN devised the idea for the series, to introduce fresh voices to the network and discover new broadcasting talent. 'We need to start looking for the next generation of Redheads and MacGregors,' was the way he put it.

The First Time
Radio 4 series in 1990 in which Martin Roberts followed the fortunes of various novices – youngsters on an ocean-going yacht, junior doctors during their first 24 hours in a large Manchester hospital, trekkers in Thailand.

Five Aside
The only daily sequence programme, on any BBC network, which does not come from London began on

Radio 5's first day in August 1990. Live from Manchester every teatime, hosted at first by MARTIN KELNER and similar to the old *Nationwide* on television, it also delivers the weather forecasts in a different way – city by city, using percentages, so instead of talking about 'scattered showers' it says 'there's a 30 per cent chance of rain'. In 1991 two new presenters, Sue McGarry (ex-BBC Radio Cumbria) and Julian Worricker (ex-BBC Radio Leicester) took over.

Five Master Photographers

Colin Ford, Keeper of the National Museum of Photography, Film and Television, interviewed, among others, Lord Snowdon and Karsh of Ottawa in this Radio 3 series in 1990.

Five To Ten

'A story, a hymn and a prayer' which went out at 9.55 a.m. on the Light Programme from Monday to Friday from 1950–70, proving that even in the middle of busy weekday mornings the BBC wished to remind its listeners of the Christian heritage to which most of them claimed allegiance. It later became PAUSE FOR THOUGHT, and a regular feature on the shows of RAY MOORE, TERRY WOGAN and DEREK JAMESON.

'The Fleet's Lit Up'

One of the most celebrated examples in history of why alcohol and the microphone do not go well together was this inebriated talk by TOMMY WOODRUFFE, one of the BBC's sports and outside broadcast commentators, at the Spithead Naval Review in 1935. It was such a sensation that it even inspired a West End show, *The Fleet's Lit Up*, mounted by George Black at the Hippodrome.

Woodruffe had had to spend the day of the broadcast aboard his old ship, HMS Nelson, where he enjoyed substantial and prolonged hospitality. When it came to the evening, and the ships switched on their lights, listeners all over Britain heard this commentary: 'The Fleet's lit up. When I say "lit up" I mean lit up by fairy lights. Is lit up by fairy lights. It isn't a fleet at all . . . the whole fleet is a fairyland . . . the whole fleet's lit up . . . the ships are lit up . . . even the destroyers are lit up . . . '

He continued in this vein for several minutes until his voice was faded out by HARMAN GRISEWOOD, the announcer on duty in London. 'And that is the end of our relay from Spithead,' he said, 'so now over to the Carlton Hotel for dance music . . . '

Afterwards an outraged JOHN REITH held what Grisewood recalls was 'a court-martial type of inquiry' which he says he found more remarkable than the incident itself. Woodruffe was suspended for six months, but he later commentated at the 1936 Olympics and the 1939 Cup Final.

Fletcher's Friends

Radio 2 series which began in 1988, hosted by Cyril Fletcher, in which he recalls magic moments with chums like Jack Hulbert and The Crazy Gang.

Floggit's

Light Programme comedy series set in a general store which ran from 1956–58. In the cast were Ronnie Barker, Joan Sims and Anthony Newley, but the stars were ELSIE AND DORIS WATERS.

Flotsam and Jetsam

Comedy double act which made its radio debut in 1926 and entertained audiences for most of the next two decades. High-voiced Flotsam was pianist B.C. Hilliam from Scarborough (1890–1968) and deep-voiced Jetsam was Malcolm McEachern, born in Australia of Scots parents and sometimes billed as 'Basso Supremo' (1883–1945).

Among their triumphs was a famous song, put on record in 1927, which captured some of the magic of early wireless:

Little Miss Bouncer loves her announcer
Down at the BBC;
She doesn't know his name
But how she rejoices
When she hears that voice of voices;
Absolutely tireless, sitting at the wireless,
Poor little Miss B;
It's the man who announces with such a lot of passion-in-it:
'The Daventry shipping forecast will follow in a minute'
Little Miss Bouncer loves her announcer,
Down at the BBC!

Flying Doctor

Adventures in the Australian outback, as dramatised on the Light Programme from 1958 to 1963. Australian writer Rex Rienits used his country's real flying doctor service as the basis of the series. James McKechnie had the title role; Bill Kerr played his high-spirited pilot and Bettina Dickson was the wisecracking radio operator back at base. Until 1960 McKechnie was the only non-Australian in the cast, but in that year Rosemary Miller, a New Zealander, joined as a new nurse.

Flywheel, Shyster and Flywheel

Six scripts of this historic Marx Brothers radio series, broadcast on NBC across America in the 1930s, were found by a researcher, Mike Barson, in the Washington Library of Congress in 1988.

Since no actual recordings of the shows (for which sponsors Standard Oil were said to have paid the brothers $6,500 a week) had survived, this discovery generated some excitement. The thirty-minute scripts were acquired by the BBC, adapted by Mark Brisenden, brought to life before a studio audience with the actors in costume, and broadcast on Radio 4 as a comedy highlight in 1990.

Michael Roberts played Groucho's part (the smart, wise-cracking, rogue attorney Waldorf T. Flywheel) and Frank Lazarus took the Chico role of the idiotic assistant, Emmanuel Ravelli. Both sounded exactly like the originals (and looked like them too).

FM

Frequency modulation: altering the length of the radio wave (not the height, as with AM). Used on all VHF broadcasts. Unlike AM, FM can carry stereo, and is supposed to provide greater protection against interference from electrical appliances and thunderstorms. Its disadvantage is that its range is much more limited (which is why Radio 4, the one network which would remain in a national emergency, has to maintain its LONG WAVE frequency which covers the whole of the British Isles).

FM was introduced by BBC Radio around 1960. BBC local radio stations have gone out on FM, as well as AM, since they began in 1967. Radio 1 launched its own FM frequency in 1988 and hopes to be available in FM over the whole of Britain by the end of 1992. Radio 2 became FM only in August 1990. The BBC's speedy progress towards FM was made under the impetus of the government, which is taking away the MEDIUM WAVE frequencies of Radio 1 and Radio 3 for two of the new commercial channels.

Until 1990, the police and emergency services used the main 88——108 MHz section of the FM band. They were then pushed off to another, less crowded, part of the spectrum in order to accommodate the new wave of local stations such as (in London) Jazz, Melody and Kiss. With the police no longer audible, the Home Office lifted its ban on prisoners listening to FM. Formerly they had only been allowed radios that were confined to medium and long wave. Only because the prohibition has been lifted, therefore, can prisoners now listen to Radio 2. Behind bars this is of some importance, given the popularity among prisoners of COUNTRY CLUB and FOLK ON 2, with their Country and Western music and romantic love songs.

FM was developed in 1939 by the American scientist Edwin Armstrong (1890–1954). He had already, in 1916, invented a device called the superheterodyne receiver which enabled non-engineers to tune radios – simply by turning a dial.

Folk on Friday

Presented by JIM LLOYD and produced by FRANCES LINE (who subsequently married), this began on Radio 2 in 1970 and is credited with having a strong influence on the revival of folk music which began in the 1960s and continued in the early 1970s, when Britain could boast a thousand folk clubs and artists such as Tom Paxton, Judy Collins and The Spinners played at sellout concerts.

With Fairport Convention's 'Lark in the Morning' as its signature tune, it went out live at 7 p.m. every Friday and many folk clubs would start early that evening, their members listening to the show while the radio was perched on the club bar before beginning their own entertainment. The Corries, The Yetties and the McPeake family from Belfast all appeared in early programmes.

One of *Folk on Friday*'s most popular ingredients was a club spot for new singers making their debut on the air. Among those who appeared in it were Maddy Prior, Martyn Wyndham Reid and Robin and Barry Dransfield, all of whom returned to take part in a special Radio 2 concert in 1990 marking the fact that twenty years had elapsed since *Folk on Friday* was first heard.

The programme's successor was FOLK ON 2, which continued to be hosted by Jim Lloyd.

Folk on 2

Folk music series on Radio 2 which began in 1980 when FOLK ON FRIDAY moved to Wednesday ('Folk on Wednesday' not having the same alliterative appeal). The presenter remained the same, JIM LLOYD, but the new show had less news from around the folk scene and more music. It still goes out on Wednesday nights and features both contemporary and traditional musicians.

The programme's Young Tradition Award, created by Lloyd and open to solo musicians under 25, has done much to encourage young folk artists. The first winner, in 1988, was accordion player Lynne Tocker. English concertina player Simon Thoumire won in 1989 and Ingrid Henderson from Fort William, who played the clarsach (Celtic harp) was only thirteen when she triumphed in 1990.

The Food Programme

Weekly Radio 4 programme which began in 1979, when it was billed as 'meat and drink for your Sunday lunchtime entertainment'. No longer at Sunday lunchtimes (it was pushed out in favour of DESERT ISLAND DISCS when Michael Parkinson took over) and no longer just meat and drink, either.

What used to be a lightweight magazine, half of it given over to cooking and recipes, has developed into a pungent, informative and frequently controversial programme examining food issues in the context of diet, nutrition, pesticides, marketing, impurities, hospital catering, commercially sponsored teaching aids and so on.

Food writer DEREK COOPER, who conceived the idea of the programme, has always written and presented it.

For a Later Age
Radio 3 series in 1989–90 of nine programmes of Beethoven chamber and piano music. The title was a quote from a letter written by the composer, wherein he wrote that this music was not for his own time, but 'for a later age'.

For the Young
See CHILDREN'S HOUR.

Forces' Favourites
Popular record request show on the Forces Programme in the Second World War, with a wonderful signature tune – 'When You Wish Upon a Star'. The Ink Spots, Bing Crosby and Vera Lynn were among the favourites.

JEAN METCALFE was picked from her clerical obscurity and given a disc jockey's job on it (a BBC decision she modestly describes as 'brave and reckless'), and MARJORIE ANDERSON was another who presented it. It became FAMILY FAVOURITES after the end of the war.

Forces Programme
Launched as a separate light entertainment channel for British servicemen (most of whom were then still in Britain) in 1940. It grew into the Light Programme in 1945, which in turn was renamed Radio 2 in 1967.

Fordyce, Keith (1928–)
Worked as a DJ with the British Forces Network in Hamburg, on his National Service, before going to Cambridge to read law; later a DJ on Radio Luxembourg's TOP TWENTY before switching to the Light Programme where he introduced EASY BEAT and, later, BEAT THE RECORD.

Forgotten Reputations
Radio 3 series in 1989–90, presented by John Amis, about unjustly forgotten, or tragically truncated, musical careers. Included were composer William Busch; conductor Walter Goehr; violinist Olive Zorian (Amis's former wife); Australian pianist Noel Newton-Wood, who committed suicide; soprano Margaret Ritchie; and Arnold Goldsborough, founder of the orchestra which later became the English Chamber Orchestra. All six died in the 1940s, 1950s and 1960s.

Formula Five
Radio 5 series for youngsters, presented by Sue Nelson, covering topics from CDs to software, sci-fi comics to the environment.

The Forsyte Chronicles
Epic serial of three generations of the Forsyte family, and their descendants the Cherrells, which stretched across 23 hour-long episodes on Radio 4 from September 1990 to March 1991. Unlike previous adaptations of John Galsworthy's saga of property and passion, this was based on all three of the author's trilogies. For the first time, therefore, it embraced the complete sequence of nine novels.

Between 1945–47, the Home Service broadcast a serialisation of the first trilogy, *The Forsyte Saga* (consisting of *The Man of Property*, *In Chancery* and *To Let*) which was written by Muriel Levy, directed by VAL GIELGUD and starred Ronald Simpson and Griselda Hervey as Soames and his wife Irene. A new production of these scripts, in 48 half-hour parts, began on the Home Service in July 1967 and continued until September 1968, with Alan Wheatley and Rachel Gurney in the central roles. BBC2's *The Forsyte Saga* of 1967, starring Eric Porter and Nyree Dawn Porter, was based on both the first trilogy and the second, *A Modern Comedy* (consisting of *The White Monkey*, *The Silver Spoon* and *Swan Song*) which ends with the death of Soames at the end of the 1920s.

The *Chronicles* of 1990–91, however, also included the final trilogy, *The End of the Chapter* (*Maid in Waiting*, *Flowering Wilderness* and *Over the River*) which took the story into the early 1930s: the ninth and final novel was completed only a few months before Galsworthy's death in 1933.

The *Chronicles*, whose starting point was 1886, boasted an impressive cast. DIRK BOGARDE (in his first radio drama since a production of *Doctor at Sea* in 1955, for which he received 15 guineas) was the narrator. Alan Howard played Soames, with Diana Quick as Irene, Sir Michael Hordern as Old Jolyon, Michael Williams as Young Jolyon, Amanda Redman as Fleur Forsyte and MAURICE DENHAM as James Forsyte. Fabia Drake, who played one of the elderly Victorian Forsytes (Aunt Ann) died, aged 86, on the same day that her character was buried in the studio.

The Forsyte Saga
See THE FORSYTE CHRONICLES.

The Foundation Trilogy
Isaac Asimov's powerful and majestic sci-fi saga, about a doomed galactic empire and the efforts of a great mathematician to save it from thousands of years of barbarism through a new movement called the Foundation. It was adapted (mainly by Patrick Tull) as an eight-part serial and broadcast on Radio 4 in 1973.

Foundations of Music
Celebrated evening series of mighty length, running from January 1927 to June 1936.

The Four Seasons

Former Chancellor Denis Healey presented some of his favourite music to illustrate the seasons in this four-part Radio 4 series in 1990. His choices included Beethoven's Spring Sonata, Gershwin's 'Summertime' and Yves Montand's 'Autumn Leaves'.

Fourth Column

Columnists, scribes and assorted literary gadabouts reflected on the week's events, and life in general, in this Radio 4 series hosted by Alan Coren and mounted as a summer holiday relief for LOOSE ENDS in 1990. Simon Hoggart, Christopher Matthew and Sir Clement Freud all contributed to the first show. It returned in 1991, this time chaired by Hoggart.

Fox, Charles (1921–91)

Jazz presenter, mainly on Radio 3. He began broadcasting in 1959, presenting JAZZ TODAY from 1963–88. He was jazz critic of the *New Statesman* from 1965–88 (having begun writing, for *Jazz Music* and other wartime jazz journals, in the 1940s). He presented programmes on Ragtime, Charlie Parker and Jelly Roll Morton and was a biographer of Fats Waller.

Fox FM

ILR station based in Oxford and covering Oxfordshire and West Bucks, launched in 1989. Only the second ILR station (CN.FM being the first) to go out exclusively on FM. It sets out to appeal to different age groups at different times of day: 15- to 24-year-olds from 7 p.m. to midnight, older folk from midnight to 6 a.m., all sorts from 6 a.m. to 6 p.m. Chairman is the bookseller Julian Blackwell.

Fragile Paradise

Six-part series on Radio 4 in 1989–90 with conservationist Andrew Mitchell crossing the Pacific and discussing ecological dangers.

Francis, Sir Richard (1934–)

Managing director of BBC Radio from 1982–86. His vision of a radio equivalent of BAFTA led to the creation of the RADIO ACADEMY.

Frankie's Bandbox

Frankie Howerd starred in this Light Programme comedy show, starting in 1960. BARRY TOOK and his partner Marty Feldman scripted it. Guest artists included MAX JAFFA and Rosemary Squires.

Frankly Speaking

Home Service series from 1952–1966 in which a variety of influential figures ranging from Tom Mboya to Cliff Richard were quizzed by, among others, John Freeman, George Scott and Rumer Godden.

One person who declined the honour of submitting himself to this hot seat was ALISTAIR COOKE. Neil Crichton-Miller, General Talks Producer (Sound), wrote to him in January 1962 inviting him to appear. He described it as 'quite a relaxed conversation programme' and added: 'I am sure that you would enjoy doing it.' Cooke replied from his New York home in April 1962. After apologising for the delay, he wrote: 'I quite frankly do not like doing programs [*sic*] about myself or being the victim, rather than the perpetrator, of an interview. I mean to hold on to my unvictimized status as long as possible. I am sorry about this.'

Freeman, Alan (1927–)

Australian disc-jockey who started as an announcer-presenter with 7LA, a Melbourne station, in 1952 (the first record he ever played on air was *Wheel of Fortune* by Kay Starr). After two years on Radio Luxembourg he settled in London and started on the Light Programme in 1960, presenting HOUSEWIVES' CHOICE and, from 1962, PICK OF THE POPS. It was on this show that he first uttered the line

Some DJs in the 1960s became almost as big as the pop singers they helped to make stars, and got used to being mobbed by teenage fans. Alan Freeman, who sported a Las Vegas-type ring in those days, always smiled and signed the autograph books

which was to become his trademark: 'Greetings, pop pickers!'

He became a daily presenter on Radio 1 in 1972, taking over an afternoon slot from TERRY WOGAN and spotlighting the activities of youth clubs (he used to be vice-president of the London Union of Youth Clubs). He presented the first RADIO 1 ROADSHOW in 1973 and later one of the network's longest series, THE STORY OF POP. Freeman left in 1979 and spent the next decade at Capital Radio, but returned to the BBC in early 1989 to present two shows: *Pick of the Pops*, now rather different from before, and NIGHT ROCKIN'. Nickname: Fluff. Other catchphrases: 'Not 'arf', 'All Right? Right! Stay bright!'

The French Had a Song For It

Popular *chansons* from the 1930s to the 1990s, and their leading exponents including Piaf, Chevalier, Aznavour, Charles Trenet and Jacques Brel, were featured in this six-part Radio 2 series in 1991. The presenter, Philip Bacon (axed as LBC's programme controller the previous year) was well qualified – his parents are French and his mother went to school in Paris with Juliette Greco.

French Service

French-language programmes on the BBC World Service began in September 1938, at the time of the Munich crisis, and resulted from an urgent Foreign Office request to the BBC to broadcast in French, German and Italian a broadcast by Neville Chamberlain which warned Germany of the consequences of invading Czechoslovakia or Poland.

After a frantic search for translators, the BBC complied, and the French version – read out by an announcer called Duncan Grinnell-Milne – launched what became the French Service.

In June 1940, it was used for one of the most celebrated of all wartime broadcasts, General de Gaulle's call to arms against the Nazi occupation, which effectively started the French Resistance movement. Towards the end of the year the service was used to broadcast coded messages to the Resistance: the transmitters used for this (at a transmitting station known as Skelton B) from 1943 to 1945 were still in use for broadcasting World Service programmes to North Africa in March 1990, when they were finally closed down.

Once vital to the waging of war, the French Service is today part of the mechanisms of peace. It is on the air for 1 hour 45 minutes a day in Europe, as part of a trilingual service. See BBC FOR EUROPE.

Potential audiences have increased considerably in recent years, with 75 French FM stations now broadcasting the service's news bulletins on their own airwaves.

There are also three hours a day of French programmes directed at listeners in Africa.

French Singers and Pianists

Eleven-part Radio 3 series in 1989 in which Roger Nichols recalled, with records, the careers of several major performers, starting with the soprano Germaine Lubin.

Friday Lives

Live, weekly show on Radio 4 presented by Joanna Buchan and strong on human interest. It features people from all over the country who have exciting or unusual tales to tell (drifting in the Pacific Ocean for eight days, a father donating a kidney to his teenage son, two women private eyes who specialise in tracking down errant husbands, and so on). It began in 1990.

Friday Night is Music Night

'Radio's Hall of Melody and Song' has been running on the Light Programme since 1953, which makes it one of the BBC's oldest music programmes. It was created as a vehicle for the newly formed BBC CONCERT ORCHESTRA and the brief to conductor SIDNEY TORCH was to create a Friday-night show which would 'help people relax after the week's hard work and put them in the right mood for a happy weekend.'

Torch ran it for several years and fashioned a programme which still, today, features the varied musical menu that he developed – from Stephen Sondheim to Tommy Reilly's harmonica, from film musicals to traditional tunes. He retired in 1972, but his arrangements are still regularly featured.

The show travels all over the country, playing wherever there is a stage large enough. Its regular venues include Southend, Bexhill and the Fairfield Hall, Croydon, where the silver jubilee show was staged in 1978. Programmes have been broadcast in collaboration with Belgium, Holland, Denmark, Ireland, Germany and Norway, with orchestras and artists working in one another's countries. The programme's regular home was once the Camden Theatre but is now the Golders Green Hippodrome.

Friday Play

Weekly classic drama slot on Radio 3 which ran between 1988–90. Plays included John Gielgud's *Hamlet*, first broadcast in 1948. Modern classics were not neglected: in 1989–90, more than a dozen plays were broadcast which – in the opinion of several leading theatre critics, who nominated them – reflected the cream of original British stage plays from the previous fifteen years.

They included Simon Gray's *Melon* (revised as *The Holy Terror*); C.P. Taylor's *Good*; *Jenkin's Ear* by Dusty Hughes; and *Pravda* by Howard Brenton and David Hare. In 1990 classic drama moved to a new slot, THE SUNDAY PLAY.

From Dzikowow to Willesden Green
Actress Rula Lenska's mother, Polish-born Countess Elizabeth Tyskiewicz, recounted her eventful life, which has seen the inside of German concentration camps, in this three-part Radio 4 series in 1990.

From My Post-Bag
Weekly show on the Light Programme with organist SANDY MACPHERSON playing listeners' requests which ran from 1945–64.

From Our Own Correspondent
One of the BBC's very few current affairs programmes to pre-date Suez, this began in 1955 when correspondents were confined mainly to RADIO NEWSREEL on the Light Programme. From the outset FOOC was on the Home Service, a weekly (now twice weekly) forum in which the BBC's reporters could try and convey something of life in distant lands with telling anecdotes and vivid, first-person stories.

There have been over 3,000 editions, which means about 15,000 despatches have so far been broadcast from all corners of the globe. They used to arrive on spools of tape aboard aeroplanes: now, they do so by telephone, cable and satellite.

Much controversy was generated by the BBC's decision to axe the Saturday edition for half the year from October 1989 to make way for EUROPHILE. Several foreign correspondents took the unusual step of protesting publicly, including Tim Llewellyn, who wrote to *The Times* from the Middle East.

FOOC also goes out on the World Service, although the content can be different: since 1990 it has produced its own version of the programme and in 1991 started broadcasting two editions of it each week.

'It is a programme of "postcards from the world". Like real postcards, they come at unexpected times from unlikely places, telling improbable adventures' – John Tusa.

From Pétain to Pompidou
Six-part series on French cabaret songs from the 1930s to the 1980s, presented by Richard Mayne on Radio 3 in 1989. Artists heard included Jacques Brel, Boris Vian and Juliette Greco.

From Plato to Nato
Radio 4 series tracing the history of political thought, presented by BRIAN REDHEAD in 1984.

From Raj to Rajiv
Five-part Radio 4 series in 1987 in which Mark Tully, the BBC's man in Delhi, charted India's progress in the forty years since the British left.

From Sea to Shining Sea
Six-part Radio 4 series in 1988 in which Sally Hardcastle presented a vivid, personal view of the ways in which the USA had changed in the quarter-century since President Kennedy's assassination.

From The Film of The Same Name
Radio 2 series beginning in 1989, written and presented by DICK VOSBURGH, which features famous title tunes from the movies, from *Redskin* in 1928 ('Redskin, redskin, why are you blue?') to gems like *Robinson Crusoe On Mars* and *The Blob*.

From The Weeklies
BBC World Service's view of the British weekly press, now also broadcast on Radio 5.

Front Line Family
One of the BBC's first soap operas, launched as a propaganda exercise for overseas listeners in July 1941. It was produced and scripted by Alan Melville. Since the title was applicable only to war, it was changed after victory in 1945 to THE ROBINSON FAMILY.

FTP Radio
Black music pirate station in Bristol (the initials mean 'For the People') which turned legit and won the INCREMENTAL franchise for the area in 1989. It went on the air the following April.

Funf
Farcical German spy in the wartime ITMA, whose name was his country's word for 'five'. He tended to introduce himself with a guttural *'Zis iss Funf speakink . . .'* Jack Train played him.

Funny That Way
Barry Cryer's profiles of leading practitioners of comedy, past and present, which went out on Radio 4 in 1989–90. Included were Bob Hope, John Cleese, JOYCE GRENFELL, SPIKE MILLIGAN, ALAN BENNETT, Lucille Ball, Marty Feldman, Mel Brooks and Ronnie Barker. Each show combined interviews and clips of the performer's work. Devised and compiled by Michael Pointon.

Fusspot
Bureaucratic figure of fun in ITMA, a civil servant working in the Ministry of Aggravation and Mysteries. Played by Jack Train.

G

Galton, Ray (1930–)
Former TGWU employee who met ALAN SIMPSON at Milford Sanatorium when both were recuperating from tuberculosis. Together, they wrote and performed their own comedy routines over the hospital radio, graduating to professional work with comedian Derek Roy and *Happy Go Lucky*, where they first wrote for a rising comedian called TONY HANCOCK. The genius of their partnership displayed itself best, on radio, during the years of HANCOCK'S HALF-HOUR (1954–59) and, on television, when they created the equally immortal *Steptoe and Son*.

Gambaccini, Paul (1949–)
New York-born (to a father of Italian, and mother of British, ancestry) presenter of prodigious musical knowledge and great critical acumen. Joined Radio 1 in 1973: hosted a variety of shows from ROCKSPEAK and the weekly US charts programme to appreciations of Elton John and the Bee Gees.

In 1986 he left the BBC to be the first presenter of AMERICAN COUNTDOWN, syndicated throughout ILR, and now presents a Saturday show on Capital Radio. Formerly British correspondent for *Rolling Stone* magazine, he is also co-author of *The Guinness Book of British Hit Singles*.

Gardening programmes
Founding father JOHN REITH planted these in the BBC's soil at the beginning of the 1930s. They have been a source of immense comfort for millions, and disseminated information and advice on every conceivable horticultural topic. Gardeners, a gentle and kindly breed, have been among the best loved of all broadcasters. See GARDENERS' QUESTION TIME, THE GARDENING QUIZ, C.H. MIDDLETON, FRED STREETER, FRED YULE.

Gardeners' Question Time
One of the hardy perennials of the Home Service, this began in 1947 under the title *How Does Your Garden Grow?* and, for more than thirty years, featured an unchanging team of three wise men – Fred Loads, Bill Sowerbutts and Alan Gemmell – none of whom missed a single programme in the whole of that period.

It began as the brainwave of Robert Stead, a BBC Radio talks producer based in Manchester. He thought that the nation's new enthusiasm for gardening (a side effect of the Dig for Victory campaign during the war years) could be reflected in a new series which would try to solve the problems ordinary people faced in their back gardens and on the vegetable patch.

Stead chaired the first programme, recorded in a hotel near Manchester in April 1947, which featured two nervous gardeners called Fred Loads from Burnley and Bill Sowerbutts of Ashton-under-Lyne answering questions from members of the Smallshaw and District Garden and Allotments Association. (One man was under the impression that he was taking part in HAVE A GO, and insisted on playing his cornet.)

This programme, called *How Does Your Garden Grow?*, in due course blossomed into *Gardeners' Question Time*. The final seed of its success was sown in 1950 when Professor Alan Gemmell, a precise Scots biologist of what later became Keele University, joined the team. For over thirty years, he and Loads and Sowerbutts never missed a single edition and became one of the best liked and most dedicated teams in broadcasting history. Neither personal tragedies, family crises nor sickness ever prevented any of them from turning up, wherever the recordings were made and however difficult the transport and weather were.

There cannot be a pest, disease, shrub, flower or tool which this trio did not at some time have to rake over as they faced audiences in draughty village halls, horticultural societies and allotment associations the length and breadth of the land. The country atmosphere was captured vividly on one occasion when a cow put its head through an open window and mooed.

After Fred Loads died, aged 78, in 1981 (roses were planted in his memory in Mr Middleton's Garden at the BBC), the team atmosphere had gone for ever. This was the main reason why Gemmell retired from the programme in 1982, soon after the series celebrated

1,500 editions. (He died in 1986.) Sowerbutts then retired in 1983 (and died in 1990).

The programme title was changed to *Gardeners' Question Time* in 1951 and the show was broadcast nationally from 1957 onwards. Previously it was heard in the North only. Its slot of 2 p.m. on Sunday has remained unchanged for over three decades.

There have been only seven chairmen since it began. Robert Stead (who later became Controller of the BBC's North region) presided until 1953. Then came FREDDIE GRISEWOOD (1953–61), FRANKLIN ENGELMANN (1961–72), Michael Barratt (1972–77), Ken Ford (1977-85), Leslie Cottingham and finally the present incumbent, a Welshman with the appropriate name of Clay Jones (his real name is actually David Clay-Jones) from Chepstow in Gwent.

The present team consists of Dr Stefan Buczacki of Stratford-upon-Avon, Fred Downham of Lancaster and Daphne Ledward of Spalding who rotates with Sue Phillips of Chichester. One programme in three is devoted to answering listeners' questions by post and the series is still produced in Manchester, just as it has always been.

'People say "Why have my sweet peas died?" And I say, did they decay upwards or downwards? Ah, they didn't look. What was the state of the roots? No, they hadn't looked at those either.

'And then there are the occasional baffling questions we have to deal with. One man said he had planted an apple tree and a pear tree had come up, and why was that please? He refused to admit that he hadn't planted an apple tree. What on earth can you say?' – Alan Gemmell, ruminating in 1982 on some thorny moments.

The Gardening Quiz
A cutting taken from GARDENERS' QUESTION TIME, this involves Stefan Buczacki putting questions to two teams of green-fingered celebrities, led by Irene Thomas (of ROUND BRITAIN QUIZ fame) and NORMAN PAINTING (Phil in THE ARCHERS). It began on Radio 4 in 1988.

Garrison Theatre
Saturday-night Second World War comedy series which became very popular. It helped to make Jack Warner a big name.

Gary Byrd's Sweet Inspirations
Sixteen-part Radio 1 series in 1984 in which American radio broadcaster Gary Byrd, author of a rap hit record which chronicled black achievement, traced the history and nature of Gospel music.

Gelly, Dave (1938–)
Saxophone-playing former teacher who went into journalism and broadcasting, specialising in jazz. He presented Radio 2's NIGHT OWLS from 1982–90 and the

same network's VOICES. He has also hosted music series for Radio 3 and the BBC World Service. He is a jazz and popular music critic for *The Observer* and has written two books on jazz.

General Overseas Service
The new name the BBC gave to its Empire Service in 1942. It later became part of the 'External Services', which in turn were renamed the BBC World Service in 1988.

The German Renascence
Six-part Radio 4 FM series in 1989, marking the fortieth anniversary of the creation of West Germany, which traced the rebirth and rebuilding of that country's political and economic structures after the Second World War. Germans and members of the Allied forces of occupation both recalled their experiences.

German Service
German language programmes in the BBC World Service started in September 1938, at the time of the Munich crisis. Today, the output runs to three hours a day and the BBC says that audiences throughout Germany, and in Austria, have increased sharply in recent years.

It has identified four factors in this: the dismantling of the Berlin Wall, democratic rebirth of East Germany and subsequent reunification; the first exhibition, in East Germany, of the service's work; the rebroadcasting of the BBC's German programmes on sixty commercial radio stations throughout what used to be West Germany; and the fact that the service now goes out on the cable networks of Hanover and Vienna.

The Germans
David Wheeler reported on contemporary Germany – its power, history and identity – in this six-part Radio 4 series in 1990.

Get By in Arabic
BBC radio series in 1987.

Get By in Chinese
Basic course in everyday Mandarin produced by Kathy Flower (who presented BBC's *Follow Me* television series in China in 1982) and presented by Liu Yuan and Paul Crook, broadcast on Radio 4 in 1988.

Get By in Hindi and Urdu
Radio 4 FM series in 1989 introducing listeners to two national Asian languages which have a common spoken vocabulary but different scripts. Aspects of Indian etiquette and culture were also considered.

Get By in Japanese
Radio 4 FM series in 1989 which conveyed the rudiments of one of the world's most difficult languages (as well

as some of the social niceties of Japanese culture, like checking that your socks don't have holes in them) against a background of increasing Japanese influence in Britain, especially in manufacturing in South Wales and the North-East.

Get By in Russian

Six-part Radio 4 FM service in 1990 in which Edward Ochagavia (from the BBC's Russian Service) and Ludmilla Matthews (of London University) taught basic Russian for tourists and business visitors – at an auspicious time, given *glasnost* and *perestroika*.

Get By in Turkish

Six-part Radio 4 FM series in 1989 in which Bengisu Rona and Tayfun Ertan presented the rudiments of their language for business travellers and tourists, at a time when Turkey had surged ahead as one of the most popular destinations for British holidaymakers.

Get Writing

Eight-part series on Radio 4 FM in 1990 which sought to teach the rudiments of successful writing, with helpful advice from novelists, scriptwriters and editors. It was presented by George Evans, creative writing tutor at Sutton College of Liberal Arts in Surrey.

Gielgud, Val (1900–81)

Creator of British radio drama, of which he was in charge from 1929 to 1963. He showed that sound alone did not inhibit a play's capacity to move or thrill, to inspire fear or open the floodgates of imagination, and he pioneered the techniques necessary for their successful production. Under him SATURDAY NIGHT THEATRE and WORLD THEATRE became dramatic fare for millions.

During the Second World War he showed how broadcasting could play a vital role in maintaining morale. In November 1939 he wrote that drama and features were there to make 'contributions to the preservation of civilised culture in time of war' and programmes designed to 'stir national pride . . . without descending to the jingo level'. During the war he produced one of radio's landmarks, THE MAN BORN TO BE KING.

Not all his decisions turned out to be wise. In 1953 he rejected *Waiting for Godot*, with the result that the first performance in Britain of SAMUEL BECKETT's most famous play was in a London theatre (in 1955), rather than on radio as it could have been.

As a writer, Gielgud was prolific, but is best remembered for the furore over what he called 'a trivial little comedy' – *Party Manners*, which provoked heated debate when the BBC banned a repeat broadcast because of its alleged anti-government bias.

Originally performed on the provincial stage, Gielgud adapted it for the Home Service and then produced it

for BBC Television. It went out in October 1950 but its repeat, scheduled for a few days later, was cancelled on the grounds that it was a malicious attack on the Labour Party. The *Daily Herald* attacked it as such and there were rumours that Herbert Morrison had been so offended he had telephoned the chairman of the BBC, Lord Simon of Wythenshawe, to protest. In his autobiography Gielgud recalled that (even then) he was doorstepped and telephoned incessantly by reporters.

The fuss, however, did not ensure success on the West End stage. Although Lord Montgomery of Alamein came to the first night, it did not live up to its much hyped scandalous reputation and lasted only three months.

He was the elder brother of Sir John Gielgud, whom he occasionally directed (e.g. in a SHERLOCK HOLMES dramatisation in 1954).

Gilbert and Sullivan

The complete canon of Gilbert and Sullivan's Savoy operas, which was five years in the making, was broadcast on Radio 2 in 1989. All twelve programmes featured the BBC CONCERT ORCHESTRA (with Sir Charles Mackerras the usual conductor). The displacement of BENNY GREEN and ALAN DELL for three months provoked not only hundreds of protests from listeners but also pickets outside the BBC.

Giles Cooper Awards

In honour of the dramatist GILES COOPER, these are given each year to what are judged to be the best original BBC radio plays. They have helped to launch many young writers, and given encouragement to several not so young. Winners have included RHYS ADRIAN, HAROLD PINTER, TOM STOPPARD and PETER TINNISWOOD. Non-BBC plays and those on the World Service are ineligible (a rule which ensures that the winning plays always come from either Radio 3 or Radio 4). Nominations are made by the slot editors. Judges normally include a representative of Methuen (who publish the winning plays each year), a representative of BBC Radio's Drama Department, a writer and a critic. Prizes consist of a certificate and Methuen's book. There is no prize money, but the winning plays are always aired again, which means extra royalties.

The victors include most of the leading lights of radio drama in recent years. In strictly alphabetical order, they have been:

For the year 1978:
Richard Harris (*Is It Something I Said?*), Don Haworth (*Episode on a Thursday Evening*), Jill Hyem (*Remember Me*), Tom Mallin (*Halt! Who Goes There?*), Jennifer Phillips (*Daughters of Men*) and Fay Weldon (*Polaris*).

1979:
Shirley Gee (*Typhoid Mary*), CAREY HARRISON (*I Never Killed My German*), Barrie Keeffe (*Heaven Scent*),

John Kirkmorris (*Coxcomb*), John Peacock (*Attard in Retirement*) and Olwen Wymark (*The Child*).

1980:
Stewart Parker (*The Kamikaze Groundstaff Reunion Dinner*), Martyn Read (*Waving to a Train*), Peter Redgrove (*Martyr of the Hives*) and William Trevor (*Beyond the Pale*).

1981:
PETER BARNES (*The Jumping Minuses of Byzantium*), Don Haworth (*Talk of Love and War*), Harold Pinter (*Family Voices*), David Pownall (*Beef*), J.P. Rooney (*The Dead Image*) and Paul Thain (*The Biggest Sandcastle in the World*).

1982:
Rhys Adrian (*Watching the Plays Together*), JOHN ARDEN (*The Old Man Sleeps Alone*), Harry Barton (*Hoopoe Day*), Donald Chapman (*Invisible Writing*), Tom Stoppard (*The Dog It Was That Died*) and William Trevor (*Autumn Sunshine*).

1983:
Wally K. Daly (*Time Slip*), Shirley Gee (*Never in my Lifetime*), Gerry Jones (*The Angels They Grow Lonely*), Steve May (*No Exceptions*) and Martyn Read (*Scouting for Boys*).

1984:
Stephen Dunstone (*Who is Sylvia?*), Robert Ferguson (*Transfigured Night*), Don Haworth (*Daybreak*), Caryl Phillips (*The Wasted Years*), Christopher Russell (*Swimmer*) and Rose Tremain (*Temporary Shelter*).

1985:
Rhys Adrian (*Outpatient*), Barry Collins (*King Canute*), Martin Crimp (*Three Attempted Acts*), David Pownall (*Ploughboy Monday*), James Saunders (*Menocchio*) and Michael Wall (*Hiroshima: The Movie*).

1986:
Robert Ferguson (*Dreams, Secrets, Beautiful Lies*), Christina Reid (*The Last of a Dyin' Race*), Andrew Rissik (*A Man Alone: Anthony*), Ken Whitmore (*The Gingerbread House*), Valerie Windsor (*Myths and Legacies*).

1987:
Wally K. Daly (*Mary's*), Frank Dunne (*Dreams of Dublin Bay*), Anna Fox (*Nobby's Day*), Nigel D. Moffat (*Lifetime*), Richard Nelson (*Languages Spoken Here*) and Peter Tinniswood (*The Village Fete*).

1988:
Ken Blakeson (*Excess Baggage*), Terence Frisby (*Just Remember Two Things: It's Not Fair and Don't Be Late*), ANTHONY MINGHELLA (*Cigarettes and Chocolate*), Rona Munro (*The Dirt Under the Carpet*) and Dave Sheasby (*Apple Blossom Afternoon*).

1989:
Elizabeth Baines (*The Baby Buggy*), Jennifer Johnston (*O Ananias, Azarias and Misael*), David Zane Mairowitz (*The Stalin Sonata*), Richard Nelson (*Eating Words*) and Craig Warner (*By Where the Old Shed Used To Be*).

Gillard, David (1947–)
Writer who was radio correspondent on RADIO TIMES from 1982 to 1991, contributing most of its articles on the subject. He has also been opera critic on the *Daily Mail* since 1971.

Gillard, Frank (1908–)
Former Managing Director of BBC Radio (1969–70) with a long and distinguished career as an active broadcaster. As a war correspondent he broke the news to the world of the link-up between the US and Soviet armies inn April 1945 at the River Elbe: 'the forces of liberation have joined hands'. Later he was responsible, as Head of West Regional Programmes, for conceiving ANY QUESTIONS? in 1948. Devotees of CHILDREN'S HOUR, however, have never forgiven him for killing it off when he was Director of Sound Broadcasting in 1964.

Has continued to broadcast to a ripe age. He presented a two-part profile of the BBC's founding father, *Reith Remembered*, in 1989 and a pithy portrait of CHARLES HILL in 1990, both on Radio 4.

Girls Will Be Girls
Comedy series on Radio 4 beginning in 1989 featuring sharp songs and sketches from The Bobo Girls. They consist of Sioned Williams (a former BBC Radio light entertainment producer, who left to become a producer of the Jonathan Ross show on Channel 4) and Rebecca Front (an actress who also writes the duo's songs).

Glendenning, Raymond (1907–74)
Chartered accountant who joined the BBC as an organiser on CHILDREN'S HOUR in Cardiff in 1932. Left the staff in 1945 to become a full-time sports commentator and until 1963 was BBC Radio's main commentator on football, boxing, racing and tennis. He also commentated on greyhounds, and showjumping in the 1948 Olympics. Noted as one of the fastest speaking broadcasters of all time, once clocking up over 300 words in a minute.

Global Concerns
First regular environmental series on the BBC World Service, now also going out on Radio 5.

Globe Theatre
Drama season mounted jointly by Radio 4 and the World Service since 1986, with plays going out on both to ensure worldwide audiences of millions. In 1989 the plays included *Redevelopment* by VACLAV HAVEL,

Welsh-born Raymond Glendenning was the BBC's main sports commentator for almost twenty years. His 1953 autobiography was called *Just a Word In Your Ear*. He was famous for delivering the words at breakneck speed

who, that same year, became the first president of Czechoslovakia after the ending of communist rule. Here, dramatists from whom plays have been commissioned have included Frederic Raphael, JOHN MORTIMER and ANTHONY MINGHELLA.

GLR

Acronym for Greater London Radio, BBC's talk-and-music local radio station for the capital. Formerly BBC Radio London, and relaunched as GLR in October 1988. Along with GMR and BBC Radio WM, it was then given three years to prove itself or face abolition.

Among new presenters hired were JANICE LONG and TIM SMITH. 'GLR was set up to cater for the many radio listeners in London who were fed up with "pop and prattle",' wrote managing editor Matthew Bannister at its first birthday. 'Our music policy is to play only the best, not slavishly follow the charts.' On the speech side, there are programmes aimed at four of the capital's ethnic communities: Asian, Afro-Caribbean, Jewish and Irish.

In 1989, with ILEA, the station set up a special training course at Vauxhall College, London SW8, for people between 16 and 21 to learn radio skills. (This was followed, in 1991, by the creation in White City of the West London Radio Training Centre, in association with local and central government.)

Worthy as all this was, it did not win many new listeners. The station's relative lack of popularity provoked harsh attacks from its critics, who included David Mellor, the then broadcasting minister. 'I have my eye on GLR although rarely my ear,' he said in May 1990. 'I don't find GLR an attractive listener prospect. The BBC must think hard whether it is occupying frequencies without making much use of them.' The BBC said his remarks were 'bordering on the outrageous'. Later that year the BBC announced that the station had been performing sufficiently well for it to be reprieved, and the threat to its future was formally lifted.

The Glums

See TAKE IT FROM HERE.

GMR

BBC local radio station covering the Manchester area, relaunched in 1988 from the ashes of the old BBC Radio Manchester. It tried to be brighter and snappier than its predecessor and, initially, played more music.

For many years it has broadcast what it thinks is British radio's first regular show for Chinese listeners, *Eastern Horizon*, every Tuesday evening. Aimed at the city's large community of Hong Kong descent, the hour-long programme is half in English and half in Cantonese.

Diana Goodman, now BBC correspondent in Bonn, was once a journalist on the station and breakfast host Peter Wheeler has gone on to become a television presenter.

Go, Man, Go
'The show with the most' gave a snappy rhythm to weekday lunchtimes on the Light Programme from 1958–64. Introduced by David Ede, it featured a group called The Hound Dogs, along with 'the "groovin' " guitar of Don Sanford and your "pop" requests'.

God and Caesar
MIKE WOOLDRIDGE interviewed the President of South Africa, F.W. de Klerk, the former Taoiseach of Ireland Dr Garret Fitzgerald, Sir Garfield Todd of Rhodesia, former Indian Prime Minister V.P. Singh and former New Zealand Prime Minister and Methodist lay preacher David Lange in this Radio 4 series of 1991 which explored the relationship between Church and State, religious principle and political ideology.

God's Revolution
Radio 4 serial in 1988 about the Levellers and Independents in Cromwell's New Model Army in 1647–49. Written by Don Taylor. Bernard Hepton played Cromwell.

Going Places
Early evening Radio 4 show on Fridays which covers travel and transport, from the glamour of the Paris Air Show to delays on the cross-Channel ferries, from weekend prospects on the roads to tests on exotic new cars. It goes out in a DRIVE-TIME slot so you tend to find yourself listening to it in traffic jams, not inappropriate for a travel programme.

Began in 1978, with Barry Norman the first presenter. Presented by CLIVE JACOBS from 1984 to 1990. PETER HOBDAY replaced him, briefly, when the BBC decided that the programme needed to change gear, placing a greater emphasis on business travel and more consumer involvement in road tests. BERNARD FALK then took over. After his untimely death, Jonathan Marcus, BBC Radio's transport correspondent, became the new presenter in November 1990.

Going Underground
Subterranean existences (including a family living twelve feet below the surface of the Gloucestershire countryside, a couple with a temple for pagan worship in Margate, a man with a home-made bunker, and the London Silver

Vaults) were explored by Mark Burman in this four-part Radio 4 series in 1990.

A Golden Treasury of Music and Song
Home Service series at noon on Saturdays from 1956–65.

The Golden Years
Friday night series on Radio 2 hosted by ALAN KEITH which began in 1984.

The Good Book
Twelve-part Radio 4 series about the world's most widely read (and most misquoted) book, The Bible, which BRIAN REDHEAD presented in 1986. It was later repeated on the World Service.

A Good Day Out
Bearded ladies, fortune tellers, peepshows and boxing booths: all the fun of the fair was evoked in one of four sound pictures which made up this vivid, nostalgic, Radio 4 series in 1990 on popular diversions of the 1920s and 1930s. The others were a day at the races, an outing to London and a trip to the seaside (sausage sizzlers on the beach, looking for Lobby Ludd) at Cromer.

The Good Establishment Guide
Patrick Hannan and CHRIS STUART used words and music to celebrate Parliament, the Law, the Church and Royalty in this four-part Radio 4 series in 1988.

Good Morning Sunday
Sunday morning records-and-chat show on Radio 2 closely associated with ROGER ROYLE, who presented it from 1985 to 1990. His predecessors in the slot were Paul McDowall and Nick Page.

Royle, who once presented the programme from Lapland, gained a devoted following (and improved audiences) with a warm and kindly style which avoided preachiness and radiated the sort of practical Christianity which comforts the lonely and infirm. He often said that the nicest letter he had ever received was from a listener who told him that at 7.30 on a Sunday morning the whole of Britain became one parish.

He made a feature of interviews with fellow Christians in which they talked, always optimistically and with a light touch, about the role faith played in their lives. His guests ranged from Cardinal Hume to the King of Tonga, entertainer Shirley Bassey to television cook Rustie Lee. On his final programme he was joined by Thora Hird and the Bishop of Stepney, Jim Thompson. He left to become a school chaplain in Hampshire.

Don Maclean was appointed his successor. Maclean, a Roman Catholic whose previous radio series included *Maclean Up Britain* and *Keep It Maclean*, continued a tradition of Christian comedians embodied by Roy Castle and Sir Harry Secombe. His first guest as the new regular host was Cliff Richard, to mark the singer's fiftieth birthday.

Also in 1990 the programme conducted a poll among listeners to discover their favourite hymns, and several hundred responded. The results were:

1. Dear Lord and Father of Mankind
2. How Great Thou Art
3. The Old Rugged Cross
4. The Day Thou Givest
5. When I Survey
6. Love Divine
7. What a Friend We Have in Jesus
8. O Love That Wilt Not Let Me Go
9. Great Is Thy Faithfulness
10. Abide With Me

A Good Read

Thirty-minute discussion about paperback books with a chairman and two guests, broadcast on Radio 4 during the summer when BOOKSHELF is on holiday. The chairmen have been John Hale (1979, when it began), Theresa McGonagle (1980–84), Brian Gear (1985–88) and Edward Blishen (1989 onwards).

Each invited guest – who may be doctors, scientists or politicians, as well as literary alumni – chooses two paperbacks which he or she believes worthy of the programme's title (and which have to be in print). The guests read each other's choice of books, and the chairman reads all four: the programme consists of a conversation about the four books which (hopefully) all three people have now read.

At the end of each series, the programme produces a booklist of suggested 'good reads', and sends out thousands of copies to interested listeners.

Goodier, Mark (1961–)

Disc-jockey on Radio 1, where he presents both an evening show to highlight up-and-coming acts and the weekend flagship programme TOP 40.

He started with Radio Forth at the age of eighteen (having first applied at the age of thirteen) and later worked on other ILR stations in Scotland, where he championed bands such as Wet Wet Wet and Deacon Blue long before they had record deals, by playing their demo tapes. After a spell at Metro he joined Radio 1 in 1987.

The Goon Show

Forever part of British folklore, and one of the most celebrated and influential of all radio comedies: a mix of surreal clowning, licensed anarchy and brilliant punning wordplay fashioned by its dominant creative genius, SPIKE MILLIGAN. The regular characters convey some of the flavour of the humour: ECCLES, BLUE-BOTTLE, MAJOR DENIS BLOODNOK, THE HON. HERCULES GRYTPYPE-THYNNE, NED SEAGOON, HENRY CRUN, MORIARTY, as do the titles of some of the shows: The Dreaded Batter Pudding Hurler, The Affair of the Lone Banana, The House of Teeth, Ned's Atomic Dustbin.

The word 'goon' betrayed the wartime influence on Milligan and Secombe particularly, who had first met in the North African desert: it was a word often used by prisoners of war to describe their guards, although Milligan, who invented the title, said he got it from the *Popeye* cartoons.

Began in May 1951 under the title CRAZY PEOPLE, with Milligan, Peter Sellers, Harry Secombe and Michael Bentine. It changed its name to *The Goon Show* in June 1952. Bentine left five months later. The last of more than 200 episodes, entitled *The Last Smoking Seagoon*, went out in January 1960. Transmission was on the Home Service, often with repeats on the Light a few days later. The weekly shows were normally recorded either at the Paris or the Camden Theatres in London, and WALLACE GREENSLADE was the regular announcer.

The Goons' antics often worried the senior levels of the BBC, who made several attempts to suppress it. In 1954 Peter Sellers's impersonations of Churchill were banned, as were scenes depicting the House of Commons asleep.

In 1972, Milligan, Sellers and Secombe were reunited on stage at the Camden Theatre after twelve years for what was to be the very last Goon Show, for the BBC's golden jubilee. Prince Philip, Princess Anne, Princess Margaret and Lord Snowdon were in the audience but not the Goons' devoted fan Prince Charles, who was aboard his guided missile destroyer HMS *Norfolk* in the Mediterranean. He sent a telegram saying his hair had turned green with envy.

The Goons' architect was Milligan, who invented nearly all the characters and wrote the vast bulk of it, although both Eric Sykes and Larry Stephens penned a number of episodes. The gruelling responsibility of producing brilliant comic inventiveness week after week brought about the first of Milligan's several mental breakdowns.

'It cost blood to put that show on for me. Sheer agony. It wrecked my first marriage and it wrecked my health. My nervous breakdown happened while I was on the show and I've been a neurotic ever since. I gave my sanity to that show' – Spike Milligan, 1972.

'Spike had all the sweat of writing it, but for Peter and me it was just a giggle' – Harry Secombe, 1972.

'No matter how much "fashion" in humour changes, there will always be thousands of people whose minds are attuned to the kind of mental slapstick and imaginary cartoonery that typifies Goonery . . . .It has always been one of my profound regrets that I was not born ten years earlier than 1948, since I would then have had the pure, unbounded joy of listening avidly to the Goons each week' – The Prince of Wales, 1973.

Peter Sellers, Harry Secombe, Spike Milligan and Michael Bentine found it easy to live up to the name of their programme – *Crazy People* – flanked by an all-seeing, all-hearing microphone. Things got even crazier when the programme's successor, *The Goon Show*, began in 1952

'The chemistry of Bentine, Sellers and Secombe was like a cannon, loaded and primed. All you had to do was light the fuse' – Spike Milligan, 1991.

Gorham and Swift
Radio 2 comedy series featuring Carol Gorham and Amanda Swift which started in 1989.

Gosling, Ray (c. 1940–)
One of the most distinctive and idiosyncratic of all broadcasters, with an oblique and discursive manner, a curiously sing-song voice of elusive origin, and the inquisitive approach of a loner who marvels at our follies and foibles.

Born in Northampton, he went to Leicester University but dropped out after only a year. Thereafter he became, in his own words, a 'teenage rebel' and helped to run rock bands and youth clubs in Nottingham – where he still lives. Started in broadcasting as a researcher for producer CHARLES PARKER, on subjects ranging from polo to lorry drivers, and made his debut at the microphone on a Midlands radio opt-out programme called *Shire Talk*. Went on to give several fifteen-minute talks on Radio 3 about various British towns, including Rochdale, Cheltenham and Dundee.

His biggest Radio 4 series was an investigation into *Who Owns Britain?* Others have included THE HEAVY SIDE OF TOWN; *On the Train to New Zealand*, a journey across India by rail; and *Next Door's Doorstep*, four talks about Welshness today. He once presented the ARCHIVE FEATURE and, outside the BBC, made a Sony-winning series on Liverpool for Radio City.

The most enjoyable of his series has been A TASTE OF . . . , in which each programme deals with the beauty and complexities of a particular language, which have included Arabic, Swahili and Russian. Gosling talks to various British-based teachers and bilingual experts on their various delights. The programmes do not venture abroad, but are vivid enough for one not to miss it.

Gospel Jubilee
Radio 2 gospel music show in the late 1980s which actor-singer Lon Satton, star of *Bubbling Brown Sugar* and *Starlight Express*, hosted for two series. It was closely associated with the BBC GOSPEL CHOIR OF THE YEAR competition. After it finished, singer Gloria Gaynor continued the gospel tradition on the network with her own series.

Grand Hotel
Light music series with a Palm Court orchestra running from the 1920s to 1970s, initially inspired by the presence next door to the BBC of the Savoy Hotel, with which it had the closest of musical associations.

Grand Tour
Radio 4 series in 1990 which took listeners into a foreign city through the experience of one individual, with the aim of conveying the feel of each place through a mix of words, specially made recordings, music and archive material. J.G. Ballard talked of Shanghai, Nadine Gordimer of Johannesburg, Sir Stephen Spender recalled Berlin in the 1930s and Anthony Burgess described Rome, where he used to live.

Gray, Ezeke   (1943–)
Singer of Caribbean extraction who joined Radio 1 in 1990 to present a weekly reggae programme called *The Sunshine Show*. A former Jamaican chart star, he uses the stage name The Man Ezeke. He has also worked for BBC Radio Bedfordshire since 1985 and is a community arts officer for Luton Borough Council.

The Great Bug Hunt
Four-part Radio 4 series in 1990 presented by Martin Wainwright recording his trip with an expedition of entomologists to the Indonesian island of Sulawesi.

Greek Service
Greek language programmes on the BBC World Service began in September 1939. Today, they go out for 2½ hours a day and have recently gained an extra audience through being rebroadcast on several FM stations in the country and by Greek National Radio.

A Green and Pleasant Land
Four-part Radio 4 series in 1989 in which Christopher Nicholson traced the ways in which poets and novelists have responded to the variety of English landscape, and how it has inspired their work.

Green, Benny   (1927–)
Jazz saxophonist and prolific writer and broadcaster who has been heard regularly on both Radio 2 and Radio 4 since 1965 (and sometimes on other stations, such as Jazz FM).

His output includes talks, criticism, series and discussions. He broadcasts mainly on jazz, lyricists and popular music of the 1930s and 1940s, but also on other passions including cricket and P.G. Wodehouse. He made many appearances on STOP THE WEEK; has presented a Sunday-afternoon Radio 2 show on the songwriter's art since 1978; and chaired JAZZ SCORE since 1979.

Vivid proof of his Sunday programme's popularity arrived in the shape of pickets outside BROADCAST-ING HOUSE in 1989. They gathered after the BBC announced that he and ALAN DELL were being 'rested' for several months so their slots could be taken over by the exhaustive GILBERT AND SULLIVAN series. This displacement, revealed the BBC's Annual Report, provoked 400 complaints from their supporters – one of the bigger radio protests of recent years.

Green, Michael   (1941–)
Controller of Radio 4 since 1986. Has made a welcome injection of entertainment at night, improved the Monday-morning ARCHIVE FEATURE, and introduced some fine new programmes, but his decisions to move WOMAN'S HOUR and axe MARGARET HOWARD have attracted much heartfelt protest.

Greenslade, Wallace   (–1961)
Joined the BBC staff in 1945 as a general announcer, which was his job on THE GOON SHOW. Worked on several other shows.

Greenwich Time Signal
Usually referred to as 'The Pips', and first broadcast on BBC Radio on 5 February 1924. Supplied by the Royal Greenwich Observatory every day since, both in wartime and in peace, until 1990 (first from Greenwich, but after the mid-1950s from the observatory's new home in Herstmonceux Castle, Sussex). When the observatory moved again, to Cambridge, it decided to cease production of its world famous time signal, and its last ones went out at 1 p.m. on 5 February 1990 – 66 years to the day since they were first heard under an agreement between JOHN REITH and the Astronomer Royal.

Listeners, however, have never heard any difference: the pips have continued to go out at the same time, and sound exactly the same as before, because the BBC now generates the time signal itself with equipment which it bought for £250,000 from the electronics company Seltech International based in Bourne End, Bucks. This includes three pairs of Canadian computer clocks and a rubidium oscillator made in the USA.

Smiling Through: First Pip.
'Of course it's only natural that the dear boy
should like to stand near the radio when
the Time Signal comes on.'

The word 'pip' had been used since the First World War to mean a star on an officer's epaulette, but in the BBC Yearbook of 1929 it gained another meaning too: each of the six pulses of the Greenwich Time Signal

Installed in the lower ground floor of BROADCAST-ING HOUSE, this is what now generates the pips which go out every day on the BBC and World Service, just as before. The pips are broadcast on all five of BBC Radio's national networks and go out 227 times a week (compared with only seventeen times a week for BIG BEN). Some ILR stations also generate their own pips as a time signal.

In technical terms, the time signal is a one kilohertz tone, broken into six pulses. The first five last 100 milliseconds each, while the sixth is of 500 milliseconds, and it is the start of this sixth and final 'peeep' which is the exact time point.

'Greetings, pop pickers!'
One of the most familiar of modern radio catchphrases, used by ALAN FREEMAN to introduce PICK OF THE POPS since 1962.

Gregg, Hubert (1916–)
Actor and songwriter (whose biggest hit was 'Maybe It's Because I'm a Londoner') with a weekly Radio 2 show THANKS FOR THE MEMORY. Running since 1972, it plays the popular music of the 1920s, '30s and '40s from stage (where Gregg himself first appeared professionally in 1933), theatre and cinema. Gregg was also, briefly, an announcer on the Empire Service in 1936.

Grenfell, Joyce (1910–79)
Witty broadcaster and comedienne, plus a pianist, poet, artist, devoted Christian Scientist and niece of Nancy Astor, with a long and varied life in radio.

She was the first radio critic for *The Observer* (landing the job after she happened to sit next to the then editor, J.L. Garvin, at a dinner party) from 1937 to the outbreak of the war. Then, she first worked in the canteen of the National Gallery, serving sandwiches and fruit cake while Myra Hess gave her piano recitals, and later entertained troops abroad.

She created the HOW TO. . . series with STEPHEN POTTER, which ran from 1943–62, and appeared in the panel game WE BEG TO DIFFER. She was a member of the Pilkington Committee on Broadcasting in 1960.

'Genteel herself, she made gentility the target of her wit, and in so doing immortalised certain aspects of the English character' – Richard Baker.

Stephen Potter and Joyce Grenfell, as captured by the great *Picture Post* photographer Bert Hardy in September 1946. They were recording *How To Cope With Christmas*, one of the comic *How To . . .* series which opened the Third Programme during that year

'It is rarely that wit is wholly devoid of cruelty. But it was with Joyce Grenfell' – Leader in the *News of the World*.

Grisewood, Freddie (1888–1972)

Worcestershire rector's son, educated at Radley and Oxford, whose impeccable BBC voice and kindly manner were central to the success of ANY QUESTIONS?, which he chaired from the first programme in 1948 until his retirement twenty years later.

He was held in enormous affection: stepping down in the February of 1968 after heart trouble, he made a final appearance on his eightieth birthday two months later when the programme took place in his home village of Liphook, Hampshire.

On the panel were Lady Asquith, C.A. Joyce, the Bishop of Crediton and JOHN ARLOTT, who suggested there should be a Grisewood Award for the best mannered broadcaster of the year. A poetic tribute written and recorded by TONY BENN, often a panellist on the programme, was played to the team and the audience.

Freddie, the cousin of HARMAN GRISEWOOD, worked on several other radio shows after training as a singer and joining the BBC as an announcer at SAVOY HILL in 1929. He played an Oxfordshire rustic, Our Bill, in CHILDREN'S HOUR, narrated the popular SCRAPBOOK series and during the Second World War presented recipes in KITCHEN FRONT.

In his 1952 autobiography *The World Goes By* he recalled his greatest blunder at the microphone having been when he should have read 'His Holiness Pope Pious' and it came out as 'His Holiness the Pipe'.

'He was one of a handful of men whose voice amounted to a comforting unseen presence, a strong defender of values that his hearers believed in as certainly as he did' – Peter Black, *Daily Mail*.

Grisewood, Harman (1906–)

BBC actor and announcer in the 1930s and the man who switched off the inebriated THE FLEET'S LIT UP broadcast from the Spithead Review in 1935. He rose to become Controller of the Third Programme (1948–52). Afterwards he was Director of the Spoken Word (1952 to 1955, when the post was abolished) and Chief Assistant to the Director-General, from 1955–64. He is the cousin of the late FREDDIE GRISEWOOD.

In his 1968 autobiography *One Thing at a Time* he alleged that during the Suez crisis the then Prime Minister, Sir Anthony Eden, instructed the Lord Chancellor, Lord Kilmuir, to prepare an instrument to take over the BBC and subject it to the will of the government.

Growing Pains

Poignant, authentic Radio 4 sitcom which began in 1989, written by ex-professional footballer Steve Wetton and based on his own fostering experiences, about a married couple called Tom and Pat Hollingsworth (played by Ray Brooks and Sharon Duce) who become foster parents of a boy called Jason, much to the horror of their own three children.

'The laughs come mainly from the characters, but there is a very serious subject underneath' – Ray Brooks.

The Grumbleweeds

Three Yorkshiremen (Robin Colvill, Maurice Lee and Graham Walker) who became a professional act specialising in impressions, comedy and music in 1967 and later gained a much bigger audience with a major breakthrough on Radio 2. Their series *The Grumbleweeds* (originally called *The Grumbleweeds' Radio Show*) ran from 1979 to 1988 and was followed by another series, *Someone and The Grumbleweeds*, in 1989.

Grundy, Eddie (1951–)

The cunning yokel of THE ARCHERS is the only character in the world's longest running serial to have had his own fan club (founded by a schoolteacher in 1981), and also to have released a record – the Country and Western song 'Poor Pig'.

Grundy, Stuart (1938–)

Radio 1 executive who oversees its involvement in concerts such as those for Nelson Mandela and from Knebworth, as well as its evening and weekend programmes. Joined the network for its launch in 1967, and has been there ever since. Before 1967 he was a DJ with Radio Luxembourg, after several years with the RAF and BFBS in the Mediterranean and North Africa.

He presented *Rock On* in the early 1970s and still makes occasional forays back to the microphone, e.g. to present a series on Motown in 1989.

Gruntfuttock, J. Peasemold

Eccentric and endearing old fool played by KENNETH WILLIAMS on ROUND THE HORNE.

Grytpype-Thynne, The Hon. Hercules

Character on THE GOON SHOW played by Peter Sellers. 'Son of Lord "Sticky" Thynne and Miss Vera Colin, a waitress at Paddington Station. Recreations: homosexuality.'

Gudgin, Tim (1929–)

Longserving presenter and announcer on Radio 2, who started on the Light Programme in 1954. Like many of his broadcasting generation, he entered radio via National Service – in his case the Army, followed by a spell with BFBS in Hamburg, Cologne and Trieste. He has been a freelance since 1965: other work includes television commercials for Square-Deal Surf, voiceovers for Spam and McDougall's Flour and PR consultant to the Isle of Man Government from 1973–76.

Guilty Party

Panel game on the Home Service from 1954 to 1957. A celebrity trio listened to a short crime play peppered with clues before interrogating the suspects (i.e. the actors playing the characters) to uncover the villain. Only the guilty party was allowed to lie: all the others had to tell the truth.

The three sleuths were JOHN ARLOTT (who used to be a detective sergeant), Robert Fabian of Scotland Yard and F.R. Buckley, who apparently had connections with MI5. It was later adapted for BBC-TV.

Gulf Link

See BBC TOPICAL TAPES.

Gummidge, Worzel

Heroic scarecrow created on CHILDREN'S HOUR in 1935 in a commissioned play by Barbara Euphan Todd. Hugh Wright was the first actor to play him. Worzel, who lived in Ten Acre Field, appeared on the programme until the 1950s, later transferring to television when Jon Pertwee (former star of THE NAVY LARK) played him.

Gunsmoke

That rare creature – an imported radio serial. This one was made by the American network CBS and went out on Wednesday evenings on the Light Programme around 1960. William Conrad (later the fat detective Cannon on television) starred as Matt Dillon, US Marshal. It was edited at the BBC by CHARLES CHILTON.

Guthrie, Sir Tyrone (1900–71)

Influential pioneer of radio drama in the 1920s who later enjoyed a long and fruitful association with the Old Vic from the 1930s to the 1950s. *The Flowers are Not For You to Pick* was among the plays he wrote. In 1952 he was invited to create the first Shakespeare Festival at Stratford, Ontario, which evolved into a major Canadian cultural event.

Guthrie eloquently explained the unique power of radio drama when he wrote, in 1930: 'The impressions of the microphone play are more intimate than those of the stage because neither the writing nor the playing needs to be pitched high enough to carry to the back of pit and gallery . . . they are more subtle because, received by each listener privately at home, they are not coarsened by being flung into an auditorium where individuals are fused together into one mass . . . incapable of the minute pulsations of feeling, the delicate graduations of thought, which each member of the crowd experiences when alone.'

Guyler, Deryck (1914–)

Fine comedy actor with a deep, instantly recognisable voice capable of a variety of tremors and subtleties. For eleven years he was one of THE MEN FROM THE MINISTRY, opposite RICHARD MURDOCH, and has distinguished himself on many other classic shows. He estimates he has made more than 1,000 radio appearances. A Liverpudlian, he made his wireless debut in *Round the Northern Repertories* (1937). At the beginning of the Second World War he became an instructor in the RAF police, but was invalided out with eye trouble after two years. His war years he spent in the BBC DRAMA REPERTORY COMPANY, with whom he made some 800 programmes.

In the cast of ITMA as Frisby Dyke, Percy Palaver and Sir Short Supply, 1946–49; appeared in HOW TO LISTEN, which launched the Third Programme on its opening day; partnered ERIC BARKER in JUST FANCY, when they played their two old men; was the lunar presence, The Voice, in JOURNEY INTO SPACE; and played Jesus Christ in a postwar production of THE MAN BORN TO BE KING. He played another title role in the Light Programme's enjoyable weekly whodunnit INSPECTOR SCOTT INVESTIGATES.

GWR

ILR station covering Wiltshire and Avon – stretching from Hungerford to Weston-super-Mare, and from Amesbury to Wantage. Based in Bristol, it began in 1981. Split its services in 1988. GWR FM, on its FM frequencies, beams contemporary pop for under-35s: Brunel Classic Gold, on the AM frequencies, offers golden oldies for over-35s.

The initials GWR were chosen to unite a region in which they once stood for Great Western Railway, whose locomotives used to be built at Swindon. Brunel is named after the great engineer Isambard Kingdom Brunel (1806–59), who became that railway's engineer in 1833 and also built the famous Clifton suspension bridge in Bristol.

H

A Hack in the Borders

Vivid, eventful, engrossing and dramatic Radio 4 series in 1990 in which journalist Dylan Winter gave his account of a 300-mile journey with his packhorse Molly from Prestatyn to Chepstow down the English–Welsh border – the route of Offa's Dyke. Over five weeks he encountered aggressive dogs, surly farmers, juggernauts and sheep-shearing and suffered blisters and dislocated bones, and kept his tape-recorder running for (almost) all of the time, with wonderful results.

Haldane, John Burdon Sanderson (1892–1964)

Versatile and acerbic scholar of a generation ago who did much to popularise scientific inquiry through lively and opinionated radio talks.

He was an Old Etonian polymath of a type now virtually extinct, gaining Firsts at Cambridge in both mathematics and classics and capable of holding forth with equal vigour on genetics and Thucydides. A biochemist whose prime scientific achievements lay in the mathematical exploration of evolution, he was also politically active – a communist in the 1930s, chairman of the editorial board of the *Daily Worker* in the 1940s – and famous for subjecting himself to experiments. He sat for fourteen hours in a small steel chamber to estimate the conditions as they were aboard the submarine *Thetis* when it was lost in 1939. He emigrated to India and became an Indian citizen in 1960. His sister is the writer Naomi Mitchison and VAL ARNOLD-FORSTER is his niece.

'Are you related to Professor J.B.S. Haldane?' an American visitor once asked him. 'That depends on whether identity is a relationship', answered the irascible Haldane.

Hall, Henry (1898–1989)

One of the major musical figures from the golden age of wireless. He created what is often described as British broadcasting's first chat show, which ran for over twenty years; conducted the BBC DANCE ORCHESTRA from 1932 to 1937; and made a recording of 'The Teddy Bears' Picnic' which sold a million and is still available today.

A working class boy from Peckham, he was playing the cornet in a local Salvation Army band in 1914, and developed into a talented pianist and conductor. In 1932, the year the BBC moved into BROADCASTING HOUSE, JOHN REITH invited him to take over from Jack Payne as director of the BBC Dance Orchestra, where he stayed for five years.

His 'chat show', *Henry Hall's Guest Night*, grew out of the night on Boat Race day in 1934 when Hall and the orchestra were in the studios for their regular evening show, with music hall stars Lupino Lane, ELSIE AND DORIS WATERS and ANONA WINN. Hall suggested they come along for the next edition too, and an unscripted programme gradually evolved combining music and showbiz chatter which was immensely popular. His regular greeting, 'Hello everyone, this is Henry Hall speaking', became something of a national catchphrase.

One of the shows that saw Britain through the dark days of war, and bearing a famous signature tune in 'Here's to the Next Time', it attracted stars of the calibre of Noel Coward, Danny Kaye, Gracie Fields, Bob Hope and Laurel and Hardy and ran for 972 editions until the late 1950s.

Hallam

ILR station covering the areas of Sheffield, Rotherham, Barnsley and Doncaster, on the air since 1974. In 1989, like most ILR stations, it split its output into two by launching a new golden oldie service, Classic Gold, on AM with Hallam FM remaining on FM.

Hamilton, David (1939–)

Disc-jockey whose nickname 'Diddy David' apparently derives not from his lack of physical stature, but from a former job as straight man to KEN DODD.

A scriptwriter on ATV, he was one of the last batch of Britons called up for National Service. Conscripted into the RAF and posted to Cologne where the British Forces Network was based, he came to decide that life as a teenage jock, hosting a Sunday afternoon pop show called *Hey There!*, was preferable to working as a Morse operator, even though it paid nothing.

Worked as a DJ on Radio 1 before moving to Radio 2. Quit in 1986, after thirteen years of having a daily radio programme, saying its music policy had become 'geriatric'. 'There's only so much Vera Lynn and Max Bygraves you can play,' he said. Went off to play 'grown up rock and roll' on Radio 210 in Reading. Now has a weekday and a Sunday show on Capital Gold: the latter is also carried by twenty other ILR stations.

Hams

These have had an historic connection with broadcast radio, not merely through the famous TONY HANCOCK programme. There are about 1.5 million hams throughout the world (including King Hussein of Jordan) of whom many are in Britain. The Radio Society of Great Britain, a Potters Bar-based organisation in existence since 1913, and the DTI, are keen to encourage their growth, as a natural training ground for tomorrow's electronic engineers.

'Had it not been for amateurs, wireless telegraphy as a great worldwide fact might not have existed at all. A great deal of the development and progress of wireless telegraphy is due to the efforts of amateurs' – Guglielmo Marconi, 1920.

Hancock, Tony (1924–68)

Comedy performer whose talent, truthfulness and extraordinary *alter ego* of belligerent, insecure, self-deluding Anthony Aloysius St John Hancock in HANCOCK'S HALF-HOUR – often described as the greatest radio comedy series of all – has assured him a position high on broadcasting's Mount Olympus. His battery of personal problems, however, which eventually drove him to suicide, often made life difficult for lesser mortals.

Son of a semi-professional music hall artist, he left school (Bradfield) at fifteen and soon became a stand-up comedian, learning much of his craft on stage at the Windmill Theatre. Made his wireless debut in 1941 in a light entertainment show called *A La Carte*; came to prominence in EDUCATING ARCHIE, in which he played the dummy's tutor from 1951–53. At the same time he appeared in *Happy Go Lucky*, where he first used gags and one-liners supplied by RAY GALTON and ALAN SIMPSON. The show's producer at this time, Dennis Main Wilson, later became the first producer of *Hancock's Half-Hour*. Galton and Simpson continued to write material for Hancock when he co-starred with CHARLIE CHESTER in *Calling All Forces*, which evolved into *Forces All Star Bill*, *All Star Bill* and finally *Star Bill*. The nucleus thus developed of performer Hancock, producer Wilson and writers

A fetching grin from Anthony John Hancock, better known as Tony Hancock, better known still as his radio incarnation Anthony Aloysius St John Hancock. Usually his smiles contained more self-doubt

Galton and Simpson, the team which created *Hancock's Half-Hour*.

He starred in a radio production of *The Man Who Could Work Miracles* by H.G. Wells (1956) and was a castaway on DESERT ISLAND DISCS (1957), but stage, screen and television claimed him after he found success on radio.

His death in Sydney, Australia, was the basis of a fine Radio 3 play by HEATHCOTE WILLIAMS in 1988.

Hancock's Half-Hour

The most enduring vehicle for Britain's greatest comedian, TONY HANCOCK, went out on BBC Radio from November 1954 to December 1959. It transferred to BBC Television in 1956 and thereafter ran concurrently.

It was set at one of the best known of all fictional addresses, 23 Railway Cuttings in East Cheam, and, as written by RAY GALTON and ALAN SIMPSON, recounted the escapades of those who lived there. Hancock played a bombastic version of himself in the form of Anthony Aloysius St John Hancock; Johannesburg-born Sid James was his rogue of a landlord; Wagga Wagga-born Bill Kerr played the good-hearted Australian; and the two other performers in the first series were KENNETH WILLIAMS as Snide and another South African, Moira Lister (who had worked with Hancock in a radio show called *Star Bill*) as the girlfriend.

After the first series she returned to South Africa and was replaced by Andree Melly as Hancock's new (French) girlfriend although her character was dropped after the third series. Hattie Jacques, as secretary Griselda 'Grizzly' Pugh, provided a more substantial and sentimental female presence in the fourth and fifth series – a total of 36 shows.

Other actors appeared in the series from time to time. In the final radio show, for example, called *The Impersonator*, Peter Goodwright provides the Hancock-like voice heard in the commercial for 'Harper's Cornflakes' which appears while Sid and Bill are watching television.

The snatch of tuba music at the beginning, as the star himself stutteringly intoned the title 'H-H-Hancock's Half-Hour', was composed by Wally Stott. That, and his other few bars of music which were heard over scene changes, were initially played by Harry Rabinowitz and his Orchestra.

Much has been written about Hancock's pathos and timing and the skill with which he made his pompous, lugubrious and self-important radio character into one of universal sympathy. In the annals of radio comedy, few shows are more venerated and few comedians more revered, but for those who worked with him it was often a much less happy experience.

Williams, for example, paints a picture in his autobiography of an insecure, vain and foolish performer whose nitpicking over the scripts and endless anguish over the human condition created a tense and disagreeable working atmosphere, compounded by Hancock's antagonism towards him personally when the audience began to like him. He recalled Hancock's bitter opposition to Williams's increasingly popular 'Oooh, stop messing about' catchphrase (created on the show), which Hancock dismissed as 'cardboard comedy not based on truth'.

Handley, Tommy   (1896–1949)

Much loved radio comedian, famous most of all for ITMA, who started on the stage in 1917, made his radio debut in 1924 (in a revue called *Radio Radiance*) and found it worked wonders for a flagging career.

Mischievous, but never malicious. Tommy Handley provided years of comic relief on *It's That Man Again*, the one show which everyone who lived through the Second World War can remember

His clear, direct delivery was ideal for early wireless and often he wove topical subjects into his traditional jokes – such as the new type of broadcast called the WEATHER FORECAST. Example: 'A great depression has settled over the South. My mother-in-law has arrived from the North.'

ITMA was his great achievement, and when he died (of a brain haemorrhage, the same ailment which killed another funny man, GERARD HOFFNUNG) he was greatly missed. The Director-General, Sir William Haley, broadcast a tribute to the nation; 10,000 mourners flocked to the crematorium for the funeral; and St Paul's held a memorial service.

Hanson, John   (1922–)

One of the most familiar voices on FRIDAY NIGHT IS MUSIC NIGHT, this Canadian-born (but British-reared) singer turned professional in 1947 and has been appearing on radio since 1949. He has made romantic operettas his particular forte and also sung in SONGS FROM THE SHOWS and RAY'S A LAUGH.

Happidrome

Popular comedy show of the Second World War with Robbie Vincent (Enoch), Harry Korris (Mr Lovejoy) and Cecil Frederick (Ramsbottom).

Harding, Gilbert   (1907–60)

One of the great broadcasting stars of the 1950s, cantankerous, self-opinionated, extraordinarily rude, emotional and deeply insecure.

A teacher and would-be barrister, his skill in languages led to BBC MONITORING hiring him shortly before the outbreak of the Second World War. He became the travelling questionmaster in charge of the provincial teams on ROUND BRITAIN QUIZ and after a stint chairing THE BRAINS TRUST got his big chance when he joined the battle-of-the-sexes talk show WE BEG TO DIFFER.

Had an enormous appetite for work, chairing several shows on radio, including TWENTY QUESTIONS and PURELY FOR PLEASURE, as well as becoming one of the first big television celebrities.

He was sacked from *Twenty Questions* for being drunk and disorderly on the air, calling it an 'idiotic

Gilbert Harding. His body language in this study by Baron is a clear indication of his irascible, confrontational nature

game', insulting panellist Joy Adamson (calling her 'Joy by name, but not by nature'), carrying on with a round even though Jack Train identified the object – a peony – at the seventh question, and finishing three minutes early.

The scheduled repeat of this shambles of an episode was cancelled on the orders of the Director-General, Sir William Haley, and Harding was fired from the programme, to be succeeded by the much more genial KENNETH HORNE.

In September 1960, Harding became one of the most famous subjects in John Freeman's harshly revealing interview series on BBC-TV, *Face to Face*. Harding started crying when asked about his mother, who had died. Freeman unwittingly had stumbled into one of the areas of Harding's life which caused him deep pain, his homosexuality (not believed to have had much physical expression, since his enormous consumption of alcohol probably made him impotent).

Two months later Harding was dead. He died in the doorway of a BBC building opposite Broadcasting House shortly after recording an edition of *Round Britain Quiz*, which, as a mark of respect from the BBC, was not broadcast.

'Beneath the crisp crust, it's all marshmallow' – Joyce Grenfell.

'His success defeated him, even though it never killed his hopes' – *The Times*.

'I never knew an unhappier man' – Stephen Grenfell, editor of the 1961 book *Gilbert Harding – By His Friends*.

Harper, Gerald   (1929–)

Debonair actor turned disc-jockey who sends out roses and champagne to lucky listeners in Radio 2's weekly dose of syrupy romance.

He was one of the bigger names on Capital Radio when it began in 1973 and his three-hour Sunday show, *A Sunday Affair with Gerald Harper*, ran without a break for ten years. The roses and champagne were sent to listeners celebrating special anniversaries and birthdays and doing good deeds. Bottles were even sent to The Queen and Mrs Mary Whitehouse (and accepted with thanks).

Harper quit this weekly 'piece of gaiety', as he calls it, so that he could have free Sundays for the first time in a decade. In 1988, however, when Radio 2 offered him a similar Sunday spot, he accepted and has been there ever since. Now, however, although still in the middle of the day, it lasts only 90 minutes and not three hours: but he still manages to send out an average of two to three bottles of champagne per programme.

'Mine is not a serious show. It's here to help people pass an idle hour and to let people relax and have a little fun. Champagne signifies that to me. Some people ask me why I don't give away something worthy but champagne is useless, it's ridiculous, it's fun and has a certain style and I quite like a certain style' – Gerald Harper, interviewed by the BBC, 1991.

Harris, Bob   (1947–)
'Whispering' Bob, so called for his virtually inaudible delivery on BBC2's *Old Grey Whistle Test* throughout most of the 1970s, first joined Radio 1 as a stand-in for JOHN PEEL in 1970, without any broadcasting hexperience. (He was originally a journalist and co-founded *Time Out*.) He rapidly became presenter of SOUNDS OF THE SEVENTIES, a job he held for the next five years. He returned in 1989, after a fourteen year absence during which he worked at LBC and Radio 210, to stand in for RICHARD SKINNER in a midnight slot.

'Whispering' later succeeded the late ROGER SCOTT as presenter of the late-night Sunday rock and pop show, playing The Eagles, James Taylor and suchlike mellow sounds, and later moved to midnight in the midweek.

Harrison, Carey   (–)
Writer of several radio plays, the first of which, *I Never Killed My German* (Radio 3, 1979) won a GILES COOPER AWARD. His three-part epic *The Sea Voyage* was broadcast in 1989 on Radio 3, sixteen years after being commissioned. A teacher in California, he is the son of the late Sir Rex Harrison.

Harrison, Ted   (1948–)
BBC Radio's religious affairs correspondent from 1988–89. He relinquished the job to go freelance, its pressures having proved a particular burden for someone on dialysis twice a week. (After five years on a machine, he subsequently underwent a kidney transplant, and his book *Living with Kidney Failure* was published in 1990.)

Since leaving the BBC he has been heard as a reporter on Radio 4's THE WORLD TONIGHT and also worked with pen and ink: his caricatures of, for example, bishops at synods have appeared in several publications including *The Church Times*.

Hartill, Rosemary   (1949–)
Widely admired religious affairs correspondent of BBC Radio from 1982, when she succeeded GERALD PRIESTLAND, to 1988, when she turned freelance. A member of the Church of England, she still broadcasts regularly, usually on religious topics, in series such as IMMORTAL DIAMONDS and WRITERS REVEALED.

Harty, Russell   (1934–88)
Began in radio in 1967 as a junior producer of arts programmes on Radios 3 and 4, including THE CRITICS

and *The World of Books*, leaving after two years for the lucrative glamour of television. But he returned years later and made a number of *Russell Harty's Musical Encounters*, in which he and a guest played pieces of music to surprise and delight the other. Presenting START THE WEEK (from 1987, until illness forced him off the air the following year) was his last job. He also helped to set up the ILR station Red Rose Radio, in his native Lancashire.

Hatch, David   (1939–)
One of the stars of a comedy classic, I'M SORRY I'LL READ THAT AGAIN, who has spent almost his entire working life in BROADCASTING HOUSE and managed to climb to the very top of its slippery pole.

Son of a vicar, and godson of a bishop, he shone in the Cambridge Footlights alongside John Cleese (see CAMBRIDGE CIRCUS) and then joined the BBC in 1964, primarily as a producer, at the same time as Cleese did as a writer. Became Controller of Radio 2 in 1980, Controller of Radio 4 in 1983 and Managing Director of BBC Network Radio in 1987.

Hausa Service
Hausa-language programmes on the BBC World Service go out for one and a quarter hours a day. See AFRICAN SERVICE.

Have A Go
Travelling quiz series which was one of the most popular shows ever broadcast on either radio or television. At its peak in the 1950s, when it was produced by STEPHEN WILLIAMS, it was said to attract an audience of twenty million.

People warmed to it as a celebration of ordinary folk, who were encouraged to tell heart-warming stories and share the experiences of their early lives and families. The presenter for such a venture could not have been better: the good-humoured WILFRED PICKLES, whose devoted wife Mabel also appeared on the show, giving rise to the programme's introduction . . .'with Mabel at the table'.

The show was live, but mishaps were few. One such was when a 94-year-old whose son had won the Victoria Cross used the word 'buggers', as in 'we've got the buggers on the run'.

The programme began in 1946 and after 21 years had travelled 400,000 miles. It had visited every part of Britain, including several offshore islands, and the Forces in Germany. It never went anywhere twice, having enough invitations to last for 1,500 years. But the BBC felt the show had simply run out of steam when they finished it in 1967.

'I soon realised that the quiz was less important than the stories that the people had to tell us about their lives, their hopes, fears and despairs. . . What *Have a Go* has taught me throughout these twenty years is the common decency of ordinary people, and as we say in Yorkshire, "There's nowt wrong with reet folk"' – Wilfred Pickles, 1966.

Havel, Vaclav (1935–)

The Czech playwright and former dissident, who became his country's first democratically elected president in 1990, has enjoyed a long association with British radio. Six of his plays were broadcast between 1966 and 1987 on Radio 3 and Radio 4, starting with *The Memorandum*, and the World Service produced two. During this period he spent four years in prison in his own country for sedition.

It was a measure of the bewildering speed at which change tore through Eastern Europe that when *Redevelopment*, his allegory about architects redesigning an ancient castle town, was premiered in the GLOBE THEATRE season in October 1989 (starring Martin Jarvis, Penelope Wilton and John Moffat) its author was still under constant threat from the Czech security forces. By the time it was repeated on Radio 4 the following April he was leader of his country.

Havel has one other connection with radio: according to the BBC, he has named his word processor 'Harold' in honour of HAROLD PINTER, the writer and human rights campaigner whom he much admires.

Hay, Jocelyn (1927–)

Former freelance broadcaster and writer, also head of public relations for the Girl Guides Association from 1973–78, who has done as much as anyone to raise the profile of radio in Britain and campaign for continued high standards.

She was instrumental in founding the pressure group VOICE OF THE LISTENER and some years before that, when active with the Society of Authors, conceived of and organised the annual trophies which have subsequently grown into the coveted SONY RADIO AWARDS. (See IMPERIAL TOBACCO AWARDS FOR RADIO.)

She started broadcasting, mainly talks, with BFBS when her husband was an officer in the Royal Army Ordnance Corps. When she returned to Britain in the 1950s she contributed many items on crafts and cookery to programmes such as WOMAN'S HOUR, HOME THIS AFTERNOON and THE EYE-WITNESS. Her 'Way with Red Cabbage' recipe has been preserved for posterity in the second *Woman's Hour* anthology, published in 1969.

Hay, Roy (–)

Distinguished BBC gardening broadcaster following C.H. MIDDLETON.

Hayes, Brian (1937–)

Pugnacious, trenchant, often controversial (and often downright rude) presenter who became one of London's best-known radio stars through hosting LBC's morning phone-in show from 1976 to 1990.

He was axed by the station's new director of programmes, fellow Australian Charlie Cox, to make way for Michael Parkinson. Not even a petition from the staff could save him. But he soon found work on Jazz FM and on his old rival GLR – hosting a late night phone-in. These shows, also taken by the BBC's nine other local radio stations in South and East England, have been Hayes's first regular broadcasts for the BBC, but he also sometimes appears on Radio 4 and has stood in for JIMMY YOUNG.

Before LBC, he was on Capital Radio for three years. Born in Perth, he worked in radio in Western Australia from 1956–71.

Hayes, Patricia (1909–)

Considerable character actress of stage, screen and radio, where she has played many boys (notably HENRY BONES, one half of the boy detectives in CHILDREN'S HOUR) but also starred as the sexy lady in RAY'S A LAUGH.

The Health Show

Live, ten-part Radio 4 FM series, presented by ANGELA RIPPON, which gave listeners the chance to ring in and get advice from experts and also hear how celebrities coped with their medical problems. Teeth, sleep, allergies, addiction, mid-life crises and 'unmentionables' (bad breath, piles, thrush, smelly feet) were some of the subjects in a series which tried to demystify medicine. It moved to Radio 5 in 1990.

Heard Not Seen

Radio 4 series in 1989 about children: Nick Baker talked to children about jokes (rude, sick, funny) and laughter.

Hearing Voices, Seeing Things

An allotment, a seaside caravan site and a roadside cafe were among the everyday places visited by Martyn Wiley and Ian McMillan (co-authors of THE BLACKBURN FILES) in a six-part Radio 4 series in 1990 about the ability of ordinary things to evoke extraordinary memories.

Heather Mixture

Miscellany of Scottish music with JIMMY SHAND and his Band in weekly Light Programme series.

Heaven Upon Earth

The rich ceremonies and music of Holy Week, as celebrated in the Greek Orthodox Church, were illustrated in this seven-part Radio 3 series of recordings of the liturgy's most important moments. It went out in 1989.

The Heavy Side of Town

RAY GOSLING explored the factory districts of several British towns – including Ebbw Vale and Barnard Castle – in this Radio 4 series in 1990, and reflected on the industrial traditions of a land where, despite the much trumpeted growth of Filofax culture and the service sector, a sixth of the workforce still has jobs in manufacturing.

Hello Cheeky

Comedy series which began in 1973, with Tim Brooke-Taylor, John Junkin and Barry Cryer.

Hello Playmates

(1) Catchphrase of ARTHUR ASKEY. (2) BBC comedy series starring Askey which ran for seven years, written by the partnership of Bob Monkhouse and Denis Goodwin. Irene Handl played Mrs Purvis, who had an unmarriageable daughter called Nola (Pat Coombs).

Henry, John (–)

A lugubrious 'Hallo, Everybody' was the catchphrase of this early radio comedian from the 1920s, whose voice was as you would imagine Eeyore's to be. From 1923 he performed monologues often imbued with traditional music-hall humour: 'Wireless is a very wonderful thing. Anything that'll make a woman listen must be wonderful, mustn't it?' Later, his wife Blossom joined him for comic dialogues.

Henry, Stuart (1941–)

Former drama student from Scotland who was a DJ on Radio 1 from 1967–75 until he was axed from his Saturday morning programme. Went to Radio Luxembourg the same year, and broadcast there until multiple sclerosis deprived him of the use of his limbs, so he could no longer play records. At first his wife Ollie came into the studio to put them on the turntable for him, but eventually he became too ill to carry on.

Henry is still on the Luxembourg payroll, however: he compiles a detailed and well-presented monthly bulletin crammed with anniversaries of musicians' births and deaths, and other events in the music world, at his home in the Grand Duchy. He and his wife post this journal, *RTL Database*, to all Luxembourg DJs and producers to help them assemble their programmes, so that they can see what happened in years past on any day of the month.

Henry Wood Promenade Concerts

The world's biggest, and for many the most enjoyable, festival of classical music has been run by the BBC since 1927: every summer is made more enjoyable by the fact that every concert is broadcast on radio. Today they are always on Radio 3, although the less demanding ones, such as the Last Night, used to go out not on the Third but the Light.

The Proms were created in 1895 under the conductor Sir Henry Wood (1869–1944). When his partner Robert Newman died suddenly in 1926, it looked as if the annual concerts might die with him, but REITH arranged for their continuation at the QUEEN'S HALL from 1927 onwards. This transformed the event from an essentially local festival into a national one, and also (in Sir Malcolm Sargent's time) turned the Last Night into one of the most famous of British cultural events.

Today the Proms embrace over sixty concerts in an eight-week season, performed typically by more than twenty orchestras, fifteen choirs and 160 conductors and soloists from two dozen different countries.

Modern pieces, often specially commissioned, are as much a part of the mix as old favourites. Non-classical, non-Western music has occasionally intruded, and SIMON BATES introduced a jazz Prom (Loose Tubes, at the Albert Hall) in 1987. The first Indian classical musician to appear at the Proms was Imrat Khan, the sitar and surbahar player, in 1971. Later, there were two complete evenings of Indian music (in 1981 and 1983) and in 1989 Khan, this time with his four sons, returned for an extensive recital.

A source of periodic controversy is the inclusion, on the flagwaving Last Night, of the patriotic songs 'Land of Hope and Glory' and 'Rule, Brittania'. When Sir Colin Davis succeeded Sir Malcolm Sargent in 1968 he dropped them, with the support of William Glock, the BBC's Controller of Music. But the promenaders disapproved and the songs were reinstated. In 1990 Mark Elder was dismissed as conductor on the Last Night after saying in an interview that the BBC should drop the songs if the Gulf crisis worsened, because their use could be 'callous'. He was replaced by Andrew Davis, chief conductor of the BBC Symphony Orchestra.

Hereward Radio

ILR station based in Peterborough, covering an area within a 45-mile radius of the city – North Cambs, South Lincs, North-West Norfolk, North-East Northants and Rutland. On the air since 1980. Named after the Saxon leader Hereward the Wake, who led a revolt against William the Conqueror in 1170.

Heroes

Radio 2 series starting in 1990 in which performers talk about the musicians and singers who have most influenced them. Joe Brown was the first. (Not to be confused with MY HEROES.)

Hertz, Heinrich (1857–94)

German physicist who is immortalised each day – look at the listings of any newspaper. Radio frequencies are all named after him, whether kiloHertz (kHz) or megaHertz (MHz). He is regarded as the first scientist to have detected, and then demonstrated, radio waves. This seminal work was achieved in 1887–88.

Hewat, Jonathan (1939–)

Lecturer at Bristol Polytechnic who, after a business career and then travelling round the world, began work in BBC Radio Bristol at the age of forty and gradually accumulated dozens of tapes of blunders and out-takes. He eventually sold the idea of a series to BBC Radio's light entertainment department, and CAN I TAKE THAT AGAIN? was born. He has produced several cassettes of these on-air fluffs and clangers in a series called *Bloopers*. Most of the proceeds have gone to a wireless for the blind charity.

Hey Rrradio!

Radio 1's first comedy series, in 1987. It spawned THE MARY WHITEHOUSE EXPERIENCE.

Hi, Gang!

Morale-boosting Second World War light entertainment show with Vic Oliver (the first castaway on DESERT ISLAND DISCS), BEBE DANIELS and BEN LYON whose successor was LIFE WITH THE LYONS. Special guests included Ronald Reagan.

Hi-Fi Theatre

Radio 4 slot which began in 1978 with a new production of UNDER MILK WOOD, to mark the 25th anniversary of its author Dylan Thomas's death.

Hibberd, Stuart (1893–1983)

Former soldier (serving at Gallipoli, and later in Mesopotamia and Waziristan) who became one of the most august announcers in BBC history. Joined the BBC in 1924 and became its Chief Announcer in 1927. Read the news on over 15,000 occasions, the gravest being the death of King George V in 1936. It was Hibberd who told a mourning nation in his sepulchral, velvety tones: 'The King's life is drawing peacefully to its close.' He repeated the message every fifteen minutes throughout an evening on which, as a mark of respect, the BBC cancelled all its programmes. Nine years later he announced another death which precipitated as much joy as the earlier one had caused sadness – that of Hitler.

During the General Strike of 1926 Hibberd remained at the microphone for long periods, sometimes more than an hour, reading official news and announcements. His exceptionally beautiful voice and soft manner were much

appreciated, as was the way in which he parted company from the listeners at closedown each evening. 'Goodnight everybody' – then, after a pause – 'Goodnight'. And, according to ROY PLOMLEY, he was one of the last men in London to wear spats.

He retired from the BBC in 1951, but continued for some time as presenter of SILVER LINING on the Home Service.

Hibbert Lecture

A lecture funded by a Unitarian trust and broadcast by Radio 4 which takes place usually, but not always, once a year. It began in the mid-1980s. The trust and the BBC's religious broadcasting department jointly decide who gives it.

High Flyers

Four-part Radio 4 series in 1990 in which David Walker met a quartet of public sector executives all tipped for the top. The first was Marianne Neville-Rolfe, chief executive of the Civil Service College and once described as 'the unstuffiest woman in Whitehall'. Others were Michael Bichard, Julia Cumberlege and Prof. George Bain.

A Highway to Heaven

This eight-part series on Radio 3 in 1989 was the first radio history of black gospel music: it was written and presented by Francis Wilford-Smith, a major collector of blues and gospel records and a student of the music.

Hill, Charles (1904–89)

'How are you today? How's your tongue? Is it smooth and red, or knobbly and beige with an overcoat of a muddy hue? And how's the stomach? Is it firm and steady, or somewhat warm, or a little wobbly and a trifle windy? Or was your Christmas Day so spartan that today you're fighting fit with no twinge of remorse? Well, a word on indigestion . . . '

Homely talks like these – this one was in 1943 – delivered in his fruity, rotund, man-of-the-people voice, have ensured Hill's place in broadcasting history as the RADIO DOCTOR. Although he later held Cabinet office for four years and became an influential public figure, it is as the Radio Doctor that he is most fondly remembered.

His talks, which started in May 1942 and finished in 1950, attracted some fourteen million regular listeners. Broadcast every Friday morning, just after the 8 a.m. news, the emphasis was on good health expressed in plain words. Constipation was a regular topic: Hill's favourite remedy was 'those little black-coated workers' known as prunes.

The simplicity of tone and robustness of delivery concealed great learning. Hill, born into a poor family in Islington and whose father died when he was a baby, was a qualified doctor, with a First in medical sciences from Cambridge, and was later secretary of the British Medical Association.

His association with radio continued in other forms after his career as Britain's GP of the airwaves. He became a Tory MP and Eden appointed him Postmaster-General, which put him in charge of broadcasting. Bravely, he backed the BBC's independence during the Suez crisis of 1956. Macmillan dropped him in his 'Night of the Long Knives' purge and Hill became Chairman of the Independent Television Authority (1963–67). Wilson, controversially, switched him to be Chairman of the Governors of the BBC (1967–72).

'He was a marvellous Radio Doctor, because he could get on the same wavelength as the ordinary listener' – Sir Ian Trethowan.

'Bluff, patronising, ponderous and with impregnable self-satisfaction woven into every syllable, the Hill voice combined the worst sort of pipe-smoking, beer-quaffing "common sense" with all the timeless arrogance of the medical profession' – Nigel Andrew, *The Listener*.

Hindi Service
Programmes in the Hindi language began on the BBC's Overseas Services in May 1940, as a daily ten-minute news summary. Today they are on the air for two hours a day, with news, features and current affairs for a regular audience, in India, estimated at 25 million. The service attracts 40,000 letters a year.

Hindsight
Six events from the recent past were exhumed, in this incisive Radio 4 series in 1990, by pundits who pondered their significance with various experts. Melvyn Bragg considered the influence of Rock Against Racism in the late-1970s; Robert Kee the Aberfan disaster and influx of Ugandan Asians; Charles Wheeler the killer fog of 1952; and Polly Toynbee the 1957 Wolfenden Report, which paved the way for homosexual law reform, and the Back Britain Campaign of the late 1960s.

Hippodrome
The Golders Green Hippodrome in London NW11 has been and still is used for recording many light entertainment shows, e.g. those with DAVID JACOBS and the BBC RADIO ORCHESTRA. After the BBC's Phillips Report in 1990, on cost-cutting, the BBC said it would have to decide if it made economic sense to go on using it, and the answer seems to be that it does.

A History of Piano Blues
Radio 3 series in 1988 made by Francis Wilford-Smith, who also presented A HIGHWAY TO HEAVEN.

Hit The North
Weekly youth magazine from Manchester, broadcast on Radio 5 since the network began, which promised when it started to be 'young but not naive'.

The Hitch-Hiker's Guide to the Galaxy
Melancholy, strangely affecting comedy drama with a strong cult following, written by DOUGLAS ADAMS and starring PETER JONES. SIMON BRETT produced the first episode and GEOFFREY PERKINS the rest.

Hoax
Radio 4 panel game in 1990, with a second series to be broadcast in 1991, in which three celebrities told stories, two of which were true and the third invented. (For example, Ian Wallace told of bungling in a Glasgow hotel; Maureen Lipman revealed the secret life of a man in a Manchester cafe;; and John Wells relived a bizarre experience with the army in Korea.) The fun lies in trying to sort out the fact from the fiction. It was devised by IAN MESSITER as an updated version of his earlier show FALSE EVIDENCE.

Hobbs, Carleton (–1978)
Actor who, for many, was the definitive SHERLOCK HOLMES, a role he first played on CHILDREN'S HOUR in 1952. In his honour BBC Radio gives an

The much revered actor Carleton Hobbs who, for many listeners of the 1950s and 1960s, will never be equalled in his portrayal of Sherlock Holmes. In his honour BBC Radio presents an annual award to two young drama students

annual prize, the Carleton Hobbs Award, to two promising drama students. 'Hobbo', as he was to those who knew and worked with him, was also highly regarded as a narrator and as a reader of poetry.

Hobday, Peter (1937–)

Rotund presenter of Radio 4's TODAY programme since 1982, known for his acumen in business journalism and for making disparaging remarks about his weight. He helped to launch THE FINANCIAL WORLD TONIGHT. In 1990 he briefly replaced CLIVE JACOBS in the driving seat of GOING PLACES.

Hodson, Phillip (1946–)

Pioneer of sex therapy on the air, when he launched and presented a phone-in and counselling programme on LBC in 1975. Sixteen years on, he still presents a regular lunchtime counselling programme on the station. Has also presented similar advice spots on TV-am and ITV.

Hoffnung, Gerard (1925–59)

Berlin-born artist, illustrator, tuba-player, writer, broadcaster, Quaker and clown whose early death from a cerebral haemorrhage was regarded as having robbed the comedy world of great talent.

He both looked and sounded at least twice as old as he was, partly because of premature baldness and partly through an extraordinary voice reminiscent of crusted port; so he started acting the role of a much older man from an early age.

His gifts as an eccentric and raconteur were spotted by producer IAN MESSITER, who persuaded him to appear as a panellist on ONE MINUTE PLEASE. This led to a regular spot on *Saturday Night on the Light*, in which he was 'interviewed' by fellow humorist Charles Richards in unscripted, sometimes surreal exchanges.

Hoffnung's most celebrated party piece was his brilliantly timed story about a labourer and the accident he had experienced on a building site while lowering a load of bricks to the bottom of a building with a pulley. Having apparently found the original news item in a trade paper for builders, he used it to warm up the studio audience before recordings of *One Minute Please*. It was eventually polished into the famous Bricklayer Story which most people know from his use of it at the Oxford Union in 1958. It was recorded by the BBC and is included on a cassette of Hoffnung's output released by the BBC RADIO COLLECTION.

Holding the Ring

An account of what frontline soldiers have felt, in and out of uniform, on the streets of Northern Ireland. Broadcast on Radio 4 in 1989 to mark the twentieth anniversary of troops being sent in, it was compiled by CHARLES ALLEN, who interviewed more than forty servicemen

and women, none of whom was identified beyond rank and regiment. It was the last part of Allen's series THE SAVAGE WARS OF PEACE.

Holiday Hour

'A winter programme looking back to last summer and forward to next', this relaxing fare was heard on Sundays on the Light Programme from the late 1950s. It offered 'memories of sunlit days' as well as suggestions for the coming season, and was chaired by FRANKLIN ENGELMANN.

Holiday Music Hall

Cyril Fletcher was the compere on this Home Service variety show, broadcast in the days when the Home Service was a much more varied mixture than Radio 4 is today.

Hollywood's Oscar Nights

Ten-part Radio 2 series with Chris Kelly recalling some of the most celebrated of Academy Awards ceremonies.

Holmes, Sherlock

The world's most enduring detective has enjoyed several fine radio manifestations. CARLETON HOBBS is often regarded as having been definitive, in dramatisations starting on CHILDREN'S HOUR in 1952 with NORMAN SHELLEY as Dr Watson.

This event generated a lengthy leader in *The Times*, which in October that year welcomed the news that five of the stories were being broadcast and pronounced that parents would also be likely to find them enjoyable, albeit for different reasons.

It went on: 'All earnest students will naturally be anxious to know which are the five stories chosen, and two of them, *The Red-Headed League* and *Five Orange Pips*, must surely be universally approved. Each has its affectionately treasured moment. In the first is that, pregnant with clues, in which Holmes says that he looked not at a man's face but at the knees of his trousers; in the second is one so horrific that it is a good thing that the Children's Hour is not too near bedtime. "Have you never", said Sherlock Holmes, bending forward and sinking his voice, "have you never heard of the Klu Klux Klan?" *The Naval Treaty* and *The Blue Carbuncle*, if not in the highest class, cannot fairly be criticized, but *The Three Students* seems a rather singular choice. Possibly it is chosen to enforce on the young the moral that you ought not to cheat in examinations . . . '

John Gielgud and Ralph Richardson took the roles in *Dr Watson Meets Sherlock Holmes* in 1954 (directed by the star's elder brother VAL GIELGUD) and *The Final Problem* in 1955, with Orson Welles as the evil genius Moriarty. The dramatisations were by John Keir Cross with music composed by SIDNEY TORCH.

Later, the sleuth was played on Radio 4 by Tim Pigott-Smith (in *The Valley of Fear*) and Roger Rees (in *The Hound of the Baskervilles*, 1988). In the latter, Watson was portrayed by Crawford Logan, who plays Dr Matthew Thorogood in THE ARCHERS.

In 1989 the present Radio 4 partnership of Clive Merrison and Michael Williams made its debut, starting with the first two Holmes stories *A Study in Scarlet* and *The Sign of The Four*. They then appeared in all twelve of *The Adventures of Sherlock Holmes* (1990–91, and later released on the BBC RADIO COLLECTION) and the BBC hopes they will eventually recreate all 56 short stories and four novels.

It is believed that this will be the first time that the entire Sherlock Holmes canon will have been played by the same two actors, although Michael Hardwick adapted 45 of the 56 for the Light Programme dramatisations of the 1950s and 1960s featuring Hobbs and Shelley.

William Chubb took the role in Radio 4's 1990 play *The Adventure of the Pimlico Poisoner* by Peter Mackie, with Crawford Logan again playing Watson.

Roy Marsden played Holmes, with John Moffatt as Watson, in 24 dramatisations of short stories available to passengers over headphones on British Airways' long-haul flights in the late 1980s. The plays were produced by DAEDALUS and sponsored by ICL, with the involvement of over thirty actors.

Holness, Bob (1928–)

Made his debut on the air as a radio actor with the South African Broadcasting Corporation in 1955, his parents having moved to Durban from Britain for work reasons, and has subsequently gone on to work for just about everyone.

BBC Radio shows he has presented include HOUSEWIVES' CHOICE, MIDDAY SPIN and TOP OF THE FORM and he has often deputised for others. Was one of the five comperes who launched LATE NIGHT EXTRA on Radio 2; has hosted music shows on Radio Luxembourg and the BBC World Service; and for ten years co-hosted LBC's *AM* programme with Douglas Cameron. A new Radio 2 series on Saturday evenings, *Bob Holness Requests the Pleasure*, began in 1991, with much of the flavour of the old IN TOWN TONIGHT.

Home for the Day

Sunday morning magazine programme on the Home Service, from 1953 to 1968, which was an early example of a programme designed specifically for women who went out to work and could not therefore listen to WOMAN'S HOUR. Conceived as a weekend supplement, it consisted mainly of repeat items from the programme from the previous week.

Marjorie Anderson, whose Home Service manner was as impeccable as her grooming. She presented *Woman's Hour* from 1958 to 1972 and its sister programme, *Home for the Day*, from 1955 to 1968

It was also scheduled with working mothers in mind – even in the 1950s, many women who went out to work were married with children – and its transmission time of 9.10 a.m. was chosen so that they could listen to it over breakfast with their families.

There were various comperes for the first two years, before MARJORIE ANDERSON took over in April 1955. She continued presenting it until it finished in March 1968, being immediately succeeded by WEEKEND WOMAN'S HOUR.

Home on Saturday

Ian Wallace introduced this 'selection of recorded wit, humour and music' which went out on Saturday afternoons on the Home Service.

Home Service

Created at the outbreak of the Second World War in September 1939 by a merger of the National Programme and the Regional Programme. On 30 September 1967 it was renamed Radio 4.

Home This Afternoon

Home Service magazine programme beginning in March 1964 and intended as a partner for INDIAN SUMMER and THE SILVER LINING, primarily for older listeners. Ken Sykora was the first compere, followed by JEAN METCALFE.

Home Town

Forces show in the Second World War, starring Ronald Shiner.

Home-ing In

Radio 4 series for do-it-yourself fans in 1984, partly presented by Pamela Donald (the first woman seen on BBC2 on its opening night in 1964).

Homeward Bound

Radio 3 series with light, pleasant classical music going out in the early evening when breadwinners were as described by the title. Its successor was MAINLY FOR PLEASURE.

The Honky Tonk Man

Five-part Radio 3 series in 1991 in which Francis Wilford-Smith (A HIGHWAY TO HEAVEN) discussed blues pianists, beginning with Cow Cow Davenport.

Hopkins, Antony (1921–)

Creator and presenter of TALKING ABOUT MUSIC since January 1954. (To have presented the same programme for this long a period is an achievement probably surpassed only by ALISTAIR COOKE.) Few people have done more to take ordinary listeners by the hand and guide them into the rewards and pleasures of great music. Also a conductor, composer (his work includes the scores for fifteen films), pianist, lecturer and author.

Horizon Radio

ILR station based in Milton Keynes, covering Buckinghamshire, which goes out on FM only and is aimed at younger listeners. It began in 1989. The name Horizon is of no particular significance.

Horne, Kenneth (1907–69)

Affable man of business (director of Triplex Safety Glass, chairman of Chad Valley Toys) who also enjoyed much success in showbusiness, acting as the straight man of BEYOND OUR KEN and ROUND THE HORNE, whose bawdy puns he delivered with straight-faced innocence.

Wartime service in the RAF (when he made his first radio series, ACK-ACK BEER-BEER) brought him into contact with RICHARD MURDOCH, with whom he devised MUCH-BINDING-IN-THE-MARSH. Despite its popularity, he returned to commerce until, in 1958, a stroke paralysed his left side and removed his speech.

He gave up his business career, sold his Rolls Royce, and using ideas he had worked out during his recovery, started *Beyond Our Ken*, which was soon attracting about ten million listeners. He became chairman of TWENTY QUESTIONS after GILBERT HARDING was sacked for being drunk and went on to make *Round the Horne*, which was still running when he died.

'He made everything acceptable precisely because he himself was so respectable' – Kenneth Williams.

'A kind of human maypole of radio comedy around whom zanier talents would frolic' – Russell Davies.

Hospital Radio

Patients in hospital wards were the original audiences for several of today's top radio stars, including KEN BRUCE, who first got behind a turntable and spoke into a microphone in a hospital radio studio.

The Hot Club

'Wit, spit, music and madness' were promised in this weekly Radio 2 comedy series in 1990, mixing gags, songs, sketches and a pastiche of musical styles from flamenco to Motown. The compere was Arthur Smith, assisted by a trio of singing comics – including Josie Lawrence. What it was doing on Radio 2, with its somewhat mature audience, was not clear, and it ran for only one series.

The Hot Seat

Radio 4 series in 1989 in which JOHN HUMPHRYS interviewed five top executives (including the editor of *The Independent*, chairman of Tesco and governor of Winson Green Prison) on the pressures and frustrations of life at the top.

The Houghton Weavers

'Music, comedy and a pea and pie supper, with Lancashire's best loved sons' was the promise for this Radio 2 Lancashire folk music series.

The House

Comedy-drama series on Radio 4 beginning in 1989 written by the BBC's former defence correspondent, Christopher Lee, who has also written scripts for THE ARCHERS. The first series concerned a contemporary Tory government with a wafer-thin majority. Julian Glover is the government's Chief Whip and Sarah Badel his wife, with Timothy West as an ambitious Home Secretary. The Prime Minister is referred to as 'The Sheriff', sex not specified.

A House in a Garden

GLORIA HUNNIFORD and Alan Titchmarsh guide listeners round some outstanding country houses and castles – and the grounds they stand in – in this Radio 2 series which began in 1988.

Housewives' Choice

Cheerful, neighbourly, long running and, at its peak, immensely popular record request show broadcast on the Light Programme from 1946 to 1967. Specifically aimed at women at home, at an hour when their menfolk were supposed to have just left for work, it was nonetheless nearly always presented by men – among them Godfrey Winn, Edmundo Ros, GILBERT HARDING, RICHARD MURDOCH, SAM COSTA and EAMONN ANDREWS.

The one who enjoyed the closest association with the show, however, was vocalist and bandleader George Elrick, whose bright and breezy style was heard on and off for two decades. His own gimmick developed by accident: one day he left his microphone on and was heard by millions humming along with the signature tune. Letters arrived by the sackful demanding a repeat performance and Elrick carried on humming, which became his hallmark.

Housewives' Choice grew into a national symbol of sunny, uncomplicated, let's-get-on-with-the-dusting domesticity. That mood was epitomised every morning by the catchy and optimistic signature tune 'In Party Mood', composed by Jack Strachey (who also wrote 'These Foolish Things'). La-de-da-de-da-de-da . . .

The show was conceived a few months after the end of the Second World War in Sweden, which NORMAN COLLINS, head of the new Light Programme, was visiting to look at new trends and where he came into contact with programmes aimed mainly at women.

It was launched at 9.10 a.m. on Monday, 4 March 1946 to lift the spirits of long-suffering British women in a bleak era of rationing, queuing and austerity. The very first programme, however, which featured both the Eton Boating Song and 'Greensleeves', was not noticeably jolly. Things were more cheerful the following day, Shrove Tuesday, when there was a recipe for making pancakes without eggs (dried egg had just disappeared from the shops, and fresh eggs were unobtainable) in between Bing Crosby and The Andrews Sisters.

As the requests started to come in, the mood got bouncier and more romantic. Favourites ranged from 'Don't Sit Under The Apple Tree With Anyone Else But Me' (The Andrews Sisters) to 'La Mer' (Charles Trenet) and 'This Is My Lovely Day'. Perry Como, Ruby Murray, Percy Faith, Pat Boone and Doris Day (whose 'Whatever Will Be, Will Be' was the most requested record of 1956) were among those heard, and in the 1950s the show was groaning under the weight of 3,000 postcard requests a week and commanding an audience of eight million.

The growth of rock music, popularity of the pirates, and publicity given to the advent of the BBC's new pop network all combined to weaken the programme's appeal from the mid-1960s. It was axed in August 1967, a month before the launch of Radio 1, but is still fondly remembered. The title, which has acquired the status of a timeless catchphrase, seems to encapsulate an era.

'A piece of dreamland entirely surrounded by privet hedge' – Kenneth Allsop.

How About You?

Wednesday lunchtime series on the Light Programme, with Dickie Valentine, Stan Stennett and the BBC REVUE ORCHESTRA.

'How bona to vada your dolly old eek!'

See ROUND THE HORNE and JULIAN AND SANDY.

How Far Can You Go?

Four-part Radio 4 series in 1990 in which Barry Norman considered blasphemy, hero worship and what limits there could or should be to liberty and licence.

How To . . .

Series of 29 programmes of satirical comic sketches built on a theme (*How to woo*, *How to be good at music*, *How to give a party* and so on) which were the product of the partnership of STEPHEN POTTER and JOYCE GRENFELL who first met in 1943 and established a fruitful rapport.

Affectionate observation and gentle parody of mannerisms and speech were the essence of the series, and the techniques were put to good use in *How to Listen*, broadcast on the opening night of the Third Programme in 1946.

Its sharp edge in spoofing supposedly off-the-cuff talks which were obviously scripted, and the frenzied clapping of absurd quiz shows, has not been dulled despite the passage of almost fifty years. The programme also contained a clip of a talk by the RADIO DOCTOR on one of his favourite topics, constipation: 'Some people refuse to listen to the message of the lower bowel, evidently believing that what I have I hold . . . '

A sequel, *How to Broadcast*, satirising the work of several writers and producers, was made specially for the Third Programme's fifth birthday in 1951 and the series continued until 1962. Apart from Potter (who also wrote the scripts) and Grenfell, the casts included CARLETON HOBBS, DERYCK GUYLER, ROY PLOMLEY, Betty Hardie and Ronald Simpson.

How We Lived Then

Eel and pie shops, silent films, washdays and Sunday school outings were recalled in this Radio 5 series in 1990 through a montage of voices, songs and sounds from the 1920s and 1930s. Produced in the BBC's South and East Network Radio unit, at Elstree, which specialises in this sort of vivid oral history.

How's Your Father

TED RAY sitcom on the Light Programme from April 1964. He played Father and his real-life son ROBIN RAY played his fictional son Robin. Eleanor Summerfield was his sister Ethel and Thora Hird his housekeeper Mrs Bender.

Howard, Margaret   (1938–)

Crisp, dry-humoured, stylish presenter of Radio 4's PICK OF THE WEEK from July 1974 until May 1991, during which time she chose and introduced some 15,000 items from the riches of BBC radio and television. The very last of these concerned female orgasms, taken from WOMAN'S HOUR. Howard then quipped: 'So much for coming – I'm going.'

She was told in November 1990 that her contract was not being renewed, but no specific reason was given for this. Her replacement was Chris Serle, who first came to prominence on television's *That's Life*.

She was one of ANDREW BOYLE's protégés as a reporter on THE WORLD THIS WEEKEND (1970–74) after working as an announcer on the BBC World Service (1967–69).

Howdy Folks

Comedy series of the early 1940s starring ERIC BARKER, Nan Kenway and Douglas Young.

Huddwinks

Roy Hudd series on Radio 2, which began in 1986.

Hudson, Robert   (–)

Quiet, respected, conscientious, all-round commentator, noted for his cricket (from 1951 onwards), ten Royal tours and 25 Trooping the Colours.

It was Hudson who suggested, in 1956, that there was now public appetite for ball-by-ball coverage of Test matches, with the Third Programme as the most appropriate place for it. This was eventually accepted by the BBC and Michael Tuke-Hastings, the senior cricket producer, coined the slogan 'Don't miss a ball, we broadcast them all' when non-stop Test coverage was launched with the England versus West Indies series in 1957, starting at Edgbaston.

Hudson went on to become head of radio outside broadcasts, in 1969, and was perched high up in St Paul's Cathedral as one of the radio commentators for the Royal Wedding in 1981, the year he retired.

'Hullo Children Everywhere'

(1) Catchphrase of UNCLE MAC on CHILDREN'S HOUR, which he started using in the Second World War:
his emphasis on the last word took into account all the evacuees, away from their homes and often homesick.

(2) Title of an affectionate, three-part Radio 4 series about Uncle Mac's request show CHILDREN'S FAVOURITES together with its predecessor CHILDREN'S CHOICE and successor JUNIOR CHOICE, which went out in 1988, presented by Jeremy Nicholas.

Human Rights

Five-part co-production between the Council of Europe (to mark its 40th year) and SCHOOLS RADIO, broadcast on Radio 4 FM in 1989. Dr Sheila Cassidy, a victim of torture, and many young Europeans took part, discussing what the phrase 'human rights' actually meant to them.

Humoresque

Radio 2 series in 1988 in which Tony Capstick travelled round England and presented comedy and musical talent from each of six different towns and cities.

Humour In Jazz

In this four-part Radio 3 series in 1988, Alan Plater played music where the result, if not always the intention, was to make the listener smile. He included Coleman Hawkins, Memphis Slim and Louis Armstrong.

Humphrys, John   (1943–)

One of the four main presenters of TODAY since 1987, and before that a BBC-TV foreign correspondent and newsreader. Also presented Radio 4's THE HOT SEAT in 1989 and ON THE ROPES. Vigorous, trenchant and curious.

Hungarian Service

Programmes in the Hungarian language first came out of BUSH HOUSE in September 1939. Today, they are on the air for two-and-a-quarter hours a day.

Hunniford, Gloria   (1940–)

Cheerful, fizzy, ex-cabaret singer from Portadown in County Armagh who became a radio reporter with the BBC in Northern Ireland in 1969, because the erupting troubles made life difficult for entertainers. In 1975 she started her own daily show on the station, nicely titled *A Taste Of Hunni*, and in 1982, following a successful stint as stand-in for JIMMY YOUNG the previous year, DAVID HATCH hired her to present her own afternoon show on Radio 2. She was Radio 2's first woman to host a weekday programme and has presented it ever since, blending music with showbiz interviews.

I

I, An Actor
Spoof theatrical memoir, presented as a late-night Radio 4 reading in 1989, devised by Nigel Planer and Christopher Douglas. It purported to be the serialised autobiography of an egotistical actor called 'Nicholas Craig'.

'I Don't Mind If I Do'
One of the many catchphrases from ITMA to have become part of the language, this was the way in which COLONEL CHINSTRAP could be relied on to accept another dose of his favourite hobby – drink.

I Hear America Singing
Twelve-part series on the National Programme in 1938 in which ALISTAIR COOKE traced the history of American folk songs. The title is a line by Walt Whitman.

I Play What I Like
Light Programme show in the 1950s associated with EAMONN ANDREWS and DIRK BOGARDE.

I Remember
Two Englishwomen spoke of their experiences in Russia during the 1917 Revolution, and a dangerous train journey through Siberia, in the first episode of this Home Service series which also featured Gerald Sparrow on his 25 years in Siam.

Ian Breakwell's Diary
Fourteen-part series on Radio 3 in 1990 in which artist and film-maker Ian Breakwell narrated his observations on his fellow citizens, intended to capture life's manifold absurdities.

IBA
See INDEPENDENT BROADCASTING AUTHORITY.

The Ideas and Beliefs of the Victorians
First major series on the Third Programme, conceived by its first head SIR GEORGE BARNES. It had 83 episodes.

If It's Wednesday
Radio 4 show fronted by Kenneth Robinson, with KENNY EVERETT and Monty Modlin as regular contributors.

If You Think You've Got Problems
First ever counselling series on national radio, broadcast on Radio 4 from 1971 to 1976. Members of the public were invited into the studio to discuss problems of human relationships at home and work – at the time, a revolutionary step. JEAN METCALFE was the presenter and Dr Wendy Greengross and Dr James Hemming the main panellists. Produced by Thena Heshel of IN TOUCH fame.

Ignorance Is Bliss
Quiz show hosted by STEWART MACPHERSON who was succeeded by EAMONN ANDREWS in 1950.

ILR
See INDEPENDENT LOCALL RADIO.

I'm Sorry I Haven't A Clue
This was the Radio 4 comedy series which concluded with the team's punning parade of guests being announced at a ball: 'Will you please welcome Mr and Mrs Roids – and their daughter, Emma Roids ... ' Stars were Tim Brooke-Taylor, Graeme Garden (two of the I'M SORRY I'LL READ THAT AGAIN team), Barry Cryer and Willie Rushton. Chairman was HUMPHREY LYTTELTON.

I'm Sorry I'll Read That Again
Weekly fusillade of rude, cheerful, chaotic and noisy sketches which enlivened the BBC airwaves from 1964 to 1973. Billed as 'a radio custard pie', it was thrown by John Cleese, Graeme Garden, Bill Oddie, Tim Brooke-Taylor, Jo Kendall and DAVID HATCH, who had perfected their undergraduate humour while working

John Cleese (second left) was often John Otto Cleese on the anarchic revue *I'm Sorry I'll Read That Again*. The show helped to launch many other top names, including (from left) Bill Oddie, Tim Brooke-Taylor, Jo Kendall, Graeme Garden and David Hatch

together at the Cambridge Footlights (see CAMBRIDGE CIRCUS).

Silly voices, dollops of mild smut and awful puns ('My name's Hanger-Ending . . . Cliff Hanger-Ending') could be relied upon to manifest themselves almost every week, as could references to the lunatic radio station RADIO PRUNE.

The six members of the cast reassembled in 1989 to make a one-off, 25th anniversary show broadcast on Radio 2 on Christmas Day. Bill Oddie wrote the script. Cleese played a BBC Director-General who, on discovering that shows like those of DEREK JAMESON were damaging the ozone layer, summoned BBC Radio's managing director David Hatch and ordered him to recycle lots of old programmes in order to repair the damage.

Immortal Diamonds

How six poets wrestled with their doubts, dreams and visions of God was lucidly examined by ROSEMARY HARTILL in this Radio 4 series in 1990. With the help of various academics, she discussed the unknown author of *Sir Gawain and the Green Knight* and then Milton, Blake, Browning, Emily Dickinson and Stevie Smith. The obscure title comes from a poem by Gerard Manley Hopkins.

Imperial Tobacco Awards for Radio

These were the first awards to be initiated by the Society of Authors and have grown into what are now the SONY RADIO AWARDS. They lasted for three years in the 1970s, and then PYE took over the sponsorship. The following is a complete list of the awards – all small-scale affairs, with far fewer categories than today:

For 1975–76, presented in 1976:
Original play or serial: *On a Day in Summer in a Garden* by Don Haworth. Adaptation to single play or

serial: *The Return of the Native* by Desmond Hawkins. Original comedy: *The Small Intricate Life of Gerald C. Potter* by Basil Boothroyd. Feature: *The Cookham Resurrection* by Peter Everett. Talk: *Interval Talk Introducing Movements in Sound* by Madeau Stewart. Outstanding production or direction: Richard Wortley for *The Cookham Resurrection* and *On a Day in Summer in a Garden*. Outstanding performance by an actor: Nigel Anthony for *Oscar X*. Outstanding performance by an actress: Beatrix Lehmann for *Hecuba*. Outstanding presenter: KENNY EVERETT for *The Kenny Everett Show*. Gold Award: Peter Eveerett for *The Cookham Resurrection*.

For 1976–77, presented in 1977:
Outstanding performance by an actor: Colin Blakely for *Judgement* (Radio 3). Outstanding perfomance by an actress: Rosemary Leach for *Moonshine* (Radio 4). Outstanding production or direction: *A Wall Walks Slowly*, devised and directed by Desmond Briscoe (Radio 3). Outstanding presenter: Robin Hall for *Singing Streets* (Radio Clyde). Outstanding specialist programme: John Maddox for *Scientifically Speaking* (Radio 3). Outstanding musico-documentary: *David Munrow*, by Michael Oliver (Radio 3). Outstanding documentary feature: *A Wall Walks Slowly*, Desmond Briscoe (Radio 3). Outstanding light entertainment: KENNY EVERETT for *Captain Kremmen* (Capital Radio). Outstanding talk: RAY GOSLING for *Battle for the Slums* (Radio 3). Outstanding local radio: *Singing Streets* by Robin Hall (Radio Clyde). Outstanding dramatised feature: *When Trees Were Green* by Inez Heron (Radio 4). Outstanding adapted drama: *August 2026*, adapted by Malcolm Clarke (Radio 4). Outstanding original drama: *Dead Soldiers* by Philip Martin (Radio 3). Gold Award for the single most outstanding contribution to radio: *A Wall Walks Slowly*, Desmond Briscoe (Radio 3).

For 1977–78, presented in 1978:
Performance by an actor: Denis Quilley for *Peer Gynt* (Radio 3). Performance by an actress: Sarah Badel for *A Moon for the Misbegotten* (Radio 3). Presenter: Tom Vernon for NEWS STAND (Radio 4). Specialist programme: Charles Nairn for *What Day's Christmas Anyway?* (BBC Radio Scotland). Musico-documentary: John Amis and Natalie Wheen for *Music Now* (Radio 3). Documentary feature: Chris Bryer and John Smithson for *If the Bombs Dropped Now* (Piccadilly Radio). Light entertainment: DOUGLAS ADAMS for THE HITCH-HIKER'S GUIDE TO THE GALAXY (Radio 4). Talk: John Barrett and Dilys Breese for *Elephants Can Tell Jokes* (Radio 4). Local radio: Hazel Fowlie and Andrew Monaghan for *View from Earth – The Lanthorn* (Radio Forth). Dramatised feature: Gerald Frow for *Beau Brummell, Prince of Dandies* (Radio 4). Adapted drama: Desmond Hawkins for *The*

Woodlanders, Part 6 (Radio 4). Original play: Peter Redgrove for *The God of Glass* (Radio 3). Gold Award for the most outstanding contribution to radio: ALISTAIR COOKE.

The Impressionists
Radio 2 series chaired by BARRY TOOK and featuring ventriloquist Ray Alan and actor David Jason (who did a splendid Winston Churchill).

INR
See INDEPENDENT NATIONAL RADIO.

In All Directions
Comedy series featuring PETER JONES and Peter Ustinov in the mid-1950s. See also WE'RE IN BUSINESS.

In Committee
Fascinating Radio 4 series from Parliament which provides a unique insight into the work of Select Committees, and sometimes Standing Committees, by reporting on their work and playing extracts from their proceedings.

Beginning in 1978 as *Inside Parliament*, it greatly illuminates the process by which Bills become Acts, and the ways in which changes are often made along the way. A salutary counterpoint to the noisy hullaballoo of TODAY IN PARLIAMENT.

In Concert
Weekly Radio 1 show of concerts from top and up-and-coming bands. In 1990 it moved from Friday to Saturday nights.

In Exile
Radio 4 series in 1990 with Jonathan Steinberg talking to other expatriates settled in Britain, including a White Russian, a Czech and an aristocratic Iranian woman don, on how they have adjusted to their new surroundings.

In My Life: Lennon Remembered
Ambitious, ten-part series on Radio 1 in 1990 – starting in the week in which the ex-Beatle would have turned fifty – about the man, his life, his music and the influence he exercised on the world.

The programmes contained interviews with Cynthia Lennon, Yoko Ono, Paul McCartney and Lennon's therapist and contained much detail, for example in an examination of his painful childhood in which he felt rejected by his father and his mother was killed by a car when he was seventeen.

In One Ear
Live, near-the-knuckle comedy series starring Helen Lederer, with four series from 1983–90.

In Search Of ...

Radio 4 series in 1989 in which Robert Elms presented pithy profiles of some contemporary British types, including The Yuppie and The Hooligan.

In the Hot Seat

Teenage listeners quiz personalities such as Glenda Jackson, Ian Hislop and Julian Clary in this Radio 5 series. It has been hosted by Sebastian Scott and Magenta De Vine.

In The Psychiatrist's Chair

Irish psychiatrist Dr ANTHONY CLARE started his celebrated Radio 4 series in 1981 and has so far persuaded over fifty men and women, mostly well known, to submit themselves to his questioning about their families, emotions, relationships, fears and beliefs.

About a third have been writers, ranging from SPIKE MILLIGAN (on the first programme) to P.D. James and Germaine Greer. Others have ranged from the Bishop of London to Geoff Boycott, Bruce Kent to Mary Whitehouse.

Clare's interviewing is underpinned by an understanding of human nature much greater than that of a mere journalist, and it results in memorable and often deeply painful programmes. Alan Duquesne was a murderer trapped for ever in his guilt; KEN DODD talked of the woman he had once loved; CLAIRE RAYNER broke down in uncontrollable tears (most of it was cut) when talking about her abused and miserable childhood – see MYSELF WHEN YOUNG. The programme was jointly conceived by its Hungarian-born producer, Michael Ember, and Anthony Clare, after one of his women patients asked if the bright, witty and articulate celebrities she had heard on STOP THE WEEK were, underneath it all, as insecure as she was. Her answer was a programme which, for the last ten years, has shown that anxieties and neuroses are a shared experience and that all human feet are made of clay.

The signature tune perfectly reflects the programme's reflections and poignancy. Entitled 'Conversation Piece', it is a clarinet arrangement by FRITZ SPIEGL of a piece by Mozart. It is the subject of inquiries from listeners every time the programme goes out, but is not commercially available.

In the Shadow of ...

Radio 4 series in 1990 about British communities dominated by one particular thing, whether a cathedral (Wells), a school (Oundle), tourism (Windsor) or horse-racing (Newmarket).

In Touch

Weekly Radio 4 programme for the blind which has been running since 1961. Believed to be the world's only national radio series for the visually handicapped, and certainly the BBC's longest running series for any group of disabled people (Does He Take Sugar? began in 1978).

From the beginning, In Touch has had only blind presenters. The first was the late David Scott Blackhall, who worked on the programme from its inception until shortly before he died in 1981. A former housing officer from Hertfordshire, he has been commemorated in the programme's annual £1,000 award (funded by the Patients Aid Association) to a body or individual who has made an outstanding contribution to helping the blind.

In addition, almost all the features and interviews are made by blind reporters. The programme content ranges from handy hints sent in by listeners ('Put a rubber band halfway down on pots of marmalade – it's then easy to tell them from jam') to descriptions of services and equipment and critical assessments of help available to those with little or no sight.

There are regular interviews with visually handicapped people of all ages on ways in which they have sought to overcome the problems of blindness, and regular coverage of the ways in which blind people can cope with popular activities like gardening and cooking.

Lord Denning, former Master of the Rolls, said on the programme that neither his doctor nor his optician had told him of the illuminated magnifiers he heard about on In Touch, and which had enabled him to read again without difficulty.

Since 1973 the programme team has produced a handbook, bringing together details of all the aids and services available to blind people. This has become an accepted textbook for social workers in this area and is revised each year. Like the programme's quarterly bulletin, it is also produced in braille, Moon and on tape.

The Cardiff publishers who make this book also developed a new technique for converting print to braille: this has since been installed in the House of Commons office of David Blunkett, the only blind MP, who as a result gets government papers within an hour of publication – in braille.

In Touch has been produced since 1964 by Thena Heshel, who fled to Britain with her family from her native Vienna in 1939. She received a SONY AWARD for services to radio in 1988, having built the programme up into Britain's national meeting point for everything connected with blindness and visual handicap.

In Town Today

Lunchtime successor to IN TOWN TONIGHT, starting the week after its parent folded. The presenters stayed the same: Nan Winton and Antony Bilbow.

In Town Tonight

Celebrated Saturday evening show on the Home Service, from 1933–60, in which the BBC's top presenters and interviewers talked 'to personalities who have come by

The turbulent priest Bruce Kent is one of over fifty people to have sat *In The Psychiatrist's Chair* and be questioned by Dr Anthony Clare. The series suggests that turbulence is never far from the surface in anyone, however calm the exterior

land, sea and air to be *In Town Tonight*'. These regularly included Hollywood stars of the calibre of Errol Flynn, Gary Cooper, Jane Russell and Doris Day, all of whom were featured in the 1,000th edition – a few weeks before the programme was moved to lunchtime and renamed IN TOWN TODAY.

It was so popular that there was uproar in 1937 when it was replaced, for a time, by a 26-part series called *The BBC Presents the ABC*. The signature tune was 'Knightsbridge March' by ERIC COATES.

In the 1940s it became famous for its sometimes unpredictable outside broadcast spot. This began as *Standing on the Corner* (with Michael Standing) and continued as *Man in the Street* (STEWART MACPHERSON and Harold Warrender), *On the Job* (John Ellison, then BRIAN JOHNSTON) and *Let's Go Somewhere* (Johnston).

In Your Garden
See C.H. MIDDLETON.

Incrementals
New wave of 21 local radio stations, plus an airport information service for Heathrow and Gatwick, set up by the IBA in 1989 and 1990. The first one on the air, inappropriately named, was SUNSET RADIO in Manchester.

The new stations, of whom about a quarter were ex-pirates, were designed to serve specialised 'niche markets'. They were intended to increase listener choice by appealing either to particular ethnic groups with foreign language programmes (e.g. Spectrum), or through specialist music (e.g. Jazz FM), or because they were for people in relatively small geographical areas (e.g Belfast Community Radio). Under the Broadcasting Act of 1981, they had to be in areas already covered by ILR stations. This meant they were additional, or incremental, to the existing services of broad appeal.

Most of the new stations were hit hard by the advertising slump. After a year over half had been refinanced, lost their original management, or become part of bigger ILR companies.

Independent Broadcasting Authority
Body which, in law, was the broadcaster of ILR from when it began in 1973 to the end of 1990, when it was dissolved. Since then its radio functions have been taken over by the RADIO AUTHORITY. The IBA had two Directors of Radio: JOHN THOMPSON (until 1987) and PETER BALDWIN (1987–90, who then became Chief Executive of the successor body).

Independent Local Radio
Britain's network of local commercial radio stations, which began with LBC in 1973 (forty years after most other countries got their commercial radio). From the outset it faced an uphill struggle.

The BBC was in place with four national networks, several local radio stations and the loyalty of millions. ITV had been going for nearly twenty years, taking the bulk of advertising revenue. Thirdly, ILR was fragmented, obliged (by the IBA) to pay a level of rental for transmitters which deterred it from making high profits, and required to be so broad based that it tried to please everyone. 'Forcing radio stations to be most things to most men caused collapses and unfortunate marriages,' wrote LBC's BRIAN HAYES, many years later, about the early days of severe financial difficulties.

But by the late 1980s the industry had picked itself up. Takeovers and reorganisation created a more certain financial base for many stations; there was keen interest in radio shares on the Unlisted Securities Market; and advertisers (many of whom found the cost of TV airtime prohibitively expensive) started to look at radio with such enthusiasm that the rate of growth in advertising revenue, about 24 per cent year-on-year, became the highest in Britain at one point. Revenue doubled from £69 million in 1983 to £139 million in 1988, slowing somewhat to £146 million in 1990. However, radio attracts only about 2 per cent of the national advertising cake compared with up to 10 per cent in some other countries.

In 1988–89, many ILR stations did the splits – splitting their services for up to 24 hours a day, usually putting out golden oldies or soft melodies on their medium wave frequencies while keeping their stereo FM channel for rock or contemporary hits. The splitting, in which County Sound led the way, followed the government's declaration to both BBC and ILR that it wished to end simulcasting (the simultaneous transmission of a programme on more than one frequency) and thus release frequencies for more services, widening the choice available to listeners.

At the end of the decade, in its last major act, the IBA established a number of more specialist INCREMENTAL stations in various parts of Britain. They, and all the other local stations, are now licensed by the new RADIO AUTHORITY.

'I began the decade by leaving the womb of the BBC and going into freefall running ILR's smallest station, Moray Firth Radio. I discovered that ILR didn't always stand for Indescribably Loathsome Rubbish' – Thomas Prag, managing director of Moray Firth Radio, in 1989.

Independent National Radio
Three national commercial networks being established from 1991 onwards, two on AM and the third on FM, to provide the first national competition to BBC Radio. Licensed and regulated by the RADIO AUTHORITY, and set up under the BROADCASTING ACT 1990.

The FM channel, awarded to the easy listening group Showtime in July 1991, expects to be on air by summer 1992. The first AM service will use Radio 3's medium wave frequency, expected to be surrendered around the end of 1991. This would be for 'any combination of speech and music' or mainly one or the other. The third licence, using Radio 1's medium wave frequency and expected to be more widely audible than the first AM service, would be advertised in 1993. The Act says that one of the new networks should consist mainly 'of spoken material'.

Independent Radio Drama Productions
One of the few independent programme producers in British radio, this enterprising venture was created by Tim Crook (once IRN's Old Bailey reporter) and Richard Shannon (a theatre producer) in 1987 when both were in their late twenties. In Britain its productions are heard mainly on LBC. This used to be on Sunday afternoons, in an hour-long slot repeated the following Sunday morning. When this began, in October 1989, it was claimed to be Britain's first regularly scheduled one-hour drama on commercial radio. LBC's cutbacks in 1990 reduced this drastically to 25 minutes a week – five minutes every weekday night.

Several IRDP plays, including *Frankenstein*, *The Canterbury Tales*, *Tartuffe* and an eight-hour version of *A Tale of Two Cities*, have been sold to the National Public Radio Network in the USA and won several major awards in that country. In addition, half-hour dramas about Samuel Pepys and the Great Fire of London were sold to British Airways and offered to air travellers as in-flight entertainment.

In 1989, Crook and Shannon helped to launch a competition called the New Radio Playwrights' Festival, jointly funded by LBC and Greater London Arts, to winkle out new writing talent. Contestants had to write a forty-minute play for radio and more than 200 entries were sent in. The five winning plays (four of which were comedies) were *Visi D'Arte* by Paul Sirrett; *Coffee and Tea 90p* by Tony Duarto; *Talking Shop* by Rosalynd Ward (who worked in BBC Radio!); *From Bed to Worse* by Christopher Prior and *On the Knocker* by John Caine. They were all broadcast on LBC and the authors each won £500.

Crook and Shannon followed this up in 1990 by organising the WOOLWICH YOUNG RADIO PLAY-WRIGHTS' COMPETITION, whose winning plays were broadcast on several ILR stations including Downtown, Red Dragon and Mellow.

Cassettes of several IRDP dramas, including *The Canterbury Tales* and *Mutiny on the Bounty*, were launched as an exclusive range in W.H. Smith in 1990 entitled The Drama Collection. It was an obvious rival to the BBC RADIO COLLECTION – especially as the price of a double cassette, at £5.99, was exactly the same.

Independent Radio News

Started in 1973, when ILR began, to service the whole of the ILR network with regular news bulletins. Run by LBC. Housed (in cramped conditions) in Gough Square, just off Fleet Street, until it moved with LBC into new premises in Hammersmith in 1990.

In 1988, IRN created a new advertising device called Newslink, in which – for the first time in Britain – synchronised advertising breaks were allowed within selected morning news bulletins right across the country. This extended the amount of advertising the IBA allowed commercial radio to have. It also enabled national advertisers to run their commercials in, or around, the IRN bulletins. The increased advertising revenue that resulted helped to reduce IRN's costs in providing news to the ILR network.

Indian Summer

Attractive title for weekly Home Service programme in the late 1950s and early 1960s which provided 'advice and entertainment for retired people and older people generally, and a meeting place on the air for those concerned for their welfare.' What graceful prose *Radio Times* had in those days.

The Indissoluble Union

Prophetic Radio 4 series in 1989 presented and written by GORDON CLOUGH, which examined the USSR and the nationalist ferment around its borders threatening to make it anything but indissoluble. In 1991, also on Radio 4, he provided a sequel, *Death of a Superpower*, whose title this time was not ironic. He presented an updated analysis of a country apparently tearing itself apart with demands for separatism.

Indonesian Service

Programmes from BUSH HOUSE in the Indonesian language began in October 1949. Today, this output of the BBC World Service is on the air for ninety minutes a day.

Tens of thousands of Indonesian workers, trapped in the Middle East during the Gulf crisis of 1990,

were catered for when the BBC put out programmes in their language on two new frequencies which they could tune into.

Information Please!

'The BBC's enquiry desk', was the billing for this Light Programme series. 'You ask – we answer' was its promise. Beginning in July 1964, it continued in the vein of WHAT DO YOU KNOW? and featured the same team of presenter FRANKLIN ENGELMANN, deviser JOHN P. WYNN and producer Joan Clark. It tried to answer questions of general interest, such as why Eastern music sounds strange to Western ears and how long an elephant's intestine is.

An Inland Donkey

Six-part Radio 4 series in 1990 in which writer and broadcaster David Bean followed the route of R.L. Stevenson's nineteenth-century travels through Northern Europe, as described in his early books *An Inland Voyage* and *Travels With a Donkey in the Cevennes*. (Bean made do without a donkey, unlike Stevenson who had the assistance of a beast called Modestine.)

The Innocent Ear

A simple and excellent idea inspired this Third Programme series which ran from 1959 to 1979 and was later revived. Several pieces of music – for example an overture, a suite and a set of variations – were played without being identified in any way beforehand, thus depriving listeners of their usual preconceived notion as to whether or not they would enjoy them. The composers were not announced until after each work, 'and the listener is invited to approach the music with an unprejudiced mind' in the words of *Radio Times* in 1960.

Clearly, this appeal fell on deaf ears, since the intolerance of Radio 3 listeners was still being lamented a generation later by controller JOHN DRUMMOND. Perhaps this is why he revived the programme in 1990. Robert Layton was taken on as the first presenter, playing music from his own collection and not identifying it until afterwards. The programme also provided much fun for music lovers in trying to identify the piece or at least its period, composer, or country of origin, while it was playing. (Much of the early series inn the 1960s was produced by ROBERT SIMPSON, who later wrote a tract called *The Proms and Natural Justice*, arguing against the Controller of Music's absolute and unfettered power over the Proms.)

Innovator and Visionary

Recitals by eight younger British pianists, on Radio 3 in 1990, which covered Beethoven's piano output from his earliest to last works. Each of the ten programmes contained a sonata, but also quirkier and less frequently performed pieces.

Inside Sasha
Surreal Radio 2 comedy adventure series that took place inside the human body.

Inside Science
Radio 4 FM series in 1988 in which Paul Heiney peered 'behind the scientific headlines' at topics such as radioactivity – standing on top of a nuclear reactor at Sizewell A power station and so on.

Inspector Scott Investigates
DERYCK GUYLER took the title role of the Scotland Yard detective in this enjoyable Light Programme series, created by JOHN P. WYNN, which ran from 1957–63. A crime was committed; Scott and his sidekick, Det. Sgt. Bingham (Brian Hayes, brother of PATRICIA HAYES) interviewed two or three suspects; then, while music played, there was a short intermission for listeners to decide who had dunnit before the final *denouement*.

International Assignment
Radio 4 series offering dispatches from foreign correspondents, which in 1989 changed its name to SPECIAL ASSIGNMENT and enlarged its menu to include domestic stories. (It could not be called *Assignment* as there was already a World Service programme of that name.)

International Concert Hall
Grandiose title for a show once broadcast on Sunday nights on the Home Service, featuring great music on gramophone records.

International Radio Festival of New York
One of the main international radio galas, covering both programmes and advertising, running since 1982. The judges are US radio professionals.

About 1,800 entries are submitted each year, from about two dozen countries. It is part of a larger media awards organisation, The New York Festivals, which dates back to 1957.

The BBC, with its long tradition of making high quality, scrupulously crafted programmes, has often taken prizes, as have ILR stations and even the small British outfit INDEPENDENT RADIO DRAMA PRODUCTIONS.

International Star Time
Famous stars introduced the voices of other big stars – on disc – in this Light Programme show running from 1960. Gracie Fields was the first presenter.

Interpretations on Record
Radio 3 series which takes one work from the musical repertoire (e.g. Bach's Flute Suite, Bizet's Carmen, Liszt's Piano Sonata) and plays extracts from the different recordings made of it over the last sixty years, illustrating the contrasting ways in which different artists tackle the same work.

Invicta Radio
One of the few ILR stations with a Latin name. It means 'unconquered', and is also the old Roman name for Kent. On the air since 1984, the station covers all of rural Kent with its headquarters now in Whitstable. It is one of the few ILR companies that is a PLC. Over the years it has employed about twenty DJs who started on the pirate ship Radio Caroline.

In 1989 it divided its services, like most ILR stations. Coast Classics, on AM, broadcasts golden oldies. Invicta FM, on FM, offers hits from the Top 40 and the last decade.

Invitation Concert
Third Programme series of weekly concerts held in front of an invited audience at MAIDA VALE studios, beginning in 1960.

Invitation To Dinner
Susan Marling, the PUNTERS presenter, shares meals with families from different ethnic backgrounds in this Radio 5 series which began in 1990. She has chewed the fat and broken bread with a Hindu family in Caerphilly, a Lithuanian family in Nottingham and several more, always in the family's own home and nearly always with three generations round the table.

An Invitation To Music
Music in a lighter vein, that is. This was an afternoon series on the Home Service, made in BUSH HOUSE, at the beginning of the 1960s.

IRN
See INDEPENDENT RADIO NEWS.

Islanders
Radio 4 series in 1989 about the Western Isles of Scotland, presented by DEREK COOPER.

Isle of Wight Radio
Based at Newport, and covering the Isle of Wight, this 24-hour music station (50 per cent current hits, 50 per cent golden oldies) with six full-time journalists providing local news went on the air in April 1990. It started on Easter Sunday, just as Radio Caroline had done 26 years previously, and the first record played was 'We've Only Just Begun' by The Carpenters. It was one of the new wave of INCREMENTAL stations.

ITMA
See IT'S THAT MAN AGAIN.

ITN Radio
Division of ITN formed in 1990 to bid for one of the national commercial channels set up by the

BROADCASTING ACT 1990. Its first venture, ITN Radio News, consisted of an hourly news service to some of the new wave stations like WNK and Sunrise. Each bulletin lasted two or three minutes and was beamed from ITN's London headquarters via the Astra satellite. The newscaster who read the first bulletin, in March 1990 at the launch of Jazz FM, was Sue Carpenter.

It's a Bargain
Value-for-money tips from Norman Tozer on Radio 4 in 1981.

It's a Deal
'The best site improver since the Greeks invented spectacles' was how Sid James regarded himself, in his role

of a greedy property developer, in this Light Programme comedy which started in 1961. Dennis Price was his silky associate and June Whitfield his secretary. ROBIN RAY played the office-boy, Steve.

It's All Yours
Sentimental, hands-across-the-ocean show in the Second World War in which children gave messages to their fathers or other relatives serving in the Forces overseas. One such was a nine-year-old Petula Clark, who spoke to her uncle as well as singing 'Mighty Like a Rose', a song Paul Robeson had made famous, in a girlish treble. STEPHEN WILLIAMS produced it.

'It's being so cheerful that keeps me going'
One of the rich catalogue of funny catchphrases from ITMA: this one was coined by the gloomy MONA LOTT.

It's One O'Clock
Former Light Programme show once hosted by ADRIAN LOVE.

Petula Clark was a winsome nine-year-old when she appeared on the Forces show *It's All Yours* in 1942. With her, left to right: Eileen Cuthbert, producer's secretary; Stephen Williams, producer (holding her hand); Jimmy Burking, control engineer; Jack Leon; Robin Richmond; Joan Gilbert, compere; Cecil Madden, head of the BBC's overseas entertainment unit

The ITMA company in fine fettle at a London rehearsal
in September 1948. Left to right: Joan Harben; Fred
Yule; Hugh Morton; Diana Morrison; Jack Train; Tommy
Handley; Hattie Jacques; scriptwriter Ted Kavanagh;
Deryck Guyler

It's Only Me
Light Programme comedy series starring Peter
Goodwright, which began in 1962.

It's That Man Again
The one programme which everyone who lived
through the Second World War can remember, hugely
popular for its quickfire crosstalk and array of larger-
than-life, affectionately drawn comic characters. It en-
grossed the nation on Thursday nights from July 1939
to January 1949. Its main star and pillar, TOMMY
HANDLEY, died three days after the last episode, which
was the 310th.

Characters included MRS MOPP, COLONEL
CHINSTRAP, FUNF, MONA LOTT and FUSSPOT and
among the cast were Jack Train, DERYCK GUYLER
and MAURICE DENHAM (who played the char Mrs
Lola Tickle).

ITMA invented a great number of catchphrases, which
seeped into the language: 'Can I Do Yer Now, Sir?'
(coined by Mrs Mopp); 'I Don't Mind If I Do' (Col.
Chinstrap); 'It's Me Noives' (Lefty); 'Ta-ta for now', also
known as 'TTFN' (also Mrs Mopp); 'It's being so cheerful that keeps me going' (Mona Lott); 'After you, Claude
– No, after *you*, Cecil'; 'Zis iss Funf speakink' . . .

Few shows captured public affection like ITMA.
When Handley died, and the ITMA show which had
been recorded was cancelled as a mark of respect, the
BBC's Director-General Sir William Haley made a rare
appearance at the microphone. In simple and moving
language he announced to the nation:

'Ladies and gentlemen, we cannot tonight present
ITMA. Tommy Handley, That Man, that humorous, ebullient, kindly man around whose personality
it was built and whose art held it together, is dead.

'For the men and women and children of this
generation to whom ITMA meant something that
no other show will ever mean, and who tonight
hold Tommy Handley in grateful and affectionate
memory, there will never be anyone quite like That
Man again.'

ITMA's brilliance was a combination of the star,
Handley, and the writer, TED KAVANAGH. It was
he who took the title from a phrase invented by the
Daily Express in its headlines about Herr Hitler – IT'S
THAT MAN AGAIN.

It's Your Line
One of the first main PHONE-IN programmes, presented on Radio 4 in the 1970s by SIR ROBIN DAY.

It's Your World
Series of live PHONE-INS to world leaders organised as a joint venture between Radio 4 and the BBC World Service, and broadcast on both from 1984 onwards. People telephone BUSH HOUSE from all over the world, often at considerable expense and from post offices if there is no direct dialling. Questions are sifted and selected, and lucky callers are then rung back at the BBC's expense and asked to stand by with their question.

An initiative by WOMAN'S HOUR, the original presenter was MICHAEL CHARLTON. SUE MACGREGOR anchored it afterwards. Later programmes were not always taken by Radio 4 and went out on the World Service only.

Guests have included Margaret Thatcher, Neil Kinnock, Rajiv Gandhi of India, Benazir Bhutto of Pakistan and Kenneth Kaunda of Zambia. Glasnost eventually propelled a leader from Eastern Europe to appear: Mieczyslaw Rakowski, Prime Minister of Poland, in 1989.

'One of the most satisfying things is to establish links between, say, an important guest from the Sudan and a caller in Papua New Guinea, all via London' – Neil Curry, a frequent *It's Your World* producer.

It Was On The Spaceship Venus
David Jason starred in this, which was probably the first comedy series to be set in space.

Ixion
Motorcycling correspondent of the BBC in the early 1930s, named after a mythical Greek king punished in the afterlife by being fastened to a perpetually rotating wheel.

Jack De Manio Precisely
Afternoon show on Radio 4, hosted by the ebullient ex-TODAY presenter. When it was axed in 1978 it marked the virtual end of his thirty years with the BBC.

The Jack Payne Record Show
Saturday lunchtime show on the Light Programme with Jack Payne introducing 'popular gramophone records from here, there and everywhere'.

Jackson, Jack (1907–78)
Bandleader who after the Second World War became a distinctive radio presenter, initially with a Decca-sponsored show on Radio Luxembourg. Became famous, when in charge of RECORD ROUNDABOUT on the Light Programme, for his lightning cutting between, and mixing of, comedy extracts and music. After the birth of Radio 1 he was heard on the new network on Saturday lunchtimes. The man who has stepped into his shoes with a similar show is ADRIAN JUSTE, who still has the same time slot (1 p.m. on Saturdays) which Jackson used to occupy.

Jacobs, Clive (1939–)
Presenter of Radio 4's religious magazine programme SUNDAY for eighteen years, and of its travel series GOING PLACES for six, until both programmes decided to dispense with his services in 1990. He was previously a BBC-TV journalist and co-hosted the BBC2 news programme *Newsdesk*.

Jacobs, David (1926–)
The man who once wrote that he was 'a product of the national obsession with pop music' has enjoyed a much more versatile career than that modest description suggests, and nor are his abilities confined to the velvety smoothness which some regard as his hallmark. It was Jacobs the actor who eerily intoned 'JOUR-NEY IN-TO SP-A-A-CE!' at the beginning of each episode of that wonderful adventure in the 1950s as well as playing a total of 22 other parts including a Scots radio ham in Greenland.

His first broadcast, after service with the Royal Navy, was NAVY MIXTURE in 1944. Since then BBC radio shows he has hosted include HOUSEWIVES' CHOICE, PICK OF THE POPS, ANY QUESTIONS? and its sister ANY ANSWERS?, MIDDAY SPIN and those of the BBC RADIO ORCHESTRA. He also presented a Luxembourg show which was sponsored by Bournvita and recorded on disc in London before being flown out to the Grand Duchy.

His lunchtime Radio 2 show reflects his favourite music – from the Cole Porter era of great lyrics and memorable musicals.

Jaffa, Max (1911–)
Violinist who is one of Britain's longest serving entertainers and broadcasters, dubbed 'King of the Palm Court' when he was leader of the Palm Court Orchestra on GRAND HOTEL.

He made his debut at the microphone in the 1920s, and celebrated his diamond jubilee in 1987 with a gala concert at the Queen Elizabeth Hall, heard on Radio 2, when he also conducted the BBC RADIO ORCHESTRA and was accompanied by his wife, contralto Jean Grayston.

Jaffa began a new series, *The Max Jaffa Trio*, in 1989 on Radio 2, accompanied by Alan Dalziel (cello) and Gordon Langford (piano).

Jameson, Derek (1929–)
High-profile breakfast presenter on Radio 2 whose life story of being born poor and illegitimate in London's East End, being brought up in a foster home, starting work at fourteen as a Reuters messenger boy and rising to become editor of two Fleet Street papers, the *Daily Express* (1977) and *News of the World* (1982) is brilliantly told in his autobiography *Touched by Angels*.

Although he started broadcasting in television, he owes most of his current success to a libel action he launched against the BBC in 1980 after Radio 4's satirical show WEEK ENDING savagely lampooned him as 'the archetypal East End boy made bad . . . who still believes

'Do you have any radios that don't
receive Derek Jameson?'

Radio 2's Derek Jameson, who commands fierce passions both for and against, was even more in evidence than usual in August 1990, when this *Daily Telegraph* cartoon appeared, by taking a key role in publicising the great switchover to FM

that "erudite" is a glue.' Four years later Jameson lost the High Court action and faced the prospect of his life savings disappearing because he had to pay both sides' costs, estimated at £75,000.

To help him pay off the costs, the BBC kindly gave Jameson lots of work. On radio, he was invited to be a regular on Radio 4's COLOUR SUPPLEMENT in 1985, and in November that year was hired as a holiday relief for JIMMY YOUNG. This provoked such a huge, and favourable, response – critic Jill Neville, in THE LISTENER, memorably described how she had stumbled across his 'Burglar Bill' voice – that FRANCES LINE immediately snapped him up. KEN BRUCE was shunted off the following April to mid-morning to make way for the rasping Cockney whose cheery rallying call of 'Mornin', mornin'!' has introduced the breakfast show ever since.

In 1989 (by which time he was appearing on Sky TV and earning a total, he said, of £250,000 a year) he claimed that his breakfast show received over 800 letters a week and more telephone calls than all the other programmes on Radios 1, 2, 3 and 4 put together. There was no confirmation of these startling assertions, but there is no doubting his profile and popularity - even if he is someone you either love or hate.

Japanese Service

Programmes in the Japanese language started to be broadcast from BUSH HOUSE in July 1943. They were still running at the rate of an hour a day when they were axed in March 1991, along with the Malay

Service, as part of a package of measures partly agreed with and partly imposed by the Foreign Office.

The decision saved the BBC £279,000 a year, less than it costs to make one episode of *Casualty*. Not surprisingly, it drew sharp protest from many, including Lawrence Breen, head of the Far East section of the World Service from 1977–84. 'It seems regrettable that, for the sake of a comparatively paltry sum, we should abolish what could continue to be an invaluable British asset in our dealings with the world's second largest economic power,' he wrote in a letter to *The Times*.

Jazz Club

ALAN DELL introduced this Thursday evening show on the Light Programme, featuring a variety of jazz musicians.

Jazz FM

Britain's first legal jazz station went on the air in March 1990, beaming all forms of jazz ('the only music', according to HUMPHREY LYTTELTON, 'that appeals simultaneously to the heart, the head and the feet') throughout Greater London for 24 hours a day. The first record played, which reflected the hour, was 'It's Early in the Morning' by Joe Williams.

The birth of the station was the culmination of a ten-year campaign by pianist and composer DAVE LEE, who became Jazz FM's first director of music. Lee's bid won the franchise for one of the IBA's new wave of INCREMENTAL stations. His application pointed out that London had over 120 jazz clubs and pubs but, unlike other major cities in Europe, Australia and the USA, no jazz radio station – 'a glaring gap' in the range of music available to listeners. He intended Jazz FM to become a national focus for jazz and a force actively contributing to the music's renaissance.

Aware of the tendency of some jazz fans to regard their own favourites as the only true form of the music, and dismiss the rest as impure, Jazz FM shrewdly set out to appeal to all tastes. Its idea of 'jazz' was nothing if not comprehensive. It identified over a dozen different varieties, including big band, trad, ragtime, blues, bebop, swing, Latin-American, Afro-Caribbean, vocal and instrumental standards, rhythm and blues, soul, reggae, gospel, freeform and urban contemporary dance. Mainstream music of broad appeal was promised for the daytime, with more esoteric tastes being catered for after 9 p.m., but a constant criticism of the station in its early days was that 'mainstream' meant nothing but soul and funk. Lee subsequently conceded that too much of this had been played.

The station originated its own chart of the Top 20 best-selling jazz records in London. Compiled by *Music Week* magazine, it goes out on Sundays, like all other radio chart shows. In 1990 it also launched a weekly film review spot with George

Perry of *The Sunday Times*, sponsored by accountants KPMG Peat Marwick McLintock. An increase in the power of its Crystal Palace transmitter later in 1990 expanded the area it could be heard in – as far as Dunstable in the north and Maidstone in the south.

The station nurtured its own Jazz FM Club, which had over 1,000 members within six months. For an annual subscription of £15, they receive discounts, up-to-date information on jazz events in the UK and abroad, and regular newsletters and magazines.

No other commercial radio station has ever enjoyed as much support at Westminster. Five MPs (including Labour's front bencher John Prescott) and two peers were on Jazz FM's original advisory panel. In addition, Cabinet Ministers Douglas Hurd and Kenneth Clarke have never hidden their liking for jazz and the Tory MP for Hertford, Bowen Wells – co-ordinator of the jazz lobby at Westminster – was on the original board of directors, alongside Johnny Dankworth, Lord Rayne and Ron Onions.

None of these elevated names, however, guaranteed success for the station. It failed to pull enough advertising or listeners and in February 1991 announced that it was making one-third of its staff redundant – a total of sixteen people. Lee himself stepped down and the station promised it would provide more popular jazz in a bid to increase audiences.

Jazz Parade

Five nights a week Radio 2 jazz show often presented by PETER CLAYTON, which began in April 1990 (a month after the launch of Jazz FM) and was a considerable extension of Radio 2's jazz coverage, notwithstanding its midnight hour. It features a variety of jazz styles, plus news and reviews from the jazz world.

Jazz Record Requests

Saturday show on Radio 3 dating from 1965. Presenters have included PETER CLAYTON and CHARLES FOX.

The Jazz Scene

HUMPHREY LYTTELTON introduced this Sunday night show on the Light Programme in the 1960s featuring new releases, live bands, news and views.

Jazz Score

Weekly Radio 2 jazz quiz, hosted by BENNY GREEN.

Jazz Session

Monthly survey of jazz events once broadcast on Network Three and hosted by jazz buffs like ALEXIS KORNER, BENNY GREEN and Ken Sykora.

Jazz Voices

Four-part Radio 3 series in 1989 in which composer Richard Rodney Bennett (a former jazz pianist) presented his favourite records by female jazz singers, who included Billie Holiday, Sarah Vaughan and Anita O'Day.

Jennings

Ten-year-old boy at a fictitious prep school who made his debut on CHILDREN'S HOUR in October 1948, along with his faithful chum Darbishire: their escapades, of which there were more than a hundred beginning with *Jennings Learns the Ropes*, were popular listening throughout the 1950s.

Their creator, Anthony Buckeridge, was himself a teacher at a real prep school. Because of this the stories were supposed to carry some authenticity, though for critics the boys were always insufferable prigs.

Jennings and Darbishire were played originally by David Page and Lois Somerville. Jennings was later played by child actor Glyn Dearman, who grew up to become a BBC Radio drama producer – drawing on other boyhood memories when he made DAN DARE. One of the Jennings stories was revived on Radio 5 in 1990 when it was read by the actor Stephen Fry.

'How refreshingly natural the voices of Jennings and his friends always sound! Why, in other programmes, do we so often have to make do with females painfully overacting in their attempts to portray the "fine manly little chap"?' – The Rev. Andrew Hodgson of Norwich, in a letter to *Radio Times* in 1962.

Jensen, David (1950–)

Canadian DJ (born in Victoria, British Columbia) who started in radio at the age of sixteen, presenting classical music on a Canadian FM station; then made his way to Radio Luxembourg where the fact that he was but eighteen summers old earned him a nickname which stuck: 'Kid'. He hosted *Jensen's Dimensions*, a midnight show every Friday dedicated to contemporary rock of an avant garde flavour, with plenty of Van Morrison. He was at Radio 1 from 1976–84 and since then has been at Capital.

The Jesuits

Lord Rawlinson explored the contemporary political influence of the Society of Jesus in this six-part Radio 3 series in 1988.

Jewel, Jimmy (1912–)

Comedian who appeared in several radio series of *Up The Pole* in a double act with his cousin BEN WARRISS.

The adventures of conformist prep-school boy Jennings were among the most popular items on *Children's Hour* throughout the 1950s. Recording sessions in the studio were not without their lighter moments, either, as this 1952 picture shows

Born James Marsh in Sheffield, son of variety artists, he used the name Jewel on stage and later adopted it by deed poll. He and Warriss – their mothers were sisters – were a team for 33 years, topping the bill at the London Palladium and appearing in six Royal Variety Performances.

The partnership broke up when Warriss decided he didn't want to continue with it. Since then Jewel has enjoyed a new and highly successful career as a straight actor, beginning in 1975 with Trevor Griffiths' stage play *Comedians*.

The Jewish People in the Year 2000

Philosopher Dr Jonathan Sacks, then Principal of Jews College and now Chief Rabbi (and 1990's Reith Lecturer) gave these three talks on Radio 3 in 1988 in which he reflected on the crises facing Judaism. He explored the survival of belief after the Holocaust, threats of schism between traditional and reform approaches, and trends towards secularisation and intermarriage.

Jewish Writers

Six authors, including Arnold Wesker, Bernice Rubens and Dan Jacobson, talked in this Radio 4 FM series in 1990 to Nick Kochan about what effect Jewishness had on their work.

JICRAR

Joint Industry Committee for Radio Audience Research: a body composed of representatives from advertising agencies, advertisers and ILR companies which lays down the rules for measuring the audiences for commercial radio. The figures are published by the RADIO MARKETING BUREAU, which officially commissions the research.

Essentially unchanged since 1973, the measuring system is based on diaries. Respondents make a note of their radio listening over a seven-day period from Monday to Sunday in a diary divided into segments of the day. The diary is produced by Research Surveys of Great Britain Ltd (part of AGB which compiles the weekly television ratings).

Joad, Cyril E.M.   (1891–1953)

Fabian philosopher who will be forever remembered for his catchphrase 'It all depends what you mean by . . . ' with which he prefaced some, but by no means all, of his answers on THE BRAINS TRUST. Head of philosophy at Birkbeck College, London, he did much to popularise his subject – particularly political thought – on a programme which was itself one of the most potent educating institutions of its age.

He appeared almost every week from the first edition in 1941 until April 1948 when he pleaded guilty to fare evasion at Tower Bridge court in London and was fined 40 shillings with 25 guineas costs. The BBC dropped Joad immediately, replacing him on the very next programme with Stephen King-Hall, and Joad never again appeared on the programme which he had helped to make such compulsive listening.

It did not emerge at the time, and indeed was not fully realised until the broadcast of RADIO LIVES in 1990, that the court case, far from being an isolated incident, was the result of Joad's bizarre obsession in trying to defraud the railways, to the extent of carrying pocketfuls of penny tickets about and telling lies about the station he had come from, and even scrambling over hedges and fields to avoid ticket collectors: he appeared to think that being an intellectual put him above the law.

Neither this fixation nor his empty personal life, however, should obscure the erudition of thought and clarity of speech – tying everything up into neat little packages, so that little could usefully be added – which distinguished his contribution to one of the BBC's most influential radio programmes.

John, Adrian   (1954–)

Started in radio on the QE2, as host of the ship's internal radio station, and later had a similar job at Top Shop in Oxford Street. Rejected as a DJ by both Capital and Luxembourg, but spotted by PETER POWELL. He joined Radio 1 in 1979 and later presented an early morning show on weekdays, but left in 1989 after six years of getting up before dawn and went to work for Radio Invicta in Kent.

Johnny Washington Esquire

The escapades of an American safecracker, played by BERNARD BRADEN and written by Francis Durbridge, which ran on the Light Programme from 1949. David Kossoff and Andrew Faulds (who later played the hero of JOURNEY INTO SPACE) also appeared.

Johnson, Duncan   (–)

One of Radio 1's first DJs when it was launched in 1967, a rugged-voiced Canadian who hosted CRACK THE CLUE for a short period.

Johnson, Teddy   (1919–)

First presenter of the first ever charts programme, Radio Luxembourg's TOP TWENTY in 1948. He hosted it for the next two years at a wage of £10 a week throughout, but made his debut on the station with a programme of Geraldo records. Born Edward Johnson, he was previously a dance band singer (with JACK JACKSON's band, among others) and has also worked as a presenter on Radio 2.

Johnston, Barry   (1949–)

Sunday breakfast host on Radio 5. Son of BRIAN JOHNSTON, he has followed in his father's broadcasting footsteps but not by pulling strings. Formerly a pianist, songwriter and manager of The New Seekers, he became a breakfast DJ in California in the 1980s and then worked for five years on BBC Radio Sussex before joining Radio 5 in 1990.

Johnston, Brian   (1912–)

Amiable, relaxed, jocular broadcaster known for infusing his cricket commentary with a sense of fun, and for public school mannerisms which include giving affectionate nicknames to his colleagues ('Blowers', 'McGillers', 'Cudders', 'The Boil' and so on – his own is 'Johnners').

Hired by 'LOBBY' LOTBINIERE in 1946, in BBC Radio's Outside Broadcasts. First commentating job was on the detonation of an unexploded bomb in St James's Park, which he covered from the vantage point of a ladies' lavatory.

He had his own outside broadcast spot, *Let's Go Somewhere* (the title of an earlier 1930s show featuring JOHN SNAGGE) on IN TOWN TONIGHT. This was a live four minutes in which he had a variety of assignments, from staying alone in Madame Tussaud's Chamber of Horrors to lying under a passing train. The item ran to 150 editions, from 1948–52.

Became the BBC's first cricket correspondent in 1963, after which he started commentating on the game on radio (previously he had been only on television). Dropped by BBC-TV in 1970, in a move to give its commentary team more of a specialist flavour, he promptly joined TEST MATCH SPECIAL and has been there ever since. Has a great fondness for the cakes which listeners send in.

Presented DOWN YOUR WAY from 1972–87 and has commentated at several major State occasions, including the Funeral of King George VI, the Coronation, and Royal Wedding of 1981. One of his five children is BARRY JOHNSTON, on Radio 5.

The Jonathan Ross Radio Show

Chat, comedy and music show hosted by JONATHAN ROSS, starting on Radio 1 in 1990 and live from Ronnie Scott's jazz club in Soho in front of a 300-strong audience.

'There aren't many people on radio with a "soft r", which is what my affliction is called, so that's at least one thing I've got to offer' – Jonathan Ross.

Jones, Paul (1942–)

Oxford educated actor and ex-lead singer with Manfred Mann, founding The Blues Band in 1979, who presents a weekly Radio 2 showcase of his favourite music, rhythm and blues. He plays a mixture of vintage R&B and recent releases. One show a month is dedicated to requests.

Jones, Peter (1930–90)

Voice of BBC Radio sport for 25 years, whose mastery of clear and elegant prose – often delivered under intense pressure – was manifested at State as well as sporting occasions.

A Cambridge Blue (for football), who taught at Bradfield before going to the BBC, he was the commentator at every FA Cup Final from 1968 until the year of his death, and also covered five World Cups, much tennis and boxing and two Royal Weddings.

He spoke almost non-stop for four hours on the night of the Heysel Stadium disaster in 1985. He collapsed and died on a launch while commentating on the Boat Race, the microphone still in his hand. Not one to take himself too seriously, he was once asked to recall his greatest *faux pas*. He said it had occurred during the

Sixteen years before man stepped on the moon, Captain 'Jet' Morgan (Andrew Faulds, left) was exploring its eerie mysteries on the Light Programme. *Journey Into Space* also featured David Jacobs (right) who not only intoned the title, into an echo chamber, but also played over twenty minor parts

FA Cup Final in 1985, when he had told listeners: 'At this moment the Band of the Grenadier Guards stand erect in the centre circle, their instruments flashing in the sunshine.'

'He could make a dull game bearable and an exciting one almost unbearable' – David Hatch.

'You knew for certain that his words would paint a picture. . . He was the last of the BBC's all-rounders' – Cliff Morgan.

Jones, Peter   (1921–)

Splendid comedy actor who has long been a feature of BBC Radio comedies: IN ALL DIRECTIONS, in which he partnered Peter Ustinov, WE'RE IN BUSINESS with Harry Worth, JUST A MINUTE, and THE HITCH-HIKER'S GUIDE TO THE GALAXY.

Jones, Steve   (1945–)

Started in the music business, singing 'Does Chewing Gum Lose Its Flavour On The Bedpost Overnight?' with Lonnie Donegan's band. Became a DJ, spent five years at Radio Clyde; presented a late night Saturday slot on Radio 2 until 1985; now hosts a programme on LBC.

Journey Into Space

Space adventure written by CHARLES CHILTON, which stretched over 62 episodes in the 1950s and enthralled a generation.

Originally, when it blasted off from the Light Programme in September 1953, it was intended to be no more than eight episodes, with one episode a week (on Mondays at 7.30 p.m.). But such was its immediate success that the eight episodes became eighteen and the one broadcast a week became two. By the time it finished in 1958, it had been translated into seventeen languages and broadcast from radio stations all over the world. At home, it was the last evening radio series which attracted a bigger audience than that watching television at the same time and was, therefore, a watershed in the history of British broadcasting.

The first adventure, *Operation Luna*, was set in the distant future of 1965 and told of man's conquest of the moon; the second, *The Red Planet*, was set in 1971–72 and traced the fantastic events after a space fleet led by Jet Morgan in the bright blue flagship Discovery set off on a 35 million-mile trip to Mars; and the final story was set in a *World in Peril*.

The four adventurers were Captain 'Jet' Morgan (played by Andrew Faulds, later Labour MP for Warley East); 'Doc' Matthews (Guy Kingsley-Poynter); 'Mitch' Mitchell (Don Sharpe, replaced in 1955 by David Williams); and radio operator Lemmy Barnett (originally David Kossoff, who left after a few months for a stage show and was replaced by Alfie Bass). Most other parts were played by DAVID JACOBS.

The intellectual content in terms of benign intelligence and distortions of time and space; the haunting sound effects; eerie and striking music composed and conducted by Van Phillips; all combine to make *Journey Into Space* a true radio classic.

A new, ninety-minute adventure, again written by Chilton and with John Pullen playing Jet, went out on Radio 4 in 1981. It took up where the last adventure had finished in 1958.

Operation Luna was released on cassette as a boxed set in September 1989, with a repeat on Radio 2 starting at the same time, and *The Red Planet* was repeated on Radio 2 in 1990–91.

Journey Round My People

Vivid Radio 4 series in which FERDINAND DENNIS travelled round England and looked with a quizzical eye at some of the activities of his fellow Afro-Carib-Britons, from pirate radio to dub poetry and domino-playing.

Joyce, William   (1906–46)

One of the most keenly remembered but least loved broadcasters of the Second World War, better known as LORD HAW-HAW. Hanged for high treason at Wandsworth after being captured by British troops in Germany, where he had spent the entire war broadcasting Nazi propaganda talks – prefaced by the words 'Germany calling, Germany calling' – in his strange, nasal voice.

The sentence was highly controversial and the case went to the House of Lords. Joyce, born in New York, was legally an American citizen, of Irish descent. His subsequent British passport was obtained fraudulently, but the Attorney-General (Sir Hartley Shawcross) argued that he had 'clothed himself in the Union Jack' and had presented himself in Hitler's Germany as a British citizen, which was why he was of such value to the Third Reich.

One of Sir Oswald Mosley's blackshirts, Joyce later formed his own National Socialist League to attack Bolsheviks and Jews, before leaving for his beloved Germany in 1938. He was hired, by German radio's English-speaking service in Berlin, initially to read the news, and later to present his own commentaries. It was the voice, with its hypnotic sneer, and his ardent beliefs, which won him the job.

The phrase 'Lord Haw-Haw' was coined by Jonah Barrington in the *Daily Express* fifteen days after the outbreak of the Second World War. Joyce had not even started work by then, and the broadcaster who attracted the description was either Norman Baillie-Stewart, a former Seaforth Highlander officer, or a German who speaks perfect English in a frightfully upper-class English accent, Wolf Mittler (still broadcasting today, in his late seventies).

Barrington wrote of Lord Haw-Haw on the day he invented the name: 'From his accent and personality I imagine him with a receding chin, a questing nose, thin, yellow, brushed back hair, a monocle, a vacant eye, a gardenia in his buttonhole, rather like P.G. Wodehouse's Bertie Wooster.'

Although this physical description bore no resemblance to Joyce, the nickname stuck. This was a tribute to the impact his broadcasts made, both unsettling and entertaining. He appeared to have about six million regular listeners in England, and by May 1940 German radio was introducing his talks as by Lord Haw-Haw.

What Joyce said made news. He appeared to be disturbingly well informed. How *could* he know that the clock at Banstead was five minutes slow and that the benches had been taken away from the promenade at Littlehampton? How could he be so clued up about troop movements and convoys? Proof, surely, of a shadowy Fifth Column in Britain which was somehow feeding him the information. The consensus now is that Joyce is celebrated more for what he did not say than for what he did, and that rumours bred rumours.

Joyce provoked ridicule as well as generating discomfort – comedians dubbed him 'the Humbug of Hamburg' – but he became, nonetheless, a familiar part of the nation's listening. He gained credibility from mentioning items which the BBC was often slow to report, such as bombing raids. His constant theme was the hopelessness of the British cause, and he chipped away at Britain's sense of security week after week after week.

Deciding that his broadcasts were potentially damaging to morale, the *Daily Mirror* launched an 'Anti Haw-Haw League'. It printed stickers for people to put on their wireless sets. These carried the words 'This set is Anti Haw-Haw. It hears no evil, speaks no evil', though it is not clear what effect they had on the ratings.

As the war tilted in the Allies' favour, Joyce's impact waned. His last broadcast, in a voice slurred by drink though the words are quite distinct, was made from Hamburg on 30 April 1945, on the day Allied forces entered the city. It was relayed to Britain by Radio Luxembourg, which the Germans had seized at the beginning of the war. His closing words are chilling: 'Germany will live, because the people of Germany have in them the secret of life: endurance, will and purpose.'

Joyce went to the gallows an unrepentant anti-Semite. In his last hour of life, he wrote a final letter to his wife, Margaret. 'I defy the Jews who caused this last war,' he wrote, 'and I defy the power of Darkness which they represent.' He concluded by writing 'Sieg Heil!' three times.

The term 'Lord Haw-Haw' has been used since to describe radio propagandists who try to undermine enemy morale in times of crisis, usually by insinuations rather than outright lies. After Iraq's invasion of Kuwait in 1990, for example, a man on Radio Baghdad – his honeyed tones rather marred by fractured English –

sought to plant seeds of doubt in the minds of American soldiers who had just been poured into Saudi Arabia. Naturally, he made sure he touched sensitive nerves:

> 'Your children are waiting for you, your wife is waiting for you,' he was reported (in *The Times* and *Financial Times*) to have said. 'You might have a lover. She is also waiting for you. Didn't you hear that the sand heaps in the Arabian desert are moving and they swallowed many people and will swallow you? Remember what the petrol emirs are doing with the American girls. Do you want to defend them? The Sabah family is driven away by the Kuwaiti people. What is your interest in bringing these criminals back to rule?'

The Judges
Radio 4 series in 1988 in which six judges, normally a shy and retiring breed in public, spoke to Hugo Young about the law, their work and the processes of reaching judgement. One of the subjects, Lord Templeman, explained why he is called 'Sid Vicious'. Produced by ANNE SLOMAN.

Jukebox Saturday Night
Radio 2 series hosted by Dave Dee.

Julian and Sandy
Outrageous pair of queens who provided some of the risqué element on ROUND THE HORNE each week: the mincing effeminacy of Hugh Paddick's 'Hallo, I'm Julian and this is my friend Sandy' never failed to produce gales of laughter. KENNETH WILLIAMS, too, squeezed every suggestive drop from his lines and this campest of all couples coined several new words which entered the language in the mid-1960s: 'bona' (good), 'fantabulosa' (very good), 'omipaloni' (homosexual), 'bold, bold' (bold). Like the rest of the show they loved the *double entendre*: 'Hallo, we're Bona Caterers – we handle everything'. According to the show's writer BARRY TOOK, Julian and Sandy were named after Julian Slade and Sandy Wilson, each of whom wrote a popular musical, respectively *Salad Days* and *The Boyfriend*.

J and S didn't retire when the show ended: they popped up from time to time until 1987 when they made their first and last television appearance on *Terry Wogan's Christmas Show*. The duo was brought to an end by Kenneth Williams's death the following year.

Junior Bridgebuilders
Offshoot of BRIDGEBUILDERS, this was launched in 1943 on the same North American service of the BBC and with the same object – to enable the youth of Britain and the USA to meet on a 'radio bridge of understanding'. Every week a stream of boys and girls – who included

Scouts, Guides, members of Youth Clubs and the like – made their way to the BBC's studios at 200 Oxford Street and then down to the underground studios to tell of the war, and air their views on pocket money, parents and schools.

The programme started with letters from American teenagers who had been listening to the North American service and were keen to know what life was like for youngsters their own age in a Britain at war. Vernon Blose, a sixteen-year-old from Pennsylvania, wrote to the BBC: 'I would like some information on how the war affects British young people, and I would like to have an answer from a British youth about my own age.' His answer came from a fifteen-year-old boy from Southwick, Sussex, called Albert Slater, who broadcast from Oxford Street and became one of the first of hundreds of Junior Bridgebuilders.

Sometimes the children's chatter was recorded where they lived. The BBC took a 'roving microphone' to several places, including the village school at Christmas Common, Bucks, whose children sent greetings to the small community of Santa Claus, Indiana. On another occasion the choirboys of Westminster Abbey broadcast at Easter 1944 to the choirboys of the Cathedral of St John the Divine in New York, singing Handel's 'Let the Bright Seraphim' after a few words about life in a city under bombardment.

The first time that youngsters from both sides of the Atlantic were able to talk to one another on the same programme was in December 1946. Six boys and girls who belonged to the Bromsgrove Young Farmers' Club went to the studios in Birmingham to talk to children in Schenectady, New York State, from a 4-Club (Head, Heart, Hand and Health) about a topic of common interest – livestock and farming. This went out at 5.30 on a Saturday afternoon here and also on Station WGY in Schenectady, and had the distinction of being the first programme in CHILDREN'S HOUR to be broadcast simultaneously in Britain and the USA.

Junior Choice

Successor to the children's request show CHILDREN'S FAVOURITES, this made its debut on the first day of Radio 1 – Saturday, 30 September 1967, with Leslie Crowther reading a card from a Mrs Jackie Allen in Johannesburg for her four nieces and nephews in Welwyn Garden City. Since *they* were little monkeys she wanted something by The Monkees, and got it: 'Pleasant Valley Sunday'.

Introduced by its signature tune 'Morning Town Ride', by Stan Butcher, it continued to go out on both Saturday and Sunday mornings, as its predecessor had done. Despite a strong emphasis on pop, it did not neglect silly voices and outright sentimentality. It was broadcast on both Radio 1 and Radio 2, which split at 9.55 a.m. when it came to an end.

There was one key difference between the new programme and its parent. The records played on *Children's Favourites* were those which had been requested in the greatest number: the records on *Junior Choice*, although they had to be requests, were selected by a producer.

ED ('Stewpot') STEWART, who took over from Crowther, came to dominate the programme just as DEREK MCCULLOCH had done on its predecessor, and for almost exactly the same length of time. He took over in 1968 and left in 1979, during which he gained a huge following said to attain sixteen million. Records claimed to have been made into Top Ten hits by repeated exposure on the show included 'Ernie' (Benny Hill), 'Granddad' (Clive Dunn) and 'Two Little Boys' (Rolf Harris).

The first disc Stewpot ever played was Roger Whittaker's 'Early One Morning', and on that same first show he also played 'Don't Stop The Carnival' by Alan Price. This was the song he played a year or two later for Princess Margaret's two children. She visited the BBC to meet a group of disc-jockeys and he offered to play her offspring's request on the air, an offer which was gratefully accepted.

TONY BLACKBURN took over after Stewpot, but the programme had run its course and was dropped in the early 1980s.

Junkin's Jokers

Radio 2 series in 1990 in which comedy writer and actor John Junkin talked with various funny men (like Bob Monkhouse, Keith Waterhouse and RICHARD MURDOCH) about what made *them* laugh.

Just A Minute

Long-running Radio 4 panel game which began in 1967. Guests have to talk on topics ranging from 'My Ticklish Bit' to 'Eating Winkles' for sixty seconds 'without repetition, deviation or hesitation'.

The show was devised by IAN MESSITER as a successor to his ONE MINUTE, PLEASE: modifications he made included the reduction of the team from six people to four.

Regular panellists have included Clement Freud, Derek Nimmo and PETER JONES. Necessarily, they are all brilliant raconteurs. Perhaps the most popular was the late KENNETH WILLIAMS – sulky, temperamental, always challenging. After his death in 1988, his place was filled by a succession of guests starting with Wendy Richard (of *EastEnders* fame) but was eventually filled by Paul Merton.

JIMMY EDWARDS was originally invited to be the programme's chairman, but the pilot was recorded on a Sunday and he declined to give up the polo he always played on that day. Producer DAVID HATCH therefore asked Nicholas Parsons instead. He accepted, and has done it ever since. The signature tune is

The late Kenneth Williams and Clement Freud, two of the most popular and consistently witty panellists on *Just a Minute*. They are pictured here in 1969, when the show had been running two years

'The Minute Waltz' by Chopin, and the show has been exported to over fifty countries. The 24th series began in 1991 with Freud, Nimmo, Jones and Merton.

'There can be uncomfortable moments. In one programme Clement was given the subject "Beauty" and he said that in the play *Beauty and the Beast* his wife had played Beauty. Nimmo immediately challenged. "Deviation – have you seen his wife?" The audience fell about but Clement was not a little annoyed' – Kenneth Williams.

Just Before Midnight
Fifteen-minute slot for unsettling stories which were dramatised on the Light Programme in 1964. It yielded many promising writers. Among them was TOM STOPPARD, who made his radio debut with one of the first stories featured, *The Dissolution of Dominic Boot* (a farce about a man who cannot pay an ever increasing taxi fare). Other writers whose work was broadcast included Philip Levene, Frederick Bradnum, R.D. Wingfield and Jill Hyem. It was resurrected in the late 1970s and ended in 1980 with *Here Comes the Bride* by Susan Hill.

Just Fancy
Comedy series which ran from 1951–62, written by and starring ERIC BARKER, along with DERYCK GUYLER, Kenneth Connor and Pearl Hackney. Its sketches explored with gentle whimsy the foibles of human nature and the English character, and the strongest expletive seemed to be: 'Oh, my giddy aunt!'

Just For Fun
RICHARD MURDOCH played records 'he hopes will amuse you' in this Light Programme series.

Just For You
Light Programme record show on Sunday evenings, which featured David Geary playing requests.

Just Jazz
Trad, mainstream and modern jazz records featured in this Saturday evening show on the Light Programme, introduced by STEVE RACE among others.

Just Three Wishes
Revealing little Radio 4 series beginning in 1989, in which interviewer Robert Booth turned Fairy Godfather and extracted from Diane Abbott, Jo Grimond, Brian Patten, Pam Ayres, Jessie Kesson and Jeffrey Bernard the three wishes they would make if someone could only wave a magic wand.

Just William
Richmal Crompton's ageless and mud-stained schoolboy, born in a magazine story in 1919, starred in a popular dramatised series from 1945–52 with a cast that included Charles Hawtrey and PATRICIA HAYES. He gained an entirely new and equally appreciative audience from 1986 onwards, through the talents of actor Martin Jarvis who has read 25 of the short stories on Radio 4's MORNING READING slot. Time has done little to dent their popularity or dilute their sense of fun.

His latest batch of readings, in 1990, was simultaneously released by the BBC RADIO COLLECTION and reached 74 in the cassette charts. Gallup, who issue the charts, said it was so rare for a spoken word cassette to make the charts that they could not remember any previous example.

Juste, Adrian   (1947–)
Leicester-born Radio 1 DJ whose speciality, first heard on the network in 1978, is the quickfire cutting from music to comedy clips and back again (reminiscent of the late JACK JACKSON). It requires sixteen hours in the studio to put together one sixty-minute show. Prior to Radio 1 he worked at BRMB and BBC Radio Leicester.

K

Kaleidoscope

Nightly Radio 4 arts programme which began in April 1973: playwright and biographer Ronald Harwood was the first presenter. The four items in the first episode were a review by TOM STOPPARD of the World Theatre season at the Aldwych; a story about Geoffrey Moorhouse's book, *The Missionaries*; a review of BBC-TV's *Search for the Nile*; and an analytical piece about dreams by Dr Christopher Evans.

The object of the programme, instigated by the then Controller of Radio 4, TONY WHITBY, was to cover both arts and sciences. This was laudable in theory but soon recognised as an ambitious mistake in practice. As the original editor, Rosemary Hart, recalls witheringly: 'A review of the new Van Gogh Museum in Amsterdam with research on aggressive anemones, an explanation of negative ions with a review of *Save the Tiger* starring Jack Lemmon, or Chinese acrobats at the London Coliseum combined with a talk on painless dentistry, satisfied the expectations of neither the science nor the arts-orientated audiences.' The combination was therefore dropped after only one year and science coverage was switched to a new programme, SCIENCE NOW.

Kaleidoscope then developed into a fully fledged arts series, mixing conventional reviews of first nights with longer profiles (e.g. of Ingrid Bergman) and interviews (e.g. with Graham Greene) together with live transmissions of events such as the Booker and Whitbread Prizes. The programme began to feature editions from abroad, covering events like the Cannes and Berlin Film Festivals, the Frankfurt Book Fair and the PRIX ITALIA, and claims to be the first radio arts programme to record an edition from China. Architecture was covered both in a series about the great English cathedrals and in the monitoring of contemporary buildings such as the National and the Barbican, throughout their construction until the opening nights.

Harwood, Peter France and PAUL VAUGHAN were the original presenters. More than four dozen have followed. At various times, *Kaleidoscope* was given an extra fifty minute slot on Saturdays which repeated the best items of the week under the title *Encore*. In the late 1980s the programme had a daily repeat in the afternoon and was devoting at least one show a week to events in the regions.

In 1990 the programme reversed the order of origination and repeat, so that it now goes out live every afternoon and gets repeated the same evening. The point of this was to cover first nights in a more considered, less frantic way and enable a wider range of guests to get to the studio and participate. It also reflected the fact that 75 per cent of the audience listens in the afternoon, not at night.

At the same time, every day was tailored to a particular topic: books on Monday, music on Tuesday, movies on Wednesday, theatre on Thursday and visual arts on Friday.

Kavanagh, Ted (1892–1958)

Brilliant creator of COLONEL CHINSTRAP, FUNF, MRS MOPP and all the other characters of ITMA, which he wrote for ten years.

A New Zealander who came to Britain to study medicine but instead turned to writing, he was one of the first to make use of the comic possibilities offered by the new medium of radio. He teamed up with TOMMY HANDLEY, for whom he wrote humorous monologues and revues in the 1920s. This led to their years of successful co-operation on ITMA: Kavanagh the fertile inventor and fount of ideas, Handley the master of timing who made the words come alive at the microphone.

Helped to train several others in the art of comic writing, including FRANK MUIR, DENIS NORDEN and ROY PLOMLEY. A dedicated Roman Catholic, he was awarded in 1952 a knighthood of St Gregory by Pope Pius XII.

KCBC

New INCREMENTAL station for the Kettering and Corby area of Northants, broadcasting on AM and on the air since April 1990: one of the founders was Howard Rose, former editor of the magazine NOW RADIO.

Keillor, Garrison (1942–)

Writer who captured the heart of America with his gentle idylls of the town that time forgot, Lake Wobegon, loosely based on his own Minnesota childhood in a small, quiet Plymouth Brethren community in Anoka. He is one of the few modern figures to rise to national prominence through radio.

Keillor began his radio career in 1968 as a presenter of an early morning classical programme on Minnesota Public Radio, which he continued until 1982. In 1974 he helped to create a live variety show called *A Prairie Home Companion*, which later started to be broadcast nationally. Via radio he acquired the exposure and awards which enabled him to become a bestselling author, from 1985 onwards, and he is now one of the USA's highest paid and most successful writers.

Listeners in Britain have been able to hear him read three of his books on Radio 4. The poignant LAKE WOBEGON DAYS, which built his reputation, was first read as A BOOK AT BEDTIME on its UK publication in February 1986 and because of its popularity repeated as a MORNING READING the following August. *Leaving Home*, similarly, was first broadcast at bedtime in March 1988 and repeated in the mornings the following September. In July 1990 America's modern Mark Twain was back in the breakfast slot, reading a collection of his essays, poems, stories and autobiographical musings called *We Are Still Married*.

Keith, Alan (1908–)

Presenter of YOUR HUNDRED BEST TUNES and THE GOLDEN YEARS, who started his long BBC career as a variety show compere in 1936. For six years he also presented *Among Your Souvenirs*. Born a month before ALISTAIR COOKE, he is believed to be the oldest regular voice on the national airwaves.

Kelly, Barbara

See BERNARD BRADEN.

Kelner, Martin (1949–)

Freelance broadcaster, born in Manchester. He hosted Radio 5's FIVE ASIDE for its first few months and used to present a Saturday afternoon Radio 2 show. From 1985–90 he hosted Radio 2's late-night Saturday show, in succession to STEVE JONES, which was eventually dropped to make way for THE ARTS PROGRAMME. In May 1991 he became the weekend host of a live evening show on BBC local stations in the North.

Kershaw, Andy (1959–)

Rochdale-born DJ, bubbling with enthusiasm, who has used radio to foster keen interest in the world's traditional music, from that of the Soweto townships to Cajun and a cappella. Formerly Billy Bragg's tour manager, he has a weekly show on Radio 1 which began when he filled the gap created by the death of ALEXIS KORNER in 1984.

He has twice won SONY AWARDS, did much to introduce the music of the Bhundu Boys into Britain and journeyed through Mali, one of the biggest countries in West Africa, for a memorable, three-part Radio 4 series on its music and people in 1989. Younger brother of Liz.

Kershaw, Liz (1958–)

Rochdale-born DJ who co-presents Radio 1's weekend breakfast show with BRUNO BROOKES. She joined the network in 1987 to host BACKCHAT, having started in radio presenting a 'gig guide' on an ILR station in Leeds. Elder sister of Andy.

The Keys to Creativity

Four-part Radio 4 series in 1988 in which Peter Evans discussed scientific theories about the mysteries of the creative process and the true nature of 'genius'.

KFM Radio

Pirate station in Stockport in the 1980s, its name apparently drawn from part of the town's postcode, which turned legal and opened as an INCREMENTAL in February 1990. Three months later, having failed to attract listeners and advertising, the money ran out and Signal Radio, with publishers EMAP, bailed it out and took control. The station concentrates on mainstream pop music but under its promise of performance made to the IBA 30 per cent of it has to be 'local' – written or performed within ninety miles of the town. It now also broadcasts local news at breakfast.

King Cutler

Six-part Radio 3 comedy series in 1990 featuring IVOR CUTLER and singer Phyllis King.

King, Gary (1964–)

Disc-jockey who joined Radio 1 in 1990, hosting the dawn show on Saturdays and Sundays and now in the same slot five mornings a week. Previously he was a DJ in Dublin, Luxembourg and local radio and appeared as a stand-up comic at London's Comedy Store.

King Street Junior

Radio 4 sitcom about a junior school with James Grout as the headteacher, Mr Beeston. Tom Watson and Karl Howman played two of his teaching staff.

Kiss FM

London's first legal, 24-hour, black music station, which went on the air in September 1990 at the end of a £1 million advertising campaign – nearly five years after starting life as a pirate. Appropriately, the first record played on the legal station was the reggae track 'Pirate Anthem', by Shabba Ranks.

As an unlicensed station, from 1985 to 1988, it won a keen following for its music but equally close attention from the DTI. Government figures disclosed that the station was raided, on average, more than once a month during the whole three-year period of 1986 to 1988. This apparent persecution succeeded only in making the station more successful, not less, and it became a byword for style, musical chic and entrepreneurial flair.

The station's founders included South London club DJ Gordon McNamee and George Eracleous (who also founded London Greek Radio) and its studios were in the latter's home in London N19, with transmitters on various tower blocks.

In 1988 it closed down as a pirate. This was to prepare for its bid – which proved successful at its second attempt – to win one of the new INCREMENTAL licences for London. Backed financially by Virgin, the publishing group EMAP and two printing companies, Kiss started providing a legal service of non-stop soul, hip-hop, house, reggae, blues, bhangra, salsa and R&B. ('Black music' had by this time given way to the phrase 'dance music' to denote the way its appeal had widened.) It was part of Kiss FM's case that such music formed only 4 per cent of Radio 1's output, 4 per cent of Capital Radio's and 11 per cent of GLR's, so they were adding significantly to the choice available.

The best known DJs on the new station were David Rodigan, joining from Capital Radio (where his eleven-year-old *Roots Rockers* show was claimed to be the longest running reggae show in the world), Dave Pearce who joined from GLR and ROBBIE VINCENT.

Footballer John Fashanu and TONY PRINCE were on the board of directors.

Kitchen Front
Second World War series starring ELSIE AND DORIS WATERS, and to which FREDDIE GRISEWOOD also contributed.

K-Jazz London
Pirate station operating at weekends in London in the late 1980s, dedicated to jazz. Co-founder Chris Philips later joined the programme-making team of Jazz FM.

Knight, Graham (1949–)
Former Cadburys worker who joined Radio Trent in 1975, moved to BBC Radio Derby in 1983, and since 1987 has been a weekend presenter on Radio 2.

Knight and the Music
Sunday evening series on the Light Programme, with the Peter Knight Concert Orchestra, 'Knight-Ride on the Turntable' and 'Swingalong with the Knight-Caps'.

Knox-Mawer, June (1930–)
Presenter of many Radio 4 documentary programmes, from CONCERTO to locust hunters: her husband is Ronald Knox-Mawer (1925–), who spent much of his working life as a judge in Aden and Fiji and has himself been heard in Radio 4 reminiscences.

Korner, Alexis (1929–84)
Jazzman, blues guitarist and co-founder of Blues Incorporated who presented his own Radio 1 show until his death.

The Lady in the Van
ALAN BENNETT's account of his relationship with an extraordinary eccentric called Miss Shepherd who, for fifteen years, lived in the drive of his home in Camden Town, North London, in a succession of dilapidated old vans. She died in 1989 and his four-part memoir was broadcast on Radio 4 in 1990.

Lake Wobegon Days
Loving recreation of small-town America written and read in ten episodes by GARRISON KEILLOR on Radio 4 in 1986 (originally on A BOOK AT BED-TIME in the spring, but repeated that summer as a MORNING READING, when it took off). It was later released on the BBC RADIO COLLECTION, to preserve for ever on tape its vivid evocation of the pangs, pains and joys of growing up.

Landscapes in Brass
Four series on Radio 3 in 1989 devoted to brass and wind music, concentrating on the repertoire of major original work for brass bands over the last seventy years, from Hubert Bath and Gustav Holst in the 1920s to ROBERT SIMPSON and John McCabe today.

The Langham
Grand building facing BROADCASTING HOUSE in Portland Place. It reopened in 1991 as the luxury hotel which was how it began in 1864. Then, built in the style of a Florentine palace with 600 rooms, and with the Prince of Wales among 2,000 guests at its gala opening, it set the standard for all the luxury Victorian hotels which followed it. Statesmen from Napoleon III and Haile Selassie, and celebrated composers and writers such as Dvorak and Twain, all stayed here.

It declined in the 1920s and its worst moment came in 1940 when a landmine exploded outside, puncturing the hotel's 38,000-gallon water tank which flooded much of the hotel.

After the war the BBC took over the building, using it for studios and offices, but later sold the site. The new Langham Hotel, which incorporates the little town oasis known as Mr Middleton's Garden, opened in March 1991.

Laser 558
North Sea pirate radio station on the MV *Communicator*, American-owned and registered in Panama, which operated thirteen miles off the Essex coast (near Radio Caroline's position) during the mid-1980s. JOHN CATLETT was its manager. It ended its adventure when it limped into Harwich in November 1985 after being battered by gales and blockaded by a DTI vessel, which had prevented it receiving supplies from the mainland, which would have been illegal under the 1967 act (see PIRATES).

It was aboard Laser that disc-jockey CHARLIE WOLF first made a point of broadcasting standing up, which he had learned in America, and which he later took to Atlantic 252.

Last Chance to See
Unusual Radio 4 series in 1989 about disappearing species. Author DOUGLAS ADAMS and zoologist Mark Carwardine went to Indonesia (in search of the Komodo dragon), Zaire (Northern White Rhino), Mauritius (Rodrigues Fruit Bat), New Zealand, Chile and China. It proved that wildlife programmes don't have to be visual to be effective: the array of exotic sounds and vivid, on-the-spot descriptions made just as much impact.

(The trip was not, of course, financed by cost-conscious BBC Radio, but by publishers Heinemann who commissioned the pair to go and brought out their book in due course. BBC Radio asked them to tape-record their experiences, although a producer did travel out to one of the countries.)

Late Night Extra
Show which went out on both Radio 1 and Radio 2. Five presenters launched it, including BOB HOLNESS, who stayed for seven years, and BARRY ALLDIS.

Latin Quarter
Music from Central and South America was featured in this weekly Radio 2 show in 1988–89, presented by LUCY DURÁN.

Law and Disorder
Comedy actor ERIC BARKER played Mr Trodd, managing clerk in the offices of Cheetham and Dabbe, solicitors in a small English market town, in this Light Programme sitcom beginning in 1960.

The Law Game
Legal quiz game on Radio 2 chaired by Shaw Taylor and devised by Brad Ashton. Actors recreate cases and celebrities try to figure out who won, and why. It has been running since 1976.

Law in Action
Legal series which began on the Third Programme and was resumed on Radio 4 in October 1984. Marcel Berlins often presents it.

Lawson Dick, Clare (1913–90)
Controller of Radio 4, 1975–76.

LBC
Britain's first ILR station, which went on the air on 8 October 1973 with the object of providing news and talk for the capital. Now a wholly owned subsidiary of Crown Communications, which began as an Australian company but became anglicised, and is now a PLC. LBC (London Broadcasting Company) was a 24-hour station from the beginning, but when hit by financial crisis in 1975 it reduced its output to eighteen hours a day for twelve months and imposed redundancies. However, 1975 was also the year that it mounted London's first airborne traffic report service, from a helicopter. In 1977, in conjunction with IRN, it opened commercial radio's first foreign bureaux, in Rhodesia (as it still was) and Washington. In 1978, along with the BBC, it started broadcasting from Parliament.

In October 1989, almost exactly sixteen years since it began, LBC split its frequencies in common with most other ILR stations at this period. LBC Crown FM began on FM and London Talkback Radio on AM, and they openly declared their aim of poaching sizeable chunks of the Radio 4 and Radio 2 audiences respectively. Crown was to be 24 hours of news, travel information and talk, 'aimed at an upmarket, stylish and information-hungry audience' aged from 25 to 44. BRIAN WIDLAKE was poached away from BBC Radio to present the breakfast show. Jingles were abolished.

Talkback, on the other hand, was targeted at downmarket and unstylish oldies. In the company's words it aimed to be 'a warm and good-humoured station' for those women over forty and men above fifty who enjoyed 'a less hectic lifestyle'. Phone-ins, news and audience participation, along with hosts such as PETE MURRAY, STEVE JONES, Douglas Cameron and Bob Wellings, were designed to produce a style that was 'chatty, warm and informal'.

The following spring it was realised that this split had been a failure. Talkback was holding its own but the much-hyped FM service, launched with posters proclaiming 'Keep Up With The Dow Joneses' and 'Knowledge Is Power', had failed to make any inroads into its target audience. The station therefore imported a new, young director of programmes from Sydney, Charlie Cox, and pushed out its editorial director Philip Bacon. Widlake was moved to lunchtimes and a succession of starry presenters, including editors Andrew Neil and Donald Trelford, were given his slot before ANGELA RIPPON was installed. BRIAN HAYES was stripped of the morning show he had held for fourteen years and MICHAEL PARKINSON was given it for a year. Cox explained that Parky was being hired for 'his relaxed style, humour and sense of fun'. Three dozen journalists lost their jobs in enforced redundancies, and the name of the FM service was changed from LBC Crown FM to LBC Newstalk.

Learning to Listen
Five-part Radio 4 FM series in 1989 on counselling, made by the same team (including presenter Dr Tony Lake) responsible for ROOM TO LISTEN, ROOM TO TALK.

Leave It To The Boys
Bob Monkhouse and Denis Goodwin wrote and presented this Light Programme comedy series in 1960. June Whitfield, Max Wall and Dick Bentley were also in it.

Leave Your Name and Number
Comedy series starring BERNARD BRADEN and BARBARA KELLY, on the Light Programme in 1950. Its plot was based on the idea of two Canadian performers trying to get work in London, a semi-autobiographical notion they had evolved when they made a pilot of it in 1949. The scripts (by their fellow countryman Eric Nicol) made much of the novelty, to Canadians, of rationing and poor food. Miriam Karlin, Lyn Evans and NORMAN SHELLEY were also in the cast.

Lee, Dave (1930–)
Pianist with John Dankworth's orchestra, and accompanist to Judy Garland, who composed the signature tunes for *That's Life* and I'M SORRY I'LL READ THAT AGAIN before launching his campaign for a London jazz station in 1980. Ten years later and Jazz FM was on the air. Lee had about 25 per cent of the shares and became the station's first director of music, the final arbiter of what was jazz and what wasn't. Not

Like various other performers before and since, Bernard Braden and his wife Barbara Kelly once made a series in which they played themselves. They were two newly arrived Canadians trying to break into showbusiness in *Leave Your Name and Number*, on the Light Programme in 1950

everyone agreed with his ideas of what was, however, and the station was hard hit by the recession. When it made a third of its staff redundant in early 1991, Lee stepped down as well.

'Left hand down a bit'
Catchphrase from THE NAVY LARK.

Legal, Decent, Honest and Truthful
Poking fun at advertising in this comedy series were Miriam Margolyes, Martin Jarvis and Sally Grace.

Leicester Sound
ILR station for Leics, on the air since 1984. In 1988 it split itself in two. GEM-AM, a golden oldie service which is also on Radio Trent, goes out on medium wave, and Sound-FM broadcasts contemporary pop on FM.

Lenin of the Rovers
Alexei Sayle played midfield maestro Ricky Lenin in Britain's only communist football team in this Radio 4 soccer sitcom from the 1980s. Ricky's teammates included Terry Trotsky and Stevie Stalin; John Sessions played a seedy hack working for the 'Daily Tits'; and Kenneth Wolstenholme, ex-sports commentator, played a sports commentator.

Actors Ballard Berkeley (who also played Col Danby in THE ARCHERS) and Maurice Colbourne both made their last radio appearances on the programme.

Lennox, Mike (1941–)
Former actor from Canada (he had appeared in *The Bedford Incident* and *Dr Who and the Daleks*) who was part of Radio 1's original line-up of DJs in 1967. He later returned to his native land to be a stockbroker.

Lent Observed
Six talks on Radio 4 in 1991 in which journalists with a personal faith, including JAMES NAUGHTIE and Mary Kenny, each reflected in a different way on the story of Christ's Passion.

Lent Talks
Six talks on Radio 4 during Lent, nearly always given by Christians: in 1990, however, all six were non-Christians and they reflected on the Easter story in the light of their own lives and experiences. Speakers included Dr Marietta Higgs (the controversial Cleveland paediatrician); Jill Morrell (friend of Beirut hostage John McCarthy); and Chapman Pincher (author and scourge of spies).

Let The People Sing
Amateur choral contest run by the BBC from 1957, broadcast on the Home Service.

Let's Find Out
Teenagers, nominated by their schools or youth clubs and then handpicked at auditions, asked polite questions of prominent figures such as judge Lord Birkett, astronomer Patrick Moore and *Daily Express* chief foreign correspondent Rene MacColl in this Light Programme series chaired by Peter Haigh.

Let's Spend Some Time Together
Three-part Radio 1 series in 1989 on The Rolling Stones, past and present, as they spent their 27th year together as a rock band. NICKY CAMPBELL interviewed Mick Jagger, Keith Richards, Bill Wyman and Ronnie Wood.

Letter From ...
Weekly Radio 4 series starting in 1990 which adapts the LETTER FROM AMERICA formula – a relaxed, intimate style emphasising people as much as politics – for other places in the world. A different BBC foreign correspondent delivers a talk in similar vein to that of

ALISTAIR COOKE: thus Mark Tully has delivered a Letter From Calcutta, Ben Bradshaw a Letter From Berlin and Stephen Jessel a despatch from England, Arkansas. As with its parent programme, each talk is fifteen minutes long.

Letter From America

One of Radio 4's most venerated and admired programmes, and one that has changed the least. ALISTAIR COOKE started this weekly talk in March 1946 and has never missed a single programme since. Usually written in New York, though sometimes in San Francisco or Vermont, they have covered all aspects of American life, and are celebrated as much for their precise, pithy, elegant prose as for the perceptive insights they offer with regard to life in the world's most powerful country and human affairs more generally.

The programme stemmed from a Sunday evening talk Cooke gave during the Second World War, *American Commentary*. After the war he was asked by the BBC to continue giving a weekly talk − not so political, but about anything and everything American. The BBC did not envisage a long run. Thirteen programmes were commissioned: more than 2,200 have now been broadcast.

From the days of *American Commentary* nearly half-a-century ago, Cooke has consistently refused to play up to stereotyped images. Lazy prejudices, unsupported by honest observation, have had no place in his reporting. An eloquent statement of his philosophy in this respect is contained in a letter he wrote in January 1943 to a BBC talks executive, John Pringle, after he had been criticised for a talk on Williamsburg. What Cooke said is as true today as it was then:

'I would say that I simply cannot bring myself to satisfy British preconceptions about America. I know it's difficult − when an audience expects a talk on Texas, say, to be about cowboys and buffaloes − to tell them that the best domestic architecture in the country is in the housing estates at Houston, and that there are no more buffaloes at large ... for the same reason, I think Britain loses valuable respect here by having people go on describing it in terms of fox-hunting, Wedgwood, and the village pub.

'Mrs Miniver, from this point of view, did Britain here incalculable harm by describing with perfect fidelity a tiny minority of the English and implying (for Americans at least) that this was Britain today, that these were the people of Sheffield and Liverpool, patronized and cowed by a decorative but inflexible county aristocracy.

'I can imagine nothing more mischievous to real understanding (for those who want it) than "light" talks about America of the wrong kind − i.e. talks which superficially repeat all the preconceptions about a place or person that the listening audience is likely to hold.'

Cooke always types his talk on a manual typewriter, usually on a Thursday in his Fifth Avenue apartment. He then goes into the BBC's New York studios, further south down Fifth Avenue, and dictates it on Thursday afternoon. It is flown to London and broadcast on Radio 4 on Friday evening, with a repeat on Sunday morning. After that it goes out on the BBC World Service. Cooke has had appreciative letters from listeners in more than forty countries.

Although the Letters are usually taped in the studio, illness has forced Cooke to do one or two in his study over the years and three from hospital.

'My personal interest, not to say obsession, is no different from what it was 40 years ago, which is to learn to write for talking effectively to the largest possible audience. I am not being coy in saying that I am still learning to handle an idiom that can be understood by English-speaking people of every type and class and race in many countries.

'No pleasure in work well done, in a lifetime of journalism, can compare with the evidence that comes in from the mail that you have done a talk that touched the hearts and minds of a bus driver in Dorset, a judge in Canberra, a student in Bombay, a housewife in Yorkshire, a space scientist in Sri Lanka, a high school teacher in Beijing or a nurse in Libya' − Alistair Cooke, giving *The Listener* Lecture, 1990.

Lewis, C.S.   (1898–1963)

Influential Christian philosopher, writer and don (Fellow of Magdalen College, Oxford, 1925–54) whose eight radio talks on *Christian Behaviour* in the autumn of 1942 stirred much interest. His most famous children's story, *The Lion, The Witch and The Wardrobe* was adapted for radio in 1959. Both that and his *The Magician's Nephew* went out in 1987 on SCHOOLS RADIO and were repeated as a CAT'S WHISKERS summer special on Radio 4 in 1989.

Lewis, Cecil   (1898–)

First World War pilot and author who was one of the four founding fathers of the BBC, before moving to Hollywood and becoming a scriptwriter.

Lewis Smith, Victor   (1961–)

Prankster with a brilliant gift for mimicry and music, a savage wit and an evident need to cause upset and outrage. A music graduate of York University, he spent three years as a producer of talk shows on Radio 4, becoming notorious as the man who hired Cockney comedian Arthur Mullard to stand in for LIBBY PURVES on MIDWEEK and who encouraged Ruby Wax to scream on START THE WEEK. Eventually he was sacked. Later, he contributed to LOOSE ENDS.

He gained yet more attention when, in 1989, he telephoned Radio 4's annual phone-in to its Controller, gave a false name ('Harold Coltart') and savaged MICHAEL GREEN – who was as much deceived by the call as everyone else on the programme – for broadcasting the soap opera CITIZENS.

In 1990 he had a late-night comedy series on Radio 1, called simply *Victor Lewis Smith*, which was officially billed as 'a unique combination of surrealism and bad taste' and preceded by an on-air warning that some listeners might find it offensive. The show, in which Lewis Smith was responsible for all the voices as well as the incidental music, blended jokes about soiled underpants, unflushable faeces, Chinese takeaways and one-fingered Jewish gynaecologists with spoof telephone calls made to Harrods shop assistants, security guards, receptionists and broadcasters, in which he gave false names and tape-recorded mocking conversations without the victims' knowledge and then broadcast them without their consent.

This was in breach not only of the BBC's guidelines but also his own contract with the BBC, in which he had promised to obtain permission from those whom he hoaxed. Two of his interviewees (including a BBC receptionist) complained formally to the BBC which resulted in Lewis Smith's executive producer, JOHN WALTERS, having to intervene and ask those hoaxed if the calls could be broadcast.

'Surreal, macabre and downright tasteless' – BBC publicity description of his sense of humour.

Lidell, Alvar (1908–81)

Announcer who worked at the BBC from 1932 to 1969 and announced some of the century's most momentous items, including the Abdication of King Edward VIII and the broadcast by Neville Chamberlain on the morning of 3 September 1939, telling the British people they were now at war with Germany. Despite the received English and quintessentially BBC voice, he had a Swedish grandfather and began as a singer.

Life of Bliss

George Cole starred in this popular comedy series, in which PERCY EDWARDS played a dog called Psyche.

A Life of Song

Six-part Radio 2 series in 1989 on Wally Ridley, a lifelong servant of the British music industry who helped to discover Vera Lynn.

Life With Lederer

Five-part Radio 4 series in 1990 in which entertainer Helen Lederer revealed her recipes, intended to be wise and witty, for coping with life's pitfalls.

The Queen's English was never more safe than in the hands of, and at the microphone of, Alvar Lidell. As with a number of other BBC announcers, he started his professional life as a singer

Life with the Lyons

Slick, quick, popular Light Programme sitcom with a difference: it featured a real, not fictional, family. American actors BEN LYON (who had starred in films like *Hell's Angels* alongside Jean Harlow) and BEBE DANIELS (known for stage musicals such as *Rio Rita*) came to Britain in 1935, when they had already been married for five years and basked in the title of 'Hollywood's happiest married couple'.

They decided to settle in London, raise a family and make their careers here: *Life with the Lyons*, written by Bebe and broadcast throughout the 1950s, gave listeners an insight into their lives and in particular the upbringing of their children Richard and Barbara. The couple's comic style was a kind of crosstalk similar to that of their compatriots George Burns and Gracie Allen.

In the story, the couple had a maid-housekeeper called Aggie Macdonald. She was played by Molly Weir, who

Life with the Lyons **was the most celebrated example of the phenomenon of performers playing themselves and using their real-life family relationships to underpin their comedy. Left to right: daughter Barbara, son Richard, mother Bebe Daniels and father Ben Lyon**

outside the series became famous for her recipes. Collins published a book of them in 1960.

Lift Up Your Hearts
Five-minute Christian reflection which was usually broadcast twice at breakfast time on weekdays on the Home Service. It came into being in December 1939 in response to listeners' requests for a brief thought for the day in the early morning, and continued through war and peace until 1965. It was then replaced by TEN TO EIGHT which, by contrast, was no longer exclusively Christian in content.

Light Programme
Inaugurated in 1945 by NORMAN COLLINS as the peacetime successor to the Forces Programme, this continued the same mixture of broad comedy and light music (and RADIO NEWSREEL) which had proved hugely popular for much of the Second World War. It changed its name to Radio 2 on 30 September 1967 though the essential mix continued, and does to this day.

Lighten Our Darkness
Fifteen-minute programme of evening prayers, sometimes with the BBC Northern Singers, which went out late on Saturdays on the Home Service.

Lights Out
Friday evening show which used to bring the curtain down on Fridays on the Light Programme.

Lilliburlero
Familiar throughout the world as a clarion call of the World Service, calling the faithful to the loudspeaker, this has been the signature tune of the English Service (where it immediately precedes the hourly news bulletins) since November 1943. Earlier that year it had

briefly been used as the signature tune of the Chinese Service, incongruous as that may now seem.

The music's origins are unknown, but it has been attributed to Purcell and was set to words by Orangemen in Ulster for use as a marching song.

Limb, Sue (–)
Author noted for her idiosyncratic comic inventions on Radio 4 such as UP THE GARDEN PATH, THE WORDSMITHS OF GORSEMERE and the Cromwellian comedy THE SIT-CROM.

Line, Frances (1940–)
First woman Controller of Radio 2, taking over in January 1990, having worked her way up the network from being a £6-a-week secretary typing letters for the producers of SATURDAY CLUB and EASY BEAT in 1957.

Worked as a producer in the 1960s and 1970s and was described by SHE magazine as 'the earth mother of the folk revival' for having launched FOLK ON FRIDAY – whose presenter, JIM LLOYD, she later married.

Became Radio 2's head of music in 1985 and fashioned a music policy based on melody, familiarity, excellence and breadth, aimed closely at the core audience of over-45s. Previously, she said, Radio 2 had been 'trying to entertain everyone, from 25 to dead'.

As controller, she axed ROUND MIDNIGHT and ADRIAN LOVE and introduced THE ARTS PROGRAMME, JAZZ PARADE, SOUNDS OF THE FIFTIES and the monthly CLAIRE RAYNER series about coping with traumas such as bereavement and cancer. She also resurrected RADIO 2 BALLROOM

Lines From My Grandfather's Forehead
Fine comedy sketch series starring Ronnie Barker.

Listen On Saturday
Fifteen-minute musical programme for the under-fives which went out on Saturday afternoons on the Home Service.

Listen to Britain
Golden weddings, fittings at a gentlemen's outfitters in Malvern and trips to Asda superstores were among the varied rituals reflected in this five-part Radio 4 series of contemporary sound portraits in 1990.

Listen to this Space
Nicholas Parsons hosted this Light Programme comedy series of the mid-1960s, written mainly by Anthony Marriott and Alistair Foot – years before they hit the jackpot with *No Sex Please We're British*, which became the longest running comedy in theatre history.

Listen with Mother
Few radio memories come as misty-eyed as this: no other signature tune evokes the warmth and tenderness of childhood security as powerfully as the Berceuse from Fauré's Dolly Suite. The opening words 'Are you sitting comfortably? Then I'll begin . . . ' have become so much a part of the language that they are now in the *Oxford Dictionary of Quotations*, commemorating one of the most widely known and best loved programmes in broadcasting history.

A fifteen-minute programme of stories, songs and nursery rhymes for children under five, it began in 1950. At the peak of its popularity a few years later, in its traditional slot of a quarter to two just before WOMAN'S HOUR, the audience was over one million. Later on, it was shunted round the schedules and ended up on FM only at the much less convenient time of 10.30 in the morning. Little wonder that its audience fell to below 50,000, the justification used by the BBC to switch it off for good in September 1982. This act was carried out in defiance of 400 protest letters, numerous petitions (one of them signed by 2,000 people and another by 27 professors of education pleading for it to be spared) and a campaign joined by Alan Ayckbourn, Glenda Jackson, John Cleese and MPs of all parties.

The last story ever heard was *Wriggly Worm and the Stick Insect* by Eugenie Summerfield. The pair who presented the programme for the last seven years of its existence, and brought the curtain down with a final chorus of 'Jelly on a Plate', were Nerys Hughes and Tony Aitken. Those most closely associated with the programme in its golden years were Julia Lang, Daphne Oxenford (who presented it for 21 years) and Dorothy Smith (who read the stories for 26 years).

It was replaced by a five-minute slot, on FM only, called LISTENING CORNER.

The Listener
Energetically championed by REITH, the BBC's second oldest magazine was launched in January 1929 to capture the fugitive word in print, as its mission was later described. The transcripts of broadcast talks were later augmented by arts reviews, literary pages and general features, but in 1991 it fell victim to dwindling circulation.

The first editor, in charge until 1939, was Richard Lambert. His successors were: Alan Thomas (1939–1958), Maurice Ashley (1958-67), Karl Miller (1967–74), George Scott (1974–78), Anthony Howard (1979–81), RUSSELL TWISK (1981–87), Alan Coren (1987–89) and Peter Fiddick (1989–91). In 1981 Richard Gott, features editor of *The Guardian*, was chosen as editor but the appointment was cancelled after intervention from MI5, on the grounds that he had 'ultra-Leftist' sympathies. Twisk therefore got the job instead.

Julia Lang, one of the main presenters of *Listen with Mother*. It ran for thirty-two years until, despite strong and sorrowful protest, the BBC brought it to an end in 1982

The magazine's circulation fell from a peak of over 150,000 a week in the 1950s to 79,000 in 1979 and 17,000 in 1990. When ITV withdrew from the joint ownership set up in 1988, the BBC decided it could not shoulder on its own the magazine's annual losses of £1 million, and closed it down. The last issue was in January 1991.

Listeners Answer Back
Light Programme's answer to ANY QUESTIONS?, which ran from 1961.

Listening Corner
Radio 4's successor to LISTEN WITH MOTHER.

Listening to . . .
Monthly programme on Radio 3, introduced in 1990, in which Michael Hall (who also presents many of the music editions of THIRD EAR) illuminates the complexities of a particular composer's work. He began with Stravinsky.

Literary Consequences
An entertaining if not wholly successful experiment on Radio 4 in 1990, this consisted of a late-night thriller serial, *Dead of Night*, each of whose five episodes was written by a different author.

In order they were Colin Forbes, Jack Higgins, Ken Follett, Ted Allbeury (who used to own the pirate ship Radio 390 on a disused fort in the Thames estuary) and Craig Thomas. Forbes's only instructions were to weave in three ingredients (a copper bracelet, a lake and a twelve-year-old boy) and he opened with a car explosion and murder in a lonely part of Suffolk. Each writer added his own ingredients, picking up where the last one left off, and the result was a dense jungle of treachery, intrigue, revenge, MI5, the IRA, terrorists, twin girls and butterfly tattoos. The hero, however, came through with credibility intact: Chief Inspector Roy Conway, whose investigation of the killing sent him hacking his way through much tangled undergrowth to a denouement in Berlin.

This literary device, although the BBC was apparently unaware of it at the time, had been used on radio on several previous occasions. In 1930 there was *Behind the Screen*, in which six authors took part – Hugh Walpole, Agatha Christie, Dorothy L. Sayers, Anthony Berkeley, E.C. Bentley and Ronald Knox. Each of them read his or her own instalment, and the audience was invited to send in their own solutions to the mystery to the editor of THE LISTENER. The idea for the venture came from J.R. Ackerley, one of the magazine's executives. In 1931 this was followed by a similar serial called *The Scoop*, with Clemence Dane and Freeman Wills Croft replacing Knox and Walpole.

During the Second World War, while GEORGE ORWELL was working as a talks producer on what is now the BBC World Service, he too devised and organised a serial in which each of the five parts was written by a different person. *Story by Five Authors*, set in London in the Blitz of 1940, was broadcast at weekly intervals during October and November 1942. Each author read his own instalment. In order they were Orwell himself, L.A.G. Strong, Inez Holden, Martin Armstrong and E.M. Forster. Orwell confessed disappointment with the experiment, but the story (at least on the printed page) is taut and easy to follow, since it is set in only one place and has only three main characters.

The device was resurrected again in 1964 with a Light Programme serial called *Follow That Man*. DAVID JACOBS starred as a BBC producer, Rex Anthony, caught up in a mysterious train of events. Once more, each of the episodes was written by a different writer, starting with EDWARD J. MASON. They included JOHN P. WYNN, Ted Willis, Bob Monkhouse, FRANK MUIR and DENIS NORDEN. Script editor was GALE PEDRICK.

Literary Walks

Radio 4 series in which writers discuss their books in the localities described in them, for example Alan Sillitoe in Nottinghamshire.

Literature is My Mistress – Medicine My Wife

Cumbersome title for Radio 4's seven-part biography in 1990 of Anton Chekov, a playwright (and doctor) who had many mistresses quite apart from books. David Suchet played him and MAURICE DENHAM his tyrannical father, Pavel, with Janet Suzman as Olga Knipper, the actress who became his wife.

The Litmus Test

Lively, interesting and entertaining Radio 4 panel game on science, which makes one realise how little popular physics, chemistry, astronomy, zoology and so on there is on radio.

Questions which have been asked include: 'Why do polar bears not eat penguins?' and 'Roughly how much red phosphorous is in a match head?' (None – the red phosphorous is in the strip on the side of the box.)

Little Blighty on the Downs

Satirical look at Thatcherite Britain which occupied the WEEK ENDING slot during its summer breaks at the end of the 1980s. The village of Little Blighty was a not hugely subtle symbol of Dear Old Blighty as a whole; its parish council was the Tory government in miniature; the chairman of the council was a Mrs Roberts, which just happens to be Margaret Thatcher's maiden name. It starred Jo Kendall.

Living With . . .

Radio 4 series in 1989 in which close colleagues of the first four postwar Prime Ministers talked to Peter Jenkins about them.

Living With Betty

Radio 2 comedy series about the ups and downs of two people, Betty and Bill (Barbara Windsor and Glynn Edwards). It was written by Arline Whittaker.

The Living World

Always made in Bristol for Radio 4, this started out as a monthly wildlife programme in 1966 and turned weekly three years later, continuing like that until 1987 (during which time it spawned THE NATURAL HISTORY PROGRAMME). Today, it usually goes out in two series a year and is based on one of its original ingredients, nature trails, with programmes taking the form of guided walks with a little added science and ecology. The presenters most closely associated with the programme have been, and still are, Peter France and Derek Jones.

Lloyd, A.L. (Bert) (1908–82)

Self-taught Londoner who spent much of his life searching out folk songs in different parts of the world, from the sweaty shearing sheds of New South Wales to whaling songs learned when he was a deckhand in the South Atlantic, and who used radio to make them much more widely known.

He worked on *Picture Post* from 1938–50 and at the beginning of that period co-wrote BBC Radio's *The Shadow of the Swastika*, a propaganda series dramatising the rise of Nazi Germany. As a freelance folklorist after 1950, he became an authority on and singer of folk music from many countries.

He gave radio talks on the music of the countries he had visited, from Argentina to Romania, and used folk songs to illustrate talks on historical subjects, such as Nelson. He collaborated with CHARLES PARKER on some of his RADIO BALLADS, including *The Ballad of John Axon* (1958), *Song of a Road* (1959) and *Singing the Fishing* (1960). Lloyd also wrote travel programmes for schools in the 1950s and 1960s and worked as a translator. With his wife Charlotte he translated Brecht's *Mother Courage*, broadcast on the Third Programme in 1955.

His programme *The Folk-Song Virtuoso* on the Third Programme in 1966, presenting outstanding singers and instrumentalists from all over the world, attained cult status. Bootlegged copies circulated for years afterwards. In 1990, Radio 3 at last got round to repeating the programme, whose contents ranged from a double-voiced singer from Mongolia to the lament of a Gaelic fisherman in Connemara.

Lloyd, Jim (1932–)

Former actor and Tyne Tees announcer who started to arrange folk concerts and is now Britain's leading broadcaster on folk music, presenting Radio 2's FOLK ON FRIDAY (1970–80) and then FOLK ON 2 (from 1980 onwards).

On Radio 4 he wrote and presented (in 1985) a ten-part series on this century's folk revival, *Music from the People*, and has also presented a folk series on the BBC World Service called *Musical Islands*. Is a former director of the English Folk Dance and Song Society. Married to FRANCES LINE, whom he met shortly before they made *Folk on Friday* together.

Lloyd, John (1951–)

Best known for award-winning television comedy (he started *Not The Nine O'Clock News*, was first producer of *Blackadder* and a founder of *Spitting Image*) but, like so many, took his first steps in radio. Joining the BBC as a radio producer in 1974, he made about 400 shows, including much of QUOTE . . . UNQUOTE, THE NEWS HUDDLINES and THE NEWS QUIZ.

The Local Network

Conceived as a national showcase for the work of BBC Local Radio, this began on Radio 4 in April 1986 and ended in 1991. Paul Heiney was the first presenter, but was succeeded the following year by Neil Walker and David Clayton. It was made in the studios of BBC Radio Newcastle and tackled some unusual topics, among them silence, walls, tunnels, school songs and public toilets.

Lofthouse, Marjorie (1944–)

Birmingham-based presenter of a variety of Radio 4 programmes. In 1984 she started an annual competition to find Britain's most enterprising small businesses (see ENTERPRISE) and since 1988 has presented PRELUDE on Sunday mornings. She has also hosted Midlands editions of WOMAN'S HOUR, and is seen on television.

London Calling

The magazine sent out to the four corners of the world for listeners to the BBC World Service. The magazine started in September 1939, taking its title from the original way in which the BBC used to call up the five areas of the world which took the Empire Service from 1932 onwards: 'This is London calling . . . the Australasian region', and so on.

The magazine was produced continuously throughout the years of the Second World War, its elegance and literacy a lasting tribute to those who worked on it. When surface mail became regarded as too unreliable in 1957, an airmail edition on flimsy paper was introduced. When that became too expensive, it turned into a monthly magazine, printed on normal paper, in 1963.

London Greek Radio

Former pirate station in North London, co-founded by Cypriot-born George Eracleous (a club DJ whose stage name was George Power) who also co-founded Kiss FM. During its pirate years from 1983–88 it was raided about 300 times by the DTI, almost certainly a record, and in 1988 was fined £14,000 – the largest fine ever imposed on an unlicensed station.

Like many pirates, it voluntarily closed down in 1988 in order to turn legal and won the INCREMENTAL franchise for Haringey jointly with WNK, going on the air in November 1989.

Today it broadcasts Greek music and news for eleven hours a day, in the mornings, early evenings and small hours. WNK is on the air for the other thirteen hours, although one of those thirteen hours is given over to Turkish programmes following representations made by the Turkish community that they wanted airtime too.

London Greek Radio's main audience is found in the Haringey, Camden, Edmonton and Enfield areas of North London. In early 1991 it had plans to launch its first non-Greek programme, going out in English for the younger Cypriots in its audience who have not grown up with fluency in the language of their parents.

London Lights

Wednesday evening show on the Light Programme with a variety of comperes from 1958–62 introducing 'the stars, the music, the discoveries, the shows' – exciting stuff which tended to mean TEDDY JOHNSON, Jon Pertwee, Rawicz and Landauer and so on.

London Royal

Soap opera on the BBC World Service set in a fictional, four-star family hotel overlooking Hyde Park. Kim Braden (daughter of BERNARD BRADEN) played a chambermaid. It ran from 1984.

The Long Hot Satsuma

Brisk Radio 2 sketch show with Barry Cryer, Graeme Garden and Alison Steadman, which began in 1989.

Long, Janice (1955–)

Liverpool-born former Laker Airways hostess who started in radio in 1980 as a station assistant on BBC Radio Merseyside, eventually hosting her own show for teenagers called *Street Life*.

She came south as Radio 1's second woman DJ in 1983, but resigned acrimoniously in 1988 when she was offered a less attractive slot, which would have moved her from weekdays to weekends, on her return from maternity leave. She joined GLR as breakfast presenter in 1989 and has been heard as a contributor to series on Radios 4 and 5.

A Long, Long Tale A-Winding

Six-part Radio 4 FM series in 1990 in which Michael Barber examined the attractions and characteristics of serial novels, such as Anthony Powell's *A Dance to the Music of Time* and Lawrence Durrell's *The Alexandria Quartet*.

Long Wave

Broadcasts in the range 148.5 to 283.5 kHz. Radio 4 goes out on long wave (on the frequency once used by the old Light Programme), as does Atlantic 252. See also AM.

Looking Eastwards to the Sea

Rich, engrossing account, told in six parts on Radio 4 in 1990 by John Keay, of the pioneering voyages of the East India Company for spices.

Looking Forward to the Past

Light, seven-part Radio 4 history series in 1990 in which chairman Robert Booth and his guests talked on topics ranging from Henry VIII's sex life to Oscar Wilde's last words.

Loose Ends

Full of braying, brittle young voices and a chic metropolitan flavour, this Saturday morning talk show has now been running on Radio 4 since 1985. Ex-producer

Ian Gardhouse recalls that it was created simply to fill the gap left by the move of PICK OF THE WEEK from Saturday to Sunday.

NED SHERRIN has always chaired the proceedings (apart from once when impressionist Rory Bremner stepped in – he was so good that no-one spotted the difference) with a group of laughing acolytes who have included Craig Charles, Carol Thatcher, Robert Elms, Victoria Mather, Emma Freud and VICTOR LEWIS SMITH.

Although originally conceived as a filler, the show quickly acquired a cult following and was perceived

Ned Sherrin Rools – sometimes – on *Loose Ends*, although his pupils continue to show off. Red Saunders's picture of the 1988 class for the cover of *Radio Times* shows Craig Charles (catapult), Richard Jobson (whites), John Walters (rugby ball), Robert Elms (pouting), Victor Lewis Smith (boater), Victoria Mather (applying make-up) and Emma Freud (averting face)

as the spearhead of Radio 4's attempts to woo the yuppie audience. Sir Antony Jay, co-author of *Yes, Minister*, is also associated with it: he appeared on the first programme, the 100th and the 200th.

Sherrin does not, incidentally, write his opening monologue buzzing with waspish puns. This is the work of Pete Sinclair, main writer on *Spitting Image* and co-author of AT HOME WITH THE HARDYS.

'This programme often seems to me a bit like Plato's Symposium: a forum where bright young things are encouraged to show off by a disreputable old philosopher with a penchant for saucy questions' – Sue Limb.

Lord Haw-Haw
See WILLIAM JOYCE.

The Lord Of The Rings
One of the longest and most ambitious pieces of drama ever mounted on radio, this 26-part adaptation (by Brian Sibley and Michael Bakewell) of J.R.R. Tolkien's epic account of the struggle to save Middle Earth from the Dark Lord was broadcast on Radio 4 in 1981.

Ian Holm played Frodo, Michael Hordern Gandalf, Robert Stephens Aragorn and John Le Mesurier Bilbo Baggins. It was repeated, this time in thirteen 55-minute episodes, in 1982.

Loss, Joe   (1909–90)
Britain's best known and most enduring bandleader also broadcast regularly from the 1930s, and appeared on MUSIC WHILE YOU WORK during the Second World War. Vera Lynn made her radio debut on one of his programmes. She was introduced to him by Wally Ridley, whose story was told in Radio 2's A LIFE OF SONG.

Lott, Mona
Gloomy woman in ITMA. Anyone called Mona Lott might moan a lot, and she did. Hence her ironic catchphrase: 'IT'S BEING SO CHEERFUL THAT KEEPS ME GOING!' She was always played by Joan Harben. Political gossip of a later generation had it that Mrs Thatcher's influential press chief Bernard Ingham gave the nickname to former Foreign Secretary Francis Pym, whom he allegedly sought to undermine.

Louder than Words
Radio 4 series in 1989 in which Peter Jenkins interviewed six top people on the extent to which they had the power to translate words into action. They included the Chairman of British Telecom and the Secretary General of the European Commission.

Love, Adrian   (1944–)
Son of bandleader Geoff Love, and a veritable radio nomad. Started as a DJ on the pirate station Radio

William Joyce, pictured in his adopted homeland of Nazi Germany in March 1940, at the height of his infamous career as 'Lord Haw-Haw'. His talks exercised a strange fascination on wartime Britain and millions listened in regularly

City in 1966; moved in 1967 to the Light Programme, presenting IT'S ONE O'CLOCK; then stints on the BBC World Service and LBC; then five years as host of Capital Radio's *Open Line*. (He had a weekly spot advising callers on their emotional and sexual problems: unfortunately, as he was candid enough to reveal on the air one day, his own marriage broke up at the same time. 'It's a case of "physician, heal thyself",' was his wry comment.)

Went to Radio 1 in 1980 to develop and host STUDIO B15, TALKABOUT, MAIL BAG and ROUNDTABLE, after which he freelanced for BFBS.

He started presenting a regular weekday afternoon show on Radio 2 in 1987: nicknamed 'Love in the Afternoon', it claimed to play more records per hour than any other programme on Radio 2. Such productivity, however, did not prevent it from being axed by new broom FRANCES LINE when she took over in 1990. She seized his slot for a new series in which stage, screen and recording stars, the first being Howard Keel, presented their own choice of discs for a week at a time.

Love, who also devised Radio 2's TIME CYCLE show, went back to local radio – playing golden oldies on County Sound's breakfast show and also presenting a weekend programme on Fox FM.

Lunt, Patrick (1949–)
Announcer and presenter (e.g. of NIGHT RIDE) on Radio 2.

Lustgarten, Edgar (1907–78)
Prolific writer on homicide whose extreme enthusiasm for the subject manifested itself with the reconstruction of dozens of courtroom dramas in which, displaying some talent for mimicry, he played all the parts. Not for nothing was he known as 'Mr Murder'.

Although his first broadcast work was *Police Call*, an adaptation of a Georges Simenon story (Home Service, 1951), most of his output was in the 1960s and early 1970s – dramatic reconstructions of trials and macabre criminal cases in a succession of series on the Home Service carrying titles such as *The Great Defender*, *Advocate Extraordinary*, *The Charge is Murder* and *Accused in the Box*. To ring the changes, he also reconstructed some famous spy cases in a Light Programme series of 1964, *The Faceless Ones*.

Lyon, Ben (1901–79)
American film actor who later became a radio star. He and his wife BEBE DANIELS, who had also started in silent movies, divided their time in the 1930s between Hollywood and London. They arrived back in the UK in the fateful summer of 1939 and stayed in London through the worst days of the Blitz, during which they presented the hit show HI, GANG!. They followed this with LIFE WITH THE LYONS which also featured their two children, Richard and Barbara.

Lyttelton, Humphrey (1921–)
Old Etonian, ex-Grenadier Guardsman trumpeter and bandleader who ranks as the grand old man of radio jazz. He started presenting his first radio show in 1950. Went on to host THE JAZZ SCENE and now spins jazz records every Monday evening on Radio 2 in a slot called *The Best of Jazz*. Also chairs I'M SORRY I HAVEN'T A CLUE.

M

Macaulay, Dame Rose (1881–1958)
Novelist, writer and broadcaster (notably on THE CRITICS) who was also radio critic on *Time and Tide*.

McCartney on McCartney
Ambitious Radio 1 series in 1989, consisting of eight one-hour programmes, in which the ex-Beatle and hugely successful songwriter and rock performer talked to MIKE READ about his life, from his Liverpool childhood, through the years of Beatlemania to the era of Wings. It also played virtually every McCartney hit in recent years.

McCulloch, Derek (1897–1967)
The voice of Larry the Lamb and much more besides: a revered presenter who will forever have a place in the hearts of the children who grew up with him and raced home from school to listen to his CHILDREN'S HOUR.

Although the victim of serious injury (losing a lung and an eye in the Great War and a leg in a road accident in 1938) he enjoyed a solid, successful BBC career, joining it as an announcer in 1926, becoming an Organiser of *Children's Hour* in 1933 and its director in 1938. His golden age as UNCLE MAC followed.

In the Second World War he started his practice of finishing the programme with the words 'Goodnight children – everywhere', whose emphasis on the last word was a simple act of companionship for an audience that was so scattered: evacuees in the countryside, boys and girls in bombed cities and others yet to be freed in occupied Europe.

Although he left the BBC in 1950, he returned in 1954 to host CHILDREN'S FAVOURITES, live every Saturday morning, for the next ten years. He also remained as chairman of NATURE PARLIAMENT, one of his creations. He was the subject of *This Is Your Life*, then still a BBC show, in March 1964 – a month before *Children's Hour* was dropped.

'He was like a benevolent uncle. He wouldn't work today, but he was dead right for his time' – Jeffrey Archer.

MacGregor, Sue (1941–)
One of Radio 4's most respected interviewers, whose red hair belies a cool manner. Her tone can vary from firm to friendly, but never descends to the familiar. Started broadcasting in South Africa, where she was raised; trained as a reporter on THE WORLD AT ONE; presented WOMAN'S HOUR from 1972–87; in 1987 joined TODAY as one of its four regular presenters, the first regular female presenter since LIBBY PURVES left in 1982. Also has her own series, CONVERSATION PIECE, in which she has interviewed many interesting men and women of her choice since starting it in 1978.

A youthful Sue MacGregor, then the presenter of *Woman's Hour*, preparing for its fortieth birthday in 1986. She had celebrated her own five years previously

McKay the New

Comedy series on Radio 2 beginning in 1989 in which Michael Fenton-Stevens plays the title role of a man left a huge Scottish castle by a long lost uncle and who has to find £500,000 to pay off the debts. Denise Coffey, Jon Glover and Hugh Paddick play the (unpaid) staff. The writers are John O'Farrell and Mark Burton.

Mackenzie, Sir Compton (1883–1972)

The novelist and man of letters, perhaps best known for *Whisky Galore*, was also the first person to present a programme of records on British radio, in 1924. See DISC JOCKEY.

McLelland, Charles (1930–)

Controller of Radio 2 from 1976–80 (and of Radio 1 from 1976–78) during which time he axed both PETE MURRAY and WAGGONERS' WALK. Afterwards he was BBC Radio's Deputy Managing Director.

MacNeice, Louis (1907–63)

Poet and classical scholar whose prolific radio output during and just after the Second World War made him one of the most respected and influential cultural figures of the period.

In 1940 he returned to London from a lecturing job at Cornel University in the USA. Rejected by the Royal Navy because of poor eyesight (like his contemporary SIR GEORGE BARNES, first Head of the Third Programme), he joined the BBC instead to write in support of the war effort. Scores of talks, adaptations, features, translations and verse – his own as well as that of others – followed, most of it with a strongly moral content.

He wrote over seventy features in the war, many of which he also produced. The two biggest were *Alexander Nevsky* (1941), based on Eisenstein's film, in which Robert Donat took the title role and music was by Prokofiev; and *Christopher Columbus* (1942, to celebrate the 450th anniversary of Columbus's trip to America) in which Laurence Olivier played Columbus and William Walton provided an original score.

After the war, in which MacNeice also made programmes about the Allies and D-Day, his best known production was THE DARK TOWER, an imaginative fantasy about suffering and salvation broadcast on the Home Service in January 1946. Its title was drawn from Browning's poem *Childe Roland To The Dark Tower Came*.

MacNeice said that it was 'concerned with real questions of faith and doubt, of doom and free will, of temptation and selfsacrifice', and likened its allegorical nature to that of *Everyman* or *The Pilgrim's Progress*. A new production was recorded in 1956, with Richard Burton as the leading character Roland.

Macpherson, Sandy (1897–)

BBC's Theatre Organist for many years, with a warm, friendly and engaging manner which endeared itself to countless listeners. He was especially remembered for his musical companionship in the early days of the Second World War: while most of the BBC was reorganising itself at new premises outside London, he stayed on and played almost continuously, broadcasting 45 programmes in two weeks.

Born in a small town in Ontario, Canada, he served in the Canadian Army before becoming a professional musician, moving to London in 1928 and becoming a familiar figure seated at the organ of the Empire, Leicester Square.

He was one of the first to broadcast from the BBC organ after it was installed in 1936 and succeeded Reginald Foort as BBC Theatre Organist two years later.

After 1945 his popularity continued with sentimental and long-running Light Programme request shows such as FROM MY POST-BAG and THE CHAPEL IN THE VALLEY, usually introduced by his signature tune 'I'll Play to You'. Real name: Roderick Macpherson.

MacPherson, Stewart (1908–)

Winnipeg-born broadcaster who began as an ice hockey commentator and arrived in Britain in 1937. After service as a BBC war correspondent, he was the first presenter of DOWN YOUR WAY and chairman of IGNORANCE IS BLISS and TWENTY QUESTIONS. As a leading ice hockey and boxing commentator, he struck up a memorable relationship with BARRINGTON DALBY. Returned to Canada in the 1950s for family reasons and continued his career in his native town.

McWhinnie, Donald (1920–87)

Influential champion of highbrow drama when he was Assistant Head of BBC Radio's Drama Department in the 1950s. He took the lead in producing SAMUEL BECKETT and other European dramatists.

Madden, Steve (1953–)

Regular presenter of NIGHT RIDE and THE EARLY SHOW on Radio 2, where he has been an announcer since 1983.

Magic Moments

British television soaps, the after-shave revolution which apparently began in 1957 with the launch of Old Spice, *The Sun*, eating out and package holidays have all been examined in this Radio 4 series beginning in 1990 in which Nigel Fountain, co-founder of *City Limits*, traces the growth of things we now take for granted.

Maida Vale

Studios of BBC Radio in Delaware Road, London W9, in use for decades and which in 1990 were developed

Curiously, there were two Canadian-born broadcasters with an almost identical name who became nationally famous on radio in the 1940s. This one is organist Sandy Macpherson, not to be confused with sports commentator Stewart MacPherson

as high quaality music and drama studios after the BBC decided not to move its radio headquarters to White City. The BBC also said there would be a 'more vigorous hiring out policy'.

Mail Bag
Radio 1 show hosted by ADRIAN LOVE.

Mainly For Pleasure
Or, music while you commute. One of Radio 3's most popular series, going out five days a week in the early evening DRIVE-TIME slot. It stems from HOMEWARD BOUND and continues to play classical music of a lighter, more familiar sort. Clarinettist Jack Brymer hosted the first programme in 1980: presenters since (there has never been a regular) have ranged from RICHARD

BAKER to Natalie Wheen. Composer Sir Michael Tippett, featured on the tenth anniversary programme in 1990, played the Dire Straits record 'Brothers in Arms' – one of the rare occasions when pop music has been heard on the network.

Make 'Em Laugh
Radio 2 series in 1989 celebrating the leading talents of film comedy, from both sides of the Atlantic, over the past half-a-century. Narrated by Bernard Cribbins, it featured Billy Wilder, Woody Allen, Mel Brooks, Eddie Murphy and Robin Williams, plus the *Carry On* team, Ealing Studios and Peter Sellers, as well as the writers, directors and character actors who have sometimes stolen scenes from bigger stars.

Malay Service
Programmes in the Malay language on the BBC World Service started in 1941. They were on the air for fifteen minutes a day (the smallest output, along with Nepali, of any of the 37 foreign language services at BUSH HOUSE) when they were axed in March 1991,

along with the Japanese Service, as part of a package of financial measures agreed with the Foreign Office. The scrapping of the Malay Service saved the BBC £80,000 a year.

Man About Town
Influential critic James Agate came to life in this four-part Radio 4 series in 1990, based on his life in London during the 1930s and 1940s as recorded in his nine volumes of diaries, aptly entitled *Ego*. His words were read by Timothy West.

The Man Born To Be King
Dramatised story of Christ written by Dorothy L. Sayers (a clergyman's daughter who also created LORD PETER WIMSEY) broadcast in twelve parts on CHILDREN'S HOUR between December 1941 and October 1942, going out between 5.15 and 6 p.m. on Sundays.

Produced by VAL GIELGUD, to whom the printed version of the plays was dedicated by the author, it became one of the most famous and fiercely debated issues in BBC history up to that time.

Two major controversies attended the project while it was still in preparation. First, there was an internal BBC row. The programme selected to broadcast the plays, CHILDREN'S HOUR, wanted to alter Sayers's text in a way which, she believed, would dilute their power and effect. She tore up her contract and returned the pieces to the BBC. The project did not collapse at this point only because the BBC Religious Broadcasting Department, which had commissioned the plays in the first place via its head Dr James Welch, gave her Gielgud as the producer (with whom she had successfully collaborated before) and this placated her.

The second row broke out after Sayers, at a London press conference, read out some passages from her scripts which used colloquialisms interpreted by some newspapers as 'slang'. Scores of complaints were received by the BBC, the Lord's Day Observance Society protested and questions were asked in the House of Commons by Sir Percy Hurd, Tory MP for Devizes.

The BBC, aware that this was very probably the first time in Britain since the Middle Ages that Christ had been portrayed in a public play, eventually allowed the Religious Advisory Committee to veto the scripts. When the first play went out, much of the criticism was seen to be misplaced. But when Gielgud was given an OBE in the New Year's Honours, less than a fortnight later, he joked to Sayers that it stood for 'Order of the Blasphemous Enterprise'.

Robert Speaight took the title role in the plays, which contained strong echoes of the turbulent conflict in which the world was then embroiled. They required impressively large casts: 35 was the smallest.

The play cycle was repeated, each time on the Home Service, in 1949, 1951 and 1965. In a fresh production, DERYCK GUYLER played Christ. Adapted by Raymond Raikes, it made another outing as a Radio 4 Sunday serial in 1975, this time with new music composed by Roberto Gerhard.

The Man Ezeke
See EZEKE GRAY.

The Man In Black
Sinister storyteller played originally by VALENTINE DYALL, who from 1943 introduced APPOINTMENT WITH FEAR's late-night plays in cold, hushed tones, designed to make flesh crawl and spines shiver. Then, from 1949, *The Man In Black* was used as the title for a series of macabre stories which included R.L. Stevenson's *Markheim* and M.R. James's classic *Whistle And I'll Come To You*.

The sepulchral-voiced narrator was revived in the mid-1980s, this time played by Edward de Souza, when Radio 4 mounted a new series of tales of mystery and horror called FEAR ON FOUR.

Man of Action
Engaging Radio 3 series from the 1970s, in which a well-known person reflected on his life and illustrated it with his favourite music.

Mandarin Service
(BBC World Service) See CHINESE SERVICE.

Manna to Microwave
Brilliant title for this Radio 4 series in 1990 in which food writer and actress Madhur Jaffrey traced the development of cookery in several cultures over the past 8,000 years.

Mansell, Gerard (1921–)
Head of the Home Service and Radio 4 from 1965–69, where he presided over the birth of THE WORLD AT ONE as well as the controversial policy document BROADCASTING IN THE SEVENTIES. Managing Director of the BBC External Services from 1972–81. He is the author of the definitive history of the World Service, *Let Truth Be Told*.

Many a Slip
Amiable and long-running panel game blending intelligence and humour, education and entertainment, invented by IAN MESSITER. Chairman ROY PLOMLEY read out a number of items each of which contained up to a dozen errors of fact, consistency, grammar or syntax. Two teams – initially Eleanor Summerfield and Lady Isobel Barnett versus RICHARD MURDOCH and David Nixon – pressed buzzers when they believed they had spotted the mistakes. If they were right they scored

Robert Speaight (centre) took the title role in *The Man Born To Be King*, whose controversy helped to take the nation's mind off the war. He is flanked by Dorothy L. Sayers and Val Gielgud

points but if they were wrong their opponents got the points.

In the middle of each programme, in the ancient tradition of a musical interlude, STEVE RACE played carefully composed mistakes on a piano, such as wrong notes and false titles. Fingers hovered over buzzers once again.

Marcher Sound

Wrexham-based ILR station for Chester, Deeside, South Wirral and Wrexham, on the air since 1983. In 1989 it did what most ILR stations were doing and split itself into two wings. MFM (chart music) is on FM and Marcher Sound (golden oldies) on medium wave. One hour a night on weekdays on the AM service is in Welsh. The station's title derives from the fact that the region used to be called Wales and The Marches.

Marching And Waltzing

Weekday afternoon series on the Home Service, moving to Radio 2 after 1967.

Marconi, Guglielmo (1874–1937)

Radio's founding father. Born in Bologna of an Italian father and Irish mother, he came to Britain when the Italian government displayed little interest in his work, which is why his key discoveries were made in England.

In 1895 he discovered that an antenna would assist both the transmission and reception of radio waves, whose existence had been demonstrated by HEINRICH HERTZ seven years before. In December 1901 he broadcast a signal across the Atlantic – from Poldhu in Cornwall to St. John's in Newfoundland, using balloons to lift his antenna, and this day has often been thought of as the one on which radio was invented. He formed the first company which made radio equipment and received the Nobel Prize for Physics in 1909.

In February 1920 he began two daily programmes from Chelmsford that constitute Britain's first public radio broadcasts, going on to broadcast Dame Nellie Melba's historic concert from Chelmsford in June 1920 (see DAILY MAIL). There was then a pause because the Postmaster-General intervened to stop these broadcasts, on the grounds that they interfered with other communications.

In 1921, his company received a licence from the Postmaster-General allowing it to make regular public broadcasts from a hut at Writtle, outside Chelmsford. These were mounted from February 1922. It was here that Britain's first radio drama was broadcast, a reading of Rostand's *Cyrano de Bergerac*, plus a variety of other programmes including records. The brilliant pioneer P.P. ECKERSLEY, later the BBC's first chief engineer, was its guiding spirit.

Marconi's company opened a London station within a few months, whose call sign was 2LO, and it was from here that the fledgling BBC started broadcasting in November 1922.

His widow, the Marchesa Marconi, opened 'The Story of Radio' exhibition at the BBC RADIO SHOW in 1988 and the company her late husband founded still operates in Chelmsford to this day.

Market Forces
Four-part Radio 4 series in 1989 exploring the purpose and value of marketing, presented by Jenny Cuffe.

Markov, Georgi (1929–78)
One of the few people to have been murdered for what they have said on radio talks, Markov was a Bulgarian who defected to Britain in 1969 and worked for the BBC's Bulgarian Service at BUSH HOUSE. He also had critical talks broadcast on Radio Free Europe, in Munich.

In 1978, as he was going home, he was stabbed in the thigh with an umbrella while waiting for a bus by Waterloo Bridge. Four days later he died. The inquest heard that he had been injected with a tiny metal pellet 1.52 mm in diameter. It contained ricin, a lethal poison derived from the castor oil plant. Nobody was ever charged, but there has always been much speculation that it was the work of the Bulgarian security services.

That appeared to be confirmed when, in 1989, the then Foreign Office minister William Waldegrave accused the Bulgarian government of being 'an instigator' in the killing. The present Bulgarian regime has also indicated that it believes the murder was political. Markov's memoirs were published posthumously under the title *The Truth That Killed*.

Marriott, Bryant (1936–)
Controller of Radio 2 from 1983–89, during which time its music policy was overhauled (largely by FRANCES LINE). An Oxford contemporary of Dudley Moore, for whom he sometimes played the drums in the early days

of Moore's piano trio, he formerly worked as a producer of a variety of popular Radio 2 music shows.

Marshall, Arthur (1910–89)
Modern languages master at his *alma mater*, Oundle, whose evident gifts for parody at school concerts led a radio producer to invite him, in 1934, to take part in a comedy programme.

Thus began a connection with radio which lasted altogether for over fifty years, in which he was famous in the 1930s and 1940s for comic send-ups of stories about girls' schools. These took the form both of readings of stories he had written himself, on the Angela Brazil model, and dramatic sketches in which he played roles like that of the hearty schoolmistress, Miss Pringle. The most celebrated of his creations, introduced in 1944, was the equally hearty Nurse Dugdale of Hornsey Ride Hydro.

He was a regular ANY QUESTIONS? panellist for many years, generally doing a comic turn in his distinctively high-pitched voice, and also wrote for the *New Statesman* for 46 years.

Marshall, Howard (1900–)
BBC Radio's leading commentator at sporting and national occasions in the 1930s, chosen to describe both Coronations (1937 and 1953) and much acclaimed for his cricket commentaries between 1934–45. His deep, mellow, attractive voice was also heard in grimmer times – he was a war correspondent and accompanied the D-Day landings in Normandy.

Martin-Jenkins, Christopher (1945–)
The BBC's cricket correspondent, from 1974–91. Despite his efforts, failed to win a Blue at Cambridge, but has spent all his subsequent professional life either writing about, or broadcasting on, the game he loves. Joined *The Cricketer* straight from university (and has been its editor since 1981) and the staff of the BBC in 1970. His history of the broadcasting of cricket in Britain, *Ball-by-Ball*, was published in 1990. In 1991 he joined the *Daily Telegraph*, and was succeeded as cricket correspondent by former England fast bowler Jon Agnew.

The Mary Whitehouse Experience
Weekly late-night comedy show on Radio 1, starting in 1989 as a spin-off from HEY RRRADIO! It combined pungent satire and stand-up comedy from David Baddiel, Steve Punt, Hugh Dennis and Rob Newman.

Like many radio comedies, it eventually transferred to television. The same quartet made a pilot shown on BBC2 in 1990 and a six-part series in early 1991, a co-production between the BBC and Spitting Image.

Dubbed the *Not the Nine O'Clock News* for the 1990s, the original radio time slot was midnight. Such was its popularity, even at that late hour, that the following year it was moved forward to 7.30 p.m.

The show is clearly a backhanded tribute to the impact which Mrs Whitehouse (the Clean-Up Television campaigner who is now president of the National Viewers and Listeners Association) has made on British life. The BBC did not ask Mrs Whitehouse for permission to use her name, however, and she has not communicated her feelings about its use to them.

Mason, Edward J. (1913–71)

Prolific scriptwriter, telling stories that have entertained millions. He and Geoffrey Webb (who died in the early 1950s) wrote the whole of DICK BARTON – SPECIAL AGENT! and then brought THE ARCHERS into being with the first script and most of those that followed. Mason wrote 3,000 Archers scripts in all. He also devised, with TONY SHRYANE, the programmes MY MUSIC, MY WORD! and GUILTY PARTY.

Born into a working-class home in Birmingham, he left school at fifteen and went to work at the chocolate factory in Bournville, not writing for radio until he was in his early thirties. One of his sons played Roger Travers-Macy, first husband of Jennifer in THE ARCHERS.

Matthew, Brian (1928–)

Coventry-born DJ who started in radio with British Forces Network in Hamburg in 1948, then went to RADA to become an actor. Started SATURDAY CLUB in 1957 (originally called *Saturday Skiffle Club*, the Skiffle being dropped within three years) followed by EASY BEAT in 1960. As host of both these shows on the Light Programme, he helped to wean a generation of youngsters on wholesome pop music. This may have been in the mind of Princess Margaret when she accused him of 'starting all the pop DJ lark' at a lunch one day in the Governors' Suite at Broadcasting House. Matthew's response to her comment was that it was 'flattering, but inaccurate'. Matthew's love and knowledge of theatre proved useful on Radio 2's popular ROUND MIDNIGHT, the arts and music magazine four nights a week, which he hosted throughout its twelve-year existence from 1978 to 1990. It was dropped by FRANCES LINE, who changed the late evenings to bring in a new magazine show hosted by KEN BRUCE and a new arts strand at the weekend.

Although his programme was dropped, Matthew himself was not. He landed a job which took him back to his salad days in the golden age of pop. In March 1990 he became the new, regular host of SOUNDS OF THE 60s.

Matthews, Al (1942–)

Black New York folk singer and actor who presented two Radio 1 shows in the 1970s, a Friday evening programme and DISCOVATIN'.

Mayo, Simon (1958–)

After a spell on BBC local radio stations, Mayo joined Radio 1 in 1986 and two years later succeeded MIKE SMITH as presenter of the breakfast show, probably the most coveted slot on the network. He also presented SCRUPLES.

Meaning in the Blues

Sex, love, migration, superstition, gambling, the Depression and New Deal were among the themes in American blues songs examined in this ten-part Radio 3 series in 1990, presented by Paul Oliver.

He interviewed veteran blues singers, played records of their music and made the point that, until the 1950s, when it started to influence rock, blues was performed exclusively within black America.

Medicine Now

Radio 4 series on all aspects of medicine, presented since it began in 1980 by Geoff Watts, who comes armed with a degree in zoology and a PhD in biomedical research.

Medium Wave

Broadcasts in the range 526.5 to 1606.5 kHz. Radio 5 and Radio Luxembourg use it, as do all the ILR 'golden oldie' services. See also AM.

Meet The Huggetts

Comedy series with Jack Warner, brother of ELSIE AND DORIS WATERS, which ran from 1953–61. It was a spin-off from the cinema's popular comedy drama of 1947, *Holiday Camp*, which had introduced the Huggett Family. Warner's co-star in that, Kathleen Harrison, also played his wife in the radio show.

Mellow

Name of INCREMENTAL in Tendring, Essex, which began in 1990 as an easy listening station aimed at oldies.

Melodies For You

Pleasant Radio 2 record programme concentrating on light classics, which began in 1986. RICHARD BAKER presents it on Sunday mornings. His three-week holiday in 1990 enabled actor Tom Conti to make his debut as a DJ, and he took the opportunity to play his favourite romantic music.

Melody Radio

'No chat, no quizzes, no phone-ins, no horoscopes, no agony aunts and no prattling DJs' was the promise of this easy listening FM station which began in London in July 1990, aimed at the capital's over-35s and in

Listeners throughout the 1950s enjoyed meeting the salt-of-the-earth Huggetts, particularly Kathleen Harrison as Ethel and Jack Warner as her husband Joe. Vera Day was the second of six actresses to play their nubile daughter Jane. All three went to Margate in 1954 for *Picture Post* photographer Bert Hardy

particular the affluent over-50s in the core audience of Radio 2.

Talk is at a minimum (the posters promised 'Radio without the speakers') and presenters are anonymous. There were initially only five commercials per hour, much less than what was allowed, but then the station is wholly owned by the multi-millionaire tycoon Lord Hanson (a radio presenter and producer for the Central Mediterranean Forces during the Second World War).

The emphasis was, and still is, on playing as much melodious music as possible, ranging from Sinatra to 'Stranger on the Shore', with light opera, stage and film themes and classic songs and instrumentals. The first record on the air was 'Strike Up The Band', played by the Royal Philharmonic Orchestra.

One of the INCREMENTALS, it operates from studios in Knightsbridge and is managed by Radio Clyde under the personal stamp of its managing director James Gordon. The station manager, Sheila Porritt, is only the second woman station manager in ILR.

'Melody Radio is Largactil by ear, non-stop Muzak, interrupted only by commercials, the odd name check and treacle-toned news bulletins' – Nigel Andrew, *The Listener*.

'Melody is the stereo equivalent of a flotation tank' – Robert Hanks, *The Independent*.

Memories For You
Requested tunes played in strict tempo by Victor Sylvester's Ballroom Orchestra in a series heard on both Light and Home.

Memories Of You
Radio 2 series in 1988 in which Chris Ellis recalled the triumphs and tragedies of great stars like Alice Faye, Gracie Fields and Paul Robeson.

The Men From the Ministry
Affable Light Programme sitcom in which, for most of its life, RICHARD MURDOCH and DERYCK GUYLER were the two timorous and incompetent civil servants forever trying to placate their irritable Whitehall boss Sir Gregory. It was written by its producer, Edward Taylor.

When it began, in 1962, Wilfrid Hyde White appeared opposite Murdoch as Roland Hamilton-Jones, head of the General Assistance Department. Murdoch played Richard Lamb.

In 1966 Hyde White departed (in the story, Mr Hamilton-Jones was moved to the Ministry of Expansion, where they got two biscuits with their tea) and Guyler took over. The series carried on until 1977.

As a spoof on government bureaucracy, it paved the way for BBC-TV's *Yes, Minister*, though with nothing like the same bite. The humour suggested that civil servants were bumbling buffoons, rather than devious plotters determined to thwart their democratically elected masters. Their bungles included putting a woman into space by mistake and landing the War Office with 20,000 left boots.

The programme was introduced on the air each week as 'a weekly tribute to that faithful army of public servants who direct our lives and whose function is illustrated by their ancient crest: two crossed memos and a bowler hat carrying a can.'

Mercia Sound
Coventry-based ILR station, covering that city as well as Warwicks and South-West Leics. On the air since 1980. In a joint operation with sister station BRMB, it launched Xtra-AM on its medium wave frequency in 1989, with chart pop provided on its FM frequencies by Mercia-FM.

Meridian
World Service arts magazine dating from 1981, with a strong international remit. Radio 5 has carried it for a domestic audience since 1990.

Merry-Go-Round
Celebrated Second World War comedy series, which had input from all three armed services. After the war it split into three separate programmes, each of which reflected the humour and ethos of a different service: STAND EASY (Army), MUCH-BINDING-IN-THE-MARSH (RAF) and *Waterlogged Spa* (Royal Navy).

Messiter, Ian   (1920–)
Surgeon's son from Dudley who has spent much of his life in radio and light entertainment: he created JUST A MINUTE (inspired by a frightening experience he suffered as a thirteen-year-old schoolboy at Sherborne), MANY A SLIP and FAIR DEAL, and also a number of television games.

He had to sack GILBERT HARDING from the chairmanship of TWENTY QUESTIONS for being drunk on air. He started with the BBC in 1942, placing needles on the grooves of gramophone records. His candid and readable autobiography *My Life and Other Games* was published in 1990.

Metcalfe, Jean   (1923–)
Skilful presenter with a girl-next-door touch, whose potential was noticed when she was working as a typist on the newly created Forces Programme in 1940. She was promoted to play records on its request show FORCES' FAVOURITES in 1941, where she carried on after 1945 when it became FAMILY FAVOURITES on the Light Programme.

This was where she met her future husband, CLIFF MICHELMORE – on the air. She was at the London end of the programme and he, a former Squadron Leader in the RAF, presented it from the Hamburg end. After eighteen months of talking together on the air they finally met, in 1949, and married in 1950. (Michelmore quipped that 'it was love at first hearing'.) Later, she presented WOMAN'S HOUR and IF YOU THINK YOU'VE GOT PROBLEMS.

Metro Radio
ILR station covering Northumberland, Tyne and Wear and Co. Durham since 1974. Based in Newcastle upon Tyne. In 1989, JIMMY SAVILE joined the team of presenters with his famous Sunday lunchtime show SAVILE'S TRAVELS, which was then syndicated to 30 per cent of ILR. The same year saw the station's split into Great North Radio and Metro FM. The first, a golden oldie service for 35- to 54-year-olds, is on the AM frequency, and the second offers chart pop on the FM frequencies. Metro is a title closely associated with Newcastle: it is the name of the city's underground system and of its giant shopping complex, claimed to be the biggest in the Western hemisphere.

Michelmore, Cliff   (1919–)
Presenter who will forever be associated with FAMILY FAVOURITES: he met his future wife JEAN

The Men From the Ministry were always a drain on Whitehall's resources, but added considerably to the stock of national laughter. Deryck Guyler (left) and Richard Murdoch

METCALFE on the air when they were both presenting it. Although he became a major BBC-TV star in the late 1950s and 1960s, through presenting *Tonight*, he has not turned his back on radio and his more recent series have included WATERLINES.

Midday Music-Hall
Weekday lunchtime series on the Light Programme featuring different BBC orchestras – most of them, like the BBC NORTHERN DANCE ORCHESTRA, sadly axed long ago.

Midday Spin
Radio 1 show hosted variously by CHRIS DENNING, DAVID RIDER, DAVID JACOBS and TERRY WOGAN.

Middleton, Cecil Henry (1887–1945)
Son of a head gardener on a large Northamptonshire estate who, in 1931, began broadcasting the BBC's first regular gardening series, THE WEEK IN THE GARDEN. He had been introduced to the BBC by the Royal Horticultural Society after the BBC asked it to recommend an expert.

Mr Middleton, as he became known, became a national institution mainly through his second series IN YOUR GARDEN, which he presented every Sunday from 1934 and throughout the Second World War until his death. It continued until 1970, with

C.H. Middleton, the BBC's first and much commemorated gardening broadcaster. Ten years after his death, a secluded West End garden was named after him: the gate to that garden now forms the entrance to the BBC's Written Archives Centre in Caversham

ROY HAY introducing it on Network Three in the 1960s.

Mr Middleton was also a regular panellist on THE BRAINS TRUST and contributed to the war effort with his tireless support for the government's 'Dig for Victory' campaign.

Both Mr Middleton and another respected man of the soil, FRED STREETER, made frequent broadcasts from the pretty, walled garden next door to 12 Cavendish Place near BROADCASTING HOUSE. This dates from the 1760s and ranked as one of the oldest private gardens in the West End before becoming part of BBC premises. In 1955 it was commemorated as 'Mr Middleton's Garden' when an imposing wrought-iron gate was erected in his memory.

The BBC no longer owns the site, which is part of THE LANGHAM hotel, but it is still preserved as a patio garden complete with seats, trees and flower beds. The gate has been transported to Berkshiree, where it now frames the entrance to the BBC WRITTEN ARCHIVES CENTRE, a move which would surely have pleased him greatly.

Midweek

Morning chat show on Radio 4 whose original presenter, when the show went out on Thursdays, was Desmond Wilcox. When it moved to Wednesdays he was unavailable, so RUSSELL HARTY stepped in. He was succeeded by Irishman Henry Kelly for a couple of years before LIBBY PURVES took over in 1984.

Midweek Choice

Two-hour assortment of different pieces of music, all requested by listeners, on Radio 3 every Wednesday morning. Generally presented by Susan Sharpe, it is a midweek offshoot of YOUR CONCERT CHOICE on Sundays.

Milligan, Spike (1918–)

Radio, humour, and the rest of our culture would be immeasurably the poorer without the creative genius of this Irishman who wrote nearly all of THE GOON SHOW, and suffered dearly because of it. Real name: Terence Milligan.

The Million Pound Radio Show

Comedy series written and performed by Nick Revell and Andy Hamilton, who have also made a name for themselves in television, where they appeared on *Friday Night Live* and *Who Dares Wins*.

Mind Your Own Business

Comedy series on Radio 2 centred on the clash between a brilliant but reckless tycoon, Jimmy Bright (Bernard Cribbins) and a stony accountant, Russell Farrow (Frank Thornton). Annette Crosbie, as their secretary Nan, acts as referee. In 1988, when the show began, the economy was booming and plots were about expansion and expenditure. By its fourth series in 1991, storylines centred on problems, redundancies and the desperate search for sales.

Minghella, Anthony (1954–)

Leading playwright and former drama lecturer at Hull University who writes for radio, as well as television and the stage, to great effect. His best-known radio play, *Cigarettes and Chocolate* in 1988, about a woman who retreats into silence while her friends seek to break through the barriers of non-communication, won a SONY and a GILES COOPER AWARD. Michael Billington said in *The Listener*: 'He has written a major state-of-the-nation play about our fragmented lives, our petty infidelities, our adoption of this or that cause and our ultimate indifference to real suffering. It proves that radio drama, just as much as theatre, takes the moral temperature of the culture.'

Mining the Archive
Weekly Radio 3 series beginning in 1990 which was the network's first systematic attempt to harvest the musical riches of the BBC SOUND ARCHIVES, mainly historic recordings from the 1940s, 1950s and 1960s. The first programme included wartime recordings (of Elgar, Smetana and Brahms) made by the BBC SYMPHONY ORCHESTRA under Sir Adrian Boult.

Mission Investigates
Atlantis, black holes, ESP and genetic engineering were among the scientific conundrums explored in this spoof private eye series for youngsters, on Radio 5 in 1991. Brad Lavelle played the programme'e hero, Ed Mission. Made by an independent production company, Rewind.

The Mix
Weekly youth magazine programme on Radio 5, made in London (unlike the youth magazine shows on the other nights of the week).

Mixing It
Innovative Radio 3 series co-presented by jingles composer Mark Russell and Robert Sandall, rock critic of *The Sunday Times*, straddling both classical and rock and featuring music which often gets neglected, being regarded as neither one nor the other.

The first programme, in 1990, set the style with music by both the Kronos String Quartet and Peter Gabriel (from the latter's soundtrack for Martin Scorsese's film *The Last Temptation of Christ*).

The programme fulfils a longstanding wish of JOHN DRUMMOND to mount a series of direct appeal to younger listeners, and he said it was 'for anyone with open ears'. It goes out live every other Monday night.

Molestrangler, Dame Celia and Binky Huckaback
Two vivid fictitious characters from ROUND THE HORNE with strangulated upper-middle-class voices, played by Betty Marsden and Hugh Paddick. She was a caricature of a certain type of theatrical and he an ageing 'juvenile' with absurdly exaggerated elocution. Together, they often played FIONA AND CHARLES.

Monday Night at Eight
Variety show which began in the 1930s, originally starting life an hour earlier as *Monday Night at Seven*. It blended music, comedy, puzzles and a detective slot in the shape of *Inspector Hornleigh Investigates*.

Monday Night At Home
Ian Wallace, of MY MUSIC fame, introduced this 'selection of recorded wit, music and humour' which ran on the Home Service. IVOR CUTLER was among those who took part.

The Monday Play
Radio 4's Monday night drama which, traditionally, is the most searching and ambitious of the network's plays each week.

Monday night has been a regular drama slot for more than 25 years (Robert Bolt's *A Man For All Seasons* started life as a Monday night play on the Home Service) though the title 'Monday Play' was not introduced as its official title until 1971, when it was first used for *The Seagull* by Chekhov.

The plays were often repeated in the afternoons to gain a bigger audience, which sometimes led to problems. *Excess Baggage*, an award-winning play about the loneliness and boredom of Army wives by Ken Blakeson, had its scheduled repeat cancelled in 1988 because MICHAEL GREEN thought its bad language would offend Saturday afternoon listeners. Frederick Harrison's play *The Cassandra Generation*, set during the Falklands War, suffered the same fate in the same year.

Money Box
Radio 4 series hosted by Louise Botting which helps listeners to find their way through the maze of personal finance and investment.

Moore, Ray (1942–89)
Liverpudlian who made his radio debut on a show called *Pop North* in 1966, joining Radio 2 the following year and eventually becoming the network's much loved early morning presenter. A heavy smoker (sixty a day, and he often referred to it), he was forced to retire from the microphone in 1988 after developing throat cancer. His journal, kept in his last months, was published posthumously along with his widow Alma's story of their life together under the title *Tomorrow – Who Knows?* Again, posthumously, he was honoured with a FERGIE AWARD in 1989.

The Moral Maze
One of the first religious series to go out in a peak weekday slot as opposed to the usual Sunday, this incisive and rewarding Radio 4 programme beginning in 1990 and chaired by Michael Buerk examines the moral questions behind topical news stories. Its panel can call three witnesses for cross-examination.

Panellists have included Prof. Jennifer Temkin of Buckingham University, fellow academics Roger Scruton and Norman Stone, Rabbi Hugo Gryn, Museum and Galleries Commission chairman Lord Morris, *Guardian* columnist Edward Pearce and *Times* writer Janet Daley.

Moran, Johnny (–)
One of Radio 1's original team of DJs at the birth of the station in 1967, presenting SCENE AND HEARD for eight years.

179

Moray Firth

One of the smallest ILR stations in terms of audience size (only 220,000 people live in its area) but one of the biggest as far as geography goes. It covers a coastal strip some 200 miles long, from John O'Groats to Fraserburgh, at the northernmost tip of the British mainland. On the air since 1982 and based in Inverness.

Volunteers present all the evening output, from 7 p.m. For example Syd Atkinson, a retired British Rail manager, presents *Down Memory Lane*, a programme of 1940s dance music mixed with local tales from places like Elgin and Wick. An Episcopalian minister, Len Black, is a part-time producer and roving reporter. Programme controller Brian Anderson won national notice for his programmes from China in summer 1989 (he was arranging a pop series when he got caught up in the turmoil of Tiananmen Square) and now has a regular spot on Radio Shanghai.

More Barnes People
See PETER BARNES.

Moriarty, Count Jim
Villainous character on THE GOON SHOW played by SPIKE MILLIGAN. Not to be confused with Professor Moriarty, arch-enemy of SHERLOCK HOLMES.

Morning Concert
One of the nicest ways of being woken up that mortal man has yet devised, this goes out every day of the week at 7 a.m. on Radio 3.

Morning Edition
Radio 5's breakfast show, presented by Sarah Ward and Jon Briggs. Signifying that this is a sports channel, it carries both a daily racing preview and even news for anglers.

Morning Has Broken
Originally, when this Sunday-morning Radio 4 programme began, it was assembled from hymns already sung on SUNDAY HALF HOUR. It now has other music as well as hymns, and ends with a few minutes of bell-ringing called BELLS ON SUNDAY. Presenter is Jack Hywel Davies.

Morning Music
Morning show on both Light and Home, which featured a variety of long gone BBC orchestras like the REVUE, MIDLAND LIGHT and SCOTTISH VARIETY, plus Cecil Norman and the Rhythm Players and so forth.

Morning Reading
Unofficial title of Radio 4's 8.45 to 9 a.m. slot from Monday to Friday when Parliament is in recess, which has featured memorable and often magnificent serialisations of an array of books. They have included James Hilton's *Lost Horizon*, Walter Lord's *A Night to Remember*, about the sinking of the Titanic, Christopher Matthew's DIARY OF A SOMEBODY (1979), Alec McCowen's *McCowen on St Mark* (1980), PETER TINNISWOOD's TALES FROM A LONG ROOM (1981) and GARRISON KEILLOR's LAKE WOBEGON DAYS (1986). Adrian Mole, the immortal adolescent created by SUE TOWNSEND, made his broadcast debut here and ALAN BENNETT scored a notable success with the stories of Winnie-the-Pooh as did Martin Jarvis with JUST WILLIAM – which made history when it was the first speech tape to make the cassette charts.

The slot enjoys the biggest audience of any of the radio readings (about one million), which is unsurprising since it falls in the morning DRIVE-TIME period when audiences are at their biggest and most attentive. It exerts a considerable effect on sales, both of the books themselves and of cassettes of the readings, often released at the same time by the astute BBC RADIO COLLECTION.

Morning Service
Radio 4's Sunday-morning church service, ranging from Parish Mass to Holy Communion. Its time has varied: it used to be 9.45 a.m., was moved to 10.30 a.m. in 1964 (after the omnibus edition of THE ARCHERS) and is now at 9.30 a.m. (immediately before the omnibus edition).

Morning Story
Venerable programme in which, each day, an actor used to read a fifteen-minute short story of about 2,200 words. It began in the late 1940s on the Light Programme and traditionally its slot was at 11 a.m. From 1972 to 1973 it was moved to 1.15 p.m. and given a new name – not lunchtime story but *Today's Story*. It reverted to the morning and then in July 1973 switched from Radio 2 to Radio 4, where it remained until moving to the afternoons in September 1991.

Morris, Johnny (1916–)
Endearing and popular broadcaster who has entertained millions of children over the last forty years. Although most famous for his BBC-TV series *Animal Magic*, and as 'The Hot Chestnut Man' before that, he began on radio as a discovery of the BBC in Bristol, where he first appeared in the West of England Home Service.

His talent for mimicry has extended to seagulls, steam engines, squeaking signs, dogs, tiresome children and all sorts of other things in the human comedy, and radio has been much the richer for his presence.

Born in Wales of Gloucester stock, he had several jobs before coming to the Wiltshire village of Aldbourne as the bailiff of a farm. The BBC's Desmond Hawkins (later the Controller of the BBC's South and West region) also lived in the village and came to know and appreciate him as a larger-than-life local character. He introduced him cautiously to BBC Radio in Bristol in small acting parts, although Morris recalls that his very first broadcast was a talk on April Fools' Day 1946 called *Folly to be Wise*, and that Hawkins compiled and produced it.

From this he graduated to talks about rustic life, a series called *The Plug in the Wall* and another early 1950s series called *Pass the Salt*, portraits of other people's jobs. This started life as a regional feature on the Home Service but later went national on the Light Programme under the title *Johnny Comes to Town*, where it was given a good slot after THE BILLY COTTON BAND SHOW on Sunday afternoons.

In June 1957 came the first of his *Johnny's Jaunts*, in which the BBC sent him round the coast by caravan, bicycle and foot from the Bristol Channel to Cornwall and round as far as Lymington. Later jaunts took him to the Mediterranean and Istanbul, and the series transferred to television.

Mortimer, John   (1923–)
The QC and writer has had a long association with radio, which is where he made his debut as a playwright (with *The Dock Brief*, on the Third Programme in 1957). His radio debut, though, was two years before that when he adapted his own novel *Like Men Betrayed* on the Light Programme. More than twenty of his works have been broadcast, including *A Voyage Round My Father* (1963) and *Rumpole of the Bailey* (1980, starring MAURICE DENHAM).

Mosey, Don   (1924–)
Yorkshireman who graduated from Fleet Street cricket writer to sports producer and commentator, specialising in cricket, golf and rugby. BRIAN JOHNSTON's nickname for him: 'The Alderman'.

His on-air remarks from India in 1981–82, when the England cricket side was touring, provoked many complaints to the BBC. He didn't like the heat, food, taxis or the quality of Indian engineering since the passing of the Raj. He was not sent to cover the following winter's Test tour of Australia. This was said to be unconnected with his remarks, but not everyone believed that.

The Motor Way
Sitcom on the Light Programme from 1962, about life in a small garage. It capitalised on the success of television's *Dixon of Dock Green* by casting the same two stars: Jack Warner was the owner of the firm, Jack Turner, and Peter Byrne his nephew Peter Turner. DERYCK GUYLER played the foreman, Crocker. This 'logbook of a garage owner' was written by Lawrie Wyman.

Motoring And The Motorist
Weekly half-hour magazine series on Network Three. From 1959–61 it was produced by David Glencross, now chief executive of the Independent Television Commission.

Moult, Ted   (1926–86)
Farmer, broadcaster, actor and Everest double glazing salesman helped by radio to become a popular personality in the late 1950s and 1960s, but whose life ended tragically at his own hands.

Appearing as a contestant on BRAIN OF BRITAIN in 1958 led to regular appearances on other radio and television shows and he presented HOUSEWIVES' CHOICE in 1961. After years as a panellist and character actor, he auditioned for the role of Dan Archer, ageing patriarch of THE ARCHERS, in the mid-1980s. Although the part went to Frank Middlemass, he was given a new role of pig breeder Bill Insley. He shot himself in 1986. In the story, his character simply sold up and moved away.

Movie-Go-Round
Stars, clips, festivals and studios were all included in this 'sound approach to the cinema', a film round-up which Peter Haigh introduced every Sunday afternoon oon the Light Programme. Jack Hawkins appeared on the first show in September 1956. Based at MAIDA VALE, and founded by Trafford Whitelock, it broadcast clips from about 400 films in its first four years.

Peter Noble contributed 'Around the British studios': in those days there were enough to keep him occupied. The rousing signature tune, just right for the programme's title, was 'The Carousel Waltz'.

Movie Matinée
Thirty minutes of clips from the soundtrack of a new film on release in the cinema. DESMOND CARRINGTON and Spencer Hale were the presenters, on Saturday afternoons on the Light Programme.

Mr and Mrs North
BERNARD BRADEN and BARBARA KELLY played an American couple who solved mysteries in this series of 1950.

Mr Ros and Mr Ray
Show starring musicians Edmundo Ros and Ray Ellington. The latter and his quartet, which he founded in 1950, played on THE GOON SHOW.

Mrs Dale's Diary
Much loved soap opera about a middle-class doctor and his family which began on the Light Programme in January 1948 and ended on Radio 2 in April 1969. By then it had changed its name (in

'While we're waiting, is it all right if I listen to Mrs Dale's Diary?'

Mrs Dale's Diary came to represent a placid and un-troubled middle-class world. One unexplained curiosity of this *Punch* cartoon, however, is that it was published in August 1968, more than six years after the programme had changed its name to *The Dales*

February 1962) to THE DALES, a change that took place when Dr Jim Dale and his wife Mary moved from their South London suburb of Parkwood Hill to the expanding new town of Exton somewhere in the Home Counties.

This was a serial in which, for a long time, everyone remained in a time warp. Among the reactions from listeners was this letter in 1961 to *Radio Times*, from a Mrs Angela Campling of Northampton:

'It puzzles me that although Bob and Jenny's twins are now by my calculations at least three and a half years old they still use cots, high chairs, etc, and are generally treated like babies. They could almost be at nursery school, like my own child who is only a few months older. Perhaps, like the other characters in *Mrs Dale's Diary* – Mrs Freeman, particularly – they are destined never to grow older?'

'It is the only way of knowing what goes on in a middle-class family' – reported comment of The Queen Mother.

Mrs Feather
Scatty comedy character of the 1930s, created by actress Jeanne de Casilis.

Mrs Mopp
The char with the bottomless bucket in ITMA, played by Dorothy Summers. Her name, as well as her catchphrase

'CAN I DO YER NOW, SIR?', have both passed into the language.

Much-Binding-in-the-Marsh

Peacetime child of MERRY-G0-ROUND, this was set on a fictitious RAF station-turned-country club in the late 1940s and was reputed to be King George VI's favourite programme.

KENNETH HORNE and RICHARD MURDOCH both wrote and starred in this example of an early sitcom, having met one another in the Air Ministry during the Second World War, when Murdoch was a Squadron Leader under Wing Commander Horne.

They were joined by SAM COSTA, representing other ranks, and MAURICE DENHAM as Dudley Davenport. Both these had catchphrases which were

guaranteed to produce a round of welcoming applause from the studio audience. Costa's was the solicitously polite: 'Good morning, sir, was there something?' while Denham scored a hit with his 'Ooh, I say, I am a fool!'

The show also introduced the practice of assembling families with punning names, later a regular feature on both I'M SORRY I'LL READ THAT AGAIN and I'M SORRY I HAVEN'T A CLUE. Example: 'Here comes Mr and Mrs Cobean . . . and their son Harry Cobean.' The show ran from 1947–53 and its famous signature tune was written by SIDNEY TORCH.

Popular at the Palace, it also had admirers in other corridors of power more than a generation later. Five days after the outbreak of the Gulf War, at a time when episodes were being repeated at 11 p.m. on Radio 4 each week, an official of 10 Downing Street contacted the Controller of Radio 4, MICHAEL GREEN, in the hope of obtaining copies of what had been broadcast, indicating that John Major was a fan.

The BBC RADIO COLLECTION promptly brought forward the release of its cassette containing four vintage

Much-Binding-in-the-Marsh, **loved by Royals and commoners alike. Left to right: Kenneth Horne; Dora Bryan; Richard Murdoch, who co-founded and co-wrote it with Horne; Sam Costa; Nicholas Parsons**

episodes, which it had been planning anyway, and sent a copy of this to a grateful Prime Minister.

Muir, Frank (1920–)

Self-taught son of a ship's engineer from New Zealand, brought up in London's East End, who started writing for Forces radio while serving in the RAF in Iceland during the Second World War. Demobbed, he joined the agency of TED KAVANAGH where he met DENIS NORDEN. The two men forged a successful partnership which has endured more than four decades, first as witty comedy writers (responsible for TAKE IT FROM HERE) and later as performers on the panel games MY WORD (since it began in 1956 until the present day) and MY MUSIC (ditto, since 1967). Muir also wrote for THE ACCORDION CLUB in the late 1940s, developed WHACK-O! on television, was on ONE MINUTE PLEASE in 1952 and broadcast a series called FRANK MUIR GOES INTO . . . which was researched and written by SIMON BRETT.

Murder Most Foul

Nick Ross narrated this six-part series of drama documentaries on Radio 4 in 1991 about celebrated murder cases of the past, drawn from that supposedly nostalgic period when police cars still had bells and Scotland Yard detectives always wore trilby hats.

Murdoch, Richard (1907–90)

Officer, gentleman and fine comedy actor whose radio career spanned nearly sixty years. He was noted for three great partnerships: with ARTHUR ASKEY, who called him 'Stinker', in BAND WAGGON; with KENNETH HORNE in MUCH-BINDING-IN-THE-MARSH and with DERYCK GUYLER in THE MEN FROM THE MINISTRY.

Disinclined to make any concessions to age, he joined the JUST A MINUTE team at the age of 82. His Radio 2 series in 1987, *A Slight Case of Murdoch*, recalled some of his great moments. He died doing what he liked best – playing golf.

Murray, Pete (1928–)

Disc-jockey of vast experience. From 1950–55, while on Radio Luxembourg, he lived in the Grand Duchy. Was one of the first presenters to use the f- - - word on the air, in 1953. A truculent technician put on the wrong programme: instead of DAN DARE it was piano music by Felix King. Murray turned to music publisher Roy Berry, with him in the studio, and exclaimed: 'Oh Gawd, he's put on the wrong f- - - - - - programme!' Within half-an-hour, as Murray recalled in an official Radio Luxembourg publication in 1979, the *Daily Mirror* were on the phone: 'I denied everything, of course, and told them I'd said "flipping". Luckily they hadn't heard it themselves – someone had phoned them up.'

In between these excitements, Murray hosted TOP TWENTY. Later, having joined the BBC, he hosted PETE'S PARTY on the Light Programme. One of Radio 1's original team of DJs when it was launched in 1967, he presented *Pete's People* for two years before switching to Radio 2 and OPEN HOUSE, where he was the host for more than ten years. He was dropped in 1983 for being 'out of date'. Snapped up by LBC, and has been there ever since.

Murrow, Ed (1908–65)

Legendary broadcaster whose descriptions, in plain and graphic words, of the air raids on London in the early part of the Second World War were heard by millions of his fellow Americans.

His nightly 'This (pause) is London' radio broadcasts about bombing and blackout were regarded as playing a very considerable part in enlisting US sympathy for Britain as it stood, for much of the time alone, against Hitler's Germany, and in bringing home to Americans the suffering of the British. Later he flew in RAF bombers on raids on Berlin and other German cities. His wartime reporting brought him the OBE, a rare honour for an American.

Murrow was one of the founding fathers of the broadcasting giant CBS: its Director of Talks (1935–37), European Director (1937–46) and Director of Public Affairs (1946–47). He built a reputation as a defender of civil liberties and as someone who insisted that dissent should never be confused with disloyalty.

In 1961 President Kennedy appointed him Director of the United States Information Agency, putting him in charge of, among other things, the output of VOICE OF AMERICA.

Music And The Ordinary Liistener

Influential early BBC series presented by Sir Walford Davies which gave many listeners their first insights into the joy of great music.

Music Box

'Gay and spontaneous' was what this Light Programme series was designed to be, according to its producer John Fawcett Wilson. It went out live after HOUSEWIVES' CHOICE, from 1959 onwards, compered by TIM GUDGIN. Informal music was provided by a sextet and various singers.

Music By . . .

Six-part Radio 2 series in 1991 in which Roy Pickard interviewed film composers such as Elmer Bernstein, Miklos Rozsa and Richard Rodney Bennett.

Music For Guitar

Former Radio 3 weekly programmme devoted to guitar music, axed by JOHN DRUMMOND in 1988.

Music For Organ
Former Radio 3 weekly programme devoted to organ music, axed by JOHN DRUMMOND in 1988.

Music For Sweethearts
The Romance in Rhythm Orchestra, conducted by Johnny Pearson, featured in this Light Programme series beginning in 1960.

Music From The Movies
Tim Rice presented this three-part Radio 2 series in 1990, featuring the BBC CONCERT ORCHESTRA playing music from movieland.

Music Hall
Popular Saturday-night variety series and one of the first radio shows made in front of a studio audience. Comedians, singers and other music hall acts all had to appear in proper costume and make-up. Vic Oliver (later the first castaway on DESERT ISLAND DISCS) and SANDY POWELL both appeared on it during the 1930s.

Music in Mind
One of Radio 4's few music programmes: this one goes out on Saturday nights, usually presented by Brian Kay.

Music In Our Time
Programme devoted to the work of serious contemporary composers, now on Radio 3. It was started in 1942 by Sir Arthur Bliss. Inevitably, the programme has always had an austere reputation. People tend to like the old and familiar, not the new and unfamiliar.

Music of The Masters
Umbrella title for Saturday afternoon series of concerts on Network Three, around 1960.

The Music of Work
Radio 4 series in 1985 presented by Kevin Crossley-Holland which displayed a variety of people singing at their work, from salt cutters in Ethiopia to honey gatherers in Sarawak.

Music Programme
Separately named daytime section of the frequency carrying the Third Programme, which went out only at night. It was introduced in 1957. Originally on Sundays only, it was extended to seven days a week in 1965.

After this the early evening part of the output, devoted to further education, was henceforth called *Study Session* (except on Saturdays when it was *Sport Service*). The one frequency therefore carried a network divided into three parts: Music Programme, Study Session, Third Programme. (The Music Programme became part of Radio 3 in 1967, but the Third continued to enjoy its separate identity until 1970.)

Music Questions
A panel of musicians, such as Charles Mackerras, responded to listeners' questions in this Home Service series.

Music Through Midnight
Weekday late-night Light Programme show with top artists, record requests and leading DJs in the 1960s.

Music To Remember
Weekday evening series on the Home Service from 1953. Its concerts were performed by different BBC orchestras but always devoted to the mainstream, indestructible classics such as Beethoven, Mozart and Tchaikovsky.

Music Weekly
Sunday-morning programme on Radio 3 which from 1975–90 was presented by Michael Oliver, freelance music journalist and critic. In 1990 it started to go out live when it also acquired a new presenter, composer and former Radio 3 music producer Peter Paul Nash, and started two new slots: *Critics' Choice*, looking at musical events over the forthcoming week, and an exploration of classical music radio stations in other countries.

Music While You Work
This non-stop medley of popular tunes, played by a different band each day, began in the dark days at the end of June 1940 – between the fall of France and the Battle of Britain – as a ploy to keep workers contented and therefore productive. The tone was set by the stirring ERIC COATES signature tune, 'Calling All Workers'.

The twice daily broadcasts (one for the night shift) were designed to raise spirits and maintain morale and were played to the factory workers over their tannoy systems. For a time it went out not only every weekday but on Sundays too. By 1945 over 9,000 factories were tuning in.

The first broadcast went out on both the Home Service and Forces Programme and was given by Dudley Bevan at the BBC Theatre Organ. Other orchestras that week included Geraldo and his Dance Orchestra, Geiger and his Orchestra, Jimmy Leach and his Organolists and the BBC Military Band.

Launched in war, the programme carried on happily in peacetime, and continued until 1967: the last show (which again featured Jimmy Leach) went out on the last day of the Light Programme.

To celebrate its fiftieth anniversary in 1990, the show was resurrected for a week on Radio 2. It opened with the Phil Tate Orchestra – heard on the programme many times over a seventeen-year period – which had reassembled itself specially for the occasion. A year later it returned for a six-part series, again on Radio 2.

The Musician Speaks
Fortnightly fifteen-minute forum on the Third Programme beginning in 1960 in which musicians became critics and reacted to recent musical events. The first edition featured two items on Schoenberg.

My Country Right or Wrong
Hours before this Radio 4 series on MI5, MI6 and the Whitehall intelligence community was due to start in December 1987, the Attorney-General applied for an interim injunction against it on the grounds of possible breaches of national security. The High Court granted this and the series was duly banned. In June 1988, after the BBC had shown the government all the quotes uttered by former intelligence officers, the injunction was lifted and the three-part series was transmitted uncut.

It was notable for leading to the punishment of a man simply for talking to it. Mike Grindley, from GCHQ in Cheltenham, said he was a Chinese linguist and had worked there for 26 years. He declined to say what his duties were. Nevertheless, his employers fined him £500 for giving this interview.

Presenter Paul Barker memorably described secrecy in Britain as 'like a Dickensian pea-souper, curling round and infecting every aspect of the way this country is currently run'.

My Heroes
Fifteen programmes on Radio 4 in 1987–90 (the initial trio broadcast under a marginally different title, *My Hero*) in which Cliff Morgan interviewed people, including Robert Kee and Richard Harris, about those who had most deeply influenced them.

My Music
Long running, unchanging and deliberately timeless musical quiz on Radio 4 (although it has also gone out on Radio 2), which started in 1967. It was devised by TONY SHRYANE and EDWARD J. MASON as a sister show to their MY WORD. The chairman has always been STEVE RACE.

The original teams were DENIS NORDEN and Ian Wallace (the man who made famous Flanders and Swann's song 'Mud, Mud, Glorious Mud' in the 1950s) versus FRANK MUIR and David Franklyn. The latter, a former principal bass at Covent Garden, had to answer the very first question, which concerned the chords at the end of De Falla's *Ritual Fire Dance*. After his death in 1973, Owen Brannigan stood in at a few days' notice before fellow singer John Amis became the permanent replacement later that year.

This clever line-up of one comedian and one musicologist in each team has continued ever since, and Race – who has now devised well over 10,000 questions – and Wallace have never missed a single programme. The show has been adapted for BBC2, visited several music festivals and gone out on the BBC World Service.

It is recognised in the BBC that the show appeals particularly to more senior people: hence the cruel joke one sometimes hears about its studio recording. 'What has no teeth and 49 legs?' Answer: the front row of a *My Music* audience.

'I'm the resident philistine. I perform comic songs in the hope that the lyrics will detract from the fact that I can't sing' – Denis Norden.

My Top Ten
Radio 1 series with musical celebrities, who have included violinist Nigel Kennedy, picking their personal Top Ten as part of THE STEREO SEQUENCE.

My Top 12
Radio 1 series once introduced by ANDY PEEBLES and BRIAN MATTHEW.

My Word
Veteran Radio 4 panel game based on words and phrases, running since 1956. Devised by TONY SHRYANE and EDWARD J. MASON.

The first series pitted FRANK MUIR and Isobel Barnett against DENIS NORDEN and Nancy Spain, with a stern JOHN ARLOTT as umpire. He was replaced by Jack Longland, Director of Education for Derbyshire, followed by John Julius Norwich and MICHAEL O'DONNELL.

In 1989 Muir and Norden were still going strong and by now their respective partners were Dilys Powell and Lady Antonia Fraser. The show goes out on the BBC World Service and has been sold to forty countries. It has also transferred to television, where it appeared on BBC1.

'Do you know, he can't pass a second-hand bookstall these days without leafing through almost every volume on show. He's always hopeful of finding a new volume of words and phrases. Here is an example – *Slang and Country Sayings*, published in 1860. Guess how many clues he got out of that one? You're right, he didn't!' – an exasperated Mrs Mason, interviewed in *Radio Times* in 1960.

Myers, Pete (1940–)
One of Radio 1's original line-up of DJs who launched the station in 1967. He presented LATE NIGHT EXTRA.

Myself When Young
Radio 2 series which started in 1989 in which novelist and agony aunt CLAIRE RAYNER talks to celebrities ranging from Ken Livingstone and John Stalker to Dame

For eighteen years the panellists on *My Music* have remained unchanged. Left to right they are Ian Wallace, Denis Norden, Frank Muir and John Amis. At the piano is Steve Race, who somehow has devised over 10,000 questions to put to them

Alicia Markova and Cleo Laine about their early years – school, hobbies, family, first sins and first romances. Each guest can choose four pieces of music and a clip of archive news from their childhood.

The programme has a most unusual origin: Rayner's harrowing ordeal at the hands of DR ANTHONY CLARE when she appeared on IN THE PSYCHIATRIST'S CHAIR. His persistent questioning about her childhood, in which she was apparently beaten and abused by her parents, made her break down in agonised crying and reduced her to 'jelly', as she later put it. Some of this was heard on the programme, but most of it was cut. She did not, however, disclose to Clare the worst secrets of her childhood, a box she prefers to keep locked even from members of her own family.

The experience made her realise that the childhood memories of the famous can be of considerable public interest. Soon afterwards, therefore, she approached FRANCES LINE, then head of music for Radio 2, and proposed a light, enjoyable series in which well known folk could reminisce about their formative years. Her idea was accepted, and she became its presenter.

N

The Name's The Game
Radio 2 comedy game devised and hosted by Roger Kitter, running since 1982. Barry Cryer and Duggie Brown captain rival teams who have to identify mystery characters, both real and imaginary, from a set of cryptic clues.

National Anthem
God Save The Queen generally brings Radio 4 to a close each night, just as it did the Home Service, and has been in constant use in this way since October 1939. However, it was dropped at the outbreak of the Gulf War on 16 January 1991. The BBC said that not formally closing the network would enable it to react to important developments overnight, and that it was only a temporary measure which would resume when hostilities ceased. It changed its mind within days: 48 hours after *The Sunday Times* disclosed that the Anthem had been dropped, it was put back again.

National Programme
The BBC's service which replaced its original 2LO, in 1930. In that same year an alternative was provided by the new Regional Programme. The Home Service replaced both at the outbreak of the Second World War in September 1939.

National Radio Awards
Believed to be the first annual awards for radio programmes and programme-makers, and sponsored by the DAILY MAIL in the 1950s. The winners, who received Silver Mikes, were the people's choice: they were chosen by the public partly through ballots and partly through panels of listeners in various cities.

The following is a complete list of awards made, beginning in January 1950.

1950:
Best actress: Gladys Young. Best actor: James McKechnie. Light show: TAKE IT FROM HERE. Voice of the Year: STEWART MACPHERSON.

1951:
Best variety series: EDUCATING ARCHIE. Actor: James McKechnie. Actress: Gladys Young. Voice of the Year: RICHARD DIMBLEBY.

1952:
Radio personality of the year: WILFRED PICKLES. Outstanding programme: TAKE IT FROM HERE.

1953:
Outstanding actor: Howard Marion-Crawford. Outstanding actress: Gladys Young. Personality of the year: GILBERT HARDING. Most entertaining programme: EDUCATING ARCHIE. Most promising new programme: AL READ. Most popular musical entertainer: Tom Jenkins.

1954:
Personality of the year: GILBERT HARDING. Outstanding actor: James McKechnie. Outstanding actress: MARJORIE WESTBURY. Most popular musical entertainer: Tom Jenkins. Most entertaining programme: THE ARCHERS/TAKE IT FROM HERE. Most promising new programme: *The Name's The Same*.

1955:
Outstanding actor: Richard Williams. Outstanding actress: MARJORIE WESTBURY. Personality of the year: JEAN METCALFE. Most entertaining programme: THE ARCHERS. Most promising new programme: HELLO PLAYMATES. Most popular musical entertainer: Cyril Stapleton.

The awards appear to have stopped after that, but were resurrected as a joint venture with the BBC for the BBC RADIO SHOW in 1988. Personality: TERRY WOGAN. Best contemporary programme, and best drama series: THE ARCHERS. Radio 1 personality: STEVE WRIGHT. Radio 2 personality: JOHN DUNN. Best current affairs programme: JIMMY YOUNG. Best radio journalist: BRIAN REDHEAD. Comedy prize: BARRY TOOK, for ROUND THE HORNE. Best sports commentator: BRIAN JOHNSTON. Best light entertainment show: THE NEWS HUDDLINES. Best specialist music programme: THE PROMS.

The Natural History Programme

Puffins and pythons, bottle-nosed whales and the beast of Exmoor are all discussed with the same intelligence and enthusiasm on this weekly Radio 4 series which emerged from the loins of THE LIVING WORLD.

In 1973, listeners were sending in so many questions to that series (e.g. 'Why are flies so good at seeing attempts to swat them but so bad at spotting spiders' webs?') that it floated off the question element in the form of a separate programme, *Wildlife*, which ran until the end of 1985. It was immediately succeeded in 1986 by the weirdly named *The Nat Hist Programme*, an abbreviation which was thankfully soon expunged when the title became what it is now. Originally thirty minutes long, it got extended to its present 45 minutes in 1987.

The programme is intended to show the various relationships of *Homo sapiens* to the rest of the natural world in a magazine format. Ulsterman Fergus Keeling, who has a PhD in gerbil behaviour, has presented it from the beginning: his original partner Lionel Kellaway is now a roving reporter and has been succeeded by Jessica Holm, who also has a PhD – in red squirrel ecology.

The Naturalist

Sunday lunchtime programme introduced by Maxwell Knight which ran on the Home Service.

Naturalists' Notebook

Network Three series replaced by NATURE NEWS in 1960.

Nature News

Monthly round-up on Network Three from 1960, edited and introduced by John Hillaby.

Nature Parliament

Part of CHILDREN'S HOUR from 1946 onwards, invented and chaired by UNCLE MAC, in which naturalists tried to answer listeners' questions. Normally the panel consisted of Peter Scott, Hugh Newman and James Fisher.

Naughtie, James (1951–)

Scots journalist who in 1988 moved from being chief political correspondent of *The Guardian* to succeed SIR ROBIN DAY as anchorman of THE WORLD AT ONE. In 1990 he also started presenting Radio 3's OPERA NEWS. Other work has included a Radio 4 series on his native land, A NEARBY COUNTRY.

His crisp and incisive style attracted much hate mail when he started on Radio 4. Some listeners called his Scots accent 'alien' and urged him to return north of the border, but this early antagonism has not persisted.

Naughton, Bill (1910–)

County Mayo-born playwright, brought up in Lancashire, who left school at fourteen for a job in a weaving shed, later working as a lorry driver and coal heaver. He made his radio debut with *Timothy* (Home Service 1956) and went on to contribute about fifteen more plays on Light, Home and Third. The most enduring of these were *Alfie Elkins and his Little Life* (Third Programme, 1962) and *All in Good Time* (Radio 3, 1973). Both were successfully adapted for the stage and then cinema.

The first, which was produced by DOUGLAS CLEVERDON, became the film *Alfie*, with Michael Caine taking the role originally created on radio by Bill Owen. The second was turned into *The Family Way* with Hayley Mills and Hywel Bennett. Another of his radio plays to follow this route was *My Flesh My Blood*, basis of the film *Spring and Port Wine*.

The Navy Lark

Longest running comedy in British radio history until WEEK ENDING came along, this affectionate spoof on the Senior Service ran from 1959 to 1977 with its weekly antics aboard HMS *Troutbridge*.

The motley crew included Stephen Murray as NUMBER ONE, Leslie Phillips as a silly ass of a Sub-Lieutenant whose parrot cry was 'LEFT HAND DOWN A BIT', and Jon Pertwee as a Petty Officer. Some actors doubled up. Ronnie Barker, years before attaining fame on television, was (Un)Able Seaman Fatso Johnson as well as Lieut-Cmdr Stanton. Tenniel Evans, great-nephew of Sir John Tenniel who drew the original illustrations in *Alice in Wonderland*, had three roles – Able Seaman Goldstein, the crusty Admiral and the Governor, Sir Willoughby Todhunter Brown.

Matelots of all ranks made it a favourite. For their 21st birthday party, the WRNS requested a special performance. It took place at the Royal Festival Hall in the presence of the Queen Mother. The First Sea Lord, Sir Charles Lambe, once visited the studios during rehearsals.

The popularity of the programme was matched by that of its signature tune for harmonica and orchestra: 'Trade Wind Hornpipe', composed by Tommy Reilly and James Moody.

'I caused more damage to Naval property than the Navy had done in two world wars' – wry reminiscence of Leslie Phillips, in 1987.

Navy Mixture

Wartime variety show running from 1943–47: DAVID JACOBS made his radio debut on it in 1944, and JIMMY EDWARDS appeared on it a little later.

A Nearby Country

Three-part Radio 4 series in 1990 in which JAMES NAUGHTIE looked at the law, church and education of his native Scotland.

The Navy Lark was for many years the longest running comedy show in British radio history. Back row: A.B. Johnson (Ronnie Barker), C.P.O. Pertwee (Jon Pertwee), L.T. (Michael Bates), A.B. Goldstein (Tenniel Evans). Centre: Lieut. Murray (Stephen Murray), Capt. Povey (Richard Caldicot), Sub Lieut. Phillips (Leslie Phillips). Front: Wren Chasen (Heather Chasen) and Wren Cornwell (Judy Cornwell)

Nepali Service
Programmes in the Nepali language on the BBC World Service are on the air for about twenty minutes a day (the smallest output of any of the World Service's foreign language services).

Network Chart Show
Rundown of Britain's top-selling records broadcast since 1984 on every ILR station except one every Sunday evening (from 5 to 7 p.m.), gaining a weekly audience of four million. It was ILR's first networked show, other than news bulletins.

Presented by DAVID JENSEN, it has been sponsored since 1985 by Nescafé – who now spend £700,000 a year on it. Its claimed success in reaching 20 per cent of all 10- to 24-year-olds in Britain was said by Nescafé to be 'a vital part of our campaign to make coffee more fashionable and more relevant to young people'.

The show is taken by about a dozen other countries, including Denmark and New Zealand.

The one station that refuses to take the show is Radio Mercury. It is reluctant to promote Jensen as he is one of the stars of Capital Radio, which can be heard in Mercury's area and thus competes for both listeners and advertising revenue.

Network Three
Daytime service on the frequency which carried the Third Programme at night, introduced in 1957, its purpose

being to attract those many listeners for whom the words 'Third Programme' meant a forbidding and inaccessible land occupied by eggheads. It had programmes on chess, nature study and even do-it-yourself (BUILDING MATTERS) as well as music and the arts.

Never The Same Again

Powerful Radio 4 series, on the air since 1989, in which Jenni Mills talks to people who have had to live with trauma. In what must be one of the most painful conversations ever to have been heard on radio, the parents of eleven-year-old Susan Maxwell talked of how they had lost her to an unknown murderer in 1982. Novelist Marianne Wiggins, wife of Salman Rushdie, spoke of how her life had been turned upside down after he was threatened and had to go into hiding, and others who have appeared include a teenager who discovered she had a spinal tumour.

The New Gods

Radio 4 series of the late 1980s in which theologian Keith Ward, Professor of History and Philosophy of Religion at King's College, London, examined five new religious movements popular in post-war Britain.

News

The BBC opened with a news bulletin on 14 November 1922, read by its first Director of Programmes Arthur Burrows, and news has formed a central part of the BBC's service ever since, in both peace and war. Its ubiquitous nature in recent years, on BBC and non-BBC stations alike, has not always found favour with listeners.

News is the skeleton on which Radio 4 is built, starting with *News Briefing* at 6 a.m. and continuing with a string of programmes festooned through the day: TODAY, THE WORLD AT ONE, PM, THE SIX O'CLOCK NEWS and THE WORLD TONIGHT. Radio 2 carries bulletins on the hour, round-the-clock; Radio 1 on the half-hour, plus NEWSBEAT and NEWS 91; Radio 5 twelve times a day. Radio 3 is a sanctuary: only five bulletins a day.

For which bulletins are preserved, see BBC SOUND ARCHIVES.

See also IRN, BBC WORLD SERVICE, and under individual programmes and presenters.

Newsbeat

The name of Radio 1's two fifteen-minute news bulletins, at lunchtime and teatime, when they began on weekdays in 1974. They interspersed jingles and pop trivia with a round-up of news stories presented in breathless haste. In 1990 the afternoon edition was replaced by the beefier *News 90*, now NEWS 91.

Roger Gale, former Radio Caroline DJ and now a Tory MP, was one of the first producers of *Newsbeat*,

which ranks as the most popular of all BBC Radio's news programmes.

The News Huddlines

Popular, topical, quickfire weekly comedy show on Radio 2 starring Roy Hudd (whose radio career began in the 1960s on WORKERS' PLAYTIME) and June Whitfield. SIMON BRETT and JOHN LLOYD jointly produced the first series, in 1975.

Newshour

Highly regarded news programme, in English, broadcast every night on the BBC World Service since November 1988. It was the first news programme from BUSH HOUSE to contain both straight reporting and background analysis.

At first it went out at 10 p.m. GMT, which reached breakfast listeners in the Far East and teatime ones in the Caribbean. However, it was also too late for most people in Africa, the Middle East and India. In April 1991, therefore, it moved forward an hour to 9 p.m. GMT and a second edition of the programme started eight hours earlier at 1 p.m. GMT. A third edition is planned in January 1992 at 5 a.m. GMT, which will unite evening listeners in, say, San Francisco, with breakfasters in Bulawayo and Zanzibar.

Newsreel

World Service news magazine which succeeded the veteran RADIO NEWSREEL in 1988. Its signature tune is an electronic reworking of its parent programme's 'Imperial Echoes'.

News 91

Radio 1's first news magazine since it began in 1967, and its first bulletin to be thirty minutes long. Lively, arresting and twice the length of the afternoon NEWSBEAT which it replaced, it was launched in January 1990 and presented by SYBIL RUSCOE and ALLAN ROBB. It was Radio 1's longest ever regular speech programme and national radio's first new daily news show for twenty years.

The News Quiz

Popular Radio 4 game show which began in 1977, with Barry Norman its first compere (just as he was on BREAKAWAY). He was succeeded by BARRY TOOK, journalist Simon Hoggart and then Took again. The show was the idea of JOHN LLOYD, who produced the first series. Later it was adapted for television and called *Have I Got News For You?*.

News Stand

This has changed its remit, though not its channel. When it began, on Friday nights on the Home Service, it looked at the dailies through the eyes of William

Hardcastle and later Walter Taplin. THE WEEKLY WORLD scrutinised the weeklies. That has now gone, so it is *News Stand* which has inherited its job of turning the pages of *Psychic News*, *Meat Trades Journal* and so on. The results, on Radio 4 every Saturday morning, are often very engaging.

In 1987, when its production was transferred to the special current affairs department, its format was changed to allow interviews (of editors, for example) and more detailed discussion of a particular theme. Martin Wainwright is a frequent presenter; others have included Nicholas Comfort and Hugh Prysor-Jones.

Night Owls
Show which used to run from midnight to 1 a.m. on Radio 2, presented by DAVE GELLY.

Night Ride
One of the programmes in Radio 2's through-the-night service, introduced in 1979. It and the rest of the output until 4 a.m. tends to be presented by the network's in-house announcers. The voices of such as JEAN CHALLIS, PATRICK LUNT, John Terrett and Andrew Lane have, in this way, become familiar, friendly and reassuring for the lonely and insomniac, and those for whom the night hours hold no comfort.

Night Rockin'
Midnight heavy metal rock show presented on Radio 1 by ALAN FREEMAN on his return to the network in 1989.

The Night Sky
Monthly talk describing the stars and other heavenly bodies visible during the course of that month, which ran on Network Three.

Nightbeat
Full of echoing footsteps and moody menace, shadows of sound in smoky clubs and dark streets, the hero of this *radio noir* series is ace Chicago Star reporter Randy Stone. His night shift drags him into hazardous adventures among the Windy City's low life. He never seems to write many stories, but he rescues a lot of dames.

Originally broadcast on a US network from 1950–52, these Chandleresque stories started here – one of BBC Radio's handful of imported programmes – on the opening night of Radio 5 in 1990. Stone, the hard-bitten hack with the soft inside, was played by Frank Lovejoy (1912–62), a tough guy actor who also starred in movies of the period such as *I Was A Communist For The FBI*.

Nightingale, Anne (1943–)
Husky-voiced lady from Brighton who, having drifted into radio from newspaper journalism via interviews for

Anne Nightingale from Brighton was 27 when, in 1970, she became the first female disc-jockey on Radio 1. But her show was in the evening, and it was another nineteen years before a woman was entrusted with a daytime slot

SCENE AND HEARD and the magazine programme POP INSIDE, became Radio 1's first woman DJ. (Though not until JAKKI BRAMBLES in 1989 was a woman given a daytime slot.) Her Sunday evening request show, originally intended as a three-month filler, has been running since 1982.

No Longer Known At This Address
Well researched Radio 4 series in 1990 in which presenter Hugh Prysor-Jones and producer John Forsyth (the same team which made A YEAR OF DYING DANGEROUSLY) reported on the increasing numbers of people going missing – not the Lucans or Lamplughs, but the debtors, defaulters and disorientated, the illegal immigrants and bail jumpers, who simply detach themselves from normal society.

'No more curried eggs for me!'
Catchphrase of MAJOR BLOODNOK in THE GOON SHOW.

No Strings Attached

Eight-part Radio 2 series in 1988 devoted to groups who specialise in unaccompanied singing. It began and ended with The Swingle Singers, who have led the way in a cappella harmony since their formation in 1962.

No Time for Nursery Rhymes

Six-part series co-produced by the BBC and UNICEF, on Radio 4 in 1989, in which Tessa Shaw looked at the rights of children in the light of the Convention of the Rights of the Child, then being considered by the United Nations.

Norden, Denis (1922–)

One half of the extraordinarily productive comedy partnership with FRANK MUIR, co-writers of TAKE IT FROM HERE, BREAKFAST WITH BRADEN and *Bedtime with Braden* and fellow panellist on MY WORD (since 1956) and MY MUSIC (since 1967).

A Norfolk Man

Six conversations on Radio 4 in 1989, each one between JOHN TIMPSON and a prominent Norfolk man, who included a farmer, historian and cleric. The title could just as well refer to the interviewer: Timpson, although born in Harrow, has had a lifelong affection for the county (where he now lives) ever since he was a district reporter in Dereham early in his career.

Northants Radio

ILR station based in Northampton, covering Northants and parts of Leics and Warwicks, on the air since 1986.

Northsound Radio

ILR station based in Aberdeen, on the air since 1981. It covers an area from Peterhead in the north to Inverbervie in the south. NICKY CAMPBELL started here.

Now Radio

Lively weekly magazine for the radio industry founded in 1987 by Howard Rose, now at KCBC.

Now Read On

Six-part Radio 5 series in 1991 in which bookworm Phil Rickman investigated what people really read, as opposed to what they claimed to read.

Number One

Stephen Murray's character in THE NAVY LARK.

Nursery Sing-Song

Regular ingredient of CHILDREN'S HOUR from 1938–60, consisting of stories and songs for the wee ones. The singer Doris Gambell was closely associated with it.

Ocean Sound
ILR station based in Fareham, covering Portsmouth, Southampton and the Winchester area. Started in 1986. Launched The Light FM (1987), The Gold AM (1988) and Power FM (1988).

Odds Against
Radio 4 series in 1989 in which Nick Baker profiled four lone campaigners: Bob Borzello (who has now succeeded, having written over 1,000 letters to the Press Council, in diluting much of the racist reporting in newspapers), Stuart Holmes (anti-tobacco), Mona McNee (a passionate believer in teaching reading phonetically), and John Owen (implacable foe of the Channel Tunnel).

O'Donnell, Michael (1928–)
Presenter of RELATIVE VALUES since it began in 1987, and chosen for his sympathetic family doctor's ear. He is a qualified GP, a former editor of *World Medicine* and a member of the General Medical Council, as well as a writer and broadcaster who has contributed to STOP THE WEEK and chaired MY WORD.

An Odyssey Round Odysseus
Four-part series on Radio 4 in 1989, tracing Odysseus's homeward journey from Troy to Ithaca through the Greek islands. It was presented by Oxford classics don Oliver Taplin and made on location in Greece and Turkey, with Brian Glover playing the poet Homer in a strong northern accent.

The series was more an analysis of Odysseus's enduring appeal than a straightforward recreation of one of literature's epic journeys, and many found it difficult to follow.

Off the Treadmill
Thoughtful Radio 4 series in 1989 suggesting that Britain sends too many people to jail and that we may be able to learn lessons from other European countries in dealing with crime and criminals in non-custodial ways.

Presented by John Alderson, former Chief Constable of Devon and Cornwall and later an SDP policy adviser.

Ogden, Nigel (1955–)
Versatile, Northern-born organist who has presented THE ORGANIST ENTERTAINS since 1980. He made his debut on BBC Radio Manchester.

'Old Ones, New Ones, Loved Ones, Neglected Ones . . . '
Reverent words with which ALBERTO SEMPRINI softly introduced his long-running SEMPRINI SERENADE.

Old Stagers
Liberace and Evelyn Laye were among the showbiz stars of yesteryear profiled in this series which began on Radio 4 in 1981 and later switched to Radio 2. Peter Cotes, theatre director and writer, scripted some of the programmes.

Old Wine In New Bottles
Weekday afternoon show on the Light Programme, featuring the BBC WEST OF ENGLAND LIGHT ORCHESTRA.

The Omar Khayyam Show
Comedy series on the Home Service which began in 1963, written by and starring SPIKE MILLIGAN, in his first major radio appearances since the ending of THE GOON SHOW, and produced by CHARLES CHILTON. It starred Bill Kerr, John Bluthal, Barry Humphries (many years before Dame Edna), Brian Wilde and Bob Todd. The music was by George Chisholm 'and his Jolly Jazzers'.

On Parade
Crisp title for Radio 2 series on British military bands – their music, history and traditions – which BRIAN JOHNSTON presented in 1990. Among those featured were the bands of the Grenadier Guards, Scots Guards and Royal Artillery.

On Stage, Everybody
Sunday night Light Programme show launched by Evelyn Laye in 1960, featuring the BBC REVUE ORCHESTRA, which reflected the musical shows of the day.

On The Air
Radio 2 quiz game which harvests the great names and programmes from the long history of wireless. Devised and presented by DAVID RIDER, and running since 1984. Panellists have included PERCY EDWARDS, MARGARET HOWARD and BRIAN MATTHEW.

On the Ropes
Interesting Radio 4 series, beginning in 1989, in which JOHN HUMPHRYS interviews people who have in some way fallen from grace or lost their way, but bounced back. They have included Derek Hatton, former Liverpool politician; Jeffrey Archer, former MP; Audrey Slaughter, who lost most of her money when her magazine *Working Woman* folded after eighteen months; Arunbhai Patel, entrepreneur; Ron Brown, the Labour MP involved in a lurid court case; Count Nikolai Tolstoy; Sock Shop founder Sophie Mirman; and Anthony Simonds-Gooding, brutally deposed chief executive of the satellite television company BSB.

On Your Farm
Thirty years ago this went out at Wednesday lunchtimes on the Home Service, as a serious agricultural round-up. Today, it has changed its day, time and format, and also transformed itself into one of radio's great treats.

Sunday mornings on Radio 4 sees an interviewer tuck into a hearty breakfast with a farmer and his wife (farmers rarely seem to be bachelors, for some reason) then discuss their farm with them round the kitchen table.

The farms, as well as the breakfasts, vary: they can be anywhere from Battle to Bavaria or, on one occasion, in the Mississippi Delta. If one doesn't often hear the sizzling of sausages, there is usually a discreet background rattle of cups and saucers.

On Your Marks
Three-hour show for youngsters aged up to fourteen which has gone out on Saturday mornings on Radio 5 ever since it was launched in 1990. Hosted by Mark Curry. It has a news and current affairs quiz, *Marks out of Ten*, a regular forum for strong views, *Platform Five*, a cooking slot called *Curry in the Kitchen* and music requests.

Once Upon a Time
Lewis Carroll's *Alice in Wonderland* and Oxford; John Masefield's *The Box of Delights* and his birthplace in Ledbury, Herefordshire; Kipling's *Puck of Pook's Hill* and Sussex; and Kenneth Grahame's *The Wind in the Willows* and Pangbourne, were some of the literary landscapes explored in this six-part Radio 4 series in 1990. Christina Hardyment and MARJORIE LOFTHOUSE examined the inspiration which real places had exercised on the authors of these classic children's books.

One Minute, Please
Forerunner of JUST A MINUTE, also devised by IAN MESSITER, and based on a humiliating ordeal he experienced as a thirteen-year-old schoolboy at Sherborne. A Latin master called Parry-Jones punished him for gazing out of the window and day-dreaming by insisting that he stand in front of the class and for sixty seconds repeat what he had just said – without hesitating or repeating himself. As he was unable to do this he was then caned, in front of the whole class. Out of this painful episode emerged, in 1951, the highly successful show which is not only still running on Radio 4 under its new name but has also been heard on radio, and adapted for television, in many other countries.

The first programme, with ROY PLOMLEY as compere, pitted GILBERT HARDING, KENNETH HORNE and Reggie Purdell against Yvonne Arnaud, Valerie Hobson and Nan Kenway. The programme's chief discovery was to be GERARD HOFFNUNG, who made his debut on the show and first recounted his famous Bricklayer's Story on it.

Messiter's first suggested title of *Just a Minute* was rejected by the BBC as too slick, and he did not inaugurate it until he presented the show on South African radio later in the 1950s. Later, on Radio 4, *One Minute, Please* finished and *Just a Minute* succeeded it.

1, 2, 3, 4, 5
Radio 5 series for toddlers launched when the network began. It features rhymes, finger games, quizzes and a soap (*Wiggly Park*, by Keith Faulkener) and goes out twice every weekday.

Open House
Long-running Radio 2 series, hosted by PETE MURRAY.

Open Mind
Only one British politician per programme was the rule of this Radio 4 discussion series which began in 1988, aiming to 'say something concrete and new each week', look at current topics in a fresh way, and transcend the tedious wrangles of party politics.

It aims to discuss issues before they erupt into news stories and claims to have ventilated one of the first serious suggestions of German reunification, in a programme chaired by Edward Mortimer, long before it looked likely. Animal rights, genetic engineering, Islam and the West and the absence of a black middle class have been among other subjects discussed. Hugo Young and John Lloyd are the two other columnists who take it in turns to chair the conversation.

Open University

Over 100,000 people in Britain have gained Open University degrees using radio, television and correspondence. For more than twenty years, radio has been broadcasting courses in Socrates and linear algebra, Jews and Christians in Renaissance Venice and the geography of malaria, often at odd hours of the day and night. These are linked to students' textbooks. In addition, they provide fascinating listening for others who like to eavesdrop on the erudite, and learn.

Radio has been central to the idea of the OU. Discussion about its possible role in higher education tuition began in the 1920s and the cover of RADIO TIMES for 13 June 1924 carried the headline 'A Broadcasting University'. It was not until the early 1960s that proposals were crystallised, however, by which time several major countries had already embarked on 'distance' teaching of various kinds.

In 1962 educationist Michael Young suggested in *Where* magazine 'an open university'; in 1963 Harold Wilson, in a speech in Glasgow, proposed a 'University of the Air' as a consortium of existing universities using radio, TV and correspondence to bring their tuition to adults in their own homes. After he became Prime Minister in 1964, Wilson asked Jennie Lee, his Arts Minister, to turn the idea into reality. One new university, rather than a consortium of existing ones, emerged.

The first students were admitted in 1971, which is also when the first programmes began on BBC2 and BBC Radio. The first radio programme was *Science – Introduction to the Foundation Course*, on Radio 3. It was followed, two days later, by Radio 4's *Open Forum*, a magazine for students and staff which still goes out each week throughout the OU year.

In 1975, there were 100 twenty-minute programmes broadcast each week. But students began to show a marked preference for audio cassettes, which were sent out with the printed course material and could be played at any time. The number of radio programmes has therefore declined sharply, and in 1990 there was an average of sixteen twenty-minute programmes each week.

In 1990 all OU programmes were switched to Radio 5, and the OU plans more faculty-based rather than course-related programmes to encourage what it describes as 'a wider eavesdropping audience'.

Opera News

Monthly Radio 3 round-up of news and opinion from the opera world, presented by JAMES NAUGHTIE. It began in April 1990, intended to convey the scale, glamour and intense excitement of opera and reflect its growing popularity (especially among the young).

Hence the choice of Naughtie, a journalist albeit an opera-loving one: his crisp, urgent, topical style was just what was deemed necessary for the new programme, a deliberate move away from the languid, distant tone more associated with Radio 3 presenters.

Opinion

Short, Sunday-night series on Radio 4 in 1990 in which controversial subjects were tackled from unashamedly partisan positions. Rastafarian poet Benjamin Zephaniah and South Yorkshire's Chief Constable Richard Wells presented contrasting viewpoints on the police. Designer Vivienne Westwood attacked the dominance of commercialism over scholarship in museums, and ex-IRA member Shane Paul O'Doherty and civil rights activist Eamonn McCann spoke on violence and Ireland.

Opportunity Knocks

Years before this famous talent show arrived on television, it was running on Radio Luxembourg in the early 1950s and with the same host, Hughie Green. It was recorded on disc in London before being flown out to the Grand Duchy.

ITV made it a part of their schedules for over two decades, from 1956–77. In 1987, BBC-TV – still then being run by the astute showman Michael Grade – bought the rights to the show and resurrected it, hiring Bob Monkhouse as compere.

Options

Umbrella title for BBC Radio's adult education programmes on Saturday and Sunday afternoons when they were gathered there, on Radio 4 FM, from 1985 until June 1990, before education switched to Radio 5.

During that period the slot was host to about 170 series and fifty one-off programmes covering subjects as diverse as Renaissance music, microcomputers, crime and punishment and having a baby, as well as language courses in Turkish, Chinese, Hindi, Urdu and Russian.

Options bowed out with a menu on its last day that included *When in France* (French for holidaymakers), *Education 2000* (the future of adult education) and GET WRITING.

Orchard FM

ILR station covering Somerset, South Avon and North-West Dorset, based in Taunton where the cider apples grow. It began in 1989 and broadcasts mainly classic hits of the 1960s, 1970s and 1980s.

Orchestral Portraits

Record series hosted by ALAN DELL on the Home Service.

Opportunity Knocks **began on the Light Programme in 1949, moving to Radio Luxembourg the following year. Evidently enjoying themselves are, left to right, compere Hughie Green and his talent-spotting assistants Sheila Sim and Pat McGrath**

The Organist Entertains
Radio 2 series devoted to organ music which began in 1969. Presented by NIGEL OGDEN for many years.

Origins
Radio 4 history series which included a six-part look at the development of British cathedrals from St Augustine in 597.

Orton, Joe   (1933–67)
One of the discoveries of the BBC, to whom he sent an unsolicited script called *The Boy Hairdresser*. It shocked the female readers at the BBC, but a young John Tydeman, who had joined from Cambridge not long before and rose to become head of radio drama, spotted its potential.

He persuaded Orton to make changes in it, and helped to get him a top-class literary agent. Kenneth Halliwell – Orton's lover, and later his killer – came up with a new title which was *The Ruffian on the Stair*. Tydeman directed this on the Third Programme in 1964. It was Orton's first play, and the only one he ever had broadcast on radio. Later works, such as

Entertaining Mr Sloane, were turned down partly on the grounds that they were too visual.

Orwell, George   (1903–50)
Worked for two years as a talks producer and commentator in the Eastern Service of the BBC World Service, and modelled his most famous novel, *Nineteen Eighty-Four*, on aspects of censorship and bureaucracy he encountered at BROADCASTING HOUSE. For the wartime serial which he devised which he began and E.M. Forster finished, see LITERARY CONSEQUENCES.

Other Minds
Series of six Radio 3 conversations in 1990 between Lewis Wolpert and other scientists.

Ottoman Adventure
The eight-part story of Irish novelist Joseph Hone's travels in Turkey, read on Radio 4 in 1990.

Out of Order
Light-hearted political quiz with two rival teams captained by Tory MP Julian Critchley and Labour MP Austin Mitchell, 'Mitch 'n' Critch' as they are known in the trade. Both of them seem to enjoy more success as journalists than as politicians. The chairman is Patrick Hannan. It started on Radio 4 in Wales in 1988 but now goes out over the whole country.

Out on the Floor

The thirty-year history of the disco was traced in this three-part Radio 1 series in 1990 by JEFF YOUNG, beginning with JIMMY SAVILE who apparently claims to have invented it when he first invited people to come to a hall to listen to records rather than a live band – entertaining them by means of two turntables, thereby ensuring non-stop music.

Savile's claim was disputed. People who wrote to RADIO TIMES pointed out that dual turntables were in fact exhibited at the RADIO SHOW in 1933, advertised in *The Gramophone* in 1931 and illustrated in the BBC Handbook of 1929.

Outlook

'Conversation, colour and controversy', from Britain and around the world, are the ingredients of this World Service magazine series mixing both serious and lighter items. It now goes out on Radio 5 as well, like many other World Service programmes.

Since it began in 1966, it has been presented from all over the world and often by John Tidmarsh, one of its regulars who has been on it from the start. He started in journalism as a sports reporter on the *Western Daily Press* in Bristol and switched to the BBC in 1956 as a holiday relief on RADIO NEWSREEL.

Outside broadcasts

Have been mounted since the earliest days: the first was of Mozart's *The Magic Flute* from Covent Garden in January 1923. Later that month came the first outside broadcast of after-dinner speeches – at a Burns Night dinner. The first live broadcast of music from the Savoy Hotel was in April 1923.

The Outside Broadcasts Department was created by Gerald Cock in 1925, succeeded by the influential SEYMOUR DE LOTBINIERE in 1935. The first live sports commentary was of the England v. Wales rugby international, at Twickenham in January 1927, by 'TEDDY' WAKELAM (also see LANCE SIEVEKING). The following Saturday saw the first soccer broadcast, Arsenal v. Sheffield United at Highbury, again by Wakelam.

A few months later came the first cricket report (see SIR PELHAM WARNER). The first racing commentator (1928) was R.C. Lyle, racing correspondent of *The Times*, whose first big broadcast was that year's Derby, won by Felstead. The first major soccer commentator was George Allison, in the 1930s, but this was in an era when the game feared that people wouldn't pay money to come to matches if they could hear them free on the radio. The Football League refused to allow the BBC to broadcast any League matches throughout the 1930s, a ban which remained until after the war.

The first woman commentator was Thelma Carpenter, an amateur snooker champion, who commentated on a snooker match in 1936. The BBC's first sports correspondent (1959) was PETER BROMLEY; its first football correspondent (1963) was Brian Moore; its first cricket correspondent (also 1963) was BRIAN JOHNSTON. BBC Radio's first tennis correspondent was Gerald Williams.

In due course Radio 2 became the main national conduit for sports coverage, with about 700 hours a year, until Radio 5 took nearly all sport under its wing in 1990.

The Ovaltineys

Fondly remembered show for children, sponsored by the malted milk drink, which started on Radio Luxembourg in 1935 and went out on Sunday evenings between 5.30 and 6.30 p.m.

After more than 200 shows it stopped at the outbreak of the Second World War, when the Grand Duchy was occupied by Germany, but was revived in 1946 and ran for several more years.

Children were able to join a club, The League of Ovaltineys, which had its own rule book, secret codes and Seven Rules. By 1939, five million of them had joined (when Radio 4 launched a similar venture, the CAT'S WHISKERS Club in 1988, about 4,000 joined, which gives some idea of the scale of radio's decline).

Ovaltiney comics were given away free with *Chuckler* and *Dazzler*, and touring concert parties all helped to promote the League, the programme, and of course the drink.

Songs broadcast on the show have reverberated through the years:

> And now the happy Ovaltineys
> Bid you all adieu
> And don't forget your Ovaltine
> It's very good for you.'

The spirit and music of Luxembourg's show were revived in a nostalgic Ovaltine commercial on ITV in the 1970s, showing a man walking briskly through the rain, back home to his smiling wife and apple-cheeked children by the fireside, listening to the wireless.

P

Painting, Norman (1928–)

Former tutor in Anglo-Saxon at Exeter College, Oxford, who has been in THE ARCHERS longer than anyone else. He has always played farmer Phil, ever since the programme began as a Midlands experiment in May 1950. Under the pseudonym Bruno Milna, he has also written about 1,200 scripts for the programme.

In the 1950s he had many scripts broadcast on CHILDREN'S HOUR. Among them was *The Boy and the Seven Wonders*, a seven-part serial in 1957 about the adventures of an Egyptian boy called Toto, born just before Christ.

Painting of the Month

An early example of an imaginative series with its own 'tie-in' merchandising, though vulgar phraseology like that would not have been recognised at the time. From 1960 onwards, the Home Service mounted a series of talks on the first Sunday of the month in which art academics and gallery keepers would discuss a favourite work: the first programme featured National Gallery director Sir Philip Hardy talking about Uccello's *St George and the Dragon*. Paintings by Rubens, Rembrandt, Watteau and Manet were also discussed in that first year.

Listeners were able to purchase a set of full-colour reproductions of all the pictures, with each one being posted out shortly before the broadcast, so that they could study them in their armchairs while the talks were taking place. This service cost the princely sum of 2 guineas a year. A programme well worth resurrecting.

Parade of the Pops

'A review of this week's popular music and prediction of hits to come', this went out on weekday evenings on the Light Programme in the early 1960s, often featuring Bob Miller and the Millermen.

Paradise Street

Comedy series of the 1950s starring SPIKE MILLIGAN, Hattie Jacques and Max Bygraves, set in the East End. Its catchphrase 'A good idea – son' involved audience participation: the performers shouted the first three words and the studio audience shouted back 'son'. This two-way device was later employed by Bruce Forsyth ('Nice to see you – to see you nice') as well.

Parker, Charles (–1980)

Creator, with husband-and-wife folk singers Ewan MacColl (1915–89, who also wrote 'The First Time Ever I Saw Your Face') and Peggy Seeger, of the eight RADIO BALLADS, which broke new ground in documentaries.

For the first time, they allowed people to speak for themselves about their own lives, without actors or narrator to filter and interpret their experiences. Their stories were told with the help of actuality sound, and folk song or jazz to create the twentieth-century equivalent of ancient folk ballads.

Much of Parker's work is kept at the Central Reference Library in Birmingham, including some 5,000 tapes plus files and papers. GILLIAN REYNOLDS was a founding trustee of his archive.

Parodies Lost

As the title suggests, a literary entertainment. Chaired by Jenni Murray on Radio 4, it allows contestants to decide their own fates. Each episode is written by a different writer, who have included SIMON BRETT and Wally K. Daly, in a different genre.

Party Pieces

Quirky, irreverent, ten-minute political lampoon conceived by Kenneth Baker MP (then a Tory backbencher) and running on Capital Radio since October 1979. He and Ed Boyle, former political editor of LBC, formed a company to produce the programme each week and sell it to Capital.

The show consists of sharply edited and very funny extracts culled from the taped proceedings of both Commons and Lords. Many of the backbenchers who have presented it on air have won ministerial office, whereupon they have promptly stopped presenting it. These include Baker himself and David Mellor. On the other side of the House, MPs who have presented it include Chris Price, Ken Livingstone and Rosie Barnes.

Pashto Service
Programmes in the Pashto language broadcast from BUSH HOUSE, which now go out for an hour a day. In the late 1980s, the service gained an increasing audience among the Afghan refugees in the camps of the North-West Frontier region of Pakistan, reaching 600,000 people by 1989. This was reflected in the mailbag: the service received 14,917 letters that year, 70 per cent more than the year before.

Paul Temple
One of radio drama's popular classics, heralded by one of the most potent of all signature tunes – Vivian Ellis's 'Coronation Scot', with its promise of travel, glamour, mystery and danger. (It was not, however, the original signature tune, which was Ravel's 'Sheherazade'.)

Francis Durbridge created this smooth and leisurely sleuth, three years after he left Birmingham University, in *Send For Paul Temple* in April 1938. Paul was the son of Lieutenant-General Ian Temple and born in Ontario; he had come to England at the age of ten and gone to Rugby and Magdalen College, Oxford. He had published his first detective novel when he was 22 and gone on to write three dozen more.

An interest in criminology led to him helping Scotland Yard investigate several puzzling real-life cases, and in one of them he met a Fleet Street journalist called Louise Harvey, who wrote under the name Steve Trent. They were married at St Mary Abbot's, Kensington, and lived in style in Evesham with Paul collecting first editions when he wasn't out solving baffling crimes. Of course, there was a London *pied à terre* as well.

This set-up of chic married couple playing detective, like *The Thin Man* which preceded it and *Hart to Hart* which followed, proved a huge success. The adventures ran for three decades, with six actors playing Paul: Hugh Morton (1938–39); Carl Bernard (1942); Barry Morse (1945); Howard Marion Crawford (1946); Kim Peacock (1946–51) and Peter Coke (1954–68). Two actresses played the devoted Steve: originally Bernadette Hodgson and then MARJORIE WESTBURY from the second series in November 1938 until the last one in the spring of 1968.

The original *Send For Paul Temple* was one of the BBC's first serials and also helped establish the radio drama career of Martyn C. Webster, who produced the Temple serials for more than 25 years.

Pause for Thought
Religious slot on Radio 2 which evolved from FIVE TO TEN and has talks, songs, recollections or favourite hymns. Running since 1970, it now consists of three

separate broadcasts each morning. The first, always recorded, goes out at 1.30 and 3.30 in the small hours and was introduced in 1990 to comfort the lonely, anxious or insomniac. The second, at 6.45, is usually recorded. The last, always live and commanding by far the biggest audience, is at 9.15 on DEREK JAMESON's show. Among those who have appeared on this slot are RABBI LIONEL BLUE and ROGER ROYLE.

Paxton's America
The first series to start on Radio 2 after it turned into an exclusively FM network in August 1990 was this six-part portrayal of current US folk music, presented by Tom Paxton.

PC49
Archibald Berkeley-Willoughby, the amiable, ex-public school, Hendon-trained London bobby, was British fiction's first uniformed copper – as distinct from all the plain-clothes detectives and private investigators – to reach the ranks of national heroes.

A radio original, he starred in more than 100 adventures from 1947 to 1953, and won such affection that he also appeared in two films, several books, advertisements for Silmos Lollies, cartoon booklets produced by the Government in an effort to increase production, a board game called *Burglars*, a jigsaw puzzle called *PC49 and the Organ Grinder's Monkey* and, most notably, as a strip cartoon in the pages of *Eagle*. PC49 was the star of page three in the first issue of *Eagle*, in April 1950, and continued to thrill readers of the greatest ever boys' paper until March 1957, when he was replaced by Mark Question.

Whether in the cinema, on radio, or on the printed page, Archie devoted his time to catching the louts, touts, spivs and crooks who infested his manor in mythical Q Division. Although his superiors never saw fit to promote him to sergeant (unlike the similar George Dixon in *Dixon of Dock Green*, which began on BBC-TV nine years later) Archie saw to it that being a constable was a noble calling, foiling the villainy of thugs like Knocker Dawson, Slim Jiggs and The Shadow, and recovering countless hauls of hidden swag. 'My Sunday helmet!' was the nearest he came to an oath, though 'Out you go, Fortynine' (uttered by Det. Sgt. Wright) and Archie's 'Yes Sarge! Good morning all!' were the two other exclamations that turned into national catchphrases.

PC49 was created by an Australian crime reporter, Alan Stranks, who came to England in the 1930s. He conceived the idea of a series about an ordinary bobby on the beat, the backbone of the Metropolitan Police, from a Scotland Yard sergeant in 1947. He took the project to BBC Radio variety producer Vernon Harris, and the two of them fashioned what was to be a highly successful show, both charming and exciting.

Behind the scenes in Broadcasting House's golden age – pre-CD, pre-microchip, pre-cassette. The lady and her gramophones are helping to assemble *Paul Temple and the Curzon Case*, 1949

Archie was played by Cheshire-born, ENSA-trained Brian Reece; Wright by Eric Phillips; Det. Insp. Wilson by Leslie Perrins and Archie's fiancée Joan Carr (later his wife) by Joy Shelton.

Each adventure was a self-contained episode – the first being *The Case of the Drunken Sailor* – and went out initially at 9.30 p.m., but they proved so popular with youngsters that they were repeated at the considerably earlier time of 7 p.m. Archie married Joan in 1952 and by the following year she had presented him with a son and heir. The happy event was reflected in *The Case of the Blue Booties* in March 1953, the first of thirteen adventures that formed 49's last radio series.

The two movies in which Archie appeared were *The Adventures of PC49* (1949) and *A Case for PC49* (1951). Stranks and Harris wrote both, but actors Reece and Shelton appeared only in the second.

Pedrick, Gale (1905–70)
Radio critic (e.g. of the London *Star* in the 1940s) who later became a broadcaster. He was the original presenter of PICK OF THE WEEK.

Peebles, Andy (1948–)
Specialist music presenter on Piccadilly Radio from 1974–78, and a DJ on Radio 1 ever since. He has a sad scoop to his name – a lengthy interview with John Lennon two days before his murder in New York in December 1980, subsequently used as a tribute broadcast on Radio 1 and now out on cassette. (It was not the last interview Lennon ever gave, because he gave

one to RKO on the day of his death, but it was the last for British audiences.)

Peel, John (1939–)

Cotton broker's son from The Wirrall (not Liverpool) whose real name is John Ravenscroft. Schooled at Shrewsbury, he worked on radio stations in Texas and Oklahoma in the Beatles era before changing his name to the snappier Peel when he returned to become a pirate DJ on Radio London in 1967. He joined Radio 1 a few months later.

Through his TOP GEAR programme he championed both new bands, helping to establish Cream and Pink Floyd, and new musical styles including flower-power, punk and hip-hop. This enthusiasm for innovation is as much a hallmark as his lugubrious vocal monotone, its strong Liverpudlian accent an affectation dating from Beatlemania days.

His slot has moved around. *Top Gear* was originally on a Saturday, but from about 1975 he presented shows during the week. In 1990, however, he moved at his own request back to the weekends, prompted by his increasing hatred of commuting to London from his home in Suffolk and spending twenty hours a week in his car.

Peel is the one remaining DJ from the original Radio 1 line-up of 1967 still broadcasting on the network today and, in Sue Lawley's words, has had 'an uninterrupted reign as the intelligent voice of pop'.

Pen to Paper

Two Radio 4 series in 1990 of new writing, both prose and poetry. They were edited by Liz Rigbey, former editor of THE ARCHERS. More than 100 writers had their work broadcast, read by forty actors.

Pennine

Bradford-based ILR station covering that city, plus Huddersfield and Halifax, and which is also heard in Leeds and Keighley. It started in 1975. In 1989 it split its services, with a golden oldies service, Classic Gold, on medium wave and Pennine FM for younger listeners on its FM frequencies.

The station was a founder member of the Bradford Fire Disaster Appeal, which helped to raise £4 million for the dependants of the devastating fire at the city's football ground.

People and Plagues

Four-part Radio 4 series in 1989 in which Geoff Watts looked at the efforts of doctors and scientists (some of whom had bravely used themselves as guinea pigs) to combat some of history's worst diseases.

People Today

Weekly series on the Home Service in the early 1960s which featured extended interviews with interesting, unusual individuals. Several of the programmes were produced by David Glencross, now chief executive of the Independent Television Commission, who at that time was a BBC Radio talks producer in the Midland Region of the BBC.

Perkins, Geoffrey (1953–)

Talented young producer of light entertainment shows such as THE HITCH-HIKER'S GUIDE TO THE GALAXY and QUOTE . . . UNQUOTE, who has subsequently moved on to television.

Persian Service

Programmes in the Persian language first came out of BUSH HOUSE in December 1940. Today, on the air for 1 hour and 45 minutes a day, they form an important link between Iran and Britain: after the severing of diplomatic relations in 1989, following Ayatollah Khomeini's call for the death of Salman Rushdie, the service remained one of the few direct channels of communication between the two countries.

Personal Choice

Radio 2 series in which celebrity guests present their favourite music. Denis Healey chose both *West Side Story* and *La Traviata*.

Personal Obsessions

Series first transmitted on BBC Radio Scotland and then on Radio 4 in 1990 in which collectors explained the fanatical pleasure they gained from their various collections.

A Perspective for Living

Six-part Radio 4 series in 1991 in which Bel Mooney spoke to people about the different ways in which experience of death had affected their lives.

Among them was Anna Haycraft, better known as the novelist Alice Thomas Ellis, whose son Joshua died at the age of nineteen, and Tory Party chairman Chris Patten, who talked of his mother's early death and how the end of that relationship altered his perception of his role as a father.

Pet Subjects

Radio 4 series about owners and their pets, among them a collection of eighty spiders and a Stilton-eating rabbit, introduced by Fergus Keeling of THE NATURAL HISTORY PROGRAMME in 1990. The origin of the series was controversial: the rabbit's owner, Keith Wooldridge of Lewisham, claimed he had put up the idea and took out a summons against Radio 4 at Bromley County Court. He won his case in March 1991 and the BBC was ordered to pay him damages and costs.

Pete's Party

'Sunday night get-together round the gramophone' on the Light Programme circa 1960, hosted by PETE MURRAY.

Peter Calls The Tune

Saturday evening show on the Light Programme with Peter Haigh playing records.

Petticoat Line

Funny, all-female version of ANY QUESTIONS?, in which listeners' letters were treated to a feminine, and mildly feminist, point of view. For fourteen years, ANONA WINN chaired a panel which always included the earthy Renee Houston (who was rationed to saying 'bloody' three times per show, according to its producer IAN MESSITER) and often had *Observer* columnist Katharine Whitehorn and Sheila Van Damm.

The show was Anona Winn's conception. At first she envisaged it as a more serious venture to be called *The Ombudswomen*, with the panel dispensing advice in response to listeners' problems. In the event it was given a lighter and more comedic touch.

Phillips, Frank   (1901–)

Professional singer for over ten years (1923–35) who then became a BBC Radio announcer of the proper, old-fashioned school. Among the momentous events he announced to listeners was the dropping of the atom bomb on Hiroshima in 1945.

Phone-ins

Although there was at least one phone-in programme in the 1930s (when BBC-TV's first Director of Television, Gerald Cock, appeared live in the studio in December 1938 and answered viewers' questions by telephone) the term itself, according to the OED, was not in use until 1968 in the USA and 1971 in Britain. The first regular phone-in series on British radio is believed to have been that on BBC Radio Nottingham in 1968.

The 1970s was the decade of the phone-in. Cheap to produce, they were a godsend for local radio, which often made much of a feature of them. (See PHILLIP HODSON, BRIAN HAYES and JAMES WHALE.) In addition, they promised instant controversy, a contribution to democratic debate and – if someone important was in the studio – access to the powerful.

On Radio 4, phone-ins were pioneered by the late producer Walter Wallich, a refugee from Germany in the 1930s. He helped to introduce IT'S YOUR LINE and WHATEVER YOU THINK. Their successor was TUESDAY CALL, which became CALL NICK ROSS. ANY ANSWERS?, previously based on letters, was turned into a phone-in in 1989.

Today, phone-ins are now widespread throughout BBC, ILR and the World Service, which mounted its first one in 1982. They are used for a variety of purposes from questioning Prime Ministers (see IT'S YOUR WORLD and RUSSIAN SERVICE) to solving sex problems (on LBC) to arranging marriages (on the Asian station Sunrise). The station which held out the longest against them was Radio 3, but even that now succumbs once a year to enable listeners to question its Controller.

Sometimes phone-ins have been used to embarrassing effect. Denis MacShane, then a reporter on BBC Radio London, was sacked in 1976 after he posed as a listener and rang a phone-in on his own station to make a hostile remark about Tory politician Reginald Maudling. And in 1989 prankster VICTOR LEWIS SMITH posed as a listener in Doncaster when he telephoned the annual 'Call the Controller' phone-in to Radio 4 boss MICHAEL GREEN and, apparently apoplectic with rage, savaged him for broadcasting the soap opera CITIZENS. Highly skilled with voices, he used a false name when he rang and fooled everyone in the studio.

The 1980s, on American radio, saw the growth of an ugly new breed of phone-in presenter – obnoxious individuals who disagreed with callers as a matter of course and subjected them to verbal abuse. The phenomenon was explored in Oliver Stone's 1989 film *Talk Radio*.

Piccadilly Radio

ILR station in Manchester, which began in 1974. In the 1980s it diversified, and set up its subsidiary PPM RADIO WAVES to pioneer sponsored and syndicated programming. In 1987 it was banned by the IBA from offering car stickers as prizes in a quiz – with copies of *Spycatcher*, the controversial book on MI5 written by Peter Wright which the Government tried to ban, attached.

It split its services in 1988, like most ILR stations, launching a new service called Key 103 on FM. In 1989 it was taken over by the Miss World Group led by Owen Oyston. One of the broadcasters to have been launched by Piccadilly is Andy Crane, the children's television host, who had his first broadcasting job here as a £5-a-week Sunday helper.

Pick of the Pops

Started on the Light Programme in October 1955, with FRANKLIN ENGELMANN making a choice of 'current popular gramophone records'. (Not until ALAN FREEMAN took over did it broadcast the Hit Parade.) After only a handful of shows he was succeeded by ALAN DELL, then DAVID JACOBS, who was its host at 10.40 p.m. on Saturday nights. In 1961 it was incorporated into TRAD TAVERN with Freeman as the presenter, with his soon-to-be-immortal rallying call of 'Greetings, pop pickers!'

Not an Oxbridge senior common room, but a drone of correctly dressed BBC announcers in December 1951. Clockwise from bottom left-hand corner: Frank Phillips, Alan Skempton, Robert Dougall, Colin Doran, Alvar Lidell, Colin Marson and Robin Holmes

The formula he soon introduced was new releases and possible hits in the first half of the hour-long show, and the Top Ten, broadcast in reverse order in a spirit of increasingly frantic excitement, in the second. This countdown was punctuated by feverish bursts of the signature tune 'At the Sound of the Swinging Cymbal'.

Pick of the Pops, which under Freeman moved to Sunday afternoons, was therefore the BBC's first programme to broadcast a rundown of the charts, and the formula it adopted has been copied in virtually every charts show since. The show transferred to Radio 1 on the day after it began in 1967. In 1979 Freeman departed for Capital Radio, but returned to the BBC ten years later.

Today he is still there on Sundays, greeting his pop pickers just as he did thirty years ago when he first coined his other catchphrase 'All right? Right! Stay bright!' The show, however, is different. Because the charts now have a spot to themselves (hosted by MARK

GOODIER later the same day) the new look *Pick of the Pops* features three different Top Twenties culled from the last thirty years, and therefore packs in sixty records over the two-hour show.

Pick of the Week

Radio 4's amusing, well assembled collection of items from the previous seven days' output on BBC radio and television (national, regional and local), began in 1959 with GALE PEDRICK its first presenter.

In the first 52 editions he included 840 items – Hancock to Handel, Lord Boothby and Anthony Newley. This was about sixteen items per programme, which had risen to about twenty by 1990. But the material to choose from has expanded enormously. The number of national radio networks has risen from three to five, and of television channels from one to two; there are also three dozen local stations, none of which existed in 1959.

Nancy Wise made the selection after Pedrick, although John Ellison was the presenter. Then MARGARET HOWARD took over, as both presenter and selector, in 1974. MICHAEL GREEN appeared not to care for her approach, and eventually reduced the length of the programme from an hour to 45 minutes, then the number of her appearances a year from 52 to 40, then dropped her annual *Pick of the Year*. Finally, her contract was not renewed and she was replaced by Chris Serle in 1991. This decision upset not only her, but large numbers of listeners who had come to regard her as someone whose judgement as to what was worth listening to again was unfailingly reliable.

Pickles, Wilfred   (1904–78)

Halifax-born actor in the 1930s who became a BBC newsreader in the Second World War despite his strong Yorkshire accent, a familiar teatime voice for youngsters throughout the North for his Pleasant Journey walks on CHILDREN'S HOUR from 1942–63, and a national celebrity when he hosted the vastly popular quiz show HAVE A GO. He also presented WHERE ARE YOU NOW?

Wilfred Pickles and his wife Mabel, national celebrities as hosts of *Have a Go*, relaxing one evening in their flat in November 1953, photographed by Bert Hardy of *Picture Post*

Pictures From The Past

Six oral history documentaries recalling aspects of yesteryear, on Radio 4 in 1990. Subjects ranged from hot metal newspaper presses to the sort of grand hotels in which orchestras played in dining rooms. One episode, *We'll Eat Again*, recalled wartime diet: paraffin in cakes, whale meat, rationing, the black market.

The Piddingtons

Highly publicised conjuring act who gave their name to a sensational series in 1949–50. Sidney Piddington and his wife, former actress Lesley Pope, appeared to read one another's minds, but were too subtle to claim that. 'Telepathy or not telepathy? You are the judge' was how they concluded each show.

On one occasion, Lesley, flying in a BOAC Stratocruiser with over fifty journalists around her, identified the contents of two envelopes which had been filled by a studio audience sitting in front of her husband in the West End. On another, she was submerged in a diving bell when she correctly identified a card

drawn from a deck by *New Statesman* editor Kingsley Martin.

Controversy raged as to what was happening. Some people speculated that they had miniature radio transmitters concealed between their teeth, others that they did it by code. In his autobiography, IAN MESSITER, who produced their programmes, hints that he knows the secret but has no intention even now of spilling the beans.

At the height of their fame, some people suggested they used their 'clairvoyance' in a more serious cause, e.g. reading Stalin's mind (this was at the time of the Berlin airlift). When Lesley appeared on ONE MINUTE PLEASE, some listeners expressed the view that her success stemmed from her ability to read ROY PLOMLEY's mind and know what was coming.

Sydney-born Piddington (1918–91) first gained an interest in telepathy when he was held for three years in Changi, the Japanese prisoner of war camp. He devised a mind-reading act with fellow Australian POW Russell Braddon (later a frequent panellist on ANY QUESTIONS?), which they performed as part of the camp's entertainment. After the war, in 1947, he and his wife presented their 'telepathy' act on Australian radio, before bringing it to Britain, where they topped the bill at the London Palladium as well as starring on the BBC.

The Pilgrim's Progress

John Bunyan's classic allegory about the difficulties of Christian life was first heard on radio in 1943, adapted by Edward Sackville-West with music by Ralph Vaughan Williams. A new version, with Sir John Gielgud as Christian, was made in 1977 using the same score: it was repeated in 1988.

Pillars of Society

Radio 4 series examining the power and composition of some famous British institutions, which began in 1987 with the Royal Shakespeare Company. Since then Marks & Spencer, the Royal Opera House, Westminster Abbey, RSPB, Jockey Club, Co-op, Bank of England, Oxford University, Freemasons and soccer referees have been among the pillars scrutinised.

Pinter, Harold   (1930–)

Playwright who is among the most eminent to have been set on the road to success by BBC Radio, which started him off with a £60 commission, resulting in *A Slight Ache* (Third Programme, 1959). About twenty plays have followed, both full-length works and shorter pieces. They have included *The Caretaker* (Third, 1962) and *Landscape* (which had its world premiere on Radio 3 in 1968, starring Peggy Ashcroft, after the Lord Chamberlain banned its production on stage without cuts). *The Birthday Party* was broadcast on Radio 4

in 1970, three years after it was first submitted and rejected: *No Man's Land* was rejected in 1976 and again in 1980.

On one of two special evenings to mark his sixtieth birthday, Radio 3 broadcast his play *Betrayal*, in which he himself appeared in the cast alongside Michael Gambon and Patricia Hodge. This was the first time Pinter had worked as an actor on Radio 3, although he had acted on the Third Programme in 1951.

Pinter is now renowned as much for his political campaigning as for literary achievements – see VACLAV HAVEL.

Pips

See GREENWICH TIME SIGNAL.

Pirates

From the North Sea in the 1960s to council estates in the 1990s, unlicensed stations have been part of British radio for nearly three decades. White and black alike, they have exercised much influence on the shape and style of legitimate radio.

The original generation of offshore pirates launched broadcasters such as TONY BLACKBURN, JOHN PEEL, KENNY EVERETT and DAVE LEE TRAVIS, practices now taken for granted such as DJs working their own turntables, and led directly to the creation of Radio 1. The second generation of ethnic pirates created stations such as Kiss FM and London Greek Radio which are still broadcasting (legally) and whose existence has greatly widened listener choice.

The maritime variety, beginning with Radio Caroline in March 1964, were anchored in international waters – mainly those of the North Sea, chosen because the low-lying coast of Eastern England offered no hindrance to radio signals. Broadcasting slick, pacy pop music to a nation whose existing radio services largely ignored it, the pirates attracted millions of young listeners within a few weeks and consequently much advertising.

However, Harold Wilson's government set its face against the pirates, and proceeded to drive them from the air. TONY BENN, then Postmaster-General, publicly attacked them as 'a menace' and accused them of stealing copyright and endangering ship-to-shore radio.

Advertising on them, and replenishing them from the mainland, were banned under the Marine Etc. Broadcasting (Offences) Act which became law in August 1967 – six weeks before Radio 1 started up. Most of the pirate ships gave up although Caroline defied the new legislation and continued to broadcast, under many difficulties. The Act was later used against the 1980s pirate ship, *Laser 558*. See also entries for individual pirate stations.

After the abortive 1980s experiment in COMMUNITY RADIO, frustration once again grew at the tiny

'We shall not stand idly by!'

The North Sea pirates captivated millions but infuriated Whitehall. At the time of this Vicky cartoon in the *Evening Standard* (10 December 1965), John Stonehouse was the Postmaster-General threatening to drive them off the air. His successor, Tony Benn, carried the job through to its conclusion

number of radio stations permitted in this country and the reluctance of those that did exist to cater for all tastes. Hence the explosion in black pirate radio stations which pumped out reggae on the FM band in the mid-1980s. There were about four dozen in London alone by 1987–88, broadcasting music from illicit transmitters in council towerblocks, and linked both musically and financially to clubs where the DJs also appeared. Illegal ethnic stations also sprang up, such as London Greek Radio and Sina. The DTI's Radio Investigation Service took action against these under the Wireless Telegraphy Act 1949, which governs the use of the radio spectrum and, in general, makes it an offence to instal or use wireless telegraphy (i.e. broadcasting) equipment without a licence.

Pirate stations had to close down by 31 December 1988, because the Home Office announced that anyone convicted of pirate offences after this date would be banned from operating a legal radio station for five years.

Most obeyed the law and closed down. Several, like London Greek Radio, Kiss FM and WNK, found it paid off when they were awarded INCREMENTAL franchises in 1989–90. But their illegal place on the dial was taken by a third generation of pirates, with names like Centreforce, Stomp and Climax FM, broadcasting 24-hour acid house music. Once again, they have claimed to meet a demand for very tightly targeted black music such as house and want to stand outside the framework of legal regulation.

Plain Tales from the Raj
Radio 4 series of CHARLES ALLEN.

Play The Game
WYNFORD VAUGHAN-THOMAS chaired this panel game on the Light Programme, on which KENNETH HORNE, Iris Ashley and Charmian Innes were panellists.

Playback
Programme in Radio 4's ARCHIVE FEATURE, beginning in 1991, in which performers, producers or writers recall some of the great radio shows of the past in which they were involved. It started with an appraisal of MRS DALE'S DIARY by Charles Simon, the last actor to play Dr Dale. STEPHEN WILLIAMS followed with a look back at HAVE A GO, which he produced for eighteen years.

Playhouse
Name given to the Monday afternoon drama slot on Radio 4 from autumn 1990. The plays are popular, mainstream, ninety-minute narratives. Previously this slot had been used for the repeat of SATURDAY NIGHT THEATRE two days before, but when that made way for THE FORSYTE CHRONICLES, it had to be occupied by something else.

Plomley, Roy (1914–85)
Creator of the seemingly indestructible DESERT ISLAND DISCS in 1942, but noted for other achievements too. An announcer on commercial radio stations in France, including Radio Normandy; escaped to Britain in June 1940; wrote many plays and also compered several shows, including THE ACCORDION CLUB, WE BEG TO DIFFER, ONE MINUTE PLEASE and MANY A SLIP.

Plummer, Josephine (–1990)
One of the guiding spirits behind CHILDREN'S HOUR in its heyday, joining the programme in 1943 under DEREK McCULLOCH and becoming its deputy head under DAVID DAVIS in 1953.

She produced many of its finest dramas, including the highly acclaimed THE BOX OF DELIGHTS, and was also responsible for putting on air the stories of the schoolboy detectives NORMAN AND HENRY BONES.

Plymouth Sound
ILR station whose title is an adroit, perhaps inevitable pun, since Plymouth Sound is also the name of the patch of water under Plymouth Hoe. On the air since 1975 and based in the city, it covers both Plymouth plus South-East Cornwall and parts of South-West Devon. In 1991 it split its services, following the example of most ILR stations.

PM
Racy, rather breathless account of the day's news on Radio 4 at 5 p.m. on weekdays which has the feel of an evening paper: it usually manages to reflect the lighter side of life as well as weighty events. It also has a daily letters slot for listeners' views. Presenters have included Valerie Singleton, Robert Williams, Hugh Sykes and Frances Coverdale. It has been running since 1970.

Poet of the Month
Monthly Radio 3 series beginning in 1989 in which a contemporary poet is given the chance to select, and read from, both his own work and that of others of his choice. The first three poets so honoured were Thom Gunn, C.H. Sisson and Czeslaw Milosz. Others during the first year included Seamus Heaney, Fleur Adcock and Charles Causley.

Poetry
Since March 1924, when John Drinkwater delivered the first poetry reading on British radio, this has always maintained a presence on the air. See under individual programmes.

The Poetry of Popular Song
A quartet of underpraised lyricists (Al Dubin, Johnny Burke, Herman Hupfield and Gus Kahn) was celebrated by Roy Dean in this four-part Radio 4 series in 1990.

Poetry Please!
Poems requested by listeners are the main ingredient of this weekly Radio 4 series which began in 1979. After ten years of being only ten minutes, it doubled its length: the longer format has widened its scope considerably, and entire editions have been given over to single poems such as Matthew Arnold's *The Scholar Gypsy* and Kipling's *The Ballad of East and West*.

When it was only ten minutes long, each programme featured, on average, four poems. The average now is seven. All of them stem from the requests of listeners, who so far have asked for 7,000 different poems (particular favourites include *Abou Ben Adhem* by Leigh Hunt, *High Flight* by John Gillespie Magee and *The Highwayman* by Alfred Noyes).

Since 1989 the programme has had its first regular presenter – poet and former English teacher Simon Rae, also the author of a topical poem in *Weekend Guardian*. The programme now also features a guest poet once a month, who reads and discusses some of his own work as well as that of others.

The requested poems are often read by actors, but the programme also draws heavily on the extensive poetry library in the BBC SOUND ARCHIVES.

Some editions have been performed in front of an audience, such as the 500th which was recorded at the 1990 Salisbury Festival.

Polish Service
Programmes in the Polish language were first put out by the BBC on 7 September 1939 – a week after Hitler's troops attacked Poland and four days after Britain declared war on Germany. As with so much of the BBC's wartime output, the Polish service provided an invaluable link with the Allies because its news was untainted by Nazi censorship.

During the Cold War, like other World Service programmes beamed to Eastern bloc countries, its broadcasts were often subjected to jamming. The final period of jamming, carried out by the USSR, lasted from the imposition of martial law in 1981 to January 1988.

Today the Polish Service broadcasts for nearly four hours a day, two-thirds of which is news and current affairs and one-third features. The lifting of jamming, yet another sign of the East—West thaw, was followed in September 1989 by an exhibition in Warsaw to mark fifty years of BBC broadcasts to Poles in their own language. It was the BBC's first ever exhibition in Poland. The *glasnost* spirit continued in 1990 when the World Service welcomed several Polish broadcasters to England for six-week training courses, barely two years since the ending of jamming.

The training schemes (paid for by the British government) were formally endorsed by the new Polish Prime Minister, Tadeusz Mazowiecki, himself a long-time listener, and contributor, to the Polish Service. They were followed by similar training courses for broadcasters from Hungary (1990) and Czechoslovakia (1991).

Pop Inn
Lunchtime 'record rendezvous' heard on the Light Programme each week, with discs and guest stars.

Pop Inside
Magazine show from Brighton presented by ANNE NIGHTINGALE.

Pop of the Form
Radio 1 contest between secondary school teams answering questions on pop music. It borrowed its name from the now defunct TOP OF THE FORM.

Pop Over Europe
European radio link-up for popular music in the 1960s, introduced here by KATIE BOYLE (or Catherine Boyle as she was then) on the Light Programme.

Pop Score
Radio 2 panel game in which KEN BRUCE is the questionmaster. Team captains have included ALAN FREEMAN and Helen Shapiro.

Pop Shop
Weekday lunchtime show on the Light Programme introduced by BRIAN MATTHEW.

Popalong
George Melly once hosted this Light Programme music series with the likes of Carole Deene and Rog Whittaker.

Portuguese Service
Programmes in the Portuguese language were first broadcast by the BBC in 1938 for Latin America, and in 1939 for Portugal. Today, there is also a Portuguese service for Africa which, like the one available for listeners in Portugal, is on the air for 105 minutes a day. Programmes for Brazilian audiences are on the air for slightly less, 75 minutes a day. See also BBC RADIO JERSEY.

Posters of the Moulin Rouge
Four plays by John Peacock on Radio 4 in 1989, each concentrating on one character from the series of posters painted by Toulouse-Lautrec to depict Paris's 'palace of pleasure'. They included a washerwoman who became famous in the can-can, Yvette Guilbert, the singer with black gloves played by Julie Covington, an amateur male dancer and a woman who began and ended her life in an asylum.

The Postscript
Celebrated Sunday evening talks in Britain's darkest hour delivered to great effect by J.B. PRIESTLEY on the Home Service, immediately after the 9 p.m. news.

Potter, Gillie (1888–1975)
Wesleyan minister's son who worked as a comedian on both stage and radio in the 1920s and 1930s, and on radio long after that. His genteel, literary humour often concerned itself with the impoverishment of the aristocracy (he was an expert on heraldry) and the most memorable of his inventions was Lord Marshmallow of Hogsnorton, where the drive gates were tied with string and the entrance was through a gap in the hedge. He tended to open his broadcasts with what became a popular catchphrase: 'Hello England, this is Gillie Potter talking to you in English.' (Real name: Hugh Peel.)

Potter, Stephen (1900–69)
Best known as the inventor of Gamesmanship and One-Upmanship and as author of their particular Bible, *The Art of Winning Games Without Actually Cheating*, Potter was a staff producer at BBC Radio from the 1930s to the 1950s and did much to shape features and documentaries into their present form.

He was responsible, with JOYCE GRENFELL, for the influential HOW TO . . . series of gentle satires, one of whom (*How to Listen*) was chosen to launch the Third

Programme in 1946. *How to be Good at Games* went out in 1947, in the same year that *Gamesmanship* was published, although Potter had first used the word in a letter to Francis Meynell in 1931 about a tennis match against two difficult opponents.

Powell, Peter   (1951–)
West Midlander who started in radio on his area's BBC Radio Birmingham, before joining Radio Luxembourg in 1974 (he hosted its celebratory 55th birthday show in 1989) and then Radio 1 three years later.

He presented a Sunday mid-morning show and the weekend breakfast show and developed a reputation as a talent spotter, giving air time to Duran Duran and Spandau Ballet before they had hits.

Strongly associated with the RADIO 1 ROADSHOW, which he helped to present each summer, and often acknowledged for his ability to entertain and control a large crowd. He left Radio 1 in 1988 to concentrate on his own management company.

Powell, Sandy   (1900–82)
Comedian who created one of radio's earliest catch-phrases, 'Can you hear me, Mother?', which he coined at the end of the 1920s. His mother was in showbusiness, and put him on the stage at the age of seven.

In an early comedy sketch on radio, Powell was supposedly broadcasting home from the North Pole and the famous question was simply a line in the sketch, which he repeated three or four times. It caught on overnight and was soon on people's lips everywhere.

Powell exercised a strong influence on fellow Northerner PETER TINNISWOOD, who made a radio documentary about him.

The Power of Patronage
Robin Oakley, political editor of *The Times*, lifted some of the veil of secrecy surrounding the honours system, and the appointment of bishops, judges and members of quangos, in this fascinating and fact-filled Radio 4 series in 1991.

PPM Radio Waves
Now defunct subsidiary of Piccadilly Radio which pioneered syndicated programmes in Britain from 1987 onwards, bringing in sponsors (like Pepsi, Midland Bank and Budweiser) to finance the making of pop programmes like AMERICAN COUNTDOWN and ROCKLINE which were then offered for sale throughout ILR. The sponsors received liberal mentions of their name and an appealing image. PPM was started by Simon Cole in 1987: he and a fellow director, TIM BLACKMORE, resigned after the Miss World takeover of their parent company Piccadilly Radio in 1989. The two men formed a new production company, UNIQUE BROADCAST-ING, which bought PPM from Miss World along with

its programmes, so Cole and Blackmore continued to run the shows they had created.

Prelude
Classical music programme for dawn risers on Radio 4 every Sunday morning, presented by MARJORIE LOFTHOUSE.

Premiership
Three interviews with Lord Home, Edward Heath and Lord Callaghan, on Radio 3 in 1989, in which the ex-Prime Ministers discussed the necessary skills for 10 Downing Street.

Premios Ondas
Annual international contest for popular, regular radio series, held in Spain. It started in 1954 and is run by the commercial Spanish broadcasting network SER. The judges look for fresh ideas as well as presentation, production and technical quality, and awards are in the shape of a silver Pegasus. ILR programmes, and BBC, have often been successful.

The Press Gang
Light-hearted Radio 2 show running from 1986 to 1989 with GLYN WORSNIP quizzing guests on their knowledge of the week's stories in the popular press. After illness forced his departure, Gyles Brandreth took over as questionmaster, but Worsnip proved a hard act to follow and the show was axed a few months later.

Pride of the Pacific
Adventure stories written by Rex (THE FLYING DOC-TOR) Rienits, broadcast on the Light Programme in 1964.

Priestland, Gerald   (1927–91)
Quaker and former foreign correspondent who was BBC's religious affairs correspondent from 1977–82. His Radio 4 series *Priestland's Progress*, a spiritual journey, won a SANDFORD ST MARTIN AWARD.

Priestley, J.B.   (1894–1984)
Regular broadcaster on, and writer for, radio from the mid-1930s onwards, with over sixty broadcast works to his credit in the drama field alone. They included verse programmes, serials, adaptations of his books, and plays, including those which explored the nature of time such as *I Have Been Here Before* (National Programme, 1938) and *Dangerous Corner* (Home Service, 1940). His popular domestic drama *An Inspector Calls*, later made into a film, went out on the Home Service in 1950.

Priestley's greatest radio hour lay not in drama, however, but in the talks he gave to a nation at war. In his Sunday evening POSTSCRIPT series he invariably caught and articulated the national mood – resolute, phlegmatic, determined to see it through. 'This, then, is a wonderful moment', he said in one talk, 'for us who are here in London, now in the roaring centre of the battlefield, the strangest army the world has ever seen, an army in drab civilian clothes, doing quite ordinary things ... but nevertheless a real army, upon whose continuing high and defiant spirit the world's future depends.'

Priestley started the talks in June 1940, but was dropped in October that year after Conservative hostility to his recognisably socialist sympathies. He was reinstated in January 1941, but only for a short period. His talks were collected and published in *All England Listened* (1967).

'It was as a representative Englishman that he became in Sunday evening broadcasts in the dark days of 1940 second only to Winston Churchill as the spokesman of England's determination and faith in herself' – Obituary in *The Times*.

'I didn't see then and I don't see now what all the fuss was about. To this day, middle-aged or elderly men shake my hand and tell me what a ten-minute talk about ducks on a pond, or a pie in a shop window meant to them, as if I had given them *King Lear* or the *Eroica*. I have found myself tied, like a man to a gigantic balloon, to one of those bogus reputations that only the mass media know how to inflict' – Priestley's own appraisal of his wartime broadcasts, quoted in *The Times* on his death.

Prima Donna

Records of great singers presented by Philip Hope-Wallace on Friday evenings on the Home Service.

Prince, Tony (1946–)

Perhaps the only jockey ever to become a disc-jockey, 5ft 4in Prince once shared a room with Willie Carson, when he was apprenticed to Gerald Armstrong at Middleham on a six-year apprenticeship at 4s. 6d. a week. He left after six months, breaking into showbiz at a Butlin's holiday camp in North Wales where the drummer in a band called Rory Storm and the Hurricanes, whose name was Ringo Starr, suggested he enter a talent contest. Prince came second. He started singing in his native Oldham, later becoming a club DJ. He worked on Radio Caroline North before joining Radio Luxembourg in 1968, where he stayed for over ten years.

Prix Italia

Illustrious set of international radio (and now television) prizes, founded in 1948 and first held on the Isle of Capri. It opened its doors to television from 1957 onwards.

The Prix Italia is unique among broadcasting prizes in that its jurors (who listen to the programmes in translation, if needs be) are all practitioners, and from all over the world. Programme makers are therefore judged by their peers. The contest is held in a different Italian venue each year. The BBC has excelled in the contest: from 1948 to 1955 every Prix Italia for drama was won by the FEATURES DEPARTMENT under Laurence Gilliam.

The Professionals

Former *TV Times* editor Richard Barber launched this Radio 4 series in 1991, in the Monday morning archive slot, in which people in different professions look at the way their jobs have been seen and done in the past. Labour MP Tony Banks has written and presented another in the series, on politicians.

Profile

Diana Lamplugh, Raymond Briggs and Denis Noble have all been featured in this Radio 4 series which began in 1977. In recent years the programmes have shrunk from 25 minutes in length to fifteen minutes.

Proms

See HENRY WOOD PROMENADE CONCERTS

Public Affairs

Rachmanism, the Oz trial, the Crichel Down affair, the John Poulson saga, the inquiry at William Tyndale School and the Belcher case, were the six post-war *causes célèbres* examined in this Radio 4 documentary series in 1990. Each one was chosen to illuminate a particular issue. These were, respectively: slum landlordism, the obscenity laws, Ministerial responsibility, corruption in public life, progressive education and improper political influence. David Wheeler wrote and presented.

Pull the Other One

Radio 2 comedy series which is an updated version of DOES THE TEAM THINK? (producer Edward Taylor made both). David Frost is the chairman and the panel who tell lots of gags in the guise of answering listeners' questions include KEN DODD and Frank Carson.

Punters

The programme 'with listener power', as the BBC likes to describe it: a Radio 4 series presented by Susan Marling in which punters, i.e. members of the public, are invited to find the answers to questions which have been puzzling them (e.g. Can I legally be buried in my garden? Why are crisps so expensive?) which often take them on fascinating trips through the thickets of officialdom and authority. The BBC's journalists help to guide them through the jungle.

Some punters have embarked on more serious quests for enlightenment, and in at least one instance this has resulted in change: a woman called Vicki Stone, whose daughter was killed in a road accident, queried the law that permitted newly qualified teenage drivers to supervise other teenagers. As a result of her labours, and the publicity given to them by the programme, the law was changed.

Punters was the clear inspiration for a similar show of do-it-yourself investigations, *Them and Us*, launched by BBC1 in July 1990.

Purely For Pleasure
Weekly record show on the Light Programme, in which GILBERT HARDING was the disc-jockey. An unlikely choice, but he drew praise.

Purves, Libby   (1950–)
Presenter of Radio 4's MIDWEEK since 1984; was a TODAY reporter from 1976–79 and a presenter from 1979–81. Is also one of the team of SUNDAY presenters.

Pye
Long-established Cambridge company, now part of the Dutch conglomerate Philips, which was the first British firm to put a transistor radio on the market, which it did through a subsidiary company called Pam (Radio & Television) Ltd in 1956.

The original firm of W.G. Pye & Co. was founded in Cambridge in 1896 by William George Pye, an instrument maker with the Cavendish Laboratory, and specialised in making scientific instruments for schools and laboratories. Wireless sets were first made in 1920. When the arrival of the BBC boosted demand from the end of 1922 onwards, Harold Pye (W.G.'s son) drove round Cambridgeshire in his bullnosed Morris, advertising his new product with leaflets handed out to the radio dealers of the day – cycle shops, electrical retailers and garages.

Pye's first portable radio was introduced in 1925 and cost £30 12s. 6d. (a fortune for the time), and its famous 'Rising Sun' motif started to be used on sets from 1927 onwards.

The company's later diversification embraced two-way radio for tanks, which became standard equipment for Allied forces in the Second World War, television, hi-fi and aircraft landing systems. It merged with EKCO in 1960 and was taken over by Philips in 1967.

Pye Radio Awards
These ran for three years, 1979–81, in succession to the IMPERIAL TOBACCO AWARDS FOR RADIO. They continued to be organised by the Society of Authors. When, in 1981, PYE decided to end its sponsorship, there followed a gap of one year before SONY took over in 1983. The following is a complete list of the Pye awards.

1979:
Performance by an actor: David Suchet for *The Kreutzer Sonata* (BBC World Service). Performance by an actress:

Maureen O'Brien for *By Grand Central Station I sat down and wept* (Radio 3). Personality: ROGER COOK of CHECKPOINT (Radio 4). Best production: David Spenser for *Strands* (Radio 3). Documentary/current affairs programme: John Theocharis for *Spring of Memory* (Radio 3). Sports personality: Fred Trueman for TEST MATCH SPECIAL. Original comedy script: John Howard and Derek Graham for *That was the West that was* (BBC Radio Bristol). Talk: Arthur Wood and Arthur Berry for *Lament for the Lost Pubs of Burslem* (BBC Radio Stoke). Specialist programme: John Theocharis for *Spring of Memory* (Radio 3). Dramatised and illustrated feature programme: Angela Carter for *Come unto these yellow sands* (Radio 3). Adaptation to single play or serial: Tom McGrath for *The Hardman* (BBC Radio Scotland). Original single play or serial: Shirley Gee for *Typhoid Mary* (Radio 4). Gold Award for most outstanding contribution to radio: HENRY REED.

1980:
Performance by an actor: Norman Rodway and Warren Mitchell for *Faith Healer* (Radio 3). Performance by an actress: Yvonne Bryceland for *Boesman and Lena* (Radio 3). Personality: TERRY WOGAN. Production: David Spenser for *Equus* (Radio 4). Best local radio programme: *Go Freight* (Metro Radio). Sports personality: JOHN ARLOTT. Programme, or series of programmes, for young listeners: DOUGLAS ADAMS for THE HITCH-HIKER'S GUIDE TO THE GALAXY (Radio 4). Original comedy script: WEEK ENDING (Radio 4). Talk: Michael Elkins for *A Jew at Christmas* (Radio 4). Magazine, current affairs or discussion programme: Kevin d'Arcy for *Right to Work* (Radio Orwell). Illustrated or dramatised feature programme: Alan Haydock for *Dunkirk 1940* (Radio 4). Adaptation to single play or serial: Denys Hawthorne for *How Many Miles to Babylon?* (Radio 4). Original single play or serial: Catherine Lucy Czerkawska for *O Flower of Scotland* (BBC Radio Scotland). Gold Award for outstanding service to radio over the years: Alfred Bradley.

1981:
Performance by an actor: Terry Molloy for *Risky City* (Radio 3). Performance by an actress: jointly to Marcella O'Riordan for *The Old Jest* (Radio 4) and Maureen Beattie for *Can You Hear Me?* (BBC Radio Scotland). Production: Patrick Rayner for *Manderston* (Radio 4). Best local radio programme: *Hartley Colliery Disaster* (Radio Metro). Programme or series for young listeners: TALKABOUT (Radio 1). Contribution to a light entertainment programme (writer or performer): Alexei Sayle for *Alexei Sayle, Community Detective* and *The Fish People* (Capital Radio). Scripted talk or report: RAY GOSLING for *Skelmersdale* (Radio 4). Current affairs documentary or feature programme: JAMES CAMERON for *James Cameron and the Korean*

War (Radio 4). Arts or history documentary or feature programme: Peter Everett for *The Ballad of Belle Isle* (Radio 4). Personality: Tom Vernon. Sports personality: BRIAN JOHNSTON. Adaptation of a drama: Liane Aukin for *Between the Acts* (Radio 3). Original play or serial (author): Valerie Windsor for *Variation on a Snow Queen* (Radio 4). First play by a new writer: Nick Dear for *Matter Permitted* (Radio 3). Gold Award for the most outstanding contribution to radio over the years: DOUGLAS CLEVERDON.

Q

Queen's Hall

Much loved musical centre outside BROADCASTING HOUSE which was used for the PROMS until its destruction by bombs in May 1941. Great figures who played or conducted here included Rachmaninov and Toscanini, and it was also where the BBC SYMPHONY ORCHESTRA gave its first concert, in 1930. On the site today stands Henry Wood House, which accommodates one of the BBC's main libraries and some of its offices.

Queen's Hall Light Orchestra

One of the BBC's main orchestras of its golden age, run for many years by SIDNEY TORCH.

Quiz Kid

Radio 1 contest in the 1970s which ALAN FREEMAN chaired.

Quiz Party

Light Programme series featuring a miscellany of quizzes, chaired by Michael Miles in the early 1960s. Pensioners and Services personnel made up the studio audience and had a chance to try their talents as actors or bandleaders. Spots included the 'Yes–No Interlude', 'Who, When and Where?' and 'Turn Back the Clock', a musical quiz featuring songs of the past.

Quizzes

The first British radio quiz is believed to have been on CHILDREN'S HOUR in November 1937, in the form of a spelling contest between different regional teams. Among later manifestations were TRANSATLANTIC QUIZ, ROUND BRITAIN QUIZ, DOUBLE YOUR MONEY, HAVE A GO and QUIZ PARTY.

Quote . . . Unquote

Radio 4 panel game which has been running since 1976, invented and chaired by NIGEL REES. Peter Cook, Jacky Gillott, BENNY GREEN and Ian McKellen have been among the panellists. It has also been broadcast on Radio 2 and the BBC World Service.

Race, Steve (1921–)

Presenter of MY MUSIC on Radio 4 and a variety of musical programmes on Radio 2, where he used to be a regular host of shows featuring the BBC RADIO ORCHESTRA. Also a composer, e.g. of the music in a 1966 production of Rostand's comedy *Cyrano de Bergerac* starring Ralph Richardson.

He started his professional life as a pianist, playing with Harry Leader's Band, and going on to play for bandleaders Cyril Stapleton and Lew Stone and work as an arranger for the Ted Heath Band and Judy Garland. His fifty years in broadcasting were celebrated on a special edition of the JOHN DUNN programme in March 1991.

Radio Academy

Founded in 1984 as a forum for all those working in British radio, conceived mainly by SIR RICHARD FRANCIS. It organises regular seminars and meetings and an annual Radio Festival, and publishes a quarterly journal. First based in Bristol, it moved to London in 1989 and now has over 900 members.

Radio Active

Bright, barbed and funny Radio 4 comedy series of the 1980s, mocking the frantic antics and clichéd claptrap of a local radio station. It generally hit its targets with unerring accuracy. Producers included Jamie Rix, son of former farceur Sir Brian.

'It singlehandedly introduced millions of listeners to the idea that a lot of what they were listening to elsewhere was very silly' – Russell Davies.

Radio Aire

ILR station based in Leeds, starting in 1981, whose main claim to national fame is that it launched the belligerent JAMES WHALE. In July 1990, following the example of so many other ILR stations, it started to split its services. Magic 828, on its medium wave band, plays golden oldies for 35 to 54-year-olds while Aire FM is aimed at younger listeners.

Radio Allotment

Wartime programme which encouraged people to Dig for Victory, going out live from a real allotment in Park Crescent about 400 yards from BROADCASTING HOUSE.

Radio and Music

Fortnightly magazine with a controlled circulation launched by the EMAP group in June 1989, concentrating on playlists, marketing, industry news, DJs and music programming. Publication was suspended at the end of 1990 because of insufficient advertising.

Radio Atlanta

Britain's second pirate radio ship began in May 1964, in international waters off Harwich and fourteen miles from RADIO CAROLINE. Two months later the rivals merged. Caroline then sailed north to the Isle of Man and became RADIO CAROLINE (NORTH) while Atlanta renamed itself RADIO CAROLINE (SOUTH).

Radio Authority

Set up by the BROADCASTING ACT 1990 to replace the IBA as the new supervisory body for all non-BBC radio in Britain, with a 'light touch' the weight of which has still to be measured. Its job is to license and regulate not only INR and local radio, but also hospital radio, student radio, and special event, cable and satellite radio.

LORD CHALFONT was appointed (by the Home Secretary) as the first chairman, and he in turn appointed PETER BALDWIN the first chief executive. Barrister Mrs Jill McIvor was made deputy chairman and there are five other members: management consultant Richard Hooper, former Labour MP John Grant, ex-journalist and advertising copywriter Mrs Margaret Corrigan, lecturer Ranjit Sondhi, and Michael Moriarty, head of the Broadcasting Department at the Home Office from 1981-84, now retired.

Radio Ballads

See CHARLES PARKER.

Radio Borders

Last of the conventional (i.e. non-INCREMENTAL) ILR stations, this Melrose-based FM station went on the air in January 1990, serving the central Scottish Border country and North Northumberland. Its output, for a target audience of 25 to 55-year-olds, is 75 per cent music, concentrating on melodic hits from the 1950s to 1980s, and 25 per cent speech.

Radio Broadland

ILR station covering Norfolk and North Suffolk, based in Norwich, which began in 1984.

Radio Caroline

Britain's first pirate radio ship, rightly credited with launching all-day music radio in this country and forcing the BBC to start Radio 1.

It went on the air on Easter Sunday, 29 March 1964, with these words from disc-jockey SIMON DEE: 'Good

morning, ladies and gentlemen. This is Radio Caroline broadcasting on 199, your all-day music station.' Three weeks later it was claiming seven million listeners. After merging a few months later with RADIO ATLANTA, Caroline sailed north and dropped its anchor off the Isle of Man, becoming Radio Caroline (North). Atlanta, broadcasting from *MV Mi Amigo*, became Radio Caroline (South). It was this pincer action, operated from both ends of Britain, which dented the Light Programme and Radio Luxembourg.

Radio Caroline (South) was a cornerstone of the Swinging Sixties. Millions of pop-mad youngsters grew up with groovy, exciting young DJs like TONY BLACKBURN, EMPEROR ROSKO and DAVE LEE TRAVIS, all of whom made their radio debut on Caroline. (A lesser known DJ on the ship was Roger Gale, later an editor on the TODAY programme and NEWSBEAT and, since 1983, a Conservative MP.)

The man behind Britain's first pirate ship was a 27-year-old Irishman, Ronan O'Rahilly, who described himself as a Roman Catholic anarchist. He claimed that he named the station after the daughter of President Kennedy, assassinated the previous October; cynics suggested he was trying to curry favour with the Chancellor of the Exchequer, Reginald Maudling, who also had

---

'The Tower of Power' was the name given to another pirate station, but it could also have applied to Radio Caroline's enormous aerial during much of the 1980s. The ship was the *Ross Revenge*, a converted trawler which once belonged to the Ross Frozen Food fleet

a daughter called Caroline. Among his investors was Jocelyn Stevens, then editor of the chic magazine *Queen*.

Beloved by its fans, for whom it was a potent symbol of freedom and rebellion, Caroline was held in great suspicion by the political establishment. After all, it was not *controlled*. It could, if it wanted, beam seditious propaganda. It also stood for untamed commercialism (TONY BENN, then Postmaster-General, has since described it as early Thatcherism) and it evaded royalties and interfered with designated frequencies.

The Marine Etc. Broadcasting Offences Act of 1967, by banning British companies from advertising on them, made it virtually impossible for the North Sea pirates to carry on. Caroline was the only one to try, and became the one child of the 1960s that refused to grow up. JOHNNIE WALKER was the leading DJ to stay aboard, most of the others defecting to the lucrative respectability of the BBC.

It closed its offices in Chesterfield Gardens, Mayfair, and moved its headquarters to Holland (and later to an accommodation address in Spain). In 1968, in a dispute over unpaid bills, it was boarded by a group of Dutchmen – a pirate ship raided by pirates – and put off the air. Saved by supporters, it went back on the air from 1973–80 when it hit a sandbank and sunk.

O'Rahilly then bought a converted Icelandic trawler, *Ross Revenge*, once part of the Ross Frozen Foods fleet. On this Caroline has been broadcasting, on and off, since 1982, with 7,000 albums and 7,000 singles aboard. The October 1987 hurricane destroyed its mast so the ship fashioned a replacement from its cod liver oil pipes.

It was raided by the DTI, in association with Dutch authorities, in August 1989. Effectively this put it off the air, although it was broadcasting again for part of 1990. Supporters of the ship, who regard it as something of a temple, have claimed the raid was in breach of international law. They have begun a legal action, in both Britain and Holland, with the object of winning substantial compensation. The ship, now rusty and forlorn and still moored fifteen miles off Ramsgate, has been silent since the autumn of 1990.

Caroline has always acted as a floating launchpad for DJs, national ones in the 1960s and the local variety in the 1980s: many ILR stations, such as Radio Invicta in Kent, have hired ex-Caroline presenters. See also PIRATES.

Radio Caroline (North)
See RADIO CAROLINE.

Radio Caroline (South)
See RADIO CAROLINE.

Radio Circle
Popular club, formed within CHILDREN'S HOUR, which ran from 1923–33 and organised a variety of fundraising charity schemes all over Britain. At its peak over 150,000 children were members. Its work in helping poor, sick and disadvantaged children was continued by the programme's regular appeals, particularly the Christmas one 'for Children in Need of Help', which grew into the annual CHILDREN IN NEED jamboree of today.

Radio City
(1) Pirate station which began in May 1964 on a fort on Shivering Sands, nine miles off Whitstable. Its name was then Radio Sutch and it was owned and run by the singer Screaming Lord Sutch, who launched it with £5,000. Renamed Radio City in September 1964, it was nicknamed 'The Tower of Power' because of its 200-ft high aerial. ADRIAN LOVE began as a DJ here, in 1966.

(2) Liverpool-based ILR station broadcasting to Merseyside, Cheshire, some of North Wales and much of Lancashire since it began in 1974. City FM is its round-the-clock music service aimed mainly at under-35s and City Talk is a speech-based service on AM on the air during the daytime. It was launched in October 1989 and offers news, guest interviews, phone-ins, competitions and advice features.

The station had a key role, in 1988, in organising what it claimed to be the biggest concert by a solo artist ever staged in Britain – that of Michael Jackson at Aintree Racecourse, before 125,000 people, in the farewell performance of the European leg of the singer's world tour. City acted as co-promoter and organised advertising posters, tickets and on-air competitions for 'the tickets you can't buy!' The station's directors include Alan Bleasdale and Ian St John.

Radio Clyde
ILR station for Glasgow since 1973, and the first to be established outside London. Its managing director has always been James Gordon, a Glaswegian who used to teach Latin and Greek before becoming political editor of Scottish Television and moving into a new career in broadcasting. He is widely regarded as one of British radio's wisest senior figures.

The station was the first new building in Clydebank Business Park, the old home of Singer Sewing Machines which once employed 20,000 people. 'I like to think', wrote Gordon in 1990, 'that Radio Clyde has played its part in restoring self-confidence to a city which had begun to despair.'

Clyde has also played its part in maintaining standards in radio. It is the one and only ILR station always to have had a full-time drama producer. From 1973–88 this was Hamish Wilson, now at BBC Radio Scotland, and since then Finlay Welsh, who has already won a PREMIOS ONDAS award. It has also been one of the very few stations to have broadcast live sports commentaries each week, and is noted for its soccer coverage in what is a football-mad city. Every Saturday in the football season it brings live coverage of an out-of-town match, whether the team involved is Celtic or Rangers, and has also accompanied Scottish teams at matches throughout the world.

Like so many ILR stations, the station divided itself, in 1990, into two separate services. Clyde 1, on FM, broadcasts music for 20 to 40-year-olds and Clyde 2, on AM, melodies for more mature folk.

STEVE JONES was one of its original presenters, staying five years. Richard Park, who spent thirteen years at Clyde, the last six of them as music controller, is now programme controller at Capital, and regarded as the best in the business.

Radio Data System

A radio signal you can't hear, beamed on FM and automatically retuning your radio – if it's an RDS set – to the strongest signal. So drivers no longer have to fiddle with the dial, a blessing on long journeys. It also provides a visual readout on a panel identifying the station which is playing (for example, 'RADIO 4', 'INVICTA') so that the listener knows, without having to wait for some identifying sound or the words of an announcer, what he or she is listening to. RDS is able to provide local travel information which, if the listener wishes it and programmes the radio accordingly, will cut into what he is listening to.

For all these reasons RDS has been hailed by British radio, most of whose stations now broadcast RDS as standard practice, as 'user friendly', 'fumble free' and representing 'the greatest improvement in radio sets since the transistor'.

Unfortunately, however, users are few and far between because RDS sets are few and far between. RDS radios are fitted as standard on some cars. Otherwise you have to buy them and get them fitted. Many are now on the market and prices begin at about £200. About 40,000 drivers are estimated now to have RDS radios. But a portable RDS radio, an eagerly awaited concept first promised in 1988, has run into problems.

The concept of RDS originated in Sweden about 1978 and its development was taken up by the BBC and other European broadcasters. There is now one European specification (defined by the European Broadcasting Union) which is a pleasing example of European technological co-operation in practice. In Britain, the first manufacturer to put an RDS set on sale was Volvo, as a fitted car radio in April 1988.

Radio Doctor

See CHARLES HILL.

Radio England

Pirate ship off Frinton from 1966–67 which, like most pirates of the time, broadcast pop music. Uniquely,

however, it shared the vessel with another station called BRITAIN RADIO which put out softer, middle-of-the-road melodies. The two stations operated from separate studios but shared the same mast. JOHNNIE WALKER started his radio career below the decks.

Radio Essex

Pirate station in the mid-1960s, operating from a disused fort in the Thames estuary, which was beamed at East Anglia. It was started by a Southend businessman and his wife and offered easy listening by day and pop by night.

Radio Fiona

Pirate station run on and off for eighteen years (1969–87) by two brothers in Letchworth, Herts, broadcasting to the North Herts and East Beds area using a transmitter which had formerly belonged to the US Navy.

Radio 5

'Dumping ground', 'mish-mash' and 'treasure chest' were some of the phrases used for BBC Radio's fifth national network which began at 9 a.m. on Bank Holiday Monday, 27 August 1990. It is a mixture of sport, bedtime stories, serials for teenagers, youth magazines, SCHOOLS programmes, language courses and adult education. It is also the first domestic network to include World Service programmes such as OUTLOOK and MERIDIAN in its regular output.

The first voice to be heard on the network was that of a five-year-old boy, Andrew Kelly from Blackpool, who was discovered when RADIO GOES TO TOWN arrived in his. He piped up: 'Hallo, good morning, welcome to Radio 5.' Both this and the whole of the opening show, TAKE FIVE, were recorded. The show was hosted by BRUNO BROOKES and the first record he played was the recent pop-rap hit 'Thunderbirds Are Go', by M.C. Parker.

The network goes out on the old medium wave frequencies of Radio 2 and was conceived in response to the Government's radio policy, first spelled out in its Green Paper of 1987, which required the BBC to end simulcasting and surrender two frequencies, to make room for new stations and give listeners more choice.

Radio 5 therefore became the new home of all the sport formerly carried on Radio 2 medium wave, and Radio 2 turned into an FM-only service on the same day. It also carries the schools and adult education programmes which had previously gone out on Radio 4 FM (see OPTIONS). It will also take TEST MATCH SPECIAL from Radio 3.

Radio Forth

Edinburgh-based ILR station, on the air since 1975, which serves East Central Scotland, from St Andrews to Berwick. In 1990, like most ILR stations, it split its output – launching a golden oldie service, Max AM, on medium wave with Radio Forth FM remaining on FM. The former MP Margo MacDonald, now working in television, hosted a Sunday morning show on the station, *Dial Margo*, in the 1980s.

Radio 4

What the Home Service has been called since 30 September 1967, and one of Britain's greatest possessions. Its skeleton is made up of NEWS programmes but COMEDY, DRAMA, TALKS and a wide range of FEATURES provide the tissues and muscles. No-one would quibble with the BBC's claim that it is 'Britain's leading speech channel'.

The Radio 4 Debates

Series of formal debates staged at universities and learned institutions, broadcast on Radio 4 and chaired by BRIAN REDHEAD. They were believed to be the first specially organised radio debates held at British universities for more than twenty years.

The first series, in 1989, opened at the Oxford Union with Lord Peston and Prof. Denis Noble proposing 'that the nation is failing to invest in the future of the universities', which Robert Jackson and Sir Douglas Hague opposed. The second series in 1990 began with students, barristers and judges debating the proposition 'Our system of justice serves the interests of the strong' (proposed by Anthony Lester QC and Helena Kennedy and opposed by John Laws and Lord Justice Farquharson) in the Inner Temple. The third series in 1991 opened with 'The British public cannot have confidence in our present system of policing', proposed by John Alderson (former Chief Constable of Devon and Cornwall) and opposed by David Owen, Chief Constable of North Wales.

Radio 4 Generation

Two hundred people aged between 18 and 23 when they were first selected (by the BBC's Broadcasting Research Department) to be a roughly representative slice of their generation in terms of region, sex, class and employment. This was in 1987 when they were all first-time voters in that year's general election.

Since then they have been wheeled out for a variety of Radio 4 discussions (e.g. on the relevance of the Seven Deadly Sins, in a series called *Towards 2000* chaired by JOHN HUMPHRYS in 1988) intended to find out what the country's youngsters think. Radio 4 intends to monitor them and their opinions until they reach middle-age.

Radio Free Europe

American station based in Munich which has been beaming anti-communist propaganda into the Soviet bloc since 1951. Funded by US Congress since 1972,

when it was revealed that the station had been funded by the CIA.

Radio Fun

(1) Comic in 1930s with stars such as ARTHUR ASKEY on the front cover.

(2) A twelve-part history of BBC radio comedy, written and presented by RUSSELL DAVIES, broadcast on Radio 4 in 1988 and given a second outing on Radio 5 in 1990.

Radio Goes to Town

Five-year nationwide travelling show and exhibition, centred on a festive Big Top, which started its travels in May 1989. It promotes all aspects of BBC Radio (and the BBC's career prospects) at a time when it is under increasing competition and mounts all manner of live shows from the local Corn Exchange, Market Square and so on. Up to 136,000 visitors have been attracted during one stay, and many towns and cities have been visited. SANDRA CHALMERS is the organiser.

Radio Harmony

Poles, Asians and Irish all have their own music on this appealingly-named INCREMENTAL station for different ethnic groups in Coventry. It began, on FM, in August 1990.

Radio International

Cleverly conceived radio series which was like a Euro-Pick of the Week: it played extracts from soaps, cat food commercials, interviews, etc, from the bewildering array of European radio stations. They were translated and introduced by foreign nationals of the countries concerned. Each of the nine programmes concentrated on a different country, which included Italy, Spain and France, and the series went out on Radio 4 FM in 1989.

Radio Jackie

Land-based pirate station (one of the few) in the late 1960s.

Radio Journalists Trust

Body set up by the BBC in 1988 as one of several measures designed to encourage recruitment of people from Asian and Afro-Caribbean backgrounds.

Radio Liberty

American station based in Munich, under the same ownership and management as Radio Free Europe, which has been beaming anti-communist propaganda into the Soviet Union since 1951.

Radio Licence

Introduced on 1 November 1922, thirteen days before the BBC went on the air. The price, 10 shillings, remained unchanged until 1946 when it was increased to £1. It went up again to 25 shillings in 1965, and was abolished in 1971. On that same date, combined radio and television licences (first introduced in 1946) were also abolished and TV-only licences came in. Since 1971, therefore, no licence has been required for a radio set.

Licence figures offer a graphic illustration first of radio's rapid rise in national popularity and then of its devastating eclipse by television. The number of radio licences rose from 26,000 in 1922 to two million in 1926 and four million in 1932. By 1950 there were 11.82 million radio licences and fewer than 344,000 for radio and TV combined. By 1960, the number of radio licences had slumped to 4.48 million while radio and TV combined had risen astronomically to 10.47 million. By 1970, another decade having passed, the process was complete: radio-only had fallen to 2.28 million while radio and TV together had jumped to 15.61 million.

A year later the radio-only licence was killed off. Several European countries, however, among them Germany, Holland, Belgium and Switzerland, still see the merit in issuing separate radio licences.

Radio Link

Believed to be the first *regular* British programme which linked people in different countries in live, topical discussions on subjects of mutual importance, something the world now takes for granted. It went out each month on the Home Service, from 1956, chaired by Robert Mackenzie in London.

Radio Lives

Excellent Radio 4 series which presents vigorous, detailed, warts-and-all biographies of radio luminaries from the past, intending to reveal 'the real person behind the famous voice'. C.E.M. JOAD, singer Gracie Fields, opinionated scientist J.B.S. HALDANE, STEPHEN POTTER, GILBERT HARDING and writer-politician A.P. Herbert were featured in 1990, and UNCLE MAC and Lady Isobel Barnett were among those in the 1991 series.

Radio London

Pirate station which began at Christmas 1964, moored off Frinton. Operating from a former US minesweeper fitted out in Miami, it offered slick and polished competition to Radio Caroline (which by now covered the whole country, from two ships) with an Americanised style and catchy, self-promoting jingles like 'Big L' and 'Wonderful Radio London'.

JOHN PEEL made his British radio debut on the station and TONY BLACKBURN made his name on it, describing it twenty years later as 'the best station we've ever had in this country'. The first and last voice to be heard on the station was that of Paul Kaye.

Radio Luxembourg

The world's most famous commercial radio station, which has helped to train some of the best-known names in broadcasting: DAVID JACOBS, PETE MURRAY, JIMMY SAVILE, JIMMY YOUNG, JOHNNIE WALKER, NOEL EDMONDS, MIKE READ and PETER POWELL are among those to have spent some of their early careers broadcasting on Luxembourg, following in the footsteps of STEPHEN WILLIAMS who was the first DJ in 1933.

Luxembourg took the lead in developing sponsored programmes with popular shows such as THE OVALTINEYS. It also made a point of mounting its top attractions like George Formby and Gracie Fields on a Sunday, when the demand for light entertainment was greatest. For this was the day the BBC, created by a high-minded Calvinist keen to observe the Fourth Commandment, was at its most serious and sombre and closed down early.

This tradition of Sunday entertainment continued after the Second World War (during which the Germans invaded and occupied the Grand Duchy and used the station to relay the Nazi propaganda broadcasts of WILLIAM JOYCE). OPPORTUNITY KNOCKS, sponsored by Horlicks, was first broadcast on Sunday afternoons. TOP TWENTY, sponsored by Outdoor Girl lipstick, was also broadcast on a Sunday starting with its first programme in 1948. It set the pattern for all future chart shows by going out on this day of the week, which explains how the day of rest came to be the day of rock'n'roll as well. Other big attractions included TAKE YOUR PICK, sponsored by Beecham's Pills. Warren Mitchell, who later achieved household fame as Alf Garnett, was among the early postwar DJs but lasted only a few weeks.

The late 1940s to early 1960s was Luxembourg's golden age. Audiences were in the millions. Advertisers such as football pools tipster HORACE BATCHELOR and evangelist Garner Ted Armstrong became household names. 'Two-O-Eight – your station of the stars!' was the way Luxy billed itself. For pop fans there was nothing else, apart from the weekly SATURDAY CLUB and PICK OF THE POPS on the Light Programme.

Inevitably, the audience shrunk when new sources of pop arrived on the dial: North Sea pirates in 1964, Radio 1 in 1967 and ILR stations such as Capital from 1973 onwards. Today, still broadcasting each evening on its famous wavelength of 208 metres on medium wave which it has used since 1951 (it was on long wave before that), it claims an audience of around a million. It has speech, documentaries and religious slots from 6.30 p.m. and music from 7 p.m. onwards.

In August 1990, Luxembourg launched a new radio channel, carried only on the Astra satellite. Called RTL International, this all-day pop service, incorporating

Beneath the smoothly conformist appearance of Stephen Williams was an adventurer who broke new ground. He took a leading role in much early commercial radio before becoming Radio Luxembourg's first DJ in December 1933

the existing evening output, was aimed primarily at Scandinavia, although it goes out in English.

See also ATLANTIC 252.

Radio Mercury
Crawley-based ILR station, covering Surrey, North Sussex and West Kent, on the air since 1984 (and 1985 for Horsham). It also owns, and conceived of, Airport Information Radio serving Gatwick and Heathrow.

Radio Newsreel
Began in July 1940, initially for the North American audience and later also broadcast to the Pacific and Africa. It started to be broadcast domestically in November 1947, two months before the assassination of Gandhi of which it brought an eye-witness account.

The bracing military march used as its signature tune ever since 1940, 'Imperial Echoes', was abolished and electronically rejigged under JOHN TUSA's modernising regime in 1988, when the programme became NEWSREEL.

Radio Normandy
First radio station to beam commercials and sponsored shows to British listeners, when it began at Fécamp in France in 1931 (under its original name Radio-Normandie), run by Captain Leonard Plugge. STEPHEN WILLIAMS was one of its pioneers.

Radio Northsea International
Pirate ship jammed by the DTI in 1970.

Radio 1

Britain's first national pop station was born when TONY BLACKBURN placed the needle on 'Flowers in the Rain' by The Move, at 7 a.m. on Saturday, 30 September 1967. Its conception was in the mid-1960s, when the evident demand for pirate radio jolted the BBC out of its apathy and forced it to provide a pop service of its own.

Radio 1's original line-up of 22 disc-jockeys in 1967 was, alphabetically: MIKE AHERN, BARRY ALLDIS, TONY BLACKBURN, PETE BRADY, DAVE CASH, CHRIS DENNING, PETE DRUMMOND, KENNY EVERETT, BOB HOLNESS, DUNCAN JOHNSON, MIKE LENNOX, JOHNNY MORAN, PETE MURRAY, PETE MYERS, JOHN PEEL, MIKE RAVEN, DAVID RIDER, KEITH SKUES, ED STEWART, DAVID SYMONDS, TERRY WOGAN and JIMMY YOUNG. Only one is still broadcasting on the network today.

Radio 1 had plenty of people who were brash outsiders, not marinated at all in the ways of the BBC – both disc-jockeys like Blackburn and Peel and executives such as STUART GRUNDY and JOHN WALTERS. Nonetheless, a more accurate name for the new station would have been Radio One-and-a-Half. Lack of funds and needletime limitations meant that Radio 1 shared most of the day with Radio 2 and on its first day only 5 hours and 35 minutes consisted of its own programmes. Not for many years was separation achieved.

Radio 1's traditional 'pop-and-prattle', gushing and uncritical about the discs it put on the turntable, has

The faces that launched a thousand discs: Radio 1's original line-up of DJs on its opening day. Top row: Tony Blackburn, Jimmy Young, Kenny Everett, Duncan Johnson (sitting), Robin Scott, Controller of Radio 1, David Rider (loud shirt), Dave Cash, Pete Brady, David Symonds. Middle row: Bob Holness, Terry Wogan, Barry Alldis, Mike Lennox, Keith Skues, Chris Denning, Johnny Moran, Pete Myers (dark glasses). Front: Pete Murray, Ed Stewart, Pete Drummond, Mike Raven, Chris Denning (glasses), John Peel undergone considerable change. Today the station puts a greater emphasis on album tracks and has much more speech, ranging from comedies (such as HEY RRRADIO, THE MARY WHITEHOUSE EXPERIENCE and VICTOR LEWIS SMITH), news (see NEWS 91) and occasional documentaries which have aired harsh views on the state of contemporary pop.

There is a good reason for the network's efforts to become more adult orientated: the number of 16 to 25-year-olds (the core of Radio 1's audience) is expected to fall by over two million from 1988 to 1996. Widening Radio 1's appeal is therefore necessary to avoid dwindling audiences in the years ahead.

To this end, and to sharpen the network's identity as it limbered up for likely competition from a national commercial pop channel, Radio 1 unveiled its first ever policy document, *Music Radio for the 1990s*, in May 1990.

This spelled out its manifesto for the decade ahead: optimistic determination to retain both its public service principles and the size of its audience, plus a support for new music, a desire to have a 24-hour telephone helpline, further experiments with non-musical programmes and presenters from 'a variety of backgrounds'.

Radio 1's public service element is most clearly reflected in its campaigns. These date back to 1979 and the first Action Special, which gave information to school leavers on jobs, training and further education opportunities. Its formula of short, on-air bulletins supported by off-air advice and literature, was subsequently used in Radio 1's annual Drug Alert campaigns and others it has organised on AIDS, debt, homelessness and sexual

Radio I's DJ line-up exactly twenty years later, in 1987. Back row: Bruno Brookes, Robbie Vincent, Mike Read, Dave Lee Travis, Mike Smith, Andy Kershaw, John Peel, Gary Davies, Simon Bates, Liz Kershaw, The Ranking Miss P. Centre: Peter Powell, Janice Long, Adrian Juste, Steve Wright, Adrian John, Simon Mayo, Andy Peebles (standing). Front: Anne Nightingale, Jeff Young, Nicky Campbell, Ro Newton

and emotional problems. All these have concentrated on straightforward information, rather than bludgeoning the audience with shock horror. The neatly-named Rhythm 'n' Booze programmes covered alcohol, with listeners describing what drink did to their love lives, wallets and driving.

The Action Specials remain the biggest of these activities: in 1990 there were 10,000 telephone inquiries in five days, answered by over a thousand staff from local education authorities, voluntary agencies and careers and training experts.

Until 1988, Radio 1 had no FM frequency of its own. By 1990, 75 per cent of Britain could hear Radio 1 in FM and the target was 96 per cent by the end of 1991. The medium wave frequency is being surrendered for one of the new commercial networks in 1993.

Radio 1 started rocking round the clock, broadcasting 24 hours a day, on 1 May 1991, with BOB HARRIS the first to whisper through the night.

Radio 1 Roadshow

Annual summer extravaganza of outside broadcasts at seaside resorts, which travels thousands of miles round the coast of Britain in nine weeks.

Created by JOHNNY BEERLING in 1973, and launched by ALAN FREEMAN in Newquay, the first Roadshow consisted of a caravan and trailer towed by a Range Rover. They broadcast from the front of the caravan and sold T-shirts from the back.

By 1990 it had swollen to embrace two articulated lorries, a travelling satellite ground station and a mobile record library. Its role had also widened, from a series of fun-filled summer shows to a major promotional jamboree for the network, especially useful in plugging the switchover to stereo FM in recent years.

The BBC likes to bill the Roadshow as 'the biggest free show of the summer' and says that 750,000 people flock to see it and join in each year. Despite its increasing size, it has two unchanging ingredients, quite apart from the general gaiety, cheers and odd bucket of water which gets thrown about: the Mileage Game (in which participants have to guess how many miles the Roadshow has travelled since its last appearance) and the Bits and Pieces quiz (when contestants have to guess from snatches of records the titles of ten pop songs).

Radio Orwell

ILR station based in Ipswich, covering East Suffolk and North Essex, on the air since 1975.

Radio Paris

Commercial station in France in the 1930s also known as Poste Parisien, which beamed sponsored programmes into Britain. ROY PLOMLEY worked on it.

The Radio Programme

Weekly Radio 4 magazine series, looking at all aspects of the wireless world. It began in 1986 and has always been presented by Laurie Taylor, the loquacious University of York sociology don.

Radio Prune

Comic creation of I'M SORRY I'LL READ THAT AGAIN.

Radio Radio

(1) Name of a Radio 1 series in 1986 skilfully blending words and music which interviewed six DJs, including KENNY EVERETT, PAUL GAMBACCINI and NOEL EDMONDS, about their early influences, innovations and love of radio.

(2) Name of a venture launched by Richard Branson in 1988 which, using the Eutelsat satellite, provided music-and-chat shows throughout the night for whichever ILR stations wanted to take them for their own listeners. The service was free and Radio Radio intended to recoup the cost by selling airtime to advertisers. DJs included JONATHAN ROSS, JANICE LONG and JOHNNIE WALKER. This 'sustaining service', to give it its technical name, was not taken by as many stations as was hoped and most of the star names left by the end of 1988. The Miss World group of Owen Oyston took over the management, and acquired a 26 per cent stake in 1989, but the service continued to languish and in particular was not taken by any London station, so most advertising agencies were unaware of what it sounded like. It ceased in 1990.

Radio Scotland

Pirate ship in the mid-1960s, anchored five miles off Troon. Not to be confused with BBC Radio Scotland.

Radio Show

Annual London exhibition for forty years, ceasing in the 1960s just before the launch of Radio 1 and local radio, and resurrected by the BBC as a one-off anniversary gala in 1988. The first show, in 1926, was called RadiOlympia after its venue and was organised as a joint venture between the BBC and the flourishing industry of British radio manufacturers. It was the first of 30 similar exhibitions (from 1936 they covered television as well) which came to an end in 1966 when the BBC felt the industry was served adequately by shows abroad, and very few British manufacturers were still in existence.

The Corporation's 1988 revival was the BBC RADIO SHOW, at Earls Court, visited by over 93,000 people.

Radio Tay

Dundee-based ILR station covering Dundee and Perth, on the air since 1980.

Radio 3

The new name for the output of Network Three and the Third Programme (though the latter continued to have its own identity for another three years) from

30 September 1967. Its mix of highbrow talks and drama and serious European music continued largely as before, though in recent years, particularly in the regime of JOHN DRUMMOND, there have been conscious efforts to introduce more debate and vivacity, make the tone of the channel less sniffy and the musical descriptions less technical.

About 20 per cent of the output is speech, and the remainder music. About two-thirds of that is live, much of it performed by one of the BBC's five orchestras. The network mounts a public or studio concert every day and, on average, two operas a week.

About 14,000 pieces of music are played on Radio 3 every year, but over 99 per cent go out only once or twice. Only about three dozen are performed ten times or more – the great and enduring works of wide appeal such as Beethoven, Brahms, Mozart and Rachmaninov – and no piece ever seems to receive more than fourteen performances over the course of a year.

The music played on Radio 3 has often provoked heated debate. It incurs the wrath of those who feel that far too much is obscure and second-rate and mounted purely for the benefit of a small intellectual elite. LORD CHALFONT, for example, has made no secret of his view that it is not 'accessible' enough. Certainly the *range* is vast, since about 4,000 composers are heard on the network each year, and Radio 3 does not believe that good music stopped at 1900.

But going through the printouts of all the music played during 1989 and 1990 does at least show that, contrary to the frequently expressed charge that Radio 3 turns up its nose at popular classics, these are precisely what are broadcast most frequently.

The 'Top Thirty' for 1990, with the placings from the previous year in brackets where applicable, were:

First position (fourteen performances):
Beethoven Symphony No. 7 (3)
Berlioz Symphonie Fantastique
Brahms Symphony No. 4 (3)
Debussy La Mer
Richard Strauss Don Juan

Second position (thirteen performances):
Beethoven Prometheus, Overture (4)
Dukas Sorcerer's Apprentice
Glinka Ruslan and Lyudmilla, Overture (4)
Schumann Piano Concerto
Schumann Phantasiestucke (Op 73)

Third position (twelve performances):
Chopin Ballade No. 3
Chopin Ballade No. 4
Debussy Sonata for Cello and Piano
Elgar Introduction and Allegro for Strings
Mozart Marriage of Figaro, Overture (4)
Ravel Mother Goose

Schubert Symphony No. 8 (Unfinished)
Richard Strauss Till Eulenspiegel (3)

Fourth position (eleven performances):
Debussy Iberia
Mozart Symphony No. 29
Sibelius Symphony No. 2
Richard Strauss Four Last Songs (4)
Tchaikovsky Serenade for String Orchestra
Vaughan Williams Lark Ascending
Wagner Siegfried Idyll (1)

These two surveys echo the findings of a much earlier one, for the year 1975, which the BBC published in 1978. Then, too, it was similar works which were heard most often: Beethoven's Emperor Piano Concerto and Schubert's 5th Symphony topped the list with fourteen performances each.

Radio 3 presented the first live concert from Buckingham Palace, in 1988. Later it was a participant in, and helped to organise, the most ambitious venture in classical music ever mounted on European radio – Mozart Day in January 1991. It consisted of ten live concerts, each from a different European city with which Mozart was associated. The concerts went out one after the other: they consisted mainly of Mozart, with a sprinkling of Haydn and Salieri. They were broadcast not only in the seven countries involved (Austria, Germany, France, Britain, Italy, Holland and Czechoslovakia) but thirteen others as well including Israel and the USSR.

Radio 355

Thriller writer Ted Allbeury's second pirate station, after Radio 390 was closed down. It was much less successful.

Radio 390

Pirate station run by novelist Ted Allbeury on an abandoned, anti-aircraft fort in the Thames estuary in the 1960s. Unlike most of the other North Sea pirates, 390 broadcast only warm, sentimental HOUSEWIVES' CHOICE-type music. DAVID ALLAN, one of its disc-jockeys, recalls that they had to dress properly, shave by the time they sat down at the microphone, and be scrupulously polite. Programmes carried names like 'Masters of the Organ' and 'Teatime Tunes'. None of this cut much ice with the DTI, however, which discovered a sandbank near the fort which meant it was no longer in international waters after all, and closed the station down.

Radio Times

Launched in 1923, in response to the refusal of newspapers to print details of BBC radio programmes, and now the bestselling magazine in Britain.

For nearly forty years the magazine ran its programme schedules from Sunday to Saturday, a reflection of

Reithian respect for the day of rest. It switched to the more secular order of Saturday to Friday, which has prevailed ever since, on 8 October 1960. From that date also another major change took place. Hitherto, television and radio listings had been in separate sections, with radio occupying four pages a day (twice as many as now) even though there were only three networks. From that date onwards, both television and radio listings were gathered together under each day from Saturday to Friday.

This system operated until March 1989 when the new editor, Nicholas Brett, once again put radio into its own section towards the back of the magazine. The listings were initially grouped network by network. After eight months they returned to a much more convenient day-by-day format after more than 1,800 written complaints from readers fed up with having to thumb the pages backwards and forwards to see what was being broadcast by the four networks on the same day. This system still prevails, with all five networks squashed into a two-page spread. On 1 March 1991 *Radio Times* started to carry details of ILR, ITV and C4 when changes to the listings laws came into operation.

Every two years, the magazine organises a 'Sounds Funny' Comedy Awards contest to discover new writers of wireless comedy, with £5,000 in prize money available. Hundreds of scripts get submitted: the winning ones are sometimes broadcast, sometimes not.

The winner of the first competition, in 1985, was builder's labourer Phil Steer (his script was called *The Collapse of the Romanov Autocracy*). Husband-and-wife team Gavin Petrie and Jan Etherington won the 1987 contest with *Two for the Show* (not broadcast, although they went on to write the hit series SECOND THOUGHTS) and Max Russell (*Punk and Prurience*) triumphed in 1989. Predating these are the magazine's drama trophies, covering television as well as radio. Each section offers £7,500 in prize money and it can be split up between the winning entries at the judges' discretion.

These drama awards were launched in 1973 and have helped to nurture several writers who are now prominent. In some cases the winning plays were transmitted with different titles and in others they led to the broadcast of different plays or series altogether.

The awards take place every two years, although there was a hiatus in the 1970s. The past winners in the radio section are:

1973–74: Peter Cator (*The Search for Hamilton Stiggs*).
1982–83: Jointly, Christopher Russell (*Swimmer*) and Stephen Dunstone (*Who is Sylvia*).
1984–85: Jointly, David Ashton (*The Old Ladies at the Zoo*) and Nick Warburton (*Conversation from the Engine Room*).

1986: Martin Crimp (*Definitely the Bahamas*).
1988: Patricia Finney (*A Room Full of Mirrors*).
1990: Trevor Hoyle (*Gigo*).

Both the comedy and the drama awards were launched by, and until 1990 run by, the musician, singer, broadcaster and events organiser Leonard Pearcey. He hit the headlines in 1971 with an elaborate April Fool's Day joke — a half-hour Radio 4 documentary on a man who did not exist, Gerald Burley, with spoof tributes and reminiscences from Yehudi Menuhin, the Bishop of Southwark, David Kossoff and Donald Swann.

Radio Trent
ILR station covering Notts and Derbyshire, with Mansfield, Newark, Derby and Nottingham the main centres of population. It began in 1975, named after its famous river. In 1988 it launched GEM-AM, a medium wave golden oldies service which is also heard on sister station Leicester Sound: its initials stand for Greater East Midlands. Trent FM, aimed at younger listeners, is broadcast on its FM frequencies.

Radio 2
What the Light Programme became on 30 September 1967. It later became BBC Radio's first network to start a round-the-clock service, and has never been off the air since 5 a.m. on 27 January 1979. In August 1990 it became the first national network to go out on FM only.

Radio 2 Ballroom
Ballroom dancing series on Radio 2 from 1973 to 1983, studio based with real dancers; resurrected in 1990 to reflect renewed interest in waltz, foxtrot and tango.

Radio 2 Top Tunes
Running from 1976–80, this had a listeners' panel of 1,000 people who voted every week as to their favourite tunes, which would then be arranged and performed by the BBC MIDLAND RADIO ORCHESTRA (under Norrie Paramor, until he died in 1979) every Saturday night.

Radio 270
Pirate ship in the mid-1960s, off Scarborough.

Radio Victory
ILR station for Hampshire which was on the air until the mid-1980s, but then lost its franchise. It was succeeded by Ocean Sound.

Radio Wyvern
ILR station covering the County of Hereford and Worcester, with its base in the latter city; on the air since 1982. Its name is a confluence of the area's two great rivers, the Wye and the Severn.

Ragas and a Republic

Four-part documentary series on Radio 3 in 1988 which opened what is for many in the West a closed book – Indian classical music. Written and presented by Roger Savage. Featured many of India's leading performers, as well as interviews with composers and scholars.

Ragtime to Rock'n'Roll

Mammoth Light Programme series in 26 parts in which BENNY GREEN wrote the first half and PETER CLAYTON the second, presented by actor Kenneth More.

The Ranking Miss P   (1959–)

Disc-jockey whose love and knowledge of reggae led to her own late-night Radio 1 show, CULTURE ROCK, in 1985, though she was dropped five years later. She now appears on GLR.

London-born daughter of a Jamaican dentist, she entered the radio world by singing jingles on her brother's London pirate station, DBC, in 1981 (and was later commissioned by BBC2 to write and sing the

Margaret Jones, better known as 'The Ranking Miss P', and one of the leading champions of reggae music. She had her own show on Radio I for five years

theme tune of the series *Ebony*). She is the sister-in-law of the late Jamaican singing star Bob Marley. (Real name: Margaret Jones.)

Rave

Youth culture magazine show on Radio 5 each week, coming from Cardiff.

Raven, Mike   (1924–)

One of Radio 1's original line-up of DJs in 1967, presenting a rhythm and blues show. Later ran a hotel in Devon.

Ray, Robin   (c. 1935–)

Frequent broadcaster on musical subjects, with series such as WAX WORKS. Early in 1990 he became a regular presenter on Radio 2, with an engaging and incisive Saturday-afternoon programme of (mainly) classical music called *Robin Ray on Record*.

He is the elder son of TED RAY, whose stage name he adopted (as did his actor brother Andrew). Like his late father, his real name is Olden.

Ray, Ted   (1907–77)

Failed comedian's son with a deep compulsion from boyhood to make others laugh – a mission in which he had supreme talent. His prowess on the violin inspired one of his descriptions of his own career, 'From Fiddling to Fooling'.

His main radio show, which ran for over ten years, was RAY'S A LAUGH, and he was also a regular on DOES THE TEAM THINK? His real name was Charles Olden: he chose the name Ted Ray from a list of American golfers. Elder son ROBIN RAY has followed in his broadcasting footsteps.

Raymondo

Chipmunk-like voice which every day on *The Jimmy Young Show* asked the same question: 'What's the recipe today, Jim?' And Jimbo would answer 'Savoury Sausage Roll', or 'Coconut Chiffon Tarts', or whatever the *plat de jour* happened to be. A few moments later the first chipmunk would be joined by another for a dual chirrup of the words 'And this (pause) is what (pause) you do . . .' to introduce the method of preparing the ingredients.

These exchanges were a feature of the J.Y. Prog. from 1967, when it began on Radios 1 and 2, to 1976 when it switched to Radio 2 only and gradually became a more serious current affairs programme, with the listener's recipe spot getting phased out and with it Raymondo's voice.

The voice was that of the programme's producer Ray Harvey (he was joined by a studio manager called Max for the duet), who created the sound by recording the messages at twice the normal speed on a BBC tape machine.

Two funny people were at the centre of a very funny show. England's Ted Ray and Australia's Kitty Bluett, pictured in 1949 just after *Ray's a Laugh* had begun on the Light Programme. It was to enjoy a successful run of twelve years

Rayner, Claire (1931–)
Agony aunt who has presented Radio 2's monthly series of social issue programmes since May 1990, which have covered cancer, divorce, bereavement, family violence, fear of crime and phobias. (This last programme contained a memorable and moving interview with agoraphobia sufferer Grace Sheppard, wife of the Bishop of Liverpool.) The programmes are supported by back-up literature and helplines manned by professionals.

Also known to Radio 2 listeners as a frequent stand-in for GLORIA HUNNIFORD and as presenter of her own series MYSELF WHEN YOUNG, which she devised after breaking down in tears when ANTHONY CLARE interviewed her about her own awful childhood on IN THE PSYCHIATRIST'S CHAIR.

Ray's a Laugh
TED RAY raised countless laughs with his long-running comedy show on the Light Programme which enlivened Friday nights from 1949–61. Australian comedy actress Kitty Bluett played his wife and Laidman Browne, a wartime player with the BBC DRAMA REPERTORY COMPANY, his employer Mr Trumble. Pat Coombs appeared as home help Ursula Prune, whose love for Ted went unrequited. Others who made appearances included Peter Sellers, who played Crystal Jollibottom.

RDS
See RADIO DATA SYSTEM.

Read, Al (1909–87)
Meat maker from Salford, joking that he came from a long line of sausages, who made his debut as a radio comedian in 1950. Within two years he had become a household name and appearances before King George VI at Windsor, and in the West End, followed. He mined a rich vein of working-class Lancashire experience to create humorous 'pictures from life' with vivid sketches of recognisable human types. Popular throughout the 1950s and 1960s, his catchphrase was 'Right monkey!'

Read, Mike (1952–)
Former guitarist and singer in Manchester clubs who, after a stint on Radio Luxembourg, joined Radio 1 in 1978 to present a Saturday evening show. Hosted its breakfast programme from 1981 to 1986 and shows such as SINGLED OUT and POP OF THE FORM after that. Has co-authored five volumes of the *Guinness Book of Hit Singles*. Made a sixteen-part series on Paul McCartney, broadcast on both Radio 1 and the BBC World Service.

Reading Aloud
Sunday evening reading slot introduced to Radio 4 in 1989 – at twenty minutes, five minutes longer than either MORNING STORY or A BOOK AT BEDTIME. It also differs more fundamentally, being confined to non-fiction. The first book to occupy the new slot was *Your Name Is Olga*, by the Catalan writer Josep Espinas, a series of letters from the author to his 32-year-old daughter who suffers from Down's Syndrome.

Really Not a Soldier
Four-part Radio 4 series in 1989 in which Rupert Westmacott (born 1892) spoke in remarkable detail and vivid recall about his fighting in the Gallipoli campaign in 1915.

Rebels
Absorbing Radio 4 series of the 1980s, profiling figures such as traitor Guy Burgess (the first) to Labour MP Bessie Braddock and American Indian leader Geronimo.

Record Express
Wednesday lunchtime show on the Home Service, introduced by Jack Train.

Record Hop

'Fast-moving music to beat those Monday blues' was KEITH FORDYCE's formula for his weekly show on the Light Programme.

Record Rendezvous

Weekday afternoon series on the Light Programme which SAM COSTA hosted.

Record Roundabout

See JACK JACKSON.

Red Dragon Radio

Taking its title from the national emblem of Wales, this ILR station based in Cardiff covers Mid-Glamorgan, South Glamorgan and Gwent. It was created by Owen Oyston in 1985 from the merger of the Cardiff station CBC (which had operated since 1980) and a Gwent station (on the air since 1983).

In 1990 Red Dragon split itself into two, like most ILR stations: the easy listening and golden oldie service on medium wave is called Touch AM and the music for 15 to 35-year-olds on FM is called Red Dragon FM.

Red Letter Days

Jack Hilton, Ethel Mannin, Jack Lindsay, Walter Brierly and Harold Heslop were the radical Left-wing writers of the 1930s and 1940s reassessed by Andy Croft for this Radio 4 series in 1990.

Red Rose Radio

Named after the emblem of Lancashire, this Preston-based ILR station covers all of that county, plus some of South Cumbria and parts of Greater Manchester and Merseyside. It has always been run by media tycoon Owen Oyston and began in 1982. In 1990 it split its services: Rock FM, on its FM frequency, plays rock music to 15 to 40-year-olds, and Red Rose Gold on AM offers golden oldies for older listeners. Lancastrians RUSSELL HARTY and Victoria Wood helped to establish the station.

Redhead, Brian (1929–)

One of the men who helps to set the nation's agenda, as a presenter of Radio 4's TODAY programme since 1975. He joined it after being sacked as editor of the *Manchester Evening News*, though his connection with radio came long before his career in newspapers: he made his first broadcast in 1941 (playing the clarinet on CHILDREN'S HOUR). He invariably hosts the general election coverage on Radio 4 and often the American presidential elections, too.

A practising Anglican, he takes a keen interest in religions in general and Christianity in particular, which has deepened since the death of his eighteen-year-old

son William in a road accident in France in 1982. Religious series he has presented on Radio 4 include THE GOOD BOOK and THE CHRISTIAN CENTURIES, and political series include FROM PLATO TO NATO and AGAINST THE STATE. He chairs THE RADIO 4 DEBATES and used to chair A WORD IN EDGEWAYS.

Reed, Henry (1914–)

Writer who contributed to radio on several fronts. He wrote the HILDA TABLET comedies on the Third Programme in the 1950s. He adapted Herman Melville's *Moby Dick* as a play in 1947 with Ralph Richardson as Captain Ahab and a score by ANTONY HOPKINS, with STEPHEN POTTER the producer. He translated seven plays by the Italian dramatist Ugo Betti, all broadcast between 1954 and 1961. He appeared on THE CRITICS and was radio columnist for the *New Statesman* from 1947–48.

Rees, Nigel (1944–)

Television man who has graduated to radio, rather than (as is commonplace) the other way round. He is best known as the deviser and presenter of Radio 4's quiz series QUOTE . . . UNQUOTE, first broadcast in January 1976 and still on the air today. Two years later he produced his first spin-off book from the programme which, with its successors, looks at aspects of the English language in a humorous way. He estimates total sales of his books at over three million.

Rees, who started in broadcasting as a graduate trainee for Granada Television at the same time as John Birt, altered tracks and began working for BBC Radio at the end of the 1960s. He introduced the BBC World Service programme TWENTY-FOUR HOURS nearly 1,000 times between 1972–79. From 1973–75 he regularly presented Radio 4's nightly arts magazine KALEIDOSCOPE. Later, he presented Radio 4's two series about newspapers, BETWEEN THE LINES (1976–78) and STOP PRESS (1984–86). He appeared as an actor in WEEK ENDING for five years (1971–76) and THE BURKISS WAY for four (1976–80).

Reflections on Australia

Six half-hour interviews conducted by MICHAEL CHARLTON on Radio 3 in 1989 in which he tried to assess his native country's achievements and character in a cooler way than the Bicentennial had generally managed the year before.

Regional Programme

Began in 1930 (in London) as an alternative to the National Programme, with other areas in Britain following with their own regional services between 1931–34. They all ceased at the outbreak of war in September 1939, absorbed with the National to form the new Home

Service. (Regional programmes were restored on the BBC in 1945, though as part of the Home Service and not the Regional Programme, which disappeared in 1939.)

Reith, John Charles Walsham (1889–1971)

Presbyterian minister's son who became the founding father of the BBC. General manager of the British Broadcasting Company (see BBC) and then first Director-General of the British Broadcasting Corporation, until he stepped down in 1938.

'The BBC's role is to bring the best of everything to the greatest number of homes', he said in 1924, and this

---

Lord Reith (second left), away from the BBC for once and seemingly wishing he had worn a looser suit. He was pictured in 1949 at Henley Regatta chatting with his son, a friend and commentator John Snagge (left). Lady Reith observes the men at a respectful distance

high-mindedness – the vision of a BBC which would inform, entertain and educate all those who wished to listen, wherever they were and whatever their financial circumstances, so that at the end of the day they could feel enriched – was the guiding spirit which shaped public service broadcasting in Britain.

The BBC has changed from monopoly to half of a duopoly to part of a competitive broadcasting market, and the commercial sector is more lightly regulated than before: but Reithian ideology, albeit in diluted form, stills underpins much of broadcasting. It was the greatest irony, though, that his own insistence on keeping the Sabbath quiet and solemn (he banned comedy on Sundays) should have been responsible for achieving the exact opposite and turning the day of rest into the day of rock'n'roll. See RADIO LUXEMBOURG.

'I never learned that life was for living' – Lord Reith, speaking to John Freeman on *Face to Face*.

Reith Lectures

Annual series of lectures named after the BBC's first Director-General. It is the one programme for which the invitation comes from the Board of Governors (via the Director-General) and is thus often regarded as the most illustrious event on BBC Radio.

The lectures have often helped to focus attention on a topic of growing importance and create a deeper understanding of difficult problems. A good example was Geoffrey Hosking's on the repercussions of the tumultuous changes in Gorbachev's USSR, delivered a year before the toppling of the Berlin Wall.

With one exception, each series has consisted of six lectures. The exception was 1989, when Jacques Darras's were partly extemporised and numbered only five. The lecturers tend to be white English males: so far there has been only one woman, two blacks and two Europeans.

The lectures have always gone out in November and December on the Home Service, or Radio 4 as it now is, but have often been repeated on Radio 3. They were inaugurated in 1948, when the philosopher Bertrand Russell spoke on 'Authority and the Individual'.

His successors, and their subjects, were: **1949** Robert Birley ('Britain in Europe'); **1950** John Zachary Young ('Doubt and Certainty in Science'); **1951** Lord Radcliffe ('Power and the State'); **1952** Arnold Toynbee ('The World and the West'); **1953** Robert Oppenheimer ('Science and the Common Understanding'); **1954** Sir Oliver Franks ('Britain and Tide of World Affairs'); **1955** Nikolaus Pevsner ('The Englishness of English Art'); **1956** Sir Edward Appleton ('Science and the Nation'); **1957** George Kennan ('Russia, the Atom and the West'); **1958** Bernard Lovell ('The Individual and the Universe'); **1959** Peter Medawar ('The Future of Man'); **1960** Edgar Wind ('Art and Anarchy'); **1961** Margery Perham ('The Colonial Reckoning'); **1962** Prof. George Carstairs ('This Island Now'); **1963** Dr Albert Sloman ('A University in the Making'); **1964** Sir Leon Bagrit ('The Age of Automation'); **1965** Robert Gardiner ('A World of Peoples'); **1966** J.K. Galbraith ('The New Industrial State'); **1967** Edmund Leach ('A Runaway World'); **1968** Lester Pearson ('Peace in the Family of Man'); **1969** Dr Frank Frazer Darling ('Wilderness and Plenty'); **1970** Dr Donald Schon ('Change and Industrial Society'); **1971** Richard Hoggart ('Only Connect'); **1972** Andrew Shonfield ('Europe: Journey to an Unknown Destination'); **1973** Prof. Alastair Buchan ('Change without War'); **1974** Prof. Ralf Dahrendorf ('The New Liberty'); **1975** Dr Daniel Boorstin ('America and the World Experience'); **1976** Dr Colin Blakemore ('Mechanics of the Mind'); **1977** Prof. A.H. Halsey ('Change in British Society'); **1978** Rev. Dr Edward Norman ('Christianity and the World'); **1979** Prof. Ali Mazrui ('The African Condition'); **1980** Ian Kennedy ('Unmasking Medicine'); **1981** Prof. Laurence Martin ('The Two Edged Sword'); **1982** Prof. Denis Donoghue ('The Arts Without Mystery'); **1983** Sir Douglas Wass ('Government and the Governed'); **1984** Prof. John Searle ('Minds, Brains and Science'); **1985** David Henderson ('Innocence and Design'); **1986** Lord McCluskey ('Law, Justice and Democracy'); **1987** Prof. Alexander Goehr ('The Survival of the Symphony'); **1988** Prof. Geoffrey Hosking ('The Rediscovery of Politics'); **1989** Jacques Darras ('Beyond the Tunnel of History'); **1990** Rabbi Dr Jonathan Sacks ('The Persistence of Faith'); **1991** Dr Steve Jones ('The Language of the Genes').

Relative Values

Series of family portraits which began on Radio 4 in 1987, always presented by MICHAEL O'DONNELL.

Replay

Tutankhamun's ceremonial trumpets, blown in 1939 for the first time in 3,000 years, was the first curious story from the past unearthed in this Radio 3 archive series beginning in 1991. It also offers insights into historical figures from those who remember them, for example the views of Bertrand Russell on his erstwhile friend D.H. Lawrence, given in a talk in 1952. It is a speech equivalent of the same network's MINING THE ARCHIVE.

Return Journey

Two dozen thirty-minute programmes were made between 1945 and 1951 in this series in which celebrated writers spoke about places they remembered from their childhoods. Dylan Thomas, for example, recalled his life in Swansea.

Return Ticket

One of the strands in Radio 4's morning archives slot, this was created in 1989 for vivid, first-person accounts. For example, Charles Wheeler recalled a fraught Royal tour to India in 1961, Harvey Thomas remembered the Brighton bomb and Rebecca Johnson described her five years of camping outside Greenham Common.

Reynolds, Gillian (1935–)

Radio critic for the *Daily Telegraph* since 1975. From 1967–74 she was radio critic for *The Guardian* and then worked as programme controller at Radio City in Liverpool for twenty months (1974–75). She was one of the founding trustees of the CHARLES PARKER Archive, in 1982. She chairs the annual Radio Festival of the RADIO ACADEMY (which she first chaired in its small-scale, pre-Academy existence) and until 1991 the SONY RADIO AWARDS committee. Is a frequent broadcaster.

Rich Pickings

Hannah Gordon and David Suchet were the readers, in this five-part Radio 4 series in 1989, of poetry and prose concerned with the eternal search for true love. Writers ranged from Jane Austen and Yeats to Robert Graves and e.e. cummings. Suchet again, this time with Jane Lapotaire, read the verse and prose during the second series, in 1990. Weather – from snow to storms – was the theme of the 1991 series, in which the readers were Rosemary Leach and Michael Fitzgerald.

Richard Baker Compares Notes

A happy meeting of musical minds on Radio 4, this series began in October 1987 under the title *Comparing Notes*. Each week RICHARD BAKER converses with singers, teachers, composers, agents, musicologists and even players. The very first guests were two clarinettists, Emma Johnson and Jack Brymer. In the programme's 100th edition, in May 1990, he compared notes with conductor and sometime organ scholar Edward Heath.

Rider, David   (1940–)

One of Radio 1's original line-up of DJs in 1967, presenting MIDDAY SPIN (for three months). Later he presented 297 editions of Radio 1's children's magazine programme *Playground*, from 1976–82. He devised, and presents, Radio 2's quiz show ON THE AIR.

Riders of the Range

Cowboy Jeff Arnold and his faithful sidekick Luke were created in this musical drama series by the great CHARLES CHILTON. It ran from 1949–53, each episode introduced by thundering hooves and ending with the bark of Rustler the dog, and gained a new audience when it was fashioned into an exciting colour strip cartoon in the boys' paper *Eagle* from 1950–62, which Chilton also scripted. (The later drawings were memorable for Jeff's smart red shirt and Luke's profusion of white whiskers.)

The show, the first British radio series to celebrate the Wild West, initially centred on a character called The Rancher (Canadian actor Cal McCord). Later characters, apart from Jeff and Luke, included the Singing Cowboy (Bob Malin), J.C. McDonald, head of the 6T6 cattle ranching outfit in Texas (Macdonald Parke) and his niece Mary (Carole Carr). Country and western music was played by a group called The Four Ramblers, one of whom was Irish crooner Val Doonican.

Riders of the Range, both on radio and in *Eagle* (where it generated merchandising activity ranging from annuals to cowboy outfits) was acclaimed for being largely true to the known historical facts in the retelling of Western stories and characters, whether Billy the Kid or the Battle of Little Big Horn. Sadly, however, not one episode of the six series broadcast has survived.

Ring-a-Ding-Ding

'Have a late-night fling', urged *Radio Times* when it first billed this Light Programme series of records and singers in the early 1960s.

Rippon, Angela   (1944–)

Plymouth-born former newspaper reporter and BBC-TV newsreader who broadcasts regularly on Radio 5 and Radio 2 and has often stood in for other presenters. Her first show of her own came in 1986 with the late-night *The Angela Rippon Show*, live from Bristol. She is also breakfast presenter on LBC.

Robb, Allan   (1961–)

Politics graduate from Aberdeen University who went into ILR and then NEWSBEAT. A Scotsman, he has co-presented NEWS 91 from the beginning and is one half of what the BBC calls 'a dynamic duo' with SYBIL RUSCOE.

Robert Parker's A to Z of Jazz

Survey of classic jazz, imported from Australia and broadcast on Radio 2 in 1988, in 26 parts – one for each letter of the alphabet.

Robertson, Max   (–)

The voice of tennis for four decades, commentating at every Wimbledon for many years until he was dropped in 1986. Famous for clear, fast speech, he began his career as an announcer in Sydney with the Australian Broadcasting Corporation in 1937. Also appeared on BBC-TV, hosting both *Going For A Song* and, for a short time, *Panorama*.

Robinson, Anne   (1944–)

Presenter of a Radio 2 show on Saturday mornings which combines aggressive feminism and excellent music (she has a particular liking for Billie Jo Spears). Men, in Robinson's scheme of things, spend their weekends lazing about with their feet up while women are always up ladders with feather dusters or organising their daughters' weddings. Punchier and more opinionated than most of her colleagues on Radio 2, she is one of the network's real stars.

The slot she occupies was originally launched in 1987 with MICHAEL ASPEL the presenter: she deputised for him early in 1988 and the show became hers later that year when he stepped down.

Rockline

Live phone-in show in which pop fans can ring their idols, broadcast by a number of ILR stations since 1987, and produced by PPM RADIO WAVES. One series

Riders of the Range **was the only radio show to be in if you liked playing cowboys. The producer Charles Chilton (right) certainly believed in giving his cast plenty of rope. Rustler is in the foreground**

was sponsored by Midland Bank. The most complex was with Huey Lewis, who was in a recording studio in San Francisco when he answered questions from listeners in Britain via a satellite 35,000 miles above the Equator.

Callers can ring 24 hours a day, seven days a week, to log the questions they would like to put. (Selected ones are then called back when the show goes on the air.) In each case the name, address, phone number and age are logged and these details build into a database available to all ILR stations, helping them to acquire a more accurate profile of their audience.

Rollercoaster
Thursday morning experimental magazine show which ran on Radio 4 in 1984, devised by the network's then Controller DAVID HATCH. Presented by RICHARD BAKER, it featured waspish humour, ex-Coronation Street actor Peter Adamson reading MORNING STORY and DAILY SERVICE moving inside a studio. The object was to arrest the mid-morning slump in audiences.

Hatch came up with a novel way of telling if people liked the experiment. Six thousand car stickers were printed and distributed. They carried the word 'Rollercoaster' over a sketch of a clenched fist with the thumb sticking out. Those who approved of the programme were encouraged to drive around with the sticker glued on their rear windscreen with the thumb up. Those who disliked it were told to invert the sticker and give it the thumbs down. The fact that *Rollercoaster* rolled into oblivion after six months indicates which way up the stickers were usually seen.

Romanian Service
Programmes in the Romanian language were first broadcast by the BBC in September 1939. By the end of 1989, they were on the air for two hours a day and claimed a regular audience of 17 per cent of the population: shortly after the uprising at the end of that year, the service boosted its output by an extra fifteen minutes a day, six days a week, a few days before the bloody Christmas revolution which toppled the hated Ceausescu regime.

Romany
One of the CHILDREN'S HOUR favourites – a Methodist minister of gypsy extraction, the Rev. G. Bramwell Evens (1883-1943), who pretended to go on nature

rambles in the English countryside with two children and a spaniel called Raq.

All the 'walks' were in fact recorded in the studio, but since this was not widely known it did nothing to diminish the love of birds and animals which Evens helped to instil in his young listeners. He started his 'Out with Romany' walks in 1933 in Manchester, and started to be heard nationally in 1938. When he died, letters of sympathy and poems of tribute poured into the programme's offices. At least one of his books is dedicated 'To My Gipsy Mother Who Gave Me My Love of Green Fields and Quiet Lanes'.

Room to Listen, Room to Talk
Series about therapy presented by social psychologist Dr Tony Lake on Radio 4 FM in 1988.

The Root of the Matter
Sunday evening series on Radio 4 examining politics away from Westminster and Whitehall, on the air since 1987. It travels to a different part of Britain each week to report on a topic of local concern, which have ranged from rural violence in Somerset to the campaign against the poll tax in Scotland.

Rosko, Emperor (1942–)
Real name Michael Pasternak. DJ on Radio 1 from 1967–76, presenting shows like *Rosko's Round Table*, when he returned to the USA to be near his father, film producer Joe Pasternak. Prior to Radio 1 he had worked as a DJ on an American aircraft carrier and aboard RADIO CAROLINE (SOUTH). He returned to Radio 1 in 1982 to present a Sunday morning show for 13 weeks.

Ross, Jonathan (1961–)
The star of Channel 4 joined Radio 1 in 1990 to host a series of live talk shows, THE JONATHAN ROSS RADIO SHOW, from Ronnie Scott's jazz club in London.

Round Britain Quiz
The nearest radio gets to crossword puzzles, this gentlemanly and long-running institution of Radio 4 began in 1947, with regional teams challenging one in London. GILBERT HARDING was a celebrated questionmaster: today's are the less volatile GORDON CLOUGH and Louis Allen. The resident London team consists of Irene Thomas and Eric Korn. The verbal brainteasers are always of a high standard.

'Two teams, each consisting of a brace of pundits in charge of their quizmaster, compete for top marks, and the questions, always of a highly complex and compound kind, are drawn from the entire field of human knowledge, which includes, as everybody knows, such matter as the Quantum Theory, "the doctrine of

the enclitic De", phrases from Early Victorian comic songs, the names and dates of Derby winners, and all else that is worth and not worth knowing' – Martin Armstrong, *The Listener*, 1951.

Round Midnight
Nightly arts and music show on Radio 2, presented by BRIAN MATTHEW throughout its whole life from 1978 to 1990. It was axed to make way for the new late-evening show hosted by KEN BRUCE. New controller FRANCES LINE (who also launched a new arts strand at this hour at weekends) was unhappy that *Round Midnight* clashed with BBC2's nightly arts round-up *The Late Show* and thought the coverage too metropolitan, which Matthew strongly denied. Line thought that the dry, sly Scot could build a bigger audience at this time of the evening. However, he was later swapped for CHRIS STUART, and the audience has yet to rise.

Round Table
Weekly Radio 1 show, among whose hosts have been ADRIAN LOVE, RICHARD SKINNER and MIKE READ, which looks at the week's new record releases.

Round The Bend
Michael Bentine starred in this Home Service comedy show, some of it produced by CHARLES CHILTON, which ran from 1957–60. JUDITH CHALMERS, Ron Moody, Clive Dunn and Benny Lee also took part.

Round The Horne
Saucy *double entendres*, corny puns, brilliant wordplay and an array of richly comic characters from DAME CELIA MOLESTRANGLER and DAPHNE WHITETHIGH to cordwangling RAMBLING SYD RUMPO and limp-wristed JULIAN AND SANDY, were the ingredients of this much loved successor to BEYOND OUR KEN.

It ran from 1965 to 1969. BARRY TOOK and Marty Feldman wrote most of the shows (50 out of 66). When Feldman left to act in a television comedy, Took stayed on and wrote the remaining sixteen shows with Johnnie Mortimer, Brian Cooke and Donald Webster.

Once again, KENNETH HORNE was the genial, fruity-voiced straight man at the centre of things. Around him revolved the same team of KENNETH WILLIAMS, Betty Marsden, Hugh Paddick and Bill Pertwee acting out fast and funny sketches which usually combined the surreal and the naughty.

Its bawdy humour and suggestive language brought controversy. The puritanical Tory MP Sir Cyril Black and Mrs Mary Whitehouse were among those who objected, and they succeeded on one occasion in changing the Biblical allusions used by J. PEASEMOLD

GRUNTFUTTOCK. But the BBC's permissive Director-General, Hugh Greene, protected the show and declined to tone it down. Years later Took asked him why he had been so supportive and Greene replied that it was because he liked 'dirty shows'.

Music was provided by the Fraser Hayes Four ('they play a little flat, but where they come from they're not allowed anything sharp', Horne joked once). Their close harmony singing was a welcome change of pace at the halfway point in each show.

One sample of humour. Aboard an African steamer heading for the interior: 'Give the old boiler a kick.' 'Yes sir!' 'Ooooooooh, thank you sir – when you're an old boiler like me you don't get many kicks.'

Roundabout
Live teatime show offering 'news, views and music' for ninety minutes every weekday on the Light Programme. It was introduced by RICHARD MURDOCH, John Ellison and McDonald Hobley, among others. It celebrated its 500th edition in 1963.

Royal Greenwich Observatory
Supplied the GREENWICH TIME SIGNAL to BBC Radio from 1924 until 1990 (initially from Greenwich itself, later from its new home in Sussex) when its production ceased after the Observatory moved to Cambridge University.

Royle, Rev. Roger   (1939–)
Vicar's son from Cardiff who became a vicar himself, reading theology at Cambridge and ordained in 1962. He was senior chaplain at Eton for five years in the 1970s before moving into broadcasting for which he felt destined – and for which he was qualified by reason of warmth, schmaltzy charm, evident love of people and a giggly but infectious sense of humour.

He presented several shows in ITV before moving into radio and hosted Radio 2's GOOD MORNING SUNDAY from 1985 to 1990. He left to be chaplain at Lord Mayor Treloar College, a school for physically handicapped children in Alton, Hampshire.

Roy's Recipes
Cookery series with music on Radio 2, presented by Sussex publican and former Black and White Minstrel Roy Jefferies in 1990. It began with a most unappetising lesson on how to make soup from pigs' trotters (after first extracting their nails). This somewhat unusual offering had the distinction of being the first cookery slot on Radio 2 since the 'What's-the-recipe-today, Jim?' item on JIMMY YOUNG.

RTM
INCREMENTAL station which started broadcasting (on FM) in March 1990 to a potential audience of 400,000 in South-East London and North-West Kent. It goes out from Tavy Bridge, in the heart of Thamesmead. This was previously the base of Radio Thamesmead, a cable-based station serving 4,000 local homes.

Rumpo, Rambling Syd
('Hello me dearios . . . Cheerio, me dearios') Folk singer played by KENNETH WILLIAMS who never failed to enliven ROUND THE HORNE with his country-side chatter about whirdling his grummits, ganderbags, nobtiddlers and spottle guards. Accompanied by Bert Weedon on a guitar, he sang works like 'The Ballad of Woggler's Moulie' and 'The Runcorn Splod Cobbler's Song'. How could anyone not giggle? Rude as they sounded, however, they were also entirely innocent: all the words were specially invented.

Ruscoe, Sybil   (1960–)
Former gossip columnist on the *Wolverhampton Express and Star* who joined Radio 1's NEWSBEAT in 1987 and now co-presents NEWS 91 on weekdays.

Russell, Tony   (1946–)
Jazz specialist who has also turned his hand to other sorts of music programmes. He was a co-presenter of Radio 2's SOUNDS OF JAZZ from 1985–90 and the writer-presenterr of *Serendipity*, a Radio 3 series on country and world music, in the early 1970s. He also appears on Jazz FM. He was a founder of *Old Time Music* magazine and from 1973–81 a director and press officer for Topic Records.

Russian for Beginners
Network Three series which began in 1959.

Russian Service
Programmes in the Russian tongue were first sent out from BUSH HOUSE in March 1946 at the beginning of the Cold War, and electronic jamming was widespread until the 1970s. In January 1987, in accordance with the new mood of *glasnost*, it ceased altogether, enabling the BBC to mount technically more ambitious programmes (such as phone-ins) and establish greater contact with its audience.

Today the Russian Service enjoys an estimated audience of some fourteen million people. Fewer than forty programme makers, all Russian speakers, are employed to supply this enormous market with their 46 hours of programmes a week.

In 1988, on the first Russian Service phone-in, Mrs Thatcher took calls from many parts of the USSR. In 1989 Paul McCartney was in the studio for the second phone-in, which attracted 1,000 calls again from all over the Soviet Union. Fourteen people got through, the youngest being a seven-year-old girl in Leningrad. The show was hosted by Sam Yossman, a DJ on the Russian

Service who presented a weekly golden oldies show called *Granny's Chest*. Rock on the Russian Service is highly popular, as reflected by the third phone-in programme later in 1989. A trio of British rock stars (representing Pink Floyd, Iron Maiden and Deep Purple) talked live to fans in the USSR in support of a charity helping victims of the Armenian earthquake.

Letters from the USSR to the Russian Service jumped from 889 in 1988 to 3,865 in 1989 and 7,140 in 1990, a dramatic increase which was ascribed to the new thaw. Although this number was much smaller than, for example, the mailbags from Burma and Indonesia (99,000 and 39,000 respectively), this is explained by the fact that all letters from the USSR had to be posted direct to Bush House in London, an expensive exercise. The other countries could send their comments and questions to a local office within their own national borders.

'If I had to attempt a single answer to the question "What did you do in the Cold War, Auntie?", I would say with due modesty: "We kept hope alive"' – John Tusa, 1990.

Sailing By
Soothing instrumental lullaby, composed by Ronald Binge, which has been used to close down Radio 4 since 1973. Broadcast immediately before the SHIPPING FORECAST, it also serves as a useful aid to mariners, telling them that the prospects for Fair Isle and Dogger are but minutes away.

Sailing Without an Anchor
Five-part Radio 3 series in 1989 in which MICHAEL CHARLTON traced the history of the USA's National Security Council from the early days of the Cold War to the period when, under the determined stewardship of Henry Kissinger, it became an alternative State Department.

Sandford St Martin Awards
These religious programme awards are given each year: television one year, radio the next. They were inaugurated in 1979 by the Sandford St Martin Trust, named after the Oxfordshire village which is the home of the Anglican layman Sir David Wills, who established it.

The Trust's aim is to recognise and promote excellence in religious broadcasting (not an easy thing to define, but the Trust emphasises spiritual, as opposed to social and political, content) and encourage Christian involvement in broadcasting. It has an Anglican base and a headquarters in Church House, but an ecumenical function.

The following is a complete list of the radio awards, excluding runners-up:

1979:
Open Award: *God in my Language* (Radio 4). Local Radio Award: *Supernatural Healing Today* (Metro Radio). Station Award: Radio Forth.

1981:
Open Award: *Guilt-Edged Religion*, from *Priestland's Progress* (Radio 4). Local Radio Award: *Walsingham* (BBC Radio Norfolk). Station Award: Beacon Radio. Discretionary Personal Award: GERALD PRIESTLAND.

1983:
Open Award: *Fire in the City* (Radio 4). Local Radio Award: *Battle of Britain Sunday* (Hereward Radio). Station Award: Beacon Radio.

1985:
Open Award: *Peace on Earth* (Radio 1). Local Radio Award: *Bethlehem Radio* (Piccadilly Radio). Station Award: BBC Radio Derby.

1987 (categories revised as from this year):
Premier Award: *Gabriel 42* (Piccadilly Radio). Merit Awards: *Church Window* (Downtown Radio); *Is There a Christian Response to AIDS?* (Radio Forth); *Out of Sequence* (BBC Radio Ulster).

1989:
Premier Award: *The Resurrection Case* (a series for Easter week broadcast as one-minute slots on Radio Clyde's breakfast programme). Merit Awards: *Fear and Faith* (BBC Radio Cumbria); TURBULENT PRIESTS (Radio 4); BBC Radio Leicester's feature on the Oberammergau Passion Play.

The awards for 1991 will be announced in 1992.

Saturday Club
Two hours on Saturday morning on the old Light Programme which weaned a generation of youngsters on squeaky clean pop music. BRIAN MATTHEW was mine host, from 10 a.m. to noon, on what was initially billed 'the best of today's "pop" entertainment'. Segments included The Jazz Cellar, Cat's Call ('disc stars you've requested'), and New to You ('spinning the latest releases'). It ran from 1957–69. The Beatles dropped in 'for a chat' on the 400th edition in June 1966, which also featured Cliff Richard and The Shadows, Billy Fury, Marianne Faithfull, Spencer Davis and HUMPHREY LYTTELTON. Some line-up!

The show was revived as a summer filler in 1990, when Matthew returned with an array of ageing pop stars like Helen Shapiro, Acker Bilk, Craig Douglas and The Swinging Blue Jeans.

Saturday Live

Weekly Radio 1 show covering the national and international rock scene, hosted by RICHARD SKINNER in 1983.

Saturday Night Theatre

For almost half a century this was one of the staples of Saturday night listening on the BBC, running on the Home Service (latterly Radio 4) from April 1943 to 1990. The first play broadcast was *The Man With No Face*, a LORD PETER WIMSEY thriller by Dorothy L. Sayers, which set the tone for a generation. Thrillers, adventures and other types of popular, mainstream, narrative drama were the essence of this ninety-minute slot, whose audience fell from over 6.75 million in 1955 to between 50,000 and 100,000 (though with another 500,000 people listening to the Monday afternoon repeat).

In autumn 1990 the BBC put THE FORSYTE CHRONICLES into the slot. It said it might reinstate a play after this mammoth serial finished and denied that *Saturday Night Theatre* had been definitely ended. However, serials are continuing after March 1991 although it is possible that a play might return in autumn 1991.

Saturday Review

Radio 3 programme over the whole of Saturday mornings, embracing *Record Review*.

The Saturday Sequence

Billed by Radio 1 as its 'flagship rock magazine', this was launched in 1987 with JOHNNIE WALKER as presenter. After he left the BBC in 1988, ROGER SCOTT took over. When he fell ill in 1989, RICHARD SKINNER replaced him, becoming the permanent host in 1990.

The Savage Wars of Peace

Radio 4 series in 1988–89 about British campaigns waged since 1945 against insurgents and terrorists in Malaya, Borneo and Northern Ireland. It featured interviews with nearly fifty soldiers, from generals to privates, recorded and compiled by CHARLES ALLEN. The presenter was Major General Sir Jeremy Moore, who had been Commander, Land Forces, during the Falklands War.

Saveen, Albert   (1914–)

First ventriloquist to have his own radio series, with a Light Programme show called *Midday With Daisy May*. The doll was originally a boy, later a girl – the first sex-change character in ventriloquism. A Cockney printer, Saveen developed the Daisy May voice by learning to use one lung at a time while recovering in hospital after being blown up by a German bomb.

Savile, Jimmy   (1926–)

Former Yorkshire miner who made his debut as an extrovert DJ on Radio Luxembourg. Joined Radio 1 in 1968 with SAVILE'S TRAVELS. Later he presented a Sunday show called *Jimmy Savile's Old Record Club*. *Savile's Travels* travelled to ILR in July 1989.

Savile's Travels

Popular and long-running Radio 1 show created by JIMMY SAVILE which now goes out on Xtra-Am, on BRMB.

Saxon Radio

ILR station based in Bury St Edmunds and covering that part of Suffolk, on the air since 1982.

Scandal!

Royal, criminal, gambling and medical cases featured in these dramatisations of nineteenth-century scandals which shocked Britain, broadcast on the Home Service in 1966.

Scene and Heard

Radio 1 show hosted by JOHNNY MORAN. ANNE NIGHTINGALE contributed interviews to the programme in its early years.

Scenes from an Armenian Childhood

Six-part adaptation of Vahan Totovents's quiet, evocative memoir of a bygone age, read by David Burke and broadcast on Radio 4 in 1989.

Schofield, Phillip   (1962–)

Always ambitious to be behind a microphone, he was ten years old when he wrote off to all the Radio 1 disc-jockeys asking for help in joining their profession. Only ANNE NIGHTINGALE replied, he says, advising him to go and get some experience. This he did, some years later, when he went to New Zealand with his parents and worked on both radio and television in that country. He now presents a Sunday afternoon show on Radio 1 in addition to his television work.

Schools Radio

A feature of BBC Radio from its earliest days. The first programme specifically for schoolchildren was in February 1924 in Glasgow (talks on Scottish poetry, history and literature) and London followed quickly. Two months later a lecture on music was broadcast to an estimated 10,000 pupils from SAVOY HILL by Sir Henry Walford Davies, in association with London County Council. Sir Henry spoke about notes and melodies, and was assisted by six boys who sang extracts from Shakespeare's songs.

Ever since then programmes for schools have formed an important part of the BBC's output, though the amount has declined in recent years partly with the

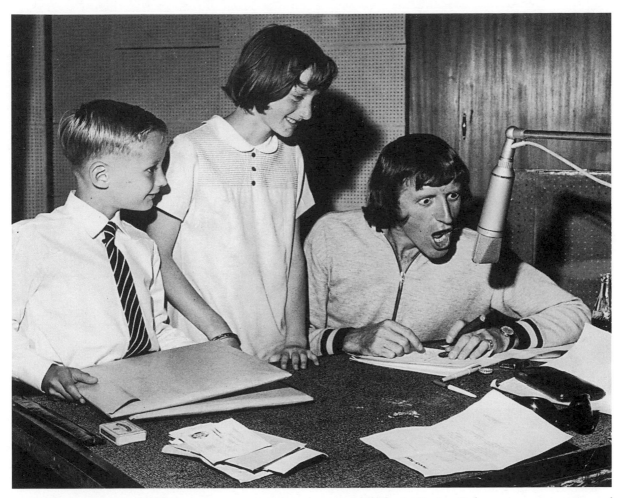

Jimmy Savile was still a provincial dance-hall manager when he became a DJ on Radio Luxembourg, where he gained big audiences and, over a period of nine years, made his name. He recorded his shows in London where, on one occasion, eight-year-old Laurence Crumby from Eltham and Sylvia Rapacchi, ten, from King's Cross, were able to see him in action

advent of the National Curriculum. Schools output was cut in half with the launch of Radio 5 (466 hours in 1989–90 down to 224 hours in 1990–91) but, at the same time, the BBC has very substantially increased the hours devoted to children's and young people's programmes.

Science Friction
While START THE WEEK had its summer break in 1990, this filled the slot: a cleverly titled series of chat shows based on vaguely scientific topics that touch people's lives, including stress, hooliganism and parapsychology. Denise Robertson, agony aunt and novelist, chaired the proceedings.

Science Now
Weekly Radio 4 series which has had more than ten presenters since it began in the 1970s (see KALEIDOSCOPE). The most recent presenters have been Peter Evans and Geoff Watts.

The Science Of Sound
Songs of the humpback whale; human speech; acoustics; the reproduction of music and the anatomy of the ear were all explored in this six-part Radio 4 series in 1990, presented by singer Toyah Willcox.

Science On The Road
Sue Cook looked at applications of science (e.g. efforts to make quieter pneumatic drills) in this Radio 4 FM series in 1988.

Science Review
Weekly round-up of science and technology events which went out on both the Home Service and Network Three, introduced by Archie Clow.

Science Survey
Weekly programme about contemporary scientific work broadcast on Network Three.

Scott, Robin (1920–)
First Controller of Radio 1, 1967–68, when he was also in charge of Radio 2, later moving into television. Real name: Robin Scutt.

Scott, Roger (1943–89)
Former Merchant Navy seaman who developed into a respected DJ and role model for his trade, only to die of cancer in the prime of life. He was one of the original team of presenters on Capital Radio when it began in 1973 and did much to introduce his idol Bruce Springsteen to British listeners.

He was poached away by Radio 1 in 1988 to present the prestigious SATURDAY SEQUENCE slot vacated by JOHNNIE WALKER. But in that year throat cancer was diagnosed, perhaps caused by his heavy cigarette smoking which he once talked about on his colleague STEVE WRIGHT's show. Two months before his death he gave a full interview about his illness to the *News of the World*, who in turn donated £10,000 to cancer research.

'He was like the Clint Eastwood of radio, always cool, always controlled' – Steve Wright.

'He was the DJs' DJ' – Alan Freeman.

Scrapbook
Evocative, nostalgic portraits of past years compiled from interviews, actuality and other recordings in the BBC SOUND ARCHIVES. FREDDIE GRISEWOOD turned the pages and Leslie Baily compiled the programmes, which became extremely popular and lasted for just over four decades. *Scrapbook for 1913*, broadcast in 1933, started the series. *Scrapbook for 1922* marked the BBC's 40th anniversary in 1962. The series ended in 1974.

'I am the proud possessor of "square eyeballs", but still feel that the good old "steam" radio has a winner in the *Scrapbook* series. It is a programme I have always listened to with great interest and I am sure there must be many more like myself who thoroughly enjoy recalling past incidents and faces' – letter to *Radio Times* in 1961 from K.C. Taylor, Exeter.

Screenplay
Radio 4 movie quiz hosted by Iain Johnstone, film critic of *The Sunday Times*, and featuring a celebrity panel.

Bernard Cribbins and Angela Douglas are among those who have taken part.

Scruples
Game of moral dilemmas which started on Radio 1 in 1988, then moved to BBC1, then back to Radio 1, where it finished in 1990. Hosted by SIMON MAYO, who put scenarios involving ethical difficulties to celebrity panellists such as pop stars, DJs and politicians. The responses provided insight into their honesty, fidelity, vanity and integrity, as well as religious commitment.

Seagoon, Neddie
Character from THE GOON SHOW, played by Harry Secombe. 'Impersonator of blue-blooded aristocracy, the entire Royal Air Force and idiots.'

Second Thoughts
Bittersweet Radio 4 comedy series, starting in 1988, starring James Bolam and Lynda Bellingham as a couple struggling to find harmony in a marriage which is second time around for each of them.

The story of Bill and Faith is a self-confessedly auto-biographical account of the lives of the husband-and-wife authors, former *TV Times* journalists Gavin Petrie and Jan Etherington, who are on their second marriages too. (Petrie's first wife, Ellen, is now married to DEREK JAMESON.) Some of their circumstances, such as Etherington's two children from her first marriage, are mirrored exactly in the series and have helped to underpin its emotional authenticity.

Rejected by BBC-TV, it was snapped up by London Weekend and turned into a sitcom with the same two stars. It began on ITV in May 1991.

'Radio is extremely good grounding for comedy writing because you are, as it were, naked. You can't rely on funny faces or falling trousers for laughs. If the words aren't funny, you're in trouble' – the authors.

Seeds of Faith
Religious slot late on Sunday nights on Radio 4, exploring different aspects of the Christian tradition. Meditation, theology, Compline, interviews and hymnody have all been featured.

Semi Circles
Sitcom on Radio 4 in 1982–83, written by SIMON BRETT some years before his much better known AFTER HENRY, about a yuppie couple and their working class neighbour.

Semprini, Alberto (1908–90)
Born in Somerset of an Italian musician father and English soprano mother, but trained in Milan under Toscanini. In the 1930s worked in Italy as a conductor, piano duettist and record executive; went into hiding in

Old ones, new ones, loved ones, neglected ones: Alberto Semprini knew them all, weaving their melodies into his romantic weekly serenade. He looked the part, too, but was actually born in Bath. This picture was taken in 1959

San Remo in the Second World War until the Allied advance into southern Italy in 1943, after which he joined the Allied forces and started to appear with ENSA, entertaining the troops. Returned to England in 1949 and carved out a successful broadcasting and variety career, the bedrock of which was his long-running SEMPRINI SERENADE.

Semprini Serenade
'Old ones, new ones, loved ones, neglected ones' were the softly spoken words with which ALBERTO SEMPRINI introduced his weekly piano recital which became one of the Light Programme's great institutions.

The eight words were an accurate description of his unchanging formula – a medley of contemporary hits, light classics, and familiar pieces from stage and films. Some critics dismissed it as musical treacle, but a loving and loyal audience lapped it up for more than 25 years, during which he made more than 700 programmes.

September Song
Seven-part Radio 4 drama series in 1991, written by Ken Blakeson, about the unlikely friendship of Ted, a mediocre schoolteacher who feels life has passed him by, and Billy, a natural comic.

Serbo-Croat Service
Programmes in the Serbo-Croat tongue were first put out by the BBC in September 1939, directed at listeners in Yugoslavia. Today, they are broadcast for about ninety minutes each day.

Seven about Seven
Seven deadly sins, seven wonders of the world, seven days in the week: LIBBY PURVES pondered the mystical

significance of the number in this Radio 4 series in 1990. It ran, of course, for seven weeks.

The Seven Ages
Radio 2 series in which people in their sixties and above – including Edward Heath, BRIAN JOHNSTON, Harry Secombe, Leonard Cheshire, Miss Bluebell and Peter Rogers, director of the 'Carry On' films – choose a record for each decade of their lives. It was the idea of its interviewer Peter Haigh, who began it in 1986: his first guest was entertainer Florence Desmond. Programmes are normally recorded in the guests' homes, in order to achieve the sort of conversation that sounds like a relaxing fireside chat.

Seven Deadly Singsongs
RUSSELL DAVIES looked at each of the seven deadly sins in turn in this Radio 2 series in 1988, with the help of well-known singers and equally well-known music. He kicked off with Lust and featured Jayne Mansfield, Mae West and Sir John Betjeman.

Severn Sound
Gloucester-based ILR station, named after the river which vies with the Thames as England's longest. On the air since 1980. In 1990 it split its services: Severn Sound, on FM, covers Gloucs, including Stroud, while Three Counties Radio, on AM, covers the larger area of Gloucs, Hereford and Worcester.

Sexuality in the Middle Ages
Three talks on Radio 3 in 1989 in which Jeffrey Richards, Reader in History at Lancaster University, examined the powerful influence of the Church on sexual conduct in medieval Europe.

Shand, Jimmy   (1908–)
Accordionist from Auchtermuchty who worked his way up from a job down the mine at the age of fourteen, became a salesman and demonstrator of the instrument and then formed his own band, giving hundreds of accordion performances since on the Light Programme.

Shelley, Norman   (1903–)
Actor famous for his Dr Watson, a role he first played on CHILDREN'S HOUR, opposite CARLETON HOBBS as SHERLOCK HOLMES.

In 1979, he was quoted as saying in the *Sunday People* that he had been asked to record Winston Churchill's 'We shall fight them on the beaches' speech for American audiences by the British Council because Churchill himself had been too busy. The claim that Shelley was used to impersonate Churchill was also made in Clive Ponting's book *1940 – Myth or Reality*, but there seems no evidence for it.

According to BERNARD BRADEN, Shelley was also the first person to say the word 'f- - -' on the Third Programme, in 1949 in a play by Ben Jonson, a distinction which seemed to amuse him greatly.

Sherrin, Ned   (1931–)
Fluent, witty, smart presenter of LOOSE ENDS and COUNTERPOINT, and sometimes a stand-in on other programmes also.

Shipping Forecast
Part of the very fabric of Radio 4, even though it is not a BBC programme at all: just like the Radio 4 WEATHER FORECASTS, it comes direct from the Meteorological Office, part of the Ministry of Defence.

It goes out four times a day, seven days a week, every day of the year: at 5.55 a.m., 1.55 p.m., 5.50 p.m. and 12.33 a.m. All go out on LONG WAVE, which alone has the power to reach ships in the middle of the North Sea and English Channel, although the first and last are broadcast on FM too.

KEN BRUCE summed up its appeal in these apt words: 'This nightly recitation of troublesome wind in Dogger and Fisher has all the calming qualities of a repeated mantra or, for traditionalists, a favourite part of the Book of Common Prayer. Its powerful narcotic effect on those listening is, as I remember only too well, just as powerful on those reading it.'

Shopping List
Five-minute morning bulletin of food news broadcast twice a week on the Home Service.

Show Band Show
Light Programme series in the 1950s on which CLIFF ADAM and his Stargazers often appeared.

Show Time
Show beginning in 1948 which acted as the OPPORTUNITY KNOCKS of its era. It featured new voices and talents from the variety world: Peter Sellers was one of them. Dennis Main-Wilson saw his stage act at the Windmill Theatre and told him he might be able to get him on this new programme. When Sellers heard nothing, he rang up the producer (Roy Speer) and pretended to be KENNETH HORNE – then a big star because of MUCH-BINDING-IN-THE-MARSH. He gave a lengthy account of Sellers' brilliance as an impressionist before dropping the deception and admitting that it wasn't Horne at all but Sellers himself.

This ingenious demonstration of his mimicry won him a much deserved appearance on *Show Time* and, shortly afterwards, he joined up with SPIKE MILLIGAN, Harry Secombe and Michael Bentine on CRAZY PEOPLE (produced by the talent spotter Dennis Main-Wilson) which was the forerunner to THE GOON SHOW.

Shryane, Tony (1919–)
Devised MY MUSIC, MY WORD and GUILTY PARTY
with the late EDWARD J. MASON, and was scriptwriter
on THE ARCHERS from 1951 to his retirement in 1979
(a total of over 7,000 episodes).

A Sideways Look
Series of quirky, intelligent, fifteen-minute talks given by
ANTHONY SMITH on Radio 4. The first was broadcast
in 1977, and they continued for more than a decade.

Sieveking, Lance (1896–1972)
One of the most influential and colourful pioneers from
the early days of radio: he was the BBC's first head
of OUTSIDE BROADCASTS and later displayed equal
energy in the DRAMA department.

Imaginative and highly talented, he made the opening
announcement at the first ever sporting occasion to
be covered by the BBC, the England v Wales rugby
international at Twickenham in January 1927. He
hired the commentator, H.B.T. WAKELAM; invited
along a blind rugby enthusiast from St Dunstan's to
sit beside Wakelam so that the commentator could
explain the game directly to him; and produced for
RADIO TIMES a squared plan of the field to help
listeners follow the action at home (hence, or so it has
been said, the expression BACK TO SQUARE ONE).
JOHN ARLOTT later described him as 'probably the
most creative pioneer of British broadcasting'.

Sieveking later moved to radio drama and the records
show he had over ninety works to his credit – mainly
adaptations, ranging from *The First Men in the Moon*
to Somerset Maugham and Evelyn Waugh.

He joined the BBC in 1924 as assistant to the Director
of Education; during the First World War he had been
a pilot, flying in Europe, the North Sea and East Africa
before getting shot down in 1917.

Signal Radio
ILR station based in Stoke-on-Trent, on the air since
1983, serving Cheshire and Staffordshire. It is named
after the fictional evening paper *The Signal* created by
one of the area's most famous sons, Arnold Bennett, in
his novels about the Potteries.

Like most ILR stations, it has split its output, but not
in the usual way. Its main service is carried on both FM
and AM but on two extra FM frequencies it has launched
Echo 96, which offers 'adult contemporary' rock and pop
for people over 25.

Anthea Turner, now a television presenter, was once
the station's record librarian.

Silver Lining
Weekly programme on the Home Service which offered 'a
message of comfort and cheer for all "in trouble, sorrow,
need, sickness or any other adversity"', introduced by

STUART HIBBERD in the 1950s after he retired from
the BBC staff.

Simon's Bug
Late-night, original and effective Radio 4 comedy series
in 1989 in which writer Richard Quick adapted his own
novel about a man called Simon who discovers more than
he bargained for when he bugs the family telephone, and
then spends most of his spare time listening to the tapes of
people's conversations, to find out if his wife is having an
affair. Hywel Bennett played Simon and Alison Steadman
his wife.

Simpson, Alan (1929–)
Former shipping clerk who teamed up with RAY
GALTON, whom he first met in hospital, to form
the most fruitful writing partnership British comedy
has ever seen, creating HANCOCK'S HALF-HOUR on
radio and *Steptoe and Son* on television.

Simpson, Robert (1921–)
Composer of considerable output who for nearly thirty
years, from 1952 to 1980, was a full-time music
producer for the BBC. He resigned over the BBC's
plan to disband five of its eleven orchestras, a plan
which was eventually amended. In 1981 he wrote
a provocative tract, *The Proms and Natural Justice*,
arguing that it was wrong for the BBC's Controller of
Music to have such total control over the content of
the Proms, and that the season should have its own,
separate, planner.

Sims, Monica (1925–)
Controller of Radio 4 from 1978–83. She was the editor
of WOMAN'S HOUR from 1964–67.

Sina
Asian pirate station based in Hounslow, West London,
running from 1984–88, broadcasting in both Hindustani
and English. Despite its illegality, the London Borough
of Hounslow bought advertising space on it on two
occasions, an acknowledgement of its ability to reach
the Asian audience within its catchment area – which
included Southall, home of the greatest concentration
of people of Indian and Pakistani descent outside
the subcontinent. The police co-operated with it on
an informal basis and when a Scotland Yard leaflet,
part of a recruiting drive for Asian policemen, was
read out on the air it drew much response from
Southall.

Run by Avtar Lit, the station turned legitimate and
successfully applied for the Hounslow INCREMENTAL
franchise. It was asked by the IBA to change its name
from Sina, which Lit describes as meaning 'power from
the heart', and chose SUNRISE instead.

Sincerely Yours
Famous Second World War Sunday-night show for soldiers, sailors and airmen, and their loved ones, presented by, and starring, Vera Lynn. It went out live from either the AEOLIAN HALL in Bond Street or from MAIDA VALE, and secured the singer's huge wartime popularity.

Sing Something Simple
Warm, smooth, cosy and sentimental Sunday-evening institution on Radio 2 founded by, and still run by, CLIFF ADAM. His troupe of singers – twelve men and four women – claim a repertoire, culled from the whole range of popular music, of more than 5,000 titles, which means that no song is heard more than once in the same year.

Cliff Adam and his singers in 1959, the year they began *Sing Something Simple*. Few programmes have changed so little, although they no longer have to wear dinner jackets and high heels

Started on the Light Programme in July 1959, initially on Fridays but soon moving to Sunday nights where it has stayed ever since. Format, style and purpose of the show have remained unchanged from the beginning. The programme was conceived with the object of persuading listeners at home to hum along, which is why three-quarters of Cliff Adam's singers are men. 'The sound of male voices is much more conducive to people joining in,' he says. The accompaniment on the first show was by accordion player Jack Emblow and his quartet, and still is today.

Over the years new tunes have been added to the repertoire, but 'Moonlight and Roses' topped a poll of listeners' all-time favourites conducted by the programme.

'When we first introduced one or two Beatles songs it was a risky undertaking because they were avant-garde. Now it's nostalgia' —— Cliff Adam.

Singer, Aubrey (1927–)
Former Controller of BBC2 who was Managing Director of BBC Radio from 1978–82.

Singled Out

Radio 1's weekly review of new single releases. Formerly presented by MIKE READ, RICHARD SKINNER took over as host in 1990. It has now been taken into ROUND TABLE.

Sinhalese Service

Programmes in Sinhalese were first broadcast by the BBC in March 1942, but were stopped as a cost-cutting measure in 1976. The ferocity of the civil conflict in Sri Lanka led to the Foreign Office authorising the BBC to revive Sinhalese programmes in March 1990, and they now go out for fifty minutes a week.

The Sit-Crom

Cleverly named Radio 4 comic historical series in 1990, written by SUE LIMB, set in Warwickshire during the Civil War and starring Joss Ackland and Denise Coffey as Sir John and Lady Firebasket.

The Six O'Clock News

Officially described by the BBC as 'the major news programme of the day on Radio 4', and certainly the most substantial, authoritative and comprehensive (with a relative lack of the speculation that infects almost all other news programmes).

Skinner, Richard (1951–)

Former reporter on the *Portsmouth News* and founder member of Portsmouth Hospital Broadcasting who joined Radio 1's NEWSBEAT in 1973, going on to present ROUND TABLE and SATURDAY LIVE. He took over THE SATURDAY SEQUENCE after the death of ROGER SCOTT.

Skues, Keith (1939–)

One of Radio 1's original line-up of DJs in 1967, who has seen many different aspects of radio in his career. He began with BFBS in Cologne, Kuwait, Kenya and Aden; then worked as a pirate DJ on Radios Caroline and London from 1964–66, and on Luxembourg; auditioned for Radio 1 and was chosen to succeed BRIAN MATTHEW as the groovy new host of SATURDAY CLUB, which he presented on the very first day of the new station.

He stayed with Radio 1 until 1974, during which time he edited THE STORY OF POP, and then quit to become programme director of the new commercial station Hallam. There he stayed until being made redundant in November 1990.

An RAF reservist, he was part of the Ministry of Defence press team during the Falklands War and was also sent to Dhahran for two stints during the Gulf War.

His nickname 'Cardboard Shoes' derives, he says, from his youthful efforts to inject personality into his shows at BFBS in Germany. This was frowned upon and he was forbidden to mention his name. Defying this injunction one day, he said to listeners: 'Monday morning, please don't snooze, hearty greetings, it's – .' Before he could finish the doggerel with his own name, in walked some top brass, and Skues, in panic, completed the sentence with the phrase which has stuck ever since.

A Slice of Life

Home Service series of light-hearted celebrity reflections on a different theme each week, beginning in March 1964. The first show was about 'The First Date' and among those who contributed was teenage actress Jane Asher, talking about her friendship with Paul McCartney. It was introduced by BRIAN MATTHEW.

Slightly Foxed

Literary quiz game on Radio 4, starting in 1989. Chaired at first by LIBBY PURVES and latterly by Gill Pyrah (ex-LBC) with questions set by David Benedictus, who runs A BOOK AT BEDTIME. Panellists who have had to demonstrate their knowledge, or lack of it, about the world of literature have included SUE LIMB, SARAH DUNANT, George Melly, Tom Rosenthal, Julian Mitchell and Denise Coffey.

Sloman, Anne (1944–)

Head of BBC Radio's special current affairs unit which has produced several well-received series. They have included *The Judges* (Radio 4, 1988) in which six judges broke their customary silence and were interviewed by Hugo Young, and MY COUNTRY RIGHT OR WRONG.

Slovene Service

Programmes in the Slovene language were included irregularly in the BBC's Serbo-Croat Service until April 1941, but then became a service in their own right. Today, they are on the air for fifty minutes a day.

A Small Country Living

Breath of fresh air on Radio 4, in which Jeanine McMullen took an unsentimental look at all sorts of rural enterprises and issues affecting the countryside. It was dropped some years ago.

Smiley, George

Bernard Hepton, an actor with an infinitely subtle voice, played John le Carré's painstaking intelligence agent in *Smiley's People* on Radio 4 in 1990.

Smiling Through

Radio 2 series devised by Cosmotheka, a Midlands singing duo who take their name from an old London music hall, celebrating the songs which kept up morale during the Second World War. It began in 1988.

Smith, Anthony (1926–)

Writer and broadcaster noted for his A SIDEWAYS LOOK talks on Radio 4.

Smith, Mike (1954–)

Breakfast presenter who has now moved into television. Started his radio career in 1975 on Radio 1, making trailers for £12 a week; on Capital Radio from 1978 to 1982; rejoined Radio 1 in 1982 and succeeded MIKE READ as presenter of the breakfast show from 1986 to 1988.

Smith, Phil (1941–)

Presenter of several Radio 4 series include *Smith and Son* (about parenthood), *Smith on the Soil*, *Smith on Old Age* (advancing years) and SMITH'S ELEGY.

Smith, R.D. (1914–85)

Idealistic Guy Pringle in Olivia Manning's *Balkan Trilogy* (played in BBC-TV's *Fortunes of War* adaptation by Kenneth Branagh) was based on the author's husband Reggie Smith, who later became a notable drama producer on the Third Programme. Among his productions were Milton's epic poem *Samson Agonistes* in 1960, which ran for 105 minutes.

Smith, Tim (1961–)

Started in radio at BBC Radio York and BBC Radio Shropshire; later presented the early morning shows on Radio 1 at the weekends and has a daily show on GLR, as well as a pop programme on the BBC World Service.

Smith's Elegy

Six programmes on Radio 4 in 1990 with PHIL SMITH looking round different churchyards.

Smokey Mountain Jamboree

Country music series on the Light Programme, billed as 'a get-together, western style, in the old barn'. Music was provided by Louise Howard, The Maple Leaf Four, Jim Hawthorn, Slim Weston and Happy Pappy.

Snagge, John (1904–)

For over half a century one of the most familiar voices on the BBC: a voice of polished mahogany, clipped and authoritative. Began as an announcer in 1928, in the days when announcers had to wear dinner jackets to read the news; was the main commentator at every Boat Race for half a century, from 1931 to 1980; called 'The Voice of London' during the Second World War; announced the D-Day landings, VE Day, VJ Day and the deaths of King George VI and Queen Mary. A career which began at SAVOY HILL ended in the era of local radio: he made more than 100 programmes in a series called *John Snagge's London* for BBC Radio London before retiring in 1981.

'I can't see who's in the lead – it's either Oxford or Cambridge' – John Snagge, in the 1949 Boat Race.

Somali Service

(BBC World Service.) See AFRICAN SERVICE.

Some of These Days

Radio 2 quiz game which takes the day of transmission as its subject, looking at some of the people, places and events which have made it notable. For example, the 1990 series began on 30 May so questionmaster CLIFF MICHELMORE asked his guests why it would have been a significant day for both Queen Victoria and Joan of Arc. (Answer: because it was the day an assassination attempt was made on Queen Victoria, and also the day Joan of Arc was burned at the stake.) Colin Sell, at the piano, provides musical clues. Guests have included Leslie Crowther, Roy Hudd, Tim Brooke-Taylor and John Junkin.

Some Parents Do 'Ave 'Em

Six-part Radio 4 series in 1989 examining commonplace (but still upsetting) problems with young children, including the traumas of sleepless nights.

Something in the City

Five-part Radio 4 FM series in 1989 in which Corinne Julius talked to people whose lives revolved around the Stock Exchange, Threadneedle Street and so on.

Something to Celebrate

Series of five programmes on Radio 4 in 1989–90 interviewing people who celebrate different events in different ways (e.g. five sisters in a convent marking 25 years of monastic life).

Something to Shout About

Early comedy series about advertising, on the Light Programme, which starred Michael Medwin as account executive Michael Lightfoot and Fenella Fielding as his secretary, Janet. Eleanor Summerfield, Warren Mitchell and Joan Sims were also in the cast. Script by Myles Rudge, with additional material by Ronnie Wolfe.

Son of Cliché

Radio 4 comedy series written by Rob Grant and Doug Naylor and starring Chris Barrie, Nick Maloney and Nick Wilton.

A Song for Everyone

The show which made a star out of Kenneth McKellar, graduate of Aberdeen University and former forester. It began in 1954 and shortly after its 100th edition in 1958 started on BBC-TV.

Songs Of Yesterday

Musical show on Saturday afternoons on the Home Service, featuring the likes of Eric Rogers and his Orchestra, Winifred Atwell and Russ Conway.

Songs We Love

Thursday morning recital of songs 'remembered from the golden hey-day of ballads and songs', sung by Mary Denise on the Light Programme.

Songs With A Story

Six-part Radio 2 series in 1989 which covered a hundred years of songs made popular in wars – from the Crimean to the Cold. It was presented by Ian Bradley.

Sony

One of the world's leading manufacturers of, and innovators in, radio. It was formed (in Tokyo) in October 1945, only two months after the nuclear bombs on Hiroshima and Nagasaki. The name was intended to combine the Latin word for 'sound' with the modern appeal in the West of the word 'sonny'. It says that a quarter of all radios purchased in Britain now bear the Sony label.

Sony's 'Walkman', the world's first personal stereo (the company again chose the name itself), became one of the symbols of its age. On sale in Japan in 1979 and the rest of the world in 1980, it originally weighed 14 oz. Ten years later it was only 6 ½ oz – with a radio in it as well, which the first ones did not have.

The company spends about £300,000 a year on sponsoring the SONY RADIO AWARDS, often regarded as the Oscars of the industry, which makes it by far the most generous patron of radio in this country.

Sony Radio Awards

First presented in 1983, these recognise excellence across the entire range of British radio programmes and attract about 700 entries each year. The trophies are normally presented at a banquet in Park Lane in April in the presence of a member of the Royal Family. Judges consist of panels of broadcasters, actors, writers and politicians.

Not all the categories have remained unchanged since the awards started, and the introduction of new ones, such as best response to a news event and best daily news programme, reflects radio's greater emphasis on immediacy.

The history of the awards goes back to the mid-1970s, when the Radiowriters Association of the Society of Authors floated the idea of a national awards scheme. JOCELYN HAY played a prominent part in this. Imperial Tobacco took up an initial three-year sponsorship in 1976 (see IMPERIAL TOBACCO AWARDS FOR RADIO) followed by PYE for a further three years.

Sony stepped in after a year's gap, and has continued ever since.

What follows is a complete record of the awards. (Each year refers to the programmes of the previous year, i.e. the 1983 awards are for programmes broadcast in 1982, and so on.)

1983:

Best light entertainment programme: RADIO ACTIVE, Radio 4. Best magazine programme: WOMAN'S HOUR, Radio 4. Reporter of the year: Michael Elkins, BBC. Best current affairs programme: THE WORLD THIS WEEKEND, Radio 4. Best children's programme: LISTENING CORNER, Radio 4. National DJ of the year: MIKE READ, Radio 1. Local DJ of the year: Tim Lloyd, Essex Radio. Best documentary/feature: *The Rent Boys*, Piccadilly Radio. Best popular music programme: TERRY WOGAN, Radio 2. Best classical music programme: *Decade – the 1800s*, Radio 3. Sports broadcaster of the year: Clive Tyldesley, Radio City. Best local radio programme: not awarded. Best community service programme: *Break the Silence*, Piccadilly Radio. Local radio personality of the year: Richard Park, Radio Clyde. Best drama production: *Over the Hills and Far Away*, Radio 4. Society of Authors Award for best drama script: *The Journal of Vassilije Bogdanovic* by Alan Plater, BBC World Service. Best actress: Mary Riggans for *Till All the Seas Run Dry*, Radio Clyde. Best actor: John Nettles for *Mirror Image*, Radio 3. Award for technical excellence: Jane Morgan for *Dark Heritage*, Radio 4. Male personality of the year: BRIAN JOHNSTON. Female personality of the year: SUE MACGREGOR. Sony Gold Award for outstanding contribution to radio over the years: FRANK MUIR and DENIS NORDEN.

1984:

Best light entertainment programme: SON OF CLICHÉ, Radio 4. Best magazine programme: THE FOOD PROGRAMME, Radio 4. Reporter of the year: Gerald Butt, BBC. Best current affairs programme: TODAY, Radio 4. Best children's programme: *In the News*, Radio 4. National DJ of the year: MIKE READ, Radio 1. Local DJ of the year: Timmy Mallett, Piccadilly Radio. Best documentary/feature: *Fat Man at Work*, Radio 4. Best popular music programme: BENNY GREEN, Radio 2. Best classical music programme: *Mr Halle's Band*, Piccadilly Radio. Sports broadcaster of the year: Charles Lambert, BBC Radio Merseyside. Best local radio programme: *Love the Bones*, Radio City. Best community service programme: *Tay Action*, Radio Tay. Best outside broadcast programme: *Water Skiing Lessons*, Wiltshire Radio. Local radio personality of the year: Susie Mathis, Piccadilly Radio. Best drama production: *Road to Rocio*, Radio 4. Society of Authors Award for best drama script: *Never in my Lifetime*, Radio 3. Best actress: Maureen O'Brien for *The Duchess's Diary* and

A Month in the Country, Radio 3. Best actor: Clive Merrison for *Luther*, Radio 3. Award for technical excellence and achievement in broadcasting: *A Concert from Seoul*, live by satellite, Radio 3. Male personality of the year: BRIAN MATTHEW, Radio 2. Female personality of the year: MARGARET HOWARD, Radio 4. Special Award for services to radio: Jimmy Gordon, Radio Clyde. Sony Gold Award for outstanding contribution to radio over the years: DAVID JACOBS.

1985:

Best drama production: *Titus Groan/Gormenghast*, Radio 4. Best drama script: *Scenes from an Execution*, Radio 3. Best dramatisation: *Titus Groan/Gormenghast*, Radio 4. Best actor: David March for *Mr Norris Changes Trains*, Radio 4. Best actress: Glenda Jackson for *Scenes from an Execution*, Radio 3. Best magazine programme: *Festival City Radio*, Radio Forth. Best current affairs programme: ANALYSIS (*Post-Recession Britain*), Radio 4. Reporter of the year: David Loyn, IRN. Sports broadcaster of the year: PETER JONES, BBC. Best documentary/feature programme: *Strathinvar*, BBC Radio Scotland. Best light entertainment programme: *In One Ear*, Radio 4. Best popular music programme: *Steve Wright in the Afternoon*, Radio 1. Best classical music programme: *Deep River*, Radio 4. Best specialist music programme: *Barbed Wireless*, BBC Radio Derby. Best local radio programme: *Kinnock and Scargill in Stoke*, BBC Radio Stoke. Best community service programming: IN TOUCH, Radio 4. Local radio personality of the year: Allan Beswick, Red Rose Radio. Best outside broadcast: *The Terry Wogan Olympic Show*, Radio 2. Award for technical excellence and achievement in broadcasting: *Hubert Gregg Says Maybe It's Because*, Radio 2. National DJ of the year: MIKE READ, Radio 1. Local DJ of the year: Timbo, Radio Mercury. Personality of the year: JIMMY YOUNG. Sony Gold Award for outstanding contribution to radio over the years: British Forces Broadcasting Service. Special Award for services to radio: Derek Chinnery, Radio 2.

1986:

Best drama production: *Hiroshima, The Movie*, Radio 4. Best actor: Ray Smith for *A Kind of Hallowe'en*, Radio 3. Best actress: Jane Asher for *Winter Journey*, BBC Radio Scotland. Best magazine programme: *Norfolk Air Line*, BBC Radio Norfolk. Best current affairs programme: FILE ON 4 (*South Africa – Reform or Revolution?*), Radio 4. Reporter of the year: Mark Jordan, Capital Radio. Sports broadcaster of the year: George Gavin, BRMB. Best documentary/feature programme: *Setting Sail*, Radio 4. Best use of comedy: DELVE SPECIAL, Radio 4. Best popular music programme: *Howard Jones at the Manchester Apollo*, Piccadilly Radio. Best classical music programme: *Symphonies and Silence*, Radio 4. Best specialist music programme: *Barbed Wireless: The A & R Man*, BBC

Radio Derby. Best local radio programme: *Goodbye Village School*, BBC Radio Wales. Best community service programming: *Clyde Action: Road Safety Week*, Radio Clyde. Best children's programming: *Say No to Strangers?*, Radio Aire. Local radio personality of the year: Bill Bore, BBC Radio Humberside. Best outside broadcast: *Live Aid Concert*, Radio 1. Radio Academy Award for the most creative use of radio: *Peace on Earth*, Radio 1. Best original script: *A Kind of Hallowe'en*, Radio 3. Best dramatisation: *Munchausen*, Radio 4. Award for technical excellence and achievement in broadcasting: FESTIVAL OF NINE LESSONS AND CAROLS, Radio 4. Radio personality of the year: Douglas Cameron, LBC/IRN. Outstanding service to the community by a local radio station: Bradford Football Disaster, Pennine Radio. Special Award for services to radio: Parliamentary broadcasting, LBC/IRN. Sony Gold Award for outstanding contribution to radio over the years: JOHN TIMPSON, Radio 4. National DJ of the year: JOHN PEEL, Radio 1.

1987:

Best drama production: *Mischief*, Radio 4. Best actor: Ronald Pickup for *The Awful Insulation of Rage*, Radio 3. Best actress: Billie Whitelaw for *Vassa Zhelyeznova*, Radio 3. Best magazine programme: LOOSE ENDS, Radio 4. Best current affairs programme: *The Aids Plague in East Africa*, Radio 4. Reporter of the year: Derek Rae, BBC Radio Scotland. Best documentary/feature programme: *Hopping Down in Kent*, Radio 4. Best use of comedy: HUDDWINKS, Radio 2. Best popular music programme: *World Popular Song Festival*, Radio 1. Best classical music programme: *The Immortal Bohemian*, Radio 4. Best specialist music programme: ANDY KERSHAW, Radio 1. Best pop music programme: THE NETWORK CHART SHOW, Capital Radio. Best local radio programme: *Aberfan – An Unknown Spring*, Swansea Sound. Best community service programming: Community Service Volunteers Compilation, Suffolk Group Radio. Local Radio personality of the year: Andy Radford, Severn Sound. Best outside broadcast: *The Mammoth Mail Coach Drive*, Radio 1. Radio Academy Award for the most creative use of radio: *Breakdown*, Capital Radio. Best original script: *The Awful Insulation of Rage*, Radio 3. Best dramatisation: *Jude the Obscure*, Radio 4. Award for technical excellence and achievement in broadcasting: *Breakdown*, Capital Radio. Local DJ of the year: DAVID JENSEN. National DJ of the year: MIKE SMITH. Radio personality of the year: DEREK JAMESON. Special Award for services to radio: BRIAN HAYES. Sony Gold Award for outstanding contribution to radio over the years: THE ARCHERS.

1988:

Best drama production: *News of the World*, BBC World Service. Best actor: Edward Petherbridge for *The Wide*

Brimmed Hat, Radio 4. Best actress: Harriet Walter for *Rhyme and Reason*, Radio 4. Best magazine programme: MEDICINE NOW, Radio 4. Best current affairs programme: *Morning Merseyside*, BBC Radio Merseyside. Reporter of the year: Lindsay Taylor, LBC/IRN. Sports broadcaster of the year: Terence O'Donohue, BBC Radio Wales. Best documentary/feature programme: *Waiting for Mrs Forbes*, Radio 4. Best use of comedy: *Crisp and Even Brightly*, Radio 4. Best popular music programme: *The Eric Clapton Story*, Radio 1. Best classical music programme: TOMTICKETATOM, Radio 4. Best specialist music programme: *Before the Blues*, Radio 3. Best pop music programme: *Elvis 10 Years After*, Radio Trent. Best local radio programme: *Oliver's Story*, BBC Radio Leicester. Best community service programme: *Roghe Sate (Good Health)*, BBC Pashto Service. Best children's programme: *It's Russel Harris*, BBC Radio Humberside. Local Radio personality of the year: Barbara Sturgeon, BBC Radio Kent. Best outside broadcast: *The Operation*, BBC Radio Cleveland. Radio Academy Award for the most creative use of radio: *Mauthausen Concentration Camp*, Moray Firth Radio. Best original script: *Village Fete*, Radio 4. Best dramatisation: *Cheap in August*, Radio 4. Award for technical excellence and achievement in broadcasting: *Viva Verdi: Part 1*, Radio 4. Outstanding service to the community by a local radio station: Campus Radio on Radio Tay, Radio Tay. *Smash Hits* local DJ of the year: JAMES WHALE, Radio Aire. *Smash Hits* national DJ of the year: MIKE SMITH, Radio 1. Radio personality of the year: ALAN FREEMAN, Capital Radio. Sony Gold Award for outstanding contribution to radio over the years: GERARD MANSELL. Special Award for services to radio: Thena Heshel, producer of *In Touch*.

1989:
Best actress: Kate Murphy for *Elephant Dances*, Radio Clyde. Best actor: Andrew Sachs for *The Heart of a Dog*, BBC World Service. Best drama production: *Cigarettes and Chocolate*, Radio 4. Society of Authors Award for best dramatisation or adaptation: *The Dippers*, Radio 4. Best breakfast show: *The Les Ross Breakfast Show*, BRMB. Best sequence programming: *Morning Call*, Moray Firth Radio. Best documentary/feature, general: *Cheltenham, the Irish Favourite*, Radio 4. Society of Authors Award for best original script: *Excess Baggage*, Radio 4. Best sports programme: *Midweek Sportsround*, BBC Radio Ulster. Best daily news programme: *210 Reports*, Radio 210. Best documentary/feature, news and current affairs: *I Want to be Normal Again*, Radio 4. Best current affairs programme: TODAY, Radio 4. Best response to a news event: Coverage of the Lockerbie air disaster on both Radio Forth and Radio 4's *Today* of 22 Dec., 1988. Reporter of the year: John Alcock, LBC/IRN. Best documentary/feature, music and arts: *Insect Musicians*, Radio

3. Best classical music programme: MERIDIAN (*Bartok Quartets*), BBC World Service. Best rock and pop programme: THE BEEB'S LOST BEATLES TAPES, Radio 1. Best specialist music programme: *Kershaw in Zimbabwe*, Radio 1. Best children's programme/programming/series: *Down Our Way*, BBC Radio Bristol. Best use of comedy: WHOSE LINE IS IT ANYWAY?, Radio 4. Best magazine programme: THIRD EAR, Radio 3. Best education programme/programming/series: *Community Matters: The Case Conference*, Radio 4. Radio Academy Award for the most creative use of radio: *The Dream*, Radio 1. Local station of the year: BRMB. Outstanding service to the community: *You and Your Benefit*, Radio 4. Local radio personality of the year: Susie Mathis, GMR. Best outside broadcast: *Give a Child a Chance – Live from Disneyworld*, Radio Aire. Best technical achievement: BBC RADIO SHOW, BBC Network and Local Radio. *Smash Hits* local DJ of the year: DAVID JENSEN, Capital Radio. *Smash Hits* national DJ of the year: BRUNO BROOKES, Radio 1. Radio personality of the year: Sue Lawley. Special Award for services to radio: John Whitney. Sony Gold Award for outstanding contribution to radio over the years: TONY BLACKBURN.

1990:
Best actress: Marsha Mason for *Visitor from Hollywood* and *Plaza Suite*, Radio 4. Best actor: Timothy West for *The Price*, Radio 4. Best drama production: *The Bass Saxophone*, Radio 3. Society of Authors Award for best dramatisation or adaptation: *A Tale of Two Cities*, Radio 4. Best breakfast show: *Breakfast Live*, BBC Hereford and Worcester. Best sequence programming: *Morning Call*, Moray Firth Radio. Best documentary/feature, general: NEVER THE SAME AGAIN, Radio 4. Society of Authors Award for best original script: *The Rime of The Bounty*, Radio 4. Best sports programme: *Capital Gold Sports Show*, Capital Radio. Best daily news programme: TODAY, Radio 4. Best documentary/feature, news and current affairs: THE INDISSOLUBLE UNION (*Cotton, Chemicals and Corruption*), Radio 4. Best current affairs programme: THE WORLD TONIGHT, Radio 4. Best response to a news event: Radio City's coverage of Hillsborough and Radio 4 *Today* programme's coverage of the Romanian Revolution (joint winners). Reporter of the year: James Miles, Radios 1, 2 and 4. Best documentary/feature, music and arts: *Dear Miss Pym, Dear Mr Larkin*, Radio 4. Best classical music programme: TASTING NOTES, Radio 3. Best rock and pop programme: *Not Fade Away – a Tribute to Buddy Holly*, Radio 1. Best specialist music programme: *Electric Youth*, BRMB. Best children's programme/programming/series: *In The News*, Radio 4. Best use of comedy: *Dick Tarrant*, Capital Radio. Best magazine programme: *Country Matters*, BBC Radio Gloucestershire. Best education programme/

249

programming/series: THE HEALTH SHOW, Radio 4. Radio Academy Creative Award: *My Dog Has Fleas*, Radio 4. Local station of the year: BBC Radio Foyle. Outstanding service to the community: FACE THE FACTS, Radio 4, and *Varying Degrees*, BBC Radio Ulster (joint winners). Local Radio personality: Gerry Anderson, BBC Radio Ulster. *Smash Hits* best local DJ: Ally Bally, Radio Tay. *Smash Hits* best national DJ: BRUNO BROOKES, Radio 1. Best outside broadcast: *The Radio 1 Around the World Challenge*, Radio 1. Best technical achievement: *Swansong*, Radio 3. Radio personality of the year: CHRIS TARRANT. Special Award for services to radio: BBC Radio Drama Company. Sony Gold Award for outstanding contribution to radio over the years: Roy Hudd.

1991:

Best sports programme: SPORT ON FIVE, Radio 5. Best daily news programme: *The Fox Report*, Fox FM. Best documentary feature, news and current affairs: *Stormclouds Over the Himalayas*, BBC World Service. Best current affairs programme: *Sunday Newsbreak*, BBC Radio Ulster. Best rock or pop programme: *Cousin Matty*, Radio City. Best specialist music programme: *The Capital Rap Show*, Capital Radio. Best documentary feature, rock and pop: *Last Night A DJ Saved My Life*, Radio 1. Best magazine programme: WOMAN'S HOUR, Radio 4. Best education programme: *Women and AIDS*, BBC Radio Sussex. Best children's programme: *A Hallowe'en Tale with Music*, BBC Radio Scotland. Best use of comedy: *Mary Whitehouse's Best Experiences So Far*, Radio 1. Outstanding service to the community: *On The Street*, BBC Radio Stoke. Best response to a news event: *Nelson Mandela Release* (*Focus on Africa*), BBC World Service. Reporter of the Year: no award made. Best documentary feature, music and arts: *Gerontius*, Radio 4. Best classical music programme: no award made. Local station of the year: Radio Borders. *Smash Hits* best local DJ: Neil Fox, Capital Radio. *Smash Hits* best national DJ: SIMON MAYO, Radio 1. Best documentary feature, general: THE TEACHERS, Radio 4. Society of Authors Award for best original script: *Different States*, Radio 4. Local radio personality: George Jones, BBC Radio Ulster. Best sequence programme: *Jeff Owen*, BBC Radio Nottingham. Best breakfast show: *Network Africa*, BBC World Service. Best dramatisation: ALL THE WORLD'S A GLOBE, Radio 3. Best drama production: *Different States*, Radio 4. Best actor: Ian Holm for *The Mystery of Edwin Drood*, BBC World Service. Best actress: MARY WIMBUSH for *The Mystery of Edwin Drood* (BBC World Service) and *The Horse's Mouth* (Radio 4). Radio Academy Award: BBC Radio Light Entertainment Department. Radio Personality of the Year: JAMES NAUGHTIE. Sony Gold Award for outstanding contribution to radio over the years: Charlie Gillet.

SOS messages

'Will Mr Raymond Brown, at present on a walking holiday in the Lake District, please contact St James's Hospital, Leeds, where his mother Mrs Dorothy Brown is dangerously ill . . . ' Messages like this, asking for relatives to get in touch with a sick person, are regularly broadcast on Radio 4 or the local radio station in the area in which the wanted person is thought to be staying. A doctor or hospital has to verify that the patient is 'dangerously ill', a phrase invariably used on the air.

Life or death messages like these have been carried since 1923. They are put out free, but only once – in the case of Radio 4, just before the 7 a.m. news or just before the 6 p.m. news.

Sound Advice

Radio 5 series hosted by Guy Michelmore (son of CLIFF MICHELMORE) which gives advice to callers, helped by the National Association of Citizens Advice Bureaux. It began in 1990.

Soundings

(1) Religious series on Radio 4 which featured a remarkably courageous confession, by former BBC economics correspondent Graham Turner, that he had spent years fiddling his expenses.

Turner, who once accused the car manufacturing plant of Cowley of being 'a skivers' paradise', revealed on the programme in 1984 that he had repaid £1,000 to the BBC which he had received, over the years, in claimed expenses: 'Taking people from the Treasury out to lunch who didn't exist, and so on.' He said he had come to a similar arrangement with the Inland Revenue after making similar admissions to them.

(2) Fortnightly series of music documentaries on Radio 3, beginning in 1990, both written and presented by Michael Oliver. Early editions covered the centenary of Jacques Ibert, Gaelic folk song and Robert and Clara Schumann.

Sounds Easy

The Sunday afternoon show of ALAN DELL on Radio 2.

Sounds Interesting

Controversial Radio 3 music series, sometimes straying into the realms of pop, presented by the late Derek Jewell in the 1970s.

Sounds of Jazz

Radio 2 jazz series – see TONY RUSSELL.

Sounds of the 50s

Saturday morning Radio 2 series which started in March 1990. It is hosted by one of the decade's singers, Ronnie

Hilton, and modelled on the highly successful SOUNDS OF THE 60s.

Sounds of the Seventies
Progressive and contemporary rock was featured in this Radio 1 series, presented in turns by JOHN PEEL, BOB HARRIS (its host from 1970–75), ANNE NIGHTIN-GALE and ALAN BLACK.

Sounds of the 60s
Saturday-morning Radio 2 show which delivers what the title promises in terms of popular records from the most nostalgic decade of them all. As soon as the signature tune starts – it has always been The Shadows' 'Foot Tapper' – the memories come flooding back.

KEITH FORDYCE was the first presenter: his successors have included Frankie Valli, Peter Asher, Duane Eddy and Jimmy Tarbuck. The one who provoked the most excited response was the eccentric but brilliant SIMON DEE. He made his debut presenting the programme's first Listeners' Top Twenty on Boxing Day 1987 and went on to host the show for most of 1988.

That Top Twenty and the two similar listeners' polls in 1988 and 1989 all yielded the same Number One favourite of the decade, Procul Harum's 'A Whiter Shade of Pale', a song whose melancholy psychedelia makes it the requiem for a vanished age (and which even got chosen by Lady Mosley as one of her DESERT ISLAND DISCS).

In March 1990, BRIAN MATTHEW became the programme's new regular presenter, some compensation for the loss of his ROUND MIDNIGHT after twelve years. He has introduced his own archive interviews into the programme, so that we can now hear what The Kinks had to say in 1965 as well as listen to their old records.

'A tidal wave of nostalgia for a large section of the country and some puzzled looks on the faces of their offspring' – Simon Dee.

Soundtrack
Radio 4 fly-on-the-wall series which tries to let the sounds and the people speak for themselves. These have included stage hypnotists, gun users, gatherers at Stonehenge during the autumn equinox, inmates at Lewes Prison and two nineteen-year-olds in their first term at Durham University. It is intended as the radio equivalent of BBC2's human interest series *40 Minutes*.

It was launched in 1988 with one of the most famous, and moving, broadcasts of recent years, in which GLYN WORSNIP revealed to the world the details of the cruel degenerative illness which had wrecked his life.

South of Sixty
Awesome, remote and ecologically vulnerable Antarctica was featured in this four-part Radio 4 series in 1988, made by an appropriately-named producer, Daniel Snowman, and reporter Bernard Jackson, aboard the British survey ship RSS *Bransfield*, visiting scientific bases around the South Pole.

South West Sound
ILR station for Dumfries, on the air since May 1990.

Southern Sound
ILR station covering Brighton, Eastbourne and Hastings on the Sussex coast, on the air since 1983 and extending its coverage to Newhaven, Lewes and Seaford in 1988 and to East and mid-Sussex in 1989.

Southern Voices
Radio 4 series in 1990 in which six academics and journalists from Latin America, the Caribbean, Ghana, India, the Middle East and the pan-Pacific bloc gave talks on Third World topics. The first was 'Sex and the Ayatollahs' by Iranian feminist Haleh Afshar.

Space Force
Son of the great JOURNEY INTO SPACE: the author of that classic, CHARLES CHILTON, wrote this six-part sequel which was broadcast on Radios 1 and 2 in 1984. The four main characters were similar to the original quartet, as was the atmosphere of the story. Actor Nicky Henson was Chipper, grandson of the original Cockney batman Lemmy who had been played by Alfie Bass.

The Spam Fritter Man
Unsuccessful BBC Radio comedy series starring Bryan Pringle.

Spanish Service
Programmes in Spanish were first broadcast by the BBC in 1938 for Latin America, followed by 1939 for Spain. Today, the BBC no longer broadcasts in Spanish to Spain and only the output for Latin America remains. In 1990, as part of a cost-cutting package, it was reduced from four and a half hours every day to three hours a day.

Special Assignment
Weekly Radio 4 programme which took over from INTERNATIONAL ASSIGNMENT in April 1989. The change of name indicated that from now on it could, if it so wanted, report on domestic issues as well as foreign ones.

Spectrum
Radio 3 science series, launched in 1988. It provides an opportunity to hear top scientists talking at length about their work, often at the frontiers of knowledge, and also aims to communicate something of the emotional as well

as intellectual excitement experienced by those engaged in making fundamental discoveries about the world – whether it be cosmic rays or *in vitro* fertilisation.

Guests have ranged from meteorologists to physicists, from Dr Jane Goodall on chimpanzees to Prof. Roger Penrose on the differences between brains and computers. The presenter is COLIN TUDGE.

Spectrum Radio

Afro-Caribbean, Arab, Asian, Chinese, Greek-Cypriot, Hispanic, Italian and Jewish listeners in London (a grand total of about 2.2 million people) are all specifically catered for in this INCREMENTAL station which went on the air in June 1990.

Based in Brent Cross, and with ex-LBC executive Keith Belcher as its programme controller, it bills itself with some justification as 'London's international station': broadcasts (a mixture of world news and specialist music) are in English for most of the day, with ethnic programmes in the afternoon and evenings. With programmes tailor-made for each community, advertisers have been openly encouraged to make their pitch to specific ethnic and racial groups.

The signature tune, however, was cunningly designed to please everyone: composers Paul Hart and David Arnold (producers of the LBC tune) assembled a theme involving the use of classical guitars, violins, sitars, mandolins, a kato, bazoukis, flutes and trombones, to represent each of the eight ethnic audiences it hoped to attract.

Spectrum's launch was attended by much embarrassment. The frequency allocated to it by the IBA (558 kHz on the medium wave) did not arrive with vacant possession – it was occupied by the seemingly indestructible North Sea pirate ship Radio Caroline, still going out loud and clear despite a DTI raid in August of the previous year.

Spectrum was given another, temporary, frequency but its launch was delayed by three weeks. When it eventually went on the air it did so via antennae slung between the lighting towers of Fulham Football Club at Craven Cottage. However, it did eventually start broadcasting on its correct frequency when Caroline finally fell silent.

Spiegl, Fritz (1926–)

Austrian-born musician (principal flautist with the Royal Liverpool Philharmonic for fifteen years) and broadcaster whose talents have graced every edition of IN THE PSYCHIATRIST'S CHAIR. He wrote the programme's poignant signature tune, taking part of Mozart's 'Les Petits Riens' and transcribing it for wind instruments. (Years before, he also helped to write the catchy signature tune for *Z-Cars*, which also featured wind instruments.) He is also a frequent presenter of *Mainly for Pleasure*.

Sport in Question

Seven-part Radio 4 FM series in 1989 in which sports personalities and administrators faced topical questions from invited audiences. Presented by Tom McNab.

Sport on Five

What SPORT ON 2 became after it transferred to the new Radio 5 network in 1990. Described by the BBC as 'Radio Sport's flagship programme', it is presented by John Inverdale.

Sport on 4

Intelligent and engrossing Saturday-morning programme on Radio 4 which always manages to relate sport to wider human concerns. Its original presenter, in 1977, was former England cricket captain Tony Lewis, who later became one of the hosts of BBC-TV's *Saturday Night at the Mill*. Ex-rugby international and former head of BBC Outside Broadcasts Cliff Morgan took over in 1986. When Radio 5 began in 1990, it was repeated on the new network the same day, with additional news, under the title *Sport on 4 Plus 1*.

Sport on 2

The sports coverage on Radio 2, constituting the majority of BBC Radio's sports output, which transferred to Radio 5 in August 1990.

Sporting Albums

Sporting heroes talk to soccer star Garth Crooks about their favourite music in this Radio 5 series which began in 1990.

Sporting Chance

Knockout sports quiz between teams from the New Towns, Armed Forces and so on, refereed by BRIAN JOHNSTON. It went out on Saturday afternoons on the Light Programme.

Sports Parade

Sports preview on Saturday afternoons on the Light Programme.

Sports Report

Sixty minute round-up of sports news and results which has gone out at the same day and time (Saturdays at 5 p.m.) for over forty years. The signature tune, 'Out of the Blue', has also remained unchanged. Making its debut in January 1948, it was originally on the Light Programme (closely associated with EAMONN ANDREWS) and then Radio 2, before transferring to Radio 5 in 1990 with the rest of Radio 2's sports coverage.

'The jaunty signature tune of *Sports Report* would summon the unpunctual from all parts of the home to hear the Everton and Liverpool scores before tea. That

Eamonn Andrews began his career as a boxing commentator on Radio Eireann and always maintained his links with the world of sport. He anchored Saturday afternoon's *Sports Report* for many years

tune, like the theme of *Desert Island Discs*, resonates with memories down the years' – John Birt, reminiscing on his Merseyside childhood in 1989.

Sportscall
Weekly quiz on Radio 5 hosted by Danny Baker.

Spotlight
'A musical focus of people, places and things the world over' on Saturday lunchtimes on the Light Programme.

Spring Into Summer
Six-part Radio 4 FM series in 1989 helping listeners to keep fit, introduced by Dr Alan Maryon Davis and part of the BBC's 'Healthcheck' campaign.

Spy-Catcher
Dramatised stories on the Home Service based on interrogator Lt-Col Oreste Pinto's wartime memoirs, starring Bernard Archard as Pinto.

SSVC (Services Sound and Vision Corporation)
See BRITISH FORCES BROADCASTING SERVICE.

St George's Hall
Headquarters of BBC Variety, just outside BROADCASTING HOUSE, until destroyed in the 1941 bombing raid which also levelled the QUEEN'S HALL next door.

Stage And Screen
Music from films and theatre played by the BBC WEST OF ENGLAND LIGHT ORCHESTRA on Thursday afternoons on the Light Programme.

Stand Easy
Light Programme show of the late 1940s, spun from MERRY-GO-ROUND, starring CHARLIE CHESTER.

Star Sound Cinema
Radio 2 movie magazine which came between MOVIE-GO-ROUND and CINEMA 2.

Star Wars
Dramatised as a thirteen-part Radio 1 serial in 1981, with Mark Hamill as Luke Skywalker.

Starlight Hour
Successful variety series which began in 1948 starring bandleader Geraldo, in which Peter Sellers and Benny Hill made early appearances. FRANK MUIR and DENIS NORDEN did some of the writing. The second series in 1949 featured BERNARD BRADEN and BARBARA KELLY – their first series on British radio – and was presented by Brian Reece, star of PC49. SPIKE MILLIGAN appeared, but received no credit. KENNETH HORNE compered a later series, on the Home Service in 1964.

Starmakers and Svengalis
Five-part Radio 1 series presented in 1989 by ALAN FREEMAN which examined some of the leading figures in pop music management, including Larry Parnes, Brian Epstein, Peter Jenner, Malcolm McLaren and Tom Watkins.

Start The Week
Monday morning chat show launched on Radio 4 in April 1970, immediately after the 9 a.m. news which has been its home ever since. Always built around plugs, it has nonetheless changed almost out of all recognition. Originally it was a light magazine, with pre-recorded inserts and music: it is now a substantial and often very impressive discussion programme covering a range of contemporary issues.

RICHARD BAKER was the first host, and the first programme contained items on Wordsworth, Swedish tax reform, pigeons and cookery with Zena Skinner. Among the early contributors were Monty Modlyn, billed as 'the roving microphone' (he once roved as far as Idi Amin, and persuaded him to play the accordion), Esther Rantzen, Mavis Nicholson and Bel Mooney. On one occasion there were thirteen guests, not all of whom spoke. It was not always the most coherent of programmes.

The most regular contributor was Kenneth Robinson, whose regular spot of a prepared talk started in 1971. His acid remarks, often directed at feminists, generated much controversy, and in 1984 the BBC formally apologised for a joke he made. A lecturer from East Anglia University was talking about an agency through which disabled people could meet prospective marriage partners. Robinson quipped: 'You can hear the wheelchairs banging together all night in some parts of the country, I know.' He was rebuked by Jimmy Hill, who was standing in for Baker, and the BBC issued an apology later in the day. Robinson also reduced ANGELA RIPPON to tears with an attack on her book about horses and so provoked Pamela Stephenson that she picked up a jug of water and poured it down his neck before the show went out.

Eventually he was dropped, precipitating his famous outburst on the air. After Baker bade him a bland goodbye, several hundred thousand listeners heard Robinson say: 'I'm not going. I've been given three days' notice after fifteen years and it's a bloody disgrace.'

Baker, too, was disappointed when his contract was not renewed in 1987. By this time the programme was all live talk and under his successor RUSSELL HARTY it became barbed, witty and unpredictable. After Harty's illness and death in 1988, several presenters were tried out including Kate Adie, Sue Lawley, George Melly and Melvyn Bragg. The latter was chosen and took over in September 1988. He and the producer, Marina Salandy-Brown, have fashioned a programme of some *gravitas*. The era of lightweight comedians is over and, although the guests are still there because they have new books, new shows, new films or new plays, the conversation is often of a formidably high calibre.

Starting from Scratch
Six talks on Radio 4 in 1990 in which Methodist minister the Rev. Colin Morris, formerly the BBC's Head of Religious Broadcasting and later its Controller in Northern Ireland, set out a commonsense case for Christianity and suggested that the quest for God should start in the place most people know best, their own experience; and that theologians, hymns and churches are but 'optional extras'.

Staying on Course
Eight-part Radio 4 FM series in 1989 which looked at the variety of 'study breaks' now available for people who wanted to take up a new interest, from beachcombing to bats, Cotswold churches to assertiveness training.

'Steady, Barker!'
Self-deprecating catchphrase of comedian ERIC BARKER.

Steps to War
Four-part Radio 4 FM series in 1989 in which Prof. James Joll looked at the rise of Hitler in the 1930s and the extent to which he revealed his plans to control and invade Europe in his testament, *Mein Kampf*.

Steptoe and Son
GALE PEDRICK adapted this television classic for radio in the 1960s. It ran on the Light Programme with the same cast.

Stewart, Ed   (1941–)
Disc-jockey who was one of Radio 1's original team when the station was launched in 1967, but best known for his eleven years (1968–79) as presenter of Radio 2's JUNIOR CHOICE, a show he made his own.

Started in radio in Hong Kong (after going there to play bass in a jazz group), returning to work as a pirate DJ from 1965 to 1967 before joining Radio 1. He has always answered to the nickname 'Stewpot'.

On *Junior Choice* he coined 'Byeeee!' as his sign-off and played chart hits as well as old faithfuls like 'Puff the Magic Dragon'.

In 1980, the year after he left the show, and now presenting an afternoon programme, he discovered that the Queen Mother was apparently among his listeners. He played an 80th birthday request for her after Princess Margaret telephoned him, he said. (Previously, on *Junior Choice*, he had played an Alan Price record for the Princess's two children.) The unusual choice of the Queen Mother, relayed by her daughter, was 'Car 67' by the group Driver 67, a warm and sentimental song about a mini-cab driver who is asked to pick up the girl who has just jilted him.

In 1981, Stewart hit the headlines in a less pleasant way when he was a victim of the sort of nightmare which besets any broadcaster with a live show. He read out the names of four soldiers serving in Northern Ireland who, he said, had requested a record, and went on to play 'Danny Boy'. But they were four of the five soldiers killed by the IRA the previous week in an attack in South Armagh. The BBC said he mistook a memo warning that the names should not inadvertently be read out on the air for a request slip, and described the error as 'unforgivable'. Both he and the BBC apologised to the soldiers' families.

He was dropped from Radio 2 in 1983 and later worked at Radio Mercury, until 1990, and made a brief return to Radio 2 at Easter 1991.

Stilgoe, Richard   (1943–)
Lyricist, pianist, compere, performer and broadcaster whose enthusiasm for the Footlights led to his premature

exit from Cambridge: 'A cloud arrived and I left under it,' he says. Made his radio debut in 1964, and now heard frequently on Radios 2 and 4. Series include THE YEAR IN QUESTION and *Stilgoe's Around*.

Stop Messing About

(1) The famous catchphrase of KENNETH WILLIAMS, which he coined in HANCOCK'S HALF-HOUR.

(2) Comedy series with Williams, Hugh Paddick and Joan Sims which began in 1969 to fill the gap left by the cancellation of that year's series of ROUND THE HORNE, created by the death of KENNETH HORNE.

Stop Press

Weekly Radio 4 programme examining the activities of newspapers and their journalists, presented by NIGEL REES (1984-86) and then GLYN WORSNIP (1986–87). Most recently Geoffrey Goodman has been in the chair.

Stop the Week

Radio 4's Saturday-evening sneer in which an assortment of metropolitan smartyboots, under the chairmanship of Robert Robinson who always manages to have the last word, all try to upstage one another and end up speaking at the same time.

It has, though, launched many talented broadcasters, who now have shows of their own: ANTHONY CLARE started IN THE PSYCHIATRIST'S CHAIR; Laurie Taylor went on to make THE RADIO PROGRAMME and MICHAEL O'DONNELL was approached to make RELATIVE VALUES.

'Sometimes I love it but sometimes I, too, want to throw something at the radio when it's on' – Michael Green.

Stop the World

Radio 2 comedy series in 1981 hosted by Francis Matthews and also featuring Sally Grace (later of WEEK ENDING), Ronald Fletcher and songs by Richard Digance.

Stoppard, Tom   (1937–)

The playwright of intellectual pyrotechnics made his radio debut on the Light Programme, when his story *The Dissolution of Dominic Boot* was mounted on JUST BEFORE MIDNIGHT in 1964. Two months later, in the same slot, came his *M is for Moon Among Other Things*. More than a dozen works have gone out since, including *Rosencrantz and Guildenstern are Dead* (Third Programme, 1967) and a complex, multi-layered, highly acclaimed play about India where he spent four years of his childhood, *In The Native State* (Radio 3, 1991). *Professional Foul* and *The Real Inspector Hound* were both produced by, and broadcast on, the World Service, and heard on Radio 4 as well, in 1979.

A Story, A Hymn and A Prayer

Short religious spot on the Light at 9.55 a.m. on Saturdays, immediately following CHILDREN'S CHOICE.

The Story of Pop

Epic Radio 1 series, in 26 parts, presented by ALAN FREEMAN and edited by KEITH SKUES in the early 1970s.

Streeter, Fred   (1877–1975)

Shepherd's son from Pulborough, Sussex, who became one of the most cherished broadcasters of his age with talks which communicated a deep and abiding love of plants.

The first, in the 1930s, was on runner beans. It attracted 200 letters. He covered most other gardening topics over the course of the next forty years, during which he worked as head gardener at Petworth and won over fifty gold medals at Royal Horticultural Society shows.

Many amateur gardeners hung on his every wireless word. 'His influence in disseminating a knowledge of the basics of gardening into millions of homes is incalculable,' said *The Times* in its obituary.

String Sound

Weekly Radio 2 show which was one of the regular outlets for the BBC RADIO ORCHESTRA.

Stringalong

Ken Sykora presented this Monday evening series on the Light Programme devoted to strings and songs.

Stuart, Chris   (1949–)

Journalist (feature writer on the *Western Mail*) and musician (composing the music for the Super Ted cartoons) before going into broadcasting (presenter of BBC Radio Wales's daily breakfast show for nine years, followed by three years in the dawn slot on Radio 2, where he succeeded the late RAY MOORE). In 1991, after twelve years as an early morning presenter, the soft-voiced and mild-mannered Stuart swapped slots with KEN BRUCE so that he now hosts the late-night show.

Stuart, Moira   (c. 1949–)

Newsreader of impeccable manner and diction, sadly lost to television. She began as an announcer on FARMING TODAY and in November 1978 became the first Afro-Caribbean to read the news on Radio 4.

Stuart, Vivien   (1957–)

Bubbly weather presenter on Radio 2's breakfast show until 1991. She was her team captain in 1969 when Torquay Grammar School for Girls won TOP OF THE FORM, a triumph which propelled her into broadcasting. She worked as a reporter on BBC Radio London and as a Radio 2 newsreader before joining DEREK JAMESON's show when it began in 1986. Their chatty exchanges enlivened the show but in 1991 she left to work as a journalist.

Studio 3
Drama slot on Radio 3 created in 1988 for new, shorter plays.

Such Rotten Luck
Radio 3 comedy series in 1989 starring Tim Pigott-Smith as a failed writer, Woodhouse Carton, with Zoe Wanamaker as the wife who supports him in his efforts. It was the first radio comedy to be written by Ronald Hayman.

Sunday
Radio 4's Sunday morning magazine programme looking at religious news and issues (mainly Christian ones) both in Britain and abroad. It was launched in 1969 on FM only, but the then Radio 4 Controller TONY WHITBY promised to put it on medium wave as well, thereby ensuring a much bigger audience, if the programme could attract an audience of 250,000. Within a few months this figure had been achieved and Whitby kept his promise.

The Rev. Colin Semper, who later became Canon of Westminster, was the first producer. Paul Barnes was the original presenter, but he left soon after for Anglia TV. CLIVE JACOBS took over in 1972 and presented it for eighteen years until 1990, when the Rev. Ernest Rea, the BBC's Head of Religious Broadcasting, declined to renew his contract on the grounds that Jacobs did not know enough about an increasingly complex area and that more specialists were needed.

Thereafter LIBBY PURVES, Trevor Barnes and Andrew Green shared out the presenting duties between them.

Sunday Edition
Sunday breakfast show on Radio 5, presented by BARRY JOHNSTON.

Sunday Half Hour
Radio 2's Sunday evening service of cheerful hymn singing began in July 1940 on the Forces Programme (in the same week as the Battle of Britain broke out) which makes it one of the BBC's longest running programmes.

It began life with a request from the British Expeditionary Force to give the troops a link with home, and the first programme came from St Mary Redcliffe in Bristol, with the first hymn being 'We Love the Place, O God'. The singing was conducted by Sir Walford Davies, Master of the King's Musick. Subsequent locations were

not always given out, for security reasons. One early programme, in August 1940, was conducted by Dr William Lloyd Webber, father of composer Andrew and cellist Julian.

The BBC's Director of Religious Broadcasting described the programme's aim as to reach, and hold, the nation's fighting men. 'All the evidence I have from the Navy is that from 7.30 to 8 on a Sunday evening, the sailors who meet on the mess deck to smoke their pipes with the chaplain are men who wish to be reminded, in a not unworthy way, of their homes and of such connections as they have with religion and the churches.'

The programme caught on within a few months and survived all the various changes to the network over the next decades: Forces to Light, Light to Radio 2, long wave to FM. From 1954–88 it also went out on the World Service. In 1990, its 50th birthday was celebrated with a special, double-length programme from Westminster Central Hall in which were gathered 2,000 hymn-singing listeners (over 3,000 applied for tickets), the BBC CONCERT ORCHESTRA and singer Stuart Burrows. It was co-presented by ROGER ROYLE, who became the programme's regular presenter later that year – when it changed to incorporate listeners' hymn requests and dedications.

Since the tradition of hearty congregational singing is much more marked in the Free Churches than Anglican or Roman Catholic, it is not surprising that the programme often comes from a Presbyterian, Methodist, Baptist or Salvation Army establishment. Ebenezer Gospel Halls, comprehensive school choirs and Winson Green prison have also been featured.

The Sunday Play
Classic drama slot on Radio 3, introduced in 1990 (previously the slot had been on a Friday). It opened with the first new radio production of *Julius Caesar* for eighteen years, with Michael Maloney as Brutus.

Sunday Soapbox
See CHARLIE CHESTER.

Sunday Sport
Sunday afternoon sports programme once on Radio 2 and now on Radio 5, which has been hosted by Charles Colville and Jonathan Legard. It transferred to the new network when it began in August 1990.

Sunrise Radio
Marriage arranging is among the ways in which this Hounslow-based station tries to meet the needs of its Asian audiences throughout a wide swathe of West London. Hundreds of Asian families have so far placed advertisements on the air seeking suitable husbands for their daughters.

A former pirate called SINA, Sunrise was the second of the new INCREMENTAL stations to go on the air, in November 1989. Just as it did when it was operating illegally, it broadcasts during the day in both Hindustani (a language understood by 99 per cent of Asians, says chief executive Avtar Lit, whether they be from India or Pakistan) and English. On Monday nights, there are programmes in Tamil, on Tuesdays in Gujerati and on Wednesdays in Punjabi. *Qwalis*, sacred Islamic songs, are broadcast on Fridays.

Unlike many incrementals, Sunrise has always run at a profit and Lit has diversified shrewdly. He and his staff run a news service covering Asian activities in the UK which is sold to several outlets, including a chain of 180 newspapers in India.

Sunset Radio
Manchester-based black music station which was the first of the ethnic and community INCREMENTAL stations to go on the air, in October 1989. Founded by Mike Shaft, ex-Piccadilly and ex-GMR, the FM station also broadcasts programmes in Indian, Greek and Chinese. Initially Shaft also presented the breakfast show, avoiding the traditional ingredients of tales from the tabloids, weather snippets, quizzes, anniversaries and jokes. 'If people want competitions and all the old prattle they can tune to something else,' he said in the first week. However, as with so many incrementals, the idealism proved ill-founded. Shaft later left after a boardroom row, and the station was refashioned.

Swahili Service
(BBC World Service.) See AFRICAN SERVICE.

Swansea Sound
Swansea-based ILR station, on the air since 1974.

Swanton, E.W. 'Jim' (1907–)
Highly respected cricket commentator who made the first live cricket commentary back to England (from Johannesburg in December 1938) and, after the Second World War in which he was a Japanese prisoner-of-war for three years, continued commentating for the BBC until 1975.

He started his career in print (on the *Evening Standard* in 1927) and has written on cricket for the *Daily Telegraph* since 1946.

Sweet and Low-Down
Six-part Radio 4 series in 1990 with Robert Cushman on New York cabaret and popular song.

Sweet Corn
'Music for modern squares' was offered in this Light Programme series with Bill Shepherd and Peter Knight directing the Sweet Corn Orchestra and Chorus. A break for records was provided in a slot called 'Corn on a Platter'.

Symonds, David (1943–)
Berkhamsted and Oxford-educated presenter of the first programme on Capital Radio, on its opening day in 1973. Has also worked, before and since, on many other stations. Hosted Sunday morning's EASY BEAT on the Light Programme in 1966 and was an announcer on Home, Light and Third: was one of Radio 1's original team of DJs in 1967, staying until 1972. Capital Radio, 1973–75. Then head of programmes for Radio Victory, 1975–76 (years before it lost its franchise) before going freelance. Radio 2 presenter, 1978–81. Morning DJ in Los Angeles, 1982–84. Radio 4 announcer and newsreader, 1985–88. A weekend DJ on Capital Gold since 1988 – back on the air on Sunday mornings just as he was a quarter of a century ago.

T

Table Talk

Dumplings, Plato's favourite tipple (home-made cider, allegedly) and erotic cakes have all featured in this short audio snack about the pleasures of food and drink which occupies ten or fifteen minutes every Sunday lunchtime on Radio 3. It is presented by Leslie Forbes, author of *A Table in Tuscany* and *A Table in Provence*. Once a month writers serve up specially commissioned short stories about memorable food.

Tablet, Hilda

Fictitious central character in HENRY REED's cultural comedies broadcast on the Third Programme from 1954 until the early 1960s. She was a composeress, played by Mary O'Farrell. The other main character, scholar Herbert Reeve (Reed's alter ego) was played by Hugh Burden. MARJORIE WESTBURY was Hilda's protegee, Elsa, and DERYCK GUYLER was the blimpish General Gland.

Take a Place Like . . .

Radio 4 travel series in which Stanley Ellis, John Grundy and Dr Juliet Barker presented portraits of towns and cities around Britain, emphasising the tell-tale signs of dialect and architecture which give places their distinctive character.

Take Five

Radio 5's weekday morning show in school holidays, featuring a joke file, music, special guests, competitions and the 'Around the World in 80 Seconds' geography quiz. It was the first programme heard on the network on its opening day, when, as a one-off, BRUNO BROOKES presented it. Various young personalities have hosted it since, including Tommy Boyd.

Take It From Here

Popular comedy series running on the Light Programme from 1948–59 which blended skits, sketches and songs and starred 'Professor' JIMMY EDWARDS, Dick Bentley and Joy Nichols.

When, in 1953, June Whitfield succeeded the latter, the show also launched a comic soap opera called THE GLUMS, which rapidly became its most popular feature. Much fun was derived from the everlasting engagement

The star trio of *Take It From Here* in its first five years: Joy Nichols, Jimmy Edwards and Dick Bentley, pictured in October 1950 during rehearsals at BBC Radio's temple of light entertainment, the Aeolian Hall in Bond Street

between the idiotic and clueless Ron (Bentley) and the eternally optimistic Eth (Whitfield) and their soppy exchange of 'Ooh Ron!' 'Ooh Eth!'

Edwards played Pa Glum, saying later that he based him on a Cockney publican whom he knew in Barnes, where he lived. Mrs Glum never appeared and never spoke (rather like 'Er Indoors of a later generation) though she did occasionally scream. Alma Cogan provided her voice. The Glums were brought back to life, for television, in 1979.

The programme introduced a pair of brilliant young writers, FRANK MUIR and DENIS NORDEN, who brought a topical edge to the series throughout its twelve years. As Muir says, 'We wrote for an audience that reads newspapers.'

Take Two
Pick-of-the-week slot on Radio 2, confined to the network's programmes, with a different presenter or critic choosing fifteen minutes of highlights from 168 hours of output each week. It began in February 1991 with KEN BRUCE's selection.

Take Your Pick
Radio Luxembourg game show hosted by Michael Miles in the early 1950s. He later presented it on ITV, where the show was produced by Associated Rediffusion, from September 1955 – the first cash quiz show on British television. It continued until the end of the Rediffusion franchise in 1968.

Talbot, Godfrey (1908–)
Fine BBC war correspondent during the Second World War; afterwards the BBC's court correspondent, 1948–69.

Tales From a Long Room
Radio 4 cricket comedy series written by PETER TINNISWOOD, starring Robin Bailey.

Tales From the South China Seas
Radio 4 series of CHARLES ALLEN.

Talkabout
Radio 1 show, hosted for a time by ADRIAN LOVE.

Talking About Music
ANTONY HOPKINS created this half-hour series in 1954. It has been running ever since, on both Home and Third, Radio 4 and Radio 3, and been sold to 44 countries. Each programme is devoted to a single musical work. Hopkins vividly illuminates it both by the words he uses to describe its origins (often with anecdotes of human interest) and by the excerpts he plays.

Several hundred editions have been made. The earliest composer he has tackled is Monteverdi: the most

modern, Peter Maxwell Davies. The very first programme examined Michael Tippett's Concerto for Double String Orchestra (a tribute to his mentor, who helped to train him).

Talking Poetry
Poetry series for children from eight upwards – more particularly those around twelve or thirteen – which is broadcast on Radio 5 each week. Presenters are Simon Rae (of POETRY PLEASE!) and Nicola Davies, a Cambridge zoology graduate and host of television's *The Really Wild Show*.

The programme contains a wide range of verse, read by children, actors and poets, and encourages young listeners to try their hand at writing it themselves (with tips from the likes of SPIKE MILLIGAN and Adrian Henri). Each edition features a guest poet, and a poetry competition in the first series was judged by Charles Causley, with the winning entries displayed on the London Underground.

Talking Politics
Steps into Radio 4's WEEK IN WESTMINSTER slot while Parliament is in recess. It started in 1970 and for many years was hosted by Prof. Anthony King of Essex University. Political journalist David Walker took over as presenter in 1989. Peter Sissons made his radio debut on the programme in 1990 when he chaired a debate on the televising of the House of Commons.

Talking Turkey
Selection by Chris Kelly of clips from some of the most dreadful films ever made, on Radio 2 in 1990.

Talks
Carefully prepared, properly written and scripted talks on a variety of subjects were strongly championed by REITH, and part of the BBC from the earliest days – a tradition which has survived, despite more recent attractions of phone-ins and chat shows.

The Corporation's records say that the first broadcast talk was by Captain E.B. Towse, VC, in December 1922. Regular weekly film, theatre and literary criticism was introduced the following summer. The 1920s saw contributions from such as James Agate and John Strachey, and J.B. PRIESTLEY, CHARLES HILL and C.S. LEWIS all helped to stiffen national resolve in the Second World War.

Perhaps the longest ever talk, by one uninterrupted voice, was when literary critic Lionel Trilling spoke for 65 minutes on the Third Programme.

Tamil Service
BBC programmes in the Tamil tongue first went out in May 1941, and today are broadcast for three hours a week. The service has mounted several ambitious drama

productions, including Tamil translations of *Hamlet* (serialised in 15 episodes) and *Pygmalion*.

Tarrant, Chris (1946–)

Former teacher in London's East End who presents what is probably London's most popular radio show: the breakfast programme on Capital FM, based on the American 'zoo radio' principle of a team of subsidiary presenters all adding to the general commotion. His broadcasting career began on ATV in *Tiswas* and, later, *OTT*.

A Taste Of . . .

Fascinating Radio 4 series in which RAY GOSLING looks at the appeal, usefulness and characteristics of other languages: so far he has sampled Russian, Urdu, Japanese, Spanish, Yiddish, Arabic and Swahili.

Tasting Notes

Showcase of six upmarket drinking songs on Radio 3 in 1989. Each song was commissioned by Wiltshire wine merchant Robin Yapp to mark his 20th anniversary in business. The composers included Sir Harrison Birtwhistle and Sir Peter Maxwell Davies and all their bibulous songs were inspired by wine-related literature from Dante to Byron.

Tea Junction

Friday afternoon Radio 4 series beginning in 1990 with Patrick Hannan and guests talking about the events of the week just finishing.

The Teachers

Fly-on-the-wall documentary series in eight parts on Radio 4 in 1990 reflecting a term at Washwood Heath Comprehensive School, Birmingham, complete with truant, scabies, Rottweilers in the playground, stink bombs, headaches with the National Curriculum and geography field trips.

It also featured the attempts of headmaster Stan Bailey to protect the school's image in the face of a barrage of complaints by residents and shopkeepers about his pupils' behaviour. The producers, Brian King and Sarah Rowlands, also produced THE DOCTORS.

Teenagers' Turn

Light Programme series whose edition of 8 March 1962 included the first radio broadcast of The Beatles – so early in their career that Ringo Starr had not yet joined (Pete Best was still the drummer) and they had not made a single record.

They were paid £26 18s, with an additional £1 14s for their four return rail fares from Liverpool to Manchester.

It was the first of over fifty music sessions at BBC Radio in which they played 88 songs, most of them never released on disc.

Telepathy

Various figures have used radio for mind-reading, both as scientific experiments and as an entertaining illusion. The earliest example of the first was Sir Oliver Lodge in 1927, and the best practitioners of conjuring were THE PIDDINGTONS.

Telling It How It Was

Eight-part series on Radio 4 FM in 1989 in which Steve Humphries encouraged people to take an interest in oral history and use tape recorders to capture some of the national treasure trove of memories – of school, games, fashion, work, local stories and so on – to prevent these accounts of everyday life in the earlier part of the twentieth century from being lost for ever.

Telling Lies

Four-part Radio 4 series on deceit in 1990.

Ten O'Clock

The long established NEWS at 9 p.m. on the Home Service was axed in September 1960 and replaced by this half-hour programme which went out an hour later. The BBC said it was a better time for two reasons. It enabled the bulletin to include news of important Commons speeches in the closing stages of debates, which often did not take place until after 9 p.m., and it provided more of an opportunity to report on events from the USA because of the time difference. These arguments also found favour outside the BBC. Seven years later, in 1967, ITN decided to mount its own flagship bulletin at the same time when it launched *News at Ten*.

Ten to Eight

Successor to LIFT UP YOUR HEARTS on the Home Service, which continued as a religious slot at breakfast time but, unlike its predecessor, carried the thoughts of other faiths as well as Christianity. It ran from 1965–70 and was succeeded by THOUGHT FOR THE DAY.

Ten to Ten

Ten-minute Christian slot on Radio 4 at this time every Saturday evening: it adopted its format from FIVE TO TEN.

Test Match Special

The name of the live, ball-by-ball coverage of Test matches on Radio 3, which is transferring to Radio 5 after Radio 3 loses its medium wave frequency around the end of 1991. Every Test match that has taken place in England since 1957 has been covered ball-by-ball. By 1990, not only home Test matches were covered in this way but also many abroad, for example in New Zealand and the West Indies.

Launching Radio 3's 1989 cricket coverage were, from left, Fred Trueman, Christopher Martin-Jenkins and Brian Johnston. The scene reflected both the *Test Match Special* tradition of cakes sent in by listeners and a joke from earlier in Johnston's career when a colleague passed him a slice of cake, followed quickly by the microphone

The BBC has pointed out that when TMS transfers to Radio 5, there may be occasions when ball-by-ball coverage makes way for other sport (e.g. Wimbledon or Olympic athletics) regarded as of equal or greater importance, or for other types of programmes. This loss of the same absolute guarantee of ball-by-ball coverage in the future as has existed in the past has created controversy. It has been forced upon the BBC, of course, by the loss of Radio 3's medium wave frequency which is being surrendered for a new national commercial network.

Commentators most associated with TMS are JOHN ARLOTT, BRIAN JOHNSTON, famous for his sense of fun and the enjoyment he gets from the cakes which listeners send in, and CHRISTOPHER MARTIN-JENKINS. See also A VIEW FROM THE BOUNDARY.

'It evokes, as cricket rarely does these days, a certain idea of Englishness – nonchalant professionalism, easygoing courtesy, boyish fun, a desire to see fair play. TMS remains unashamedly fixated in an innocent past, a world of pop, tuck and practical jokes' – John Dugdale in *The Listener*, 1990.

TFM Radio

ILR station whose area stretches from Durham south to Harrogate, based in Stockton on Tees, which began as Radio Tees in 1975. It was relaunched under its present name in 1988 and in 1989 began splitting its output, launching Great North Radio on AM for older listeners and TFM on FM for the younger ones.

Thai Service

Programmes in the Thai language were first put out by the BBC in April 1941. Today they are on the air for an hour a day.

Thousands of Thai workers were trapped in the Gulf during the crisis of 1990 and most of them could speak no other language. To ensure they could keep in touch with what was happening, the BBC started to broadcast their Thai programmes on three new frequencies, all of them audible throughout the Middle East.

Thanks For The Memory
Radio 2 show presented by HUBERT GREGG. Its slow, relaxing signature tune is 'Time Was', played by Nelson Riddle and his Orchestra.

That Reminds Me
Swedish singer Elisabeth Soderstrom presented music, stories and reminiscences in this graceful Radio 4 series first heard in 1984: it returned after rather a long gap in 1991.

The Thatcher Decade
Three-part Radio 4 series in 1989 examining three features of Margaret Thatcher's first ten years as Prime Minister: the downfall of the unions; the influence of her press secretary Bernard Ingham; and an assessment (by GORDON CLOUGH) of her international standing.

These You Have Loved
Melodious and long-lasting music programme, much influenced during the Second World War by poignant and eloquent requests from the Forces, which Doris Arnold began on the National Programme one Sunday afternoon in November 1938. It contained 'The Floral Dance', 'The Blue Danube', 'The Londonderry Air' and Handel's Largo. This last piece was eventually adopted as the programme's signature tune (to use the term Miss Arnold herself hated).

During the Second World War, she presented from 24 to 52 programmes a year. Their content was largely determined by the requests which flooded in from people who wanted to hear parts of their favourite concertos, symphonies and arias which would comfort and console them, ease their grief or act as reminders of happier times.

The programmes continued regularly until 1952 and intermittently until 1957. After a six-year gap, in 1963, Doris Arnold made her 330th appearance on the programme and carried on. It then continued as the Home Service equivalent of the rather similar series YOUR HUNDRED BEST TUNES going out at the same time on the Light Programme. From 1972–77, when it came to an end after nearly forty years, the programme was presented by RICHARD BAKER on Radio 4.

Third Ear
Arts series on Radio 3, at 7.05 p.m. on weekdays, launched by JOHN DRUMMOND in 1988. The programmes usually take the form of conversations, examining a different aspect of the arts each night of the week.

Third Network
Successor to Network Three in the early 1960s, but exactly the same thing: the separately named portion of the Third Programme which went out in the afternoons and early evening, before the Third started at about 8 p.m.

Third Opinion
(1) A Radio 3 series 'of reflections on current affairs' produced in Manchester in 1981: Gerald Long, then Managing Director of Times Newspapers, was one of the speakers.

(2) Radio 3's Saturday-evening successor to CRITICS' FORUM, which began in September 1990 presented by CHRISTOPHER COOK. Unlike its predecessor it goes out live, often ventures outside London, fosters a more argumentative spirit with a frequent four-minute polemic, and does not neglect music, dance and architecture.

The first programme included items on novelist Paul Bailey and photographer Fay Goodwin. The two guest critics, A.S. Byatt and Roy Porter, reviewed Sondheim's musical *Into the Woods*, Muriel Spark's *Symposium* and BBC-TV's *Portrait of a Marriage*.

Third Programme
Created in September 1946 as an uncompromising service of highbrow speech and music (although, to show it was not entirely humourless, its opening programme was the comic *How to Listen*, in the HOW TO . . . series of STEPHEN POTTER and JOYCE GRENFELL). The first Head was SIR GEORGE BARNES. Within six months of its birth, it was suspended for sixteen days (in February 1947) because of a national fuel crisis in what was a bitterly cold winter.

In the beginning, it went out in the evenings only, but in 1953 started broadcasting at 3 p.m. on Sundays. Four years later came the first reorganisation which some critics felt was the beginning of the end of the Third's unique personality and its sense of cultural mission. Over the next thirteen years, other services (Network Three, Music Programme, Third Network) were added to the same frequency, so that its impact was inevitably diminished.

After 1967, when the whole frequency was renamed Radio 3, the Third Programme kept a separate editorial team and its output was under a separate heading in RADIO TIMES. In April 1970, however, in the wake of BROADCASTING IN THE SEVENTIES and after much heated public debate, it was absorbed into its new Radio 3 parent. The less recherché parts of its speech output went to Radio 4.

In recent years, some of Radio 3's Controllers, most notably JOHN DRUMMOND, have made much effort to make the tone of the network more friendly, draw more attention to some of its glories and swell its tiny audience (about 2 per cent of the total).

Although primarily a music channel, the network has always broadcast DRAMA, mainly the heavier

'Courage, Oona! Let us show the world that the Highbrows of Britain can TAKE IT, too!'

The Third Programme was dropped for sixteen days in February 1947 as a result of a national fuel crisis. This cartoon by Lee in the *Evening News* speculated on withdrawal symptoms among eggheads

classics and experimental work. Writers who came to prominence via the Third include HAROLD PINTER and BILL NAUGHTON. It has also broadcast thousands of scholarly TALKS.

'[It acknowledges] the fact that some listeners are fools and some are not, and that we cannot wait for the fools to catch up with their betters' – Henry Reed, 1946.

This Family Business
JOHNNIE WALKER has presented this regular Radio 5 series on the ups and downs of parenting, with reviews of children's games and a 'grouseline' for people to let off steam, since it began in 1990.

This Sceptr'd Isle
Radio 3 series in 1989 celebrating the British poetry, song and instrumental music which was inspired by a sense of national identity.

This Week's Composer
Series on the Home Service, and later Radio 3, which was succeeded by COMPOSERS OF THE WEEK in 1988.

Thompson, John (1928–)
First Director of Radio at the IBA, from 1973 – when Independent Local Radio began – until 1987. Previously he had been senior advisor on radio to the Minister of Posts and Telecommunications, the Minister who then had governmental responsibility for broadcasting. He is a former ITN newscaster and a former editor of both *Time and Tide* and *The Observer* Magazine.

Those Were The Days
Song and light music series on Saturday evenings on the Home Service from 1943, later on the Light as well, and Radio 2 after 1967. It had its 900th edition in 1961 and continued until 1974.

Thought For The Day
Religious enclave on Radio 4's TODAY programme at 7.50 each morning, in which a speaker has three minutes to 'reflect on the events of the day from a perspective of faith'. It has been running since 1970, and succeeded TEN TO EIGHT.

This is where RABBI LIONEL BLUE made his name, his Monday-morning homilies becoming so popular that he released fifty of them on a cassette in 1990. Others who have appeared include Robert Foxcroft (died 1986), the Bishops of Oxford and Stepney, and Prof. Charles Handy of the London Business School, who spoke on the morning of the San Francisco earthquake in October 1989. The Archbishop of Canterbury spoke on the morning of the massive Allied onslaught on Iraq in January 1991.

Most of the twenty regular speakers are Christian, of nearly all shades, but there are also three Jewish speakers and one Sikh. There is no Hindu or Muslim despite the rapid growths of these faiths in Britain, although the BBC has made some efforts to find an Islamic contributor.

The slot, short as it is, is no stranger to controversy – partly because what the speaker says is completely unchallenged, and also because it goes out in the sensitive *Today* programme. In 1990 Canon Eric James, director of Christian Action and a chaplain to The Queen, resigned from the pool of speakers in protest at what he claimed was continual censorship of his scripts.

He announced in *Church Times* that 'regular battles' with the BBC had come to a head over his script – intended for the opening day of the Labour Party conference – on a radical East End priest, Father John Groser (1890–1962), who said of himself that he was a socialist because he was a Christian. He was ordered to cut an approving reference to 'the spiritual value of revolt', and refused. He was replaced by a Methodist, Dr Leslie Griffiths.

The BBC responded that it was 'imperative' that the Thinkers for the Day, given their privileged position in which their remarks were never questioned, did not seem to be pushing a party political line.

'When I'm shaving I like to hear *Thought for the Day*. Often, if Rabbi Lionel Blue is on, I'll be standing there, razor poised, just listening. I think he has such a down-to-earth way of putting across a spiritual message' – John Taylor, prospective Parliamentary candidate for Cheltenham and likely to be Britain's first black Tory MP.

Through the Fire

Six-part Radio 4 series in 1989 in which Louis Teeman, a Leeds man aged 86, recalled his grim childhood, anti-Semitic encounters and his struggle to escape from a Jewish ghetto.

Ticket to Write

Punning title for Radio 4 FM series in 1989 in which John Keay looked at the work and attitudes of travel writers including Jan Morris, Paul Theroux, Geoffrey Moorhouse and many more.

Time Cycle

Devised and chaired by ADRIAN LOVE, and beginning in 1989, this Radio 2 panel game combines comedy with general knowledge, with celebrity panellists such as as Jimmy Mulville and Hale and Pace being asked to improvise important events from the past – and future.

Time For Verse

Programme of contemporary poetry originally conceived, produced and presented by Patric Dickinson, a great verse champion, in 1945. Resurrected on Radio 4 in 1979, it has since undergone a variety of formats.

Today, with Carol Ann Duffy as the presenter, it trawls the poetry and literary festivals and about 45 poets a year are heard reading their own work. Almost half of them are women, the proportion having increased steadily over the last decade. It was planning to take an active part in Radio 4's poetry festival of September 1991.

Time Travel

Radio 5 series starting in 1990 in which John Campbell discovers the past by visiting the places where major historical events (e.g. the Battle of Britain) happened.

Time Will Tell

Seven-part Radio 4 FM series in 1989 (originally made for the BBC World Service and revised as an educational programme) in which analysts and academics looked at major international topics (e.g. *perestroika*, the rise of Japan, Northern Ireland's sectarian conflict) and considered future scenarios for them in the light of historical forces.

Timpson, John   (1928–)

Presenter of Radio 4's TODAY programme from 1970–76 and from 1978–86 (during the gap he made an unsuccessful foray into television). Much celebrated for his partnership with BRIAN REDHEAD and his jovial, John Bull, yo-ho-ho sense of humour.

Chairman of ANY QUESTIONS? from 1984–87, when the incessant travelling round Britain finally got too much for a man who is fond of his creature comforts at home in rural Norfolk. Freelance Radio 4 series since then include *Timpson's England*, examining quirks of his native country.

The Tingle Factor

Radio 4 series in which famous folk (including Bernard Levin and Pam Ayres) revealed the musical moments which had given them particular pleasure. ROBIN RAY interviewed them and played the extracts.

Tinniswood, Peter   (1936–)

Liverpool-born journalist (*Sheffield Star*, *Western Mail*) who has become a popular writer of comedy for radio, particularly celebrated for his TALES FROM A LONG ROOM and the character of UNCLE MORT.

He made his debut as a radio dramatist on the Third Programme, with the comedy series *Hardluck Hall* co-written with David Nobbs in 1964. The Northern chauvinist Uncle Mort came out of a series of four novels he wrote, starting with *A Touch of Daniel*, which became popular when he started adapting the work for radio. There have now been thirteen episodes of *Uncle Mort's North Country* and another thirteen of *Uncle Mort's South Country* on Radio 4, with Stephen Thorne playing the title character.

His award-winning radio play *The Village Fete* introduced the character of Winston Hayballs, described by Tinniswood as a village poacher with a 'fat, brown, boozer's belly'. The success of the play has so far spun three series: *Winston*, *Winston Comes to Town* and *Winston in Love*.

Tinniswood has also been responsible for a number of radio documentaries, their subjects ranging from cricket and Cowes to fellow Northerner SANDY POWELL.

Tip-Top Tunes

Light music series on the Light Programme which began in 1956 with Geraldo and his Orchestra, continuing into the 1960s.

To Keep the Memory Green

Radio 4 series about the literary societies which succeed in keeping the candles burning for many British authors, including G.A. Henty, J.R.R. Tolkien, Edgar Wallace, Samuel Pepys, Dorothy L. Sayers, Jerome K.

Jerome and Sir Arthur Conan Doyle. It was presented by Humphrey Carpenter, who explored questions like: 'What is it about furry hobbits that draws together solicitors, librarians and Cambridge research students?' The series also revealed that Tory politician Kenneth Baker (creator of the radio show PARTY PIECES) was among members of The Chesterton Society.

To the Back of Not Very Far Away
Ten tales of 1960s life all written by Barry Pilton and read by Anton Rodgers, on Radio 4 in 1990.

To The Manor Born
This started life, like many successful television comedy series, on radio – as a pilot with Penelope Keith and BERNARD BRADEN. He played the entrepreneur whom Peter Bowles later portrayed on TV, but on this first occasion the character was American and distantly related to the lady of the manor.

It was produced by JOHN LLOYD, written by Peter Spence (who had for a time been writing all of WEEK ENDING, and went on to write *To The Manor Born* as a television series) and recorded at the Paris Theatre in 1979. But it was never broadcast. It was poached by BBC-TV and Keith, her star then in the ascendant from *The Good Life*, was signed up within a week to star in it.

Today
Now one of the BBC's best known, most influential and most popular news and current affairs programmes ('setting the nation's agenda', as the BBC says), this began on the Home Service in 1957 as a light magazine show to accompany breakfast. The survey of national papers, now one of the most popular items, was introduced in May 1959.

The programme has grown into the platform from which every politician in the land wants to drop a word in the nation's ear, and which Mrs Thatcher once telephoned direct from 10 Downing Street (to tell the programme that she had heard for the first time on Radio 4's *News Briefing* at 6 a.m. that Mikhail Gorbachev would not be coming to London as arranged but was flying straight home from New York because of the Armenian earthquake).

Avuncular JACK DE MANIO, relaxed and casual, presented the programme on his own from 1958–70. JOHN TIMPSON was then put in as his partner, heralding a brisker approach to the news, and De Manio left a year later, in 1971. Several people were then tried out as Timpson's partner, including Robert Robinson and Barry Norman, before BRIAN REDHEAD arrived in 1975.

He and Timpson formed one of the great radio teams. Their voices, quips and mannerisms suggested a fine balance between town and country, tenor and baritone, north and south – and also, many felt instinctively,

left and right. The partnership lasted ten years until Timpson left the programme to go freelance in 1986. Redhead's co-presenters today are JOHN HUMPHRYS, SUE MACGREGOR and PETER HOBDAY.

No other programme so consistently attracts the wrath of Tory politicians. Partly this is due to the fact that there is no longer a foil for Redhead's occasional anti-Tory barbs. It is also true that *Today* is the one programme which all politicians and editors hear, and therefore its slightest nuances are inflated into an importance they would not enjoy elsewhere. In addition, *Today* questions those in power, and the Conservatives have been in power for most of the period in which it has been a proper current affairs programme: it is therefore seen as antagonistic towards one political party.

The most famous accusation against Redhead came in March 1987 when he challenged the then Chancellor, Nigel Lawson, about whether the new jobs created in the UK were real, full-time jobs or low-paid, part-time ones. Lawson responded: 'Well, you have been a supporter of the Labour Party all your life, Brian, so I expect you to say something like that.' Redhead (who claims to be more of a Tory wet, not a socialist) then suggested a minute's silence for Lawson's presumption as to his voting habits.

Every December the programme mounts its Man and Woman of the Year poll, when listeners are urged to send in their choices on a postcard. The contest has been held every year since 1982, prior to which it was part of THE WORLD AT ONE. The winners have been:

1982: Pope John Paul II, Margaret Thatcher
1983: Bruce Kent, Margaret Thatcher
1984: Arthur Scargill, Margaret Thatcher
1985: (the year of famine) Bob Geldof, Princess Anne
1986: Terry Waite, Margaret Thatcher
1987: Gordon Wilson (who forgave the Enniskillen bombers who killed his daughter Marie), Margaret Thatcher
1988: Mikhail Gorbachev, Margaret Thatcher
1989: Mikhail Gorbachev, Margaret Thatcher
1990: Michael Heseltine, Margaret Thatcher

In 1990 there was embarrassment for the programme when it was revealedd that it had discounted the man for whom the most votes had been cast. He was a prominent Hindu politician in India, Lal Krishan Advani, leader of the Bharatiya Janata Party. The BBC said that many votes had been identically worded and arrived on identical cards, and that this pointed to an orchestrated campaign which was not in keeping with the spirit of the competition. *Today* itself carried an item on the row, which included a despatch from Mark Tully in India. It has also been said, though with no evidence, that Mrs Thatcher's repeated victories were helped by a letter-writing campaign whipped up by Young Conservatives.

John Timpson is on the left and Brian Redhead on the right, although listeners with political antennae liked to think it was the other way round. Together on *Today* from 1975–86 and one of the great radio partnerships

Today in Parliament

Late night report on Radio 4 of the debates and exchanges in both the House of Commons and the House of Lords, broadcast every day Parliament is sitting. (An accurate summary of Parliamentary proceedings is one of the few things the BBC is required to provide under its Charter and Licence.)

Radio broadcasting from Parliament was carried out on an experimental basis from 9 June to 4 July in 1975. It began on a regular basis on both BBC and ILR on 3 April 1978. (Televising of the Lords began in 1985 and of the Commons in 1989.)

Today's the Day

Six-part Radio 4 series in 1990 in which THE LOCAL NETWORK presenters, David Clayton and Neil Walker, followed some very different individuals through eventful days in their lives, from nineteen-year-old Steve Eccles

from Tyneside making his debut as 'Magnum – the high-calibre stripper' to 77-year-old Mrs Elsie McKean moving out of the house where she had lived for the past thirty years and into an old people's home in Southport.

Tokyo Rose

Name of a mythical siren of the airwaves broadcasting Japanese propaganda, in English, to US troops across the Pacific during the Second World War. Although, as the FBI later confirmed, 'Tokyo Rose' was a composite person because at least a dozen Japanese-American women were making such radio broadcasts, the idea grew among GIs that she was one person – mysterious and seductive.

One of the broadcasters was Los Angeles-born Iva Toguri (1918–) who appeared regularly on a show called *Zero Hour*. Although this subtly mocked her Japanese employers, she was prosecuted on treason charges in the USA in 1948. She was convicted on one of eight counts at the end of a trial which many regarded as a gross miscarriage of justice, and was jailed for ten years. She was released in 1956 but did not receive a full pardon until President Ford's last day in office in 1977.

Like LORD HAW-HAW, the nickname 'Tokyo Rose' has come to be used as a paradigm of a propaganda broadcaster, though during the Gulf War one such in Iraq was known as 'Baghdad Betty'.

Toleration and Freedom
Three-part Radio 3 series in 1990 in which Prof. Maurice Cranston of the LSE traced changing concepts of freedom via Erasmus, Locke and Voltaire.

Tom, Dick and Harry
Off-duty escapades of a soldier, sailor and airman featured in this Second World War comedy series.

Tomticketatom
One of BBC Radio's most brilliant music documentaries, which won three national awards as well as a PREMIOS ONDAS for its beguiling analysis of Ravel's Bolero from the point of view of those percussionists and wind players who have to play it. While they talked, the piece played on and on in the background. The programme went out on Radio 4 in 1987 to mark the 50th anniversary of Ravel's death.

Tong, Pete (1960–)
Record company talent spotter and club DJ who in January 1991 moved from Capital Radio to take over the Friday-night Radio 1 dance show from JEFF YOUNG. He first appeared on the network in 1981 on PETER POWELL's show and launched his own record label, FFRR, in 1988.

Took, Barry (1928–)
Commercial traveller's son who left school at fifteen and worked as an office boy for a music publisher. His gifts for making people laugh were first recognised in 1951, when he won a radio talent contest as a stand-up comedian, and he developed into a highly creative and successful comedy writer whose series have included BEYOND OUR KEN, ROUND THE HORNE and THE NEWS QUIZ.

Top 40
Radio 1's Sunday afternoon charts show, which BRUNO BROOKES used to present and MARK GOODIER does now. Radio 1 says that the final countdown attracts its biggest audience of the week. (See RADIO LUXEMBOURG for background as to why the show goes out on a Sunday.)

Top Gear
Influential show presented on Radio 1 by JOHN PEEL from 1967, promising 'the coolest sounds around on

Barry Took, fertile and good-humoured creator of much radio comedy. He co-wrote *Beyond Our Ken* (with Eric Merriman) and *Round the Horne* (mainly with Marty Feldman) and now chairs *The News Quiz*

disc'. It specialised in longer tracks and lesser known names and did much to help new bands win acceptance.

Top Of The Form
Long-running quiz show on the Light Programme, running from 1948–86. Immaculately behaved teams from rival secondary schools were politely if sometimes patronisingly questioned on their general knowledge by a succession of comperes. They included former IN TOWN TONIGHT presenter John Ellison, once described as 'the commentator with a smile in his voice'; Robert MacDermot; JOHN DUNN in the 1960s and BOB HOLNESS in the 1970s. Each school had to field a team of four, of different ages – under thirteen, under fourteen, under sixteen and under eighteen. In the first fifteen years, Scotland won eight times, Wales four and England three. The show, which later transferred to BBC-TV, launched Radio 2's former weatherwoman VIVIEN STUART, who captained her winning team in 1969 when she was at school in Torquay.

Top Of The Pops
(1) Thursday-night BBC1 programme now simultaneously broadcast on Radio 1.

(2) Weekly World Service show based on British chart hits and hosted by BRIAN MATTHEW since 1964.

Top Team
Light Programme series of general knowledge contests between schoolchildren throughout the Commonwealth.

Top Twenty
The first notes in the march of pop music into the Sabbath were sounded by this Radio Luxembourg show which began on a Sunday night in 1948, presented by TEDDY JOHNSON.

It was then a programme of the bestselling sheet music, and sponsored by Outdoor Girl lipstick; not until 1952, with the creation of the first pop chart in *New Musical Express*, did it develop into a programme of bestselling records.

Johnson did the show until June 1950; his successor Roger Moffatt disliked it and made way quickly for PETE MURRAY who in turn was replaced by BARRY ALLDIS. At its peak, in 1959, it was said by Luxembourg to have attracted twelve million listeners, which would put it among the most popular evening radio programmes ever heard in this country. There was, of course, no competition.

After pirates started in 1964, and Radio 1 in 1967, it lost most of its audience in common with all other Luxembourg shows. It had, nonetheless, started the trend of mounting Top Twenty programmes on a Sunday. This tradition was continued throughout the rest of radio – by PICK OF THE POPS, by Radio 1's THE TOP TWENTY SHOW and TOP 40, by ILR's NETWORK CHART SHOW and also by Jazz FM's charts programme.

Trying to buck a trend it had itself started, Luxembourg moved its chart show to Monday in the mid-1980s, in order not to compete with the mighty rivals of BBC and ILR. But audiences slipped and the station moved it back to its traditional Sunday home in October 1989.

The Top Twenty Show
Radio 1's Sunday afternoon charts show in the 1970s. Later it became TOP 40.

Torch, Sidney   (1908–90)
Creator of, and for most of his adult life associated with, FRIDAY NIGHT IS MUSIC NIGHT, for which he was dubbed 'Mr Friday Night' by one of its presenters, Jimmy Kingsbury.

Torch was also a versatile musician: a cinema organist in the 1930s at the Regal, Edmonton, a pianist in Albert Sandler's orchestra, a composer, e.g. of the signature tune of MUCH-BINDING-IN-THE-MARSH,

and a conductor, leading the QUEEN'S HALL LIGHT ORCHESTRA before taking charge of the BBC CONCERT ORCHESTRA. He started broadcasting in the 1930s and during the Second World War, while an air gunner with the RAF, he also played for the 'Double or Quits' quiz on the programme *Mediterranean Merry-Go-Round*.

Tough Cookies
Five determined women, not well known but all with stories to tell, told them to Jenny Cuffe in this conversation series in 1990 on Radio 4. They included Ghana-born Dora Boatemah, who has helped to transform a crime-ridden Brixton council estate; Sharley McLean, a campaigning Lesbian who arrived in Britain as a refugee from Nazi Germany; and Sheila Mottley, who in 1962 gave birth to a child damaged by Thalidomide.

Townsend, Sue   (1946–)
Creator of the immortal schoolboy Adrian Mole, who began life under a different Christian name altogether. Her thirty-minute play *The Diary of Nigel Mole Aged 13 3/4* went out on Radio 4 in 1982 and attracted Methuen so much that they commissioned a book. Townsend changed the boy's name to avoid confusion, and plumped for Adrian.

Her book, *The Secret Diary of Adrian Mole Aged 13 3/4* was serialised as a MORNING READING and the broadcasts were such a success that they helped to make the book a runaway bestseller. *The Growing Pains of Adrian Mole* was its sequel, broadcast on Radio 4 in 1984.

Toytown
One of the best loved parts of CHILDREN'S HOUR: 36 stories about the inhabitants of a happy, sunny, carefree land written by a book illustrator, S. Hulme Beaman. They were first broadcast in the 1930s, and many times since. Felix Felton played the Mayor of Toytown, DEREK MCCULLOCH immortalised himself as tremulous Larry the Lamb, Ralph de Rohan was Mr Grouser and NORMAN SHELLEY Captain Brass.

Tracy, Sheila   (1934–)
First woman to read the news on Radio 4, in August 1974 – eased in quietly on the midnight bulletin to avoid too many tremors. It was shortly before ANGELA RIPPON hit the headlines when she started reading the news on BBC-TV.

A former trombonist with the Ivy Benson Band, who later became one half of the female musical duo The Tracy Sisters, she also devised TRUCKERS' HOUR on Radio 2 and has introduced BIG BAND SPECIAL since it began in 1979.

Live for long-distance lorry drivers, between 1 and 2 a.m., *Truckers' Hour* played Country and Western music and requests for truckers and used Citizen's Band nicknames which they might find amusing. Tracy presented this rather louche show throughout its run in 1981–82, but eventually landed in hot water when she advised drivers over the air: 'Keep the lipstick off the dipstick'.

She says she had innocently found the phrase in a CB dictionary, and just decided to read it out, but was shortly afterwards reprimanded by a furious DAVID HATCH, then Controller of Radio 2. Shortly afterwards the show finished, and has never returned.

Trad Tavern

'The hostelry where lovers of live jazz and pop records meet' was how this Light Programme series billed itself shortly after it began. The 'tavern' was in fact the plush AEOLIAN HALL in Bond Street, which was where Chris Barber and other bandleaders went to make the jiving couples gyrate. PICK OF THE POPS started as a part of the show.

The Trade Rag

Radio 4 series examining four trade papers, including *The Stage* and *Police Review*, in 1989–90.

Transatlantic Quiz

Wartime series replaced by ROUND BRITAIN QUIZ.

Transistor

The successor to the VALVE, and one which enabled radio sets to be much smaller and sturdier, thereby putting them into the hands of the masses and making them truly portable.

Its development dates from the discovery, in 1948, of a new kind of crystal, germanium, a semi-conductor which could perform all the functions of a valve but without its bulk – because it was solid and required no vacuum. It consumed less power, produced less heat and operated at lower voltages. It was also much stronger than a valve and there was no delay while it heated up.

Three US scientists made the discovery: John Bardeen (1908–), Walter Brattain (1902–87) and William Shockley (1910–). The word 'transistor' (which refers to the fact that the device transmits current across a resistor) was coined by the American electrical engineer John Pierce (1910–) and first used in 1948.

Hearing aids were the first transistorised devices sold to the public, in 1953. But radios were close behind. The first transistor radio in the USA went on sale in 1954 (called 'The Regency') and the first transistor radio made in Britain appeared in 1956 (called 'Pam', and made by PYE).

'With so many nationalities caught up in the tide of war, the transistor radio tuned to London is a vital link for millions of people across the region' – John Tusa, when the Gulf War erupted in January 1991.

Petula Clark with Britain's first transistor radio when it was launched by its makers, Pye, in February 1956. In her left hand is one of the set's transistors. The set cost 30 guineas, a fortune in its day, but was claimed to run for five hours for only a penny

Travis, Dave Lee (–)

Mancunian who became a DJ in local clubs, toured the USA with Herman's Hermits, worked aboard RADIO CAROLINE (SOUTH) and then joined Radio 1. He succeeded NOEL EDMONDS as host of the breakfast show. He had a bestseller in 1976 with a record called 'Convoy GB', made with fellow disc-jockey PAUL BURNETT. They called themselves 'Laurie Lingo and the Dipsticks'. It reached Number 4 in the charts.

In 1990 the BBC revealed in LONDON CALLING that his World Service series, *A Jolly Good Show*, received the biggest postbag of all the English programmes – about 800 letters a month.

Treasure Islands

Literary, elitist Radio 4 series which is the only slot devoted purely to children's books on national British radio. Reviews books; profiles authors; interviews writers and illustrators and occasionally allows us to hear from children as to what they like. But this is a programme about children and not for them. The original presenter, when it began in 1987, was novelist Penelope Lively. She was succeeded in 1989 by children's writer Michael Rosen.

Treble Chance
Travelling quiz show on the Light Programme, which ran from 1962. Teams which often featured Nan Winton and WYNFORD VAUGHAN-THOMAS had to answer general knowledge questions and also identify sounds, voices, snatches of music and so on. Typical of the questions were these: Who was the last commoner to rule over Britain? If you had epistaxis, what would you be suffering from? And what would you do with a calumet? (Answers: Richard Cromwell, 1658–60; nose-bleeding; smoke it.)

Producer Michael Tuke-Hastings estimated in 1966 that during the first four years he and the panel had clocked up over 60,000 miles by road, rail and air in making the programme.

Trethowan, Sir Ian (1922–90)
Managing Director of BBC Radio from 1970–76. He sacked a Radio 1 disc-jockey (KENNY EVERETT) for his rude joke about a politician's wife but also allowed a female to read the news on Radio 4 for the first time (SHEILA TRACY). In 1977 he succeeded Sir Charles Curran as Director-General.

Trivia Test Match
Celebrity quiz based on the rules of cricket, on Radio 4. The two team captains are Tim Rice and William Rushton with BRIAN JOHNSTON as the amiable umpire. The show has been broadcast from many village cricket clubs.

The Trouble With You, Lilian
Series featuring Beryl Reid as the irascible Madge and PATRICIA HAYES as her long-suffering lodger, Lilian.

Truckers' Hour
Too rude for Radio 2! See SHEILA TRACY.

True Story
Dramatised real-life stories on the Light Programme, presented as a weekly series, featuring such heart-in-the-mouth incidents as the airline pilot who had to ditch his plane in the Pacific Ocean.

Truth To Tell
Four extraordinary but true stories told by ANTHONY SMITH on Radio 4 in 1990, with a second series coming.

T.T.F.N.
('Ta-Ta For Now') Catchphrase of MRS MOPP in ITMA.

Tudge, Colin (1943–)
Freelance broadcaster on scientific topics. A Cambridge zoology graduate, he was features editor of the *New Scientist* from 1980–84. Since then he has been closely associated with Radio 3, where he has presented two series of *Science on 3* and three of SPECTRUM. Also the author of several books on ecology, conservation and food production.

Tuesday Call
Radio 4 phone-in series which, true to its name, went out on Tuesdays and covered a variety of topics from how to treat household pests to more serious matters. Presenters included SUE MACGREGOR.

The programme which attracted the greatest number of calls was in 1985, when Princess Anne became the first member of the Royal Family to appear on a phone-in. It was also the first live radio interview she had given. More than 5,000 people tried to reach the Royal presence, but only 25 succeeded. The Princess revealed she owned three dogs, including a lurcher, and that people had told her she was 'quite good' at making scrambled eggs.

Later the programme became CALL NICK ROSS but the slot remained the same, immediately after the 9 a.m. news.

Tuning In
Trawl of the BBC SOUND ARCHIVES in three parts by Michael Bentine, one of the original stars of THE GOON SHOW, on Radio 4 in 1990.

Tuning Up
Weekend Radio 3 series aimed at younger listeners created by JOHN DRUMMOND and launched in 1990. Presented by Chris de Souza, it allows young(ish) musicians not only to play, but also to explain what, how and why they play.

Turbulent Priests
Radio 4 series in 1989–90 in which Dr Edward Norman talked to Archbishop Desmond Tutu, Rabbi Meir Kehane and Father Daniel Berrigan about the theologies which guided their beliefs and actions.

Turkish Service
The BBC has been putting out Turkish-language programmes since November 1939. Today, they are on the air for just over ninety minutes a day.

Turning Points
The day Michael Bentine saw Belsen at the end of the Second World War, poet Seamus Heaney's decision in 1972 to leave Ulster and move with his family to a tiny cottage in the Republic of Ireland, Margaret Jay's

decision to give up her job as a TV reporter to run the government's National Aids Trust ('I stopped just observing and started *doing*') – these were three of the landmarks in the lives of celebrated people explored by Bel Mooney in this Radio 4 series in the late 1980s.

Tusa, John (1936–)
Presenter of THE WORLD TONIGHT in the late 1960s who also presented TWENTY-FOUR HOURS. After seven years of anchoring BBC2's *Newsnight* he was made Managing Director of the BBC External Services in September 1986, on a six-year contract. He subsequently changed the name of the whole organisation to the BBC World Service.

Twenty Questions in 1949: Stewart MacPherson in the chair and Richard Dimbleby on the panel. Listeners, as well as the studio audience, knew that the next object was 'Forty Winks', but the team had to guess it by asking no more than twenty perceptive questions

Czech by birth: born in Zlin, he came to England with his family at the age of three and became a British citizen in 1947. Fluent, bright (a historian and author of two books) and widely admired, both inside and outside the BBC.

Twelve O'Clock Spin
Record show at noon on weekdays on the Light Programme.

Twenty Questions
Game of antique origins brought to life in 1947. Its first chairman was slick Canadian STEWART MAC-PHERSON, followed by volatile GILBERT HARDING (sacked for being drunk on air). Panellists included ANONA WINN, RICHARD DIMBLEBY, Jack Train (one of the ITMA stars), Joy Adamson and Daphne Padel.

The show was hugely popular, not least with Royalty, and ran until 1976 on BBC Radio; it also went out on Luxembourg.

Twenty-Four Hours

BBC World Service programme of comment and analysis on the day's main news stories. It dates from 1965, but reached a new, domestic, audience when Radio 5 started taking it in 1990.

20-Something

Short Radio 4 series in 1990 with Stephanie Calman looking at three people in their twenties who had turned their backs on convention.

2LO

Station opened by MARCONI in May 1922 in The Strand, London, which within months became the BBC's first radio station. From here the British Broadcasting Company (see BBC) commenced daily broadcasting on 14 November 1922, when Arthur Burrows read the first news bulletin. In February 1923, 2LO moved to bigger premises at 2 Savoy Hill, adjacent to the Savoy Hotel and just off the Embankment, and lived on until 1930 and the creation of the two BBC radio programme services, the National Programme and Regional Programme. '2LO Calling' were the words that preceded all 2LO programmes from Marconi House in The Strand, and this call-sign was also used for a short time after the move to Savoy Hill.

Two Counties Radio

ILR station for Bournemouth, on the air since 1980.

210

Reading-based ILR station covering Reading since 1976 and extending its service to Basingstoke and Andover in 1987.

Two-Way Family Favourites

'Records for Service men and women stationed abroad and their families at home' was the essence of this popular Light Programme show which went out at Sunday lunchtimes. Before 1960 it was known as FAMILY FAVOURITES. The famous presenters were CLIFF MICHELMORE and JEAN METCALFE, whose story of how they met and married is one of radio's most romantic.

U

Uncle Mac
See DEREK MCCULLOCH.

Uncle Mort
See PETER TINNISWOOD.

Under Milk Wood
The most celebrated piece of radio Britain has yet produced. Dylan Thomas's ninety-minute 'play for voices' about the inhabitants of a small Welsh village, Llareggub, bursting with some of the richest verse and ripest imagery of any poem in the language, was first broadcast in January 1954 on the Third Programme, two months after its author's death.

The producer was DOUGLAS CLEVERDON, who spent seven years persuading, cajoling and encouraging Thomas to write it. The music was written by Daniel Jones (1913–), a symphonic conductor and friend of Thomas from boyhood.

It was repeated four times, broadcast on the World Service (or General Overseas Service as it still was) six times, translated for the German Service and released as a record – all in the same year. It was repeated, on either Third, Home or Radio 4, in 1955, 1956, 1957, 1960 and 1972. Cleverdon made a new production in 1963 and, as in the original, Richard Burton played the narrator, First Voice. A third production launched Radio 4's HI-FI THEATRE slot in 1978.

It was staged at the Edinburgh Festival, in the West End and on Broadway (1956–57), televised by the BBC (1957) and turned into a film (directed by Andrew Sinclair, and starring Richard Burton and Elizabeth Taylor, 1971). It is now being turned into a cartoon film by the Welsh animation house Siriol, for screening on both BBC and S4C in 1992.

In an incomplete state, it received public readings in the USA in 1953 (in which Thomas himself participated) and was published as a book both there and in Britain in 1954, after its broadcast. It has been translated into most European languages, including Welsh, and also Japanese.

Commissioned by the FEATURES DEPARTMENT of BBC Radio, *Under Milk Wood* stemmed from a talk which Thomas gave on the Welsh Home Service in 1945 called *Early One Morning*. It needs a cast of 74 individual adult voices, as well as a chorus of children. Actors in Cleverdon's first production included Hugh Griffith (Captain Cat), Diana Maddox (Polly Garter), Philip Burton (The Rev. Eli Jenkins) and Rachel Roberts (Mrs Dai Bread Two).

The most stirring voice was that of Richard Burton, although he was not the original choice because the author himself was going to play First Voice. Nobody knows what Thomas would have been like in the radio production. But the combination of his poetry and Burton's voice is unforgettable, as in these famous opening lines:

'To begin at the beginning: It is spring, moonless night in the small town, starless and Bible-black, the cobblestreets silent and the hunched, courters' and rabbits' wood limping invisible down to the sloeback, slow, black, crowblack, fishingboat-bobbing sea ... '

'He conscripts metaphors, rapes the dictionary, and builds a verbal bawdy-house whose words mate and couple on the wing' – Kenneth Tynan, reviewing it at the Edinburgh Festival in 1956.

'One of the great events for the human ear' – Gwyn Thomas.

The Unfair Quiz
Radio 2 general knowledge game in 1988 devised and chaired by John Junkin, with celebrity guests and the accent firmly on knockabout comedy.

Unique Broadcasting Company
Formed in 1989, with Capital Radio owning 24 per cent of it, to make sponsored shows for the expanding commercial radio market. It was part of the consortium which brought Fiat-sponsored match commentaries in the 1990 World Cup on to the airwaves of 55 ILR stations.

Uncle Mac burning the midnight oil in 1946. Every year, *Children's Hour* had a 'Request Week' in which listeners were urged to send in postcards nominating their favourite items from the programme. Tens of thousands of cards poured in

Directors included NOEL EDMONDS (returning to radio after ten years in television), Michael Peacock (former Controller of both BBC1 and BBC2), TIM BLACKMORE and Simon Cole. The last two had previously been at PPM, where they had pioneered sponsored programming, and which they left after its parent company Piccadilly Radio was taken over by Miss World.

In 1990, Miss World disposed of PPM and sold its two shows AMERICAN COUNTDOWN and ROCKLINE – to Unique.

Up Before the Bench
Ludovic Kennedy looked at the daily work of magistrates, not just in dealing with lawbreakers, but also child abuse, maintenance orders, pub licensing, bar extensions and so on, in this Radio 4 FM series in 1988.

Up The Garden Path
Radio 4 sitcom written by SUE LIMB, starting in 1987, with Imelda Staunton as a teacher, Izzy Comyn, whose Christian name fits her character – dizzy. She has two loves in her life, chocolate and a married colleague called Michael (Nicholas Le Prevost).

The show was rejected by BBC-TV. Granada then snapped it up and turned it into a six-part series, with the same leading actors, for screening on ITV. This was one of five Radio 4 light entertainment shows within two years whose television potential the BBC failed to see in time. All of them were consequently seized by ITV or Channel 4. (See COMEDY.)

The Upper Hand
Radio 4 series in 1989 in which Dylan Winter looked at dentists, garage mechanics, solicitors and cleaning ladies,

four professions which (according to him) somehow manage to retain subtle control over their clients.

Urdu Service

Programmes in the Urdu language were first broadcast (see EASTERN SERVICE) in 1940. Urdu and Hindi Services began on the same day and both were aimed at the Indian subcontinent.

In the beginning they were simply daily news summaries: today the Urdu Service is on the air for about ninety minutes a day, with its predominantly news and current affairs coverage carrying an emphasis on South Asia. It attracts an audience (in 1990) of 8.4 million in Pakistan and 1.9 million in Uttar Pradesh and Delhi alone, with more listeners in the Gulf States.

Because of the Gulf audience, the service was extended by ten minutes a day as part of a thirty-minute programme along with Hindi and Bengali, going out at lunchtime to the Gulf each day during the 1991 war.

V

Valves

Developed by a British electrical engineer, John Fleming (1849–1945), who in 1904 invented a rectifier which let electricity flow in only one direction. This became known as a radio valve (or, in the USA, a 'tube') and was of key importance in enabling radios to work.

Their disadvantages were many. They had to be big enough to enclose a vacuum, which was why early radio sets were large, chunky pieces of furniture. They were fragile, frequently needed replacing, and didn't work straight away because of a delay while the filament heated up. The advent of TRANSISTORS, which replaced valves from the mid-1950s onwards, consigned these difficulties to history, even if transistor radios did not possess the richness and resonance of tone of valve sets.

In Britain, valves are still made for transmitters, but no longer for domestic radios. However, there are an estimated forty million valves still in existence, so replacements are plentiful. One of the few who still makes valve radio sets is GERRY WELLS, in a workshop at the bottom of his garden in Dulwich. He sells as many as he can build.

Vance, Tommy (–)

Radio 1 DJ who has presented his heavy metal rock show on Friday nights since 1978. Iron Maiden and Def Leppard both featured in the tenth anniversary programme. He joined the network after stints on Radio Luxembourg, Radio Caroline and Radio London. Before that he had two spells in the USA, working in radio on the West Coast.

Variations On St Louis

Radio 2 series in 1990 in which jazz musician and writer Miles Kington looked at the role of jazz composers.

Variety Bandbox

BBC variety series from the early 1940s to early 1950s. Derek Roy, Max Wall, Reg Dixon and Frankie Howerd were regulars, as was ex-painter and decorator Arthur English who played the resident comedian and Prince of the Wide Boys. His catchphrase was 'Play the music, open the cage!' – a meaningless piece of jumble he came out with one night and which stuck.

Variety Playhouse

Home Service series which in 1953 took over the Saturday-evening variety slot running since the 1920s. *Variety* began the tradition, in April 1927; shortly after *Vaudeville* took over and became established by 1928–29, continuing until late in 1933. Later it changed its title to *Music-Hall* and ran until 1952 (an edition in October 1934 contained the broadcasting debut of Vic Oliver, later the first castaway on DESERT ISLAND DISCS). A short gap was filled by *The Star Show* before *Variety Playhouse* began in 1953. It continued until 1963. ELSIE AND DORIS WATERS, ARTHUR ASKEY and Ronnie Barker all appeared on it.

The change in content in the slot also reflected the evolution of this sort of popular entertainment. Music-hall comedy acts gave way to situation comedy and character actors, and music-hall songs were succeeded by musical comedy, pop and operetta.

Vaughan, Paul (1925–)

Former chief press officer for the British Medical Association (1959–64) who left to become a freelance, straddling both arts and sciences. He has been a presenter of KALEIDOSCOPE since it started and also hosted Radio 3's *Record Review* from 1982–88. On the screen his interests are more towards science: he was the principal narrator for BBC2's *Horizon* for twenty years and has narrated other documentaries both for television and the technical film and video industry.

Vaughan-Thomas, Wynford (1908–87)

Lyrical, eloquent, versatile Welsh commentator who infused his broadcasts with Celtic passion and vivid imagery. He once described talk as 'the divine amalgam that holds civilisation together, the lovely whitewash of words poured over the asperities of life to make them bearable'.

Wynford Vaughan-Thomas, able to re-live vivid memories four years before his death. Aboard a Lancaster bomber in a night raid on the German capital, he produced some of the most memorable reporting of the Second World War

A friend of Dylan Thomas, whom he first met at Swansea Grammar School, he began broadcasting in 1937 as an outside broadcasts assistant in Cardiff and was one of those who commentated on King George VI's Coronation.

He is remembered particularly for his reporting in the Second World War. In 1943 he flew in a Lancaster bomber in a night raid on Berlin, describing the terrifying 'bullring' of searchlights and flak. He covered the Anzio landings, the Allied entry into Rome and Montgomery's crossing of the Rhine, ending up making a memorable broadcast in Hamburg from the studios which WILLIAM JOYCE had used only a day or two previously for his final, drunken, rambling address to the world – with Joyce's script and empty bottle of gin still lying on the desk.

In peace, he provided words for some of the country's greatest occasions, from VJ Night in 1945 to the Royal Wedding in 1981. He also presented Radio 4's THE COUNTRYSIDE IN ... series for many years until his death.

The Verdict Of The Court
Home Service series of reconstructions of famous trials with postscripts by Lord Birkett.

VHF
(Very High Frequency) Broadcasts which are in the range of 87.5 to 108 MegaHertz. Radio 2 goes out on VHF only, Radio 3 is expecting to from around the end of 1991, and so do many local stations, both BBC and non-BBC. Radio 1 will also become VHF-only when its medium wave frequencies suffer the same fate as Radio 3's and are taken away for an INR channel. See also FM.

Vietnamese Service
Programmes in the Vietnamese language first went out from BUSH HOUSE in January 1952. In 1990 they were increased by a quarter of an hour a day, and there are now nearly nine hours every week.

A View from the Boundary

Saturday lunchtime talk, by a celebrity who happens to be passionate about cricket, which has become a popular part of Radio 3's TEST MATCH SPECIAL. It goes out in every Test match held in England.

Ben Travers, then 94, was one of the first celebrities who appeared, during the Lord's Test against the West Indies in 1980. He reminisced fluently about great players he had known, starting with W.G. Grace in 1896.

Other speakers have included Christopher Lee, John Alderton and MICHAEL CHARLTON, and one of the most unusual was that given by blind pianist George Shearing, who explained why he always visited England for the cricket each summer and what kind of 'view' he experienced.

Viking

Hull-based ILR station for the Humberside region, on the air since 1984. In 1986 it became the first ILR station to split its services, albeit only at weekends, so that listeners could have a choice of Rugby League on medium wave or music on FM. This paved the way for a much more extensive use of the splitting device by other ILR stations, most of whom now practise it. In 1989 Viking launched Classic Gold, offering golden oldies, as its medium wave service.

Vincent, Robbie (–)

Champion of jazz-funk, soul and dance music while at BBC Radio London in the 1970s and early 1980s. He hosted a weekend soul show on Radio 1 until January 1990, then joined ex-pirate Kiss FM when it went on the air legitimately the following September, again hosting a weekend show devoted to his favourite music.

Visiting Lives

Radio 4 series on biographers, each of whom appears twice – first to talk about his own work and then, the following week, to interview a fellow practitioner about his approach. Bevis Hillier, Humphrey Carpenter, Ann Thwaite and Andrew Motion were among those who were featured.

Viva Garibaldi

Six-part Radio 4 series in 1989 in which David Bean travelled in the footsteps of Giuseppe Garibaldi, one of the key figures responsible for the unification of Italy.

Voice of America

International American broadcaster, funded by the US government, which began in 1942. Initially it broadcast only in German but now this has swelled to 43 languages (a few more than the World Service).

It works under a charter requiring it to be balanced, but also has to present statements of US policy the content of which is determined by the State Department and White House. It has admitted that, at the height of the Cold War, it felt itself to be engaged in a battle for the hearts and minds of its Eastern European audience with Radio Moscow.

Voice Of The Listener

Energetic and indefatigable pressure group formed in 1983 by JOCELYN HAY to campaign for the maintenance of high Reithian standards on radio, especially in an era of greater deregulation. It claims that it was its pressure that resulted in the World Service being broadcast on Radio 4 long wave after midnight. It was also noted for its tireless lobbying during the passage through Parliament of the BROADCASTING ACT of 1990.

In 1991 it announced that it was launching an annual award scheme for radio, with the first winners being announced in November 1991. It said there would be two awards, both based on members' votes: one for the outstanding programme or series on a national network and the other for the outstanding contributor to a national network, whether as actor, presenter or reporter.

Voice Of The People

Early phone-in series on Radio 4, organised from Pebble Mill.

Voices

Radio 2 series in which DAVE GELLY examined the style and techniques of several of the world's greatest singing stars, including Ella Fitzgerald, Louis Armstrong and Rosemary Clooney.

Voices of the Americas

Three-part Radio 3 series in 1990 drawing thumbnail sketches of some of the enduring American musical traditions including Latin, ragtime, songs from slavery and the 'great outdoors' of the prairies.

Vosburgh, Dick (1929–)

New Jersey-born, he came to Britain in 1949 to attend RADA. Has worked as an actor (e.g. on CHILDREN'S HOUR), a writer (co-writing 93 editions of THE SHOW BAND SHOW, and writing and narrating programmes on his idols S.J. Perelman and George S. Kaufman) and as a panellist (where his appearances have ranged from ON THE AIR to SCREENPLAY, on which he is a resident). He co-wrote the West End and Broadway stage hit *A Day in Hollywood, A Night in the Ukraine.*

Vox Pops

Weekday evening sequence on Radio 5 aimed at youngsters – progressively older ones as the evening goes on.

Ingredients include serials, plays and favourite stories and its programmes have included EUROMIX, SPORTING ALBUMS, IN THE HOT SEAT, FANSHAWE ON FIVE, *Cult Heroes*, FORMULA FIVE and TALKING POETRY.

A Voyage of Discovery
Enjoyable four-part Radio 4 series in 1990 in which JOHN MORTIMER talked about, and played extracts from, opera from the standpoint of someone whose discovery of its pleasures was comparatively recent.

W

Wade, David (1929–)
Radio critic for THE LISTENER (1964–67) then *The Times* (1967–89). Has also had several works broadcast on Radios 3 and 4, including adaptations, plays, schools programmes and documentaries.

Waggoners' Walk
Suburban soap opera which went out every afternoon from Monday to Friday for eleven years, from 1969 to 1980. The first story in this Radio 2 saga was written by Alan Downer and Jill Hyem, who also wrote the last episode (Number 2,824) in May 1980.

The Waiting Game
Radio 4 FM series in 1990 about pregnancy. It lasted nine weeks – one week for every month – and was presented by the indefatigable Anneka Rice, who admitted to having planned her own baby 'like a military operation'.

Wakelam, Lt-Col Henry Blythe Thornhill (1893–1963)
Former Harlequins captain who gave the first running sports commentary to be broadcast in Britain, the England v. Wales rugby international at Twickenham in 1927 (see LANCE SIEVEKING). Quick-witted and regarded as a natural in the job, he went on to make the first television commentary of a Test match, in 1938, which was England v. Australia at Lord's. Generally known as Teddy Wakelam.

Walker, Johnnie (1945–)
DJ whose rebellious streak, nurtured at school in Solihull, led him out to sea in the direction of the pirates. At 21 he started as a DJ on Radio England-Britain Radio before moving to Radio Caroline, staying aboard when it decided to defy the banning legislation of 1967, but eventually joining Radio 1 in 1969. When he quit in the 1970s he went to San Francisco, recording a weekly show there which was broadcast on Radio Luxembourg. He has also appeared on Radio Radio and Capital, and now presents a programme about families on Radio 5.

Walters, John (1939–)
Former art teacher at a Newcastle comprehensive, and trumpeter with the Alan Price Set from 1965 to 1967 (appearing on the bill at the Empire Pool, Wembley, on The Beatles' last British appearance) who joined Radio 1 at its birth as a staff producer. He left the BBC staff in 1991.

Produced most of the programmes of JOHN PEEL after 1969. Also had his own series on Radio 1 called WALTERS WEEKLY. In 1990 he had another series, *Largely Walters*, this time on Radio 4, in which he considered subjects as diverse as cannibalism and trainspotting.

Walters Weekly
Irreverent Radio 1 series in the early 1980s in which the talkative JOHN WALTERS presented a round-up of leisure and the arts.

War Report
Nightly bulletin of war reporting from Europe which ran from D-Day on 6 June 1944, through to the German surrender in May 1945. It was broadcast after the main 9 p.m. NEWS.

Warner, Sir Pelham (1873–1963)
Former England cricket captain (whose MCC teams won the Ashes in 1903–04 and 1911–12) who has a niche in radio history as the person who gave the first eye-witness description of a cricket match heard on the BBC, a close-of-play report of the match between Surrey and Hampshire at The Oval on 7 May 1927. He was at the time editor of *The Cricketer*, a post later held by CHRISTOPHER MARTIN-JENKINS.

'Plum', as was his nickname, continued to give occasional talks until the 1940s, although the BBC considered his delivery too 'melancholy' and that he was not a natural broadcaster.

War Report owed much to the skill of correspondents such as Frank Gillard. Here, assisted by Lieut. H.G. Robson of the Royal Corps of Signals who is holding the microphone, he filed his despatch from the Normandy beachhead on 18 June 1944

Warriss, Ben
See JIMMY JEWEL.

Waters, Elsie and Doris (1895–1990 and ?-1978)
Sisters who became, through radio, one of Britain's best loved comedy acts, the Cockney gossips Gert and Daisy.

They always wrote their own scripts, had the proud claim that they never used the same sketch twice and invented an array of working-class characters that included their menfolk (Bert and Wally) and Old Mother Butler. They and their five siblings, one of whom, Jack Warner, later played BBC's *Dixon of Dock Green*, were offspring of an East End funeral furnisher and the concerns and aspirations of ordinary people were always central to their work.

Making their wireless debut in 1927, the sisters graced the BBC airwaves for almost half a century. Although it was not until after 1945 that they starred in their own shows – *Gert and Daisy's Working Party*, *Petticoat Lane* and FLOGGIT'S – their heyday was during the Second World War itself, when shows like ACK-ACK BEER-BEER, NAVY MIXTURE, WORKERS' PLAY-TIME, concerts for the troops and propaganda broadcasts for the Ministry of Food made them a national institution.

Their Cockney chit-chat would usually include exhortations to 'eat more oatmeal' or 'grow green vegetables'. Indeed, their status was such that LORD HAW-HAW once said in a broadcast from Germany that 'the good folk of Grimsby should not expect Gert and Daisy to protect them from attacks by the Luftwaffe'.

Waterlines
Messing about in boats was the essence of this weekly Radio 4 magazine, hosted by CLIFF MICHELMORE.

Wax Works
Radio 4 series in 1988 in which ROBIN RAY traced the history of gramophone records, from 78s to CDs.

The Way of Life
Sunday evening religious programme in several regions of the Home Service in the 1950s and 1960s, in which 'Christians think about their faith and its living expression'.

The Way of the World
One of the earliest talk series based on the news, presented by Vernon Bartlett in the 1930s.

We Beg To Differ
A mock war between the sexes was the essence of this discussion programme between four women (JOYCE GRENFELL, Kay Hammond, Gladys Young and Charmian Innes) and two men (CHARLES HILL and John Clements, who was Kay's husband). It began in 1949. The fact that it was thought necessary for four women to take on only two men was in itself controversial. The chairman was ROY PLOMLEY. Topics discussed included 'Womanly Intuition' and 'Should Women Design Kitchens?'

After a month Hill dropped out, pleading pressure of work. He was replaced at first by the broadcaster Herbert Hodge, a former taxi-driver. GILBERT HARDING later replaced him. He made it a great success – starting him on his career as a grumpy, cantankerous, self-opinionated pundit of the airwaves which lasted many years.

Listeners did not always approve of what they heard. A withering George Bernard Shaw wrote in the *Daily Mail* in March 1950:

'A few weeks ago some distressed person wrote to the BBC asking how snoring could be cured. Four picked, clever women, some of them mothers, had to tackle this question.

'Not one of them knew the answer, which was given to me by my father 80 years ago and to the whole English-speaking world at large by George Catlin in 1861.

'The absurdity of the BBC speakers' suggestions ranged from soundproof walls and floors to the addition of snoring to cruelty, adultery and desertion as grounds for divorce.

'My father told me simply to keep my mouth shut and always breathe through my nose. I obeyed, and have never snored.'

Wear FM
Station for Sunderland, on FM, running since November 1990. It was the last of the two dozen INCREMENTALS to come on air.

Weather
The BBC's first daily weather forecast was on 26 March 1923, the beginning of one of the most ubiquitous services in the whole of radio.

Week Ending
Longest running comedy show in British radio history: a topical, satirical, Friday-night revue on Radio 4, which is repeated (despite its jokes often being far ruder than anything on television) the following afternoon.

Beginning in 1970, produced by SIMON BRETT and DAVID HATCH, the show was initially hosted by BBC-TV's *Nationwide* anchorman Michael Barratt, who on the 20th anniversary recalled his role as 'slightly embarrassing' because he hadn't known if he was meant to be funny or not.

The show had an all-male cast – a throwback to the old tradition of university revue – for the first seven years, until Sheila Steafel arrived as the first Mrs Thatcher (previously it had been David Tate with a high voice). After five years she was succeeded by Tracey Ullman (1982–83) and then Sally Grace, who alone has provided Mrs Thatcher's voice ever since (in contrast to John Major, who is played by more than one actor).

Other long running actors have included Bill Wallis, now in his 21st year (in 1991), David Jason, who was on the programme for twelve years, and NIGEL REES, who stayed for five.

In the early days the whole 25-minute show was written by one man, Pete Spence (who later wrote TO THE MANOR BORN), fresh out of university. Clearly this could not be sustained and the show has encouraged scores of comic writers over the years. It has employed hundreds of non-commissioned writers, some of them contributing only the briefest quips or one-liners, plus 65 commissioned writers, and has also had 27 producers. These have included Griff Rhys Jones and Jimmy Mulville, both of them going on to make their fortune in television comedy, and DOUGLAS ADAMS, creator of A HITCH-HIKER'S GUIDE TO THE GALAXY.

The programme blends waspish writing with skilled mimicry and pokes fun at people in power for 44 weeks a year. It was considered too sensitive to have on the air during general election time until 1987.

Like most political satire of the last decade, it used to reserve special scorn for the dominating figure of Mrs Thatcher, joking that her one orgasm in recent years was when the *Belgrano* was sunk. In 1989, BBC Enterprises brought out a cassette called *Ten Years With Maggie*, a compilation of ten years of sketches which mimicked, insulted and parodied her. The following year former Liberal leader Sir David Steel, well used to being ridiculed on the programme himself, presented a two-part documentary on Radio 4 to mark the show's 20th birthday.

Politicians seem to regard the programme as rather toothless – a good example of the old adage about imitation being the sincerest form of flattery – and even DEREK JAMESON has now lost most of his enmity. In 1980 he became the first person to sue it for libel after a savage sketch written by John Langdon described him 'the archetypal East End boy made bad' and a 'nitty-gritty titivation tout'. To the strains of Elgar's King of the Barbarians, it went on to say he was a man 'who is to journalism what lockjaw is to conversation, and who still believes that erudite is a glue.'

Four years later, at the end of a highly publicised High Court case, a jury decided that although the words were defamatory they were not malicious. Jameson lost the case and was faced with a bill of £75,000, a disaster which was to be turned into triumph when the BBC picked him up and made a highly successful broadcaster out of him.

'When it started we thought we were rather daring. We never thought it would end up as an alternative *Down Your Way*' – Simon Brett.

The Week in the Garden
See C.H. MIDDLETON.

The Week in Westminster
The world's longest running political programme began in November 1929 as a straight talk aimed specifically at women, following Parliament's decision the previous year to give the vote to women under thirty.

It went out on Wednesdays at 10.45 a.m. which was 'the time we find most busy working women can listen best, when they have their cup of tea', as the first producer Marjorie Wace wrote in a letter to Nancy Astor, the first woman MP to take her seat in the Commons. Underlining this, Director-General JOHN REITH said the programme was 'chiefly for the benefit of housewives', who were assumed to have less time to read newspapers than men. But it was not simply *for* women, it was *by* women. There were fourteen women MPs in 1929 and during the series each of them gave a live, fifteen-minute talk on what the House had been up to. The first was Mrs Mary Agnes Hamilton, MP for Blackburn.

Within two years, male MPs were sometimes being allowed into this female sanctuary and a strict rota system was introduced to maintain a balance between the political parties and keep the Whips happy. In 1941, *The Week In Westminster* shifted to a peak-time slot of 7.45 on Saturday evenings and was presented by Lloyd George's daughter, Megan Lloyd George MP. She was told by the Director of Talks to keep the programme lively as it came at 'a favourite listening time immediately preceding a highspot variety programme known as *Oi*'.

Guy Burgess, later exposed as a traitor, was a producer at one point. But instead of political talks, he wanted political access. As an early champion of the broadcasting of Parliament he wrote in a BBC memo in 1937: 'Speeches are meant to be heard and not read.' It was another forty years before those words came true.

Today, interviewees on the programme come from both Commons and Lords but are normally backbenchers, still engaged in the task set out in the 1920s of telling listeners about their week's activities. Presenters tend to be senior political commentators, such as Peter Jenkins and Robin Oakley. Robert Carvel (1919–90) was for many years the main presenter (as well as being political editor of the London *Evening Standard*) and presented a special 60th birthday edition of TWIW, whose pungent atmosphere perhaps accounts for the fact that it attracts a slightly younger audience than Radio 4's as a whole.

The Week's Good Cause
The longest running programme on British radio, and listed as such in *The Guinness Book of Records*. It has been broadcast on Sundays on the Home Service ever since it began in January 1926, initially in the evenings but now at 8.50 in the morning. (Although the first *ever* radio appeal is recorded by the BBC as having been made in February 1923, by Ian Hay on behalf of the Winter Distress League, which raised £27 6s. 6d.)

Appeals policy, though refined over the years, still follows the terms of reference established by the first Appeals Advisory Committee, in 1927: 'In general, appeals should be restricted to causes which concern themselves with the relief of distress, the preservation of life and health, and the amelioration of social conditions.' Thus, as the present statement of Policy and Practice (last revised in 1975) makes clear, charities for whom appeals are broadcast have usually to be concerned 'with the alleviation of human suffering' – which explains why animal welfare charities are seldom heard.

The amounts raised vary enormously. In 1987 the lowest was £989 and the highest £42,070. In 1988, likewise, the range was £1,141 (LIBBY PURVES, for Maternity Alliance) to £57,010 (Jocelyn Brewer, for the National Deaf-Blind League). In 1989 the range was from £1,493 (Dame Judi Dench, for the Greater London Alcohol Advisory Service) to £71,062 (Sir Richard Attenborough, for the Muscular Dystrophy Group). In 1990 KATIE BOYLE raised £2,573 for the Association to Aid the Sexual and Personal Relationships of People with a Disability (SPOD), while BRIAN REDHEAD raised £108,663 for Crisis (formerly Crisis at Christmas). (The *averages*, on the other hand, vary little each Sunday: £12,865 in 1987; £13,832 in 1988;

£11,825 in 1989 and £17,143 in 1990.) Nobody has ever put forward a satisfactory theory to explain these huge variations. The BBC says it simply does not know why they vary so much, and finds it impossible to predict the result of an appeal.

For many years, the *highest* amount ever raised by a Week's Good Cause was £89,221.44 by Cardinal Hume for the St Francis Leprosy Guild in 1980. After holding the record for ten years this was at last exceeded by the money raised for Crisis in 1990.

Weekend
See WEEKEND WOMAN'S HOUR.

Weekend Woman's Hour
Successor to HOME FOR THE DAY, and motivated by the same purpose of enabling women who had been out to catch up on some of the week's WOMAN'S HOUR on a Sunday, this ran on Radio 4 from 1968–74. It returned in 1979–81, then changed its name to WEEK-END and ran under that name until 1985. It came back as *Weekend Woman's Hour* again in January 1986 and carried on until the following November. Presenters included Sally Feldman and JUNE KNOX-MAWER.

The Weekly World
Twenty-minute review of the weeklies on Saturday mornings on the Home Service, with JOHN SNAGGE reading the extracts.

Wells, Gerry   (1929–)
Creator and curator of what is probably the world's most comprehensive museum of old radios. He has about 1,000 sets, all from the pre-transistor age, in the detached Victorian house in West Dulwich where he was born and still lives. He established The Vintage Wireless Museum in 1974, the year after his radio repair and amplifier manufacturing business went into liquidation.

Rates and electricity on the house are paid for by Paul Getty, in thanks to Wells for repairing a rare 1924 HMV prototype radiogram (in which the sound was amplified by a diaphragm, not a horn) which Getty had bought at auction. Getty has also bought land at the end of the garden on which Wells has built several sheds and workshops which house parts of his collection. At any one time some of the sets are on loan, for example to the BBC, Design Centre, other museums or television companies who want genuine props. He lets visitors tour his collection, by appointment. See also VALVES.

Welsh Rarebit
Clean, honest-to-goodness comedy show from Cardiff which originally went out in Wales only and then got promoted to the Light Programme in 1949. The BBC said that, in Wales, it had been more popular even than ITMA.

The resident comedian was Les Jones, who had started by entertaining his RAF pals with dialect sketches, and the high spot of the series were the antics of Tommy Trouble and his Friends, written by Eynon Evans. The show also featured a 25-strong male voice choir called the Lyrian Singers and, unusually, was produced by a woman, Mai Jones.

Wenham, Brian   (1937–)
Managing Director of BBC Radio from 1986-87. He was an usher at his erstwhile friend and Oxford contemporary GLYN WORSNIP's wedding, although he later axed him from *Breakfast Time* when he was BBC-TV's Director of Programmes. Now a consultant to Crown Communications, owners of LBC.

We're In Business
Home Service comedy series starring PETER JONES and Harry Worth as a couple involved in money-making schemes. Scripts were written by Jones, Marty Feldman and BARRY TOOK. Jones played Dudley Grosvenor, originally conceived by Peter Ustinov and him in their radio series IN ALL DIRECTIONS in the mid-1950s.

West Sound
ILR station in Ayr, which has been on the air since 1981.

Westbury, Marjorie   (1905–89)
Played PAUL TEMPLE's wife Steve from the second series in 1938 to the last in 1968, and also played the soprano Elsa Strauss in all the HILDA TABLET satires on the Third Programme. To mark her golden jubilee on radio, in 1983, Radio 4 mounted a production of N.C. Hunter's *Waters of the Moon* in which she played Helen Lancaster.

Whack-o!
Comedy starring JIMMY EDWARDS as the uncouth, bullying headmaster of Chiselbury school: it began on BBC-TV in 1957, transferring to the Light Programme in 1961.

Whale, James   (1951–)
Belligerent, unpleasant and egotistical presenter whose acidic skills were first displayed on Metro Radio in the 1970s and later, more notoriously, on Radio Aire from 1981 onwards, where he made a name for himself with a late-night show in which masochistic callers were humoured, abused, ridiculed and sometimes cut off before they could speak.

This eventually found him a national audience: from 1988, these radio programmes started to be televised by Yorkshire TV (who billed him as the 'Mighty Mouth') and taken by several ITV companies as an example of a new type of talk – 'confrontainment'. *The James Whale Radio Show*, as the television series was called, was networked from 1989 onwards, although Whale left Radio Aire in 1990 to concentrate on television. Real name: Michael Whale.

What Do You Know?
Quiz show on the Light Programme which began in 1953, with listeners competing for the title 'Brain of Britain' under the chairmanship of FRANKLIN ENGELMANN. It also included the 'Hear! Hear!' memory test both for listeners and members of the audience. By 1960, JOHN P. WYNN, who created and wrote the show, had devised over 12,000 questions. Maoris, Danes and Dutchmen also competed on the programme, which in 1967 was re-named BRAIN OF BRITAIN.

What If . . . ?
What if Hitler had won the war? What if Kennedy had survived Dallas? Prominent historians speculated in this Radio 4 series in 1991 on what might have happened in these two scenarios and others. Chairman was Cambridge don Dr Christopher Andrew. Those who hypothesised included Norman Stone and D.C. Watt.

Whatever You Think
Lunchtime series on Radio 4 in the early 1970s fronted by CLIFF MICHELMORE, with a phone-in format.

What's Love Got To Do With It?
Four-part Radio 1 series on love, sex and human relationships in 1988.

What's the Idea?
Those explaining their beliefs and answering questions (from various interrogators) in this Home Service series included Dr Donald Soper on pacifism, spokesmen for nudism and abortion law reform, and A.P. Herbert on his 'penny a book' campaign for Public Lending Right.

What's Your Game?
Wendy Lloyd examined the role of sport in schools in this six-part Radio 4 FM series in 1988.

When Housewives Had the Choice
Four nostalgic series broadcast on both Radio 2 and Radio 4 between 1982 and 1989. Devised by RUSSELL DAVIES who co-presented the programmes with Maureen Lipman and Julie Covington: they dipped into the archives to play extracts from HOUSEWIVES' CHOICE and tell the story of that much loved pillar of the Light Programme. Inevitably, it rekindled vivid, poignant memories of life at home during the 1940s, '50s and '60s.

When In France
Radio 4 FM series in 1990 in which actors Polly James and Olivier Pierre roamed around Paris and Brittany to provide an introduction to French language and culture.

When In Italy
Radio 4 FM series in 1989, about Italian culture, presented by Denise De Rome.

When Swing was King
Three-part Radio 2 series in 1989 in which Mel Torme traced the history of big band music from its rise around 1935 to its decline in the late 1950s.

Where Are You Now?
Weekly show on the Light Programme in which WILFRED PICKLES helped people get in touch with old friends or workmates (though not relatives). A typical example was a girl who wanted to find a wartime colleague from the A.T.S. to ask if she would be a bridesmaid at her wedding. An old soldier from the First World War found the lady who, as a schoolgirl, had knitted him socks. An even older soldier (an 83-year-old veteran of the Boer War) was put in touch with an old comrade.

Brimming with human interest, this simple but effective programme formula was resurrected by London Weekend TV in the 1980s for Cilla Black's *Surprise, Surprise*, and its theme of reuniting long-lost friends was also the basis of the East–West spectacular hosted by David Frost which launched BSB's Now Channel in 1990.

Which Way Now?
Annual information campaign on Radio 1 aimed at thirteen and fourteen-year-olds choosing their exam options, broadcast in conjunction with a booklet, helpline and careers advisers.

Whitby, Tony (1929–75)
Former Controller of Radio 4.

The White Coons Concert Party
Early variety show beginning in 1932, broadcast in an era when such a name could be judged not to create offence: TOMMY HANDLEY was one who appeared on it.

Whitethigh, Daphne
Versatile, gushing and husky creature who popped up regularly on ROUND THE HORNE, splendidly played by Betty Marsden. A cookery expert (parodying Fanny Cradock) as well as an agony aunt on 'The Round the Horne Colour Supplement', her contributions ranged from advice on how to make moose stroganoff ('Before you stuff it, make sure it's dead') to this answer given

to a Mrs J.P. of Aldershot: 'I realise that a mole on your hip is an unsightly thing, but don't worry. My opinion is that the mole is only hibernating and he'll go back to the garden when the fine weather comes.'

Who Knows?
Weekly question and answer programme on the Home Service, from 1956, with four scientists answering listeners' queries on science and technology. They were given the questions in advance, in contrast to some other panel programmmes, so were expected to come up with considered and well researched answers. These were not always purely theoretical – one physicist spent a weekend making dozens of pots of tea, to find out which kept the tea hottest. The first chairman was Sam Pollock; his first panel was Robert Boyd, Harry Collier, Peter Sykes and G.P. Wells.

Whose Line Is it Anyway?
Wonderful improvised comedy series, chaired by Clive Anderson, which made its debut on Radio 4 before both it and its co-producer Dan Patterson (who devised it with Mark Leveson) were snapped up by Channel 4.

Whose Shall Be the Land?
Three-part programme on Radio 4 in 1990 in which GORDON CLOUGH explored the prospects for South Africa's future in the wake of Nelson Mandela's release, and the search for a new society which could be shared by millionaires and squatters alike, by neo-fascist Afrikaaners and black revolutionaries.

Whyton, Wally (1929–)
Skiffle singer of the mid-1950s who moved into broadcasting and notched up 2,000 television shows for children, becoming most famous for his nightly appearances with Pussy Cat Willum. In 1965 he started *Strings and Things* on the Light Programme and has been on the network ever since, from 1967–74 in *Country Meets Folk* and since then as compere of COUNTRY CLUB.

Widlake, Brian (1931–)
Solid Radio 4 news presenter who defected to LBC in 1989 to launch its new FM breakfast show. When, six months later, it was deemed to be failing in its task of attracting a young, upmarket Radio 4 audience, he was pushed over to the lunchtime slot and starrier names replaced him. The current breakfast presenter is ANGELA RIPPON.

Wildlife
See THE NATURAL HISTORY PROGRAMME.

Wilko's Weekly
A Britain quite different from the one in the national media – quirky, parochial, full of surprises and eccentricities – was revealed in this weekly Radio 4 series in which Tony Wilkinson visited local newspaper offices throughout Britain, spending a week at each to show how it covered the news in its area. *The Warrington Guardian*, *The Cornishman*, and *The Teesdale Mercury* were among the organs he brought to life.

In 1989 he started to go further afield, looking at six varied US communities (from a declining Virginia mining town to a wine centre in California) as reflected in their local weeklies, and later going to Australia and New Zealand in *Wilko Down Under*.

Will You Still Love Me?
Radio 4 series in 1990 in which people over sixty talked about their experiences of romantic and sexual love. Tied in with fact sheets and helplines, like the other series also produced by Sukey Firth and broadcast on Radio 1.

Will You Still Love Me Tomorrow?
Charlotte Grieg, author and singer, chronicled this six-part Radio 1 series in 1990 on girl pop groups, from The Chantels and The Shangri-Las to Bananarama and Vixen. It revealed that Lala Brooks, one of The Crystals, had now donned the veil as a Sunni moslem, and that former star Little Eva was living on welfare.

Williams, Heathcote (1941–)
Poet, playwright and actor whose magnificent poem *Whale Nation* made its broadcast debut on Radio 3 in July 1988 when it was read by Roy Hutchins – three weeks before it was published in book form.

Previously, in 1987, his similar epic *Sacred Elephant* (also later published as a book) was read on Radio 3, and in 1989 he performed *Falling for a Dolphin* on the same network. Aptly, *The Sunday Times* has described him as 'the Poet Laureate of animal liberation'.

Williams' taut and painful stage play about the final moments of TONY HANCOCK, *Hancock's Last Half-Hour*, was broadcast on Radio 3 in 1988 on the twentieth anniversary of the comedian's suicide in Australia. Richard Briers played Hancock.

Williams, Kenneth (1926–88)
Wonderfully talented comedy actor and raconteur, proud owner of a voice which oozed effortless innuendo and trembled with every variation of camp imaginable. Heard to best effect in BEYOND OUR KEN and ROUND THE HORNE, he was also a panellist on JUST A MINUTE, where his famous petulance was usually contrived and always funny, for almost twenty years. Earlier, he had a much less happy time coping with the antagonism and neuroses of TONY HANCOCK when he appeared in HANCOCK'S HALF HOUR. Williams' serious side, his prodigious knowledge of English poetry, keen intellect and constant search for human truths, was displayed in

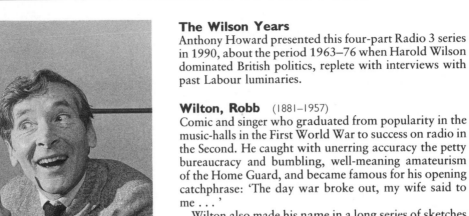

Kenneth Williams, caught in classic mode. He coined the phrase ''Ere, stop messin' about' on *Hancock's Half-Hour* and later brought to life a range of characters from Arthur Fallowfield to Rambling Syd Rumpo

a 45-minute solo programme, *The Crystal Spirit* (a line from a poem by George Orwell) in 1974.

His choice of luxury in DESERT ISLAND DISCS was Michelangelo's David. He claimed it was the 'God-like head' that appealed, not the nudity.

Williams, Stephen   (1908–)

Adventurous pioneer of commercial radio: first on a yacht voyage organised by the DAILY MAIL round the coast of England in 1928–29, broadcasting gramophone records from the deck; then Radio Normandie; then Radio Luxembourg, where he launched the English service in December 1933 and became its first disc-jockey.

During the Second World War, with the BBC in London, he directed VARIETY BANDBOX and gave nine-year-old Petula Clark her wireless debut on the Forces Programme's IT'S ALL YOURS. He relaunched Luxembourg in January 1946 but rejoined the BBC in 1948, where he spent the next 27 years. He produced HAVE A GO for most of that time.

The Wilson Years

Anthony Howard presented this four-part Radio 3 series in 1990, about the period 1963–76 when Harold Wilson dominated British politics, replete with interviews with past Labour luminaries.

Wilton, Robb   (1881–1957)

Comic and singer who graduated from popularity in the music-halls in the First World War to success on radio in the Second. He caught with unerring accuracy the petty bureaucracy and bumbling, well-meaning amateurism of the Home Guard, and became famous for his opening catchphrase: 'The day war broke out, my wife said to me . . . '

Wilton also made his name in a long series of sketches about 'Mr Muddlecombe, JP'. One of them drew a complaint from the Magistrates' Association, who felt that his portrayal of a magistrate rather the worse for drink, who requested an attractive female complainant to meet him later in a pub, was a slur on their good name. The BBC responded that the broadcast was quite clearly a farce, and that the charges before the court, such as racing tortoises within the 30 mph limit, were too fantastic for any of it to be taken seriously.

Wimbush, Mary   (1924–)

Highly regarded radio actress, on the air since 1945: her work was acknowledged by a SONY AWARD in 1991.

Wimsey, Lord Peter

Dorothy L. Sayers's gentleman detective was the subject of the first SATURDAY NIGHT THEATRE play, in 1943; quite separately, he has also been well played on Radio 4 by actor IAN CARMICHAEL.

Winn, Anona   (c. 1907–)

Australian-born broadcaster and actress who originally wanted to be a pianist, but her hands were too small. She turned to study opera under Dame Nellie Melba in Melbourne, later travelling to Britain. She worked as a singer, composer, actress, impressionist and broadcaster and enjoyed much popular success as a panellist on TWENTY QUESTIONS, and also devised PETTICOAT LINE.

Her longest run as a stage actress was in *Bless the Bride*, and Georges Guetary singing 'Table for Two' was one of the eight records she chose as a castaway in 1951. In recent years she has disappeared from public view.

Winston

Three series of this PETER TINNISWOOD comedy have so far been heard on Radio 4, starring Bill Wallis in the title role as a short, fat, hairy village poacher.

Anona Winn was one of many talents from Australia and New Zealand to make their mark on British radio. Others have included Dick Bentley, Kitty Bluett, Michael Charlton, Roger Cook, Alan Freeman and Ted Kavanagh

Wireless Willie
Very early radio character created by William Rouse in the 1920s. Example of humour: 'She was only a baker's daughter but she certainly needed my dough.'

With Courage
Home Service series consisting of hour-long dramatisations of true life stories of valour.

With Great Pleasure
Highly civilised Radio 4 series, now running for 21 years, in which a leading figure usually drawn from the arts or literary world chooses his or her favourite poetry and prose.

More than 200 such guests, including Sir John Betjeman, Jacqueline du Pré, Roy Hattersley and Gwen Ffrangcon-Davies, have revealed themselves through their reading matter in this way. The pieces are read by an actor and actress and the programme is recorded in front of an audience.

The venues vary, but often have a connection with the guest. The items also vary – Chaucer to Larkin, Austen to Yates, John Milton to Keith Waterhouse – but tend to be English, like those who choose them.

Rupert Brooke's *The Old Vicarage, Grantchester* was once such a popular choice that the producer rationed its appearance to once every two series, to avoid irritating the audience.

WNK
Tottenham-based pirate station of 1986–88 whose initials, chosen by its creator JOE DOUGLAS, denoted that it was 'wicked, neutral and kicking'. It won the INCREMENTAL franchise for Haringey (jointly with London Greek Radio) and went on the air as a legal station in 1989. It broadcasts soul and reggae for twelve hours a day, and also Caribbean news every Sunday afternoon.

Wogan, Terry (1938–)
Radio 2's breakfast presenter from 1972 to 1984, whose wit and gentle self-mockery won him a huge following and set him up for the lucrative BBC-TV career that followed. His constant references to both *Dallas* and THE ARCHERS helped to win a following for them, too. Four million daily listeners tuned in for his 'Fight the Flab' and gift of the gab, the 'Wogan's Winner' racing tip and the barbed dialogue while handing over to JIMMY YOUNG, out of which the Irishman generally emerged triumphant.

After working in a bank in Dublin, and on RTE, Wogan's first regular BBC show was MIDDAY SPIN. He was one of the original team of DJs when Radio 1 began in 1967, hosting LATE NIGHT EXTRA for two years before landing, in October 1969, his own daily show on Radios 1 and 2. In April 1972 he became Radio 2's breakfast host. Also presented WOGAN'S WORLD.

In 1989 he appeared as himself in the 10,000th episode of *The Archers*, opposite Dame Judi Dench as the timid Pru Forrest.

Wogan's World
TERRY WOGAN's first chat show, long before he started the one on television, was this weekly programme on Radio 4.

Wolf, Charlie (1959–)
Mormon disc-jockey who got a name for himself while on the pirate ship Laser 558, partly by eccentric activities such as negotiating a pay rise for himself over the air. From his native USA, he also imported the practice of broadcasting standing up, which he and his manager JOHN CATLETT later took to Atlantic 252.

Woman's Hour
Masturbation, homosexuality, the Pill, frigidity, transsexuality, impotence and flatulence – complete with sound effects – were all taboo subjects on radio until

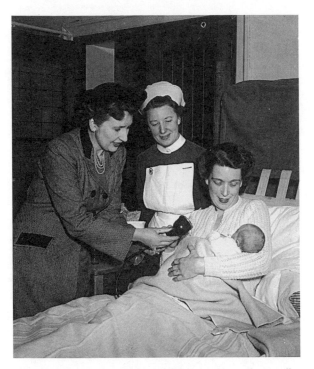

Woman's Hour has never confined itself to the studio.
Jean Metcalfe, complete with pearls, visited this London
hospital in December 1950. Among those she interviewed
was a Mrs Elizabeth Oliver of Norbury, holding her three-
day-old daughter Joan Barbara

dealing with 'keeping house, health, children, beauty care and home furnishing' with 'a short serial reading'. The first edition, on 7 October 1946 (opening with the signature tune 'Oranges and Lemons') contained a talk on *Mother's Midday Meal*, following it up with tips on *Putting Your Best Face Forward*. Other early programmes offered hints on how to catch mice and bleach black-out material. Everything was properly scripted, and speakers often wore hats in the studio.

Within a few months the programme was receiving a thousand letters a week. In the main these were requests for advice: on shyness, menstrual problems, the menopause, children's feeding. In this way the programme became, and still is, a forum for the voices and views of its listeners, a sisterhood of the airwaves, and a lifeline to those who were housebound. It was non-judgemental: a woman who helped her mother commit suicide, for instance, was allowed simply to speak about it, without condemnation. This characteristic of the programme, a calm tolerance, has also been reflected in the approach of its presenters, including JEAN METCALFE, MARJORIE ANDERSON (1958–72), SUE MACGREGOR (1972–87) and JENNI MURRAY (1987 onwards).

Domestic activities are still regularly included on the programme, but occupy a smaller proportion of the whole (just as they do in women's lives in general). There is less cookery and more current affairs. Thus, for example, in MacGregor's last programme the guests included Foreign Office minister Lynda Chalker, child-birth campaigner Sheila Kitzinger, writer Erica Jong, philosopher Lady Warnock and singer Ruby Murray.

Many items are now arranged up to the last minute, to ensure topicality, but this does not please all those listeners for whom the loss of topicality would be a small price to pay for returning to the days when the menu for each day's programme was given in advance in RADIO TIMES. (This was up to 1972, when the contents were arranged weeks in advance and each day's programme was rehearsed in the morning.)

The present head of the programme, Claire Selerie-Gray, who took over in 1987, has made it more substantial, ending items which were purely whimsical and ensuring that most serials are of novels more directly related to women's lives than in the past. The programme has been accused of being a 'flagship for feminism' and Selerie-Gray, while saying she wants to keep things fun and avoid *Spare Rib* didactics, agrees that those now running the programme have, inevitably, been influenced by the women's movement which has shaped their outlook as they have grown up.

Radio's only programme for, by and about women actually started off in 1946 with a male presenter, but since then it has usually had an all-woman team, sometimes with a token man. Its audience, however, which has slipped from three million to 500,000 over

they were brought into the open on *Woman's Hour* which, although never quite shaking off its middle-class, Home Counties tone, has not been as cosy as some have supposed.

With nearly 12,000 episodes under its girdle, however, this clever mix of Women's Institute and women's lib has certainly undergone change. When it began, in the grey days of rationing and food coupons in 1946, most women were at home: today, the majority go out to work.

It would be odd had the programme been unaffected by this fundamental shift. Its concerns are consequently now much broader, more geared to national and international affairs, and the tone less flippant. Indeed the history of the programme, through austerity, affluence, permissiveness, feminism, Thatcherism and post-Thatcherism, is almost the story of women in Britain since the end of the Second World War.

The programme was conceived by the remarkable NORMAN COLLINS, creator of the Light Programme, to help women with their domestic lives in the one hour they were presumed to have to themselves (2 p.m. to 3 p.m., while doing the washing-up). It was billed as the course of its life, is estimated to be 20 per cent male.

The first serial was the swashbuckling romance *Under the Red Robe*, by the Victorian writer Stanley Weyman, which was mounted again as part of the programme's ruby wedding celebrations in 1986. (The anniversary programme also contained an item which some found shocking and others outrageously funny – on flatulence. See SANDRA CHALMERS.)

The serial has probably been the most popular ingredient over the years. One of the programme's behind-the-scenes celebrities, who has done as much as anyone to maintain a sense of continuity, is Pat McLoughlin, its serials producer, who has chosen and adapted more than 500 books for *Woman's Hour* listeners over the last twenty years. (Of that vast total, her particular favourites are Elizabeth Taylor's *A Game of Hide and Seek*, Oswald Wynd's *The Ginger Tree*, which was read by Hannah Gordon long before it was serialised on BBC1, and Margery Allingham's *The Tiger in the Smoke*.)

There was a national furore in 1990 when Radio 4's Controller, MICHAEL GREEN, announced that from September 1991 he was moving the programme out of the sacred 2 p.m. slot which it had occupied since it began and into the mornings. He also said it would have an unspecified new look, although it would continue to be produced by the same team and (he decided later) carry on with the same title. Hundreds of listeners complained that the new slot was much less suitable and the programme's unique nature as a feminine oasis would be irreparably damaged. Green, however, argued that the mornings contained a larger potential audience.

A Woman's Work

Five-part Radio 4 FM series in 1989 which explored the changes over the last fifty years in British society's attitudes towards working women.

Women

The first programme introduced by a woman announcer, who was Sheila Borrett, was in July 1933. The first time a woman read the news was in August 1933, but this was apparently discontinued shortly afterwards. SHEILA TRACY was the first woman to read the news on Radio 4 (1974), SANDRA CHALMERS the first woman to run a local radio station (1976) and MOIRA STUART the first black woman to read the news (1978). Today, women occupy far more senior positions in radio than in television, including two of the five BBC network Controllerships.

Woodruffe, Tommy (–)

Commentator immortalised by a gaffe caused by a drop too many with his old shipmates – see 'THE FLEET'S LIT UP'.

Wooldridge, Michael (1948–)

Religious affairs correspondent of BBC Radio since 1990, and a practising Anglican. His first major series in the post was GOD AND CAESAR in 1991. He was the BBC's man in East Africa for most of the 1980s, and then its Southern Africa correspondent.

Woolwich Young Radio Playwrights Competition

Contest in 1990 co-sponsored by LBC and the Woolwich Building Society and organised by INDEPENDENT RADIO DRAMA PRODUCTIONS, which directed the ten winning plays when they were performed on LBC. Over 170 people entered. The first prize of £750 went to Emily Fuller (granddaughter of the poet Roy Fuller) for a piece of sustained menace called *Jump the Waves*, in which a woman had put paid to her husband.

A Word in Edgeways

Saturday evening talk programme which began on the Home Service in June 1965, based in London. Harold Evans, later the editor of *The Sunday Times*, and ANTHONY SMITH alternated as chairmen. In September 1966 it moved to Manchester, whereupon BRIAN REDHEAD became the conversation's choreographer. It continued for many years. Normally there were three guests: frequently they were strangers to one another, but chosen on the grounds that they had interesting things to say both on their own areas of expertise and other topics which intrigued them.

Words

Radio 3 series offering 'reflections on language', in which various distinguished academics and thinkers discuss words in their own spheres of interest. They have included Don Cupitt (theology), Ted Honderich (philosophy), Roy Porter (medicine) and Helena Kennedy (law).

Words Of Faith

World Service programme, which now goes out on Radio 5 as well, in which at the close of the day people of all religions share thoughts on their Scripture.

The Wordsmiths at Gorsemere

Gentle send-up of the Romantic poets, as indicated by the Wordsworthian pun in the title. SUE LIMB was the author. Simon Callow played Coleric and Tim Curry was Byro.

Workers' Playtime

In 1940, Ernest Bevin requested a cheerful show for the war effort in the factories. The BBC came up with this variety programme, which began in May 1941 with an edition from a Royal Ordnance factory 'somewhere in

England'. FRED YULE was one of those on the bill. Characters included MRS FEATHER.

The Works
Quirky, innovative, 'free-form' musical magazine which enlivened Friday evenings on Radio 3 from January 1989 to June 1990. Aimed partly at younger listeners, it covered an astonishing variety of topics: from the Reggae Philharmonic Orchestra to songs sung by football crowds, from buskers and bell-ringing and electronic synthesisers to hunting horns, youth orchestras and steel drums. Not everyone approved, though, of the obscure, self-indulgent way in which items were sometimes presented. Presenter and interviewer was David Owen Norris, a pianist and teacher at the Royal Academy of Music.

JOHN DRUMMOND ended the programme after only a short life because, he said, it had achieved its aims and he now wished to spread its zestful spirit more widely through the network.

'Daring if not always appreciated' – the BBC's verdict in its Annual Report for 1988–89.

The World At One
Lunchtime news programme on Radio 4 whose sharp, popular, racy style was a considerable innovation when it was launched in October 1965, the creation of its editor ANDREW BOYLE (who later exposed Anthony Blunt, via his book *The Climate of Treason*) and presenter William Hardcastle under the aegis of GERARD MANSELL.

Hardcastle, ex-editor of the DAILY MAIL, anchored the programme for the first ten years. He established its essence with probing, determined, sometimes irreverent interviewing, as well as a breathless delivery. That tradition was continued by his successors David Jessel, Nick Woolley, PETER HOBDAY, GORDON CLOUGH, SIR ROBIN DAY, Nick Worrall, BRIAN WIDLAKE and JAMES NAUGHTIE, as well as the use of eyewitness reports to provide vivid, first-hand accounts of events as they happen. ANNE SLOMAN, in the *British Journalism Review* in Autumn 1990, revealed that Robert Carvel, political editor of the *Evening Standard*, was invited to become the regular presenter in the late 1970s, but declined because he loved newspapers more.

Naughtie, the first of the nine presenters to have a non-metropolitan accent, attracted several months of hate mail from listeners, mainly in southern England, who called him 'alien' and objected to the way he elongated words such as 'says'.

The programme spawned two similar offspring (THE WORLD THIS WEEKEND in 1967 and PM in 1970) and nurtured the talents of several broadcasters including MARGARET HOWARD, SUE MACGREGOR, Nick Ross, Jonathan Dimbleby and ROGER COOK, all of whom worked as reporters on it.

The first programme, although it did have ALVAR LIDELL reading the news to show that not everything had changed, included Ian Smith speaking that morning from Heathrow Airport, the Pope speaking that morning from Rome and GERALD PRIESTLAND interviewing Patrick O'Donovan on the Pope's visit to the UN. Smith, the premier of Rhodesia, was to feature heavily that year and the programme made its mark within weeks with its scoop in reporting his declaration of UDI. It also carried an interview with Salman Rushdie on the day it broke the news of the Ayatollah's death threat in February 1989. One of its most fascinating interviews, however, was only partially broadcast – that with Neil Kinnock, in which he lost his temper and said he would not be 'kebabbed' by Naughtie for Tory blunders.

A World Dense With Promise
A portrait of a Lancashire family from 1900 to 1939 was provided in these six talks on Radio 3 in 1990 by post office clerk's daughter Rachel Trickett, who in due course became a novelist and Principal of St Hugh's College, Oxford.

World Theatre
Drama series which began in 1946 with Gilbert Murray's translation of *Hippolytus* by Euripides.

The World This Weekend
Radio 4's Sunday-lunchtime news and current affairs programme has been going since 1967 and is noted for its big political interviews, frequently quoted in the Press the next morning. GORDON CLOUGH and Nick Clarke are the presenters.

The World Tonight
Renowned for its reasoned analysis and comprehensive foreign coverage, this has been running on Radio 4 each weekday evening since 1970. Past presenters have included JOHN TUSA, Anthony Howard and Charles Wheeler, and Henry Kelly worked on it from 1976–80. Today's presenters include Richard Kershaw, Robin Lustig, Alexander MacLeod and David Sells.

It moved from 10.30 p.m. to its present slot of 10 p.m. in October 1989 when Radio 4 rejigged its late evening schedules. The editor, Margaret Budy, said it was 'the only BBC current affairs programme to send a team to every session of the European Parliament in Strasbourg, so our listeners are among the best informed on European political issues.'

Worsnip, Glyn (1938–)
Actor and presenter with a light comic touch who enjoyed a close association with BBC Radio until seized and brought down by a degenerative disease, cerebellar ataxia, which robbed him of coherent speech and then the use of his limbs.

Glyn Worsnip, who began his radio career as an actor in *The Dales* and went on to become a household name on television, later presenting the Radio 4 shows *The Press Gang* and *Stop Press*

The programme in which he came out publicly and revealed the details, which launched Radio 4's SOUND-TRACK series in 1988, drew almost 1,000 letters from listeners – one of the biggest postbags the network has received in response to a single programmme. 'People wrote to say that they had stopped what they were doing to listen; they did not go into the supermarket; they parked in laybys; they stopped the ironing; and some did not go to work at all,' Worsnip

recalled in his autobiography *Up The Down Escalator*.

The disease forced him out of all three of his radio series. He had appeared every third Monday as a wry presenter of Radio 4's Monday-morning ARCHIVE FEATURE since 1981, but had to step down in 1987. In the same year he was axed from STOP PRESS, which he had started writing and presenting the year before. He chaired Radio 2's panel game THE PRESS GANG, whose guests such as Henry Kelly, Frances Edmonds, Arthur English and Gyles Brandreth gave him much support, from 1986 until 1989, when he could carry on no longer.

Worsnip started on the radio a decade before his years of television stardom (1974–78) with Esther Rantzen on *That's Life*. He was in the cast of THE DALES and had a mildly satirical slot which he wrote himself on a lunchtime show called *This Time of Day*.

Wright, Steve (1954–)

Radio 1 afternoon disc-jockey famed for his collection of strange characters (Mr Angry, Mr Mad and so on) and voices (Mick Jagger, Keith Richards). Originally he did most of them himself, before handing over Mick Jagger, for example, to an actor.

Wright ran a radio station at his school in Essex, and later worked in hospital radio in his spare time. Joined the BBC as a researcher, then left for ILR and Radio Luxembourg, before rejoining the BBC in 1980, this time as a presenter on Radio 1.

Writers Revealed

Radio 4 series in 1989 in which ROSEMARY HARTILL conversed with seven novelists about the way religious beliefs, or the absence of them, affected their work. The interviewees were Iris Murdoch, Anthony Burgess, JOHN MORTIMER, Brian Moore, Sara Maitland, Bernice Rubens and A.N. Wilson. In a second series, in 1990, the writers who revealed themselves were David Lodge, Chaim Potok, P.D. James, Jeanette Winterson, William Trevor and Richard Ingrams. Her third series in 1991 concentrated on playwrights, including David Hare.

Wynn, John P. (–)

Imaginative creator of many BBC shows, ranging from BRAIN OF BRITAIN to INSPECTOR SCOTT INVESTIGATES and YOUR VERDICT.

The Year In Question
(1) Bland Radio 4 series hosted by RICHARD STILGOE with TERRY WOGAN and Henry Kelly.

(2) Sharp, entertaining quiz game, also on Radio 4, in which teams of journalists had to answer general knowledge questions about one particular postwar year. In the first series in 1989, recorded in the beery environs of Ye Olde Cock Tavern in Fleet Street, scribblers from eight national newspapers fought one another. *The Sun*, for reasons best known to itself, declined to enter, and was replaced by *Today*: unfortunately it found itself drawn against *The Independent* in the opening round and was soundly defeated. *The Independent* went on to beat *The Daily Telegraph* in the final. The second and final series in 1990 featured a similar knockout contest between the weeklies: in the final *New Statesman and Society* beat *The Spectator*. SIMON BATES was the referee in both series.

The Year of Dreams
Radio 4's six-part review in 1988 of turbulent 1968, presented by several commentators.

A Year of Dying Dangerously
Five-part Radio 4 series in 1989, which explored the features of all 687 homicides in the year 1986, the latest for which full details were available. This was the year of the 'Stockwell Strangler' and 'Fordingbridge Massacre' – strikingly horrible and also strikingly unusual. Presenter Hugh Prysor-Jones and producer John Forsyth (who later co-operated on NO LONGER KNOWN AT THIS ADDRESS) attempted to portray the 'typical' murder, something very different from the sensational cases that always make the headlines.

Yes, Mr Churchill
Six-part Radio 4 series in 1990 in which the former Marion Holmes talked (to JUNE KNOX-MAWER) about her life as personal secretary to Churchill – taking dictation while he soaked in his bathtub, travelling to Yalta with him, and so on.

Yesterday in Parliament
Fifteen minutes of extracts from the previous day's debates in both Commons and Lords, included in Radio 4's TODAY programme each morning during Parliamentary sessions. For background to Parliamentary broadcasting, see TODAY IN PARLIAMENT.

Ying Tong Song
Popular song from THE GOON SHOW, sung by MILLIGAN, Sellers and Secombe which got to Number 3 in 1956 and stayed in the charts for ten weeks.

Amazingly, when it was reissued seventeen years later in 1973, it again stayed for ten weeks in the charts and again got into the Top Ten, but this time reached only Number 9. Prince Charles, one of the greatest of Goon fans, wrote in 1973 that it was the only song he knew by heart.

You and the Night and the Music
Radio 2's soothing, friendly through-the-night show which started when in January 1979 the network joined up its closing time of 2 a.m. and opening time of 5 a.m. and thus became the BBC's first 24-hour network.

You and Yours
British radio's only national daily consumer and social affairs programme, which began in 1970. Early editions featured checkout prices and shoddy goods: the emphasis now is on broader issues which affect large chunks of the audience, such as transport, fostering, the cost of legal actions and debt and credit.

There is an annual *Call to Account* in which leaders of public bodies and service industries answer listeners' queries and criticisms and in 1990 the programme brought out its first book, *How to Complain*, giving information about consumer rights and featuring 200 individual cases, written by senior producer David Berry.

Presenters have included Nancy Wise, DEREK COOPER, Sue Cook, Jenni Mills, Patti Coldwell, Bill Breckon, Paul Heiney, Debbie Thrower, John Waite and John Howard.

You Asked For It

Improvised comedy series which began on Radio 4 in 1989, very obviously influenced by WHOSE LINE IS IT ANYWAY? which the BBC lost to Channel 4. Two teams displayed their wit and spontaneity in a variety of storytelling rounds prompted by a studio audience, who filled in pieces of paper asking for stories to incorporate particular lines of dialogue, unusual objects, strange obsessions and so on. The chairman was Luke Sorba and the panellists included Sandi Toksvig, Paul Merton, Josie Lawrence and Neil Mullarkey.

You the Jury

Radio 4 debates in front of a studio audience, presented by Dick Taverne, QC.

You'll Never Be 16 Again

Acclaimed Radio 4 'history of the British teenager' in 1985–86 produced by Peter Everett.

Young, Jeff (1955–)

Chemical analyst at St Thomas's Hospital, London, for eight years before leaving to join a record company. He became a DJ on BBC Radio London before making his debut on Radio 1 in 1985. Two years later he landed his own weekly show, DANCE PARTY, but stepped down at the end of 1990 to concentrate on his new job as a director of A&M Records. He was succeeded in the slot by PETE TONG.

Young, Jimmy (1925–)

Former crooner (with two Number 1 hits, 'Unchained Melody' and 'The Man from Laramie', both in 1955) who has enjoyed even greater success on the air: his voice, with its distinctive Gloucestershire burr he has never lost, has for years been one of the best known in Britain.

Made his debut on BBC radio in 1949 and first introduced records on *Flat Spin* in 1953. Two weeks presenting HOUSEWIVES' CHOICE in 1960 (a show which he first hosted in 1955) led to several years as a DJ on Radio Luxembourg, recording his shows at the station's studios just off Park Lane in Mayfair.

He was one of Radio 1's original team of DJs when the station was born in 1967 and his weekday morning show went out for several years on both Radio 1 and 2. In 1973 he joined Radio 2. On his show, he has interviewed every Prime Minister since 1964 and many world statesmen – although Reagan always said no. The programme has been broadcast live from several countries, including the USA, USSR, Egypt and Israel.

His recipe slot, always introduced by the sing-song question 'What's the recipe today, Jim?' asked by the chipmunk voice RAYMONDO, ceased in 1976 when the show changed direction to become more substantial.

It regularly features legal and consumer experts of various sorts and a political content reflected in the fact that his stand-ins have included MPs such as Ken Livingstone and Dame Janet Fookes.

Young Playwrights Festival

Season of plays by first-time writers aged from fifteen to thirty, broadcast on Radio 4 in 1988 in a bid to discover and encourage new talent. Twenty-one plays were chosen out of 1,000 sent in. Authors included Jeanette Winterson (who had already written a prize-winning novel, *Oranges Are Not The Only Fruit*) and dub poet Benjamin Zephaniah. The network was planning a second festival over ten days in October 1991.

Your Concert Choice

Sunday afternoon record programme which began in July 1954 on the Home Service, later travelling via the Music Programme to Radio 3. Trevor Harvey presented and helped to compile the first edition, which featured the Elgar Violin Concerto with Jascha Heifetz as the soloist and the LSO under Sir Malcolm Sargent. Since October 1990 the programme (which plays only complete works, not extracts) has had a regular presenter in Paul Guinery, who also writes the scripts.

All the music played is requested by listeners, as the title suggests. The programme receives about eighty requests a month, covering a wide range – all the way from Haydn symphonies and the Trout Quintet to slightly more obscure works such as Albrechtsberger's Concerto No. 1 for Jew's Harp and Mandolin.

Your Cup of Tea

Second World War series with FREDDIE GRISEWOOD.

Your Hundred Best Tunes

Gentle, quiet and serene record programme which ALAN KEITH has been presenting on Sunday evenings since 1959. It began on the Light Programme, changed to the Home Service in the 1960s, and later moved back to Radio 2. (It was originally called *The Hundred Best Tunes in the World* and changed to its present title in February 1960.)

Jerusalem, part of Mendelssohn's Violin Concerto and some Elgar were included in the first programme, and this mixture has set the tone ever since. Whether it be extracts from Weber clarinet concertos, Bellini operatic duets, arias, ballet suites or symphonies, the music is a solace and the mood comforting and confiding. Keith likes to imagine his listeners as thoughtful folk sitting round a fire on a winter's night.

He plays very little modern music, no Hindemith, no Schoenberg – 'nothing far out, you know' – but has certainly helped to popularise serious music and appears to have been one of the first presenters to play the Pachelbel Canon, Allegri's Miserere and Albinoni's Adagio, all of which are now popular classics. Despite the title, it is not a request series and the records are actually selected by Alan Keith, not his listeners. He makes a point of picking the best conductors, orchestras and soloists from the choices available in the BBC GRAMOPHONE LIBRARY.

In 1984 the programme conducted a poll of listeners' favourites. The Top Ten (with places from a previous 1976 poll in parentheses) emerged as:

1 (1) Duet 'In the Depths of the Temple' from *The Pearl Fishers*, Bizet
2 (2) Chorus of the Hebrew Slaves, Verdi
3 (4) Miserere, Allegri
4 (5) Violin Concerto No. 1, Bruch
5 (7) Canon in D, Pachelbel
6 (6) Symphony No 6 (Pastoral), Beethoven
7 (–) Piano Concerto No. 21, Mozart
8 (–) Lament 'What Is Life?', Gluck
9 (–) The Holy City, Stephen Adams
10 (8) Nimrod, from the Enigma Variations, Elgar

The series gained much publicity in 1988 when Earl Spencer, father of the Princess of Wales, stood in for three weeks while Keith was on holiday. His choice of music was perfectly in tune with the series as a whole. It

ranged from Handel's 'Let the Bright Seraphim' to 'The Seduction Song' from Mozart's *Don Giovanni*. Another stand-in (in 1990 and 1991) has been Rosalind Runcie, pianist and wife of the former Archbishop of Canterbury.

'A good deal of it is luck. I could have played an unpopular first tune and the show might have gone down the pan' – Alan Keith.

Your Verdict
JOHN P. WYNN devised and wrote this Light Programme series of dramatised legal problems, beginning in 1962. It was introduced by Ludovic Kennedy and then JOHN SNAGGE. A qualified legal opinion came from F.W. Beney QC and there were comments from a jury made up of members of the public.

Yours Faithfully
Radio 4 religious slot (five minutes long) with GERALD PRIESTLAND in 1981.

Youth Club Call
Radio 1 series presented by ALAN FREEMAN in the 1970s.

Yule, Fred (–)
Entertainer who appeared on many BBC shows.

The Zither on the Wall

Five-part series on Radio 3 in 1990, all the programmes going out over one weekend, which surveyed one of the oldest of all stringed instruments, first mentioned in Chinese texts of *c.* 1,000 BC. The music was played by Li Xiangting from Beijing, on an instrument about 700 years old.

The Zoo Man

Regular speaker on CHILDREN'S HOUR, played by David Seth-Smith from 1934–45. He was based in London, and other regions sometimes had their zoo men, too, e.g. Tom Gillespie in Scotland.

Chronology

Entries are assembled in the following order: technological developments first, because they make everything else possible; the birth of stations; other radio events of importance; the launch of programmes still running today.

Before 1920
1888   Heinrich Hertz the first to demonstrate radio waves.
1895   Guglielmo Marconi discovers the importance of antennae.
1901   Marconi sends radio signal from England to Newfoundland.
1904   Radio valve developed.
1906   AM first used, in Massachusetts.

The 1920s
1920   Marconi makes Britain's first public radio broadcast, from Chelmsford.
1922   British Broadcasting Company is formed (October) and starts daily broadcasting (November) from 2LO.
      Radio licence introduced (price 10s.).
1923   2LO moves from Strand to Savoy Hill.
      First outside broadcast (*The Magic Flute* from Covent Garden); *Twelfth Night* the first play to be heard on British radio; chimes of Big Ben first broadcast.
      Radio Times starts publishing.
1924   *Danger* is the first play to go out that is specifically written for radio; Compton Mackenzie becomes the first DJ; the Pips are broadcast for the first time; the BBC broadcasts its first schools programmes.
1925   Daventry long wave transmitter opens.
1926   *Choral Evensong* and *The Week's Good Cause* begin.
1927   British Broadcasting Company becomes the British Broadcasting Corporation, it takes over the Proms and broadcasts its first sports commentary (the England v. Wales rugby international

at Twickenham) and its first cricket report.
1928   *Daily Service* begins.
1929   The BBC broadcasts its first farming programme, a recitation of the fat stock prices; *The Week in Westminster* begins.
      The Listener starts publishing.

The 1930s
1930   National Programme and Regional Programme begin, replacing 2LO.
      BBC Symphony Orchestra created, under Sir Adrian Boult.
1932   Empire Service begins.
      BBC moves into its new home, Broadcasting House.
      First Christmas broadcast by the Monarch (King George V).
1933   Derek McCulloch starts regular Children's Hour appeals for youngsters, which eventually grow into the *Children in Need* appeal.
      Radio Luxembourg begins broadcasts to Britain (December).
1934   *Henry Hall's Guest Night* begins, often described as the BBC's first chat show; Mr Middleton, the BBC's first gardening broadcaster, starts his celebrated series *In Your Garden*.
1935   BBC Scottish Symphony Orchestra is founded.
1937   *Farming Today* begins.
1938   The Arabic Service begins, the first of the World Service's foreign language services.
      BBC Monitoring begins, initially at Evesham.
1939   FM first demonstrated.
      Home Service begins, at the outbreak of the Second World War, replacing National and Regional Programmes. The Polish Service also begins.
      BBC Drama Repertory Company is formed.
      London Calling starts publishing.

The 1940s

1940 Forces Programme begins, as does the African Service, Hindi Service and Bulgarian Service.
Sunday Half Hour and *Radio Newsreel* begin. The BBC Pronunciation Unit comes into being, as a 'temporary' replacement for the pre-war Advisory Committee on Spoken English (it now deals with 11,000 queries a year).

1941 Malay Service begins.

1942 *Desert Island Discs* begins.

1943 Japanese Service begins.
BBC Monitoring moves to Caversham.
Saturday Night Theatre begins.

1944 *Before the Ending of the Day* begins.

1945 Forces Programme renamed Light Programme; regional broadcasting resumes.
Time for Verse begins.

1946 Third Programme starts up, as does the Russian Service. Many classic shows begin, of which those still running are *Letter from America*, *Woman's Hour* and *Down Your Way*.

1947 *Round Britain Quiz* and *Gardeners' Question Time* begin.

1948 Discovery of the transistor.
First Prix Italia competition: first of the Reith Lectures.
Top Twenty, the first charts show, begins on Radio Luxembourg.
Any Questions? begins on the Home and *Sports Report* on the Light.

1949 *A Book at Bedtime* and *Morning Story* begin, both on the Light but later on the Home.

The 1950s

1950 Humphrey Lyttelton presents his first radio jazz show.

1951 *The Archers* begins.

1952 BBC Concert Orchestra is formed.

1953 *Friday Night is Music Night* and *What Do You Know?* (renamed *Brain of Britain* in 1967) begin.

1954 *Under Milk Wood* broadcast.
Any Answers? begins.

1955 *From Our Own Correspondent* and *Pick of the Pops* make their debut.

1956 *My Word* begins. Rhys Adrian and John Arden have their first plays on radio.

1957 Hausa, Somali and Swahili services begin on the BBC's African Service.
The *Today* programme begins. Samuel Beckett makes his drama debut, on the Third. Ball-by-ball Test coverage starts.

1958 BBC Radiophonic Workshop is formed.

1959 A clutch of shows that will become famous make their debut, among them *Sing Something Simple*, *Your Hundred Best Tunes*, *Pick of the Week* and *The Innocent Ear*.

The 1960s

1961 *Afternoon Theatre* and *In Touch* begin.

1962 Start of experimental transmissions in stereo. Alan Freeman takes over *Pick of the Pops*.

1964 Radio Caroline, the first offshore pirate ship, starts up. BBC Radio Orchestra begins.

1965 *Jazz Record Requests* begins.

1967 Radio 1 begins (30 September). On this day also the Light Programme becomes Radio 2, the Third Programme Radio 3 and the Home Service Radio 4. BBC launches its local radio network with BBC Radio Leicester (November). Marine etc. Broadcasting (Offences) Act comes into force, quashing the pirate ships.
Just a Minute begins, as does *The World This Weekend* and *My Music*.

1968 BBC Radio Brighton begins (now BBC Radio Sussex).
Savile's Travels begins.

1969 Prince Charles gives his first broadcast interview, to Jack de Manio on the *Today* programme.
Sunday begins.

The 1970s

1970 Kenny Everett sacked from Radio 1 for a joke about a politician's wife. BBC Radio Medway (now BBC Radio Kent) and BBC Radio Oxford begin.
Many Radio 4 series make their debut: *The World Tonight*, *PM*, *Analysis*, *Week Ending*, *Talking Politics* and *Start the Week*. Radio 2 sees the launch of *Folk on Friday* (*Folk on 2* from 1980).

1971 Radio licence abolished.
The Monday Play is introduced.

1972 *Beat the Record* and *Thanks for the Memory* begin.

1973 Independent Local Radio begins with LBC (8 October) and Capital Radio (16 October). Radio Clyde follows. Independent Radio News is born, to service ILR.
First Radio 1 Roadshow. *Kaleidoscope* and *Newsbeat* begin.

1974 BRMB, Hallam, Metro, Piccadilly Radio and Swansea Sound begin.
Science Now begins. *Black Londoners* begins on BBC Radio London.

1975 Pennine, Plymouth Sound, Radio Trent and TFM begin.

Capital Radio launches Help a London Child.
The News Huddlines begins.

1976 Beacon Radio, Downtown Radio and 210 begin.
Phillip Hodson starts the first sex therapy programme, on LBC.
The Law Game begins.

1977 *Enterprise, File on 4, The News Quiz* and *Sport on 4* begin.

1978 Radio broadcasting from Parliament begins, on both BBC and ILR.
Bookshelf, Conversation Piece, Does He Take Sugar?, Enquire Within and *Going Places* begin.

1979 Sony Walkman goes on sale.
Radio 2 becomes a 24-hour station.
Big Band Special, Breakaway and *The Food Programme* begin. The Grumbleweeds have their first show on Radio 4.

The 1980s

1980 BBC Radio Norfolk, Devonair, Hereward Radio, Red Dragon Radio, Severn Sound and Two Counties Radio begin.
Mainly for Pleasure and *Medicine Now* begin.

1981 Chiltern Radio, Essex Radio, GWR, Northsound Radio, Radio Aire and West Sound Radio begin.
The Lord of the Rings is broadcast on Radio 4.
In The Psychiatrist's Chair begins, as does Desmond Carrington's *All-Time Greats*.

1982 Moray Firth, one of Britain's tiniest stations, begins in Inverness. BBC Radio Cambridgeshire, BBC Radio Northampton, Radio Wyvern, Red Rose Radio and Saxon Radio also start.

1983 The Community Radio Association is formed, as is the pressure group Voice of the Listener.
County Sound, Marcher Sound, Signal Radio and Southern Sound begin.

1984 The Radio Academy is formed.
Leicester Sound, Radio Broadland, Radio Mercury and Viking begin.
The Network Chart Show begins on ILR and *On the Air* on Radio 2.

1985 BBC Radio Bedfordshire begins.

1986 Home Office cancels community radio experiment.

BBC Essex, Northants Radio and Ocean Sound begin.
The ABC Quiz, Back to Square One, Huddwinks, Loose Ends and *Melodies For You* begin.

1987 BBC 648 begins.
Radio 4's series on intelligence, *My Country Right or Wrong*, is subject to government injunction.
Radio 1 mounts its first comedy series, *Hey Rrradio!*
Citizens begins.

1988 Volvo is the first car to go on sale fitted with a Radio Data System radio.
The BBC Radio Collection is launched.
BBC Radio London relaunched as GLR. BBC Radio Gloucestershire begins.
Beginning of *All in the Mind, Cinema 2, Classic Albums, Composers of the Week, Drama Now, The Friday Play* and *Third Ear*.

1989 Atlantic 252 begins.
Jakki Brambles becomes Radio 1's first female DJ on weekdays.
Sunset Radio is the first of the new incremental stations, followed by Sunrise Radio, London Greek Radio and WNK. Also the start of Fox FM, CN-FM and Wiltshire Sound.
Start of *An Actor's Life For Me, Ad Lib, Age to Age* and *Europhile*.

The 1990s

1990 Radio Authority begins (December).
Radio 5 begins (27 August). On the same day, Radio 2 becomes the first national network to go out on FM only.
Many new stations start up, including Airport Information Radio, BBC Radio CWR, BBC Radio Suffolk, Choice FM, East End Radio, FTP Radio, Isle of Wight Radio, Jazz FM, KCBC, KFM, Kiss FM, Melody Radio, RTM and Spectrum Radio.
The Arts Programme, The Forsyte Chronicles, Mining the Archive, Mixing It, Soundings, Third Opinion, Table Talk and *Tuning Up* begin.

1991 First INR licence advertised.
The Listener ceases publication.
First INR licence awarded to Showtime, an easy listening service which promises to be a bright, lively competitor to Radio 2.

Picture credits